FROMMER'S
WONDERFUL WEEKENDS
FROM NEW YORK CITY

F R O M M E R ' S

WONDERFUL WEEKENDS
FROM NEW YORK CITY

BY MARILYN WOOD

Macmillan • USA

MACMILLAN TRAVEL USA
A Pearson Education Macmillan Company
1633 Broadway
New York, NY 10019

Find us online at **www.frommers.com**

ISBN: 0-02-862768-7
ISSN available from the Library of Congress

Editor: Alice Fellows
Production Editor: Lori Cates
Photo Editor: Richard Fox
Design by Amy Peppler Adams—designLab, Seattle
Digital Cartography by Raffaele Degennaro and Ortelius Design

SPECIAL SALES

Bulk purchases (10+ copies) of Frommer's and selected Macmillan Travel Guides are
available to corporations, organizations, mail-order catalogs, institutions, and charities
at special discounts, and can be customized to suit individual needs. For more information write to: Special Sales, 1633 Broadway, New York, NY 10019.

Manufactured in the United States of America.

CONTENTS

CONNECTICUT
◄○►

RHODE ISLAND
◄○►

MASSACHUSETTS
◄◌►

VERMONT & NEW HAMPSHIRE
◄◌►

NEW JERSEY
◄◌►

PENNSYLVANIA & DELAWARE
-‹○›-

MAPS

About the Author

Marilyn Wood came to the United States from England to study journalism at Columbia University. The former editorial director of Macmillan Travel, she has also worked as a reporter, ranch hand, press officer, and book reviewer. In addition, Marilyn is the author of *Frommer's London from $55 a Day* and *Frommer's Toronto,* a co-author of *Frommer's Canada,* and a contributor to *Frommer's Europe from $50 a Day.* Currently she's at work on *Wonderful Weekends* guides from San Francisco, Boston, and Washington, D.C.

An Invitation to the Reader

In researching this book, I discovered many wonderful places—inns, restaurants, shops, and more. I'm sure you'll find others. Please tell me about them, so I can share the information with your fellow travelers in upcoming editions. If you were disappointed in a recommendation, I'd love to know that, too. Please write to:

Marilyn Wood
Frommer's Wonderful Weekends from New York City
Macmillan Travel USA
1633 Broadway
New York, NY 10019

An Additional Note

Please be advised that travel information is subject to change at any time—and this is especially true of prices. We therefore suggest that you write or call ahead for information when making your travel plans. The authors, editors, and publisher cannot be held responsible for the experiences of readers while traveling. Your safety is important to us, however, so we encourage you to stay alert and be aware of your surroundings. Keep a close eye on cameras, purses, and wallets, all favorite targets of thieves and pickpockets.

Abbreviations Used in This Book:

MAP   Modified American Plan
EP   European Plan
AP   American Plan

Find Frommer's Online

Arthur Frommer's Budget Travel Online (www.frommers.com) offers more than 6,000 pages of up-to-the-minute travel information—including the latest bargains and candid, personal articles updated daily by Arthur Frommer himself. No other Web site offers such comprehensive and timely coverage of the world of travel.

SIX IMPORTANT TOPICS

Prices & Hours: Although I've made every effort to obtain correct and current prices and hours for establishments and attractions, these can change swiftly and dramatically. Changes in ownership, changes in policy, and inflation can all affect this information. For prices beyond 1999, add about 10% to 15% to the given rates per year.

Reservations: These are a must on weekends. For accommodations they should be made well in advance—in some cases as much as 3 months ahead and in exceptional circumstances as much as a year (at Saratoga, for example, during the racing meet). Dinner reservations, especially for Friday and Saturday, should also be made ahead of time.

Minimum Stays: Most places demand minimum stays of 2 or 3 nights on weekends and 4 nights on holiday weekends during high season, sometimes year-round. This information hasn't always been included, so check ahead.

Deposits: These are often nonrefundable since they're the innkeeper's only defense against folks who don't show up, especially during inclement weather. Always clarify this when you book.

Taxes: I haven't included these in the quoted rates. Percentages vary from state to state.

A Note on the Dining Listings: Where there's a heading, "Dinner Only," it means that the restaurants under this heading aren't open for lunch on Saturday or Sunday. It does not mean that they don't serve lunch at all—they may well do so on weekdays, but they're not open for lunch to weekenders.

Definitions: *Weekends* in hotel and restaurant listings always refers to Friday and Saturday nights. In attractions listings, it refers strictly to Saturday and Sunday. The term *weekdays* refers to Sunday night through Thursday night.

INTRODUCTION

By Thursday, most of us harried urban or suburban dwellers are looking forward to the weekend, eagerly anticipating a break from our work routine and the chance to get away from the tarmac—to relax, calm our jangled nerves, and rediscover who we really are. That's what this book is all about: 2- or 3-day breaks among the lakes, or in the mountains, or in the forests, or down along the shore—and all within 2 to 4 hours' driving time from the city of New York.

We often forget that the city is surrounded by many alluring yet serene hideaways and head off either for far-flung destinations, or we retreat every weekend for a few months of the year to a summer house, where we meet the same faces and view the same vistas. Why not take a risk and explore what's in your own backyard—see new faces, make new friends, and explore new places? In short, why not come weekending?

There are country markets and fairs, horse shows, music, theater, apple and oyster festivals, flower shows, antique car markets, horse races, and a multitude of other festive celebrations and events to attend. There are all kinds of unique museums and art galleries; historic homes filled with the drama and personalities of those who've lived there; whole villages that seem to exist as tranquilly today as they did 200 years ago; fascinating communities of artists and writers; ostentatious and lavish mansions by the sea where outrageous events were staged; fantastic buildings created by personalities like Frederic E. Church and Henry Chapman Mercer; and, of course, camping, hiking, fishing, skiing, rafting, sailing, or doing whatever you relish and enjoy. Or you can simply opt for a rocking chair and a cup of tea or a cocktail on a broad veranda overlooking a verdant garden or wonderful view.

And while you're enjoying all this, you can stay in 17th-century riverside inns; old sea captains' homes; luxurious hotels that once welcomed Paganini; Italianate, Greek Revival, and castlelike mansions that once belonged to robber barons; gingerbread Victorian fantasies with turrets and lacy trimmings; farms where you'll be awakened by the crowing of the cockerel; old mills; and even a caboose surrounded by quiet fields. Your choices are endless, and so are the gourmet delights—juicy sweet lobsters from New England's waters, continental cuisine served in elegant hotel dining rooms, hearty farm meals, and picnics savored at music festivals or by the ocean.

To arrange your weekend in a way that suits your particular needs and personality requires a certain amount of planning. When you have only 2 days, you need to know where you want to stay and you can't waste precious moments trekking to a well-regarded restaurant for lunch on Saturday only to find it closed. This guide has been researched and written to forestall such problems and deliver you, the weekender, from such headaches, leaving you free to concentrate on roaming and fully enjoying your weekend your way. It's designed to help you step-by-step in the planning process.

Each destination opens with a section that lists details about getting there by car or public transportation as well as estimated driving times, plus a box on special seasonal events you may want to plan your weekend around (or plan to avoid, depending on your attitude toward crowds). Getting out of the city on a Friday afternoon or evening can be a real hassle, and you may well want to choose public transport over driving. If you do decide to rent a car, book well in advance. Unfortunately, detailed road maps are really beyond the scope of this book, but you can get them by calling the Automobile Association of America, if you're a member, at 212/757-2000.

After these opening sections, there follows a brief, general introduction to the history and highlights of the place, then a detailed description of what your weekend is really all about: what to see, what to do, and what to explore. Inevitably, it's a very personal choice. When it comes to museums, you may feel like Louis Kahn, who commented (though he designed several), "I get tired immediately upon entering a museum," or, conversely, like museum director Thomas Hoving, who called museums "a place for people to battle against the blows of technology and the misery of life." You may regard the ocean in the words of Wallace Stevens as "dirty, wobbly, and wet," or you may relish sailing on it as much as Sir Francis Chichester obviously did. You may relegate sports and those who practice them to the "Toy Department," or you may enjoy the challenge of rigorous exercise.

I've described the many choices available and offered some guidance about how to organize your 2 or 3 days and highlighted what I consider the real finds of each destination. You, of course, will pursue your own interests, whether they're architecture, historic houses, antiques, graveyards, gardens, art galleries, museums, theater, birding, fruit picking, or active pursuits from swimming or windsurfing to skiing, golf, or horseback riding. These last I've covered in a section on special and recreational activities at the end of each chapter (except in certain cases where it made more sense to place them at the end of each section in the chapter). In this section I've located public sports facilities wherever possible, but I make no claims as to their quality and standards of service.

I tackle the problem of lodging next, and while I'm on the subject, I can't urge you strongly enough to make reservations—in peak summer and fall seasons, as much as 5 or 6 months in advance, *especially on weekends.* I've selected what I consider especially appealing places—an Italian palazzo, a working Mennonite farm, a converted grist mill—including a great number of inns and bed-and-breakfasts wherever they exist, grand and sometimes funky downtown hotels that often offer alluring weekend packages, and, on rare occasions, a typical motel chain for those who desire that kind of accommodation or where there simply is no other alternative. In each case, I've endeavored to convey the atmosphere and type of lodging and treatment you can expect to receive. I've listed the rates, but I urge you always to check on them when you make reservations because prices will undoubtedly have changed by the time this book reaches your hands. Do keep in mind that many inns have 2- or sometimes 3-night minimum stays on weekends and that weekend packages are offered on a space-available basis. Though this doesn't pretend to be a camper's guide, I've included some camping ideas, usually state parks and other wilderness areas. Commercial campgrounds and trailer parks aren't listed here.

Next, I cover the problem of meals. I know an English woman who built a successful restaurant around the honest, nutritious breakfast she served, one that's so difficult to find unless you know where to go—freshly squeezed juices, farm eggs, fine Canadian bacon, spicy sausage, and homemade bread and muffins. If your lodging doesn't provide breakfast, you, too, will have to search for a breakfast or brunch spot, unless you're willing to settle for the easily found Howard Johnson's, McDonald's, or Denny's. Wherever possible, I've tried to help you out, though it hasn't always been easy—and in some cases I've given up. Similarly, Saturday lunch can prove elusive—many restaurants close for lunch on Saturday— so I've tried to find the best of those available. Often, though, on a balmy Saturday you'll want to take a picnic somewhere overlooking the ocean or a river. Sadly, I've discovered that unlike France or England, where you can pull into a field and stretch out among the poppies with a fine bottle of wine, some garlic sausage, and a baguette, it's a little harder and more formal in the United States. So I've tried to direct you to state parks and other idyllic settings for your leisurely meal *en plein air* and also to the suppliers of your picnic fare.

For dinner I've described a selection of restaurants serving a diversity of cuisines for you to choose from. And in each destination I've included unique local favorites. In all cases I've relied on a mixture of my own judgment and experience as well as local recommendations. Hours and prices are all included to help your planning.

And finally, though many of the country destinations that appear in this book lack any rousing nightlife (which is precisely why you've chosen to go there, right?), I've tried to include some nightlife options, if only in a cozy, convivial bar.

T. H. White wrote, "The Victorians had not been anxious to go away for the weekend. The Edwardians, on the contrary, were nomadic." Let's be positively nomadic. And one final thing—if you feel like it, you can always rewrap this volume in a brown paper cover and rename it "Marvelous Midweek Breaks from New York City" if your working routine affords you such blissful luxury.

Either way, happy traveling!

NEW YORK

The Hudson River Valley

The East Bank: Poughkeepsie ◆ *Hyde Park* ◆ *Rhinebeck* ◆
Red Hook ◆ *Hudson* ◆ *Old Chatham*

The West Bank: New Paltz ◆ *High Falls* ◆ *Lake Minnewaska*
◆ *Hurley* ◆ *Kingston*

The Lower Hudson: Garrison ◆ *Cold Spring* ◆ *West Point* ◆
Storm King ◆ *Newburgh* ◆ *Hopewell Junction*

Distance in miles: Newburgh, 66; Poughkeepsie, 77; Kingston, 97
Estimated driving times: 1 to 2 hours

◄O►◄O►◄O►◄O►◄O►

Driving: For west-bank destinations, take the Palisades Parkway to West Point and the New York Thruway to points farther north—like New Paltz and Kingston. For east-bank destinations, you can do the same; cross the river at either Poughkeepsie or Kingston. You could also take the Taconic Parkway, for a more scenic route.

Bus: Adirondack/Pine Hill Trailways (☎ 800/225-6815) goes to New Paltz and Kingston.

Train: Amtrak (☎ 800/872-7245) travels up the east bank of the Hudson, stopping at Rhinecliff (just west of Rhinebeck). Metro-North's Harlem-Hudson line (☎ 800/638-7646) stops at Garrison, Cold Spring, and Poughkeepsie.

Further Information: For more about the east-bank areas, contact the **Columbia County Chamber of Commerce**, 507 Warren St., Hudson, NY 12534 (☎ 518/828-4417); **Dutchess County Tourism**, 3 Neptune Rd., Poughkeepsie, NY 12601 (☎ 800/445-3131 or 914/463-4000); and **Putnam County Tourist Information**, % Cold Spring Area Chamber of Commerce, P.O. Box 36, Cold Spring-on-Hudson, NY 10516 (☎ 914/265-3200).

For more about the west-bank areas, contact **Greene County Tourism**, P.O. Box 527, Catskill, NY 12414 (☎ 518/943-3223); **Orange County Tourism**, 30 Matthews St., Goshen, NY 10924 (☎ 914/291-2136); and **Ulster County Public Information Office**, P.O. Box 1800, Kingston, NY 12402 (☎ 914/340-3000 or 914/340-3566).

The Hudson River Valley

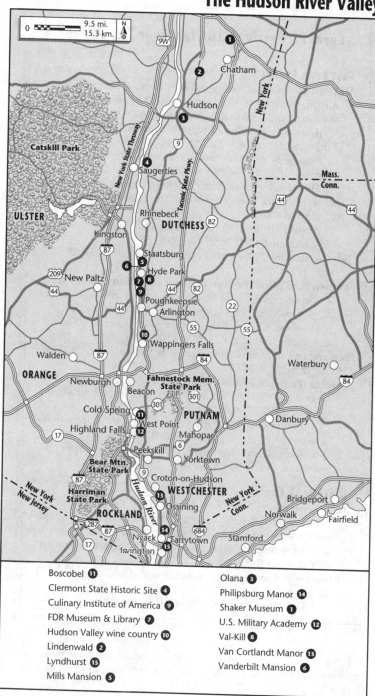

0 ┣━━━━┫ 9.5 mi.
         15.3 km.

N

9W

1 Chatham

2

Hudson

3

9

New York State Thruway

Taconic State Pkwy.

Catskill Park

4 Saugerties

Rhinebeck

DUTCHESS 82

ULSTER

Kingston

87

Staatsburg

5

6 Hyde Park

7 **8**

9

44 82

209 New Paltz

44

Poughkeepsie

Arlington

44

55

10

22

Wappingers Falls

Walden

87

84

Waterbury

ORANGE

Newburgh

Fahnestock Mem. State Park

84

Beacon

301

301

Cold Spring

PUTNAM

11

Highland Falls

12 West Point

Mahopac

Danbury

17

Peekskill

6

Bear Mtn. State Park

Yorktown

9

Croton-on-Hudson

New York New Jersey

Harriman State Park

13 Ossining

WESTCHESTER

Bridgeport

ROCKLAND

87

287

87

Nyack

14 Tarrytown

New York Conn.

Norwalk

Fairfield

17

Irvington

15

684

Stamford

Hudson River

Mass. Conn.

44

44

55

New York

Boscobel **11**	Olana **3**
Clermont State Historic Site **4**	Philipsburg Manor **14**
Culinary Institute of America **9**	Shaker Museum **1**
FDR Museum & Library **7**	U.S. Military Academy **12**
Hudson Valley wine country **10**	Val-Kill **8**
Lindenwald **2**	Van Cortlandt Manor **13**
Lyndhurst **15**	Vanderbilt Mansion **6**
Mills Mansion **5**	

Events & Festivals to Plan Your Trip Around

East Bank Events

May: **Great Hudson Valley Balloon Race,** Dutchess County Airport, Wappingers Falls. More than 30 balloons, sky diving, aerobatic shows, and more. Call ☎ 914/463-4000.

Hudson River Valley Antique Auto Show, Dutchess County Fairgrounds, Rhinebeck. Call ☎ 914/876-4001.

Rhinebeck Antiques Show, Dutchess County Fairgrounds, Rhinebeck. Call ☎ 914/876-4001.

Rhinebeck Crafts Fair, Dutchess County Fairgrounds, Rhinebeck. More than 350 craftspeople display their work. Call ☎ 914/876-4001.

Herb Fair and Plant Sale at the Shaker Museum, Old Chatham. Call ☎ 518/794-9100).

July: **Winterhawk Bluegrass Festival,** Ancramdale. Call ☎ 518/390-6211.

August: **Bard Music Festival Rediscoveries,** Bard College, Route 9G, Annandale. Series of lectures and performances concentrating on particular composers' works. Call ☎ 914/758-6822.

Dutchess County Fair, Rhinebeck (mid-August). Second-largest fair in the state. Call ☎ 914/876-4001.

September: **Columbia County Fair,** at the Fairgrounds in Chatham. Call ☎ 518/828-3375.

October: **Pumpkin Festival,** Clearwater. The sloop *Clearwater* sails the Hudson, celebrating at various riverside locations along the way. Call ☎ 914/454-7673.

Rhinebeck Crafts Fair, Dutchess County Fairgrounds, Rhinebeck. Call the fairgrounds at ☎ 914/876-4001.

Rhinebeck Antiques Show, Dutchess County Fairgrounds, Rhinebeck. Call ☎ 914/876-4001.

West Bank Events

July–September: **New York Renaissance Festival,** Sterling Forest, Tuxedo (every weekend from the end of July to the second weekend after Labor Day). A celebration of pageantry, jousting, wandering minstrels, and other fitting entertainments. Call ☎ 914/351-5171.

October: **Chrysanthemum Festival,** Seamon Park, Saugerties. Call ☎ 914/340-3000.

Oktoberfest, Kingston. Call ☎ 914/340-3000.

For general New York State information, contact the **New York State Department of Economic Development,** Division of Tourism, One Commerce Plaza, Albany, NY 12245 (☎ 518/474-4116).

◄O►◄O►◄O►◄O►◄O►

New Yorkers need only to travel to The Cloisters and Fort Tryon Park at the top of Manhattan to get a perspective on the Hudson River. You'll marvel at the beauty and majesty of this broad swath of water that travels 315 miles from the Adirondacks, where it rises as a trout stream, cuts between the Catskills and the Berkshires, flows past the bluffs of the Palisades down to New York Bay, and out into the ocean. This river has spawned many legends and mysteries, inspiring such authors as Washington Irving and William Cullen Bryant and painters like Thomas Cole and Frederic Church, whose work gave rise to one of the first schools of American painting, the Hudson River School.

Early Exploration In 1609, representing the Dutch East India Company, Henry Hudson sailed up the river aboard the *Half Moon* as far as present-day Albany. Failing to find passage beyond that point, he withdrew and dropped anchor at Athens, where he encountered Native Americans and remarked on their corn and pumpkins. In 1624 the Dutch founded the colony of New Netherland at Fort Orange (now Albany). Great estates and patroonships were later established along the fertile river valley, which is still famous for its apples, produce, dairy goods, and horticultural wonders (Rhinebeck, for example, was once the world's violet capital). The English took over the area in 1664, laying out vast estates, as the Livingston family did at Clermont.

The Revolutionary War Two-thirds of all Revolutionary War battles were fought in New York State, many along the banks of the Hudson, making the area rich in historical associations. Remnants of British General John Burgoyne's army straggled back from the Battle of Saratoga and encamped just outside Catskill. The spy Major John André, en route through the patriots' lines from a meeting with Benedict Arnold, was captured in Tarrytown and executed at Tappan Hill. General George Washington spent 17 months at Newburgh while discussing the nature of the peace. At West Point, an early garrison against the British, remnants of the chain barrier erected across the river to stop the British advance can still be seen today. During the turmoil of the revolution, the governing body of the state was forced to move about, settling briefly in Hurley and later in Kingston, where its meeting place survived the city's burning by the British and can be visited today. Many of these historical events and dramas can be experienced by visiting West Point, Newburgh, Kingston, New Paltz, and Hurley, where stone houses from the original Dutch settlements remain.

The 19th Century When Washington Irving first sailed up the river in 1800, the trip to Catskill took anywhere from 4 to 10 days, depending on the weather, but Robert Fulton's first steamboat, the *Clermont* (1807), changed all that, reducing the trip to a mere 24 hours. The river became a steamboat lane, and tall smokestacks could be seen gliding upriver, sidewheels churning and decks crowded with people headed for the Catskill Mountain resorts via Kingston and Catskill Point.

In the 19th century, the river became the very lifeline of New York City. All kinds of supplies were shipped downriver—ice blocks and bricks from

Athens; cement and bluestone for the base of the Statue of Liberty and the caissons of the Brooklyn Bridge; fruit and livestock; and, most important, anthracite coal from Pennsylvania mines, which traveled via the Delaware-Hudson Canal to Kingston and from there, down the Hudson. The river was lined with bustling ports. Kingston was the largest and busiest port; Newburgh, Poughkeepsie, and Hudson were important whaling towns.

20th-Century Changes Many of these communities have long slumbered—almost as if waiting for another call from the river to return to life, since railroads, automobiles, and airplanes stole their livelihoods. Many of these once-important towns are being revived these days, and in summer they're lively with celebrations and festivals, fairs, and all kinds of fun, both on and off the river. A maritime museum and a trolley museum are bringing the Kingston Rondout back to life; Hudson and Cold Spring Harbor have become magnets for antiques lovers. Life has returned to the Hudson—even the striped bass and the shad are running and spawning again. Naturalist John Burroughs would no doubt applaud the efforts to rescue the river from the destructive effects of pollution. For visitors, there's no better way to get acquainted with the Hudson than to take a trip on the sloop Clearwater, which leaves daily from Beacon and has brought a lot of publicity to the campaign to save this national treasure. Other cruise boats leave from Kingston, Catskill, Poughkeepsie, and Albany.

The Hudson Valley Today Visitors come to the valley to explore the river towns. They browse for antiques; attend festivals, fairs, and other special events; visit the mansions and homes of early settlers, artists, or political figures like Franklin Roosevelt and Martin Van Buren; attend parades and football games at West Point; drive through the sculpture field at Storm King; cruise on the river; hike, fish, and camp in the state parks; stay at old country inns; and enjoy the bounty of the farmlands—fruits, wines, and cheeses. All seasons bring beauty to the river valley: In spring the river is high and fast flowing, and the orchards along its banks are in full blossom along with the dogwood trees. In summer the river is filled with sailboats that tack from side to side, while other pleasure craft tow water-skiers or just cruise along, past towns celebrating summer events. In autumn the trees are radiant, and the locals congregate at country fairs or are busy in the orchards and fields collecting the abundant harvest. In the coldest winter weather the scene resembles a Dutch painting: Iceboat parties take to the river, and people go skating and walking on the ice, their breath trailing momentarily in the frigid air.

No wonder so many prominent families—the Van Cortlandts and Verplancks and later the Livingstons, Jays, Harrimans, Astors, and Roosevelts—chose to build mansions in this area. Today their homes are marvelous places to visit, providing some of the best vantage points from which to view the river—Boscobel in Garrison, Roosevelt's home at Hyde Park, the Vanderbilt and Ogden Mills mansions, Livingston's Clermont estate, and Frederick Church's Olana, which commands a view of the famous bend in the river that Church so loved to gaze upon and paint.

So why not follow in their footsteps and head for the Hudson, returning laden with stories and fresh produce, memories, and more?

THE EAST BANK

In this section I haven't included the Sleepy Hollow Restorations—Philipsburg Manor, Sunnyside, and Sleepy Hollow—because I consider these day trips from Manhattan. Instead, I begin just south of Poughkeepsie and travel all the way up the river to Hudson. On the east side of the river there are not many accommodations, so your choice is restricted to the Beekman Arms and several bed-and-breakfasts in Rhinebeck and environs. If none of these appeals to you, your best bet is to anchor on the other side around New Paltz, where the Mohonk Mountain House offers delightful accommodations and there are several outstanding B&Bs. From there, you can cross the river at either Poughkeepsie or Kingston to take in the sights on the opposite bank.

POUGHKEEPSIE

POUGHKEEPSIE ATTRACTIONS

At **Samuel F. B. Morse's Locust Grove**, on Route 9 just south of Poughkeepsie (☎ 914/454-4500), you'll discover that Morse was far more than just the inventor of the Morse Code. He also invented the telegraph, which he made out of the canvas stretchers (among other things) he used in his primary career as a painter of portraits and landscapes. Indeed, he regarded his inventions only as ways of supporting his painting career—an attitude supported in this century by the sale of his *Gallery of the Louvre* for $3.25 million. When Morse purchased the estate from the Livingstons it included an early-19th-century Georgian home. Morse hired Andrew Jackson Downing to remodel it to look like a Tuscan villa, and the Morse family lived in it from 1847 to 1901. A good interpretive tour is given of the site. One room is filled with Morse memorabilia, including a model of the first telegraph. Other rooms contain the 18th- and 19th-century furnishings of later owners, including several Duncan Phyfe pieces. Afterward, you can explore the flower and herb gardens and 4½ miles of riverfront trails. *Hours:* May to late November, daily 10am to 4pm; grounds are open year-round until dusk. *Admission:* $5 adults, $4 seniors, $2 children ages 6 to 18.

The **Frances Lehman Loeb Art Center**, at Vassar College (☎ 914/437-5632 or 914/437-5235), is housed in Cesar Pelli's dramatic series of buildings, which opened in 1993. The galleries are devoted to antiquities, European Renaissance and baroque paintings, 19th- and 20th-century European and American art, Asian art, and prints and drawings. The two sculpture courts are very appealing. The collection comprises 12,500 objects, but only 400 are exhibited in the Main Gallery. Highlights of the historic collections are the red granite head of Viceroy Merymose (1391–53 B.C.); a rhyton in the shape of a dog's head; an Eastern Han Dynasty tower (A.D. 25–220); paintings by Pieter Brueghel the Younger, Cézanne, Delacroix, and Doré; and works by John Singleton Copley, William Hamilton, and George Innes.

The 20th-century galleries include notable sculptures by Calder and Anthony Caro as well as paintings by Francis Bacon, Marsden Hartley, Georgia O'Keeffe, Jackson Pollock, Balthus, and Mark Rothko. *Hours:* Tuesday to Saturday 10am to 5pm, Sunday 1 to 5pm. *Admission:* Free.

From Poughkeepsie, detour along Route 44. Take the Taconic Parkway north to the Salt Point Turnpike, and turn right at the end of the exit. This will bring you to Clinton Corners, site of one of New York's small, picturesque wineries, **Clinton Vineyards** (☎ 914/266-5372). Proprietor/winemaker Ben Feder produces high-quality Seyval blanc table wine and Johanissberg Riesling dessert wine as well as *méthode champenoise* Seyval natural. Tours and tastings are offered on weekends year-round and on Fridays in the summer. The tasting room offers wine accessories and picnics that can be enjoyed on the grounds. To reach the vineyard, go through Clinton Corners until you come to a 10-m.p.h. sign, where the road curves to the right. Make a sharp left onto Schultzville Road and look for the vineyard sign on the left.

POUGHKEEPSIE LODGING & DINING

The **Inn at the Falls**, 50 Red Oaks Mill Rd., Poughkeepsie, NY 12603 (☎ 914/462-5770; fax 914/462-5943), belies its name because it's absolutely new and modern, from the exterior of red brick and shingles to the blond-wood reception desk. It does look out onto Wappinger Creek and the falls and is a very attractive accommodation. There are 22 rooms, 2 minisuites, and 12 suites in an L-shaped arrangement. A standard double contains a brass bed, a wing chair, a blond pine desk, and a wardrobe. Jade and dusky rose are the chosen colors. A TV/VCR, a phone in both bedroom and bathroom, an unstocked refrigerator, a hair dryer, and terry-cloth bathrobes are among the nice amenities. The toilet is separate from the bathroom.

The suites are spectacular: The Contemporary Suite has a dramatic black-tile bath with a Jacuzzi and a platform bed with a polished black headboard and dusky-rose comforter. The English Suite has a king-size four-poster bed with a crocheted canopy, a polished roll-top desk, brass lamps, a gaming table, and Queen Anne–style chairs among its antique reproductions. The country minisuite sports a Pennsylvania Dutch–style chest, a Windsor chair, and a leather wing chair. A high-ceilinged sitting room is available for guests. The continental breakfast is served in your room. Other services include laundry/valet, nightly turndown, and twice daily maid service. Guests can relax in the common room, which overlooks the creek and falls.

Rates (including breakfast): $140 to $145 double, $170 to $175 suite.

POUGHKEEPSIE AFTER DARK

Poughkeepsie's **Bardavon Theater**, 35 Market St. (☎ 914/473-2072), is one of the oldest continuously operating theaters in New York State. Today it hosts a variety of performance companies including dance, opera, and jazz plus popular Broadway and Off Broadway shows. See the ornate stucco and decorative work, which has been restored to its 1869 splendor.

HYDE PARK

HYDE PARK ATTRACTIONS

The FDR Museum & Library

You can spend a day or more at Hyde Park exploring this moving memorial to Franklin Delano and Eleanor Roosevelt, for there are several parts to the whole. First, the **FDR Museum and Library**, 511 Albany Post Rd. (☎ 914/229-8114), documents the life, political campaigns, triumphs, and tribulations of Roosevelt through a superb collection of memorabilia, letters, speeches, and documents. The collection makes for riveting viewing and reading. The most importan t exhibits are the photographs dramatizing the great and tragic moments of history—the 1945 capture of thousands of German soldiers in the Ruhr; the liberation of Paris on August 25, 1944; perfectly disciplined Allied soldiers under attack waiting to be rescued at Dunkirk; the famous picture of the abandoned baby crying in the ruins of Shanghai during Japan's invasion of China.

On a lighter note, there's also a photograph of Roosevelt's famous Scottie, Fala—in an effort to libel Roosevelt in the 1944 election campaign, certain Republicans charged that the dog had been left on the Aleutian Islands and recovered at great expense to American taxpayers. There's also a stirring multimedia exhibit on World War II that features a replica of the "Map Room," the secret communications center in the White House basement. An interactive computer exhibit allows visitors to assume the role of commander-in-chief and make tactical and strategic decisions. Roosevelt's personal side is captured in exhibits about his youth, his battle with polio, and, of course, the life and career of Eleanor, also portrayed through exhibits and displays.

Behind the museum, you can walk down to the **rose arbor and garden** where Franklin was buried in 1945 (Eleanor in 1962), then proceed to the 32nd president's **birthplace and home** overlooking the Hudson River, preserved as it was when he died. Tour the house while listening to Eleanor Roosevelt's recorded comments and anecdotes, which bring the various features and furnishings of the house to life and provide insights into the historic events that took place here—the office, for example, where Roosevelt and Winston Churchill signed the agreement resulting in the first atomic bomb, and the room where he was born on January 30, 1882.

Hours: April to October, daily 9am to 6pm; November to March, daily 9am to 5pm. Closed Thanksgiving, December 25, and January 1. *Admission* (for home, museum, and library): $10 adults, free for children ages 16 and under.

Val-Kill

From 1926, **Val-Kill**, on Route 9G (☎ 914/229-9115), was Eleanor Roosevelt's weekend and vacation place. The name means "valley stream," and here, along the banks of a small stream, Eleanor often picnicked with friends. Her husband was the first to suggest building a house at this location.

At the beginning of the tour you're shown an excellent black-and-white film that captures the amazing compassion, enthusiasm, and humanity of this great woman. Born in 1884, she was a disappointment to her beautiful mother and aunts, all belles of New York, but her ne'er-do-well father doted on her.

When she was 8 years old her mother died, and she and her younger brother went to live with their maternal grandmother; 2 years later their father died. Perhaps these early losses nourished Eleanor's humanitarianism. Soon she was sent to the Allenswood School in England, where she was encouraged in her studies by the headmistress, Mlle Souvestre. At age 18 she renewed her acquaintance with her distant cousin Franklin, with whom she'd been friends. Over the objections of his mother, she married him in 1905. The film then charts the birth of their five children and Franklin's political career until he contracted polio in 1921, when Eleanor began actively to promote his aspirations. Later, it follows them as they bring attention to the unjust conditions that prevailed among women, minorities, youth, and the unemployed.

During Roosevelt's presidency, Val-Kill became a center of Eleanor's social life and a tranquil retreat that she wrote about in her newspaper column, "My Day." After Franklin's 1945 death she withdrew to Val-Kill, but continued to involve herself in the United Nations, human rights, and politics, campaigning for Adlai Stevenson in 1956 and for John F. Kennedy in 1960. On November 7, 1962, she died at age 78, and the *New York Times* obituary eulogizing her stated that "she was a humanitarian who won over many of her critics by the greatness of her heart." Take some time to look at the photos in the theater, including an intimate moment of her picking roses.

From here, the tour of the house proceeds into the office/sitting room. The desk and some of the other furnishings were hers, including the filing cabinet crafted to look like a chest by workmen in the Val-Kill Industries furniture factory—an enterprise she helped establish to provide for farm youth and to preserve old skills.

The overwhelming response to this residence is "how simple, how home-like and unpretentious, how ordinary." The rooms are filled with mementos, bric-a-brac, and photographs. Eleanor loved to sleep on the porch overlooking the garden rather than in her bedroom. Note the bathroom mirror placement—she was 6 feet tall.

Hours: May to October, daily 9am to 5pm; November to April, Saturday and Sunday 9am to 5pm. The tour takes 80 minutes. *Admission:* $5 adults, free for children ages 17 and under.

Antiques lovers may want to travel up the road a little to the **Hyde Park Antiques Center**, 544 Albany Post Rd. (☎ 914/229-8200), where 40 to 50 dealers are located under one roof. *Hours:* Daily 10am to 5pm.

HYDE PARK DINING

Make arrangements at least 3 months in advance for one of the four dining rooms at the **Culinary Institute of America**, Route 9 (☎ 914/471-6608), the nation's leading culinary school. The school occupies a lovely 150-acre site with distant views of the river. Every year, 2,000 new chefs emerge from the 36 kitchens of this residential school attended by such legendary chefs as Alfred Portale (Gotham Bar and Grill), Larry Forgione (An American Place), Roy Yamaguchi (Roy's Restaurant, Honolulu), Bradley Ogden (Lark Creek Inn, Larkspur), and Walter Scheib, executive chef at the White House. The school has come a long way from its founding in 1946 in New Haven, Connecticut, as a local training center for veterans of World War II. It moved to the current site in 1972. For reservations, call ☎ 914/471-6608 Monday to Friday from 8:30am to 6pm. For weekends you'll need to call several months in advance;

on weeknights you may be able to secure same-day reservations if you're lucky. If you'd like to take a tour of the school, call ☎ 914/452-9600. Tours are usually given Monday 10am to 4pm for a $4 admission fee.

The French-style **Escoffier Room**, with chandeliers, is the most formal space. It features modern interpretations of classic French cuisine—like sautéed Dover sole with mushrooms in a brown butter sauce, roast duck breast and confit duck leg with black-currant sauce, and roasted rack of lamb with rösti potatoes. Lunch entrees run from $15 to $19; dinner entrees, $20 to $26. Book at least 6 months ahead for weekends.

Hours: Tuesday to Saturday 11:30am to 1pm and 6:30 to 8:30pm.

The **American Bounty**—my favorite dining room—celebrates the country's diverse cultural heritage and presents contemporary American cuisine using as many local organic ingredients as possible. For example, you might find dishes using Summerfield Farm veal and Stone Church Farm chicken as well as grilled beef tenderloin accompanied by a delicious Zinfandel sauce. Each day, the Julia Child Rotisserie prepares a special roast. There are always several soups offered, served smörgåsbord-style if you wish, along with a variety of breads and salads. You can see the chefs cooking in the glassed-in kitchen hung with copper pots. A sumptuous array of produce is displayed in front, and the walls are adorned with mouth-watering color pictures of food and ingredients. Prices run from $13 to $16 at lunch, $18 to $25 at dinner. *Hours:* Tuesday to Saturday 11:30am to 1pm and 6:30 to 8:30pm.

In the **St. Andrews Cafe**, the contemporary menu includes soups, salads, wood-fired pizzas, vegetarian dishes, and a limited selection of grilled entrees like grilled chicken breast with chilled gazpacho sauce. Outdoor dining is available in season. *Hours:* Monday to Friday 11:30am to 1pm and 6 to 8pm.

The **Caterina de Medici Dining Room** offers fixed-price menus of regional Italian specialties and seasonal selections. Among the wonderful, flavor-filled dishes you might find a Piemontese-style brook trout pan-fried with mushrooms, tomatoes, crisp pancetta, and scallions, or quail with a terrific sausage, herb, pine nut, and raisin stuffing. The prix-fixe lunch is $21.95; dinner is $27.95. *Hours:* Monday to Friday 11:30am to 1pm and 6:30 to 8:30pm.

For a convenient nearby lunch after visiting Hyde Park or Val-Kill, stop at the **Easy Street Cafe**, on Route 9 (☎ 914/229-7969), which has deli sandwiches and burgers priced under $6. *Hours:* Monday to Saturday 11:30am to 10pm, Sunday 11:30am to 9pm.

ATTRACTIONS NORTH OF HYDE PARK

Vanderbilt Mansion

Just north of Hyde Park, also on Route 9, is the "smallest" Vanderbilt residence (☎ 914/229-7770), designed by McKim, Mead, and White for Frederick Vanderbilt. He was the third grandson of Commodore Cornelius Vanderbilt, who started off ferrying fruit and vegetables from Staten Island to New York City and had amassed a fortune of $1 million by 1830. Although the house cost $660,000 and contains 59 rooms, 14 baths, and 22 fireplaces, it's considered modest (especially when you compare it to other remaining family homes—like the Breakers and Marble House in Newport, Rhode Island, and Biltmore House in Asheville, North Carolina). Frederick, in fact, received the smallest inheritance from the family because they disapproved of his marriage to Louise Anthony, a divorcée 12 years his senior, whom he'd wed in secret. Still, the house is pretty opulent, as the 45-minute tour reveals, progressing from the den through the oval main hall and walnut-paneled drawing room, where many a gala ball was held. Upstairs, Mrs. Vanderbilt's bedroom was modeled after a French queen's boudoir. Mr. Vanderbilt's bedroom features solid carved-walnut columns, a gigantic marble fireplace, and a vast bath. Frederick managed to increase his inheritance sevenfold, to a total of $80 million, and he never missed a detail, as many of the house's features indicate. For example, though the house was used in spring and autumn only, it had a central heating system, its own power plant, light dimmers, and sleeping quarters for 60 servants. After touring the house, explore the grounds north of the mansion for an unsurpassed view of the Hudson. *Hours:* Daily 9am to 6pm (last tour 5:15); winter, daily 9am to 5pm. Closed Thanksgiving, December 25, and January 1. *Admission:* $8 adults, free for children ages 16 and under.

Mills Mansion

A few miles farther north on Route 9, in Staatsburg, is the lesser-known Mills mansion (☎ 914/889-4100), reflecting the grand living style of the well-to-do in early-20th-century America. Through the trees you'll glimpse the mansion's classical proportions, embellished with pilasters, a balustrade, and statuary, located on a small bluff. The grounds sweep down to the Hudson River, making it an ideal picnicking spot. The 65-room home was built by Morgan Lewis, a Revolutionary War general and governor of New York. It later became a home for one branch of the Livingston family when Lewis's great-granddaughter Ruth Livingston married financier Ogden Mills. They enlarged and remodeled the 1832 Greek Revival house with the aid of McKim, Mead, and White. Marble fireplaces, gilded plasterwork, and oak paneling provide an opulent backdrop for ornate furnishings, tapestries, and objets d'art. Consider, though, that this was only one of the Millses' retreats—they also owned homes in Paris, Newport, New York City, and California. *Hours:* Memorial Day to Labor Day, Wednesday to Saturday 10am to 4:30pm, Sunday noon to 4:30pm; Labor Day to October, Wednesday to Sunday noon to 4:30pm. Closed November to early April. *Admission:* $3 adults, $2 seniors, $1 children ages 5 to 12.

RHINEBECK & RED HOOK

RHINEBECK AREA ATTRACTIONS

Just 5 miles up Route 9 is the delightful village of Rhinebeck, where you can enjoy a cocktail in the tap room at the Beekman Arms, browse through the stores and boutiques, see what's on at the old movie theater that runs classic and foreign films (often attended by their directors), and attend any number of special events that are scheduled during summer and fall at the Dutchess County Fairgrounds (like the county fair or the big spring and fall antiques fair). Sadly, the renowned American Craft Enterprises Rhinebeck Crafts Fair has moved on, but there's another good crafts show now in its place.

Rhinebeck boasts another exciting attraction, the **Rhinebeck Aerodrome**, northeast of the town on Stone Church Road, off Route 9 (☎ 914/758-8610).

During summer, daredevil pilots perform spectacular flying stunts, restaging mock battles in World War I triplanes and biplanes, re-creating an era when propellers still whirled and flying was truly a pioneer's pastime associated with smoke, grease, and risk. Besides viewing the thrilling air show when the "Black Baron" threatens the skies, you can take a ride in a 1929 vintage flyer and admire the many antique aircraft housed here.

Three buildings contain exhibits from the various flying eras. My favorite is the Pioneer Building, which displays Bleriot's machines, the Wright brothers' glider, the 1912 Passett ornithopter (it was built with the intention of the pilot flapping its wings and was specially constructed for use in *Those Magnificent Men and Their Flying Machines*), and a peculiar 1912 Thomas Pusher vehicle (it looks like an insect), which Cole Palen (the museum's founder) actually flew to Flushing Airport. The two other hangars exhibit planes from the Lindbergh and World War I eras, including a Waco Model 10 that cruised at 84 m.p.h. and had a 385-mile range. Among the World War I exhibits are the Sopwith 7F1, a 121-m.p.h. British fighter; the Fokker D VII, a German fighter that downed 275 Allied aircraft; the Fokker DR-1, a triplane with a 2-hour range that Baron Manfred von Richthofen (the Red Baron) favored; and the Spad in which Captain Eddie Rickenbacker achieved fame piloting as a member of the renowned "Hat in the Rug" squadron. Some are original; some were built by Palen. Sunday air shows feature World War I aircraft; Saturday shows use planes from the pioneer and Lindbergh eras. Before and after, you can fly in a 1929 open-cockpit biplane.

Hours: May 15 to October, daily 10am to 5pm. *Shows:* Mid-June to mid-October, Saturday and Sunday at 2pm. *Admission:* Museum, $5 adults, $2 children ages 6 to 10; on weekends including air show, $10 adults, $5 children ages 6 to 10.

Just south and west of Rhinebeck stands **Wilderstein**, Morton Road (☎ 914/876-4818). The house was built in 1852 for Thomas Suckley in an Italianate style, but his son updated the design in 1888 to a Queen Anne motif, complete with five-story round tower with curved windows. It's a very appealing residence. The main floor, which can be toured, was decorated by J. B. Tiffany and features many stained-glass windows. The landscaping was completed by Calvert Vaux, and the original trails and layout are still being researched and restored. There are lovely views downriver, and in summer tea is served on the veranda after 3pm. *Hours:* May to October, Thursday to Sunday noon to 4pm. *Admission:* House, $5 adults; grounds and tea, free.

RED HOOK & ANNANDALE ATTRACTIONS

The town of Red Hook, about 6 miles north of Rhinebeck on Route 9, actually possesses little of note, except a wonderful old library and an attractive lodging and dining place called the Red Hook Inn. Both **Bard College** and **Montgomery Place** are to the west in nearby Annandale, about 4 miles northwest. From Bard, the innovative liberal arts college, there are lovely views of the river. Among the landmarks on the bucolic campus, the characteristic Carpenter Gothic chapel of Holy Innocents stands out. The interior was decorated by Ralph Adams Cram. Also on campus, the **Center for Curatorial Studies** (☎ 914/758-2424) often features art exhibits worth stopping for. *Hours:* Wednesday to Sunday noon to 5pm. *Admission:* Free.

The road winds through the college campus and then past orchards and farms, breaking open occasionally to reveal magnificent vistas of the purple-hazed peaks of the Catskills to the west across the river.

A narrow, winding road that passes down through apple orchards leads to one of the great early American riverside estates: **Montgomery Place,** River Road, Route 103, Annandale on Hudson (☎ 914/758-5461). The country seat of a branch of the Livingston family, it remained in the family from 1804 until 1965. The 23-room mansion at the heart of a 400-plus-acre estate was built by Janet Livingston, the widow of General Richard Montgomery, a Revolutionary War hero who fell in the assault on Quebec in 1775, and sister of Chancellor Robert Livingston of Clermont. Originally a striking Federal house, it was redesigned in the Classical Revival style by Alexander Jackson Davis between 1840 and 1860. The original shaping of the landscape was accomplished by Alexander Jackson Downing and added to by Violetta White Delafield, who created the rose, herb, perennial, and wild gardens and laid out the evocative ellipse with its pool.

The estate is remarkably appealing because it is so complete; incorporates one of the celebrated 19th-century Hudson River beauty spots, the Saw Kill falls; and recalls another era when the Hudson River aristocracy loved to emulate the English gentry. Tours are given of the house's main floor and kitchens, and along the way you'll learn some family history. You might want to bring a picnic lunch because after the tour you can walk the trails, stopping to eat and enjoy the river and mountain views.

Hours: April to October Wednesday to Monday 10am to 5pm; November and first 2 weeks in December Saturday and Sunday only. Closed January to March. *Admission:* $6 adults, $5 seniors, $3 students.

North of Red Hook is a favorite place for locals: **Greig Farm** on Pitcher Lane off Route 9 (☎ 914/758-1234), which always has something that's in season to pick—apples, strawberries, raspberries, pumpkins—or some event going on, like the series of Fall Festivals. The farm has a nice store where you can purchase locally produced food items. *Hours:* April to December, daily 9 to 6:30pm.

RHINEBECK LODGING

The **Beekman Arms,** Route 9, Rhinebeck, NY 12572 (☎ 914/876-7077), has been serving travelers since it was established in 1766 at the junction of the road to Hudson and the road to Albany. It still possesses an authentic colonial taproom with dark-wood paneling, oak tables, and a brick hearth. People love to come here to drink and dine.

A typical guest room here may contain a canopied oak bed, an oak desk, a brass candlestick lamp, chintz or striped wallpaper, a table, and comfortable side chairs. Additional touches include a decanter of sherry, a coffeemaker, and a small selection of books. Amenities include air-conditioning, phones, TVs, and hair dryers in all rooms, plus unstocked refrigerators in all rooms except those at the Beekman itself. Some rooms also have fireplaces, and five have kitchenettes. The establishment has 59 rooms located in the main inn, the Delameter House, six guest houses, and a motel-style building behind the main inn. The most fetching accommodations are in the gothic Delameter House (1844), a few doors away. High gables with ornamented carved verge boards, a rustic porch, and bay and mullioned windows characterize this striking building fashioned by Alexander Jackson Davis, who also designed robber baron Jay Gould's Lyndhurst in Tarrytown. The eight rooms are furnished with wicker, colorful quilts, and large armoires, all in keeping with the American Gothic style of architecture. You'll also find a parlor furnished with wicker that offers a TV and comfortable seating. Swagged drapes, diamond-pane windows, a marble fireplace, and equestrian prints complete the Victorian ambience.

Behind the Delameter, several guest houses are clustered around a grassy area. The Germond (1820) has four guest rooms. Room 69 features a pencil four-poster bed standing on wide-plank floors, a country towel rack, a Wedgwood-blue rocker strategically positioned in front of the fireplace, and an adjacent parlor furnished with wing chairs, a desk, and Windsor chairs—a lovely accommodation. The Carriage House rooms have cathedral-style ceilings with crossbeams and furnishings that include a brass bed, armchairs, Windsor chairs, a pine table, and a selection of books. In the morning, coffee cake and danishes are served on the patio at the Delameter House only. The dining room under Larry Forgione has established an excellent reputation in the area for its cuisine, which features local Hudson Valley ingredients in finely prepared dishes. At dinner you might find such entrees as Adirondack free-range duck served with toasted almonds, glazed pearl onions, and wild rice; barbecue fillet of mahimahi in a pepper vinaigrette; plus such simple but tasty choices as a burger made with ground sirloin and served with either cheese or smokehouse bacon on a good sesame bun; or turkey pot pie made with free-range turkey. Prices range from $10 to $23. An appetizer I can recommend is the house-smoked salmon and potato crisp Napoleon layered with cream and drizzled with chive oil, or the potato and locally made Coach Farm goat cheese terrine with greens and rosemary oil.

Rates (including breakfast): Inn, $100 to $130; motel, $90 to $109; Delameter House, $95 to $160 double. *Dining hours:* Daily 8 to 10am; Monday to Saturday 11:30am to 3pm and 5 to 10pm, Sunday 10am to 2pm; daily 5:30 to 9:30pm.

If you can't secure a room at the Beekman Arms, try **Veranda House,** 82 Montgomery St., Rhinebeck, NY 12572 (☎ 914/876-4133; www.verandahouse.com), where Linda and Ward Stanley offer four air-conditioned guest rooms in an attractive Federal-style home. Two rooms have Shaker four-posters, while another features a brass bed. All have phones. Guests enjoy the library containing many art and architecture titles as well as a TV/VCR; a comfy living room with a fireplace; and the signature feature of the house, the veranda, which is furnished with wicker chairs. There's also a terrace with umbrella tables overlooking the garden where a full breakfast is served. Complimentary wine and appetizers are offered on Saturday evenings. *Rates* (including full breakfast): $90 to $130 double.

The **Belvedere Mansion,** P.O. Box 785, Rhinebeck, NY 12572 (☎ 914/889-8000), is a few miles south of Rhinebeck on Route 9. It stands on 10 acres atop a hill looking out over the Hudson River to the Catskill Mountains—an impressive Greek Revival mansion with a classical pediment supported by four columns at its entrance. The original was commissioned by Major John Pawling, who fought in the Revolution in 1760, but it was rebuilt in 1900 after a fire burned it to the ground. It has been restored by Patricia Rebraca with great imagination and care. There are seven lavishly decorated guest rooms in the mansion itself, all with telephones, some with fireplaces. Each has a rich color palette of its own and contains fine antique furnishings and fabrics. The most extravagant boasts a hand-painted French armoire, a large ormolu mirror, a Persian rug, and a four-poster bed dressed with a richly patterned antique silk coverlet and a Battenburg lace canopy. The Lafayette is enriched by a rare Aubusson carpet of ecru, claret, and moss green, while the Vanderbilt boasts a marquetry bed and an ebony enameled Napoléon tub and chaise longue; several possess beautiful views. Six rooms are located in the carriage house, and there are also four smaller rooms that are offered at reduced rates because of their size. All are nicely furnished, though, with Early American furniture and other antiques and folk art. The beds are covered with quilts and the pillows sport lace-fringed linens. A full breakfast is served by the fireside in the dining room or in the gazebo overlooking the fountain and pond. Facilities include an outdoor pool. *Rates* (including breakfast): Mansion, $185 to $205 double; carriage house, $105 to $155; and $75 to $95 in smaller rooms.

Rhinebeck does have some B&Bs, but they seem to come and go, so your best bet, if you're looking for this type of accommodation, would be to contact the Rhinebeck Chamber of Commerce, 19 Mill St. (P.O. Box 42), Rhinebeck, NY 12572 (☎ 914/876-4778).

RHINEBECK DINING

Besides the **Beekman Arms** (see above), for an atmospheric place for lunch, dinner, or Sunday brunch, there are several choices.

Just around the corner is **Le Petit Bistro**, 8 E. Market St. (☎ 914/876-7400), a charming and thoroughly French restaurant, right down to the lace curtains in the windows. The cuisine is classic French—but the restaurant's most popular dishes are the roast duck with black currants, the rack of lamb, and the frogs' legs Provençcale. Prices range from $15 to $24. Start with the smoked trout or pâté and finish with the crème brûlée or marquise au chocolat. *Hours:* Sunday 4 to 9pm, and Thursday to Monday 5 to 10pm.

For breakfast or lunch, head for **Schemmy's**, 19 E. Market St. (☎ 914/876-6215), a genuine old-fashioned drugstore now operating as a restaurant, coffee shop, and soda fountain. It has a fun atmosphere. *Hours:* Summer, Monday to Thursday 8am to 8pm, Friday to Saturday 8am to 10pm, Sunday 8am to 9pm. Winter hours are usually shortened to 5pm.

RED HOOK LODGING & DINING

The **Red Hook Inn**, 31 S. Broadway, Red Hook, NY 12571 (☎ 914/758-8445; fax 914/758-2239), has been pleasantly restored in colonial style. There are five rooms, all with baths and furnished with antique country pieces; some have fireplaces. In the dining room (with a blazing hearth in winter), the menu features contemporary American cuisine with traces of Thai and Italian inspiration. For example, among the main dishes you might find crispy skinned salmon with lemongrass and Thai lime leaf sauce, or roast duck confit with lotus leaf–steamed sticky rice, plus a dish like roast free-range Cornish game hen with basil, served with garlic mashed potatoes. Prices range from $13 to $19.

The innkeepers have opened a gourmet takeout called **Susan's** (☎ 914/758-0435) at the rear of the inn where they sell their house-smoked salmon and trout and their own sausages, plus charcuterie and local cheeses. This is one place to pick up some picnic ingredients.

Rates (including breakfast on weekends): $85 to $135 double. *Dining hours:* Tuesday to Saturday 5 to 10pm, Sunday 11am to 3pm and 4 to 9pm.

In nearby Tivoli (see below), **Santa Fe** (☎ 914/757-4100) is one of the most happening places in the valley and the best place to secure spicy Southwestern cuisine. What makes the food extra-special are the local ingredients, used in such dishes as the quesadilla with sun-dried tomatoes and Pine Plains Coach Farm goat cheese. Another great appetizer is the quesadilla with Baja shrimp and spinach. Among the entrees are mole poblano (char-grilled chicken breast with mole sauce); a delicious Mazatlan pork loin made with caramelized onions, mushrooms, and tomatillo sauce; or, for a change of pace, shrimp satay in a ginger-curry peanut sauce with sweet plantains. Otherwise, there are plenty of enchiladas, tacos, and burritos to enjoy. Prices range from $7 to $13. The wall and furniture colors are brilliant, and the atmosphere is lively. Entertainment is provided late on Saturday. *Hours:* Tuesday to Sunday 5 to 10pm.

RHINEBECK AFTER DARK

Upstate Films, 26 Montgomery St. (☎ 914/876-2515), shows American independent films as well as foreign-language movies and old classics. It features a great guest speaker/director series, too.

FROM RHINEBECK/RED HOOK TO HUDSON

AREA ATTRACTIONS

Tivoli

From Red Hook you can take Route 199 west to link up with Route 103, which will take you to Bard College (see the previous section). From Bard you can continue up Route 9G to the turnoff to Tivoli, a small town worth a brief stop to browse a handful of stores. The town itself has an interesting history. Originally it was meant to be a model community. It was designed by Charles Balthazar Julien Fevret de Saint Menin, a courtier of King Louis XVI who gave the streets such names as Friendship, Liberty, Plenty, and Peace. The scheme collapsed and the local squire Livingston bought the whole town in foreclosure. Several generations of Livingstons rest in the graveyard behind St. Paul's on Wood Road. Stop and linger a while at the antiques store, the bookstore, the artist's co-op, and the De Peyser gallery (in a church on Broadway).

Clermont

From Tivoli, a shaded bucolic road leads to one of the great Hudson River estates, Clermont. The **Clermont State Historic Site** (☎ 518/537-4240) is a historic park affording glorious views of the river from its gardens. It's one of the many Livingston family estates. The founder of this important family arrived from Scotland in 1673. Thirteen years later, at the age of 32, he had amassed a 160,000-acre estate along the Hudson and erected a manor. He bequeathed a 13,000-acre corner of this estate to his third son, Robert, who built Clermont. Robert's son was Robert R. Livingston (1746–1813), one of the signers of the Declaration of Independence. He also attended the Continental Congress and administered the oath of office to President George Washington.

He also helped his son-in-law, Robert Fulton, invent the first steamboat, the *Clermont*. Fulton's folly, as his steamboat was called, stopped here on its maiden voyage on August 18, 1807. It had set out 24 hours earlier from the foot of West Tenth Street in Manhattan on its journey up the Hudson to Albany. The sidewheeler made its way slowly north, "a monster moving up the river defying wind and tide and breathing flames and smoke," as one bystander wrote. After stopping overnight at Clermont, it proceeded the next morning to Albany, where it arrived at the end of its 36-hour journey.

The Clermont estate remained in the Livingston family from 1728 until 1962, when it was acquired by the state. The house has been restored to its 1730 appearance. The gardens are lovely, especially in spring when the magnolias are in bloom and the lilac walk leading to the house is glorious. The walk winds past the ice house, where ice cut from the river was once stored. The grounds provide a glorious riverside site for picnicking; for your picnic supplies, stop in Red Hook or nearby Tivoli. You can find good cross-country skiing here as well.

Hours: House, April 1 to October 31, Tuesday to Sunday 11am to 4:30pm; November 1 to December 15, Saturday and Sunday 11am to 4:30pm. Closed mid-December to March 31. Grounds, year-round, daily 8:30am to sunset. *Admission:* $3 adults, $2 seniors, $1 children ages 5 to 12.

Olana

Just south of Hudson is **Olana** (☎ 518/828-0135), artist Frederic Church's magnificently idiosyncratic home, which has been meticulously restored to even the most minute detail in an effort to recapture his vision and intention. It stands at a superb location overlooking the famous bend in the river that still looks just as it did when it was painted by the artist. Church was meticulous and planned every detail of the exterior and interior of the house as well as the landscaping. The restoration is a fitting tribute to a man who had so great a passion for design that he drew 200 sketches of the staircase alone. He also selected every tree on the property and laid out a lake at the bottom of the hill specifically to mirror and balance the Hudson.

Church (1826–1900) came from a very wealthy New England family. His father, a silversmith, paper-mill owner, and banker who was on the board of Aetna Insurance, was appalled at his son's desire to become a landscape artist and agreed to let him become apprenticed to Thomas Cole only because Cole was deeply religious. Because the decor of the house has been maintained as an authentic period creation, the many artworks are not displayed to maximum advantage, but on the walls hang many of Church's masterpieces or sketches for them—*Twilight in the Wilderness, Niagara,* the *Memorial* paintings, *Sunrise and Moonrise,* and *Pilgrim in the Valley of the Shadow of Death.*

The 37-room house was built between 1870 and 1874, soon after a visit Church made to Persia and the Near East. Inspired by Near Eastern culture, he incorporated many Persian elements into the decor—like gold- and silver-stenciled doors and richly colored and decorated patterned tiles for the fireplaces. The doorway bears the inscription "Mahaba," meaning "welcome." Throughout the house, Church exhibited his painterly instincts by his use of color—in the vestibule, a vivid purple on the walls and pumpkin on the ceiling, and in the Court Hall, a pink ceiling that's echoed by the Erastus Dow Palmer roundels on the walls.

Much of the furniture was shipped from Persia and other faraway places: for example, painted chairs from Kashmir and 10-sided tables of mother-of-pearl from Syria. The Court Hall, where the lower landing was used as a stage by the family, reflects Church's careful attention to detail. Light from the golden staircase window, which Church created by using yellow paper, gives the effect of sunshine falling on the brass banister; the ombra arch window is placed to capture the "spectacular moment in Nature"—the famous bend in the Hudson River. Toward the end of the century, Church paid several visits to Mexico, and in his studio is piled a wonderful collection of sombreros and pre-Columbian Mexican pottery. His wife used to play the piano here to stimulate his creative inspiration.

Outside, you can walk down to the informal scatter garden that blooms in harmonious confusion below the walls encircling the mound on which the house is built. Linger a while and perhaps spread out a picnic. Better yet, join one of Olana's special period picnics attended by magicians and other entertainers. Christmas is also a good time to visit, when the house is authentically decorated according to late-Victorian custom and with appropriate musical accompaniment.

Hours: House tours (mandatory), April 1 to November 1, Wednesday to Sunday first tour at 10am and last at 5pm. Reservations recommended. *Admission:* $3 adults, $1 children ages 5 to 12.

HUDSON

HUDSON ATTRACTIONS

From Olana, you can continue up Route 9G into the former whaling town of Hudson. It has a gritty air, which it has earned over the years. Settled in 1783 by whalers from Nantucket and New Bedford, by 1790, Hudson had 25 registered schooners working in sealing, whaling, and the West Indian trade. An industrial town producing machinery, woolen knits, ginger ale, shirts, and matches (plus cement from a plant outside of town), it also developed a reputation for bawdy houses. Historic homes dating from the 19th century line the main street, many with elegant doorways and elaborate cornices testifying to Hudson's earlier wealth. At the western end of the main street, Parade Hill river promenade (1795) offers great river views, but has fallen into a sorry state of decay. The other end of the street, however, is booming, having become a mecca for antiques hunters who flock to store after store brimming with beautiful, immaculate, and expensive antiques and fine art. A couple of names to look for are **Sutter Antiques** at 556 Warren St. (☎ 518/822-0729) and **British Accent** at 537 Warren St. (☎ 518/828-2800).

Another major attraction besides all the antiques stores is the **American Museum of Firefighting,** on Harry Howard Avenue (☎ 518/828-7695 for information). Although it may not seem that enthralling a prospect initially, the museum is marvelous, boasting fascinating collections and equally fascinating guides—retired firefighters like Bill Rhodes who have "lived" through much of what they explain.

This museum houses one of the largest collections of its kind in the country. Among the old fire engines are the first mobile fire wagon, which was used from 1725 to 1879, standing on wooden wheels with steel bands and an 1846 double-decker engine of hand-carved and painted wood with copper hubcaps that required 45 men to operate. Later models are steam powered, many made by La France Company in Elmira, N.Y., and used locally. Favorites include Hercules, an 1882 horse-drawn steamer built to travel on trolley tracks (it was last used in 1940) and the 1870 Clapp and Jones Steamer, built in Hudson, which vibrated (or "walked") so much that it had to be staked down or tied to a tree.

Around the walls, display cases hold uniforms, helmets, medals, badges, and other memorabilia. But the pièce de résistance appears at the end of the tour—a beautiful 1890 parade carriage with 68-inch wheels. Its reel is finished in etched mirrors and supported on each side by two silver-plated lions couchant. Over the reel stands a fireman holding a child and trumpet. The lamps and other artistic details are also elaborate.

Hours: Daily 9am to 4:30pm. *Admission:* Free.

The Daughters of the American Revolution operate a museum at the 1811 **Robert Jenkins House,** 113 Warren St. (☎ 518/828-9764). Works by Hudson River artists—Henry Ary, Bert Phillips, Arthur and Ernest Parton—are on display along with other local memorabilia, including items documenting the town's whaling heritage. *Hours:* July to August, Sunday and Monday 1 to 3pm. *Admission:* $2.50 adults, $2 seniors, free for children ages 11 and under.

For evening entertainment, the recently refurbished and reopened **Hudson Opera House** is at 327 Warren St. (☎ 518/822-1438).

HUDSON DINING

Try **Charleston,** 517 Warren St. (☎ 518/828-4990), an attractive restaurant that offers eclectic American cuisine. The menu changes frequently, but it always features a good number of local products. For example, among the popular appetizers is Rawson Brook Farm chèvre with field greens, roasted beets, and garlic croutons; smoked trout with mustard-dill sauce; and grilled portobello mushrooms on orzo salad. The cuisine is inspired by several different traditions. Among the entrees I recommend the grilled diver sea scallops with a spicy ginger vinaigrette or the seared Chilean sea bass with thyme, lemon, and caper sauce. The rack of lamb is given an extra fillip by the addition of rhubarb and fresh mint sauce. Prices range from $14 to $25. Note that on Monday nights some authentic Mexican cuisine is offered. Expect to enjoy such dishes as roast halibut with tomato, black olives, onions, garlic, and herbs or piccadillo Oaxaqueno, which are chiles poblano stuffed with a tasty mixture of pork, raisins, almonds, and sweet Mexican spices. *Hours:* Thursday 11:30am to 3pm and 5:30 to 9:30pm, Friday and Saturday 11:30am to 3pm and 5:30 to 10pm, Sunday noon to 4pm and 4:30 to 9pm.

FROM HUDSON TO OLD CHATHAM

AREA ATTRACTIONS

Turning away from the river will bring you into the communities and towns that were originally settled by Dutch and English farmers, who then amassed great wealth from the flocks of sheep and livestock that once roamed and grazed here. One of the Dutch families who made good in this farming county was the Van Buren family, and on Route 9H, 2 miles south of Kinderhook, stands **Lindenwald** (☎ 518/758-9689). This is the home to which Martin Van Buren retired, and it has been restored to its 1850–62 appearance.

Van Buren was born in 1782 in Kinderhook, where his father ran a tavern on Hudson Street. He left in 1801 to study law in New York City; there he met Aaron Burr and DeWitt Clinton, among others, who helped launch his political career. "The Red Fox of Old Kinderhook" managed to climb from state politics to the White House as the nation's eighth president (1837–1841). Lindenwald, acquired by Van Buren in 1839, is an odd-looking hodgepodge of Federal, Italianate, and Gothic Revival styles. It was once the hub of a 220-acre farm surrounded by apple and pear orchards. Van Buren's son is responsible for the way it looks today—he asked Richard Upjohn, "the great architectural oracle," to embellish the 1797 colonial original with gables, dormers, cornices, and an Italianate tower (of all the additions, the tower looks most like an afterthought).

Still, the whole has an oddly romantic air. In the entrance hall are 51 original French wallpaper panels that form a mural-like hunting scene. The Van Buren political and personal memorabilia includes busts, portraits, the accoutrements he used to maintain his immaculate grooming, and the room in which he died. He is buried in the Kinderhook Reformed Cemetery on Albany Avenue, a fitting location for a man who, in response to Queen Victoria when she asked about his roots, stated "Kinderhook, ma'am."

Hours: Mid-April to October, daily 9am to 4pm; November to December 5, Wednesday to Sunday 9am to 4:30pm. Closed Thanksgiving and December 6 to mid-April. The grounds are open year-round. *Admission:* $2 adults, free for children ages 16 and under.

Just off Route 9H in Kinderhook, the **Van Alen House** (☎ 518/758-9265) is worth visiting to see a modest Dutch home dating to 1737 and the collection of Hudson Valley paintings that it contains. The house consists of two rooms and a garret under a pitched gable, and it was the home of Helen Van Alen, who is said to have been Washington Irving's model for Katrina Van Tassel in *The Legend of Sleepy Hollow.* The house is especially lovely in spring, when a special flower festival is celebrated. *Hours:* Memorial Day to Labor Day, Thursday to Saturday 11am to 5pm, Sunday 1 to 5pm; the rest of the year, by appointment. *Admission:* $3 adults, $2 seniors and children ages 12 to 18.

From Kinderhook, winding country roads lead to several charming small towns. In the tiny hamlet of Malden Bridge, there seems to be only one commercial building, the absolutely winning antiques store, **Wonderful Things Antiques**, owned by an equally entrancing owner. Inside, wend your way around and between a brilliant assembly of extraordinarily eye-catching objects from all over the world.

On Route 9H in Claverack, stop by **Hotalings Farm Market** (☎ 518/851-9864) at any time of year. It always has a great display at harvest time, when you'll find bushels of all kinds of apples, raspberries, cherries, pumpkins, gourds, and much more.

OLD CHATHAM ATTRACTIONS

From Kinderhook it's a short trip to Old Chatham, which boasts a fine old inn and, across the street from it, a **Shaker Museum**, Shaker Museum Road (☎ 518/794-9100), formed from the collection amassed by John S. Williams. The museum consists of eight buildings, including several workshops that display the woodworking, weaving, and gardening skills of all the different communities of Shakers from New England to Ohio and Kentucky. It's not on the site of a Shaker community, and for this reason it takes a more comprehensive approach to Shaker culture and art. The study collection has more than 32,500 items from different Shaker communities. There is also a library, bookstore, and gift store. *Hours:* May to October, Wednesday to Monday 10am to 5pm; November to mid-December, the gift shop is open Saturday and Sunday 10am to 5pm for Christmas shopping. *Admission:* $8 adults, $7 seniors, $4 children ages 6 to 17.

OLD CHATHAM LODGING & DINING

Old Chatham Sheepherding Company Inn, Shaker Museum Road, Old Chatham, NY 12136 (☎ 518/794-9774; fax 518/794-9779; e-mail: oldsheepinn@worldnet.att.net), occupies a lovely 500-acre setting looking out across wooded hills and sheep-dotted pastures. The 1790s Georgian house surrounded by lovely gardens contains six guest rooms and several intimate dining rooms, which offer some of the finest cuisine in the area in a relaxed yet gracious, pampering atmosphere. The house was once the home of the renowned Shaker art collector John S. Williams, but is now owned by Tom and Nancy Clark. The accommodations are either in the main inn, the Cottage, the Carriage House, or the Barn. All have private baths and are furnished in grand style, with most featuring four-poster beds, along with original art, oriental rugs, and sumptuously upholstered furnishings. The most secluded rooms are the two cottage rooms, with private decks and lovely views over the farm. The Cotswold Suite has a working fireplace and a luxurious red tub, and can accommodate four. The Carriage House contains two super suites with working fireplaces and high beamed ceilings. Terraces look over the kitchen gardens to the hills beyond. Guests also enjoy the parlors, furnished with authentic but comfortable antiques. Guests start the day with a lavish breakfast that might include such appetizing dishes as pumpkin pecan waffles or a farmer's omelet filled with potatoes, leeks, and sheep's-milk cheese. Afternoon tea is also available.

In the restaurant, the cuisine makes maximum use of local ingredients, which are prepared simply to bring out their natural flavors by Chef Melissa Kelly. The naturally raised lamb and sheep's milk come from the adjoining farm, while the Camembert is made in the Hudson Valley along with the foie gras. Signature dishes include a wonderful tapenade-crusted rack of lamb; cedar-planked salmon in a Chardonnay–grain mustard sauce; free-range chicken breast stuffed with spinach, currants, and fresh sheep's ricotta; and a grilled New York strip steak served with Gorgonzola, onion jam, and rösti potato cake. Prices range from $18 to $24. To start with, try their own farm-fresh Camembert crisp served with cherry gooseberry chutney, venison prosciutto, and walnut levain croutons. Among the desserts, try the sheep's-milk ice cream or the candied pumpkin filled with crème brûlée.

Rates: $170 to $370. *Dining hours:* Sunday 10am to 2pm and 5 to 9pm, Wednesday to Saturday and Monday 5:30 to 9:30pm.

CHATHAM AFTER DARK

The **MacHaydn Theater** (☎ 518/392-9292) in Chatham (not Old Chatham) is one of the finest summer stock theaters around. It features musicals from Memorial Day to Labor Day. Call for schedules and ticket information.

East Bank
Special & Recreational Activities

Antiquing: The greatest concentrations of stores are in Millbrook, in Hyde Park at the **Hyde Park Antiques Center,** in Rhinebeck at the Beekman Arms barn, and (the star of them all) along the main street of Hudson.

Ballooning: Blue Sky Balloons, 246 Mountain Rd., Pleasant Valley (☎ 914/635-2461), charges $175 per person for a 1-hour hot-air balloon ride. Best time to go is between April and October, although they do operate the rest of the year provided that the weather is cooperating. **American Balloon Works** operates out of Kinderhook (☎ 518/766-5111).

Boating: Row and paddleboats can be rented in **Lake Taghkanic State Park,** Route 82, in Ancram (☎ 518/851-3631); and **Taconic State Park,** Rudd Pond Area, off Route 22 in Millerton (☎ 518/789-3059), where rowboats are available.

Camping: The best camping is in the state parks, open from mid-May to October: **Lake Taghkanic State Park,** Route 82, Ancram, NY 12502 (☎ 518/851-3631), offers 51 sites, swimming, fishing, and boat rentals; **Taconic State Park,** Copake Falls area, Route 344, Copake Falls, NY 12517 (☎ 518/329-3993), has 112 sites that stay open until mid-December, plus swimming and fishing; the **Rudd Pond area,** also in Taconic State Park, on Route 22, Millerton, NY 12546 (☎ 518/789-3059), has 41 sites and the most facilities, including a camp store and recreation building; **Margaret Lewis Norrie State Park,** Route 9, Hyde Park, NY 12538 (☎ 914/889-4646), offers fishing and a children's area. The basic fee for all is around $13 a night.

Canoeing/Kayaking: Atlantic Kayak Tours, 320 W. Saugerties Rd., Saugerties, NY 12477 (☎ 914/246-2187), offers a variety of kayaking tours in the Hudson Valley and elsewhere on the East Coast. It also provides instructional classes.

Cross-Country Skiing: You can enjoy this at **Clermont, Olana, Lake Taghkanic State Park,** and **Mills-Norrie State Park.**

Fishing: At **Lake Taghkanic** (☎ 518/851-3631); at **Taconic State Park,** both the Rudd Pond and the Copake Falls areas; and at **Norrie State Park** (☎ 914/889-4646).

Fruit Picking: Philip Orchards, Route 9H, Claverack (☎ 518/851-6351), for apples, pears, and plums; **Greig Farm**, on Pitcher Lane, north of Red Hook off Route 9 (☎ 914/758-5762), for asparagus, peas, raspberries, strawberries, blueberries, apples, and cut-your-own flowers.

Golf: Dinsmore Golf Club, right off Route 9 in Staatsburg (☎ 914/889-4071 or 914/889-4751), with a panoramic view of the Hudson, charges $10 for nine holes, $19 for 18 holes; **James Baird State Park Golf Course**, Freedom Road, Pleasant Valley (☎ 914/452-1489), offers an 18-hole course and a driving range and charges $20 on weekends for a round.

Hiking: James Baird State Park, LaGrange; **Norrie Point State Park**, Hyde Park; **Lake Taghkanic State Park**, Route 82, Ancram. For more information on the state parks, contact the Taconic Region, Staatsburg, NY 12570 (☎ 914/889-4100), or the main office at New York State Office of Parks, Recreation and Historic Preservation, 1 Empire State Plaza, Albany, NY 12238 (☎ 518/474-0456).

Picnicking: Along the banks of the Hudson are several magnificent picnicking spots, all granting views over this river. Starting at the farthest south, there's the **Mills mansion** in Staatsburg, 5 miles south of Rhinebeck, where you can pick up your supplies in one of the many delis or super-markets. Just north of Rhinebeck in Germantown, at Clermont, is **the home of Robert R. Livingston**, where the rolling parklands and gardens are open from 8:30am to sunset daily, year-round. Pick up supplies in nearby Red Hook (there's a deli on the corner at the main crossroads). Finally, at **Frederic Church's Olana**, you can picnic high on a hill overlooking the bend in the river that he made famous. Olana even organizes occasional period picnics at which people arrive dressed in costume and are entertained in a 19th-century manner with magicians, jugglers, and so on.

Skiing: Catamount Ski Area in Hillsdale (see the "Central Berkshires & Pioneer Valley" chapter, later in this book).

Swimming: Lake Taghkanic, Taconic State Park—Rudd Pond, and Copake Falls areas.

Tennis: Call the individual chambers of commerce for information. Most public schools open their courts to the public in the evenings and on weekends. Public parks sometimes have courts, too. In Hudson you can play at **Hudson's Columbia-Greene Community College** by the Rip Van Winkle Bridge.

THE WEST BANK

The west side of the Hudson River offers several towns that are gateways to the Catskill Mountains. Here you'll find an assortment of accommodations, ranging from bed-and-breakfasts and motels to the impressive Mohonk Mountain House. But first, let's examine the things there are to see and do.

NEW PALTZ, HIGH FALLS &
LAKE MINNEWASKA

AREA ATTRACTIONS

At its western edge, New Paltz boasts **Huguenot Street,** a National Historic Landmark District that incorporates the "oldest street in America with its original houses"—five stone houses, all built before 1720 above the banks of the Wallkill River. The original land grant was made by royal patent to a group of French refugees in May 1677.

The most notable house is the **Hasbrouck House,** an outstanding example of Flemish stone architecture, built in 1712 by Jean Hasbrouck, who is reputed to have served in the British army and to have been a friend of Governor Edmund Andros. (The kitchen was the scene of many a cockfight.) For over 250 years these houses have passed from one generation to the next of the original Duzine, the 12 men who founded this community. They named it *Die Pfalz* after the temporary refuge they had found in the Palatinate during years of exile from their native France. The historic district also includes the French church and burying ground, plus a Federal-period house and late Victorian house. *Hours:* Saturday and Sunday 10am to 4pm. *Admission:* $3 adults, $2 seniors, students, and children ages 5 to 12.

The Hasbrouck house is usually included on the tours given by the **Huguenot Historical Society,** 18 Broadhead Ave. (☎ 914/255-1660 or 914/255-1889), which maintains the district. Tours are given from early May to October 31 from Tuesday to Sunday. There are three tours: The complete tour takes 3 hours and visits all six houses and the church; it leaves only at 9am and 1pm and costs $10 for adults, $9 for seniors, and $5 for children ages 5 to 12. The regular tour takes 2 hours, visits two houses and the French church, leaves between 9am and 2pm, and costs $6 for adults, $5 for seniors, and $3 for children ages 5 to 12. The one-house tour leaves between 9am and 3pm and costs $3 for adults, $2 for seniors, and $2 for children ages 5 to 12. Tours start from Deyo Hall.

The society also maintains the **Howard Hasbrouck Grimm Gallery** and a museum, both open to the public free of charge. *Hours:* Memorial Day to October 1, Wednesday to Sunday 9:30am to 4pm; October 2 to 31, Saturday and Sunday 9:30am to 4pm; the rest of the year by appointment.

At the **D&H Canal Museum,** on Mohonk Road in neighboring High Falls (☎ 914/687-9311), you can view the brief history—from 1828 to 1898—of the 108-mile-long Delaware-Hudson Canal, built in 1825 to ship coal from Pennsylvania to the Hudson River and from there to New York City. By the 1870s its role was usurped by the railroads. Maps, photographs, dioramas, working models of canal locks, and a replica of the suspension aqueduct by John Roebling (of Brooklyn Bridge fame) tell the story. If you like, you can walk to locks 16 to 20, which were built in 1847 when the canal was enlarged to accommodate 140-ton boats. Each lock dropped the canal an average of 12.6 feet. Ask for information at the museum. *Hours:* Memorial Day to Labor Day, Monday and Thursday to Saturday 11am to 5pm, Sunday 1 to 5pm; May and September to October, Saturday and Sunday 1 to 5pm; November to April, Saturday 9am to 5pm. *Admission:* $2 adults, $1 children ages 6 to 13.

A little farther up the road, the **gristmill** at the base of the falls is another fun place to visit.

From New Paltz, it's a short distance along Route 299 to the brilliant turquoise **Lake Minnewaska** (☎ 914/255-0752), set atop the Shawangunk Mountains and rimmed by a forest of high hemlocks. A resort once functioned here. Today it's a state park open for day use only, providing opportunities for hiking, swimming, canoeing, and picnicking. Entry to the area is $4 on weekends. In winter, you can ski 40 miles of cross-country trails, past frozen waterfalls and streams, between snow-covered hemlocks to points with views over the Hudson Highlands, Berkshires, and Catskills. Ski rentals are available.

AN EXTRA-SPECIAL NEW PALTZ LODGING

Perched on the shore of a turquoise-blue lake high in the Shawangunk Mountains on 2,200 spectacular acres, the historic **Mohonk Mountain House**, New Paltz, NY 12561 (☎ 800/772-6646 or 914/255-1000; fax 914/256-2100; www.mohonk.com), is an attraction in itself. It's such a beautiful, inspiring place that if you don't enjoy a wonderful weekend here you should check your vital signs. A 2-mile drive through curving, wooded lanes brings you to a large, rambling, primarily stone structure capped by towers that looks out over the Rondout Valley. From the rockers or mission settees on the veranda, which wraps around the back, you can gaze across the crystalline mountain lake, surrounded by craggy rocks and dotted with gazebos, and contemplate the stillness of eventide. This is the last of the many fine resorts that once dotted the area and attracted wealthy vacationers. It has retained its Victorian flavor, with shuttered windows, oak pieces, and mantels in the 261 rooms, and old-fashioned bathroom fittings, including tubs that actually come with footstools. The grounds are a delight any time of year, but especially in summer, at spring blossom time, and in early June, when the surrounding acres are aglow with pink and white mountain laurel. A magical spot where visitors are asked to drive slowly and quietly up the approach road "to harmonize with nature," the whole place exudes a sense of tranquillity, contemplation, love of nature, and reverence for life.

In short, it still bears some resemblance to the original idea of its Quaker founders and teachers, Albert and Alfred Smiley, who established the house in 1869 as a place where "like-minded people can gather to savor the earth and the sky." Their educational mission continues today in more than 40 programs that are operated during the year. These programs cover a variety of subjects: nature, holistic healing, mystery writing, film, food, jazz, gardening, hiking, tennis, dancing, and much more. In summer there's even a 6-week-long festival of the arts. Mohonk also offers a tremendous range of activities— six tennis courts, racquetball, platform tennis, horseback riding (April to October), nine-hole golf, swimming, boating, canoeing, fishing, lawn bowling, putting, croquet, snowshoeing and ice-skating in winter, and 85 miles of nature trails, including 35 miles of cross-country skiing trails.

Some of the famous visitors here include John Burroughs, Andrew Carnegie, and presidents Teddy Roosevelt, William Taft, Rutherford Hayes, and Chester Arthur. This was also the site of the famous conference on Indian Affairs and International Arbitration between 1883 and the outbreak of World War I. Photographs of these gatherings and of prominent visitors line the corridors.

Meals are served in the incredible oak-columned and -ceilinged dining room that seats 500. The food is well prepared and there's plenty of it. The menu, which features about eight entrees, changes daily. You'll find such dishes as steamed halibut with lemon caper cream, veal chops with tequila-lime butter sauce, strip steak with port wine sauce, and other flavorful dishes. Appetizers and desserts are equally appealing. Though there's no bar, liquor is available at dinner. Guests also enjoy wares sold in the old-fashioned ice-cream parlor and soda fountain.

Rates (including breakfast, lunch, afternoon tea, and dinner): $305 to $425 double with sink, $450 to $575 double with bath; $450 to $515 suites/junior suites; $360 to $450 rooms with balcony and fireplace. For children ages 4 to 12, add $65. There are special charges for some activities. You can be met at the Adirondack Trailways at New Paltz or at the railroad station in Poughkeepsie. On most weekends 2- or 3-day minimum stays are required.

new PALTZ AReA Bed & BReAKFASTS

The old stone house known as **Baker's**, 24 Old Kings Hwy., Stone Ridge, NY 12484 (☎ 914/687-9795; fax 914/687-4153), off Route 209 just south of town, was built in 1780 and commands a magnificent view that has remained unspoiled since the days when the highway was the primary east-west route (before the canal was constructed). The house then served as a stopping place for travelers; Doug Baker and Linda Delgado continue that tradition today. This is the seventh house that Doug has restored with care and artistry; he even installed the Rumford-style fireplace, which has a high inner hearth and fire box and a tiny 5-by-5-inch-hole flue opening. The house is furnished with Early American hutches, 18th-century Dutch-German wing chairs in the parlor, and other Early American and Federal pieces.

There are six guest rooms, all with private baths, and one suite with a sitting room, TV, and wood-burning stove. They have beamed ceilings, wide-board floors, stencil decorations, and cannonball beds with real down comforters. Linda, who teaches and functions as a counselor at the local college, turns out fine breakfasts of juice, fresh fruit, and a variety of dishes like venison medallions, ham poached in homemade maple syrup, smoked trout, and the more usual egg dishes. Attached to the side of the house is a solarium/greenhouse where they've installed a hot tub. The pond provides skating or swimming and also some nice black bass. Chickens, ducks, and geese roam the property, while cows graze peacefully on the adjacent 20 acres. *Rates* (including breakfast): $108 double, $148 suite.

Captain Schoonmaker's B&B, 913 Rte. 213, High Falls, NY 12440 (☎ 914/ 687-7946), is situated on 8½ acres with two waterfalls and the remains of a stone gristmill. It occupies a 1760 stone house that has been immaculately restored. Current innkeepers Judy and Bill Klock offer four guest rooms in the post-and-beam barn, each with a private balcony overlooking the trout stream. The rooms share two baths. In the evenings, wine is served by the fire in the solarium, which was created around an old well whose stone now serves as a coffee table. A full breakfast is also served in the handsome dining room, which has the original fireplace. *Rates* (including breakfast): $100 double.

Just outside New Paltz, **Ujjala's**, 2 Forest Glen Rd., New Paltz, NY 12561 (☎ 914/255-6360; fax 914/256-1409; www.ujjalasbnb.com), offers accommo-dations with a distinctly personalized flavor, for Ujjala herself specializes in holistic health and teaches stress management—but only if you feel you need it, of course. Boy, is she kidding! A stay at her sunny Victorian home nestled among apple, pear, and quince trees on 4½ acres should amply restore your spirit. All the rooms (two with bath, two with shared bath) are prettily decorated and greet you with a bowl of fruit and nuts upon your arrival. The large skylit living room has a fireplace and a sitting room. The large country kitchen with an outside deck for summer breakfasts is filled with plants and life—in fact, the whole house is. Ujjala also tends a bountiful vegetable garden. Breakfast usually offers fresh fruits, granola, homemade bread, omelets, and crêpes. To get there, take Route 208 south off Route 299 for 3½ miles, passing Dressel farms on the right. Take the second right onto Forest Glen Road. The house is the second on the left. *Rates* (including breakfast): $100 with private bath to $95 shared bath, $120 in winter for fireplace room.

Jingle Bell Farm, 1 Forest Glen Rd., New Paltz, NY 12561 (☎ 914/255-6588), occupies a lovely 1776 stone house with dormer windows. It's owned and operated by Julie Christman, who took up innkeeping after a celebrated career as a cabaret artist giving performances in all the great New York hotels and with Perry Como and Kate Smith at Carnegie Hall. She also performed thousands of "jingles" for all kinds of advertisements, hence the name of the farm. There are four beautifully decorated rooms. The Master Room is the most elaborate and features an unusual scallop-shell art deco bed plus loads of books. Upstairs, the Rose Room contains a brass bed, whereas the Canopy Room sports a canopied bed and chintz-rose decor. A hand-painted cottage set graces the Cottage Room. Guests can relax in two elegantly furnished parlors with fireplaces and pianos. A full breakfast featuring a main dish like omelets and pancakes is served by candlelight. The beautifully landscaped pool is a lovely haven in summer. *Rates:* $125 to $135 double.

STONE RIDGE & HIGH FALLS LODGING & DINING

The **Inn at Stone Ridge,** P.O. Box 76, Stone Ridge, NY 12484 (☎ 914/687-0736), occupies a beautifully mellow Dutch colonial stone mansion known as the Hasbrouck House, set on 40 acres of lawns, gardens, and woods. The guest rooms are furnished with antiques. The public areas include a large guest parlor featuring a full-size billiard table, a sitting room with a library, and a TV room. Milliways Restaurant offers modern American cuisine served either in the formal dining room or in the tavern and Jefferson Room. About 10 main courses, each using super-fresh ingredients, are well prepared in a traditional way with the occasional Asian accent. For example, there might be lemongrass-marinated free-range chicken breast with ginger-lime dipping sauce, or New York strip steak with shiitake-Madeira sauce. In season, expect to find such dishes as roasted pheasant with apple and corn relish. The fish dishes are also special, like the grilled halibut Florentine with braised fennel. Prices range from $16 to $25. The Sunday buffet brunch (with omelets and other egg dishes cooked to order) is a good value at $17. The tavern menu offers a full selection of sandwiches plus such popular items as nachos, quesadillas, and chicken pot pie. *Rates:* $70 to $105 double with shared bath, $155 suite with shared bath, $135 double with private bath. *Dining hours:* Wednesday to Saturday 11:30am to 2:30pm, Sunday 10:30am to 2:30pm; Wednesday to Sunday 5 to 10pm.

At the **De Puy Canal House**, Route 213, High Falls (☎ 914/687-7700 or 914/687-7777), dining is treated as an art. This landmark 1797 stone house was built by Simeon De Puy, who catered to the needs of the barge workers and is recalled by memorabilia throughout the tavern rooms with their polished wide-plank floors and multiple fireplaces. Here Chef John Novi has been able to combine his two great passions—history and food. Since 1969, when he opened this revered restaurant, he has helped put Hudson Valley cuisine on the map and earned himself four stars from the *New York Times*. He uses a lot of local, organically raised ingredients and prepares them in exciting, inventive ways. The menu is always seasonal and well balanced, offering a selection of game, fish, shellfish, veal, and other meats along with a vegetarian option. You might start your meal with one of several superb soups—caramelized leek and three-mushroom (shiitake, portobello, and straw)—or a delicious pâté made with smoked salmon, capers, and mango and served with sweet-and-sour rhubarb sauce and yellow pepper puree. Among the 10 or so entrees there might be grilled beef tenderloin and 2-year-old-brandy black fig served on porcini-mushroom sake sauce, or quail served with blackberry and white cherry on two-berry barbecue sauce, or frito misto with steamed lobster scallop and bluefish served traditionally with fried chocolate pudding on a Creole sauce. Prices range from $21 to $32. Several prix-fixe menus are offered—a $35 three-course, $46 four-course, and a $58 seven-course. The most luscious dessert is the chocolate-brandy soufflé with chocolate-custard sauce. *Hours:* February 14 to December, Thursday to Saturday 5:30 to 9:30pm, Sunday 11:30am to 2pm (brunch) and 4 to 9pm.

For a weekend lunch or a casual dinner, try the **Egg's Nest**, Route 213, High Falls (☎ 914/687-7255). Giant sandwiches are the specialty at this 19th-century canal house, which has uneven floors. You'll see hanging from the low ceiling everything from a watering can and an old pair of beaten-up shoes to a miniature of the Red Baron's plane. You can't get your hands around the deli sandwiches, so filled are they with turkey, ham, corned beef, or whatever else you ordered. Other specialties include fish-and-chips, zesty chili, pizza with a variety of toppings, and dishes like enchiladas with black-bean sauce and pasta with chiles, tomatoes, and chicken. Prices range from $6 to $10. *Hours:* Sunday to Thursday 11:30am to 11pm, Friday and Saturday 11:30am to midnight.

The **Northern Spy Cafe**, Route 213, High Falls (☎ 914/687-7298), offers what can only be described as around-the-world cuisine. Among the entrees might be roasted duck with cranberry-cinnamon glaze, steamed ginger shrimp, pork chops with mole sauce and mashed sweet potatoes, and shell steak with apple-butter barbecue sauce. The menu is rounded out by a selection of pasta/noodle dishes, pizzas, burgers, and salads. Prices range from $7 to $16. The restaurant offers an extensive wine list. In summer, the favored spot is the outdoor patio. *Hours:* Monday to Thursday 4:30 to 10pm, Friday and Saturday 4:30 to 11pm, Sunday 9:30am to 3pm (brunch) and 4:30 to 10pm.

NEW PALTZ DINING

The **Locust Tree Inn and Golf Course**, 215 Huguenot St. (☎ 914/255-7888), occupies a pretty setting at the head of a fir-lined drive that winds past a duck pond. The restaurant occupies a stone house dating to 1759 and an addition built in 1847. Of the restaurant's three rooms, the most appealing is the low-beamed tavern, where Delftware is displayed on both sides of the mantel. The menu changes weekly, but among the specialties might be seared scallops in lemon-shallot beurre blanc, veal in Gorgonzola and sun-dried tomato wine sauce, or rack of lamb in a port wine sauce. Prices range from $15 to $22. This place is lovely for summer dining outside on the patio overlooking the golf course. A traditional Sunday brunch ($12) is a good bet, too. *Hours:* Tuesday to Friday 11:30am to 2:30pm and 5:30 to 10pm, Saturday 5:30 to 10pm, Sunday 11am to 2pm (brunch) and 3 to 8pm.

Other choices include the **Wildflower Cafe,** 18 Church St. (☎ 914/255-0020; open Wednesday to Monday noon to 3pm and 5 to 9pm), for healthy and vegetarian fare; **Barnaby's,** 16 N. Chestnut Street (☎ 914/255-5542 or 914/255-9831; open Tuesday to Friday and Sunday 4:30 to 9:30pm, Saturday 11:30am to 10:30pm), for burgers, salads, sandwiches, and pasta dishes, all under $6, and dinners from $8 to $17; and **Bacchus,** 59 Main St. (☎ 914/255-8636), open Sunday to Thursday 11:30am to 9pm, Friday and Saturday 11:30am to 10pm), for Mexican fare as well as seafood and continental dishes, served in a pine-and-plants atmosphere.

HURLEY & KINGSTON

AREA ATTRACTIONS

From Stone Ridge you can travel Route 209 via Hurley to Kingston. **Hurley** was the state capital for a month in 1777, when the Council of Safety, then the state's governing body, retreated here from the advancing British. After the American Revolution it became a major stop on the Underground Railroad and is noted for being the birthplace of Sojourner Truth. The prime reason for a visit here is to view the 10 privately owned **Dutch stone houses** on the second Saturday in July, when they open their doors to the public. You'll see details like the iron "witch catcher" hanging in the chimney of the Polly Crispell House and the bullet holes puncturing the shutters on the stone porch of the Ten Eyck House.

Kingston was once an important town. It was the first capital of New York State, where the first state constitution was adopted, and where the first governor, DeWitt Clinton, was sworn in. The original settlement was destroyed by the Esopus tribe of Native Americans in 1653. To ward off similar attacks, Peter Stuyvesant ordered a stockade built; today in this **Stockade District** you'll find the city's finest homes—17th-century stone houses as well as Federal, Victorian, Italianate, Romanesque, and art deco buildings. They constitute a veritable walking tour through American architectural history. Although the town has seen better days, it still has a flavor of history and is on the upswing. The best way to explore Kingston is to walk around the stockade area.

The first Senate met in what was then the simple stone home of Abraham Van Gaasbeek in fall 1777 before the British attacked and burned Kingston. Today the **Senate House,** 312 Fair St. (☎ 914/338-2786), is one of the few buildings that survived the British sacking. The interior contains many Dutch features, like Delft tiles and a beehive oven.

The adjacent **museum** relates the story of the birth of the New York State government and also displays major works by John Vanderlyn and other artist-members of this Kingston family. The collection includes sketches for such monumental works as *Versailles* (currently in the Metropolitan Museum of Art) and for *Landing of Columbus,* which hangs in the rotunda of the Capitol in Washington, D.C. It also possesses works by such prominent American artists as Ammi Phillips, Joseph Tubby, and Thomas Sully. The site also includes the **Loughran House,** an 1873 Italianate house at 296 Fair St., which features temporary exhibits. *Hours:* Mid-April to October, Wednesday to Saturday 10am to 5pm, Sunday 1 to 5pm. *Admission:* $3 adults, $2 seniors, $1 children ages 5 to 12.

In the 19th century, Kingston became a thriving commercial port. The Cornell Steamship Company made its headquarters here and shipped supplies downriver to New York City, while a steady tourist flow made Kingston one of the gateways to the Catskills. After a long decline, activity has once again returned to the Rondout Landing. The **Trolley Museum of New York,** 89 E. Strand (☎ 914/331-3399), gives rides along the waterfront. The **Hudson River Maritime Museum,** 39 Broadway (☎ 914/338-0071), exhibits photographs, models, and artifacts relating to the history of Rondout Creek. You can go aboard a replica of the **Half Moon,** the ship in which Henry Hudson first explored the river. *Hours:* Daily 11am to 5pm. *Admission* (including the *Half Moon*): $4 adults, $3 seniors and children ages 6 to 12; museum alone, $2 adults, $1 children ages 6 to 12.

In its golden years, the port bustled with steamers, sloops, tugs, and freighters, especially from 1828 to 1898, when the D&H Canal was operating and coal was shipped from Pennsylvania into the Rondout and then elsewhere. Steamboats like the *Mary Powell* (1861–1917), the most famous and fastest on the river, made daily round-trips to Manhattan. After the canal closed in 1898, shipyards continued to operate, building ships for World Wars I and II, but thereafter the decline became permanent.

From the Rondout, boats leave the pier at the foot of Broadway for afternoon, sunset, and dinner cruises on weekends. A fun cruise aboard the *Lindy* is operated in conjunction with the Maritime Center. It crosses the river to Rhinecliff, stops at the Rondout lighthouse for a guided tour, and then returns to the Rondout. The $9 charge for adults ($7 for children) includes admission to the museum, the *Half Moon,* and the lighthouse. The *Rip Van Winkle* takes passengers on a 2-hour sightseeing cruise that is accompanied by music. For information on this and other cruises, call or write **Hudson River Cruises, Inc.,** P.O. Box 333, Rifton, NY 12471-0333 (☎ 914/255-6515 or 914/255-6618). The cost ranges from about $12.50 to $17 for adults, and cruises normally operate between May and October.

SHOPPING

One store you won't want to miss is **Anyone Can Whistle,** 323 Wall St. (☎ 914/331-7728), which offers terrific musical gifts in all price ranges and displays a full range of musical instruments—string, reed, and percussion—from around the world. The place is fun, educational, and even magical. It sells the famous Woodstock chimes.

On the Rondout are many shops for browsing as well as an ice cream and cookie store.

KINGSTON LODGING

The best accommodations choices are across the river in Rhinebeck at the Beekman Arms, at the Mohonk Mountain House, or one of the B&Bs around New Paltz on the west side of the river (see above). Or you can anchor in nearby Woodstock, which is about 20 minutes away.

KINGSTON DINING

Schneller's, 61 John St. (☎ 914/331-9800), in Kingston's stockade area, has been here since 1955, when Robert and Hannelore Schneller opened a meat market. It's a fun place to go for German sausages and schnitzels, plus such dishes as sauerbraten and German-style pork chops braised with sauerkraut and apples. Prices range from $11 to $19, the last for the wurst sampler, which includes four different wursts served with potato salad, sauerkraut, red cabbage, and two potato pancakes with applesauce. These hearty dishes can be accompanied by a selection from the 25-plus varieties of fine beer. The dining room, upstairs from the retail fish-and-meat store, is decked out with beer steins and similar decorations. You can enjoy outdoor dining in summer. *Hours:* Monday to Tuesday 11:30am to 3:30pm, Wednesday to Saturday 11:30am to 9pm, Sunday noon to 5pm.

Down at the Rondout on the river are several choices. The **Armadillo Bar & Grill,** 97 Abeel St. (☎ 914/339-1550), offers somewhat mildly spiced Southwestern cuisine in a colorful atmosphere. The tables and chairs are brilliant blue, pink, and turquoise, and the usual Southwestern accents—cacti and desert-bleached skulls—set the scene. All the traditional favorites are on hand—chimichangas, quesadillas, enchiladas, chiles rellenos, and fajitas, priced from $12 to $17. Try the chicken enchilada with almond and dried tart-cherry mole sauce or the grilled shrimp with adobo marinade. *Hours:* Tuesday to Sunday 11:30am to 3pm and 4:30 to 10pm.

The Golden Duck, 11 Broadway (☎ 914/331-3221), serves good Chinese cuisine in a light, modern atmosphere. A carved gilt arch leads into the dining room. A popular combination includes soup, an egg roll or chicken wings, and an entree. There are other combinations available, or you can choose à la carte. The great specialty is Peking duck ($28), carved tableside and served with pancakes, or any of the duck dishes—crispy duck, duckling Hunan style, or Mongolian duck. Crispy chicken, shrimp Imperial, chicken with cashews, orange beef, and beef Szechuan are other favorites. Prices run from $8 to $28. *Hours:* Monday to Thursday 11am to 2:30pm and 3 to 9:30pm, Friday 11am to 2:30pm and 3 to 10:30pm, Saturday 3 to 10:30pm, Sunday 3 to 9:30pm.

The Sturgeon Wine Bar, 23 Broadway (☎ 914/338-5186), has an extensive selection of wines by the glass. *Hours:* Sunday to Thursday noon to 2am, Friday and Saturday noon to 4am.

There's an outdoor cafe on the waterfront. Other dining choices can be found nearby along or off Route 28 in Woodstock, Bearsville, and Mount Tremper or north along Route 9W to Saugerties, all only 20 to 30 minutes away from Kingston. For details, see "The Catskills," earlier in this book.

KINGSTON AFTER DARK

Kingston's **Ulster Performing Arts Center,** 601 Broadway (☎ 914/339-6088), which was built in 1927, has been renovated and is the largest performing arts facility between New York City and Albany. It offers a broad range of entertainment—from rock to classical concerts, and drama as well as comedy and musicals. Tickets range from $20 to $35.

The West Bank
Special & Recreational Activities

Boating: There are a number of marinas along the Hudson River, but boat rentals are scarce. Your best bet is the **Great Hudson Sailing Center** in Kingston (see "Sailing," below). **Riverview Marine Services,** 101 Main St. in Catskill (☎ 518/943-5311), has powerboat rentals from $135 for a half day on weekends.

Camping: Open from mid-April to mid-October, **Beaver Pond,** Harriman State Park, R.F.D., Stony Point, NY 10980 (☎ 914/947-2792), has swimming, fishing, and boating facilities (☎ 914/947-2444 for rentals) and 52 campsites. For more information, contact the **Palisades Interstate Park Commission,** Bear Mountain, NY 10911 (☎ 914/786-2701).

Fruit Picking: *High Falls:* **Mr. Apples,** Route 213 (☎ 914/687-9498), for apples and pears. *New Paltz:* **Dressel Farms,** Route 208 (☎ 914/255-0693), for apples and strawberries; **Wallkill View Farm,** Route 299, a mile west of New Paltz (☎ 914/255-8050), for pumpkins only. *Stone Ridge:* **Davenport Farms,** Route 209 (☎ 914/687-0051), for strawberries only.

Golf: *Accord:* **Rondout Country Club,** Whitfield Road (☎ 914/626-2513), charges $40 on weekends for its 18 holes. *High Falls:* Nine-hole **Stone Dock Golf Course,** Berme Road (☎ 914/687-9944), charges $10.50 weekends. *New Paltz:* **New Paltz Golf Course** (☎ 914/255-8282), charges $14 for nine holes; **Mohonk Mountain Golf Course,** Route 299 (☎ 914/255-1000), charges $10 midweek and $13 weekends to play their nine holes.

Hiking: Bear Mountain State Park and **Harriman State Park** offer a network of trails. Contact the **Palisades Interstate Park Commission,** Bear Mountain, NY 10911 (☎ 914/786-2701). For the Appalachian Trail, contact the **Appalachian Trail Conference,** P.O. Box 807, Harpers Ferry, WV 25425 (☎ 304/535-6331), the national organization for the entire trail from Maine to Georgia. For information on those sections of the trail in New York and New Jersey, contact the **New York–New Jersey Trail Conference,** 232 Madison Ave., New York, NY 10016 (☎ 212/685-9699). **Black Rock Forest** on Route 9W, just northwest of West Point, has marked and unmarked trails. **Crow's Nest** is in the Storm King section of Palisades Park on Route 9W south of Storm King Mountain.

Horseback Riding: In New Paltz, **Mountainview Stables** (☎ 914/255-5369) offers guided trail rides for $20 per hour.

Skiing: Cross-country in **Bear Mountain** and **Harriman state parks.** Also, great trails at **Mohonk Mountain House** (☎ 914/255-1000).

Tennis: Contact the individual towns' chambers of commerce for information about using school, college, and park courts in the region. The **Woodstock Tennis Club,** Zena and Sawkill roads (☎ 914/679-5900), is also open to the public. The fee is $32 an hour.

THE LOWER HUDSON

AREA ATTRACTIONS
Garrison & Cold Spring

A wonderful weekend can be constructed around a stay at one of the several inns located in Garrison or Cold Spring on the east side of the Hudson River, or nearby, and from there you can explore both sides of the river.

Garrison was used as a setting for the Barbra Streisand film *Hello, Dolly!* and possesses a lovely park along the river, complete with a gazebo affording views of the majestic cliffs and river in either direction. Stop in at the **Garrison Arts Center,** Depot Square (☎ 914/424-3960), the artisans' workshops near the railroad tracks, and the station that now houses a theater, The Depot. *Hours:* Daily noon to 5pm.

From Garrison it's a short way north to more crowded **Cold Spring,** where you can browse in the antiques stores lining both sides of the main street.

One of the loveliest mansions on the Hudson, **Boscobel,** Route 9G (☎ 914/265-3638), was built in the early 19th century by States Morris Dyckman. It contains fine collections of porcelain, silver, furniture, crystal, and rare books and commands spectacular views of the Hudson. The flower, herb, and vegetable gardens and orangerie are particularly enchanting, especially when the roses are in full bloom. *Hours:* April to December, Wednesday to Monday 10am to 4pm. *Admission:* Mansion and grounds, $7 adults, $6 seniors, $4 children ages 6 to 14; grounds only, $4 adults and seniors, $2 children ages 6 to 14.

West Point, Storm King & Newburgh

Across the river on the west side, the **U.S. Military Academy** was founded at West Point in 1802 and has been turning out eminent leaders, both military and civilian, ever since—Robert E. Lee, Ulysses S. Grant, George S. Patton, and Dwight D. Eisenhower, to name just a few. The best time to visit is spring or fall, when you can view the cadets on parade or attend one of the football games or other sports events. The museum displays military regalia, medals, and other objects relating to military history. From West Point's location on a high bluff above the river, you can look down to Constitution Island and at Trophy's Point see the remnants of the iron chain that was stretched across the river to stop the British advance. For information on parade times, contact the visitor center at ☎ 914/938-4011. For tickets to athletic events, call ☎ 914/446-4996 or write the Director of Intercollegiate Athletics, West Point, NY 10996.

Near West Point, you might want to visit the **Brotherhood Winery** in Washingtonville (☎ 914/496-3661). The vineyard claims to have the largest underground cellars in the nation. On weekends there's an art gallery and shops to browse. Tours cost $4 and are given May to the end of December, daily from 11:30am to 4pm; January to April, weekends only from noon to 4pm.

From West Point, take the Storm King Highway to Cornwall, visiting the **Storm King Art Center,** Old Pleasant Hill Road, off Route 32, Mountainville (☎ 914/534-3115), a 500-acre park where more than 120 modern sculptures, many of them monumental, stand starkly against the horizon. Among the artists represented are Alexander Calder, Alice Aycock, Mark di Suvero, Henry Moore, Louise Nevelson, Isamu Noguchi, Richard Serra, and David Smith. Special exhibitions are on display indoors. Tours are given daily in summer at 2pm; call for a calendar of other events. *Hours:* April 1 to November 14, daily 11am to 5:30pm (indoor galleries, from mid-May); June to August the park is open until 8pm on Saturday with free admission after 5pm. *Admission:* $7 adults, $5 seniors, $3 students and children ages 5 to 12.

From here you can go into **Newburgh** to visit **Washington's Headquarters,** 84 Liberty St. (☎ 914/562-1195). Washington commanded his troops from this location during 1782–83, the crucial period when peace with the British was being concluded. Your visit begins in the **Museum Building,** which offers an audiovisual program and several exhibits recalling the events of 1782–83, when, even though General Cornwallis had surrendered at Yorktown, Washington and his troops stood ready for battle in the Hudson highlands, while the British continued to control New York City. The **Hasbrouck House,** which was Washington's headquarters for 16½ months, has been furnished to reflect the period and the events; you'll find a mix of utilitarian folding furniture and elegant appointments—from quill pens and camp beds to Martha Washington's decorative sewing.

On April 19, 1783, Washington gave the order for a "cessation of hostilities," and a monument commemorates this event. In the critical months afterward, Washington dealt with serious problems of supply, pay, and morale among his troops and also had to handle a contentious Congress.

Washington also faced down the Newburgh Conspiracy, which called for an army mutiny and a takeover of the government to settle claims for back pay and pensions. Washington quelled the movement in a dramatic speech he made to the troops at the **New Windsor Cantonment,** Temple Hill Road (☎ 914/561-1765), about 4 miles from Newburgh. Today some of the buildings that were here have been reconstructed (there were 700 of them, housing 8,000 troops) and are used for ceremonies, demonstrations, and other reenactments of historic events. The biggest celebration is on Washington's birthday in February. The other historic site that can be visited is **Knox's Headquarters** in Vails Gate. *Hours:* Mid-April to October, Wednesday to Saturday 10am to 5pm, Sunday 1 to 5pm. *Admission:* $2 adults, $1 children.

GARRISON LODGING & DINING

The Bird & Bottle, Route 9, Garrison, NY 10524 (☎ 914/424-3000; fax 914/424-3283), a tiny double-porched colonial home set in the woods, has only four rooms for rent. The floors creak and slope, the iron door latches are original, and in your room a fire will be laid in the hearth and someone will come up to light it. The whole place is highly evocative. The small tavern room is delightful. A four-course prix-fixe dinner ($37 to $54, depending on the entree) is served in a romantically low-lit paneled dining room. It might begin with grilled garlic shrimp in red-and-yellow-pepper vinaigrette, or richly flavored Gorgonzola and mascarpone fritters coated in bread crumbs and crushed macadamia nuts and served in a honey-mustard sauce. Among the 10 or so entrees there might be pan-fried chicken breast filled with Brie and apples and served with a Calvados brandy sauce, pan-seared tuna with pickled ginger and balsamic syrup, or roasted pheasant with orange and pot demiglacé. The champagne brunch is a similar four-course affair priced from $17 to $24 depending on the main selection. In addition to typical brunch egg dishes expect to find, say, pasta with sautéed seafood in tomato-basil coulis or grilled sirloin with a Burgundy sauce. *Rates* (including dinner and breakfast): $240 to $270 double. *Dining hours:* Thursday to Saturday noon to 2:30pm, Sunday noon to 2:30pm, Wednesday to Saturday 6 to 9pm, Sunday 4:30 to 7pm.

Xavier's, at the Highlands Country Club on Route 9D, Garrison (☎ 914/424-4228), is the area's consistently recommended dining spot. Waterford crystal and fresh flowers grace the tables. The $75 prix-fixe meal has two menus. For example, the five-course menu might start with an Asian lobster salad with mango and orange, followed by either charred smoked salmon with fresh horseradish or braised rabbit. After a refreshing Cabernet sorbet, you might enjoy a roast baby poussin with grilled foie gras and parsnip puree, then a delicious dessert like hot pistachio soufflé swathed in dark chocolate sauce. Coffee and petits fours complete the meal, which is accompanied by a choice selection of wine for each course, starting with a kir royal made from champagne and cassis. Reservations are required, and no credit cards are accepted. *Hours:* Friday and Saturday 6 to 9pm, Sunday noon to 2:30pm (brunch).

COLD SPRING LODGING & DINING

At the foot of Main Street, **Hudson House**, 2 Main St., Cold Spring, NY 10516 (☎ 914/265-9355; fax 914/265-4532; www.hudsonhouseinn.com), looks across to the Storm King bluffs. It was built in 1832 to accommodate passengers disembarking from steamboats at the first stop between Albany and New York City. The once-forlorn place has been delightfully transformed into a comfy, countrified lodging where lacquered wine decanters serve as bedside lamps and cookie cutters as wall decorations. The 11 guest rooms are comfortably old-fashioned, none with phone, TV, or air-conditioning. The second-floor rooms open onto a broad balcony; the third-floor rooms are tucked under the mansard roof. The doors have iron latches; the sconces are Shaker style.

The favored summer dining place is the riverside porch. An additional summer dining area is under a colorful canopy with fresh-flower trimmings. The dining room has plank floors, tables set with gingham cloths, and chairs upholstered in blue. The menu is seasonal. Entrees might include duck served with a sauce of sour cherries and fresh thyme, filet mignon with fresh shiitake mushrooms sautéed in cognac and finished with demi-glacé, or pan-roasted salmon fillet with a ginger-sesame soy. Prices run from $17 to $25. There are several alluring desserts offered, like bananas Foster (flamed with rum and served warm over vanilla ice cream) and chocolate soufflé accompanied by raspberry sauce. The **Half Moon Tavern** is prettily furnished with wing chairs in front of the fireplace, pale-blue Windsor chairs, and blue chintz. There's music in the tavern on Friday evenings from 8pm. The bountiful breakfast of scones, fresh fruit, and such entrees as Belgian waffles, stuffed pancakes, or eggs Benedict makes for a good start to the day.

Rates (including full breakfast): May to November, $160 double, $170 to $210 suite; December to April, $115 midweek; $135 weekend. *Dining hours:* May to October, Thursday to Monday noon to 2:30pm, Wednesday to Sunday 6 to 9pm; November to April, Saturday and Sunday noon to 2:30pm and 6 to 9pm. Closed in January.

At **Plumbush,** Route 9D, Cold Spring, NY 10516 (☎ 914/265-3904), which was once the home of Marquise Agnes Rizzo dei Ritti, you'll find romantic, candlelit dining in rooms where the elegant ambience is established by the wood-burning fireplaces, gilt-framed paintings, and fresh flowers. The classic cuisine with a hint of Swiss style reaches a high standard. You can select from an à la carte or a prix-fixe menu. The first highlights steaks and chops, while the second offers 10 or so entrees, which might include medallions of pork with apples and chestnuts, breast of duck with brandied plum glacé, or butterflied squab chicken with orange and mustard sauce. Prices range from $27 to $29 à la carte and $32.50 to $35 prix fixe. Most of the appetizers—from marinated fresh seafood salad to venison sausage and mushroom vinaigrette—appear on both menus. At a recent meal, the duck with a brandied-peach sauce, served with rösti potatoes, was perfectly crisp, not fatty; the turban of sole stuffed with crab meat was delicately moist. Among the desserts, the Swiss apple fritters, Sacher torte, cherry Napoleons, and orange Grand Marnier soufflé are all recommended.

Plumbush also has three rooms (including a suite) with bath available. Each is tastefully decorated in Victorian style: iron-and-brass beds, Empire chests, potted ferns, wicker pieces, marble-top tables, and so on—remarkably fine rooms for an establishment that's first and foremost a restaurant. A continental breakfast is included.

Rates: $135 double; $160 suite. *Dining hours:* Wednesday to Sunday noon to 2pm and 5:30 to 9:30pm.

A HOPEWELL JUNCTION BED & BREAKFAST

From Cold Spring, take Route 301 to Route 9 north to Route 82, which will bring you to Hopewell Junction, a trip of 25 to 30 minutes.

At **Le Chambord,** 2075 Rte. 52, Hopewell Junction, NY 12533 (☎ 914/221-1941), gracious accommodations and a well-respected dining room are combined. Antiques abound throughout the high-ceilinged 1863 Victorian residence. The hallway has a magnificent Victorian sideboard that once belonged to the Astor estate on Long Island, plus one of the largest old-fashioned wine coolers in existence—it was once originally used as the refrigerator for the family that lived here, with a block of ice in the center. The nine large, high-ceilinged guest rooms (all with bath) are eclectically furnished with antiques from various periods. Room 2 mixes American and French; room 8 affects an Empire style. Some have reproduction Queen Anne furniture, too. The third-floor rooms, tucked under the eaves, are particularly cozy. The 16 rooms in the addition (Tara) are minisuites furnished with fine fabrics. All rooms have a TV, a push-button phone, and air-conditioning.

A continental breakfast is served either in the dining room or on the flower-adorned terrace. The dining room has an excellent reputation. Pink napkins, white tablecloths, Villeroy and Boch china, lace-ruffled curtains, small crystal chandeliers, and a fireplace make for an elegant setting. At dinner you might begin with sautéed shrimp and Maine crab cakes with a roasted red pepper rémoulade, Camembert en croûte, or carpaccio of beef with aged Asiago. The entree choices are well balanced and might include pecan-and-herb-crusted salmon served with a plum tomato and Pernod sauce; duckling with raspberry sauce; and pan-roasted veal chop served with pancetta and dried apricots in a chanterelle mushroom sauce. Prices range from $20 to $34. Extravagant soufflés, double-chocolate pâté, and crêpes Suzette are the prime dessert choices. Downstairs, the **Marine Bar** is especially inviting in winter, when a fire blazes in the copper-sheathed hearth. The tapestry-covered sofas are comfortable. Portholes and an authentic ship's wheel are the marine touches. *Rates* (including breakfast): $135 double. *Dining hours:* Monday to Friday 11:30am to 2:30pm and 6 to 10pm, Saturday 6 to 11pm, Sunday 3 to 9pm.

Lower Hudson
Special & Recreational Activities

Antiquing: Cold Spring is well known for its antiques stores, which line both sides of the main street.

Boating: Fahnestock State Park, Route 301 (R.D. 2), Carmel, NY 10512 (☎ 914/225-7207), has a rowboat-rental facility.

Camping: Fahnestock State Park, Route 301 (R.D. 2), Carmel, NY 10512 (☎ 914/225-7207), is open all year, offering swimming, fishing, boat rentals, and 81 campsites.

Golf: Garrison Golf Club (☎ 914/424-3604) charges $75 on weekends for their 18-hole, par 72 course.

Hiking: Hudson Highland State Park, just north of Cold Spring, has great hiking. The **Manitoga Nature Preserve,** just south of Garrison, has 4 miles of hiking trails. **The Appalachian Trail** cuts right through Fahnestock State Park, Route 301, (R.D. 2), Carmel, NY 10512 (☎ 914/225-7207).

The Catskills

Catskill ◆ *Cairo* ◆ *Hunter Mountain* ◆ *Windham*
◆ *East Windham* ◆ *Margaretville* ◆ *Beaverkill Valley*
◆ *Pine Hill* ◆ *Shandaken* ◆ *Phoenicia* ◆ *Mount Tremper*
◆ *Woodstock* ◆ *Saugerties*

Distance in miles: Port Jervis, 68; Catskill, 115; Shandaken, 120
Estimated driving time: 1½ to 2¼ hours

Driving: Take the Lincoln Tunnel to Route 3 west to Route 17 north. Then take the New York State Thruway north to the exits for Kingston, Saugerties, and Catskill.

Bus: Adirondack Trailways (☎ 800/225-6815) travels to Hunter Mountain, Kingston, Woodstock, Shandaken, and Margaretville.

For skiers there's special transportation to Hunter Mountain from Manhattan, Westchester, New Jersey, and Long Island. Call ☎ 800/552-6262.

Train: Metro North stops at Tuxedo, Harriman, and Port Jervis. For information, call ☎ 800/638-7646 or 212/532-4900.

Further Information: For more about New York State in general, write to the **Division of Tourism,** New York State Department of Commerce, One Commerce Plaza, Albany, NY 12245 (☎ 518/474-4116).

For specific information about the Catskills, contact the **Greene County Tourism Association,** P.O. Box 527, Catskill, NY 12414 (☎ 518/943-3223); the **Hunter Mountain Lodging Bureau,** P.O. Box 335, Route 23A, Hunter, NY 12442 (☎ 518/263-4208); **the Ulster County Public Information Office,** P.O. Box 1800 CR, Kingston, NY 12401 (☎ 914/340-3000); the **Ulster County Chamber of Commerce,** 7 Albany Ave., Suite G3, Kingston, NY 12401 (☎ 914/338-5100); the **Delaware County Chamber of Commerce,** 114 Main St., Delhi, NY 13753 (☎ 607/746-2281); or the **Woodstock Chamber of Commerce,** P.O. Box 36, Woodstock, NY 12498 (☎ 914/679-6234).

Events & festivals to Plan Your Trip Around

February–April: Maple Sugar Festivals, especially the **Greene County Maple Sugar Festival**, Windham. Call ☎ 518/943-3223 for information.

June: Strawberry festivals, early June.

July: Hunter Mountain German Festival. Call ☎ 518/263-3800.

August: **Hunter Mountain Celtic Celebration.** Call ☎ 518/263-3800.

"When the weather is fair and settled, they are clothed in blue and purple and print their bold outline on the clear evening sky; but sometimes, when the rest of the landscape is cloudless, they will gather a hood of gray vapours about their summits, which, in the last rays of the setting sun, will glow and light up like a crown of glory." Thus wrote Washington Irving of his beloved Catskill Mountains. Irving was certainly not their only herald, for one of the artists that painted them, Thomas Cole, wrote home from Europe that "neither the Alps, Apennines, nor Etna himself have [sic] dimmed in my eyes the beauty of our own Catskills." Thoreau put it even more dramatically when he said of the landscape, "it was fit to entertain a traveling god."

Even today, there are parts of the Catskills that look like the Austrian or French Alps—the mountains are majestic, and the fast-running rivers, streams, brooks, cascading waterfalls, and deep quiet can leave a visitor dumbfounded by the natural beauty. This is the Catskill area around **Shandaken**, **Margaretville**, **Roxbury**, **Stamford**, the towns nestled along the Esopus Creek and the eastern branch of the Delaware River—**Mount Tremper**, **Phoenicia**, **Glenford**—and the northern fringes of **Greene County**. It attracts skiers, mountaineers, hunters, hikers, canoers, and others who relish nature and the outdoor life. The southern Catskills, around **Monticello**, **Fallsburg**, and **Liberty**, was the area nicknamed "the Borscht belt" that once sheltered the resorts that nurtured and developed so many American comedians and actors and delivered them to the TV and entertainment industry. Today most of those once-famous resorts have shuttered their doors; as a consequence, the focus of this chapter is on the northern Catskills, the natural playground for the nature and adventure lover.

From the mid-1800s until the advent of the motorcar, the Catskills were the playground of the wealthy and eminent. The first resort hotel was built in 1824; from then on the Hudson Day Line brought thousands of tourists to the mountains, depositing them at Catskill Point, which became a bustling port and passenger terminal. Horse-drawn carriages and hacks, eagerly awaiting the arrival of the ferry steamers from New York, transported visitors all over the county, though the most dramatic trip was aboard the Catskill Mountain Railroad to Palenville, where the Otis Elevating Railway (installed in 1894) scooped visitors up the face of the mountain to the Catskill Mountain House. (The gash in the mountainside can still be seen from Route 23A.) From the

The Catskills

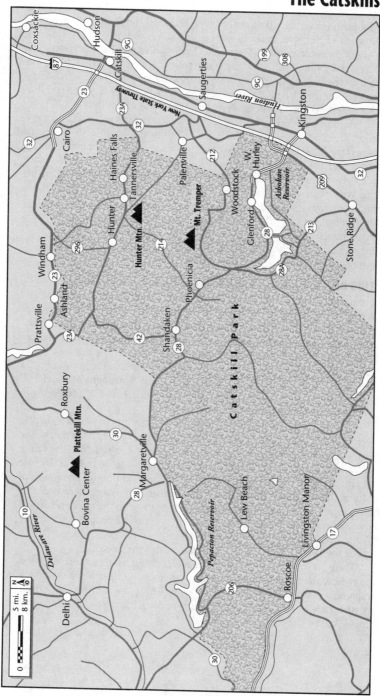

Mountain House the whole sweep of the Hudson River from north of Albany to south of Kingston could be seen against the backdrop of the mountains. Other visitors continued on to the Hotel Kaaterskill or more remote resorts. The Kaaterskill, built in 1881, was absolutely palatial and could house 1,200 guests in a three-story building shielded by soaring columns with a French Renaissance tower at each end. It fell victim to fire in 1924, a more dignified end than that experienced by the Mountain House, which was demolished in 1963.

For today's weekend visitor, the Catskills offer a supreme outdoor experience. You can ski at Hunter, Windham, or Belleayre; hike through the wilderness of the forest preserve; climb or ride to the summits of mountains granting vistas over five states; fish the Wallkill, Beaverkill, and Esopus rivers; canoe the Delaware; swim in the lakes; or soar above the mountains from Ellenville and Wurtsboro. The landscape itself is the prime attraction, though you'll also find numerous festivals and events to attend, like those at Hunter in summer or the chamber concerts at Woodstock; but the greatest thrills and rewards await the active person willing to traverse, explore, and challenge these brooding, mysterious mountains from dawn to dusk. A typical weekend could be centered on Woodstock, Saugerties, or Windham.

TWO DRIVING ROUTES THROUGH THE NORTHERN CATSKILLS

From Catskill, Route 23A brings you through some of the area's most dramatic scenery as it snakes around between the mountains and forests, cut by cascading waterfalls and gulleys, past **Kaaterskill Falls**, through Palenville, all the way to Hunter Mountain. Then take Route 296 to Windham, where you can choose either to loop back along Route 23, going over the dramatic **Point Lookout** with a five-state view into Catskill, or continue west along Route 23 to **Grand Gorge**, turning down Route 30 past the **Burroughs Memorial** all the way to Margaretville for a final loop back along Route 28 (detouring to Woodstock) into Kingston.

From Kingston, take Route 28 to Route 375, the turnoff into Woodstock. Return to Route 28 and take it to Winchells Corner. Turn left for a quick look at the **Ashokan Reservoir.** Cross the reservoir and turn right and then right again, looping along Route 28A, which will return you onto Route 28 near Mount Tremper. Turn left on Route 28 and continue through the towns of Mount Tremper and Phoenicia (both of which have some decent dining choices), all the way to Shandaken and Margaretville to the upper reaches of the Delaware. The scenery is beautiful all the way, and from here you can take Route 30 along the Pepacton Reservoir down to Hancock, where you can canoe the Delaware, or to Roscoe, trout capital of the Catskills.

There are, of course, many possible routes through the mountains. Unless you know the Catskills intimately, don't attempt shortcuts along dirt roads, especially at night, and always travel with plenty of gas. If you get off the beaten track, you can go for miles seeing nothing but trees and streams and could well be stranded for a long time.

The sections that follow have been organized according to the first route above.

CATSKILL & CAIRO

AREA ATTRACTIONS

Since Kingston was discussed in the Hudson Valley chapter, this chapter begins with Catskill, which has three or four mostly family-oriented attractions.

The 140-acre **Catskill Game Farm**, off Route 32 (☎ 518/678-9595), specializes in keeping and raising hoofed creatures, so you can see rare wild horses (Przewalski) in their natural surroundings. Kids love to pet the llamas, donkeys, sheep, and lambs; watch the antics of the chimpanzees; and ride the elephants. Peacocks wander freely about the grounds, stopping by the many food stands on the chance of receiving a treat. Bringing the makings of a picnic is a great idea. The full tour takes about 2 hours. *Hours:* April 15 to October, daily 9am to 6pm. *Admission:* $13.50 adults, $9.50 children ages 4 to 11.

Although it's not open to the public, in this depressed town stands the **home of Thomas Cole,** one of the great artists of the Hudson River School. He lived from 1836 to 1848 in a house just south of the junction of routes 23 and 385, on a property that originally extended down to the Hudson River. Among his most famous paintings are *Sunny Morning on the Hudson, View from Tivoli, View from Kaaterskill Falls,* and his allegorical series, *The Course of Empire.* Cole was married in this house in 1836.

Also in Catskill, you can play out a western fantasy by going to **Western Playland,** Route 32 just 2 miles north of the game farm (☎ 518/678-5518), the scene of melodrama shows in which kids from the audience take part, circus acts, and thriller rides for young kids, plus pony rides. *Hours:* Late June to Labor Day, daily 10am to 6pm; May 28 to late June and Labor Day to Columbus Day, Saturday to Sunday 10am to 6pm. *Admission:* $8 per person.

For more active pursuits, head for the **Funtastic Family Fun Park,** on Route 32 in Cairo (☎ 518/622-3330), half a mile south of Route 23. There are two go-cart tracks (one for adults and one for kids), miniature golf, pumper boats for kids ages 2 to 7, a fun and wet water balloon game, an arcade, and a picnic area. *Hours:* Summer, daily 10am to 10pm; spring and after Labor Day, Saturday to Sunday 10am to 10pm. Tickets are 75¢ each; on average you'll use four tickets per ride/attraction.

HUNTER MOUNTAIN

AREA ATTRACTIONS

At 4,025 feet, **Hunter Mountain,** Route 23A, Hunter (☎ 518/263-4223), is the second-highest mountain in the Catskills and the best ski area within a short distance of the city. Although it attracts thousands of skiers on weekends, Hunter handles them expertly and efficiently. The vertical rise is 1,600 feet. Hunter has 53 trails and 14 lifts and tows able to accommodate 16,900 skiers per hour. It boasts the best snowmaking capacity in the area (100%) and offers three mountains featuring terrain for all ability levels. You'll find base and summit lodges, eight dining facilities, and good nursery facilities. The price is reasonable—weekdays $39 per day, weekends $46 per day (lower rates from mid-March to closing). Rentals are available. Snowboarding is permitted, and there are also six snow chutes (each almost 1,000 feet long) and tube tow lifts for the latest sport to hit the ski scene—snow tubing. For snow information, call ☎ 800/FOR-SNOW. For quick access, take the Hunter Express Bus from Manhattan, Westchester, New Jersey, or Long Island—call ☎ 800/552-6262.

In summer, Hunter Mountain hosts a couple of colorful festivals, notably the **German Alps Festival** (late July) with beer, Hummel figurines, brass bands, Punch and Judy, and other entertainment. The mid-August 5-day **Celtic celebration** mixes Irish, Welsh, and Scottish music, entertainment, dancing, food, and drink. For festival information, call ☎ 518/263-3800.

Hunter is also the site of World Cup and Norba **mountain-bike racing**. The lift-serviced trail network provides exciting challenges for mountain-bike enthusiasts of all levels. Bike rentals are available. Even if you're not a mountain biker, while you're here ride the chairlift to the summit for a magnificent vista.

Between Hunter and Windham, just north of Tannersville in Jewett, architecture buffs may want to see the incredible **Ukrainian Church and Grazhda** (☎ 518/263-3862) on Route 23A. It's built in the traditional manner, without nails; the interior is hand-carved—a magnificent piece of craftsmanship indeed.

For cross-country skiing, **Mountain Trails**, Route 23A (P.O. Box 198), Tannersville, NY 12485 (☎ 518/589-5361), offers 35km of groomed, track-set, marked trails that are patrolled. Facilities include a warming hut, snack bar, sales and rental shop, and ski instruction. Admission is $12 per day.

HUNTER MOUNTAIN AREA LODGING & DINING

Although plenty of ski lodges cater to the needs of skiers, I'll list only a couple of particular favorites. If these are full, try the **Hunter Mountain Lodging Bureau,** Route 23A, Hunter, NY 12442 (☎ 518/263-4208), for more information.

For easy ski-on/ski-off access to the slopes you can't beat the **Liftside Condominiums** (☎ 518/263-3707), which are right on the mountain and offer slopeside views from each unit's deck. Each has a full kitchen, washer/dryer, fireplace, TV/VCR, phone, and whirlpool bath. One-bedroom units sleep up to four people, two-bedroom units up to six. *Rates:* weekend packages that include lift tickets start at $109 per person in a three-bedroom condo.

The **Scribner Hollow Lodge,** Route 23A, Hunter, NY 12442 (☎ 800/395-4683 or 518/263-4211), is a fun place primarily because of its themed rooms. You might stay in one of the futuristic duplexes, with mirrored ceilings and walls, ultramodern white and beige furnishings, and a bathtub area with a waterfall; or perhaps a hunting lodge might be more to your taste—with a large bearskin rug (complete with the animal's head), cozy cabin walls, beams, and a stone fireplace. Other options include penthouse and Southwest adobe themes. All the rooms are equipped with air-conditioning, TV, and telephone; some have Jacuzzi tubs, fireplaces, balconies, and VCRs. Even the indoor pool area is specially designed to look like an underground grotto with waterfalls. Facilities include a restaurant, outdoor pool, and tennis court, plus massage service. The regular rooms are less fun, but they're cheaper. *Rates* (MAP): $82 to $135 per person double, $135 to $235 per person special suites. Subtract $25 per person per night for room only. Two-night minimum stay on weekends.

The Red Coat's Return, Dale Lane, Elka Park, NY 12427 (☎ 518/ 589-6379 or 518/589-9858), is 10 miles from Hunter in the heart of the Catskill Game Preserve. Here, as the name suggests, you'll find traces of old England, most clearly in the publike lounge and adjacent dining room. The menu offers about eight traditional favorites like sirloin with green-peppercorn sauce, duck with apples, and chicken breast with artichokes and mushrooms, priced from $13 to $21. There's usually a roaring fire in the lounge's stone fireplace, antiques scattered about, and a cozy library room; these contribute to the warm, comfortable atmosphere of this Edwardian home overlooking fields, forests, and Schoharie Creek. The 14 guest rooms (most with bath) have been decorated with oak pieces and beds covered with fluffy down comforters, conveying a pleasant, homey touch. The surrounding 18 acres have trails and trout streams. *Rates* (including breakfast): $90 to $105 double. *Dining hours:* Friday to Monday 6 to 9:30pm.

Situated on 12 acres, the **Eggery Inn,** County Road 16, Tannersville, NY 12485 (☎ 518/589-5363; fax 518/589-5774), occupies an old farmhouse built in 1900, which was converted into a boarding house in the 1930s before being taken over and restored by the current owners in 1979. It has 15 guest rooms (all with baths, TVs, telephones, and air-conditioning) furnished in country style with wall-to-wall carpeting, chintz wallpaper, and somewhat old-fashioned country furniture. Rooms on the third floor have views of Hunter Mountain. On arrival, guests enter a cozy living room warmed by a woodstove. There's a TV, books, a player-piano, and old comfy furniture, some of it Mission-style. Guests are served breakfast and dinner in a dining room that has panoramic views of Hunter and the mountains. Guests select from a menu at breakfast offering omelets, French toast, and more. The dining room has a fireplace, and numerous plants enliven the decor. At dinner the fare is such typical American favorites like prime rib, chicken cordon bleu, veal Marsala, and poached salmon. The front wraparound porch is a favorite place for relaxing. *Rates* (including breakfast): Weekends $105 to $120 double, weekdays $100.

Four miles from Hunter, the **Swiss Chalet,** Route 23A (☎ 518/589-5445), has an alpine decor—plenty of hutches, cuckoo clocks, and pine. The cuisine is also Austrian-Swiss inspired. For example, the menu offers Wienerschnitzel, wiener rossbraten, sauerbraten, and Zurischer schnitzel (with cream and mushrooms). Dishes are priced from $15 to $24. For dessert, classics like apfelstrudel, peach Melba, and pear Hélène are offered. *Hours:* Daily 5 to 8:30pm.

The **Last Chance Cheese and Antiques Cafe,** Main Street (☎ 518/ 589-6424), is a country store selling gourmet items like cheese, pasta, coffee, tea, and more. The cafe can accommodate 90 people and offers a variety of oversized sandwiches, several soups, cheese platters, and fondue, priced from $4 to $10. *Hours:* Monday to Thursday 10am to 7pm, Friday to Saturday 10am to 9pm, Sunday 10am to 8pm.

WINDHAM

This ski area lies about 7 miles north of Hunter. It was once a private club, catering to well-to-do skiers, where many political and business leaders skied, and it still has the classiest atmosphere of the local resorts. There's good skiing from the 3,050-foot summit down a 1,550-foot vertical on 33 trails, 97% of them covered with human-made snow. The six chairlifts (including two high-speed quads) have a lift capacity of close to 12,000 skiers per hour. Lessons, rentals, a ski shop, and a cafe are all available. The mid-mountain Wheelhouse lodge is an attractive place to picnic or enjoy the views. The White Birches Ski Touring Center offers 15 miles of groomed trails through lovely terrain. There's also a large snowboard park and a children's learning center. Lift rates on weekends are $42 for adults and $36 for juniors (age 13 and over); midweek rates are $34 and $29, respectively. For information, contact **Ski Windham**, C.D. Lane Road, P.O. Box 459, Windham, NY 12496 (☎ 800/754-9463 or 518/734-4300). A shuttle bus operates from the metro area. For information call ☎ 516/360-0369 or 718/343-4444. Windham also offers lodging packages at the Windham Arms Hotel (see below), costing anywhere from $65 to $160 weeknights and $100 to $310 weekends. Their central reservations office can also place you in slope-side condos and town houses.

WINDHAM & EAST WINDHAM LODGING

The town is well kept and contains many appealing Victorian homes, some of which have been converted into accommodations for visitors.

The **Windham Arms Hotel,** Main Street, Windham, NY 12496 (☎ 518/734-3000; fax 518/734-3000), is owned by Ski Windham. The lobby glows in winter with a blazing fire. The 50 or so modern rooms (with baths, color TVs, and phones) are located in a two-story building with balconies. Amenities include room service and laundry/valet. Facilities include two dining rooms, an outdoor pool, a family recreation center, a putting green, a movie theater, a tennis court, and croquet. *Rates:* Weekends $105 to $160 rooms, $210 to $310 suites; weekdays $77 to $115 rooms, $130 to $160 suites; respectively. MAP rates and special packages also available.

The **Windham House,** Route 23 (R.R. 1, Box 36), Windham, NY 12496 (☎ 518/734-4230), is a small resort with a stately 1805 Greek revival house at its nucleus. A double porch and soaring Ionic columns give the exterior a grand look while inside old timbers, plank walls and floors, and Hitchcock chairs, give the interior immense character. The rooms are furnished in a somewhat old-fashioned way, although you'll find an occasional characterful detail—a wooden butter bowl and ladle along with a marble-topped stand in Room 18; a spool bed and washstand in Room 2-C. Some rooms are in the carriage houses. Some have only sinks, but most have baths; all have TVs and telephones. The loft of the old barn on this former farm now serves as a place for evening entertainment. The fields have been turned into a nine-hole golf course. There are swimming and tennis facilities and a 2-mile hiking trail. *Rates:* AP $320 to $470 per person per week, $80 to $110 per person daily; winter, $120 to $135 per room plus continental breakfast. Closed Columbus Day to December.

At the **Albergo Allegria Bed & Breakfast,** Route 296, Windham, NY 12496 (☎ 800/625-2374 or 518/734-5560; www.albergousa.com), two grand

Victorian houses have been connected by a new section that was carefully designed to imitate the gingerbread, brackets, and stained glass of the originals. There are 20 rooms, all with tiled bathrooms, hair dryers, TV/VCRs, and phones. They are nicely furnished with dusky-pink carpeting and brass beds covered with lacy pink eiders and pretty bed ruffles. In most there's plenty of room—enough for tables and chairs and a chest of drawers. Dried-flower arrangements add a country air. The Carriage House boasts five luxury suites furnished with king-size beds under skylights in the high cathedral ceilings. Additional amenities include double whirlpools, gas fireplaces, mini-refrigerators, CD/tape players, and candles. There are two sitting rooms with fireplaces, a few books, and polished wood floors covered with braided rugs. The one upstairs has a more Victorian feel, thanks to wicker, rattan, and Eastlake furnishings. Breakfast is served at oak tables in the dining rooms or out on the patio under a colorful awning. The Albergo is right across from the Windham Country Club's 18-hole golf course, which is ranked number 3 in the state by the PGA. *Rates* (including breakfast): Fall/winter, weekends $115 to $235 double, weekdays $75 to $160 double; summer, weekends $95 to $160 double, $75 to $135 double; off-season, weekends $75 to $95 double, weekdays $65 to $85 double.

The **Point Lookout Mountain Inn,** Route 23 (P.O. Box 33), East Windham, NY 12439 (☎ 518/734-3381), takes full advantage of a magnificent view over New York, Connecticut, New Hampshire, Vermont, and Massachusetts. Most of the motel-style rooms have decks, and all have TVs and baths. Guests can also relax in the Great Room, either basking in the hot tub or lolling around the wood stove in front of the TV. There's also a pool table and video and board games. Dining facilities include a dining room, cafe-deck, and taproom all sharing the spectacular view.

In the Bella Vista Restaurant at dinner about half a dozen pasta and risotto dishes are offered, from scampi in fresh tomato and wine sauce with linguine; to a risotto verde that incorporates artichokes, spinach, onions, and zucchini with white wine and Romano cheese. Additional entrees might include blackened steak with citrus butter, pork tenderloin with an apple-infused pan gravy, or grilled salmon with honey-mustard sauce. Prices range from $14 to $18. More than 30 beers and a dozen wines by the glass are on hand, plus a selection of California and Italian wines. For breakfast you can select from a long list of fillings for omelets or frittatas, as well as pancakes.

Rates (including breakfast): Christmas to early March, $135 to $145 double; the rest of the year, $95 to $125 double. *Dining hours:* Sunday to Thursday 11am to 9pm, Friday and Saturday 11am to 10pm. November and March to May, weekends only. Closed 2 weeks in early spring.

WINDHAM AREA DINING

Given Windham's history as an enclave for the wealthy, it's not surprising that it offers some of the finest cuisine in the Catskill Mountains at **La Griglia,** Route 296, Windham (☎ 518/734-4499). The dining rooms are warm and welcoming with their rough-hewn pine walls and post-and-beam construction. Each has a wood stove and attractively set tables. Among the more enticing appetizers are eggplant fritters stuffed with mozzarella-anchovy butter and fresh basil, smoked trout with horseradish, or mussels steamed with garlic in a light tomato sauce. These can be followed by a choice selection of entrees—scaloppine of pork sautéed with garlic, tomato, and fruit juice and layered with apples; chicken with prosciutto, mushrooms, and sparkling wine; sliced fillet of beef sautéed with Barolo, green peppercorns, and mushrooms. Prices range from $15 to $29. A good choice for Sunday brunch, too. On Wednesday and Thursday evenings the restaurant features a long seafood menu listing such dishes as lobster, scampi, calamari, and much more. *Hours:* Summer, Saturday noon to 3pm, Sunday 11am to 3pm, Wednesday to Monday 4 to 10pm; ski season, Saturday noon to 3pm, Sunday 11am to 3pm, daily 4 to 10pm.

Vesuvio, Goshen Road, Hensonville (☎ 518/734-3663), offers an elegant setting for some good Italian cuisine. Although such traditional favorites as veal francese and veal parmigiana are available, try the signature chicken della casa, which is made with a sauce flavored with sausage, cherry peppers, garlic, lemon, and white wine. Assorted seafood dishes including a delicious seafood combination of lobster, mussels, calamari, and clams in a marinara sauce are also offered. Prices run $14 to $22. *Hours:* Summer and winter, daily 5 to 10pm. Closed Wednesday in spring and fall.

At **Chalet Fondue**, Route 296, Windham (☎ 518/734-4650), you can cozy up to the Swiss alpine stove while waiting for a table in one of four dining areas—the Wine Cellar, which features two enormous wooden wine barrels; two stucco-style characterful rooms; or the solarium. Here you can feast on jaegerschnitzel, sauerbraten, Wienerschnitzel, wursts, and more, finishing with a fine Black Forest cake or apfel kuechle. Other signature dishes are the veal and beef fondue and the champagne cheese fondue. Prices run $12 to $22. *Hours:* Winter, Wednesday to Saturday and Monday 5 to 10pm, Sunday 2 to 10pm; summer, Wednesday to Saturday 5 to 10pm and Sunday 2 to 10pm; fall and spring, Thursday to Sunday 5 to 10pm.

Theo's, Route 23, Windham (☎ 518/734-4455), offers continental cuisine with a hint of Greek flavor. On the menu are Greek-style lamb chops and also some Italian dishes, along with seafood. Prices ($10 to $30) include soup, salad, a main course, a dessert, and coffee. The atmosphere is simple and homey. *Hours:* Thursday to Tuesday noon to 11pm and Wednesday 3:30 to 11pm. Closed Wednesday in spring and fall.

A GREENVILLE B&B HIDEAWAY

The **Greenville Arms**, South Street, Greenville, NY 12083 (☎ 518/966-5219; fax 518/966-8754), is indisputably an isolated hideaway and has been used as such by many a celebrity in search of rest and anonymity. Cupolas and dormers crown the roof of this lovely Victorian house, built in 1889 for William Vanderbilt and now operated by Eliot and Tish Dalton as a country inn. There are 14 rooms, all with air-conditioning, private baths (four rooms and one suite in the main house and nine in the carriage house). The most pleasant is probably Old Will's Room, which contains a canopied bed and wing chairs set against rose wallpaper; it has the added attraction of a balcony. Miss Penny's Room contains a four-poster bed, an oak dresser, and a cozy reading nook.

There's a comfortable sitting room on the ground floor and a TV/VCR room on the second floor. Fine paintings can be found throughout the house. Out back is a lovely, secluded outdoor pool you'd never expect to find, a lawn for croquet and other games, and 7 acres with a bubbling stream and

A Scenic Drive

From South Kortwright, drive over the mountains to Bovina. The climb up affords beautiful views, and the drive across the top takes you past black-and-white Holsteins and grazing horses against green fields, silos, and rust or gray barns topped with weather vanes.

Bovina Center is a tiny community with a firehouse, a community hall, and a one-room museum filled with local memorabilia—clothes, pictures, agricultural implements, and photographs.

wooded trails. The proprietors also offer workshops, an annual series of classes in painting and drawing. Bicycles are available.

A full breakfast is served in the dining rooms, both with floor-to-ceiling brick fireplaces. Guests are also served a three-course dinner. A different main course is available each night—say, chicken francaise on Tuesday accompanied by vegetables, or roast pork loin on Wednesday. On weekends there are four selections ranging from baked salmon in saffron Chardonnay sauce or filet mignon in red wine with portobello mushrooms. During the week (Monday to Friday), the meal costs $25; on Saturday and Sunday, when guests have a choice of four entrees and four appetizers, the price is $36.

Rates (including breakfast): $130 to $170 double.

FROM WINDHAM TO MARGARETVILLE

If you're following the second itinerary outlined in the section "Two Driving Routes Through the Northern Catskills," above, from Windham take Route 23 west to Grand Gorge. Here you can either take Route 30 south to Margaretville or continue on Route 23 to the attractive town of Stamford. From Stamford, Route 10 south travels through Hobart to Delhi. A scenic side trip (see the box "A Scenic Drive") through horse-and-farm country along routes 5 and 6 to Bovina Center and New Kingston will eventually return you to Route 28 just west of Margaretville. You'll have completed a small loop touching on Schoharie and Delaware counties.

If you travel down Route 30 toward Margaretville, you'll pass naturalist **John Burroughs's Memorial,** just outside Roxbury, on Burroughs Memorial Road. You can sit here and quietly reflect on nature in this Catskill Mountain pasture as Burroughs did when he was a boy. Later, when he became a renowned naturalist/philosopher whose books had changed the way many Americans looked at their natural world, he still returned here for inspiration. Today Burroughs stands out as a brilliant environmentalist who wrote as early as 1913, "We can use our scientific knowledge to poison the air, corrupt the waters, blacken the face of the country, and harass our souls with discordant noises, or we can mitigate and abolish all these things."

SHOPPING & ANTIQUING

You can stop and browse in Margaretville, which has a large antiques center on the main street where you might find a bargain. From Margaretville take Route 28 east toward Woodstock. En route, there is another fine antiques store called the **Blue Barn** (☎ 914/688-7668) operated by Fay Storm, who has a great eye for what's fine and aesthetic.

Continue along Route 28 and you'll arrive at a small shopping complex where you can view the **Kaatskill Kaleidoscope** at Mt. Pleasant Road, Mt. Tremper (☎ 914/688-5300). Shows are given daily from July 4 to Labor Day. The complex features a good gourmet food store and some other emporiums.

LODGING & DINING AROUND HOBART

A warm and friendly welcome will greet you, and some unexpected facilities will surprise you at **Breezy Acres Farm**, Route 10 (R.R. 1, Box 191), Hobart, NY 13788 (☎ 607/538-9338), just less than 2 miles south of Stamford on Route 10. Joyce and David Barber love having guests at their 300-acre crop farm. Joyce serves a hearty breakfast—enough to carry you through the whole day—of fresh fruit, muffins, and eggs. For example, you might enjoy baked apples, pumpkin muffins, and French toast with homemade bread, accompanied by their own delicious maple syrup and bacon. Guests are free to gather in the sitting room, a typically homey room with a sofa and chairs. And there's a pleasant TV room with a leather sofa and chairs, display cases filled with Winchester commemoratives, and a couple of deer trophies, including a mule deer taken in Wyoming.

There are three guest rooms, all with baths. One has solid-oak furniture crafted by Joyce's great-great-grandfather, including a fine headboard that required each tiny spindle to be lathed individually. Another has wall-to-wall carpeting, a peach- and jade-colored quilt on the carved-oak bed, and louvered closets. The other rooms have polished wood floors. Joyce usually places nuts or some other small treat in the rooms. Guest may use the hot tub, and there's a Ping-Pong table in the garage—or you can just relax on the porch.

Rates (including breakfast): $80 double weekends, $65 double weekdays.

The **Hidden Inn**, Main Street, South Kortwright (☎ 607/538-9259), is a fine old white clapboard house with a prominent pediment supported by Corinthian pillars. Family-run, it offers a small lounge with a fireplace and three plain country dining rooms: the Colonial Room, with a wood-burning fireplace; the Sunset Room, where the tables are set with burgundy napkins; and the Kortwright Room, used locally for meetings and weddings. On Friday and Saturday there's a "surf and turf" buffet. The regular menu is short and simple, listing such favorites as veal parmigiana, duck à l'orange, chicken piccata, surf and turf, and steaks. Prices run from $10 to $17. *Hours:* Monday to Saturday 5 to 9pm, Sunday noon to 7pm (may be closed Monday to Tuesday in winter).

BEAVERKILL VALLEY LODGING

The **Beaverkill Valley Inn**, Beaverkill Road, Lewbeach, NY 12753 (☎ 914/439-4844), located in a wonderful wilderness spot, makes a marvelous, unpretentious retreat. Built in 1895 especially for sport fishers, the white clapboard inn with a wraparound porch stands on the banks of the famous Beaverkill fishing creek, which attracts fly-fishers the world over. It's close enough to the stream that at night the gentle sound of flowing water will lull you to sleep. The emphasis in the restoration of the old building has been on solid comfort—really comfortable armchairs and sofas in the sitting room, real logs burning in the fireplace, plenty of books about the Catskills for readers to peruse, and ceramic lamps on the tables.

This is the kind of place you look forward to coming home to after a good day's fishing—where you can relish a good meal in the oak-furnished dining room, relax or play cards in the games room in front of a blazing fire, enjoy a game of billiards downstairs in the plushly furnished billiard room, or lounge on the porch swings. Also on the property are two tennis courts and an indoor pool housed in a converted barn, which also features (can you believe it!) a self-service ice-cream parlor. The grounds are well kept, the lawn has a finely trimmed smooth croquet court, and there are 6 miles of Beaverkill waters for private fishing in spring and fall. The pond is perfect for skating and there are miles of trails for cross-country skiing and summer hiking. The stained-glass panels found throughout the first floor are quite beautiful, especially the one in the sitting room. They were created by Cynthia Richardson, an artist from Massachusetts. The room rates include three well-prepared meals a day. At dinner splendid hors d'oeuvres are set out in the lounge and are followed with such dishes as thick lamb chops served with brandied carrots or sautéed risotto-stuffed portobello mushrooms. The kitchen is very obliging—they will accommodate special dietary requests and even supply box lunches for guests.

The inn has 21 guest rooms. The rooms in the inn itself are not large because space was used to add some baths during the renovation. Most have iron-and-brass beds, colorful quilts, oak dressers, chairs, side tables, and solid-wood closets. Additional, somewhat simpler accommodations are available at the Quill Gordon Lodge, which some people prefer because it's almost austere, has a huge fireplace, and has always been a fishing lodge. Finally, the house has a wraparound porch furnished with wicker and swings for total relaxation.

Rates (AP): $270 double without bath, $340 double with bath.

MARGARETVILLE, PINE HILL & SHANDAKEN LODGING & DINING

In the center of Margaretville, the **Binnekill Square Restaurant** (☎ 914/586-4884) is built over the narrow creek. The dining rooms have a combination of butcher block, stained glass, and comb-back Windsor chairs. The menu features a variety of beef, veal, seafood, and chicken dishes, priced from $12 to $20. *Hours:* Thursday to Saturday noon to 2pm, Tuesday to Saturday 5pm to closing, and Sunday noon to closing.

Albert Pollack (who owns a chain of movie theaters) and interior designer Gisele took over the **Shandaken Inn**, P.O. Box 36, Golf Course Road, Route 28, Shandaken, NY 12480 (☎ 914/688-5100), in 1972. At the time it was meant to be a quiet retreat from city life, but as more and more friends came to visit, they decided to continue the practice of having only their friends, friends' guests, and referrals stay with them for weekends in very proper houseguest fashion. Consequently, the inn requires no advertising.

Originally a dairy barn, the house has experienced several incarnations, from a golf clubhouse to a ski lodge to a country inn. Gisele has tastefully decorated it by installing a glowing copper bar, decorating the stone fireplace with copper pans and utensils, and scattering about all manner of antiques—decoys, samplers, and basketry—that impart a delightful country air to the comfortable sitting areas. Each of the 12 guest rooms has been decorated individually, but rather simply, some with wicker.

A typical weekend might begin with your arrival on Friday in time for dinner, prepared by Gisele, at 8:30pm. The ingredients would be fresh local produce—striped bass, filet mignon, and rack of lamb, accompanied by appetizers, salads, and desserts (such as her classic raspberry tarts—the kind that only the French seem to know the secret of baking). For the rest of the weekend you can relax, go skiing, or pretty much do whatever you like, returning in the evening for cocktails, dinner, and an informal soiree with other houseguests. There's also a tennis court and an outdoor pool. No children are accepted.

Rates (including breakfast and dinner): Weekends only, $195 to $245 per day per couple (lower price is for room with shared bath, the higher for room with fireplace).

The impressive 1896 **Birch Creek**, Route 28 (P.O. Box 323), Pine Hill, NY 12465 (☎ 914/254-5222), is set on 23 wooded acres and approached via a long tree-lined road making it a gem of a hideaway where you can walk among fir and pine and spot deer, wild turkeys, and other wildlife as you go. When you enter the house, you'll come into a long center hall/sitting area warmed by a wood-burning stove and furnished with Empire-style furniture, wicker, and other large pieces of Victoriana. The hall leads to a large wraparound porch furnished with Adirondack chairs that overlook the creek. There are seven guest rooms, all with private bath, some with TV. Most are simply huge, like the Champagne Room, which boasts a brass bed, a large armoire and couch, and an equally large bath with a tub for two and a shower. Other rooms might feature spindle or wicker or antique Victorian beds and suitable furnishings. Upstairs, guests may use the book-filled library with fireplace and glass bookcases. The vintage billiards room contains a tournament-size pool table, a piano, and plenty of board games for entertainment. Guests have access to a refrigerator. A full breakfast is served in the dining room. *Rates* (including breakfast): $95 to $155 double.

The **Auberge des 4 Saisons**, Route 42, Shandaken, NY 12480 (☎ 914/688-2223), has been well known for its cuisine ever since Edouard (Dadou) LaBeille, a waiter at Le Pavillon, Henri Soulé's legendary Manhattan restaurant (now closed), established this hunting lodge in 1954. The classically French menu changes frequently. Among the appetizers might be duck terrine with Cumberland sauce, smoked salmon marinated with vodka and dill, or a delicious local goat cheese in puff pastry with wild mushrooms and a cabernet jus. The entrees might include duck with Grand Marnier sauce, roasted rack of lamb with rosemary jus, and filet mignon with a flavorsome bordelaise sauce. Prices range from $16 to $22. The desserts are usually such classics as crème brûlée and seasonal fruit tarts.

The inn has 28 rooms (all with showers or baths, TVs, and phones). There are nine rooms in the inn building that are on the small side. The chalet contains another 19 larger rooms furnished with two double beds. There's also an outdoor pool and tennis court. Belleayre is only 6 miles away. *Rates* (MAP): $185 to $235 double. *Dining hours:* June to September, daily 5:30 to 9:30pm; the rest of the year, Friday to Sunday 5:30 to 9:30pm.

DINING IN PHOENICIA

Sweet Sue's, Main Street, Phoenicia (☎ 914/688-7852), is a great breakfast place for raspberry, blueberry, and peach pancakes or four-grain pancakes like whole wheat and fruited oatmeal, plus bountiful egg dishes. For luncheon, the soups are soul-satisfying, the sandwiches are prepared on home-baked whole-grain bread, and the pastas and vegetarian dishes are also good. It's down-home and simple. In summer, you can dine on the outdoor patio. Prices range from $4 to $7. Note on weekends, especially at breakfast, expect lines. *Hours:* Daily 7am to 3pm.

MOUNT TREMPER LODGING & DINING

La Duchesse Anne, at the corner of Route 212 and South Wittenberg Road (P.O. Box 49), Mount Tremper, NY 12457 (☎ 914/688-5329 or 914/688-5260), is a very inviting 1850 Victorian house with white clapboard siding, green shutters, and a porch gaily hung with flower baskets and set with Adirondack chairs. There are 10 rooms with shared baths, 2 with private baths, and an apartment. The rooms are on the small side, but are adequately furnished. The parlor/dining room is striking, with Victorian antiques, plus comfortable seating and spacious tables set in front of the bluestone fireplace. Classical music adds to the serenity at breakfast. The dining room is well known locally for good country French cuisine. Among the entrees, priced from $15 to $22, you might find roast duck with orange sauce, a Breton fish stew, and filet mignon with shallots and garlic butter. *Rates* (including breakfast): $70 to $75 double without bath, $100 double with bath; $130 apartment accommodating four. *Dining hours:* Monday to Thursday 5:30 to 9pm, Friday 5:30 to 11pm, Saturday 10am to 2pm and 5:30 to 11pm, Sunday 11am to 3:30pm and 5:30 to 9pm. Closed Wednesday in winter (and possibly Tuesday or Thursday as well).

The **Zen Mountain Monastery**, P.O. Box 197, Mount Tremper, NY 12457 (☎ 914/688-2228), offers bunk accommodations in dorms to those who are seriously interested in Zen. The daily schedule runs from 4:45am wake-up and dawn meditation to evening meditation. *Rates:* $195 to $270 double for a weekend retreat.

Onteora the Mountain House, Box 356, 96 Piney Point Rd., Boiceville, NY 12412 (☎ 914/657-6233), is a "land in the sky" indeed, with incredible panoramic views of the surrounding mountains and the Esopus River valley below. It's set back down a winding lane surrounded by acres of forest. This magnificent retreat was built by mayonnaise mogul Richard Hellmann, who retired here in 1930 after his doctor had warned him that he had six months to live if he did not retire and move to the country. Guests love to warm themselves in front of the fire that burns on cold days in the massive riverstone fireplace in the Great Room. Beyond is a 40-foot covered porch built in Adirondack style using sturdy tree trunks for the columns and railings. There are four rooms and a suite. The rooms are compact and cozy and are furnished with platform beds and a sink. Four, including the suite, share 2½ baths in the corridor. The suite has a glass-enclosed sunroom and a gas-burning fireplace to add to its attractions. Located upstairs, Mombaccus is the most private room. It also has a private bath and a bay window looking out over the Ashokan Reservoir. A full breakfast is served either on the dining porch or out on the southern deck. Downstairs there's a comfortable games room and TV lounge. Facilities also include a sauna. *Rates:* Memorial Day to October 31, $120 to $165; otherwise $105 to $150.

WOODSTOCK

AREA ATTRACTIONS

Woodstock lies at the foot of the Ohayo and Overlook mountains, and its scenic location attracted artists at the turn of the century. In 1902 Ralph White-head, who had studied at Oxford University with John Ruskin, established the Byrdcliffe Art and Crafts Colony on 1,000 acres he had purchased on the north side of the Woodstock Valley. Shortly thereafter, the Art Students League opened its summer school in Woodstock, and in 1910 the Woodstock Artists' Association was founded. In 1916 Hervey White, who had worked under Whitehead at Byrdcliffe, established his own colony, the Maverick, and launched summer open-air festivals of song and dance. Today the summer Sunday afternoon Maverick concerts (☎ 914/679-2007 or 914/672-6482) are among the oldest chamber-music concert series in the nation. Sadly, the landmark Woodstock Playhouse that opened in 1937 burned down in the 1980s; funds are being raised to build a modern facility, and a covered performance area has already been constructed.

Woodstock, of course, is the town that gave its name to a whole generation when 400,000 people came to celebrate the Woodstock Music Festival in 1969. Though the festival actually took place about 60 miles west in a farmer's field in Bethel, Woodstock became its moniker, and a second Woodstock was held in 1994, this time in neighboring Saugerties, about 20 minutes north, again drawing attention to the region.

Today, most of the early organizations remain; the Art Students League has been replaced by the **Woodstock School of Art** (☎ 914/679-8746 or 914/679-7558). From May to October, the famous **Byrdcliffe Arts and Crafts Colony** offers residences and studios to artists, craftspeople, musicians, and writers. The Byrdcliffe Barn is the site of extensive programming during the summer, including classes and performances. You can obtain a pamphlet outlining a walking tour of the arts and crafts colony from the Woodstock Guild.

The town is crowded on summer weekends and still has a 1960s hippie air. They still hang out on the green, and there's usually an aspiring singer entertaining with a guitar.

SHOPPING

The main street is lined with an eclectic mix of clothing boutiques, New Age shops, candle stores, crafts shops, and more utilitarian stores selling books, hardware, wine, and health food.

Among the highlights are **The Golden Notebook,** 29 Tinker St. (☎ 914/ 679-8000), an excellent bookstore run by an extremely helpful and knowledgeable proprietor and staff that seems to cram an amazing amount of stock onto its shelves. Similar expertise about wine is dispensed by **Woodstock Wines and Liquors,** next door. Survey the beautiful kilims stocked at **Anatolia Tribal Rugs and Weavings** (☎ 914/679-5311), tucked away behind Tinker Street; also back here is **Dharmaware,** selling Eastern religious books and statues of gods and goddesses as well as meditation cushions and clothes from Asia. Other stores to look for are **Blue Mountain Villager,** routes 375 and 212 (☎ 914/679-4118), selling country furniture plus draperies, blinds, wallpaper, and other interior design accessories; **The Gilded Carriage,** 95 Tinker St. (☎ 914/679-2607), for everything for the art of setting a table, including French Quimper and Italian majolica; **Mirabai Books,** 23 Mill Hill Rd. (☎ 914/679-7819), which specializes in spiritual and metaphysical books; the **Woodstock General Store** (☎ 914/679-8140), appreciated by those suffering from acute nostalgia; and **Reader's Quarry** (☎ 914/679-9572), for a broad selection of secondhand books and first editions at excellent prices.

There's still a handful of galleries in town and nearby. Stop in at the **Woodstock Artists' Association,** 28 Tinker St. (☎ 914/679-2940), for their changing exhibits and lectures. *Hours:* Monday and Thursday to Friday noon to 5pm, Saturday to Sunday noon to 6pm.

Also contact the **Woodstock Guild,** 34 Tinker St. (☎ 914/679-2079), which, besides holding classes and workshops, operates the Kleinert Arts Center, which offers year-round contemporary exhibits and musical and other performances. *Hours:* Wednesday to Monday 11am to 6pm.

The guild also operates the **Crafts Shop,** 34 Tinker St. (☎ 914/679-2688), which sells fine regional crafts. *Hours:* Friday to Monday 11:30am to 5pm.

Other galleries of note are **Lily Ente** (☎ 914/679-6064); **James Cox,** 26 Elwyn Lane (☎ 914/679-7608); and in nearby Shady, **Elena Zang,** 3671 Rte. 212 (☎ 914/679-5432), which sells some eye-catching and beautifully crafted ceramics and fine arts and sculpture, including works by local artist Mary Frank.

Outside of Woodstock, off Route 28, a shopping stop crafts lovers won't want to miss is **Crafts People** (☎ 914/331-3859), owned and operated by craftspeople and housed in several buildings. They sell some beautifully designed glass and ceramics as well as jewelry and other craft items. From Kingston, take Route 28 west to the West Hurley traffic light and turn left on Basin Road. Follow the signs from there. *Hours:* Summer, daily 10am to 6pm; winter, Friday to Monday 10am to 6pm.

NEARBY ATTRACTIONS

In the heart of the mountains, Woodstock is also home to Buddhist monasteries and other inspirational retreats. For example, at the top of Meads Mountain Road you'll find the **Tibetan Buddhist monastery** (☎ 914/ 679-4271), easily identified by the prayer flags blowing in the wind out front. Tours are given of the flamboyantly painted temple on Saturday and Sunday, and you can also visit the bookstore, which sells statuary and other religious objects.

Just outside Woodstock, in High Woods, on the way to Saugerties, **Opus 40** (☎ 914/246-3400) is a monumental environmental sculpture carved out of an abandoned bluestone quarry by sculptor Harvey Fite. It covers more than 6 acres and is made of thousands of tons of finely fitted bluestone; it was constructed over a period of 37 years by Fite, who taught art at Bard College. At the center of it stands a 9-ton monolith. Fite had meant the entire sculpture to be a backdrop for his large stone carvings, but the backdrop took over and he removed the carvings to the surrounding lawns, woods, and pools, where they can still be seen. *Hours:* Memorial Day to October, Friday to Sunday noon to 5pm. Call ahead, because Saturday is often reserved for musical and other special events. *Admission:* $5 adults, $4 seniors and students, free for children ages 11 and under.

Saugerties is an attractive Victorian town with several antiques stores worth browsing, plus an old-fashioned cinema. It's also home to a year-round tennis camp. Once a prosperous riverfront town, it achieved recent fame when it hosted the second Woodstock Festival.

While you're here you may want to visit the **Saugerties lighthouse** (☎ 914/247-0656), which has a museum. It's open on weekends from Memorial Day to Labor Day from 2 to 5pm. The caretaker's two-bedroom apartment can be reserved in advance for overnight accommodations on weekends. *Rates:* $100 double.

WOODSTOCK LODGING

Right on the main street, tucked behind a shady garden, **Twin Gables**, 73 Tinker St., Woodstock, NY 12498 (☎ 914/679-9479; fax 914/679-55638; www.twingableswoodstockny.com), is homey and attractive and retains the ambience of the time during the 1940s when many artists lodged here. There are nine rooms, three with bath and six with air-conditioning; the remaining six share 2½ baths (bathrobes are provided). The many paintings by Woodstock artists gracing the rooms add an authentic accent. Guests settle into the living room to chat or read or take advantage of such additional amenities as the TV, refrigerator, or phone. *Rates:* November to Memorial Day, $55 to $80; Memorial Day to October, $65 to $90.

WOODSTOCK & NEARBY DINING

On Woodstock's main street, **Joshua's Cafe,** 51 Tinker St. (☎ 914/679-5533), can be trusted to serve large portions of healthy Middle Eastern fare. The menu is very extensive and main courses include shish kebab, kilic sis (skewered swordfish with tomatoes, celery, mushrooms, and peppers), batata charp (potato pies filled with vegetables or meat), and paella couscous (clams, mussels, chicken, sausage, shrimp, peas, tomatoes, and onions). Dishes are priced from $5 to $18. At brunch 10 or so omelets are offered, from fried bananas and melted cheese to sautéed onions, potatoes, tomatoes, and parsley, along with a dozen egg dishes, whole-grain pancakes, and challah French toast. A small place—1960s style, with polished wood tables and chairs—Joshua's is always crowded with an interesting-looking artsy crowd. *Hours:* Sunday to Thursday 11am to 9pm, Friday to Saturday 10am to 1am.

Another town veteran is **Christy's,** 85 Mill Hill Rd. (☎ 914/679-5300), which has been serving locals since 1935. It has a cozy atmosphere, with a beamed ceiling, double fireplace, and a small bar in the back. The food is good for the price and consists of traditional dishes like roast pork and stuffed fillet of sole. Prices range from $10 to $16. There's outdoor dining in summer. *Hours:* Tuesday to Sunday 4:30 to 10pm.

Just outside of town, a more atmospheric choice is the **Blue Mountain Bistro,** Route 212 and Glasco Turnpike (☎ 914/679-8519), located in a renovated 18th-century barn. You'll find three intimate dining rooms and a spacious bar with classic zinc counter. The cuisine is French Mediterranean, but what makes the place unusual is the collection of almost 30 tapas that are offered. You can enjoy, for example, everything from Spanish potato-and-onion tortilla and chickpea salad to Swiss chard with pine nuts, salmon cakes, or oysters on the half shell. Among main courses there might be a flavorsome free-range chicken roasted with thyme, rosemary, garlic, and lemon. The house specialty, salmon en papillote, is a wonderfully moist fish that has been baked in parchment with lemon, leeks, fresh herbs, and orzo. Prices range from $13 to $21. For dessert try the Catalan version of crème brûlée, which is flavored with vanilla, lemon, and fennel. *Hours:* Tuesday to Sunday 5 to 9pm.

Bois d'Arc, at the corner of Zena and Sawkill Roads (☎ 914/679-5995), is at the top of the dining list in Woodstock. It's located in an attractive 1760 stone building away from the center of town. Inside the decor is warm and cozy. Beamed ceilings and tile floors, plus some inspirational metalwork crafted by the chef, set the tone. The tables are covered with sparkling white cloths. Chef James Jennings uses local ingredients in fresh, exciting contemporary dishes. Depending on the season, you might start with roast pumpkin soup richly flavored with cinnamon, apple, and clove; or corn-crusted calamari with cilantro, lime, and aïoli. Expect to find about six or so main dishes, which will always include a vegetarian option. There might be mustard-seared tuna in a lemon and chive beurre blanc; Black Angus fillet with demi-glace; or two roasted quail with a delicious oyster, sage, and walnut stuffing plus a cinnamon maple glaze. Prices range from $16 to $23. *Hours:* Thursday to Tuesday 6 to 10:30pm.

Mountain Gate, 4 Deming St. (☎ 914/679-5100), offers decent Indian cuisine. The atmosphere is more comfortable than that at most traditional Indian restaurants—cane-seated Breuer chairs and dark-green tablecloths combined with golden napkins. The service can be slow and erratic, though. The menu offers all the usual favorites, priced from $10 to $18. Spice lovers will want to try the lamb, beef, or chicken vindaloo; the tandoori fish and the lobster malabar are other specialties. A full range of vegetarian dishes is also available. *Hours:* Sunday to Thursday 5 to 10pm, Friday to Saturday 5 to 11pm.

The famous bakery, **Bread Alone** (located out on Route 28 in Boiceville) has a store at 22 Mill Hill Rd. (☎ 914/679-2108), selling its great breads (try the seven-grain health loaf) plus sandwiches, pizza, salads, and pastries and cakes. The breads are first-class, but the pastries are rather disappointing. *Hours:* Sunday to Thursday 7:30am to 6pm, Friday to Saturday 7:30am to 7pm.

Just out of town, on Route 212 about 3 miles east of Woodstock, **New World Cooking** (☎ 914/246-0900), serves some of the best cuisine in the area. The emphasis is on spicy Caribbean and Asian-style dishes. Jerk chicken and jerk pork come smothered with a spicy sauce, the black sesame-seared salmon is dressed with a pineapple-sage vinaigrette, and the ropa vieja or Cuban pot roast has a tangy flavor. Barbecue dishes are similarly piquant, and if you want more heat, several hot sauces are on the table. The menu also offers several vegetarian dishes, like the New World seitan steak, which is served with a choice of tomatillo salsa or jerk sauce, plus wood-grilled dishes and sandwiches. Prices range from $7 to $18. Ten wines are available by the glass; bottle prices are reasonable and the selections appropriate to the food. The restaurant occupies an old barn, and the decor is colorful and funky. Diners can enjoy the chefs working in the open kitchen. *Hours:* Monday to Saturday 5 to 11pm, Sunday 11am to 3pm.

Good Chinese cuisine is found at **The Little Bear** (☎ 914/679-8899), in nearby Bearsville, where you can dine on Hunan, Peking, Cantonese, and Szechuan fare on a patio overlooking the creek (illuminated at night) or inside in a woodsy atmosphere. It's especially haunting in fall, when a series of lit pumpkins is placed along the banks of the creek. Try the spicy, delicious General Hso's chicken or shrimp or the Trio of Delights, a combination of three dishes—shrimp, beef, and chicken in different styles. Prices range from $9 to $15. *Hours:* Sunday to Thursday noon to 10:30pm, Friday to Saturday noon to 11pm.

Another recommended Bearsville restaurant, right next door and on the creek, is the **Bear Cafe**, Route 212 (☎ 914/679-5555). It's legendary around Woodstock for having been created in 1971 by Albert Grossman, rock impresario and manager to such musical artists as Bob Dylan and The Band; Janis Joplin; and Peter, Paul, and Mary. The food is excellent, but some people may find the place too noisy. If you want to relax and have a quiet conversation, this isn't the place—on weekends you really do have to shout if you want your dining companions to hear you. It has a barnlike air, with cathedral ceilings and plenty of wood beams. The nice thing about the place is that it offers two menus—a lighter, lower-priced cafe menu featuring sandwiches, salads, and appetizers as well as a more fulsome menu. Among the entrees may be pan-seared salmon with tomato concassé and smoked roasted tomato nage, filet mignon with port-garlic sauce and Stilton cheese, and pan-roasted natural chicken with green peppercorn sauce and garlic mashed potatoes. For dessert, plump for the key lime pie. Prices range from $13 to $21. There are at least a dozen wines served by the glass, plus a selection of tequilas, single malts, single-barrel bourbon, and cognacs. *Hours:* Wednesday to Monday 6pm to closing.

Just 10 minutes from Woodstock, **The Terrapin**, 250 Spillway Rd., West Hurley (☎ 914/331-3663), is my all-time favorite place to dine in the area. It's located in a historic building. There's a tiny bar up front and two simply decorated dining rooms furnished with polished wood tables. It opened in late 1998 and soon attracted a loyal crowd that appreciates the intensely flavored dishes prepared by chef Josh Kroner and Tamara Hunter. Kroner honed his skills at Mesa Grill in New York City and likes to combine Asian, Italian, and American cuisines in dishes that feature the products of the Hudson Valley. All of the appetizers are flavorsome, from the wonderful roast garlic soup with red chili croutons to the barbecued duck quesadilla with mango avocado salsa enhanced by the addition of red onions and fontina cheese. The Hudson Valley foie gras with pecan stuffing makes a wonderful combination of textures, too. Kroner knows how to prepare fish dishes that blend flavors without overpowering the core ingredient. Try, for example the pan-roasted sea bass with an orange balsamic sauce or the horseradish-crusted tuna served with miso aïoli. To finish, order the warm cocoa cake with liquid chocolate center. It's addictive. Prices range from $14 to $19. *Hours:* Wednesday to Sunday 5:30pm to closing.

SAUGERTIES LODGING & DINING

Some of the region's best dining is found at **Cafe Tamayo**, 89 Partition St., Saugerties (☎ 914/246-9371). It occupies a handsome Victorian building, and diners can choose to dine either up front in the bar area, complete with a beautifully carved and mirrored mahogany bar, or in the rooms behind. In summer the garden is also open—a lovely flagstone patio complete with fountain and umbrella tables. The atmosphere is casually elegant. The menu changes seasonally, but whatever dishes appear will use the freshest ingredients, many of them locally and organically raised in the Hudson Valley. They are carefully prepared by Chef James Tamayo to bring out the natural flavors. You might find chicken paillard seasoned with spices and served with a piquant tomato and basil sauce, calves' liver enriched by a Madeira sauce, or grilled lamb that's been marinated in onion, garlic, lemon juice, and oil to produce a delicious au jus. Prices range from $14 to $22. The menu suggests wines to accompany each dish and offers them all by the glass. Among the appetizers, the smoked salmon and potato pancake is a favorite house specialty. So, too, is the Coach Farm goat cheese coated with bread crumbs, fried, and served with a roasted red pepper puree and mâche. The desserts are not innovative, but the lemon tart with sesame crust is my choice for the end of a wonderful meal. The wine list is extensive, and many of the selections are available by the glass. There are also two rooms available if you want to stay overnight. *Hours:* Thursday to Saturday noon to 2:30pm, Wednesday to Saturday 5pm to closing, Sunday 11:30am to 3pm and 5pm to closing.

Bluestone Country Manor, Box 144, W. Camp, NY 12490 (☎ 914/246-3060), is set on 3 acres with views to the east of the distant Berkshires and to the west of the Catskills. The house was built in the 1930s and features fine architectural details such as hardwood floors inlaid with teak. There are four comfortably furnished rooms including a carriage house suite. Guests have plenty of space for socializing and relaxing from the living room with its brick fireplace to the sunroom/library and wicker-furnished front porch. A full breakfast is served either in the dining room or on the front porch. *Rates:* $89 to $109

Total Tennis, 1811 Old King's Hwy. off 32 north (Box 28), Saugerties, NY 12477 (☎ 800/221-6496 or 914/247-9177), is one of the few East Coast tennis camps. It has 13 clay and 7 all-weather outdoor courts, plus 5 indoor courts for year-round play. If you come here, expect to enjoy up to 5 hours of tennis instruction, which can be tailored to beginners, intermediate, and advanced players. Guests relax in the living room and library at the rustic lodge, which is warmed by a fire on cold days. Three meals a day are served in the lodge dining room. There are 43 basically furnished rooms located in several different buildings. Additional facilities include an outdoor pool and a nine-hole golf course one-quarter mile down the road. *Rates:* Weekend packages including meals, lessons, and accommodations start at $350 in fall and $375 in summer.

```
                The Catskills
           Special & Recreational Activities
```

Boating: In Catskill, **Riverview Marine Services,** 103 Main St. (☎ 518/ 943-5311), rents canoes for $15 for 2 hours or $25 a day and also 16- to 20-foot powerboats for use on the Hudson River. The latter start at $130 for a half day.

Camping: Backpackers can camp anywhere on state-owned land in the Catskill Forest Preserves and State Reforestation Areas as long as the site is designated or at least 150 feet from the trail, road, or body of water and below 3,500 feet altitude. They can also use the lean-tos provided along the trails.

North Lake, on Route 23A, 3 miles northeast of Haines Falls, NY 12436 (☎ 518/589-5058), open from May 1 to late October, offers 187 sites plus spectacular scenery, swimming, fishing, and canoe and boat rentals on two lakes. Camping costs $18 a night. It's wise to make reservations.

There's also camping at **Devil's Tombstone,** Route 214, Hunter (☎ 914/688-7160), from May to Labor Day. There are only 24 sites, making for a quieter scene. The charge is $11 a night.

Other New York Environmental Conservation camping areas, charging around $14 to $15 for camping and most open from May 1 to at least September 30, are at **Beaverkill,** R.R. 3 (P.O. 243), Roscoe (☎ 914/ 439-4281), offering swimming and fishing; **Kenneth L. Wilson,** Wittenberg Road, Mount Tremper (☎ 914/679-7020), with swimming and fishing, has camping until Columbus Day ($14 a day); **Mongaup Pond,** De Bruce Road, north of De Bruce (☎ 914/439-4233), with swimming, fishing, and rowboat and canoe rentals ($15 a day), offers camping until mid-December ($14 a night); and **Woodland Valley,** 1319 Woodland Valley Rd., near Phoenicia (☎ 914/688-7647), which stays open for camping until Columbus Day ($11 a night), has 72 sites.

Contact the **Bureau of Preserve Protection and Management, New York State Department of Environmental Conservation,** 50 Wolf Rd., Room 412, Albany, NY 12233-4255. The central Conservation Authority number is ☎ 914/256-3099. For reservations at any New York State campground call ☎ 800/456-2267. Reservations can be made 11 months in advance. From May 23 to September 1, campsites in the Catskill State Forest Preserves can be reserved at least 8 days in advance through Ticketron for stays of 3 to 14 nights.

Canoeing: Canoeing-camping can be enjoyed along 75 miles of the Delaware from Hancock to Port Jervis. For information, contact **Lander's River Trips,** Route 97 (P.O. Box 376), Narrowsburg, NY 12764 (☎ 914/252-3925), which rents canoes, kayaks, and rafts for $27 to $30 per day and runs canoe-camping or canoe-lodging packages. Two-day/two-night packages (including dormitory lodging and one dinner) start at $69 per person; camping packages start at $48 per person. Children ages 12 and under are half price. Free transportation is included.

Silver Canoe Rentals, 37 S. Maple Ave., Port Jervis, NY 12771 (☎ 914/856-7055), rents canoes and rafts for $22 per day.

Esopus Creek also offers canoeing, kayaking, and tubing opportunities. Bring your kayak, canoe, or tube and board the **Catskill Mountain Railroad** open train, P.O. Box 46, Shokan, NY 12481 (☎ 914/688-7400), which will take you from Mount Pleasant to Phoenicia, where you can ride the river back to your car. It's usually a bit of a bumpy ride because the water's not very deep. Trains operate weekends from early July to Labor Day from noon to 4pm on the hour. The round-trip cost is $6 for adults and $2 for children ages 4 to 12. Tubes can be rented in Phoenicia.

Atlantic Kayak Tours, 320 W Saugerties Rd., Saugerties, NY 12477 (☎ 914/246-2187), offers a variety of kayaking tours in the Hudson Valley and elsewhere on the East Coast. It also provides instructional classes.

Cross-Country Skiing: Belleayre Mountain, Highmount (☎ 914/254-5601), and **Frost Valley YMCA Camp,** Oliverea (☎ 914/985-2291), offer beau-tiful, well-groomed trails; Hunter Mountain's area is at Mountain Trails at Hyer Meadows, Route 23A Tannersville (☎ 518/589-5361), which has 35km of trails. In Haines Falls, Vilaggio Resort has 14km of marked trails and offers rentals. In Windham, **White Birches Ski Touring Center** off Route 23 (☎ 914/734-3266) has 15 miles of groomed trails, a cozy warming lodge with two fireplaces, plus hot food. In Rosendale, **Williams Lake Hotel** (☎ 914/658-3101) has 15km of varied trails.

Fishing: Roscoe, at the junction of the Beaverkill and the Willowemoc rivers, is known locally as Trout Town. The Esopus Creek is one of the Northeast's most famous angling rivers, known for its rainbow, brown, and brook trout. Other fine waters include the Beaverkill, Plattekill, Rondout, Sawkill, and Woodland Valley creeks. You can also fish in the Ashokan and Rondout Reservoir, but special permits, in addition to the regular fishing license, are required (call ☎ 914/657-2663 for permit). Shad and bass are also found in the Hudson River. At least two fly-fishing schools operate in the region. The most famous is the **Wulff Fishing School,** P.O. Box 948, Livingston Manor, NY 12758 (☎ 914/439-4060), which is operated by Joan Wulff, an international fly-fishing champion who writes regularly for *Fly Rod and Reel Magazine* and has authored several books. The school offers weekend courses (April to June only) for $425 instruction only. Book as soon as possible just to get on the waiting list.

Fruit Picking: For information, contact any one of the county public information offices or local chambers of commerce.

Golf: Windham Country Club, South Street (☎ 518/734-9910), has 18 holes, par 71. Greens fees are $36 weekdays and $45 weekends.

Hiking: Trails abound in the Catskills. Hiking-trail maps of the region can be purchased at the Golden Notebook or Catskill Art Supply in Woodstock. Closest to Woodstock is the trail that leads to the summit of Overlook Mountain. To access it, take Rock City Road from the center of Woodstock and Meads Mountain Road to a parking area opposite the Tibetan Buddhist monastery. An accessible trail up Mount Tremper starts on the old state highway about a mile east of Phoenicia. The **Wittenberg-Cornell Slide Trail** gives access to Slide Mountain, the highest peak in the Catskills. It offers wonderful rewards at any time of year. Access is either from the Woodland Valley Campground just outside Phoenicia or from Route 47 near Winnisook Lake. The trail is under 10 miles, but is strenuous and crosses three mountains.

Horseback Riding: *Delhi:* **Hilltop Stables,** New Road, Bovina Center (☎ 607/832-4342), charges $10 per hour and also offers overnight trail rides (groups only). *Tannersville:* **Silver Springs Ranch,** Route 16 (☎ 518/589-5559), offers 1- and 2-hour trail rides starting at $25 per person. Reservations are needed for 1-day and overnight trips.

Skiing: The best is undoubtedly at **Hunter Mountain** (see earlier in this chapter), but there are other choices, notably the already-mentioned **Windham and Belleayre,** P.O. Box 313, Highmount, NY 12441 (☎ 914/254-5600 or 800/942-6904 for snow info), which is good for beginners and experts. The vertical rise is 1,404 feet. There are 33 trails, nine lifts with a capacity of 9,000+ people an hour, and 87% snow-making capacity.

Soaring & Hang Gliding: Centers for this are on the southern edge of the Catskills at Wurtsboro and Ellenville. For hang gliding, contact the **Mountain Wings Hang Gliding Center,** 150 Canal St., Ellenville (☎ 914/647-3377), which provides introductory hang gliding programs ($125) and 2- and 6-day training programs. It also offers the newest, most exciting form of foot-launched flying—paragliding—which uses parachutes that are launched like a hang glider. **Wurtsboro Flight Service, Inc.,** Wurtsboro Airport, Route 209, Wurtsboro, NY 12790 (☎ 914/888-2791), offers complete courses for beginners in soaring as well as sailplane rentals for the rated pilot. You can take a 15- to 20-minute demonstration ride for $32.

Tubing: Enjoy a bumpy ride along the Esopus. Tube rentals are available from the **Town Tinker,** Bridge Street, Phoenicia (☎ 914/688-5553). The cost is $15 per person for a tube with a seat. A deposit is required.

Saratoga Springs

Saratoga Springs ◆ *New Skete* ◆ *Lake Luzerne*
◆ *Lake George* ◆ *Friends Lake*

Distance in miles: 186
Estimated driving time: 3 hours

◄o►◄o►◄o►◄o►◄o►

Driving: Take the New York State Thruway to Albany, then I-87 to Exit 13 north. Take Route 9 north.

Bus: Both Greyhound (☎ 800/231-2222) and Adirondack Trailways (☎ 800/225-6815) go to Albany and Saratoga Springs.

Train: Amtrak's *Adirondack* stops in Saratoga Springs. For information, call ☎ 800/872-7245.

Further Information: For more about the area's festivals and events and about Saratoga Springs, contact the **Greater Saratoga Chamber of Commerce,** 28 Clinton St., 2nd floor, off Church Street, Saratoga Springs, NY 12866 (☎ 518/584-3255).

For Albany information, contact the **Albany County Convention & Visitors Bureau,** 52 S. Pearl St., Albany, NY 12207 (☎ 518/434-1217).

◄o►◄o►◄o►◄o►◄o►

Events & Festivals to Plan Your Trip Around

January–February: Winter Carnival Weekends at Lake George.
April–November: Harness racing. Call ☎ 518/584-2110.
June–September: The Performing Arts Festival. Contact SPAC, Spa State Park, Saratoga Springs, NY 12866 (☎ 518/587-3330 in season, 518/584-9330 off-season). Tickets go on sale in early May.
Late July to Late August: The Saratoga Race Meeting. Call ☎ 518/584-6200 for dates.

Normally the population of Saratoga Springs is a modest 25,000, but in summer it swells to 75,000 for the party centering on the old Victorian Clubhouse at the Saratoga Race Course. The races are on, the steeds are running, and Saratoga is the place to see the silks flashing by and the horses' flanks sweating in the sun, to feel the air of increasing excitement as the horses fly out, their hoofs pounding on the turf. It's August and this is the month to visit Saratoga, unless you dislike crowds and celebrations. People also come for the now-famous arts festival that begins in June—a unique affair blessed with two national companies as regular visitors: the New York City Ballet and the Philadelphia Orchestra. During both of these events the hotels and motels are full, with people staying as far away as Albany and even farther south. The large Victorian residences on North Broadway are filled with house parties and house guests as "the season" swings into high gear.

A Special Ambience

Although Saratoga has experienced some ups and some severe downs during its history, it has nearly always had a special summer ambience. Today you can still easily see why this spa became such a great social mecca in the 1800s and early 1900s. The park and the springs were always, and still are, prime attractions; casino gambling, and the excitement and glamour it engendered, was another; horse racing was still another plus. Grand hotels sprang up. Large Victorian summer cottages were constructed, and people flocked here at the turn of the century. It became de rigueur for the American barons to migrate to Saratoga for at least a part of the summer.

Gideon Putnam built the first hotel in 1803, and soon crowds were coming to take the waters, as many as 12,000 by 1825. They came to drink, inhale the steam, or bathe in the waters (which you can still do); if they had no physical complaints, they simply drank the waters in fashionable drink halls with elegant Greek Revival columns and long colonnades, while strolling to the lilting strains of bands and orchestras. By 1840 the era of the grand hotels had fully arrived, the most famous Saratoga examples being the Grand Union and the United States, vast and palatial. Sadly, neither has survived to today. The United States was torn down in 1946, the Grand Union following in 1952.

The Casinos & Racetrack

In 1861, John Morrissey, a sometime U.S. heavyweight boxing champion and a congressman from New York City, boldly opened the first casino so he could indulge his own passion. Two years later he built the racetrack, thus making Saratoga a veritable playground for the rich and famous. Among the most colorful patrons were Diamond Jim Brady and his companion, actress Lillian Russell. Brady, a railroad equipment salesman and steel car magnate of prodigious girth and appetite, was known to drink gallons of fruit juice along with a daily diet of three dozen oysters in the morning and eight dozen more at night, plus eggs, steaks, chops, joints of beef, several lobsters and crabs, and whole fowls accompanied by vegetables, salads, and desserts. His eminently suitable companion carried her 200 well-corseted pounds with such charm that she was able to capture five husbands. Less flashy were the Whitneys, Vanderbilts, and Morgans, who came to romp here until 1907, when reformers closed the casino and Saratoga embarked on a roller-coaster phase.

Saratoga Springs

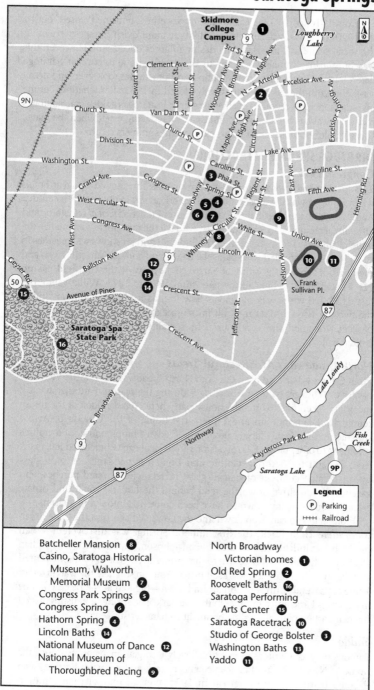

Legend
- Ⓟ Parking
- ┼┼┼ Railroad

Batcheller Mansion ⑧
Casino, Saratoga Historical
  Museum, Walworth
  Memorial Museum ⑦
Congress Park Springs ⑤
Congress Spring ⑥
Hathorn Spring ④
Lincoln Baths ⑭
National Museum of Dance ⑫
National Museum of
  Thoroughbred Racing ⑨

North Broadway
  Victorian homes ①
Old Red Spring ②
Roosevelt Baths ⑯
Saratoga Performing
  Arts Center ⑮
Saratoga Racetrack ⑩
Studio of George Bolster ③
Washington Baths ⑬
Yaddo ⑪

From 1910 to 1913 the casino and the racetrack remained closed, but by the 1920s the resort was thriving again. Many more lavish cottages were built; the social scene was populated by dashing figures once again. However, this was only a brief renaissance, for in the 1930s the ambience of Saratoga deteriorated. Gamblers, bookies, pimps, and prostitutes took over, and decay settled in until the casinos were finally closed in 1951 after a national crime investigation. Only racing kept alive the spirit of Saratoga's golden era. Saratoga's recent revival has been built around the 24-day racing meet, when the magic and splendor of those languorous, extravagant summers return.

SARATOGA SPRINGS ATTRACTIONS

Congress Park

This lovely 33-acre park, just off Broadway, was surrounded by great hotels when Saratoga was the most renowned American spa in the late 19th century. At the center of the park stands Daniel Chester French's *Spirit of Life* statue and fountain, a memorial to Spencer Trask, who led the movement to revitalize the mineral springs. Today you're likely to find craft and art shows where ladies in veiled hats once strolled with parasols. Bandstand concerts are still given and they help recapture the spirit of Saratoga's heyday. At the **Canfield casino** (☎ 518/584-6920), built in the park from 1870 to 1871, Willie Vanderbilt lost $130,000 while waiting for his lady friends to dress for dinner. Today, the two top floors are set up with museum exhibits, although the ballroom has been retained and is still used by socialite Marylou Whitney for her annual ball.

North Broadway's Architectural Treats

From Congress Park, go back out onto North Broadway to view the Victorian homes or "cottages" built for brief stays during the season. Fantasize what it must have been like to attend a house party here. You can look at the house rented by Diamond Jim and Lillian, the home of the Cluetts of Arrow shirt fame, the Gaines family home, the Ogden Phipps house, and houses belonging to other racing folk. Styles vary from Jacobean to bracketed Italianate, from Federal to Victorian Gothic and French Renaissance. As you pass by you'll catch glimpses of stained glass, turrets, vine-covered porches, and gazebos. If you drive down the road behind the houses, you'll find ornate carriage houses, many of which have been converted into living quarters.

From here you can drop down into the Lower Village, past the Olde Bryan Inn, where High Rock, the first mineral spring, was discovered. When the Mohawk Indians carried Sir William Johnson, superintendent of Indian affairs, on a litter from Johnstown to the springs in August 1771, he was cured and the springs' reputation was established. You can still take the waters today. There are several springs in and around town—Big Red at the racetrack, one in Congress Park, and a number in the spa park. The springs are distinguished by their carbonation and saline or alkaline characteristics.

Yaddo

Famous now as a writer's retreat, this lovely Georgian mansion was once the home of New York City financier Spencer Trask and his wife, Katrina, who decided to turn it into a retreat in 1926 after all four of their children died from illnesses. Among the artists, writers, and songwriters who've found inspiration here are Carson McCullers, Philip Roth, Saul Bellow, Ned Rorem, Leonard Bernstein, Virgil Thomson, Malcolm Cowley, Katharine Anne Porter (who supposedly wrote *Ship of Fools* here), and Truman Capote (who wrote *Other Voices, Other Rooms* here). Although you can't go inside the gray stone mansion, you can visit the fountains and rose garden—complete with a pergola covered with rambling roses—and the peaceful Japanese rock garden. Garden tours are given on Tuesday, Saturday, and Sunday. Call ☎ 518/584-0746 for information.

The Racetrack

If you visit during the 24-day meet, you'll want to have breakfast at the clubhouse, resplendent with ivied window boxes, while you watch the horses exercise. Even if the races aren't on, a visit to the racetrack is a must. It's the oldest thoroughbred track in the country—the first race was run in 1863. When John Morrissey formed the first racing association, he didn't think it would be that popular because it was created during the Civil War. But it was a great success and has been ever since. Famed for several stunning racing upsets, it's known as "the graveyard of favorites." In 1919, Man o' War, bested only once before, was defeated at Saratoga by a horse aptly named Upset. In 1930 the Travers Triple Crown winner, Gallant Fox, fell victim to Jim Dandy, the 100-to-1 shot. Secretariat was also upset here in 1973. Post time is usually 1:30pm.

The most famous race, the Travers Stakes, is the occasion for a whole week of spectacular events—parades, craft shows in Congress Park, golf and tennis tournaments, and concerts. The Whitney Handicap and the Saratoga Cup are also run in the season.

Note: When planning your trip to Saratoga, try to make it at the beginning or end of the second week of August, when you can share the eager anticipation in the Humphrey S. Finney Pavilion, as tuxedoed auctioneers preside over the yearling sales. Some people swear that this is *the* most exciting event in Saratoga. See for yourself. For additional information, call ☎ 518/584-4700.

SARATOGA SPA STATE PARK

Noted hydrotherapist Simon Baruch helped plan the 2,000-acre park as a spa, and his son, Bernard, finished it in 1935. Inside the park are 26 springs—primarily laden with sodium, lithium, and potassium—plus a 9-hole and an 18-hole golf course, the Olympic-size Peerless Pool, eight tennis courts, the Gideon Putnam Hotel, and the Victoria Pool, favored bathing place of dancers and artists who appear at the arts center, whose natural amphitheater is in the park. The New York City Ballet performs here in July, the Philadelphia Orchestra in August. A buffet is served before performances in the **Hall of Springs** (☎ 518/583-3003). There's a nominal entrance fee for cars (around $4). For information about the park, contact the **Park Superintendent's Office**, P.O. Box W, Saratoga Springs State Park, Saratoga Springs, NY 12866 (☎ 518/584-2000).

The Lincoln Baths

The Lincoln Baths (☎ 518/583-2880) in the park are among the highlights of any visit. Although the bathhouse looks like a utilitarian hospital—a far cry from a typically luxurious modern spa—the treatment given here is euphoric and is certainly one of the best buys in Saratoga. For about 20 minutes you lie back in a tub, up to your neck in hot, brown mineral water; it's like sitting in bubbling seltzer with a pillow at your head and a stool at your feet. The masseur then wraps you in hot sheets and gives you a head-to-toe massage before tucking you into bed for a short nap. The whole process takes about an hour. You'll emerge feeling relaxed, content, and totally rejuvenated as you walk out into the beautiful park setting. Everyone should be entitled to this experience at least once a week. Aromatherapy, reflexology, facials, and body wraps are also provided. Prices are $16 bath, $30 for a 30-minute massage, $60 for an hour. *Hours:* Summer, Thursday to Monday 8:30am to 4:40pm; the rest of the year, Thursday to Sunday 8:30am to 4:40pm. The last bath is given at 3pm. In summer you need to book at least 2 weeks in advance for a massage, not for a bath.

The **Roosevelt Baths** (☎ 518/584-2011) are currently closed for renovations.

OTHER SARATOGA SPRINGS ATTRACTIONS

The **Regent Street Antiques Center,** 153 Regent St. (☎ 518/584-0107), is in Skidmore College's first college building, constructed in 1903 (named Skidmore in 1922). It houses 20 antiques dealers plus the Museum of Antiques and Art, several private collections of stoneware, Hummel figurines, bottles, canes, and (when I visited) a local collector's exquisite scrimshaw and ivory carvings. The rest of the building is occupied by dealers displaying clocks, glass, music boxes, jewelry, weathervanes, architectural salvage pieces, silverware, Victorian furniture, and other antiques and collectibles. You can spend hours browsing here. Best of all, it's open year-round. *Hours:* Daily 10am to 5pm. Closed New Year's Day, Thanksgiving, and Christmas. *Admission:* Free.

Even for those who aren't particularly interested in architecture, the **Batcheller Mansion** on Circular Street, at Whitney Place, appeals to the fantasy in all of us with its scalloped gables and Chambord-style towers capped with minarets, all built in 1873. It has been magnificently restored and now operates as an inn (see "Saratoga Lodging," below).

The **National Museum of Thoroughbred Racing,** Union Avenue (☎ 518/584-0400), displays racing silks, equine art, trophies, and memorabilia of legendary names in turf history. *Hours:* Summer, Monday to Saturday 10am to 4:30pm, Sunday noon to 4:30pm; August, daily 9am to 5pm. *Admission:* $5 adults, $3 seniors and children over age 5.

The **Historical Society Museum of Saratoga Springs** and the **Walworth Memorial Museum** (☎ 518/584-6920) are located atop the casino building and contain exhibits relating to the history of Saratoga, plus a series of period rooms. *Hours:* Summer, Monday to Saturday 10am to 4pm, Sunday 1 to 4pm (July to August, daily 9:30am to 4:30pm); winter, Thursday to Sunday 1 to 4pm. *Admission:* $3 adults, $2 seniors and children age 12 and under.

The **polo games** are also exciting, usually scheduled throughout August on Tuesday, Friday, Saturday, and Sunday. Contact the Saratoga Polo Association, P.O. Box 821, Saratoga Springs, NY 12866 (☎ 518/584-3255 or 518/584-8108).

Dance lovers will want to view the **National Museum of Dance** (☎ 518/584-2225), in the Washington Bath building, on South Broadway (Route 9) in Saratoga Spa State Park. Modern, jazz, ballet, and other dance forms are explored through a variety of exhibits. *Hours:* Tuesday to Sunday 10am to 5pm. *Admission:* $3.50 adults, $2.50 seniors and students, $1 children under age 12.

A NEARBY ATTRACTION

Some 20 miles or so north in Glens Falls, the **Hyde Collection**, 161 Warren St. (☎ 518/792-1761), is well worth seeing. Housed in an Italian Renaissance–style villa built in 1912, the collection includes works by Botticelli, da Vinci, Rembrandt, and Rubens, and by such later painters as Cézanne, Picasso, Renoir, and van Gogh. Americans represented in the collection include Thomas Eakins, Childe Hassam, Winslow Homer, and James Whistler. These are displayed along with handsome Italian Renaissance and 18th-century French antiques, all collected by Louis Fiske Hyde and Charlotte Pruyn Hyde in the early part of this century. The galleries are arranged around a two-story skylit courtyard studded with sculpture and plants. *Hours:* May to December, Tuesday to Sunday 10am to 5pm; January to April, Thursday to Sunday. January to April, Thursday to Sunday only. *Admission:* Free.

SARATOGA LODGING

The **Gideon Putnam**, Saratoga Springs, NY 12866 (☎ 518/584-3000), is *the* place to stay. Certainly the setting in Saratoga Spa State Park is beautiful, but I prefer the Adelphi or a similar smaller accommodation. This 1935 redbrick Georgian structure offers spectacular views, whatever the season. A tree-lined circular drive that seems more appropriate for a coach-and-four than a car leads up to the Corinthian-columned portico, giving entry to a grand marbled, mirrored, chandeliered lobby. The parlor suites opening onto large, bamboo-furnished screened porches are the most desirable of the 132 rooms. The other rooms are quite ordinary, decorated in dark blue or rust with large floral-print curtains, candlewick bedspreads, and reproduction antiques. TVs and phones are standard. All rooms are gradually being refurbished.

The Georgian Dining Room, with handsome hand-painted wallpaper, is elegant for dinner. It offers contemporary American cuisine with such dishes as grilled chicken breast Dijon with a thyme jus, pan-seared duck breast with apple ginger glaze, and crab cakes with sweet chili aïoli. Prices range from $19 to $25. The typical $17 Sunday buffet brunch—a spread of scrambled eggs, lasagna, ham, beans and carrots, and so on—is popular, but somewhat over-rated. You'll need a reservation. The hotel gives you immediate access to all the park's facilities: eight tennis courts, a 27-hole golf course, three outdoor pools, and cross-country skiing (in the Victoria Pool building). Bicycles can also be rented.

Rates: August, $260 to $475 double; mid-April to mid-November (excluding August), $140 to $200; mid-November to mid-April, $105 to $175. Special packages available.

On the main street, the **Adelphi**, 365 Broadway, Saratoga Springs, NY 12866 (☎ 518/587-4688; fax 518/587-0851; www.adelphihotel.com), is the most atmospheric fantasy place here. Dating to 1877, it is a survivor from that legendary opulent era when social life consisted of walks to the springs, after-noon garden parties, and high-fashion promenades, followed by gala balls in the evening. The facade is graced with tall, slender columns that rise three stories high and are capped by delicate gingerbread fretwork. Inside, the lobby is quintessential Gilded Age. Under the lofty 14-foot ceilings supported by square fluted wood pillars stand an assortment of Victorian sofas and chairs, each beautifully upholstered in the finest brocades and fabrics. My favorites are the French polished Empire couch secured from the Schuyler mansion and the camelback sofas in the center. Stenciled walls, large flower arrangements, fringed lampshades, and one or two potted palms complete the Victorian ambience.

Gregg Siefker and Sheila Parkert bought the Adelphi more than a decade ago after it had stood empty for 10 years. They've gradually restored it, filling it with wonderful authentic period furnishings. The only pieces original to the hotel—it had been stripped—are the front desk and the valanced, draped, and tasseled floor-to-ceiling mirror. Sheila has decorated all 39 rooms in her special, inspired style with antique rugs and furniture and swag curtains. All have baths, phones, air-conditioning, and TVs. One or two front rooms have balconies overlooking the sweep of Broadway. Here are just a few favorites: Room 19, a small suite with candy-striped wallpaper in pink and jade, contains a Victorian acorn bed adorned with a spectacular oriental tent. Complementary furnishings include gilt-framed pictures and a sink with a pink marble surround. The sitting room has a dusky-rose carpet, a settee, and overstuffed comfy chairs. Suite 16 has a mix of Mission and Adirondack furnishings set against geometric-patterned wallpaper, plus a fabulous paneled bath with an old-fashioned tub and separate shower. Suite 3 is large, boasting a private balcony furnished with wicker and a Victorian-style fireplace with a grate. The curtains are valanced, the wallpaper is brocade, and chairs are slipcovered (so is the bathtub); white damask covers the sofa. The parlor is filled with Stickley and assorted Victorian furnishings and artifacts. Room 1 is typical—the bed has an inlaid headboard, the pillows are damask with lace trim, brocade molded wall panels adorn the walls, the curtains are valanced, the sofa is brocade, and the desk is elegant French style. The pièce de résistance is the Riviera Room, complete with murals of the region. Throughout, statuary, quilts, Victorian pictures, prints, and engravings abound. A favorite quiet corner is the third-floor "Turkish cozy," a tented sofa created by Sheila, with Mughal-style paintings and luxuriously covered cushions.

During the season, a continental breakfast is served out in the piazza, where Adirondack chairs are set under a colored awning surrounded by roses, pansy-filled urns, and other flowers. At the Cafe Adelphi, among camelback sofas, draped chintz banquettes, and gilt mirrors, you can enjoy cocktails, exotic coffees, and wines. The ballroom, opulently arrayed with scarlet drapes and valances, is reserved for special celebrations and weddings. The classically landscaped pool set in a secluded garden with a large pergola and lattice-work fences is a wonderful place to relax.

Rates (including breakfast): July, weekends $140 to $215 double; racing meet weekends, $215 to $340 double; weekdays $170 to $310; May, June, September, and October, weekends $120 to $190; May to July and September and October, weekdays $105 to $165.

The **Batcheller Mansion Inn,** 20 Circular St., Saratoga Springs, NY 12866 (☎ 518/584-7012; fax 518/581-7746; www.batchellermansioninn.com), is an extraordinary architectural treasure. This 1873 house with minarets, towers, and turrets was built for Judge George S. Batcheller, a brigadier general in the Union army and a diplomat who employed the finest craftsmen to create this fantasy home. The restoration has taken close to 20 years to complete—the house's integrity has been maintained while modern amenities like air-conditioning and efficient heating and plumbing have been added.

It has been carefully decorated to reflect accurately the late 1800s. Each of the nine rooms comes with a TV, phone, refrigerator, and bath (some with a Jacuzzi). Among the most dramatic is the Diamond Jim Brady, large enough to contain a regulation-size pool table, a king-size canopied bed, a large desk/study area, and a sitting area; the bath has a double Jacuzzi and shower. Another eye-opener is the Katrina Trusk, with its own circular porch, a king-size canopied bed, and a bath containing an old-fashioned tub plus a tiled shower. The wallpaper design in the Rip Van Dam depicts 4,000 horses, all racing around this tower room tucked under the mansard roof.

The common areas are equally lavish. The library offers plush velvet sofas on oriental rugs, glass-fronted bookcases, and a 48-inch TV. Breakfast is served in the Victorian dining room on tables set with lace and fine crystal and china. The living room's focal point is the marble fireplace. Potted ferns, gilded mirrors, a grand piano, and a variety of comfortable seating completes the effect. The kitchen is flooded with so much light from its 20-foot-tall windows that some guests prefer to take their breakfast here. Two porches, one affording views of Whitney Street, the other well located to catch the last rays of the evening sun, make ideal relaxing spaces.

Rates (including breakfast): Summer weekends, $160 to $260 double; racing season, $250 to $400 double; other times, slightly less.

Saratoga now has a fine modern hotel downtown, the **Sheraton Saratoga Springs,** 534 Broadway, Saratoga Springs, NY 12866 (☎ 518/584-4000). All 240 guest rooms are attractively furnished, each equipped with air-conditioning, TV/VCR, two telephones, unstocked refrigerator, coffeemaker, and hair dryer. The furniture consists of antique Queen Anne and other reproductions. The High Rock Steakhouse and pub offers pasta, grilled steaks, and such dishes as oven-roasted salmon with white wine and fresh herbs. It's served in an Adirondack hunting lodge ambience. Prices range from $12 to $19. The lounge swings on Thursday, Friday, and Saturday with live entertainment. The indoor pool has a pleasant patio for sunning; there's also a health club containing Universal equipment. *Rates:* September to July, $169 double, from $200 minisuite. August, from $309 double. *Dining hours:* Daily for breakfast, lunch, and dinner.

The **Inn at Saratoga,** 231 Broadway, Saratoga Springs, NY 12866 (☎ 800/274-3573 or 518/583-1890; fax 518/583-1890; www.theinnatsaratoga.com), has 38 large rooms, each with TV, phone, air-conditioning, and a spacious bath. Color schemes vary from dark blue and beige to dusky rose and jade. The tasteful furnishings include chintz or striped wallpapers, a free-standing full-length mirror, pelmeted drapes, comfy chairs, and a circular table with floor-length cloth; a desk and chest of drawers are tucked into a foyer.

The dining room and adjacent bar are elegant, with chintz wallpaper, potted ferns, French-style chairs, and white tablecloths providing a formal Victorian ambience. The cuisine is contemporary American. Among the appetizers might be sesame seared salmon served with vegetable nori rolls and a citrus soy sauce, or delicious mushroom ragoût, which is a medley of mushrooms flamed with brandy and port wine in a thyme-scented cream, served over puffed pastry, mixed greens, and toasted pine nuts. Entrees might include chicken francese with a lemon-Chardonnay sauce, veal sautéed in burnt orange oil and finished with Grand Marnier, the juice of an orange, and fresh oregano. Prices run from $16 to $26. On weekends a pianist entertains in the bar with its bamboo club chairs, marble bar, and glass-topped, cloth-draped tables. A serene garden dining area is also available.

Rates (including continental breakfast, except July to August): $90 to $160 double; racing season, $255 to 350 double. Weekend package available. *Dining hours:* Sunday to Thursday 5 to 9pm, Friday to Saturday 5 to 10pm.

The **Union Gables Bed & Breakfast,** 55 Union Ave., Saratoga Springs, NY 12866 (☎ 518/584-1558), is a handsome 1901 Queen Anne Victorian complete with a witch's cap turret and a wide covered veranda where wicker chairs invite guests to relax. Each of the 10 spacious rooms has a bath, air-conditioning, a TV, a phone, and a refrigerator stocked with Saratoga waters. The rooms are nicely furnished, but not in an overly fussy or pretentious way. Each is decorated with a different palette. One might have broad, strawberry-colored striped wallpaper and a bed with a draped effect while another features a darker, more masculine hue. The furnishings are comfortable and include at least two armchairs. Guest can also relax in the parlor living room. Additional facilities include an outdoor hot tub, exercise room, tennis court, and bicycles. It's located 1 block from the racetrack on a street lined with similar handsome Victorian homes. *Rates* (including continental breakfast): $90 to $210 double, depending on season.

Painted in seven different colors, the **Westchester House,** 102 Lincoln Ave., Saratoga Springs, NY 12866 (☎ 518/587-7613; www.westchesterbbsaratogany.us), certainly stands out—its cupola, gables, and fretwork are striking. It was built in 1885 and features the original handcrafted chestnut moldings and wainscoting and the elaborately carved fireplace that's the focal point of the parlor. The seven rooms are attractively furnished with oriental rugs on the hardwood floors and lace curtains at the windows. You might find a brass bed in one and a handsome inlaid French bed decorated with ormolu in another. All have private baths, telephones, and air-conditioning (though they also have ceiling fans). Fresh flowers and chocolates add an extra little touch. Stephanie Melvin, one of the innkeepers, is an opera singer, so it's hardly surprising to find a baby grand piano in the parlor. Breakfast includes freshly squeezed juice, home-baked breads, and fresh fruit. *Rates* (including breakfast): Summer, $105 to $160 double; racing season, $205 to $260 double. Special packages available at other times.

Saratoga Bed & Breakfast, 434 Church St., Saratoga Springs, NY 12866 (☎ 518/584-0920), consists of two buildings: the 1860 wood-frame Farmhouse and the 1850 House, a brick Federal that stands on lawns sloping down to a creek. Noel and Kathleen Smith have patterned their B&B on those they've stayed at in Ireland, and they provide warm hospitality. In the Farmhouse, the rooms have been furnished with maple and oak, the beds covered with locally made quilts; two rooms have fireplaces. The 1850 House contains four more lavish suites, individually decorated with walnut and mahogany antiques and equipped with a gas fireplace, TV, and phone. They've been lovingly decorated with family heirlooms, such as the cradle Kathleen's mother brought from Ireland. Noel, a former restaurateur, goes out of his way to cook up marvelous country breakfasts, while Kathy is the socializer of the team. *Rates* (including breakfast): May to October, $75 to $105 double in the Farmhouse, $130 to $155 double in the 1850 House; racing season, $105 to $155 double in the Farmhouse, $205 to $235 double in the 1850 House. November to April, $75 to $105 double in the Farmhouse, $120 to $145 double in the 1850 House.

Although the **Saratoga Downtowner,** 413 Broadway, Saratoga Springs, NY 12866-2245 (☎ 888/480-6160 or 518/584-6160; fax 518/584-2907), looks like a conventional motel, it's exquisitely kept and you'll probably get a surprise when you walk in. After you register at the desk, taking a few steps will lead you to rooms set around a long, narrow indoor pool—a welcome blessing in the summer heat. The 41 color-coordinated rooms are large and well furnished. All have air-conditioning, TVs, telephones, and unstocked refrigerators. Breakfast of homemade muffins and coffee or tea is always available—help yourself. *Rates* (including continental breakfast): September to June, $60 to $80 double; July, $80 to $90 double; racing season, $130 to $165 double. Packages available.

The **Carriage House Inn,** 178 Broadway, Saratoga Springs, NY 12866 (☎ 518/584-0352), has large units with fully equipped kitchenettes, furnished in typical motel style. The top-floor rooms have canopy beds and such extras as fireplaces and Jacuzzis. All have air-conditioning, TV, telephone, coffeemakers, and unstocked refrigerators. *Rates:* Summer, $75 to $109 double; August, $189 to $309 double; winter, $69 to $179 double.

NEARBY LODGING

The Mansion, 801 Rte. 29 (P.O. Box 77), Rock City Falls, NY 12863 (☎ 518/885-1607), 7 miles west of Saratoga Springs, has been lovingly restored and decorated by innkeepers Tom Clark and Alan Churchill. An Italianate villa complete with a central cupola, it was built in 1866 as the summer home of industrialist George West, owner of the Empire and Excelsior Mills as well as several other paper mills and textile factories. He was the inventor of the paper bag—his greatest claim to fame. The five rooms are furnished with handsome Victorian pieces and floral fabrics and wallpapers, but they're not decorated in pretentious "museum" style. The first-floor suite has its own sitting room. There are two parlors where guests can gather and relax (one furnished in Eastlake, the other in Empire), a library, and a second-floor sitting room. Particularly striking is the parlor that has a dramatic mirrored mantel, a Victorian sofa, and a plush oriental rug. Guests may use the porches. Breakfast also sets this establishment apart: A five-course breakfast is served to guests at individual tables between 7 and 9am. A well-landscaped pool is on the 4 acres of grounds. *Rates* (including breakfast): Racing season, $175 double weekdays, $195 double weekends; rest of the year, $105 double.

If you're looking for a real farm experience, **Agape Farm Bed & Breakfast,** 4894 Rte. 9N, Corinth, NY 12822 (☎ 518/654-7777), is for you. It's about 13 miles from Saratoga (16 miles from Lake George) and offers accommodations in a farmhouse surrounded by 33 acres of woods and fields, complete with a trout stream. There are six simple, comfortably decorated rooms (all with bath). Available for weekly rental is a cottage that sleeps four and has a fully equipped kitchen and a TV. Guests can gather around the piano for a sing-along if they're in the mood, stroll the fields gathering cackleberries or raspberries in season, feed the horses and chickens, relax on the wraparound porch, go birding, or indulge in other country pursuits. *Rates* (including breakfast): $75 to $160 double or cottage for two.

SARATOGA & AREA DINING
Breakfast & Lunch

When in Saratoga, the place to enjoy breakfast is at the **racetrack**, even though it can be expensive, with items priced up to $16.

Another good breakfast spot is **Bruegger's Bagel Bakery**, 453 Broadway (☎ 518/584-4372). It also serves an assortment of bagels and bagel sandwiches for under $5—eat inside or outside on the deck on Broadway. *Hours:* August, Monday to Saturday 6am to 7pm, Sunday 6am to 5pm; the rest of the year, daily 6am to 7pm.

The place to be seen lunching is the **Turf Terrace**, but unless you've booked months in advance, forget it.

Lunch & Dinner

43 Phila St. Bistro (☎ 518/584-2720), provides a sleek dining ambience for some exciting contemporary cuisine. French posters and art decorate the walls, and the warm peach/terra-cotta color scheme is lit by track lights. The menu changes daily, but dinner items will likely include cumin-spiced rack of lamb with an ancho lime aïoli, Szechuan-crusted breast of duckling with an orange marmalade sauce, and filet mignon wrapped in smokehouse bacon and served with a Zinfandel reduction. Each dish brims with flavor. Prices run $27 to $35. To start, try the grilled jumbo shrimp with tamarind sauce or the mussels in a Thai lemongrass broth. Hot jazz, blues, or classical music plays in the background. The wine list is international, including selections from Argentina, Spain, and Australia, with an emphasis on California varietals. *Hours:* Monday to Thursday 6 to 10pm, Friday and Saturday 6 to 11pm; fall, Thursday to Saturday 11:30am to 3pm; winter, Monday to Saturday 11:30am to 3pm.

The **Olde Bryan Inn,** 123 Maple Ave., at Rock Street (☎ 518/587-2990), supposedly Saratoga's oldest building, is named after Alexander Bryan, a Revolutionary War hero who spied on General John Burgoyne, thus directly contributing to the victory at the Battle of Saratoga in 1777. He purchased the inn in the late 1780s, and the place certainly possesses a well-seasoned air. In cold weather the red glow from the two fireplaces (one at each end of the polished-wood dining room) makes you feel warm and welcome. In the adjacent bar another fire roars beneath a picture of Leda and the Swan, and you can sit cozily ensconced beneath the old beamed ceiling. In summer, you can enjoy alfresco dining in the courtyards. Making up the menu are salads, sandwiches, omelets, and burgers (most under $8), plus a selection of entrees, like prime rib, Cajun blackened steak, sesame-crusted salmon baked in white wine and laced with wasabi aïoli sauce, and an old-fashioned turkey dinner accompanied by stuffing and cranberry sauce ($12 to $18). *Hours:* Daily 11am to 10:30pm. No reservations are taken.

Locals rely on **Sperry's**, 30½ Caroline St. (☎ 518/584-9618), to deliver good, honest food in down-home surroundings. The dinner menu offers such favorites as chicken Dijon and veal piccata plus specials like Cajun barbecued catfish; grilled breast of chicken with plum tomatoes, red onions, artichoke hearts, basil, olives, and feta cheese; or rack of lamb with garlic-rosemary demi-glace. Prices range from $13 to $25. For an appetizer try the Thai-style cured salmon with a soy-ginger dipping sauce or the grilled portobello mushrooms and chèvre cheese. *Hours:* Monday to Saturday 11:30am to 3pm and 5:30 to 10pm, Sunday 5 to 9pm.

If you like pasta, you'll like **Wheatfields**, 440 Broadway (☎ 518/587-0534), which serves up pasta in every conceivable manner. In fact, the menu is divided into vegetarian, meat, seafood, and stuffed pastas. There's paglia e fieno, spaghetti puttanesca, two kinds of lasagna, and fettuccine with shrimp and sea scallops—close to 30 different kinds of pasta in all. Even the regular soup on the menu (besides the soup of the day) is pasta fagioli. Prices range from $9 to $16. *Hours:* Daily 11:30am to 10pm (until 10:30pm Friday and Saturday)

Hattie's, 45 Phila St. (☎ 518/584-4790), is no longer presided over by Hattie Mosley, though she still drops by occasionally to check on the place. It's changed little since she turned it over to younger hands, for this is still the place where dancers, musicians, and other visiting stars love to gather. Their photographs, notes, and tokens of appreciation that cover the walls give thanks for a home away from home, serving good, fresh food and lots of it. Hattie who was born in Louisiana in 1900, settled in Saratoga Springs over 50 years ago, and began serving the spiciest barbecue and Southern fried chicken and ribs to happy customers. Hattie's still serves these dishes, only now these favorites are supplemented by crayfish étouffée, jambalaya, and bourbon shrimp Mandeville made with Cajun seasonings. Prices range from $10 to $16. Start with a rich, flavorsome chicken and sausage or seafood gumbo or the spicy shrimp rémoulade. In summer the brick patio and courtyard is a favorite cocktail spot. *Hours:* July and August, 8am to 11pm; September to June, Wednesday to Sunday 5 to 10pm. Reservations needed in season.

Scallions, 404 Broadway (☎ 518/584-0192), is a busy little place serving great salads, sandwiches, and hearty entrees in a sleek ambience of black-and-white tile, green bentwood chairs, and painted lemon tables. In the back the display case is filled with salads—chicken and sun-dried tomatoes, crabmeat, shrimp, and more—and desserts to go. Among the desserts, my favorites are the chocolate-chip-and-walnut pie or any of the cheesecakes, locally made by New Skete monks. Among the entrees are several chicken dishes—garlic, walnut pesto, and wild mushroom, for example. Soups and sandwiches complete the fare. Prices run $8 to $15. This is a good place to pick up the makings for a picnic. *Hours:* Monday to Saturday 11am to 9pm, Sunday 11am to 8pm. Closed Sunday and Monday in winter.

Not a particularly pretty place, **Gaffney's**, 16 Caroline St. (☎ 518/587-7359), nevertheless offers an eclectic mixture of Mexican, Italian, and continental dishes in a bistro atmosphere. Lunch specialties include chicken or beef tostadas, enchiladas, sandwiches, and pastas. Dinner fare is less casual: You'll find veal Marsala; linguine al pesto; chicken sautéed with mushrooms, white wine, and lemon; and more. Prices range from $10 to $19. It's pleasant to dine in the patio/garden, where music is featured in July and August. *Hours:* Monday to Saturday 11:30am to 3pm and 5:30 to 10:30pm, Sunday 10:30am to 3pm.

For lakeside viewing, seek out the **Waterfront**, 626 Crescent Ave. (☎ 518/583-2628), which has two decks literally hanging out over the water. The place is plain and tavernlike, with large windows and a fireplace for cooler months. Sandwiches, nachos, salads, and pasta, plus dishes from the barbecue—steaks, burgers, and seafood items like baked stuffed shrimp—are the choices here ($6 to $18). To find it, take Union Avenue to Crescent Avenue and turn left at the sign. *Hours:* Daily 11:30am to 10pm.

The Weathervane, on Route 9 south of Saratoga Springs (☎ 518/584-8157), is famous—and rightly so—for a 1-pound lobster dinner for only $10, served with a baked potato. *Hours:* Daily 11am to 9:30pm.

Dinner Only

In recent years one of the places to dine in Saratoga has always been **Chez Sophie** (☎ 518/583-3538). You can still dine here, but you'll have to repair to 2853 Rte. 9 in Malta Ridge, just south of Saratoga, a quarter of a mile south of Exit 13. Here, in a classic 1940s diner, you can sample fine cuisine made with the freshest local ingredients and garden herbs. Sophie learned to cook when she was growing up on the Belgian-French border. Husband Joseph C. Parker's fluid metal-and-wire sculptures fit neatly into the ambience. The menu changes daily, but always features a fish of the day and eight or so entrees (priced from $21 to $29), such as duck breasts with an apricot and green peppercorn sauce; pork tenderloin braised in balsamic vinegar; poussin roasted with tarragon in a Madeira and cream sauce; and the house special, a superb rack of lamb with natural juices. Start with the house-cured salmon in white wine olive oil and fresh sage, escargots bourguignonnes, or pâté de la maison. There are 15 or more wines by the glass, plus a large selection of Belgian and Dutch beers. *Hours:* February to December, Tuesday to Saturday 5pm to closing. Reservations are essential.

At the **Springwater Inn,** 139 Union Ave. (☎ 518/584-6440), the tables are set with pretty Libby's glass lanterns and burgundy napery, with burgundy Victorian chairs alongside. The restaurant has two areas—a more formal room with tables set in front of a Federal-style fireplace and a more casual skylit room overlooking Union Avenue. The food is continental. You might start your meal with the shiitake mushroom ravioli with roasted-pepper coulis and follow with venison with a Merlot sauce or duckling with a raspberry demiglace. Prices range from $16 to $25. Lighter fare is offered in the atmospheric wood-paneled taproom, which combines old English and Adirondack styles. *Hours:* July to August, daily 5 to 11pm; mid-February to June and September to December, Tuesday to Sunday 5 to 10pm. Closed January to mid-February.

Ye Olde Wishing Well, 4 miles north on Route 9 (☎ 518/584-7640), a real racing hangout, has all kinds of racing memorabilia and track/turf paintings donated over the years by owners and trainers. The stone fireplaces and low ceilings epitomize Saratoga's country charm. Softshell crabs, prime rib, filet mignon, roast turkey, veal Oscar, and lobster are the favorites here, priced from $17 to $30. *Hours:* Racing season, daily 5 to 11pm; February to December, Tuesday to Friday 5 to 10pm, Saturday 5 to 11pm, Sunday noon to 9pm.

At **Panza's Starlight Restaurant,** Route 9P at the south end of Saratoga Lake (☎ 518/584-6882), the Panza family has built a fine culinary reputation over the years by giving customers a genuine welcome and exquisite Italian/ continental cuisine served in a simple, unpretentious atmosphere. Pastas, veal dishes (piccata, Marsala, and parmigiana), chicken, and seafood make up the menu. Try the steak au poivre, which is finished with a brown sauce enriched with brandy or the scallops in a Pommery cream sauce or the signature home-made sausage platter, which is served with fire-roasted peppers and sweet onions. In addition to the traditional pastas like linguine with white clam sauce there's a penne served with smoked salmon, sun-dried tomatoes, and artichoke hearts in a vodka cream sauce. All entrees are served with a relish tray, a salad, spaghetti or potato, and a vegetable. Prices range from $15 to $19. *Hours:* July to August, daily 5 to 10pm; rest of the year, Thursday to Saturday 5 to 10pm, Sunday 2 to 9pm. It may close December to February, so check.

SARATOGA AFTER DARK

Skidmore College provides films, concerts, and lectures during the school year. For information, call ☎ 518/584-5000.

Besides the New York City Ballet, which performs in July, and the Philadelphia Orchestra, which performs in August, the **Saratoga Performing Arts Center** hosts the Newport Jazz Festival in June, theater presentations, and a number of special guests in concert; past performers have included Judy Collins, Elton John, and many others. For information, call ☎ 518/587-3330.

In addition, the **Baroque Music Festival** is held in nearby Greenfield on weekends during July and August. For information, call the Foundation of Baroque Music Studio (☎ 518/893-7527).

Harness racing (☎ 518/584-2110) can be enjoyed between May and mid-November and on weekends from January to March. For information, contact **Saratoga Harness Racing,** Nelson Avenue, Saratoga Springs, NY 12866. Or you might attend a **polo game,** usually played Tuesday and Friday to Sunday at 6pm during August. For information, contact the Saratoga Chamber of Commerce.

There are plenty of cocktail spots: the **Olde Bryan Inn,** 123 Maple Ave. (☎ 518/587-9741); **Professor Moriarty's Dining and Drinking Salon,** 430 Broadway (☎ 518/587-5981); **Gaffney's,** 16 Caroline St. (☎ 518/ 587-9791); and **Parting Glass,** 40–42 Lake Ave. (☎ 518/583-1916), for a bit of the Irish. For a piano bar (during racing season only), try **Siro's,** 168 Lincoln Ave. (☎ 518/584-4030).

A SIDE TRIP TO NEW SKETE

A trip to the **New Skete Monastery** in Cambridge (☎ 518/677-3928) will take you through Washington County, the countryside Grandma Moses portrayed so vividly in her now-famous landscapes. You'll travel past russet-red barns, yards filled with scurrying chickens and pigs, and rolling hillsides where horses are quietly grazing, until you reach the monastery high on a hill overlooking the quiet valley. Here, Greek Orthodox monks paint eggs and icons; make sausages and cheeses; smoke poultry, bacon, and hams; and bake delectable cheesecakes—Kahlúa, chocolate, and a simple deluxe, priced from $16—for which people travel miles. The monks are also noted dog trainers and operate good kennels.

You can purchase their goods, their poetry, and contemplative writings in the store before going up the hillside to the small onion-domed chapel, built by the monks themselves (the dome is made of Styrofoam, fiberglass, and polyurethane). This is a retreat for all faiths, and there's room for three or four guests in shared rooms with bunk beds and spartan furnishings. No radios, no tape recorders, and no alcohol are allowed.

While you're in Cambridge, visit **Hubbard Hall** (☎ 518/677-2765), a terrific old Victorian turreted building that now houses the Valley Artisans Market, filled with ceramics, wood carvings, art, and basketry. Stuffed animals, candles, and other country items are found next door in the Village Store and Co-op. *Hours:* Monday to Saturday 10am to 5pm.

From Cambridge, Route 40 north takes you to another typical country site: the **Log Village Grist Mill Museum,** Route 30, 2 miles off Route 40, in East Hartford (☎ 518/632-5237). I must admit that this mill was not a major destination on my visit, but I spent several hours there, fascinated and charmed by Floyd Harwood's enthusiasm and natural gift for teaching. A retired shop teacher, Floyd rescued and spent 5 years restoring the mill as a retirement project, remaking the parts from old patterns. The mill now works—you can go down and watch the 17-foot-diameter, 10-ton wheel with its 54 buckets (each holding 450 pounds of water) driving the original 1810 French burr stones that have natural pockmarks for good grinding. Corn and wheat are ground. The original stove, plus the desk with records, kept from 1874, are in the mill.

In the nearby mill barn Floyd displays a collection of old farm machinery and household items, gas and steam engines, a dog-powered churn, and all kinds of woodworking tools, including a 150-year-old treadle wood lathe, an old band saw originally advertised in the 1922 Sears Roebuck catalog, and a scroll saw advertised in an 1888 catalog. In the room above are pump organs, sewing machines, washing machines, calendars, antique clothes, and much more reflecting the daily life of earlier eras. Anyone interested in early newspapers and antique books will want to look at his collection of old newspapers, agricultural books, and calendars.

Hours: Memorial Day to October, Saturday 10am to 6pm, Sunday noon to 6pm; weekdays by appointment. *Admission:* $2.50 adults, 50¢ children.

NORTH TO THE LAKES

LAKE LUZERNE

Lake Luzerne is a small and serene lake about 20 minutes from Saratoga, southwest of Lake George. From here you can take trips to Great Sacandaga Lake, go antiquing, attend the Friday-night rodeo in Lake Luzerne, go horseback riding and lake swimming in summer, or enjoy cross-country skiing in winter.

Lamplight Inn, 231 Lake Ave., Route 9N (P.O. Box 70), Lake Luzerne, NY 12846 (☎ 800/262-4668 or 518/696-5294; www.lamplightinn.com), 18 miles from Saratoga and 10 miles from Lake George, occupies an 1890 home on 10 acres. It's only a block away from Lake Luzerne. In 1984 proud owners

Gene and Linda Merlino took over this grand home and restored it. Each of the 12 rooms (with bath and air-conditioning) is individually decorated with chintz wallpapers, quilts, and lace curtains. Some have gas-burning fireplaces. Room 2 has a mahogany canopied bed. Room 10 is decked out in forest green, peach, and white, with a draped white-iron canopied bed as the focal point. Two rooms are located in what used to be the caretaker's house, which stands beside a brook and contains a living room and two upstairs bedrooms. The bedrooms are equipped with gas fireplaces, telephones, TVs, and air-conditioning. In addition, there are five very attractive suites in the carriage house, all of which have gas fireplaces and Jacuzzi tubs in the bedroom. Four of them also have private porches. Guests can relax in the extra-large comfortable sitting room, with two wood-burning fireplaces, a TV, high beamed ceilings, chestnut wainscoting, and a keyhole staircase. The wraparound porch with a swing is great for unwinding in summer. The grounds are pretty and the whole place is surrounded by majestic white pine. In summer there are wooded nature trails to explore; in winter they're great for cross-country skiing. A full breakfast of eggs, cereal, and fruit is served at tables set with damask cloths, pink napkins, and fine china.

The dining room offers a romantic ambience and good, freshly prepared cuisine. The menu changes seasonally, but might feature such dishes as medallions of venison with sun-dried tomatoes, red wine, and shallot demi-glace; salmon steamed in parchment paper with fresh vegetables; or breast of chicken with andouille sausage in a saffron cream sauce. Beer and wine available. Prices range from $16 to $23.

Rates (including breakfast): Late July to Labor Day, $130 to $199 double; May to July and September and October, $108 to $175; November to April, $105 to $165. *Dining hours:* Summer, 6 to 9pm Thursday to Sunday; fall/winter, Friday and Saturday only. No children under age 12 are allowed.

LAKE GEORGE'S ULTIMATE RESORT

The Sagamore, P.O. Box 450, Bolton Landing, Lake George, NY 12814 (☎ 518/644-9400), lies resplendent on Lake George ensconced on 70-acre Sagamore Island, surrounded by crystalline blue waters and tree-covered mountains. The colonial revival white clapboard building with green shutters has been restored to its earlier magnificence. When it opened in 1883 it served as a focal point for social and recreational activities for the exclusive folks who'd built summer mansions on the island. Damaged by fire in 1893 and again in 1914, it was completely reconstructed in 1930. Old age didn't catch up with the grande dame until 1981, when it closed its doors. Now it combines 19th-century charm and luxury with 20th-century technology, making it a world-class resort.

Although the landward approach presents a hodgepodge of standardized condominium clusters, the hotel really should be viewed from the water. From the stylish oriental-accented lobby, step out onto the semicircular veranda, supported by 20-foot-high classical pillars, that overlooks the mountains and lake. Here you can enjoy tea at 3:30pm or cocktails to piano accompaniment among the potted palms. Pathways and stairs lead across terraced lawns to the lake, where you can sunbathe on a series of wooden decks or on the beach. The indoor pool and pool terrace are also down here. The *Morgan,* a special wooden lake cruiser, operates from here, sailing at 11am, 2:30pm, and 7pm for dinner. In winter its hull is protected from ice by a circle of warm-air bubbles.

The hotel's premier dining room, Trillium, offers an elegant setting of plush pink chairs, tables draped with magnolia-colored damask, and fine china for both Sunday brunch and dinner (entrees run $18 to $32). Appetizers might include crusted jumbo lump crab cakes served in a yellow tomato coulis or house-cured gravlax with dill and orange with a hint of mustard and chive oils. The dozen or so entrees are hard to choose from—breast of duckling with a fresh berry sauce, roasted halibut in lemongrass tomato broth, grilled fillet of beef tenderloin with truffled mushroom sauce, and roasted rack of lamb marinated in tandoori spices and served in a wonderful minted Merlot sauce. Prices range from $18 to $32. For a delirious dessert experience, select the chocolate elegance, which consists of flourless chocolate cake, chocolate mousse, chocolate ganache, and brandied cherry sauce, or the vanilla crème brûlée with hazelnut japonaise.

There are 100 guest rooms in the main building and 240 in "cottage/lodges" plus some condo units. The rooms in the main building are furnished with pencil four-posters and half-posters, peach wallpaper and carpeting, botanical prints, wing chairs, and candle stands (plus a TV, a phone, and air-conditioning); baths are tiled and feature mahogany towel bars and shower curtain rods. Most of the cottage suites have small balconies with wicker rockers; fireplaces, modular couches, TVs, and Adirondack-style chairs set the tone inside. An open kitchen with an electric stove and refrigerator and a bath and bedroom complete the layout.

Myriad facilities are available: a games room, a beauty salon, a gift shop, an art gallery, a spa (massage, facials, loofah scrub room, and Universal-equipped exercise room, sauna and steam, whirlpool), an indoor/outdoor pool, two indoor and five outdoor tennis courts, racquetball, movies, an 18-hole par-70 golf course, cross-country skiing, ice-skating, and a toboggan run. Use of canoes and rowboats is free. Besides the dining and entertainment facilities already mentioned, there's an attractive plush pub/restaurant, Mister Brown's, Van Winkle's for jazz and dancing, and the Adirondack-style Club Grill, perhaps the most appealing of all, located on the mainland up on Federal Hill at the golf club. Free round-trip transportation is provided to the golf course and to Gore Mountain and West Mountain for downhill skiers.

Rates: July to August, $285 to $355 double; spring/fall, $175 to $200; winter, $125 to $140; $150 to $440 suite, depending on the season and the view. MAP available.

FRIENDS LAKE

Only 30 minutes north of Lake George and a mere 20 minutes from Gore Mountain, this unspoiled lake has a couple of fine inns on its shores.

Sharon and Greg Taylor took over **Friends Lake Inn**, Friends Lake Road, Chestertown, NY 12817 (☎ 518/494-4751; fax 518/494-4616; www. friendslake.com), in 1982 and restored the 1860s building to its former glory (in the 1920s there used to be six inns on this small lake). From the dining porch and the front rooms there's a restorative lake view. There are 14 individually decorated rooms, most featuring four-posters with quilts, combined with attractive wallpapers and curtain fabrics, oak chests and dressers, and other country pieces. The larger junior suites have sitting areas and feature Waverly fabrics, four-posters, and Jacuzzi tubs. The most spectacular rooms are the Adirondack lodge suites, which have large riverstone fireplaces with raised hearths, plus cedar timbers and maple floors, and are furnished with locally made Adirondack-style beds. There are 16 rooms total, all with baths. Cottage accommodations are also available in adjacent buildings. Each of these has a deck, a wood-burning stove, a fully equipped kitchen, and simple, homey furnishings.

In the dining room, solid-cherry square columns support the stamped-tin ceiling; the wainscoting and a fire in the brick hearth make it cozy in winter. In summer the screened-in porch is the best dining place. The cuisine is new American and features such local ingredients as Hudson Valley foie gras. Dinner might begin with roasted pancetta-wrapped quail stuffed with wild mushroom risotto and served with a Marsala-scented compote of caramelized pearl onions and figs. Among the 10 or so entrees there might be horseradish-encrusted salmon with a maple Marsala sauce, prime tenderloin with a caramelized shallot port glaze, or an oriental pot au feu made with chicken medallions in a coconut and lime broth plus soba noodles and shiitake and straw mushrooms. Prices range from $17 to $29 (a lower-priced bistro menu from $7 to $11 is also available). A couple of vegetarian dishes are always available, too. The excellent wine list offers more than 1,200 selections including 25 to 30 by the glass.

A super special breakfast is served featuring such items as locally smoked Oscar's bacon and eggs Benedict or mango crêpes with raspberry coulis.

For relaxing, the sitting room affords a TV with VCR, and some board games, plus the opportunity to loll in front of the fire. There's a bar with a view of the lake and umbrella-shaded tables outside. Guests also enjoy the gazebo and the outdoor hot tub. The grounds have 30km of groomed trails for hiking, biking, and cross-country skiing, and there's swimming and canoeing at the lake. Rafting, fishing, and hunting trips are led by the inn's very own Adirondack guide.

Rates: MAP $195 to $285 (the higher price for lakeview rooms with Jacuzzi) double; wide selection of special packages available. *Dining hours:* Sunday 4 to 9pm, Monday to Thursday 5 to 9pm, Friday and Saturday 5 to 10pm.

Saratoga Springs
Special & Recreational Activities

Antiquing: Plenty of antiques shops can be found in town and the surrounding area. For example, try driving Route 29 west or east. Or pop south to Ballston Spa.

Boating: Rowboat and canoe rentals may be available at **Ballston Lake** beside the Good Times Restaurant (☎ 518/399-9976). **Saratoga Lake** is also a good boating spot.

Golf: There are two golf courses in **Saratoga Spa State Park**—an 18-hole championship course (☎ 518/584-2008), which charges $20 on weekends, and a par-27 9-hole course (☎ 518/584-2007), which charges $10 on weekends.

Picnicking: At the track, your best bet is at the **Top O' the Stretch** picnic area. Otherwise, **Saratoga Spa State Park** is ideal.

Skating: There's an illuminated rink in **Saratoga Spa State Park** for speed and ice-skating.

Skiing: Cross-country skiing can be enjoyed in the **Saratoga Spa State Park.** Headquarters is at the spa park office (☎ 518/584-2535). Downhill skiing is available at **West Mountain** (☎ 518/793-9431), where there are 22 trails and three chair lifts. A day pass on weekends is around $35. Take I-87 north to Exit 18W.

Swimming: Two pools are available in the **Saratoga Spa State Park**—one Olympic-size, the other, the Victoria Pool, a favorite with the dancers and other performers at the Arts Center. A beach and a pool also exist at **Kaydeross Amusement Park** on the edge of the lake.

Tennis: Saratoga Racquet Club (☎ 518/587-3000) has courts available for $18 an hour. There are also courts in **Saratoga Spa State Park** and in **Saratoga** on Division Street.

The Hamptons

Westhampton Beach ◆ *Quogue* ◆ *Hampton Bays*
◆ *Southampton* ◆ *Water Mill* ◆ *Bridgehampton*
◆ *Wainscott* ◆ *East Hampton* ◆ *Amagansett*

Distance in miles: Westhampton, 81; Hampton Bays, 90; Southampton, 96; East Hampton, 106

Estimated driving time: 2 to 4 hours, depending on Long Island Expressway traffic

Driving: Take I-495 (Long Island Expressway) to Exit 70 (Route 111 south), then take Route 27 east.

Bus: The Hampton Jitney offers express service—and they mean it. Despite the odds of beating the traffic back on Sunday night, their drivers are given instructions about all the side roads and back routes, and they often arrive in the city to standing ovations from passengers. Reservations are required. Call ☎ 800/936-0440 or 516/283-4600 from Tri-State area codes. The jitney leaves from 86th Street between Lexington and Third, from 69th Street and Lexington, from 59th Street and Lexington, and from 40th Street between Lexington and Third.

Train: The Long Island Rail Road from Penn Station stops at each of the Hamptons. Call ☎ 718/217-5477 for timetable information.

Further Information: For more about New York in general, contact the **Division of Tourism,** New York State Department of Economic Development, One Commerce Plaza, Albany, NY 12245 (☎ 518/474-4116).

For general information about Long Island, contact the **Long Island Convention and Visitor's Bureau,** 350 Vanderbilt Pkwy., Suite 103, Hauppauge, NY 11788 (☎ 516/951-3440).

For specific information, contact the **Hampton Bays Chamber of Commerce,** Montauk Highway (P.O. Box 64), Hampton Bays, NY 11946 (☎ 516/728-2211); the **Greater Westhampton Chamber of Commerce,** 173 Montauk Hwy. (P.O. Box 1228), Westhampton (☎ 516/288-3337); the **Southampton Chamber of Commerce,** 76 Main St., Southampton, NY 11968 (☎ 516/283-0402); the **East Hampton Chamber of Commerce,** 79A Main St., East Hampton, NY 11937 (☎ 516/324-0362).

Events & Festivals to Plan Your Trip Around

July: Fireworks at East Hampton Main Beach (after 9pm on July 4 or on closest weekend).
    East Hampton Ladies Village Improvement Society Fair (usually the last Saturday). Call ☎ 516/324-1220.
August: Westhampton Beach Art Show (early August). Call ☎ 516/288-3337.
Clothesline Art Sale, Guild Hall, East Hampton. Call ☎ 516/324-0806.
Artists and Writers Baseball Game, East Hampton (mid-August). Call 516/324-0362.
Hampton Classic Horse Show, Bridgehampton (late August to early September).
September: Shinnecock Indian Reservation Powwow (Labor Day weekend). Contact the Shinnecock Nation Cultural Center Museum Complex (☎ 516/287-4923).
October: Hamptons International Film Festival (late October). Call ☎ 516/324-4600.
December: Annual Tour of Historic Inns and House, East Hamp-

In Paris they're promoted as New York's Riviera; in a *New York* magazine article in the mid-1980s, journalist Marie Brenner acidly described them as "suburbia by the sea." Of course, I'm talking about the legendary Hamptons, seven or so villages clustered along Long Island's South Fork, with access to miles and miles of white-sand Atlantic beaches backed by undulating dunes—a miracle coastline for uptight urban dwellers. The beaches here are certainly as good as any in the world, which is one reason to come to the Hamptons. The other reason is to participate in the social season, a fashion scene that *Women's Wear Daily* regards as trend-setting and sees fit to comment upon.

The Hamptons didn't always engender such opposing opinions and tart commentary. Since their founding in the mid–17th century by colonists from New England, most of these villages on the east end of Long Island remained quiet farming towns—at least until the late 19th century, when they began to attract urban emigrants. As early as 1890 a journalist observed that on the South Fork people wore fancy blazers, dressed up a good deal, played tennis, and attended hops. The resort image didn't really coalesce until the 1920s, when the automobile emerged as a popular mode of transportation and the Maidstone Club opened its bathing facilities.

The scene really hasn't changed that much. The game is still tennis (along with some other pastimes), people still dress up a good deal and wear fancy blazers, but their hops tend to be a little more camp and far more frenetic. Today's celebrity-studded scene, however, can be traced more directly to the mid-1940s, when Jackson Pollock and Lee Krasner arrived and were soon followed by the de Koonings, Frank O'Hara, Larry Rivers, Nick Carone, and Barney Rosset, who in turn were followed by waves of celebrities who still lend a distinct cachet to the area—Betty Friedan, Woody Allen, Craig Claiborne, Charles Addams, E. L. Doctorow, and many more. The Hollywood crowd soon followed. Steven Spielberg, Sidney Lumet, Alan Pakula, Kim Basinger and Alec Baldwin, Kathleen Turner, and Chevy Chase were among the first film actors and directors to summer here. They were soon joined by Robert DeNiro, Alan Alda, and moguls like David Geffen, Barry Diller, and the late Steve Ross, plus Billy Joel, Barbra Streisand, Kevin Costner, and Danny Aiello. The fashion crowd arrived, too—Calvin Klein, Isaac Mizrahi, and Donna Karan. Their homes appear in *Architectural Digest* and other glossy magazines, their social lives are recorded in the gossip columns—inevitably there's a certain "Peeping Tom" quality to any visit to the Hamptons. Being seen and trying to see are an important part of the scene for some.

When Jackson Pollock arrived, the potato fields were intact and land sold for a high-priced $1,000 an acre. Today that same land sells for anywhere from $100,000 an acre and more, and jagged glass-and-wooden houses, standing starkly on the flatlands behind the sand dunes, have replaced the potato fields. Designer-labeled hordes descend every summer, clogging the streets with their Mercedeses, Jaguars, and de rigueur BMWs and Acuras. And with those 200,000-plus summer visitors have come the required gourmet food markets, boutiques, restaurants, and nightclubs that shatter the night's quietude. For those who wish to ignore the scene, the beaches remain; for those who relish participating in the scene, a better one can't be found outside New York City. The only real problem is the Long Island Expressway and Route 27. My advice is to hole up here permanently for the entire summer—never mind weekending!

Friday Night Hassles

If you have time only to spend the weekend, take heart. There are those who take pride in not having to punish themselves by driving anywhere on Friday night—they're the lucky ones. Those who have to leave on Friday night have their ways of beating the traffic—leaving early, leaving late, taking one route instead of another. My best advice is to check the *New York Times*, which publishes a map of potential bottlenecks where roadwork is being done. Stay tuned to your radio and hope for the best.

If you're headed all the way to the East End, you'll probably suffer hunger pangs en route. You can either stop at the diner at the Hampton Road turnoff into Southampton; wait until you reach Water Mill and drop into **Meghan's Saloon** (☎ 516/726-9657), a pubby bar/restaurant serving some great burger combinations; or wait until you reach East Hampton's **O'Mally's** (☎ 516/324-9010). Of course, there are plenty of other possibilities along the way.

Long Island

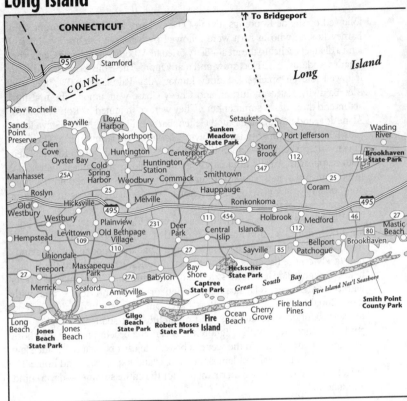

↑ To Bridgeport

CONNECTICUT

Long Island

CONN.

New Rochelle
Sands Point Preserve
Bayville
Lloyd Harbor
Northport
Setauket
Port Jefferson
Wading River
Glen Cove
Oyster Bay
Cold Spring Harbor
Huntington
Centerport
Sunken Meadow State Park
Stony Brook
Brookhaven State Park
Manhasset
Roslyn
Old Westbury
Hicksville
Westbury
Plainview
Levittown
Old Bethpage Village
Hempstead
Uniondale
Freeport
Massapequa Park
Merrick
Seaford
Amityville
Babylon
Bay Shore
Captree State Park
Heckscher State Park
Great South Bay
Fire Island Nat'l Seashore
Smith Point County Park
Long Beach
Jones Beach State Park
Jones Beach
Gilgo Beach State Park
Robert Moses State Park
Fire Island
Ocean Beach
Cherry Grove
Fire Island Pines
Huntington Station
Woodbury
Commack
Smithtown
Hauppauge
Ronkonkoma
Holbrook
Medford
Coram
Central Islip
Islandia
Sayville
Bellport
Patchogue
Brookhaven
Mastic Beach
Deer Park
Stamford

East End Bed & Breakfasts   For B&B accommodations throughout the East End, contact **A Reasonable Alternative, Inc.,** 117 Spring St., Port Jefferson, NY 11777 (☎ 516/928-4034).

WESTHAMPTON BEACH, QUOGUE & HAMPTON BAYS

There are those who say the Shinnecock Canal divides the more socially conscious Hamptons—Southampton and East Hampton—from the less socially conscious Hamptons. Westhampton Beach, closest to New York City, attracts a fast-paced crowd as well as a sizable number of blue bloods. Down along Dune Road, rows and rows of modern, angular multifaceted glass-and-wood structures stretch along the beachfront. Here, on weekends as you drive past, you'll catch the echoes of many a party and pass the crowds and cars that jostle around the nightclub spots. Neighboring Quogue has a much quieter, low-key approach to life (even though the name means "ground that shakes like thunder"); around the corner across Tiana Bay, Hampton Bays has the most down-to-earth reputation of all and attracts families and avid fishermen.

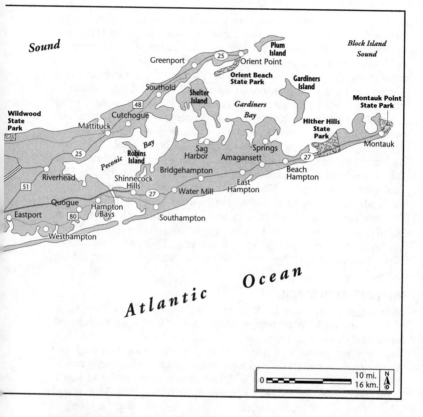

WESTHAMPTON BEACH LODGING

The **Dune Deck on the Ocean**, 379 Dune Rd. (☎ 516/288-3876; fax 516/288-2511), has 64 typically modern rooms that are fully equipped (air-conditioning, TV, telephone, and unstocked refrigerator), many with ocean views and some with balconies. Plus, you have the opportunity to dine at one of the most romantic and most highly rated restaurants in the Hamptons—Starr Boggs (☎ 516/288-5250). *Rates:* Memorial Day to Labor Day, weekends $145 to $325 double, weekdays $95 to $185; off-season rates are slightly less.

The **Westhampton Beach, Bath and Tennis Club,** 231 Dune Rd., Westhampton, NY 11978 (☎ 516/288-2500), gives you access to a full range of facilities—10 tennis courts, saltwater swimming pool, exercise room, and, most important, the beach. *Rates:* Memorial Day and mid-June to Labor Day, $170 to $460; May 1 to mid-June and Labor Day to mid-October, $120 to $300.

QUOGUE LODGING

The **Inn at Quogue,** 47 to 52 Quogue St., Quogue, NY 11959 (☎ 516/653-6560 or 212/371-3300), is one of the few accommodations that con-tributes to the town's reputation as a quiet, stylish enclave. A mile from the beach, this 210-year-old home has 18 rooms (including two cottages), all tastefully furnished with a country combination of pine, quilts, chintz wallpapers, and an occasional wicker piece. Across the street are nine more rooms in the East House, which dates back 175 years. The rooms here are more modern-looking than those in the main house. There are also some motel units surrounding the pool. Some of these have kitchens/kitchenettes. All have phones, and some have air-conditioning and color TV. The restaurant (☎ 516/653-6800) has a fine reputation and a menu that changes daily. Herbs come from a garden out back. Dinner specialties may include salmon with warm tomato compote and basil butter or sirloin steak with bordelaise sauce. Prices range from $19 to $30. Also available are beach passes, bikes, and discounted membership at a nearby health club with indoor tennis courts. *Rates* (including continental breakfast in summer): In season, $185 to $335 double weekends, $140 to $255 midweek; off-season, $140 to $290 double weekends, $105 to $215 midweek. The motel units are at the low end of the price range. Inn closed January to mid-April. *Dining hours:* Summer, Monday to Thursday 5:30 to 9pm, Friday and Saturday 6 to 10pm, Sunday noon to 3pm and 5:30 to 9pm; spring/fall, Friday and Saturday 6 to 10pm, Sunday noon to 3pm and 5:30 to 9pm. Restaurant closed January to mid-April.

WESTHAMPTON DINING

Starr Boggs at the Dune Deck Hotel, 379 Dune Rd. (☎ 516/288-5250), is the dining hit in Westhampton Beach, at least for the summer crowd. Sensational views of the dunes and ocean add an extra romance to the place. The menu features about a dozen entrees. The dishes are simple in their preparation, but use the finest local ingredients. There might be almond-crusted flounder with lemon-herb butter and basil-crusted swordfish in red pepper coulis and balsamic syrup. For a signature appetizer select the Virginia crab cake, served with a fine rémoulade and black-eyed pea salad. A couple of steaks are also usually offered, like a sirloin served with a Cabernet jus. Prices range from $21 to $30. *Hours:* Summer only, daily 11:30am to 2:30pm and 5pm to closing; spring, Thursday to Sunday 11:30am to 2:30pm and 5pm to closing. Closed in winter.

HAMPTON BAYS DINING

Villa Paul, 162 Montauk Hwy. (☎ 516/728-3261), has survived the fashions and trends and remains an institution frequented by local businesspeople and others who appreciate the reliable, good Italian cuisine. The traditional favorites are available—veal parmigiana, veal Marsala, saltimbocca, and scampi with white wine, garlic, and butter, plus steaks and local duckling with apple-raisin stuffing and a sauce of the day. Prices range from $16 to $21. *Hours:* Daily 4:30pm to closing.

  Tully's, 78 Foster Ave. (☎ 516/728-9111), which also operates a fish store next door, assures that the fish served here is some of the freshest around. It's not fancy, and the fish is simply prepared, but that's all that's required when it's this fresh. Come for the steamers, mussels, oysters, shrimp, steamed lobster, and grilled fish priced from $12 to $25. *Hours:* Mid-March to mid-November, daily 5pm to closing.

| **Hampton Bays & Westhampton Beach** |
| Special & Recreational Activities |

Bicycling: The Hamptons are ideal for biking because the area is very flat, with only some minor hills in Sag Harbor. Shelter Island in particular is a favorite touring ground.

Boating: The **Shinnecock Fishing Station**, 22 Shinnecock Rd. Hampton Bays (☎ 516/728-6116), rents 10-foot boats with outboards for $50 for a half day and $80 for a full day. **Atlantic Bait and Boat Rentals**, 215 Atlantic Avenue, East Moriches (☎ 516/878-3902), rents boats for $85 a day, and jet skis for $40 for half an hour and $75 an hour.

Fishing: One open boat, the *Shinnecock Star* docks at the Indian Cover Marina and charges $45 per person. The *Capt. Clark III* (☎ 516/728-9084) is available for charter and charges $350 for up to six people.

Horseback Riding: **Hidden Echo Ranch**, Route 24, Hampton Bays (☎ 516/668-5453)—take Exit 65 off Sunrise Highway north 1½ miles—offers 30-minute and 1-hour trail rides for $20 and $30, respectively. Special sunset rides are also arranged. **Sears Bellows Stables**, Route 24, Exit 65N off Sunrise Highway (☎ 516/723-3554), offers trail rides, including a special 30-minute ride for families and children costing $20. One-hour rides cost $30 and a 1½-hour ride that goes by the Sears Bellows lake costs $40.

Soaring: **Sky Sailors, Inc.,** at the Suffolk County Airport, Building 313, Rust Avenue, Westhampton Beach, NY 11978 (☎ 516/288-5858), offers several flight packages, including a trip for two. Prices depend on how high you go and range from $70 to $170.

Tennis: Call the chambers of commerce for information about high school tennis courts that are open to the public in Hampton Bays and Westhampton.

SOUTHAMPTON

SOUTHAMPTON ATTRACTIONS

Founded in 1640 by colonists from Lynn, Massachusetts, Southampton was the first English colony established in New York State. It became a famous resort about a century ago, when a summer colony was established here by 200 wealthy and socially prominent New York families. Their impressive estates can still be seen along Halsey, Captain's, and Coopers Neck lanes, and the oceanfront Meadow Lane, South Main Street, and Gin Lane. They built the Meadow Club, on Meadow Lane, with its grass tennis courts and shingle-style clubhouse. You can explore the town very well by securing a **walking-tour map** from the Southampton Chamber of Commerce at 76 Main St. (☎ 516/283-0402). To some, Southampton means money and high society, and a glance at the prestigious shop names on Job's Lane will certainly confirm that impression.

The **Parrish Art Museum,** 25 Job's Lane (☎ 516/283-2118), is the town's cultural center and boasts significant collections of William Merritt Chase and Fairfield Porter artworks. The museum schedules a variety of art exhibits through the year, featuring juried shows and local art festivals, plus themed exhibits relating to the artists prominent on the East End during the last 50 years, from Willem and Elaine de Kooning and Roy Lichtenstein to John Chamberlain and Franz Kline. Besides art exhibitions and lectures, the museum offers concerts in the garden on several Saturday nights during summer. Bring a blanket. The gardens are a lovely, restful haven, enhanced by several della Robbia works. *Hours:* In season, Monday to Tuesday, Thursday, and Saturday 11am to 5pm; Sunday 1 to 5pm. Off-season, Monday and Thursday to Saturday 11am to 5pm, Sunday 1 to 5pm. *Admission:* Donation suggested.

The **Halsey House Museum** (1648), South Main Street (☎ 516/283-3527), is the oldest English saltbox in the state and furnished appropriately with authentic period furnishings. *Hours:* Mid-June to mid-September, Tuesday to Sunday 11am to 5pm. *Admission:* $2 adults, 50¢ children ages 6 to 12.

The **Southampton Historical Museum,** 17 Meeting House Lane (☎ 516/283-2494), provides an overview of local history from the times when the Shinnecocks inhabited the area, before the Puritans arrived in 1695, through the railroad era and the development of the "summer colony." At the museum visitors can see the home of whaling captain Albert Rogers, which was built in 1843 in a Greek Revival style. In 1899 the Rogers home was bought by Samuel Parrish, an attorney and former mayor of Southampton; Parrish also founded the art museum when he donated his collection of Italian art to the community. The first floor is dedicated to the Shinnecock Indian collection, whaling exhibits, and temporary exhibitions. On the second floor of the museum you'll find antique dolls and toys, plus antique rifles and powder horns along with quilts and toleware. Clustered around the main building are several other buildings: a traditional wigwam; a one-room schoolhouse (where you can see the hickory sticks used to discipline the children); several outhouses; a corncrib; a tavern; a barn where agricultural, fishing, and domestic tools are displayed; and several other buildings. *Hours:* Mid-June to mid-September, Tuesday to Sunday 11am to 5pm; winter, by appointment. *Admission:* $3 adults, $2 seniors, 50¢ children ages 6 to 11.

Southampton is also the site of the **Shinnecock Indian Reservation,** where the famous powwow is held on Labor Day weekend.

SOUTHAMPTON LODGING

Obviously, your first choice would be to stay with friends who have a house, preferably south of the highway. If this cannot be arranged, then there's at least one very attractive alternative.

Marta Byer and Martin White have created some of the most original, inspired accommodations in the Hamptons at the **Village Latch Inn,** 101 Hill St., Southampton, NY 11968 (☎ 516/283-2160), only minutes from Job's Lane and a mile from the beach. Set behind a privet hedge, the handsome clapboard building was once the annex of the Irving Hotel, at one time the area's premier accommodation. Throughout the house you'll come upon all kinds of fascinating collectibles Marta has gathered on travels around the world, particularly dolls and puppets arranged in strikingly original ways—a doll's head cupped in a bird's nest, another doll seated on a small chair, an open parasol on the stair landing—and in the parlors you'll find an intriguing assemblage of Marta's artworks.

Each of the main house's 24 rooms is furnished individually. Room 68 has a pair of comfy wing chairs and a fireplace. Room 58's centerpiece is a sleigh bed, while one of the spacious suites offers a bedroom with a handsome bed covered with a hand-woven quilt, an oak chest and rocker, and a sitting room with wicker chairs in front of the fireplace.

Marta has spent the last few years carefully restoring and decorating several historic houses that now stand on the 5 acres behind the main house. Each one is more appealing than the next. For example, the 100-year-old Homestead now has nine rooms and eight baths; the spacious shared living room is filled with leather and Victorian couches. A large Regency dining table is set close to the kitchen, which has a fireplace, a brilliant Mexican tile floor, and a vast Garland range. From the Homestead guests can step out into the "spa," located in a Victorian-style greenhouse furnished comfortably with wicker. On the other side of the spa, another house has been beautifully transformed with plush furnishings and objects from around the world— masks, puppets, and other objets d'art from Africa's Ivory Coast, South America, and India.

Between the main house and the other houses stretches a large lawn for croquet, a pool with a privet hedge providing privacy, and a tennis court. Bikes are available for rent. A full breakfast of bagels, ham, cheese, yogurt, fruit, and homemade breads and cakes is served in the dining room with its brilliant-green director's chairs. An ultra-comfortable sitting room with a fireplace filled with plants and appealing objects completes this very inviting accommodation.

Rates (including breakfast): Peak season, $185 to $285 double, $235 to $385 suite/duplex; off- and shoulder season, $135 to $235 double, $205 to $235 suite/duplex. Open May through November.

The **Southampton Inn,** 91 Hill St., Southampton, NY 11968 (☎ 516/283-6500; fax 516/283-6559), offers 90 modern rooms, fully appointed with cable TVs and telephones with data ports. They are decorated in a country motif using patchwork quilts, pine and painted furniture, and sisal carpeting. The bathrooms feature decorative tilework and contain turn-of-the-century-style pedestal sinks. Facilities include an outdoor pool, two tennis courts, and dining facilities. *Rates:* Summer, weekends $339 double, midweek $159 double; spring/fall, weekends $199, midweek $139; winter, weekends $149, midweek $139.

SOUTHAMPTON DINING

Basilico, 10 Windmill Lane (☎ 516/283-7987), is a study in cream and sage. It affects a distinctly Tuscan air with its rough-cast walls and terra-cotta tiles, rush-seated chairs, and tall green plants. The menu offers a limited number of pasta, seafood, and meat dishes, plus pizzas. There might be rigatoni alla buttera (with tomatoes, cream, sausages, cheese, and peas), which you can have as a main course or as an appetizer, followed by sautéed sole served on a bed of spinach with a mustard butter, or chicken breast sautéed with sun-dried tomatoes and escarole. Several vegetarian dishes are usually offered plus daily specials. Prices range from $15 to $24. *Hours:* Monday to Thursday 5:30pm to closing, Friday noon to 3pm and 6pm to closing, Saturday noon to 3pm (brunch) and 6pm to closing, Sunday noon to 3pm (brunch) and 5:30pm to closing.

Savanna's, 268 Elm St. (☎ 516/283-0202), has remained at the top of the dining scene. The space is unpretentious and tucked away in a historic building in a remote neighborhood at the edge of town. The frequently changing menu offers Southern coastal cuisine. You might find pan-seared Chilean sea bass with herbs and a sun-dried tomato sauce, or grilled king salmon accompanied by sautéed broccoli rabe, toasted red peppers, rosemary potatoes, and a warm basil tomato salad. The chicken comes from North Sea farms and might be wood oven–roasted, with garlic and rosemary served in its own juices. Long Island duck, glazed with sweet orange and ginger is similarly wood oven–roasted. Several pasta dishes, plus wood-oven pizzas are also offered. Prices range from $15 to $34. The appetizers are very special, too—steamed local mussels with roasted tomato garlic broth; or wood oven–roasted portobello mushrooms with organic greens, arugula, roasted pimento vinaigrette, balsamic oil, and crumbled Gorgonzola. The pièce de résistance among the desserts is the pecan pie with vanilla crème Chantilly and bourbon-caramel sauce; the gâteau of Valhrona extra-bitter dark chocolate on toasted vanilla sauce is not far behind. On Sunday you can enjoy a country breakfast featuring dishes made with organic eggs, nitrate-free bacon, and homemade sausages and country ham. Prices range from $8 to $15. *Hours:* Summer, daily 11am to 3pm and 5:30 to 10pm; winter, Wednesday to Sunday 5 to 9:45pm, Saturday to Sunday 10am to 2pm.

People continue to flock to **John Duck, Jr.,** at Prospect and North Main streets (☎ 516/283-0311), for the reliable duckling with apple-raisin dressing. The decor is unpretentious. Other menu items—sauerbraten, Wienerschnitzel, scampi, soft-shell crabs, prime rib, and steaks—are served with soup and coleslaw and priced from $14 to $26. In addition, many daily specials are offered. *Hours:* Tuesday to Sunday noon to 10:30pm.

The Red Bar Brasserie, 210 Hampton Rd. (☎ 516/283-0704), throws open its windows during the summer. It's a thoroughly modern dining room featuring brasserie-style cuisine like steak with pommes frites and pan-roasted chicken with mashed potatoes. Other dishes are inspired by Asian or other traditions, like the grilled peppered tuna served with steamed bok choy, shiitakes, and ponzu sauce; or the roast Long Island duck with fresh figs and port wine. A couple of pasta dishes round out the menu. Prices range from $18 to $29. Among the starters there are several shellfish dishes like the local oysters with a mignonette sauce, plus salads and soups. *Hours:* July to August, Sunday to Thursday to 10pm, Friday and Saturday to 11pm; mid-March to June and September to mid-January, Thursday to Sunday 5:30pm to closing.

Barristers, 36 Main St. (☎ 516/283-6206), has been here for 20 years or more, which testifies to the quality-to-price ratio of its food, the appeal of its menu, and the comfort of its casual ambience. At night, the lunch menu of salads, sandwiches, and burgers (all under $8) is supplemented by specials like seared fennel-crusted salmon topped with a caper-pimento butter, or grilled pork medallions in a mushroom gravy; all are priced from $13 to $20, with most averaging $16. The pleasant, shaded courtyard is a favorite for summer dining. *Hours:* Daily 11:30am to 4pm and 5:30 to 11pm.

The other famous in-town lunch spot is **The Driver's Seat**, 62 Job's Lane (☎ 516/283-6606), offering sandwiches, burgers, salads, and omelets that can be enjoyed inside or outdoors. At dinner such entrees as New York strip steak and shrimp teriyaki or chicken piccata are priced from $15 to $20. *Hours:* Monday to Thursday 11:30am to 11pm, Friday to Sunday 11:30am to midnight.

Le Chef, at the corner of Main and Nugent streets (☎ 516/283-8581), is a pleasant restaurant where the tables sport crisp, white cloths and bentwood chairs. This place is good for lunch, when salads, sandwiches, and quiches are available. The three-course prix-fixe dinner offers excellent value at $20. You might start with pâté de campagne or snails with garlic butter, then follow with sea bass cooked Cajun-style with a salsa of tomatillo, cilantro, jalapeño, and avocado, or sliced breast of duck with orange and ginger, or else a delicious pan-seared rack of lamb with rosemary, sage, and mint. Finish with cheesecake or crème caramel or pay extra for the crêpes with French vanilla ice cream accompanied by sliced strawberries and chocolate sauce. *Hours:* Daily noon to 3pm and Sunday to Thursday 5:30 to 10:30pm, Friday and Saturday 5:30 to 11:30pm.

Southampton
Special & Recreational Activities

Beaches: For beach information, contact the **Parks and Recreation Department**, 116 Hampton Rd., Southampton, NY 11968 (☎ 516/283-6011). Parking permits are required and may be purchased at all town beaches upon proof of residency. Nonresident permits are available at certain beaches. Call for details.

Bicycling: Rotations, 32 Windmill Lane, Southampton (☎ 516/283-2890), rents bikes for $25 a day.

Golf: There are fine courses on the East End, but in Southampton you'll have to settle for the **Golf Range** on North Highway (☎ 516/283-2158), where buckets cost $4 and $7 depending on the size.

Picnicking: Picnic hampers can be filled at the **Village Cheese Shop**, 11 Main St. (☎ 516/283-6949); **Loaves and Fishes**, 50 Sagg Main St., Sagaponack (☎ 516/537-0555), which offers special lunchbox menus; or more modestly at **Ted's Market**, 264 Hampton Rd. (☎ 516/283-0929), which specializes in creating well-stuffed heroes, and **Southampton Deli**, Hampton Road and North Highway (☎ 516/283-1774).

Tennis: Sandy Hollow Tennis Club, Sandy Hollow Road, County Road 52 (Exit 8 off Route 27; ☎ 516/283-3422), offers a seasonal membership for $850; it has 14 Hartru courts. **Southampton High**, on Narrow Lane (☎ 516/283-6800), has courts open to the public. For additional public courts, call the Chamber of Commerce at ☎ 516/283-0402.

Windsurfing/Sailing: Windsurfing Hamptons, 1686 North Hwy. (County Road 39; ☎ 516/283-WIND), has windsurfers and sailboats for rent. Instruction is given. Windsurfers cost $35 for 2 hours; a Sunfish costs $85 per day.

WATER MILL, BRIDGEHAMPTON & WAINSCOTT

AREA ATTRACTIONS

A few miles east of Southampton, the village of Water Mill is on the edge of Mecox Bay. The **Water Mill Museum**, Old Mill Road (☎ 516/726-4625), displays early American tools and features craft demonstrations, an operating waterwheel, and a working gristmill, plus historic photographs and temporary exhibitions. The watermill windmill was moved here in 1814 from North Haven, hauled by 12 yoke of oxen, and was used until 1887. *Hours:* Mid-May to late September or mid-October, daily 11am to 5pm, Sunday 1 to 5pm. *Admission:* $2 adults, $1.50 seniors, free for children.

Quite a lot of literary figures hang out in Bridgehampton, and their literary gossip flies around the bar at Bobby Van's (see below). There are several antiques stores on Main Street and a landmark windmill built in 1820.

Bridgehampton also has a **historical museum** at the **Bridgehampton Historical Society** (☎ 516/537-1088), on Main Street, which has a blacksmith's shop on the grounds and another building housing antique engines and farm machinery. *Hours:* June to Labor Day, Thursday to Saturday noon to 4pm.

The constant roaring of engines that can be heard from May to early November on most weekends emanates from the **Bridgehampton Race Circuit**, Millstone Road (☎ 516/725-0888). Bridgehampton has one of the few public golf courses—the **Poxabogue Golf Course**, Montauk Highway (☎ 516/537-0025), which charges $20 greens fees.

WATER MILL DINING

The **Station Bistro**, Station Road (☎ 516/726-3016), is a very inviting place with banks of colorful window boxes. Located in the station, the restaurant seats only 40 people, and the menu is appropriately limited and carefully prepared using the freshest ingredients. It always features such items as fish and stew du jour in addition to, say, sliced loin of lamb with niçoise sauce, rotisserie-style roasted chicken with Dijon tarragon jus, and Long Island duck with a wonderfully tart cherry sauce. Prices range from $21 to $25. To start there might be a flavorful lobster and corn bisque enhanced by some fire-roasted peppers, or wonderful sesame ginger crab cakes with tomato rémoulade, or duck pâté with curry mustard sauce. The desserts change, but if the chocolate cup filled with white-chocolate mousse and a touch of raspberry sauce is offered, order it. Ditto for the lemon mousse with raspberry sauce. Prices run $18 to $26. The room positively glows and the service is always winning. *Hours:* Summer, daily 6 to 10pm; rest of the year, Thursday to Sunday 6 to 10pm.

Tucked away in Water Mill Square, **Mirko's** (☎ 516/726-4444) makes a strong statement for the chef/owner who hails from the former Yugoslavia. It's a cozy restaurant with a patio. Botanical prints grace the cream-colored walls; lace curtains hang at the windows. The menu offers continental cuisine leavened with an occasional specialty from the Balkans—for example, Croatian stuffed cabbage might be among the appetizers. You might also find an inventive portobello mushroom pizza with caramelized onions, sun-dried tomatoes, prosciutto, and Pecorino Romano; or delicious grilled shrimp and bacon with a sauce of lemon, pepper, white wine, and shallots. To follow, there'll be about eight entrees plus some pasta and risotto dishes. Seasonal examples may include pan-roasted striped bass with a tomato, fennel, and saffron broth; herb-roasted pork tenderloin with green apple compote, charred tomato, sweet and sour shallots, and balsamic sage sauce; or roasted duck breast with honey lime vinegar sauce. For dessert, the caramelized oranges with Grand Marnier over vanilla ice cream hits the spot, but chocoholics may prefer the chocolate sorbet or the white- and dark-chocolate-mousse terrine. Prices run $19 to $32. In summer you can dine in the lovely covered patio or in an open courtyard. In winter the fireplace adds to the ambience. *Hours:* Summer, Sunday to Tuesday and Thursday 6 to 10pm, Friday and Saturday 6 to 11pm; winter, Thursday to Sunday 6 to 10pm. Closed January and February.

Meghan's Saloon, Montauk Highway (☎ 516/726-9657), is a convenient place to stop on Friday nights on your way to the East End.

BRIDGEHAMPTON LODGING

The **Bridgehampton Motel,** Montauk Highway (P.O. Box 623), Bridgehampton, NY 11932 (☎ 516/537-0197; fax 516/537-5436), is the brain child of Martha Stewart's daughter, Alexis, and it certainly has shock value when you compare it to the genteel country inns and homes of the area. You can't miss the low-slung building with brilliant jade shutters. At the back of the parking lot is a nicely landscaped pool with a lawn alongside with decorous iron lawn chairs. Inside, it's modern with a vengeance. All 10 rooms have cable TV/VCRs, CD/cassette players, air-conditioning, phones, and stocked minibars (without alcohol). Furnishings are starkly modern, but the amenities emphasize comfort—Frette sheets, down comforters and pillows, and terry-cloth bathrobes. It's a matter of taste whether you warm to the retro-1950s decor. Tea and coffee are available in the mornings. *Rates:* Summer, weekends $255 double, midweek $145 double; spring/fall, weekends $155 double, midweek $125 double. Closed winter.

BRIDGEHAMPTON DINING

Karen Lee's, 2402 Montauk Hwy. (☎ 516/537-7878), draws raves from both locals and visitors. The room is simple, and there's an outdoor porch for dining. The cuisine is well spiced, and the ingredients are fresh. Though the menu changes daily, some dishes appear regularly. Start with a big bowl of mussels with tomatoes, tarragon, and garlic; or the escarole with Vermont goat cheese, sweet peppers, and sherry vinaigrette. Among the dozen or so main courses the fish dishes shine—Maine halibut on a potato pancake with wilted spinach and fried leeks; or grilled jumbo sea scallops with braised artichokes, fried beets, and Pernod. The meat dishes also have interesting accompaniments, like the tiny French beans and blackberries that arrive with the duck with basil walnut wild rice. Prices range from $19 to $31, the most expensive item being the rosemary- and sage-crusted rib-eye steak served with Parmesan mashed potatoes and sautéed spinach. There's an extensive wine list, including a decent selection by the glass. *Hours:* Summer, Monday, Wednesday, and Thursday 6 to 10pm, Friday and Saturday 6 to 11pm, Sunday 5:30 to 9:30pm; fall/winter, Thursday 6 to 10pm, Friday and Saturday 6 to 11pm, Sunday 5:30 to 9:30pm.

Made famous by Truman Capote and other literary lights, **Bobby Van's,** Main Street (☎ 516/537-0590), provides a good bar, tasty food in comfortable surroundings, and plenty of gossip (you can meet everybody here). The cuisine is eclectic, inspired by Asian and Mediterranean traditions. Among the 10 or so entrees you'll find such dishes as skillet-seared tuna in a tomato coriander broth accompanied by couscous salad and pickled ginger and wasabi; rack of lamb rubbed with chipotles and served with mango salsa; or orechiette with lobster, sun-dried tomato, asparagus, and roast garlic laced with white truffle oil. Steaks, including a luscious porterhouse round out the menu. Prices range from $19 to $34. The restaurant is a good choice for brunch, too, when you can secure sandwiches, pasta, and other dishes along with the usual egg favorites like French toast and eggs Benedict. *Hours:* Summer, daily noon to 4pm, Sunday to Thursday 5:30 to 11pm, Friday and Saturday 5:30 to midnight; winter, daily noon to 4pm, and Sunday to Thursday 5:30 to 10pm and Friday and Saturday 5:30 to 11pm.

95 School Street (☎ 537-5555)—small, plain, and tasteful—serves some powerfully good food. The chef uses local ingredients whenever possible, like the grilled Jurgielewicz farm duck breast that might be served with a fresh blueberry-strawberry sauce, or the pan-roasted Iacono chicken served with garlic mashed potatoes and sautéed greens. The fish dishes are extraordinary and fresh—the halibut baked in parchment with spinach, fennel, tomato, and onions, seasoned with fresh herbs and Pernod, is just what this wonderful fish deserves. The sautéed softshell crabs are made even more vivid with leeks, tomatoes, and capers. Vegetarians will appreciate the platter of grilled portobello mushrooms, spinach-potato pancake, corn pudding, garlic mashed potatoes, vegetable burrito with fresh tomato salsa, and rice. Prices range from $19 to $27. Even the appetizers are thrilling—crispy calamari with spicy tomato puree, crab cakes with cilantro lime sauce, and seaweed salad. This is another favorite celebrity hangout. *Hours:* Sunday to Thursday 6 to 10pm, Friday and Saturday 6 to 11pm

The **Candy Kitchen,** at the corner of Main and School streets (☎ 516/537-9885), is everyone's breakfast and newspaper pickup spot. *Hours:* Daily 7am to 7pm (to 9:30pm in summer).

WAINSCOTT DINING

Alison's by the Beach, 3593 Montauk Hwy. at Townline Road, Sagaponack (☎ 516/537-7100), is the sibling of its namesake in Manhattan. It offers some superb cuisine. The ambience is comfortable country—blue-and-white-striped curtains, country cushions, stucco, and gabled walls. Start with a wonderful petite bouillabaisse made with potatoes, fennel, mussels, and saffron rouille; or the smoked Scottish salmon served with horseradish crème fraîche, greens, potatoes, and brioche. Among the seven entrees, some have a comforting bistro style like the steak (glazed with bordelaise sauce) and frites; or the roast chicken with braised cabbage, artichokes, and black trumpet mushrooms. All the dishes bring out the intense flavors of the fine ingredients, whether it be sautéed halibut with escarole, treviso, and garlic herb bouillon; or the risotto of caramelized fennel and chanterelles with bacon and rosemary. Prices range from $24 to $32. *Hours:* Summer, Sunday noon to 3pm and daily 5:30 to 10pm; winter, Thursday to Monday 5:30 to 10pm.

Around Bridgehampton
Special & Recreational Activities

Beaches: The beach at the end of Job's Lane requires no sticker.

Golf: Poxabogue, Montauk Highway, Bridgehampton (☎ 516/537-0025), has nine holes and charges $20 greens fees.

Kayaking/Windsurfing: Main Beach Surf and Sport, Wainscott (☎ 516/537-2716), rents canoes and kayaks for $45 for a half day. They also arrange kayaking tours. The **East Coast Adventure Tour Company,** 41 Oak Lane, Amagansett (☎ 516/267-2303), also operates a series of kayak tours focusing on wildlife as well as treasure hunts and other similar pastimes. Rentals start at $12 per hour and include free transport to local beaches.

Tennis: The **Bridgehampton High School** courts, on Montauk Highway, are open to the public (☎ 516/537-0271) when school is not in session.

Windsurfing: To rent a windsurfer call ☎ 516/668-4185.

EAST HAMPTON

EAST HAMPTON ATTRACTIONS

East Hampton was once voted the most beautiful village in the United States by the readers of the *Saturday Evening Post,* and you can easily see why. At one end of the town, stately elms arch over the street and the Village Green, their branches reflecting in the still water of the old pond, while at the other end of town the old cedar-shingled Hook Mill stands on a grassy knoll as it has since it began grinding in 1806. Along Main Street stand lovely 18th- and 19th-century buildings that represent the town's venerable architectural heritage dating from 1649.

Note that East Hampton Town is a political entity that runs from the eastern border of Southampton Town to Montauk Point— including East Hampton village, Amagansett, and Montauk. The best way to explore the village is to pick up a **walking tour** at the Chamber of Commerce, 79A Main St. (☎ 516/324-0362; open Monday to Saturday 10am to 4pm), in a passageway that runs from Main Street to the parking lot behind.

On the other side of the town pond, south cemetery, and the Village Green stands the **Home Sweet Home Museum,** 14 James Lane (☎ 516/324-0713), so called because it was the boyhood home of John Howard Payne (1791 to 1852), actor, dramatist, and author of "Home Sweet Home," a song he wrote in Paris in the 1820s when he was homesick for this very house. *Hours:* Memorial Day to mid-December, Monday to Saturday 10am to 4pm, Sunday 2 to 4pm; by appointment at other times. *Admission:* $4 adults, $2 children.

Next door, the **Mulford Farm**, 10 James Lane (☎ 516/324-6850), built in the 1650s, is the most intact 17th-century property in the village. Costumed interpreters demonstrate 18th-century chores in the house and barn; the period garden contains plants used in cooking and medicine. *Hours:* Summer, daily 10 to 5pm; by appointment at other times.

The **Guild Hall**, 158 Main St. (☎ 516/324-0806), is East Hampton's cultural center, site of exhibitions featuring well-known and emerging contemporary artists, many of them associated with the region. You might find exhibits of works by such artists as Julian Schnabel and Basquiat. The galleries are open evenings before performances that are given in the John Drew Theater. The Guild Hall also presents year-round programming—plays, a writer's series, a music series, and related educational classes and activities. *Hours:* Summer, daily 11am to 5pm; winter, Wednesday to Saturday 11am to 5pm, Sunday noon to 5pm.

Across the street, the **East Hampton Library**, 149 Main St., is worth a visit just to see the reading room's luxurious comforts. At the same address stands the **Town House** (☎ 516/324-6850), the first town meeting hall and one-room schoolhouse. It provides visitors with an interactive history class from about 1860 led by a costumed interpreter.

Next door, the **Clinton Academy**, 151 Main St. (☎ 516/324-6850), built in 1784, was the first chartered secondary school in New York State, but it now features a changing collection of artifacts and furnishings culled from homes on eastern Long Island.

Hours: Town House and Clinton Academy, July to August, daily 1 to 3pm; Labor Day to October and Memorial Day to June, Saturday to Sunday 10am to 5pm. *Admission:* $4 adults, $2 seniors, $2 children ages 6 to 12.

Art lovers will want to make an appointment to see the **Pollock-Krasner house and studio**, 830 Fireplace Rd. (☎ 516/324-4929), where Jackson Pollock (1912–56) worked. He and fellow artist Lee Krasner purchased the 1¼-acre farm overlooking Accabonac Creek in 1945; here he created innovative works that stunned the art world and made him a leader of the abstract expressionist movement. In the converted barn that served as his studio, visitors can see a photo essay chronicling the evolution of his art as well as the artists' milieu, including the paint-laden floor. The house can also be visited. It remains much as Krasner left it and contains prints by both artists, plus their furniture and personal library. *Hours:* May to October, Thursday to Saturday 11am to 4pm by appointment only. *Admission:* $5.

Beyond the junction of Main Street and Newtown Lane, on a brilliant green lawn stands the lovely and fully functioning **Hook Mill** (☎ 516/324-0713), which began grinding in 1806 and continued until 1922 (it's still in working order). The burying ground behind the mill contains some headstones dating back to 1650 that are ideal for rubbing. Bring large paper and charcoal or chalk. *Hours:* June to Labor Day, daily 10am to 4pm. *Admission:* $2 adults, $1 children.

Today East Hampton is the center of "Hollywood East" thanks to such part-time residents as Steven Spielberg, David Geffen, Sidney Lumet, and other film actors and directors. It has also become the focal point of the prestigious Hamptons International Film Festival.

EAST HAMPTON LODGING & DINING

For authentic and exquisite lodgings coupled with friendly, unassuming hospitality, the only choice is the **1770 House**, 143 Main St., East Hampton, NY 11937 (☎ 516/324-1770; fax 516/324-3504). More than 20 years ago, Mr. and Mrs. Sidney Perle took it over and restored this beautiful old beamed home, filling it with their carefully selected personal collections: tall Morbier clocks, mantel clocks, and wall clocks of all sorts (Sidney's passion), plus eclectic objects that enliven and fill a room with character. Today their daughter Wendy brings her own talents to both the kitchen and the house.

All eight guest rooms are furnished with a distinct aesthetic sense—from the No. 11 attic room with twin beds, to the No. 10 suite with a private entrance. The latter has a hand-carved oak bed, a fainting couch, an oak fireplace, and a breakfront displaying some of the Perles' china collection. In the garden room (No. 12), richly decorated in blue, a leaded-glass window looks out on spring daffodils, while a sled sits at the foot of the canopied bed.

Rates (including breakfast): May 1 to October 31, $160 to $290 double; November 1 to March 31, weekends $130 to $260, midweek $105 to $130.

The **Maidstone Arms**, 207 Main St., East Hampton, NY 11937 (☎ 516/324-5006, fax 516/324-5037), is a long-standing local favorite, conveniently located across from the town pond and Village Green, only a short distance from Main Beach. This white clapboard building with green trim has the casual but semiformal ambience of a venerable beach house—wicker chairs and tables are on the front porch, and rhododendrons blossom in the garden out back.

It offers 12 bright, smartly decorated guest rooms, four suites, and three private cottages with working fireplaces and terraces. Each has a private bath, air-conditioning, a TV, telephone, and hair dryer. They are eclectically and individually furnished with antiques, including brass-and-iron beds, canopied beds, or Shaker four-posters with country quilts. The furnishings might include a butler's table and wing chair or a candle stand and club chair with bull's-eye mirror over the mantel, if the room has a fireplace. Suite 61 is particularly attractive, tucked under the eaves and flooded with sun from the skylight.

The restaurant has a sterling reputation and attracts a number of celebrities to its two dining rooms. The most intimate room features a nautical theme with paintings of ships and vintage model sailboats, a fireplace, and a small bar. The larger dining room is accented by a collection of authentic antique plates, which are paired with trompe l'oeil versions on the opposite wall. Both are warmed by fires in winter. The restaurant's reputation rests on consistently well-prepared contemporary American cuisine with a Pacific twist. Among the most popular dishes are the stir-fried tiger prawns with Thai black-bean sauce, the seared prime rib eye with port wine Stilton cheese sauce, and rack of lamb with roasted garlic herb orzo. Another signature dish is the marvelous lacquered duck. Prices range from $20 to $29. The favorite appetizer? Try either the house's own rum-smoked salmon with dill crème fraîche and green and red Tobbiko caviar, presented in a mille-feuille; or the port-braised New York foie gras with macerated cherries. As far as desserts go, go for the signature dish, a rich mille-feuille of espresso, mascarpone, and chocolate.

The Water Room, a comfortable sitting-room bar, complete with humidor for cigar fanciers, opens to the garden, where lunch and dinner are also served in summer. Guests can relax here and enjoy a game of backgammon, chess, a good book, or simply enjoy some peace and quiet and a glass of wine. In winter the room is warmed by a wood stove. A continental breakfast is served to inn guests; a heartier English breakfast is also available in one of the dining rooms.

Rates (including continental breakfast): $185 to $235 double, suites from $305, cottage $350 to $375. *Dining hours:* Monday to Friday noon to 2:30pm, Saturday and Sunday 11am to 2:30pm; Monday to Friday 6 to 10pm, Saturday and Sunday 6 to 10:30pm. Closed usually 2 weeks in March.

You can't miss the rambling, green-shuttered, white clapboard **Huntting Inn**, 94 Main St., East Hampton, NY 11937 (☎ 516/324-0410), sheltered by some very old elms and maples in the heart of the village. It was named after the Reverend Nathaniel Huntting, who called it home in the 18th century until it became an inn in 1751. The 19 guest rooms are furnished individually, with unpretentious pieces. You might find a white-painted queen-size bed with a duvet, a Victorian-style chair and armchair, and a small secretary with a Queen Anne chair, all set against a chintz background. Some rooms have brass beds with oak desks and chairs; others have wicker pieces. Room 201 possesses a delicate, peach-colored fainting couch, while Room 211 overlooks the English-style herbaceous garden, where a brick path winds among the bright colors of the foxgloves, lavender, lupines, poppies, daisies, and roses. All rooms have air-conditioning, TVs, and telephones. A wood-paneled cocktail lounge with a spectacular, long carved-oak bar and the famed Palm restaurant are on the ground floor. This branch of the famous steak house, which first opened in Manhattan in the 1920s, is a popular mecca for entertainment figures and other glamorous or moneyed folks. The portions are notoriously large, and the quality of the steaks absolutely prime. *Rates* (including breakfast): In season, $235 to $360 double, from $510 suite; off-season, $205 to $260 double, from $350 suite.

The **Hedges Inn**, 74 James Lane, East Hampton, NY 11937 (☎ 516/324-7100), occupies a classic old clapboard house with chocolate-colored shutters just down from the town pond. This property was granted to William Hedges in 1652 and remained in the family until 1923. It has an inviting air: Geranium-filled window boxes brighten each of the five front windows, a brick path lined with flowers leads to the front door, a crazy-paved patio fringed with flower boxes beckons you to its white wooden chairs and umbrella tables, and a small parlor with a TV and fireplace is available for guest use.

The rooms feature country furnishings. You might find a carved wooden bed combined with a side table draped with fabric and set against chintz wallpaper. The 11 rooms are large, with a bath, air-conditioning, and solid-wood closet doors. Several have fireplaces. Room 2 contains a king-size brass bed, two draped side tables, a chest, and comfortable chairs. The bed in Room 1 sports a pretty eyelet lace eider; there's also a Windsor chair and a chintz couch that opens into a bed. Crabtree & Evelyn soaps, bath cubes, shampoo, and other amenities are placed in each bath, and a nighttime chocolate is set on the pillow.

A breakfast of croissants, danishes, and muffins is served in a small, bright dining room, where the plank floors and oak chairs give a country feel. So do the flower displays—when I visited, half a dozen great sunflowers worthy of van Gogh's brush. The restaurant, the **James Lane Cafe**, specializes in traditional American/Italian cuisine. Prices run from $16 for spaghettini with fresh tomatoes, garlic, and basil to $30 for a 16-ounce sirloin drizzled with melted Gorgonzola. The rest of the menu consists of dishes like grilled swordfish served with black olive and sun-dried tomato tapenades, horseradish-crusted and plank-roasted salmon, and whole grilled chicken served with frites. The best place to dine is on the elegant flagstone terrace, furnished with tables with market umbrellas. The interior dining room is sunny and bright and made even more so with its bleached wood decor.

Rates (including breakfast): Memorial Day to September, $235 to $360 double; the rest of the year, $160 double. *Dining hours:* Mid-May to early October, Monday to Thursday 5:30 to 10pm, Friday and Saturday 5 to 11pm, Sunday 4 to 10pm. Closed after Labor Day to mid-May.

Outside of town at Three Mile Harbor you can stay at Jerry Della Femina's resort complex, **East Hampton Point Cottages**, 295 Three Mile Harbor Rd. (P.O. Box 847), East Hampton, NY 11937 (☎ 516/324-9191). The one- and two-bedroom cottages are individually decorated in a country style and feature a living/dining room, a kitchen, and a skylit bathroom with a whirlpool. Standard amenities include air-conditioning, TVs, telephones, coffeemakers, unstocked refrigerators, and hair dryers. Facilities include a tennis court and a pool.

The **East Hampton Point Restaurant** (☎ 516/329-2800) offers dining outside overlooking the marina or inside in the mirrored dining room. It's inspirational at sunset. The cuisine is fresh, and the menu is limited. Depending on the season, there'll likely be about nine dishes available, ranging from steamed lobster and marinated and grilled tuna steak with a balsamic vinaigrette, to pancetta-wrapped veal chop with sweet pepper jus and roasted Rocco farm chicken with a lemon-rosemary gravy. There's usually a pasta selection, too. Prices range from $18 to $27. Appetizers concentrate on shellfish and fish selections, like Maine salmon and crabmeat cake with an avocado tartare sauce and bell pepper puree, tuna sashimi, or a selection of chilled shellfish (oysters, clams, and shrimp). In season, transportation is provided to and from East Hampton.

Rates: May to September, $235 to $360 one-bedroom cottage, from $420 two-bedroom cottage; March to April and October to November, $135 to $260 one-bedroom cottage, $295 two-bedroom cottage; December to February, $110 to $235 one-bedroom cottage, from $270 two-bedroom cottage. *Dining hours:* Summer, Sunday to Thursday noon to 10pm, Friday and Saturday noon to 11pm; spring/fall, Friday and Saturday 5:30 to 10pm, Sunday noon to 4pm. Restaurant closed December to late April.

MORE EAST HAMPTON LODGING

The Pink House, 26 James Lane, East Hampton, NY 11937 (☎ 516/ 324-3400), is a very hospitable and comfortable place. The house was built in the mid-1800s for a whaler captain, and it's located by the town pond and

Village Green, a short walk from the village center. Owner Ron Steinhilber is an architect with a fine eye for interior decoration and has made this an aesthetically pleasing lodging. Throughout the house are interesting objects and marvelous watercolors painted by his grandfather. The rooms are well furnished with fine antiques, but always with a concern for comfort. Each is individually decorated and has a bath, a phone, and air-conditioning. The Garden Room holds a pencil four-poster; the Country Room offers window seats and wicker furnishings; the Attic Room is the standout, with deer trophies, a saddle, and blankets. As for the public spaces, the sitting room is inviting with a fireplace, books, a TV, and a good music collection; the wicker seating on the front porch with its hanging baskets is great for whiling away an afternoon, and the secluded pool in back has plenty of grass around it for lounging. Start the day with a full breakfast, served inside or on the back porch, that might include house specialties like sourdough French toast and banana-walnut pancakes. A wonderful choice for a rejuvenating escape. *Rates* (including breakfast): Summer, $295 to $355 double; spring/fall, $175 to $305 double; winter, $155 to $205 double.

What makes **Centennial House**, 13 Woods Lane, East Hampton, NY 11937 (☎ 516/324-9414), extra-special is the quality of its decor and its 1¼ acres of secluded gardens complete with a pool. Near the Village Pond, this gracious home was built in 1876. The downstairs parlors are very comfortably and beautifully furnished. The chairs and sofas are upholstered with glazed chintzes and silk damasks; the windows are similarly draped with valances; the walls support prints and art or ormolu mirrors like the one above the marble hearth. There's even a grand piano for those who wish to entertain. In the five rooms upstairs, guests will find lavish extras like down-filled comforters, fresh flowers, sweets, cordials, silver bowls of potpourri, and terry-cloth bathrobes along with standard amenities like phones, baths, and air-conditioning. Two rooms have fireplaces. All are beautifully furnished with antiques, including claw-foot tubs in several of the marble bathrooms. The Rose Room contains an unusual corkscrew four-poster with a canopy; the Master Room has a private entrance and overlooks the gardens and pool area. My favorite room is the Loft on the third floor, tucked under the eaves at the top of a steeply winding staircase. If you're seeking complete privacy, there's also a three-bedroom, two-bath guest cottage with kitchen, dining area, and fireplace. An elaborate, candlelit full breakfast is served in the dining room, richly decorated with Schumacher and Scalamandre silk. The gardens are lovely—shaded by venerable trees, roses and perennials. The pool is well landscaped and is an inviting alternative to the beach crowds in summer. *Rates:* Summer, weekends $$235 to $405 double; winter, weekends $160 to $285 double. There's a 25% discount off these rates for weekday stays.

Even though the **J. Harper Poor Cottage**, 181 Main St., East Hampton, NY 11937 (☎ 516/324-4081; fax 516/329-5931), is located right in town, this English manor-style house has a romantic air thanks to the secluded garden in the back. Among its more distinctive architectural features are the tall chimneys, cozy mullioned windows, the carved angels that grace the lintels of the entrance, and the skylit colonial revival staircase. The interior has wonderful hand-hewn oak beams and large fireplaces, plus a wealth of arts and crafts ornamentation. The five rooms have been luxuriously decorated using William Morris–design wallpapers and velvets or similar fine fabrics for the drapes and furnishings. The beds are arts-and-crafts-style replicas. All of the rooms have TV/VCRs, computer/fax jacks, and safes. Four have wood-burning fireplaces. Guests can relax in the paneled great room, which has a brilliant tile fireplace and very comfortable seating arrangements. In summer a full breakfast is served on an outdoor terrace made even more beautiful by the 200-year-old wisteria. In addition to fresh fruit and other baked goods, there will always be two hot dishes like omelets and pancakes or waffles. Facilities include a fully stocked bar with wines available by the glass and by the bottle. *Rates:* June to September, weekends $325 to $450, midweek $250 to $375; October to May, weekends $205 to $305, midweek $160 to $260.

At the early- to mid-18th-century **Bassett House,** 128 Montauk Hwy., East Hampton, NY 11937 (☎ 516/324-6127; fax 516/324-5944), friendly Michael Bassett caters to guests at a long refectory table in the kitchen, where he'll prepare whatever you like for breakfast (within reason). Music fills the sunken parlor, where guests gather to read one of the many volumes in the bookcase or cozy up to the Franklin stove in winter. There are 12 rooms (9 with bath, 1 with whirlpool). Michael has painstakingly collected the furnishings at auctions, and he's spent many hours stripping paint from the original woodwork. His handiwork shows most exquisitely in the ground-floor room with plank floors and wormy-chestnut paneling on the walls and ceiling; a couch in front of the fireplace and a small rolltop desk set the tone. Other rooms vary in size and ambience, from a small single with enough room for a sink, a table, and a closet to a large double with an adjacent dressing room furnished with a hand-painted Victorian bed, ladder-back chairs, and a wrought-iron standing lamp. Two have fireplaces. *Rates:* $125 to $155 double with shared bath, $135 to $260 double with private bath.

132 North Main, East Hampton, NY 11937 (☎ 516/324-2246), offers an eclectic assortment of 13 accommodations. The seven rooms in the main house (two with bath) are typically homey and often small and basic. The nicest is a double immediately off the wide deck that's covered with flowers and plants. It contains a double bed covered with a colorful quilt, two side tables, an oak chest, and a wicker folding chair. The cabanas by the spectacular private (thanks to the trees) pool are the choice accommodations because of their location: sliding doors open poolside, and the furnishings are simple in these cedar cabins—a double bed/couch, a refrigerator, and a bath. Midway between the main house and the pool, a small cottage shelters a studio with a fully equipped kitchen and a living room/bedroom heated by a wood-burning stove. Muffins and coffee are available at breakfast—help yourself. The grounds between the buildings are prettily landscaped and make you feel like you are in the country. *Rates* (including breakfast): May to September 15, weekends, $160 to $180 double without bath, $160 to $245 double with bath; weekdays, $120 to $180 double. Closed in winter.

The **Mill House Inn,** 33 N. Main St., East Hampton, NY 11937 (☎ 516/324-9766), is operated by friendly Katherine and Dan Hartnett. The Dutch colonial, with a front porch overlooking the windmill green across the street, was built in 1790. All eight guest rooms have private baths (four with a Jacuzzi, six with gas fireplaces), air-conditioning, phones, and TVs. Each room is decorated in a different color scheme. The Rose Room for example, features rose-patterned wallpaper, wall-to-wall rose carpeting, plenty of lace, a fireplace, and a Jacuzzi. Furnishings range from wicker and pine to painted armoires. There's a parlor with a fireplace for relaxing. *Rates* (including continental breakfast in summer, larger breakfast off-season): May to October, $260 to $410 double. November to April, $160 to $335 double.

EAST HAMPTON DINING

For breakfast, sandwiches, and snacks at any time of day, head for the **Windmill Deli**, Main Street and Newtown Lane (☎ 516/324-9856), which sports a couple of tables outside; it's also a good spot to pick up the city newspapers. The best hamburgers are found at **O'Mally's** saloon, 11 E. Main St. (☎ 516/324-9010)—a good Friday-night revival spot. *Hours:* Daily 11:30am to midnight.

For serious dining go to the lovely **Maidstone Arms** or the **East Hampton Point Cottages,** listed above, in addition to the choices below.

Nick & Toni's, 136 N. Main St. (☎ 516/324-3550), remains the star of the current dining scene, and consequently it's hard to secure a table unless you're a member of the celebrity crowd. It is, of course, a stylish place that wins for its food, ambience, and service. The scene is electric, made so by the rush of writers, Hollywood stars, and others who can afford to drop in every weekend to see and be seen. Certainly the restaurant has an immediate appeal with its terra-cotta tile floors, French cafe chairs, and upfront bar displaying a broad selection of grappa. The dining room is artfully designed, with sculptural objects used as fetching accents. The new American cuisine, using local ingredients whenever possible, positively shines. It's fresh, bursting with flavor, and healthful. Among the appetizers you'll find several salads, like French bean salad with prosciutto and spice almonds, or phyllo-wrapped goat cheese with mâche and plum tomato vinaigrette. Among the six or so main courses might be pan-roasted local striped bass with arugula, grilled oyster mushrooms, Parmesan, and summer truffle vinaigrette; boneless loin of lamb with grilled garden vegetable salad, black olives, and white bean hummus; and grilled rabbit with Pommery mustard. For an intensely flavored treat, try one of the wood-burning oven specials, like the free-range chicken with roasted potatoes, pancetta, garlic, and rosemary; or the fillet of rouget with tomato saffron, baby potatoes, lemon, and herbs. Desserts are equally winning, like the white chocolate cheesecake with key lime sabayon and passion fruit coulis. Prices range from $17 for pasta dishes to $30. *Hours:* Summer, Monday to Thursday 6 to 10:30pm, Friday and Saturday 6 to 11pm, Sunday 11:30am to 2:30pm (brunch) and 6 to 11pm; spring/fall, open the same hours but Thursday to Sunday and in winter Friday to Sunday.

Della Femina, almost diagonally across from Nick & Toni's at 99 N. Main St. (☎ 516/329-6666), is the other port of call for stars, and the portraits here prove it, with those of owner Jerry Della Femina and his wife, Judy Licht, at the center. The discretion displayed by the small brass plaque that marks the restaurant is matched by the serenely neutral decor. The bilevel space is handsomely appointed in a Tuscan manner with tile floors, light maple chairs set at tables covered with white cloths, and little decoration except for such natural accents as wheat-sheaf bouquets.

The menu is limited, and the cuisine is highly rated. To start, you might celebrate with the wonderful grilled Hudson Valley foie gras that is served with a banana pancake, caramelized pineapple, and pineapple rum glaze; or less extravagantly with the local organic arugula, tomato, and goat cheese salad in a garlic vinaigrette. You can follow with one of 10 or so main courses: a pasta dish like orecchiette with shrimp and tomatoes flavored with garlic, basil, tomato water, and crushed red pepper; delicious roasted cod in a black truffle vinaigrette; or striped bass in a tapenade sauce. Many of the meat dishes are made with organic poultry, as is the grilled squab with a summer truffle jus. Prices range from $23 to $35; there are also 6-, 8-, and 10-course tasting menus priced at $57, $75, and $90. The desserts are equally lavish and memorable—like the chocolate and banana tart with dark-chocolate ice cream or the terrine with crunchy dark chocolate and peanut butter. *Hours:* Daily 6pm to closing. Closed Monday after Labor Day.

Peconic Coast, 103 Montauk Hwy. (☎ 516/324-6772), has become another crowd pleaser. It has a warm country, yet elegant air. Tables are spacious and set against brick and salmon-colored walls. Dramatic floral bouquets and single orchids add a touch of romance. The menu changes nightly, but it will offer selections to satisfy every mood and taste. The fish dishes are the restaurant's pièce de résistance—items like salmon roasted on a bed of spaghetti squash tossed with herbs and grilled portobello mushrooms, served with chive sauce; or striped bass on a bed of porcini mushrooms in a white wine sauce. Some of the dishes feature organic ingredients like the chicken with lemon, sage, and garlic; others add a creative twist to the tried-and-true, like the duck breast with foie gras, apples, and blood orange glaze. Comfort dishes like meat loaf with mashed potatoes and mushroom sauce, and burgers round out the menu. Pizzas cooked in a wood-burning oven are also available, featuring such toppings as spinach and Gorgonzola, or roasted peppers, roasted garlic, black olives, artichoke hearts, chèvre, and thyme. Prices range from $9 to $28. Save room for the sinful chocolate pudding served in a martini glass. There are at least eight wines by the glass to accompany your meal. *Hours:* Sunday to Thursday 6 to 11pm, Friday and Saturday 6pm to midnight.

New York's famous **Palm** (☎ 516/324-0411) is located at the Huntting Inn, 94 Main St. Oak banquettes and brass accents in the dining room and an enclosed porch provide a conservative setting for their renowned 4-pound lobsters, huge 18-ounce steaks, and portions of prime rib. Less awesome fare includes veal Marsala and française, along with broiled chicken and shrimp sauté. Prices range from $17 to $31. The experience conjures up another time and place (the original was opened by Pio Bozzi and John Ganzi in the roaring twenties), but it's good when you're in that kind of mood. *Hours:* Summer, Sunday to Thursday 5 to 10pm, Friday and Saturday 5 to 11pm; winter, Sunday to Thursday 5 to 9pm, Friday and Saturday 5 to 10pm.

Santa Fe Junction, 8 Fresno Place, off Railroad Avenue (☎ 516/324-8700), brings the Southwest to the Hamptons and does a pretty good job of it. The cuisine offers more than just typical chile- and cheese-daubed dishes. Here you'll find appetizers like quesadillas made with barbecued duck and wild mushrooms, tamales topped with smoked wild mushrooms, and chorizo in a Madeira sauce, or delicious cornmeal-coated oysters with a rémoulade sauce. The main courses are similarly refreshing and surprising: mesquite-grilled pork loin with a pineapple salsa, filet mignon with roasted shallots and chili Madeira sauce, and blackened tuna taco served with mango salsa. The fajitas are the house specialty. The seafood version made with marinated shrimp, scallops, and tuna with cilantro pesto and roasted peppers is super. Prices range from $15 to $21. The walls are decorated with those desert sun–bleached skulls, photos of the Southwest, and Native American patterns; the tables are set with burgundy cloths and cacti, and the jade banquettes are evocative of the Southwest. *Hours:* Daily 5:30pm to closing.

Michael's at Maidstone Park, 28 Maidstone Park Rd., The Springs (☎ 516/324-0725), offers some good value cuisine for the Hamptons in a down-home, country casual atmosphere. In summer the emphasis is on local seafood—broiled flounder, blackened mako with tomato salsa, sesame-seared tuna steak with wasabi and pickled ginger, plus such dishes as chicken parmigiana and duck with orange cranberry sauce. Prices range from $14 to $30, the last for filet mignon and lobster tails. The restaurant offers a $17 prix-fixe menu including soup, salad, and dessert, as well as a $16 early-bird menu from 4:30 to 6pm. *Hours:* Sunday to Thursday 5 to 10pm, Friday and Saturday 5 to 11pm.

The Laundry, 31 Race Lane (☎ 516/324-3199), has been a favorite hot spot ever since it opened in 1980 under the auspices of several celebrity owners who attracted a celebrity crowd of such local lights as Joseph Heller, Robert Benton, Lauren Bacall, Alec Baldwin, and Kim Basinger. It's still a popular place, but the locals appreciate it best when they can enjoy a good meal in a casual atmosphere after all the weekenders have departed. The most popular appetizers are the cornmeal-fried oysters and the chicken quesadilla. The entrees range from roasted free-range chicken with rosemary and garlic to grilled salmon with fennel and cherry tomato vinaigrette. Prices range from $14 to $28. In summer, ogle the crowd and the always-decorous flower arrangements; in winter, nod off in front of the fire. *Hours:* Sunday to Thursday 5:30 to 11pm, Friday and Saturday 5:30pm to midnight.

AMAGANSETT

AMAGANSETT ATTRACTIONS

Only 4 miles to the east, Amagansett seems far less concerned with social events than does East Hampton. There are only a dozen or so stores along Main Street, including a farmer's market. A block away, **Atlantic Avenue Beach**, a favorite singles' gathering spot, is known as Asparagus Beach because everybody stands, showing themselves off to maximum advantage.

More seriously, the **East Hampton Town Marine Museum**, on Bluff Road (☎ 516/267-6544), houses displays about the East End's fishing, whaling, and nautical heritage. Two discovery rooms for infants and toddlers house rotating exhibitions. At the back of the museum, kids can ring ships' bells and clamber over a fishing trawler jungle gym that's moored in the sand. *Hours:* July 4 to Labor Day, daily 10am to 5pm; mid-May to July 3 and Labor Day to December, Saturday and Sunday 10am to 5pm. *Admission:* $4 adults, $2 seniors and children ages 2 to 12.

AMAGANSETT LODGING

The Mill Garth, Windmill Lane (P.O. Box 700), Amagansett, NY 11930 (☎ 516/267-3757), a 100-year-old lemon-yellow clapboard house, has its own windmill and offers an astounding assortment of decently kept rooms with charmingly idiosyncratic furnishings. These are located in the old original farmhouse or in cottages around the property. The suites in the main house have a living room, a bedroom, a kitchenette, and a bath. Among the cottages, my favorites are the English Cottage, with a private little garden area out back, an eat-in kitchen, two bedrooms (one with a four-poster bed), and a remarkable, octagonal paneled living room; and the Carriage House, which contains a huge living room with exposed beams and fireplace, two bedrooms, two baths, and a private patio. Also attractive is the Dairy House with its skylit living room, screened breezeway, and private patio. None have a TV or a phone. Bikes are available; baby-sitting can usually be arranged. The beach is about a mile away, and the grounds are quite lovely. *Rates* (including continental breakfast): $145 to $195 studio for two, $175 to $280 suite for two, $235 to $310 cottage for two.

Gansett Green Manor, Main Street (P.O. Box 799), Amagansett, NY 11930 (☎ 516/267-3133), offers secluded cottage/apartments, each with a private picnic area with an umbrella-shaded table and a grill. Each is nicely furnished and contains a bedroom, a living room, a kitchen, a bath, and a TV. The pebbled pathways are prettily landscaped and everything is meticulously maintained. *Rates:* In season, $185 to $360 double (the higher prices are for the two- and three-bedroom cottages); from October 1 to May 1, they are rented for the season.

AMAGANSETT DINING

Restaurants may come and go, but **Gordon's**, on Main Street (☎ 516/267-3010), continues to offer carefully prepared and served food in unpretentious surroundings. The only concessions to decor are a few hanging plants in the window and a central crystal chandelier, yet at night the low-lit room looks especially inviting. Specialties include scampi, fillet of sole meunière, veal piccata or Marsala, mignonette of beef bordelaise, and excellent salads, including arugula that's grown in the backyard. Prices run $20 to $27. *Hours:* In season, Tuesday to Sunday 6pm to closing; off-season, Tuesday to Saturday noon to 2pm and 6pm to closing. Closed February.

Mount Fuji, Montauk Highway (☎ 516/267-7600), offers truly fine sushi in a typical Japanese ambience decorated with lanterns, sake drums, and dress kimonos. In addition to the sushi, a full Japanese menu is served— teriyaki, tempura, noodles, and other dishes. Prices range from $10 to $20 (the sushi-sashimi combination). *Hours:* Monday to Thursday 11:30am to 3pm and 5 to 11pm, Friday and Saturday 11:30am to 3pm and 5pm to midnight, Sunday 5 to 11pm.

Estia, 177 Main St. (☎ 516/267-6320), is a comfortable place to repair for breakfast, lunch, or dinner. By day it's a luncheonette complete with a counter and red vinyl stools, where you can secure an omelet that's made with such spiffy ingredients as portobello mushrooms and Coach Farm goat cheese. At night the lights are dimmed, and the place is transformed into a bistro serving consistently good food. It's famous for its pasta, made on the premises and served with a variety of sauces. The pasta and the salads are served in huge bowls, with portions large enough for three. Start with the turtle rolls—quesadillas that are filled with avocadoes, beans, tomatoes, onions, cheese, and sour cream; or the amazing Thai-spiced ravioli filled with shrimp and spring vegetables. Follow with a pasta of your choice and a sauce selection (there are about a dozen—my favorite is mushrooms barbaresco made with portobello mushrooms, garlic, tomato, and red wine). Or there are such dishes as herb-roasted chicken served with mashed potatoes and green beans, or local flounder with a potato crust served with greens from the garden. Prices range from $9 to $18. For breakfast you can choose from an array of omelets and egg dishes, plus some eye-opening tortilla dishes. The wine list offers more than 20 selections. *Hours:* Summer, Sunday to Thursday 7:30am to 2:30pm and 5:30 to 9pm, Friday and Saturday 7am to 2:30pm and 5:30 to 10pm; winter, daily 7am to 2:30pm and Wednesday to Sunday 5:30 to 9pm.

AFTER DARK IN THE HAMPTONS

The volatile, electric night scene changes from season to season. Your best bet is to check the listings in the *East Hampton Star* or pick up one of the many local papers, like *Dan's Paper* (free in supermarkets) and *Hamptons Magazine* to see what's happening. Here's a rundown on spots open at press time—it's anyone's guess whether they'll survive to see another "season."

In Hampton Bays, the **Canoe Place Inn**, Montauk Highway (☎ 516/728-4121), has live bands and a DJ, plus pool and video pinball. In Westhampton Beach, **Casey's** (☎ 516/288-5828), on Montauk Highway, features Top-40 sounds and has attracted a youngish crowd; on Dune Road in East Quogue, **Summer's** (☎ 516/653-5777) was the most happening singles' scene at press time.

In Southampton, the beautiful people head to **Jet East**, 1181 N. Sea Rd. (☎ 516/283-0808); a less rarified crowd crams into the **Tavern**, 125 Tuckahoe Lane (☎ 516/287-2125). The Post House morphed into Palm Beach–style **Club Colette** at 136 Main St. (☎ 516/283-1717). A youthful crowd flocks to the massive **Life's a Beach**, 54 East Montauk Hwy., Southhampton (☎ 516/726-1999). Wainscott's **The Swamp**, Montauk Highway at East Gate Road (☎ 516/537-3332), caters to the gay crowd as it has done for decades.

In Bridgehampton people continue to make **Bobby Van's**, Main Street (☎ 516/537-0590), their stylish watering hole. In East Hampton, the old Danceteria received a Zen Tuscan makeover and became **NV Tsunami**, 44 Three Mile Harbor Rd. (☎ 516/329-6000). In Montauk **Kenny's Tipperary Inn**, West Lake Drive (☎ 516/668-3754), draws crowds to its live Irish music evenings.

Perhaps the longest-running live music venue is in Amagansett—**Stephen Talkhouse**, 161 Main St. (☎ 516/267-3117). Here, locals actually mix with visitors dancing to all kinds of sounds, from reggae to rock.

Other entertainment? The **East Hampton Cinema** (☎ 516/324-0596 or 516/324-0448) offers an eight-screen complex where matinees are shown daily during summer. This is a good refuge from the rain.

East Hampton & Amagansett
Special & Recreational Activities

Beaches: Access to beaches is rather complex. Parking permits are issued by both the village and the town (which stretches all the way to Montauk), but village permits may not be used at town beaches and vice versa. For information about town beaches, contact the Town Clerk's office at the Town Hall, Pantigo Road, East Hampton (☎ 516/324-4142 or 516/324-4143). For information about village beaches, contact the beach office at Main Beach (at the end of Ocean Avenue) or the Village Hall, 1 Cedar St., East Hampton (☎ 516/324-4150). Don't park without paying a fee or obtaining a permit—you'll certainly be fined and your car could be towed. You can park at **Main Beach** and in Amagansett at **Atlantic Avenue Beach** without a sticker, but you must pay a fee. Check with your accommo-dations about securing temporary stickers. **Georgica Beach** in East Hampton is where the stars mingle with the society set; more of the same can be found at **Gibson Lane Beach** in Sagaponack. **Cryder Beach** is the "power beach" for Southamptonites.

Bicycling: Bermuda Bikes, 36 Gingerbread Lane, East Hampton (☎ 516/324-6688), rents bikes for $20 a day or $28 for 24 hours.

Boating: Uhlein's, Montauk Harbor (☎ 516/668-3799), is the only place that rents boats. See chapter 5, "Montauk," for information.

Picnicking: Lavish picnic ingredients can be found at the **Barefoot Contessa,** 46 Newtown Lane, East Hampton (☎ 516/324-0240), where even potato salad can set you back several dollars. But it's worth the visit for the luscious displays and for the people-watching. **Amagansett Farmer's Market,** 367 Main St. (☎ 516/267-3894), is a feast for the eye, offering a veritable banquet of fresh, baked, and prepared goods. Less exotic picnic fare can be found at the **Windmill Deli** on Main Street in East Hampton or at **Dreesen's Exelsior Market,** 33 Newtown Lane, East Hampton (☎ 516/324-0465).

Tennis: Three town courts are located at the **Springs Recreation Area,** off Old Stone Highway; four courts are available at **Abraham's Path Park,** Abrahams Path, Amagansett. **Behind the East Hampton high school** on Long Lane, about a dozen courts are open to the public for a nominal fee. Some courts are open to the public at the following: **Buckskill Tennis Club,** Buckskill Road (☎ 516/324-2243); **East Hampton Racquet Club,** Buckskill Road (☎ 516/324-5155); and **Green Hollow Tennis Club,** Green Hollow Road (☎ 516/324-0297). Rates for the last three will range from $25 to $40 an hour.

Montauk

Downtown Area ◆ Montauk Point Lighthouse

Distance in miles: 124

Estimated driving time: 2 to 4 hours, depending on Long Island Expressway traffic

Driving: Take the Long Island Expressway to Exit 70, taking Route 111 south to Route 27 east.

Bus: The best bet is the Hampton Jitney. Reservations are required. Call ☎ 800/936-0440 or 516/283-4600 from Tri-State area codes.

Train: Take the Long Island Rail Road from Penn Station (☎ 718/217-5477).

Further Information: For more about New York in general, contact the **Division of Tourism**, New York State Department of Economic Development, One Commerce Plaza, Albany, NY 12245 (☎ 518/474-4116).

For specific information about Montauk, contact the **Montauk Chamber of Commerce**, Montauk Highway (P.O. Box 5029), Montauk, NY 11954 (☎ 516/668-2428).

For general information about Long Island, contact the **Long Island Convention and Visitor's Bureau**, 350 Vanderbilt Pkwy., Suite 103, Hauppauge, NY 11788 (☎ 516/951-3440).

Events & Festivals to Plan Your Trip Around

June: Blessing of the Fleet, Town Dock (early June). Call ☎ 516/668-2428.

July: Shark Tag Tournament, Montauk Marine Basin (mid-July). Call ☎ 516/668-5700.

August: Concert at Deep Hollow Ranch. Call ☎ 516/668-2744.

October: Full Moon Bass Tournament at the Marine Basin. Call ☎ 516/668-5700.

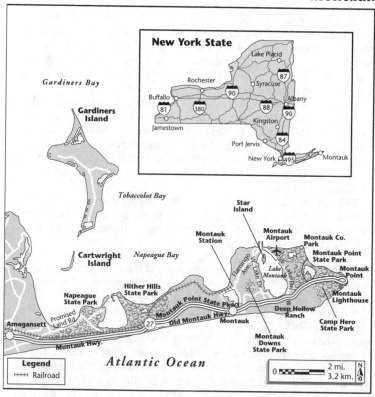

Montauk is different from the rest of the Hamptons. Once you get out of East Hampton and onto Old Montauk Highway, the two-lane road rolls along beside the dunes and the ocean as if cutting through a Marsden Hartley painting. Suddenly Montauk huddles below you like some isolated western frontier town. Compared to the frenetic chic of East Hampton and Southampton, Montauk remains the Cinderella left behind for family-style vacationing. It has a far less contrived air—there are no boutiques here, only the sea, the gulls, the gorse and beach plum, and the sand and the sky—all of which are sometimes blotted out by the mysterious mist that rises off the ocean and rolls in to blanket the area.

Besides the landscape, Montauk has some of the most romantic history in the area. It is almost an island—surrounded by water on three sides and on the fourth by Hither Hills State Park. In fact, you go "on" and "off" Montauk, a local expression that has been used ever since the English settlers bought the land from the Montaukett Indians in 1655. Adrian Block was the first European to set foot on Montauk. Lord Gardiner, who moved across from Saybrook in Connecticut, was the first to take possession of his land grant, which has remained in the Gardiner family since 1639.

Cattle Ranchers & Herders   The **Old Montauk Highway** was traced out in the 1700s by Hampton ranchers, who in spring and summer grazed horses, sheep, and cattle on the 15,000 acres patterned with 2,000 acres of lakes and ponds. Animals were driven here from as far west as Patchogue; the cattle drive was quite an event until well into the 1900s, when volunteer cowboys rode alongside the herd. Teddy Roosevelt and his Rough Riders fit in very well with the 29,500 veterans of the Spanish-American War, who came here to recuperate from disease caused by contaminated food and water.

Three houses were built for the herders, and they remained the only build-ings—except for the lighthouse, which was built in 1796 and has stood here ever since. **First House** was built in 1774 and burned down in 1909; **Second House,** now a museum run by the Historical Society (☎ 516/668-5340), with an interesting herb garden in back, was built in 1797 (the original had been erected in 1746). *Hours:* Thursday to Tuesday 10am to 4pm. *Admission:* $2 adults, $1 children.

Third House was first built in 1742, although the present structure dates from 1806. The houses also served as inns for the hardy travelers who braved the mosquitoes and the atrocious roads to come for the fine fishing (which still draws thousands) and game shooting.

19th-Century Developers In 1879 the heirs of the early proprietors sold Montauk for $151,000 to Arthur W. Benson of Bensonhurst, who brought railroad magnates and his cronies from Standard Oil out for visits. They built a few "cottages" at the point, calling themselves the Montauk Association. In 1895, Benson sold 5,500 acres to Austin Corbin and Charles M. Pratt, who brought the Long Island Rail Road from Sag Harbor out to Montauk and had dreams of making the town a major port of entry for the whole country. Those dreams were never realized; the dreams of another man, Carl Graham Fisher, were also dashed (thank goodness), for he wanted to turn Montauk into a northern version of Miami Beach. He laid out the town and built the golf course, the polo field, the Manor, the tall office building in town (now condo-miniums), indoor tennis courts, and a theater. The Surf Club and Yacht Club were established, as well as the casino on Star Island. He also opened the jetty into Lake Montauk. His dream collapsed along with the stock market in 1929.

Native American Legends Several legendary characters and romantic tales are attached to the area—pirates and bootleggers lying off Montauk Point waiting to bring their illicit cargo ashore, legends of Native Americans and their burial grounds. One such tale reveals the relationship that developed between the sachem of the Montauketts, Wyandanch, and Lion Gardiner, proprietor of Gardiner's Island and one of East Hampton's founders. Wyandanch and Gardiner had gone through the rite of blood brotherhood, and when the Narragansett Indians came down from Rhode Island and carried off Wyandanch's daughter, Gardiner arranged for her ransom. For this, in 1659 Wyandanch gave Gardiner much of the land that's now Smithtown. Native American Stephen Pharoh, known as Stephen Talkhouse, who thought nothing of walking to Brooklyn, was exhibited by P. T. Barnum as the greatest walker of all time. Another Native American associated with the area was Samson Occom, a Mohegan who came from Connecticut to the Montauketts to preach. He wrote hymns that are still sung today and raised, in England, the £12,000 sterling with which Dartmouth College was founded in 1769.

MONTAUK ATTRACTIONS

For beach and seascape lovers, Montauk offers an incredible variety of things to do (see "Montauk Special & Recreational Activities," later in this chapter) and many things to see.

The **Montauk Point Lighthouse** (☎ 516/668-2544) was built in 1797 by order of George Washington at a cost of $23,000. It stands 108 feet high, and its flashing lantern is visible for 25 miles. Originally it stood 297 feet from the cliff's edge; now, because of erosion, it's only 50 feet away. The antique lens was donated by the French in 1860 and has been operating ever since. The light that marks the craggy shoreline stands strongly isolated against the sea and sky, surrounded by masses of wild dogwood roses that ramble all over the terrain. *Hours:* In summer, it's usually open from 10:30am to 5pm or 6pm with extended hours on weekends and holidays; winter hours are usually weekends only from 11am to 4pm. *Admission:* $4 adults, $3.50 seniors, $2.50 children ages 6 to 12.

Montauk Harbor is always alive with commercial fishing activity, and it is also the site of a shopping complex that attracts many browsers. The harbor at Montauk holds more fishing records than any other single port in the world, and in 1986, excitement ran through the whole East End when two world shark records were broken within a few days of each other. Crowds gathered to view the 17-foot-long great white shark weighing 3,540 pounds, caught by rod and reel.

The town consists of a strange, amorphous collection of motels and shops clustered around the Florentine-looking **tower-folly** built by Carl Fisher. Just east of town, the famous **Manor** stretches along the bluff. Today it's a resort-condominium.

MONTAUK LODGING

The **Montauk Yacht Club, Resort, and Marina,** 32 Star Island Rd., Montauk, NY 11954 (☎ 516/668-3100), has a sea resort air. The property is located on an island with its own 232-slip marina, with a lighthouse towering above. Dining facilities include a classic, outdoor, cabana-style bar at waterside. Luxury detailing extends to the decor of the 107 rooms, where louvered doors lead to the tiled baths with robes and oversized fluffy towels. The closets are large, and the furnishings are modern and upbeat. Most of the rooms have private terraces. The extensive facilities include two outdoor pools and one indoor pool, a fitness center with saunas and massage, lighted tennis courts, and bicycles. Deep-sea fishing trips can be arranged from the dock.

Sunday brunch in the **Lighthouse Grill** is lavish, offering everything from lobster to steak Diane, pastas, omelets, crêpes, and waffles, all made to order. There's also a fresh oyster and clam bar. The favored portion of the dining room affords a spectacular water view. The regular dinner menu might feature such fish as tuna, mahimahi, mako shark, and salmon, which can be grilled, herb-seared, or blackened. Local lobster, steaks, and such dishes as pork loin smoked and served with mango and papaya relish are also available. Prices range from $19 to $38. The several excellent seafood appetizers include sesame tuna served with black-bean dipping sauce, and an unusual grilled shrimp cocktail with ginger whiskey sauce (although you can opt for the traditional sauce). Note that every night except Wednesday a $17.95 prix-fixe menu is offered. Wednesday is given over to a seafood extravaganza, when tables are laden with steamed lobster, garlic mussels marinara, cioppino, a full raw bar, and similar fare. Reservations are vital in summer. **Breeze's Cafe** serves breakfast and lunch in a bright, airy atmosphere. The fare consists of burgers, sandwiches, salads, and wraps. Around the corner, another patio overlooks a small bay beach.

Rates: Early April to late May and October, $159 to $209; late May to early July and Labor Day to early October, $209 to $259; early July to Labor Day, $259 to $309. *Dining hours:* Breeze's Cafe, daily until 3pm; the Grill, daily 6 to 10pm.

Gurney's Inn Resort and Spa, Old Montauk Highway, Montauk, NY 11954 (☎ 516/668-2345 or 516/668-3203), is directly "on the brink o' the beach" overlooking the Atlantic Ocean. It's always crowded with wealthy, overstressed urbanites and suburbanites, and corporate executives attending meetings. Some units overlook the parking lot, while cottages are directly on the ocean beach. The Captain's Quarters cottage features such luxuries as two double beds; a color TV; a phone in the living room and bedroom; two baths; a dressing room; a 30-foot terrace; a corner double divan in the living room; and a butler's pantry with a sink, a refrigerator, and an electric range. The Crow's Nest has all of the above plus a fireplace. In several buildings, terraced into the hillside, there are time-share units that have been completely soundproofed and furnished in a modern manner, featuring beds with light-oak mirrored headboards, oak partitions supporting a collection of brass objects, a phone in the bath, a personal doorbell, and a refrigerator tucked under the vanity. All units at the resort have TVs with free HBO, a phone, a coffeemaker, a refrigerator, and a tiled bath with amenities.

The famous attraction, of course, is the spa, using sea water for therapies and treatments in luxurious Roman baths and a large, heated indoor swimming pool with floor-to-ceiling windows opening out to the ocean. Guests may use the pool, Finnish rock saunas, Russian steam rooms, Swiss showers, and fitness and exercise rooms. All kinds of therapies are available, from European-type spa therapies to acupuncture to biofeedback. The spa is open to the public for a daily charge of $20.

The premier dining room, the **Sea Grille,** overlooking the ocean, offers classic modern American cuisine with a distinctly Italian accent. Among the 15 or so entrees, you might find veal alla Toscana (with pancetta, tomato, eggplant, basil, and mozzarella in a tomato sauce); duck breast marinated in tequila, lime, and peach nectar and served with a peach glaze; or potato-crusted salmon served with horseradish dill sauce. Prices range from $22 to $30. To start, choose among grilled portobello mushrooms, a chowder of the day, or local oysters on the half shell; to finish, sample any of the luscious desserts—pecan pie, tiramisu, amaretto cheesecake, or chocolate chiffon cake. A four-course $25 menu is offered every night from 5:30 to 6pm. The **Caffe Monte** is the casual, all-day dining spot offering a menu priced from $9 to $17. Spa cuisine is also available: low in calories, salt, fat, sugar, cholesterol, and refined carbohydrates.

Rates (including breakfast and $25 per person credit for dinner and $9.95 credit for breakfast): Memorial Day to mid-October, $330 to $390 double; additional person $105; mid-October to April, weekends $320 double, midweek $310; April to late May, weekends $360 double, midweek $340. *Dining hours:* Daily 7:30 to 10am and 11:30am to 10pm.

In town, **Montauk Manor,** Edgemere Street (R.D. 2, Box 226C), Montauk, NY 11954 (☎ 516/668-4400; fax 516/668-3535), occupies a Tudoresque manor house on Signal Hill surrounded by 12 acres. It was built in 1927 as a luxury resort hotel by Carl Fisher; today it's a restored National Landmark. When you enter the vaulted lobby with its massive beams, rounded arches, and stone floor, you'll feel as if you're stepping into a medieval baronial hall. The 140 accommodations are studios or one- or two-bedroom units with kitchens. Many are duplexes with two baths, terraces, and private patios. The furnishings are typically modern and the rooms are all equipped with air-conditioning, TV/VCRs, telephones, and coffeemakers. There's a restaurant on the premises, **Il Farole** (☎ 516/668-4400), between the building's two wings; it provides alfresco dining on the terrace in summer. The limited menu offers such Italian classics as linguine alle vongole, rigatoni primavera, and veal Marsala, plus such dishes as poached salmon in Grand Marnier sauce and grilled lamb chops with Chianti barolo sauce. Prices range from $15 to $23. To start, choose the prosciutto with assorted seasonal fruits, or the antipasti. Facilities include a fitness center, indoor and outdoor pools, three tennis courts, and a squash court. Complimentary jitney service is offered to the beach. *Rates:* Mid-June to mid-September, $155 to $195 studio, $185 to $260 one-bedroom suite; mid-September to late October, $105 to $135 studio, $119 to $195 one-bedroom suite; April to mid-June, $95 to $115 studio, $119 to $170 one-bedroom suite; late October to March, $95 to $109 studio, $109 to $150 one-bedroom suite. *Dining hours:* Daily 7am to 10pm.

One of Montauk's nicest accommodations right next door to Gurney's is **The Panoramic View,** Old Montauk Highway, Montauk, NY 11954 (☎ 516/668-3000; fax 516/668-7870), set on 10 acres that have been carefully landscaped to create privacy and serenity through the abundant use of pine shrubs. The grounds are immaculately kept and always blazing with seasonal colors—begonias, scarlet pimpernels, flame flowers, and the like.

The management is extremely friendly and obliging, offering a variety of accommodations to suit most tastes in buildings that are terraced into the hillside at different elevations. Barbecues are conveniently tucked away around the property. Highpoint and Point of View are older looking, but pleasantly furnished in country colonial furnishings; Salt Sea is closest to the 1,000-foot ocean beach; Valley View is an ultramodern three-story unit with less charm and privacy, also furnished in colonial-country decor. The games room is located inside this building, and the kidney-shaped outdoor pool is very convenient. Three beach homes with two bedrooms, two baths, a living room with a fireplace, a porch, and a patio are also available. All rooms are air-conditioned and have individually controlled heat, a kitchenette, a color TV, and a phone. The only drawback for beach buffs is the steep steps cut into the hillside that go down to the ocean. No children under age 10 are accepted.

Rates: In season, $102 to $224 1½-room unit, $188 to $266 2½-room suite, $485 cottage for four; early April to late June and mid-September to early November, $92 to $130 1½-room unit, $114 to $138 2½-room suite, $278 cottage for four.

For a smaller and quieter retreat stay at **Peri's Bed & Breakfast,** 206 Essex Street, Montauk, NY 11954 (☎ 516/668-1394). Located in a Tudor-style residence, it has three guest rooms, all with private baths. Azure walls greet you in the Fez room, which also has an impressive wrought-iron canopied bed. Mosquito netting creates a tented effect above the bed in the Millennium room, which also has such decorative accents as a large, carved and gilded mirror. The Marais has its own private deck and is romantically decorated with eclectic antiques. What makes a stay extra appealing, however, are the spa treatments—massage, reflexology, facials, and other body treatments—which can be combined with aromatherapy. *Rates:* In season, weekend $150, midweek $120; off-season, weekend $105, midweek $90. Two-bedroom suite in season, weekends $290, midweek $200; off-season, weekends $230 and midweek $170.

Sadly, more and more condominiums are going up along the dune approach to Montauk, their boxlike construction obscuring the dunes and the ocean. Most are managed and rented out. They often make ideal accommodations for two couples traveling together because they usually offer suitelike accommodations. There's really very little to distinguish one from the other (unless you're planning to buy, of course). All have immediate access to the beach.

The most attractive of these (to my eye) is **Sea Crest,** Old Montauk Highway, Amagansett, NY 11930 (☎ 516/267-3159), which has a more rustic appearance than some of the others. The best accommodations are in the second-floor units, which have balconies providing ocean views. Other buildings are clustered closer to the pool area. Accommodations are studios or, one- or two-bedroom efficiencies each with air-conditioning, TV/VCR, telephone, hair dryer, and an equipped kitchen. The grounds are pleasantly landscaped with shrubs and conifers, and barbecues are available in one area. Facilities include an outdoor pool, two tennis courts, handball, shuffleboard, and basketball courts. *Rates:* May to June, $100 to $135 studio, $85 to $170 one-bedroom unit; $110 to $250 two-bedroom unit; July to late July, $195 to $245 studio, $165 to $305 one-bedroom, $230 to $430 two-bedroom; late July to Labor Day, $235 to $300 studio, $200 to $355 one-bedroom, $280 to $500 two-bedroom; January 1 to April and mid-October to December 31, $80 to $110 studio, $70 to $145 one-bedroom, $90 to $160 two-bedroom.

Windward Shores, Old Montauk Highway (P.O. Box L), Amagansett, NY 11930 (☎ 516/267-8600), is equidistant from Amagansett and Montauk. Here, studio apartments and suites are arranged around a central grass courtyard and pool. Many have oceanfront and ocean-view locations. The open-design units are very modern, each featuring a fully equipped kitchen (an electric stove, refrigerator, dishwasher, and toaster) opening into a skylit living room with a pull-out couch, a TV, and a dining area; a spiral staircase leads to a double bedroom, all furnished in beige. From the decks you can literally jump down onto the Napeague dunes bordering the ocean. Two all-weather tennis courts and an outdoor pool complete the facilities. *Rates:* Mid-July to Labor Day, weekends $250 to $505 double, weekdays $215 to $460 double; late June to mid-July, weekends $225 to $445 double, weekdays $160 to $370 double; early May to late June and Labor Day to early October, weekends $120 to $230 double, weekdays $90 to $165 double; early October to early May, weekends $89 to $175 double, weekdays $75 to $135 double.

At **The Hermitage,** Old Montauk Highway (P.O. Box 1127), Amagansett, NY 11930 (☎ 516/267-6151), the units are furnished individually by their owners. All have balconies, two bedrooms, a living and dining room, and full kitchen facilities. There's a pool and also access to the beach—beach chairs, umbrellas, and towels are provided. Two tennis courts complete the scenario. *Rates:* Late July to Labor Day, weekends $440 to $540 double, weekdays $395 to $505 double; late June to late July, weekends $340 to $455 double, weekdays $300 to $410 double; mid-May to late June and Labor Day to early October, weekends $150 to $240 double, weekdays $110 to $180 double; mid-March to mid-May and early October to January, weekends $100 to $165 double, weekdays $85 to $115 double.

Driftwood on the Ocean, Old Montauk Highway (P.O. Box S), Montauk, NY 11954 (☎ 516/668-5744), is an ideal family place with direct access to the beach from motel-style units sheltered from the ocean by the dunes. A concrete-surrounded pool and two tennis courts are set behind the parking area, while a children's playground and games are set still farther back on the property. Accommodations range from cottages and two-room suites to studio efficiencies with dining, sleeping, and sitting areas, plus a small kitchenette. Furnishings are Scandinavian modern and all have cable TVs with HBO, refrigerators, telephones, and private baths, plus a conveniently located barbecue grill. *Rates:* Late July to Labor Day, weekends $230 to $270, midweek $140 to $200; July weekends $190 to $230 double, midweek $125 to $180; May, June, and Labor Day to late October, weekends $105 to $160 double, and midweek $90 to $115 double.

Wave Crest I Apartments, Old Montauk Highway (R.F.D. 1, Box 86), Montauk, NY 11954 (☎ 516/668-2141), offers several types of accommodations in several buildings terraced into the hillside overlooking the ocean. Each unit has a TV, a VCR, a phone, and air-conditioning. Beach Dune Place contains simple units, where the decks are only 20 feet from the ocean—it's like having a cottage on the beach. Some 20 or 30 feet back, Water's Edge has rooms with kitchenettes. In Panorama, pleasant efficiencies have TVs, phones, and Scandinavian Formica-topped furniture; a sink, electric burners, and a refrigerator are housed in one compact unit. There's also an indoor pool. *Rates:* Late July to Labor Day, weekends $155 to $180 double, July, weekends $150 to $170 double; early to late June and Labor Day to late September, weekends $100 to $125 double, midweek $80 to $100 double; late April to early June and October, weekends, $85 to $109 double, midweek $70 to $85 double. Closed November to March.

The **Sun Haven Motel,** Montauk Highway, Amagansett, NY 11930 (☎ 516/267-3448), is another good family accommodation. The motel-style units face toward the restaurant across a tarmac roadway that leads to the tennis courts and ultimately to beach access. A line of conifers and other shrubs screens the units nicely; in front of every other doorway a pleasant graveled niche has been created for relaxing on chaise longues or at umbrella-shaded tables. The rooms are adequate, featuring industrial carpeting, modern couches, wire chairs, rattan beds with print bedspreads, TV, telephone, and refrigerators. A functional indoor pool and tennis courts complete the facilities. *Rates:* Mid-June to Labor Day, $140 to $185 studio, $205 to $260 one- or two-bedroom; rest of the year, $100 to $145.

At the **Surf Club,** P.O. Box 1174, Montauk, NY 11954 (☎ 516/668-3800), each of the 92 units is a duplex with a kitchen opening onto the living room, a deck overlooking the pool, and a skylit stairway leading to either one or two small bedrooms and bath. All have TVs, air-conditioning, and phones. There's a private beach, of course. The units are constructed around an outdoor pool protected by a chain-link fence. Two tennis courts and a bathhouse with steam baths are offered. *Rates* (rooms for two to four): late June to late July, weekends $260 to $370 double, weekdays $235 to $325 double; late July to Labor Day, weekends $305 to $500 double, weekdays $255 to $440 double; mid-May to late June and Labor Day to early October, weekends $135 to $225 double, weekdays $105 to $175 double; mid-April to mid-May and early October to mid-November, weekends $80 to $120 double, weekdays $75 to $110 double.

Ocean Beach Resort at Montauk, 108 South Emerson Ave., Montauk, NY 11954 (☎ 516/668-4000), has accommodations in two long, two-story beachfront buildings. All are sleekly modern studios with efficiency kitchens, air-conditioning, TVs, and telephones. Some have balconies. There's also a glass atrium with an enclosed pool. *Rates:* June 30 to Labor Day, $130 to $210 double; Memorial Day to late June and Labor Day to October 1, $105 to $185 double; rest of the year, $70 to $125 double.

Charm exudes from **Lenhart's,** Old Montauk Highway (at Cleveland Drive), Montauk, NY 11954 (☎ 516/668-2356), a cluster of secluded cottages landscaped into the hill; conifers, shade trees, roses, and flowering shrubs create a tranquil country air. The accommodations are in studios or one- and two-bedroom cottages, each with a color TV, air-conditioning, and a kitchen. Even the pool is sheltered by a hedge and softened by a grass surround. *Rates* (weekends): Late July to Labor Day, $155 to $195 studio, from $200 to $240 one-bedroom cottage; late June to late July, $140 to $175 studio, from $180 to $215 one-bedroom cottage; April to late June and Labor Day to late October, $105 to $130 studio, from $130 to $150 one-bedroom cottage; November to March, $100 to $110 studio, from $130 cottage.

For clean, well-run, family-owned motel accommodations, try the **Blue Haven Motel,** West Lake Drive (P.O. Box 781), Montauk, NY 11954 (☎ 516/668-5943), which has 30 air-conditioned units, including some with fully equipped kitchenettes and two-room apartments with full kitchens. All the rooms have TVs, coffeemakers, and refrigerators, plus phones for outgoing calls. There's a sparkling-clean outdoor pool. Owners Tom and Monica Brennan will arrange fishing trips and pick you up at the train or bus stop or at the airport. *Rates:* Mid-June to October, weekends $130 double, weekdays $98 double; April to mid-June, weekends $80 double, weekdays $65 double. Three-day minimum stay in season.

MONTAUK DINING

In the last few years, Montauk has acquired some choice dining spots. A really spectacular brunch is served at the **Montauk Resort and Marina** and at **Gurney's Inn** (see above).

Harvest on Fort Pond, 11 Emery St. (☎ 516/668-5574), commands a view of the lake and in summer offers elegant water-view dining at tables set on a brick terrace. The dining room is a light and airy space, but what wins people's hearts is the inspired and superb food. The chef blends flavors with great success. You might find grilled salmon with cucumbers, dates, and walnuts or roast pork with a hazelnut crust and Grand Marnier sauce. Swordfish steaks are marinated in white wine and rosemary. For an appetizer try the grilled shrimp wrapped in pancetta. Pasta dishes, including a divine fusille with bacon, scallops, and mushrooms, plus pizzas (Gorgonzola, sausage, broccoli, and tomato) and salads, round out the menu. Portions are meant to be shared, and the waiters will advise you about this at this very friendly restaurant. Prices range from $24 to $32 ($12 for pizza). *Hours:* Tuesday to Sunday 5:30pm to closing.

Dave's Grill, 468 Westlake Dr. (☎ 516/668-9190), is a small restaurant down on the marina next to where the Viking party boats dock. The room is cozy, with a low ceiling and comfortable booths and seafaring accoutrements; there's also a small, awning-sheltered patio for water-view dining. The food is first rate, showing traces of Asian influence and concentrating on seafood, not surprisingly, for fresh ingredients are available right there at the dock. The signature dish is the cioppino chock-full of clams, mussels, lobster, scallops, calamari, and shrimp. Although the menu changes weekly you might find grilled yellowfin tuna with a plum wine and ginger reduction, or horseradish-crusted halibut with a tarragon beurre blanc. For meat eaters, the marinated pork chops are served with a luscious apple chutney, and there's usually a filet mignon with perhaps a peppercorn sauce and steak frites. I heartily recommend starting with the shellfish sampler of oysters, clams, and shrimp served with cocktail, mignonette, and Creole rémoulade sauces. Prices range from $17 to $26. For dessert most people go for the Chocolate bag, a "paper bag" made of Belgian chocolate, filled with vanilla ice cream and whipped cream and placed in a pool of raspberry sauce. For me, the bread pudding in hot bourbon sauce makes me want to come back. *Hours:* Wednesday to Monday; winter, Thursday to Sunday 5:30pm to closing.

The famous place that everyone knows about is **Gosman's Dock Restaurant,** West Lake Drive (☎ 516/668-5330), where a series of restaurants feed hordes of people during summer, while herring and black-backed gulls soar and whirl above. Here, 1- and 2-pound lobsters are the prime attractions among an assortment of softshell crabs, flounder, bluefish, bass, oysters, scallops, and clams, priced from $14 to $43 (for a 3-pound lobster). Fancier specials also appear on the chalkboard—like yellowfin tuna with ginger and soy, bluefish Cajun-style, or sole with dill-Dijon. From the open but covered dining rooms you can watch the boats coming into dock—fishing trawlers, lobstermen, and pleasure craft, with seagulls whining and whirling hungrily above. *Hours:* Memorial Day to Labor Day, daily noon to 10pm; mid-April to May and September to Columbus Day, Wednesday to Monday noon to 10pm.

The **Topside Deck,** perched atop one of the Gosman buildings (☎ 516/668-2447), offers a great vantage point and is fine for casual lunches like grilled swordfish sandwiches and grilled tuna melt. Fresh lobster is available all day. Takeout counters below turn out an endless stream of lobster rolls, steamers, and so on to customers who take their goodies to colorful, umbrella-shaded tables and feast while watching the harbor activity. The fish market is open daily from 10am to 6pm during the season. The best time to catch the fleet unloading the day's haul is 5 or 6pm at Gosman's Dock. *Hours:* Memorial Day to Labor Day, daily noon to 10pm; mid-April to May and September to Columbus Day, Wednesday to Monday noon to 10pm.

For a dash of Italy in Montauk, **Luigi's,** Euclid Avenue (☎ 516/668-3212), complete with checkered tablecloths and a sprinkling of chianti bottles, serves a variety of veal dishes, including veneziana with artichoke hearts, as well as classic scungilli and calamari marinara or Diavolo and the ever-popular chicken parmigiana. Entrees run $11 to $24. *Hours:* Summer, daily 5 to 10pm; spring, Friday to Sunday 5 to 10pm. Closed mid-October to March.

Tucked away on the edge of the dunes, **The Lobster Roll,** on Route 27 (☎ 516/267-3740), is a local favorite that has the ambience of a waterfront shanty. Here, you can sit outside and enjoy some fresh seafood as you gaze out across the dunes stretching into the distance. Or you can take a seat inside among the nautical clutter of nets, glass floats, and ship's lanterns. Crab, lobster, or shrimp rolls; fried clams, scallops, or soft-shell crabs; steamers; and fish-and-chips are just a few of the goodies that attract the crowds. Prices run $7 to $18. *Hours:* Summer, daily 11:30am to 10pm; after Labor Day, Saturday to Sunday 11:30am to 10pm. Closed late October to early May.

MONTAUK AFTER DARK

Montauk's hot spots include those listed in the "After Dark in the Hamptons" box (see "The Hamptons," earlier in this book), plus the **Montauk Resort and Marina** (☎ 516/668-3100) and **Gurney's Inn** (☎ 516/668-2345), where there's dancing and musical entertainment nightly in summer.

Montauk
Special & Recreational Activities

Beaches: Montauk's beaches fall under the jurisdiction of East Hampton Township. See "East Hampton Special & Recreational Activities," in "The Hamptons," earlier in this book.

Birding: During summer, environmentalists and naturalists lead daily nature walks spotting birds and flowers. On these walks you'll be on territory where the first cattle ranches were established in the United States. Walks leave from the **Third House,** East Lake Drive (Deep Hollow Ranch).

Boating: Uhlein's, Montauk Harbor (☎ 516/668-3799), rents 16- to 31-foot boats for fishing and waterskiing for anywhere from $120 per hour to $275 for a half day. They also rent kayaks for $25 an hour, $60 a half day, and $80 a day.

Camping: The best and most popular camping is found at **Hither Hills State Park,** where sites are near the dunes. They're not for the camper in search of seclusion though—competition for reservations is so fierce that even if you can get through to the reservation number (☎ 800/456-2267), you may find all the sites taken. Reservations are allowed up to 90 days in advance. The average cost is $16 per day, and there's a minimum stay of 7 days in summer. Open from late April to November. For information, contact **Mistix Corp.,** P.O. Box 9029, Clearwater, FL 34618 (☎ 800/456-2267). The campground office at the park (☎ 516/668-2554) doesn't handle reservations.

Cruises: The **Viking** line (☎ 516/668-5700) operates a variety of special cruises during the summer, most notably to Martha's Vineyard, Block Island, and New London. They also offer an annual fireworks cruise and an annual wine-tasting cruise, both in July. Casino cruises also run throughout the season.

Fishing: Montauk is an angler's paradise, where 11,000 vessels and 75 charter boats hold many of the world records for sportfishing. Party and charter boats leave from **Montauk Marine Basin,** West Lake Drive (☎ 516/668-5700), mostly for shark or bluefish. An annual shark-fishing tournament is held (usually mid-July) when trophies as large as 1,000 pounds are brought in.

    Viking Starship, Inc., P.O. Box 730, Montauk, NY 11954 (☎ 516/668-5700), sails daily for half- and full-day and/or night fishing for porgie, bass, bluefish, and tuna. The price ranges from $25 to $55 depending on the fish. For example, a trip for bluefish costs $40, for fluke only $25. Fishing tackle is available aboard. The *Marlin V* (☎ 516/668-2517) is another party boat. Smaller charter boats include the *Blue Fin IV,* P.O. Box 2084, Montauk, NY 11954 (☎ 516/668-9323), which charges $375 and up for parties of six and leaves from the Viking Dock; and the *Irish Rover* (☎ 516/668-1010), which docks at Captains Cove Marina on West Lake Drive.

Golf: The 18-hole, par-72 championship **Montauk Downs Golf Course** (☎ 516/668-5000) was designed by Robert Trent Jones and is one of the top 50 public courses in the United States. Greens fees are $25 weekdays and $30 weekends.

Horseback Riding: Ride in the footsteps of Teddy Roosevelt on a 1½-hour trail/beach ride for $40. Open year-round, but by reservation only. Contact **Deep Hollow Ranch,** Montauk Highway (☎ 516/668-2744).

Picnicking: Pick up supplies at **Gosman's Dock** seafood store, which sells gourmet items and salads as well as seafood. Other sources include **Herb's Market,** Main Street (☎ 516/668-2335), open Sunday, and **Ronnie's Deli and Grocery,** Main Street (☎ 516/668-2757).

Sailing: Sailboat rentals can be found at **Puff 'n' Putt** (☎ 516/668-4473).

State Park: Guided nature tours are given through **Hither Hills State Park** during summer. For information, call ☎ 516/668-2461.

Tennis: The **Hither Hills Racquet Club** (☎ 516/267-8525) has six courts available by the hour ($30) or the season. Facilities include a ball machine. Also try the **Harborside Motel and Tennis Club,** West Lake Drive (☎ 516/668-2511), where courts rent for $10 per hour. **Montauk Downs State Park,** South Fairview Avenue (☎ 516/668-5000), has six clay courts available for $10 per hour.

Swimming: Montauk Downs State Park, South Fairview Avenue (☎ 516/668-5000), has a pool if you don't like the beaches. It closes Labor Day.

Whale Watching: This is one of Montauk's unique attractions (at least for Long Island). A scientific research crew leads 4- to 7-hour trips in search of these magnificent creatures plus dolphins, sea turtles, and sea birds. Boats leave from the **Viking Dock** in Montauk. The cost is around $36 for adults, $31 seniors, and $18 children ages 12 and up. Note that seasickness medication is recommended. From January to mid-May seal-observation cruises also operate. Guided walks along the Montauk beaches are given. The visitor center in Riverhead, where animals are rehabilitated, is open weekends from 11am to 4pm. For information, contact **Riverhead Foundation for Marine Research and Education,** 431 E. Main St., Riverhead, NY 11901 (☎ 516/369-9840).

Sag Harbor & Shelter Island

Sag Harbor ◆ *Shelter Island*

Distance in miles: Sag Harbor, 106; Shelter Island, 110
Estimated driving time: 2 to 4 hours, depending on Long Island Expressway traffic

Driving: For Sag Harbor, take the Long Island Expressway to Exit 70, and pick up Route 27 east; turn left in Bridgehampton along the Sag Harbor Turnpike. For Shelter Island, take the bridge out of Sag Harbor down Route 114 to the blinking light and turn right for the North Haven ferry. Or you can take the Long Island Expressway to Route 25 to the Greenport Ferry.

Bus: The Hampton Jitney will take you to Sag Harbor (check off-season). For information, call ☎ 800/936-0440 or 516/283-4600.

Train: The Long Island Rail Road (☎ 718/217-5477) stops in Bridgehampton or East Hampton. If you come via the North Fork, it also stops in Greenport.

Further Information: For more about New York in general, contact the **Division of Tourism**, New York State Department of Commerce, One Commerce Plaza, Albany, NY 12245 (☎ 518/474-4116).

For general information about Long Island, contact the **Long Island Convention and Visitor's Bureau**, 350 Vanderbilt Pkwy., Suite 103, Hauppauge, NY 11788 (☎ 516/951-3440).

For specific information about Sag Harbor, contact the **Sag Harbor Chamber of Commerce**, 459 Main St., Sag Harbor, NY 11963 (☎ 516/725-0011).

For Shelter Island, contact the **Shelter Island Chamber of Commerce**, P.O. Box 577, Shelter Island Heights, NY 11965 (☎ 516/749-0399). During July and August, information is dispensed at the windmill on Long Wharf in Sag Harbor.

Events & Festivals to Plan Your Trip Around

September: The Triathlon—people come from all over to compete in this race that combines swimming, bicycling, and running. It's sponsored by Southampton Hospital, but held in Sag Harbor, usually the weekend after Labor Day.

Harborfest celebrates the ocean and shore with everything from clambakes, whaleboat races, a regatta, clam chowder and other food contests, and a slew of kids' entertainments. Usually the third weekend in September.

To me, Sag Harbor has always seemed the most real of the South Fork's towns, still rooted in its whaling past, less pretentious and less obsessed with chic than its East Hampton and Southampton neighbors. Sadly, that's changing. The boutiques and condos have arrived, and the stores displaying expensive gourmet items and the proverbial bar/restaurants done with light oak and brass are opening along Main Street. Still, nothing can really detract from the fine architecture of the town's 18th- and 19th-century homes or from the view across Gardiner's Bay from the main downtown dock.

SAG HARBOR

SAG HARBOR ATTRACTIONS

Like the earlier-settled Hamptons, Sag Harbor was first colonized by the English from Connecticut, who arrived and built a thriving town that was a major port even before the American Revolution, second only to New York. In 1693, a bell for Southampton was landed here. Trade between Sag Harbor and the West Indies was initiated between 1760 and 1770. In the first session of the U.S. Congress, President George Washington approved the act establishing Sag Harbor as an official Federal Port of Entry, appointing Henry Packer Dering as Sag Harbor's first Customs master.

The first **Custom House** (1789) in New York was located here, on Garden Street (☎ 516/692-4664), and can be visited today. All the cargo was cleared here, duties were paid, and mail was dropped. The house has been meticulously restored according to Dering's household inventory and reveals the lifestyle of a fairly affluent Long Island family between 1790 and 1820. *Hours:* June to September, Tuesday to Sunday 10am to 5pm; October, Saturday to Sunday 10am to 5pm. *Admission:* $3 adults, $1.50 seniors and children ages 7 and up.

During the American Revolution, the town was occupied by the British, who established their headquarters at what's now the American Hotel on Main Street. Many Long Islanders fled to Connecticut. On May 22, 1777, Lieutenant Colonel Meigs led a number of patriots across the sound from

The Hamptons, Shelter Island & the North Fork

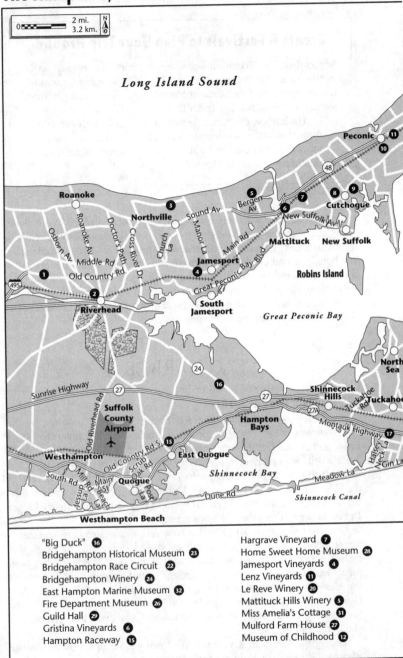

Long Island Sound

Peconic 🕚
🔟

Roanoke

Northville ❸
Sound Av

Bergen Av ❺

Cutchogue ❽ ❾

❼

New Suffolk Av

❻

Mattituck

New Suffolk

Jamesport ❹

Robins Island

South Jamesport

Great Peconic Bay

Riverhead ❷

North Sea

Shinnecock Hills

Tuckahoe

Suffolk County Airport

Hampton Bays

Westhampton

East Quogue ⓯

Quogue

Shinnecock Bay

Shinnecock Canal

Westhampton Beach

"Big Duck" ⑯
Bridgehampton Historical Museum ㉓
Bridgehampton Race Circuit ㉒
Bridgehampton Winery ㉔
East Hampton Marine Museum ㉜
Fire Department Museum ㉖
Guild Hall ㉙
Gristina Vineyards ❻
Hampton Raceway ⓯

Hargrave Vineyard ❼
Home Sweet Home Museum ㉘
Jamesport Vineyards ❹
Lenz Vineyards ⓫
Le Reve Winery ⑳
Mattituck Hills Winery ❺
Miss Amelia's Cottage ㉛
Mulford Farm House ㉗
Museum of Childhood ⑫

124

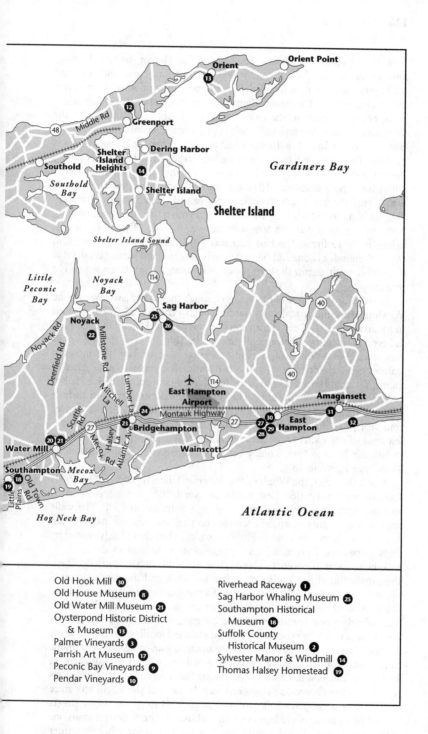

Old Hook Mill **30**
Old House Museum **8**
Old Water Mill Museum **21**
Oysterpond Historic District
   & Museum **13**
Palmer Vineyards **3**
Parrish Art Museum **17**
Peconic Bay Vineyards **9**
Pendar Vineyards **10**

Riverhead Raceway **1**
Sag Harbor Whaling Museum **25**
Southampton Historical
   Museum **18**
Suffolk County
   Historical Museum **2**
Sylvester Manor & Windmill **14**
Thomas Halsey Homestead **19**

New Haven in 13 whaleboats. They raided Sag Harbor, burned 12 brigs and sloops at Long Wharf, seized 120 tons of hay, corn, and oats and 12 hogsheads of rum, and killed 6 people and took another 90 prisoner. Two monuments on Union and High streets commemorate this daring raid.

After the Revolution, the town continued to thrive on trade with the West Indies and became an increasingly cosmopolitan community, with a newspaper, the *Long Island Herald,* established in 1791. When the War of 1812 was declared, Dering was put in charge of the Sag Harbor arsenal and the populace overcame the 1813 British attack. The war brought hardship and interfered with trade, and a disastrous 1817 fire made economic recovery difficult. It wasn't until the late 1820s that the port regained its importance, primarily because of increased whaling. By 1845 it had grown into the largest whaling port in the state and fourth largest in the world, with a fleet of 63 vessels belonging to 12 firms. The best year was 1847, when 32 ships brought in 605,000 pounds of bone and 68,000 barrels of sperm and whale oil valued at $1 million. In all, during the brief period of whaling, $25 million was brought into the port.

To recapture the flavor of this era, go through the whale's jawbone into the **Whaling Museum,** at Main and Garden streets (☎ 516/725-0770), housed in a marvelous Greek Revival mansion that was designed and built by Minard LaFever. Besides the whaling equipment, the ship models, the log books describing 4-year trips, and a great collection of scrimshaw, the museum features guns, children's toys, and other items, all crammed into a series of rooms. You could spend several hours here looking at a portrait of Sag Harbor in 1860, a tricycle from the same date, an exquisite cameo carved on a whole shell, or the Native American artifacts excavated locally. At the end of your visit you'll discover the differences among a bark, a brig, a ship, and a schooner (if you didn't know already). *Hours:* May 15 to September, Monday to Saturday 10am to 5pm, Sunday 1 to 5pm. *Admission:* $3 adults, $2 seniors, $1 children ages 6 to 13.

Across the street, the **Whaler's Presbyterian Church** (☎ 516/725-0894) also dates from this period. Designed by LaFever in 1844, it was once crowned by a five-story tower that was destroyed by a hurricane in 1938. The walls slope in the manner of ancient temples on the Nile, and the parapets are decorated with rows of whaler's blubber spades, which were finely crafted by ships' carpenters. *Tours:* Call for an appointment at the number above.

When oil was discovered in Pennsylvania, the whaling industry declined. The population of Sag Harbor dwindled to 2,000, and the nearly deserted village languished until the Fahys opened a watchcasing factory in the 1890s. The labor used was largely Jewish, and for this reason **Temple Adas Israel,** Long Island's oldest Jewish temple and congregation, was built in 1898. It's well worth a visit to see the Gothic stained glass and locally carved altar piece. At about the same time the town was beginning to gain some fame as a resort. Later, the town attracted writers like John Steinbeck, who set out from here on his famous *Travels with Charley* trip. The tradition continues—many writers and artists have chosen Sag Harbor as their home, and you might recognize one of them playing softball in the local park. History, tree-lined streets flanked by all kinds of old homes (from saltboxes to Greek Revival mansions to Victorian gingerbread confections), a lovely harbor where summer visitors dock and live aboard their yachts, and sunsets over bay beaches all make Sag Harbor a place to go down to the bay again.

SAG HARBOR LODGING

The **American Hotel,** Main Street, Sag Harbor, NY 11963 (☎ 516/725-3535; fax 516/725-3573; www.theamericanhotel.com), operates in a thoroughly Victorian atmosphere. Wicker chairs stand on the front porch, and the front parlor is filled with Victorian-style sofas and other pieces. The bar is dark and cozy, particularly in winter, when a fire burns; in summer, an overhead fan hanging from the stamped-metal ceiling hums quietly. Classical music in the background adds to the atmosphere. The rooms, reached by a separate entrance, are individually decorated in an antique elegant style. All have air-conditioning, stocked minibars, two telephones, and hair dryers. Room 2 has a sleigh bed set against candy-striped wallpaper, Room 6 features several Eastlake pieces, and Room 5 contains a high, carved Victorian bed with a crocheted coverlet, an oak dresser, and wicker chairs. Fresh flowers grace every room.

The dining room is well known, particularly for its extensive (60+ pages) wine list. There are several dining areas: the formal chintz room with a fireplace, where tables are set with crisp white linens; the skylit porch/conservatory, decked out with white metal chairs, rambling plants, and Mexican tile; and a third dining room in the rear. The menu changes daily, but always includes luxuries like caviar and foie gras to start. About a dozen main courses are offered, such as sesame-crusted tuna in ginger lemongrass nage, a luscious orange spice lobster sauté, slow-roasted duckling with citrus ginger bigarade, or grilled lamb chops with fresh mint sauce. The most extravagant dish is the shellfish platter featuring lobster, oysters, clams, mussels, and other shellfish. Prices run from $23 to $36.

Rates (including continental breakfast): Weekends $185 to $260 double, weekdays $140 to $200 double. *Dining hours:* Daily noon to 3pm and 5:30 to 11pm. Closed Thanksgiving and Christmas.

Other lodgings are scarce in Sag Harbor. The one downtown motel, **The Inn at Baron's Cove,** West Water Street, Sag Harbor, NY 11963 (☎ 516/725-2100), has been converted into modern time-sharing units, although you may have some luck getting a rental. Second-floor units offering a view of the bay and the bridge are light and airy; furnished in light oak with Breuer chairs, they feature a sleeping loft. All have air-conditioning, TVs, phones, and kitchenettes. Some have private patios and decks with good views of the harbor. Facilities include a tennis court and an outdoor fenced-in pool. *Rates:* In season (July to August), weekends $260 to $385 double, weekdays $160 to $255 double; shoulder season (May, June, September, and October), weekends $180 to $245 double, weekdays $89 to $119 double; off-season (November to April), weekend $85 to $115 double, weekdays $79 to $109 double.

SAG HARBOR DINING

Breakfast/brunch with the best view is enjoyed at **B Smith's** (see below), but you'll have to wait until noon. Most everyone in Sag Harbor heads for **The Paradise** on Main Street (☎ 516/725-6080).

On the wharf, **B Smith's** (☎ 516/725-5858), owned by the famous fashion model, commands a magnificent view over Sag Harbor marina out into Gardiner's Bay, one of the finest views in the whole of the Hamptons. In summer the large deck is filled with happy visitors relaxing waterside. The dining room has a Mediterranean ambience, appropriate to its waterfront location. Cuisine focuses on seafood and has a distinct Caribbean-Southern flair. At dinner you'll find such dishes as pan-fried pork chops with fried plantains, jerked halibut, and pan-fried sweet chili prawns in a red curry gravy served with caramelized plantains. There are a few pasta dishes, like linguine with cockles, green garlic, and herbs. Prices range from $18 to $28. *Hours:* Daily noon to 4pm and 6 to 10pm. Closed November to April.

At the **All Seasons Cafe**, 5 Bay St. (☎ 516/725-9613), past the small front bar area with windows looking out onto the dock lies a pretty dining room with a cathedral-style ceiling and rush-seated gatebacks set at tables spread with mauve cloths. The cuisine fuses a variety of traditions. Among the eight or so entrees there might be pan-seared blackened tuna with a creamy horse-radish sauce, or grilled rack of lamb served with white-bean hummus and warm roasted red pepper–calamata olive salad. Prices range from $19 to $30. To start, there's a delicious callaloo, which is a Caribbean-style spinach-potato soup sweetened with coconut milk, spiced with cilantro and jalapeño; or fresh tuna served with a cilantro lime aïoli sauce. The brick patio, arrayed with tables sporting pink cloths and turquoise chairs, is a pleasant place to dine. *Hours:* Wednesday to Sunday 6pm to closing.

Spinnaker's, 63 Main St. (☎ 516/725-9353), is a popular casual local spot for luncheon sandwiches and salads and such main dishes as crab cakes. The look is brick and brass, and the food is okay for the price. *Hours:* Sunday to Thursday 11:30am to 10pm, Friday to Saturday 11:30am to 11pm.

Sen, Main Street (☎ 516/725-1774), is a tiny restaurant, possessing only half a dozen or so polished wood tables. The menu offers typical Japanese dishes including superb fresh sushi-sashimi—eel, fluke, salmon roe, mackerel, uni, squid, and more. Individual pieces range in price from $2 to $4. Traditional dishes like beef negimaki, shrimp tempura, and chicken yakitori are also available as well as large bowls of chowder (lobster, clam, salmon, and mussel), plus one or two curried dishes. Prices range from $14 to $35 (the last for the deluxe sushi-sashimi). *Hours:* Thursday to Monday noon to 2:30pm and 6 to 9:30pm.

For Dinner Only

Locals (if you can count as locals those who come from as far away as Hampton Bays) swear by **Il Capuccino**, Madison Street (☎ 516/725-2747), a warm, comfortable place serving excellent, fairly priced food. The garden salad, tossed in a garlic dressing and served with croutons sprinkled with cheese, is superb; the special fish of the day might come with horseradish sauce; pastas, about a dozen of them, include a tasty tortellini with roasted pistachios and Alfredo sauce; and stand-bys like veal parmigiana and Marsala are available. Prices range from $13 to $18. Red gingham, red-glass candle-holders, and jazz in the background give the place a lovely glow. *Hours:* Summer, Monday to Thursday 5:30 to 10:30pm, Friday to Saturday 5:30 to 11pm, Sunday 5 to 10pm; winter, Sunday to Thursday 5 to 10pm, Friday to Saturday 5 to 10:30pm.

Tucked away, the **Inn at Mill Creek**, 590 Noyac Rd. (☎ 516/725-1116), is another favorite overlooking the busy scene, hoist, and boats at Mill Creek. The decor is simple—light oak and blue napery—and the food is fresh and a good value. The menu offers a traditional selection of steak and seafood, priced from $15 for chicken Marsala to $25 for twin lobster tails. Other dishes include broiled flounder, duck with orange sauce, chicken cordon bleu, veal parmigiana, and prime rib. During the week the price includes a trip to the salad bar. To start, try the clams on the half shell or shrimp cocktail. *Hours:* Summer, Monday to Saturday 6 to 10pm, Sunday 5 to 10pm; off-season, Thursday to Saturday 6 to 9pm, Sunday 5 to 9pm. Closed Thanksgiving to Easter.

SAG HARBOR AFTER DARK

The major cultural entertainment is provided by the **Bay Street Theatre**, at the Wharf, now in its seventh season. In the past it has premiered productions that went on to Broadway and other international venues—plays that starred such greats as Eli Wallach and Anne Jackson, Maria Tucci, Mary Cleere Haran, Dianne Wiest, and Mercedes Ruehl. For tickets and information, call ☎ 516/725-9500. The season runs from mid-June to the end of August, with spring performances by cabaret artists and other singers.

There's a downtown **cinema** in Sag Harbor. Or, more interesting is **Canio's Bookstore** on Main Street (☎ 516/725-4926) and also down at the wharf (☎ 516/725-4462), which hosts weekend poetry readings and other literary events in the early evening. It's also a delightful place to poke around during the day.

The Corner, Main Street (☎ 516/725-9760), is a real down-home hangout. But most nightlife action is found elsewhere, along Route 27 from Southampton to East Hampton.

Sag Harbor
Special & Recreational Activities

Beaches: Long Beach in Noyac is a narrow beach stretching along the bay and open to nonresidents for a fee.

Birding: The Morton Wildlife Refuge, on Noyac Road (cross the bridge, along the bay beach, and turn right by the Salty Dog restaurant), is managed for migratory shorebirds with emphasis on two protected shorebirds—the piping plover and least tern. There are plenty of other shore- and songbirds to spy, as well as pheasant, deer, and osprey. This is an ideal place for fishing and hiking on nature trails. For information, contact the Refuge Manager, **Wertheim National Wildlife Refuge**, P.O. Box 21, Shirley, NY 11967 (☎ 516/286-0485).

Boating: For boat rentals, see "Montauk," earlier in this book.

Cruises: The *American Beauty* leaves from Long Wharf on 90-minute nature cruises every day in summer at 11am and at 1 and 3pm. It also offers sunset cruises and charters. Prices range from $16 adults and $8 children ages 5 to 12 for the nature cruise and from $20 to $25 per person for the evening cruises.

Fishing: In the **Elizabeth Morton National Wildlife Refuge**, there's good bay fishing for weakfish in summer or bluefish in fall.

Hiking: The **Elizabeth Morton National Wildlife Refuge**, where waterfowl, songbirds, mammals, and even birds of prey congregate, is lovely for nature rambles and picnicking on the small beach. For a permit, contact the Refuge Manager, **National Wildlife Refuge**, R.D. 359, Noyac Road, Sag Harbor, NY 11963 (☎ 516/725-2270). From Route 27, go 2 miles north on North Sea Road, then 4 miles east on Noyac Road. Also good for clamming, oystering, and scalloping.

Picnicking: Any of the beaches or the **Elizabeth Morton Wildlife Refuge** make great picnicking spots. For gourmet supplies, **Provisions**, at Bay and Division streets (☎ 516/725-3636); for deli and other German specialties, drop in at the **Cove Deli**, 283 Main St. (☎ 516/725-0216). For more mundane fare, there's always the supermarket across from the post office.

Sailing: **Tompkins Yachts** at Sag Harbor Yacht Yard on Bay Street (☎ 516/725-5100) offers sailing instruction including a 2-day weekend course for $375. They also rent sailboats. Half-day prices range from $70 to $95 weekdays and $80 to $130 on weekends; full-day prices range from $120 to $160 weekdays and $135 and $210 weekends. Charters also available.

Tennis: Try the courts at **Mashashimuet Park** on Main Street.

SHELTER ISLAND

From Sag Harbor, it's only a short ferry ride across the bay to the rolling wooded hills and miles of white-sand beaches of Shelter Island, first settled by Quakers fleeing persecution in New England. Today it's an unspoiled haven for bicycling, hiking, horseback riding, and boating—and the residents aim to keep it that way.

From downtown Sag Harbor, cross the bridge and follow the signs to the ferry (turning right at the blinking light). Ferries leave North Haven from 6am to 11:45pm (until 1:45am during July and August and on fall weekends). For information, call ☎ 516/749-1200.

Once you're off the ferry, following Route 114 will take you all the way through Shelter Island Heights, where the island's few stores and restaurants are located, to the rim of Dering Harbor, where another ferry leaves for Greenport on the North Fork (see "The North Fork & North Shore," later in this book).

SHELTER ISLAND LODGING

At the eastern tip of the island you'll find Ram Island, so called because it looks a little like a ram. It's attached by a very narrow spit of land, so the approaching road appears more like a causeway. The island's most appealing lodging, the **Ram's Head Inn**, Shelter Island, NY 11965 (☎ 516/749-0811), is here on 4 acres overlooking Coecles Harbor. In this green-shuttered shingled colonial, a group of scientists, including Albert Einstein, gathered in 1947 for the first Shelter Island Conference on the Foundation of Quantum Mechanics. Country furniture and candlewick spreads are found in the 17 rooms (13 with bath). The grassy backyard, with shade trees and rosebushes, and a terrace furnished with tables with umbrellas sweeps down to a private beach, where two sloops, two Sunfish, a paddleboat, and a two-person kayak are available for guests. A tennis court is also available. A bar/recreation room with an upright piano affords more entertainment, while the chintz dining room serves the best cuisine on the island.

The menu changes seasonally, but among the eight or so main courses might be grilled yellowfin tuna with shiitake-apricot sauce; as well as such local specialties as honey and meaux mustard–glazed breast of duck with greens, ripe olives, and cherry tomatoes; and fillet of beef with roasted garlic potato puree served in a blood orange–tarragon veal reduction with pickled cherry peppers. Prices range from $23 to $30. To start, I recommend the coconut-grilled shrimp, or the mussels with saffron, garlic, and preserved lemons in a basil and Arborio broth. The desserts are simple and seasonal.

Rates: April to October, $120 to $160 double; November to March, $90 to $105 double. *Dining hours:* May to October, daily noon to 3pm and 5 to 9:30pm; November to April, Thursday to Saturday 5 to 9:30pm, Sunday noon to 3pm (brunch) and 5 to 9:30pm.

Since new management from the Ram's Head took over the **Chequit Inn**, 23 Grand Ave. (P.O. Box 292), Shelter Island, NY 11965 (☎ 516/749-0018), the guest rooms and dining room have been spruced up. The rooms in the main building are pleasantly furnished with wall-to-wall carpeting, beds covered with white spreads and decorated with lacy treatments behind the headboard, lace curtains, and floral wallpapers. The furnishings are often painted white, and there's comfortable seating and good bedside lighting for reading. The rooms across the street in the Cedar House still show signs of wear, but they're looking a lot better than they used to, since they've been spruced up with repainted floors and wood paneling to provide a much lighter look.

The inn is the island's focal point and social center. People enjoy breakfast, lunch, and dinner in the dining room on the covered veranda or out on the terrace surrounded by flowering hydrangea and shaded by an enormous maple tree. Dinner prices range from $16 to $20 for such dishes as roast loin of pork with apples and shallots; grilled salmon over lentil-and-lobster ragoût; or fettucine with smoked chicken, spinach, and Gorgonzola.

Rates: $90 to $160 double, from $160 suite. *Dining hours:* Summer, daily noon to 3pm and 6 to 10pm; rest of the year, Friday to Sunday 6 to 10pm.

Overlooking Crescent Beach, the rambling **Pridwin**, 81 Shore Rd., Crescent Beach, Shelter Island, NY 11965 (☎ 516/749-0476), offers guest rooms plus an array of activities—swimming in the bay or the pool, windsurfing, rowing, bicycling, Sunfish sailing, pedalboating, hydrobiking, and tennis on three courts. It's a somewhat old-fashioned summer place, well suited to families. Wicker chairs and couches line the 40-foot-long lobby; there are 40 rooms in the main building (those with even numbers face Shelter Island Sound), all with a bath and furnished very plainly in an old-fashioned way. Six suites make ideal family accommodations. Behind the main building are eight pleasant cottages (three with fireplace)—some studios, others one-bedrooms, but each with a kitchen or kitchenette, air-conditioning, TV, and a private deck. Breakfast, lunch, and dinner are served on the deck in summer; there's dancing 3 nights a week, and the Pridwin's special Wednesday cookout is a popular island event. *Rates:* Late June to Labor Day, $134 to $194 double, MAP $170 to $230 double, $194 to $214 cottage, MAP $230 to $250 cottage; spring/fall, $79 to $119 double, $89 to $129 cottage; winter, $79 to $109 cottages only (no MAP).

Closer to the Heights, the **Dering Harbor Inn**, 13 Winthrop Rd. (P.O. Box 3028), Shelter Island, NY 11965 (☎ 516/749-0900; fax 516/749-2045), occupies a grassy knoll overlooking the harbor. The main building has "late motel"–style rooms, some with private patios, cable TV, and air-conditioning. Other buildings around the property offer two-bedroom/two-bath units and one-bedroom/one-bath units with a water view; these have kitchen facilities. All rooms have air-conditioning, TVs, phones, and coffeemakers. There's an outdoor pool enclosed by a hedge, tennis courts, and a full dining room with a flagstone chimney fireplace. *Rates:* Summer, $175 to $250 studio or one-bedroom unit, $355 to $405 two-bedroom unit; spring and fall, $140 to $210 studio or one-bedroom unit; $305 to $325 two-bedroom unit. Closed mid-October to mid-May.

Also at Crescent Beach is the modern **Shelter Island Resort Motel**, 35 Shore Rd. (P.O. Box 255), Shelter Island, NY 11965 (☎ 516/749-2001), where each room has a sundeck, air-conditioning, a color TV, and a phone— and you're right across from Crescent Beach. Some units have kitchenettes. Paddleboats are available. *Rates:* Late June to Labor Day, weekends, $265 to $275 double, weekdays $140 to $160 double; late May to late June and Labor Day to early October, $225 to $245. Closed late fall/winter.

Despite its name, the **Olde Country Inn**, 11 Stearns Point Rd. (☎ 516/ 749-1633), is actually a modern building, though it has been well designed to give the appearance of age. The front door is leaded glass with a fanlight and it leads into a small lobby area where guests register at the antique desk. The eight air-conditioned guest rooms (all with bath) are furnished with a mix of antiques and antique reproductions, their oak floors covered with oriental rugs. Breakfast is served in a light and airy dining room or on the back patio and consists of crêpes, apple waffles, French toast, and omelets that are cooked to order. There's also a year-round restaurant that offers three intimate dining rooms plus a small, L-shaped bar with polished wood tables and a brick fireplace. The dinner menu offers nine or so entrees ranging, for example, from Long Island duckling served with a cherry sage sauce and seafood risotto made with scallops, shrimp, and squid to steak au poivre and rack of lamb with ratatouille Provençal. Prices run $17 to $25. The appetizers concentrate on local and other shellfish dishes, plus such items as asparagus and marinated tomatoes in vinaigrette. Guests may also use the sitting room, furnished with a grand piano and comfortable seating. *Rates* (including breakfast): Summer, $165 to $205 double; winter, $105 double. *Dining hours:* Thursday to Sunday 6 to 9:30pm.

Annabelle's Hideaway Belle Crest Inn, 163 N. Ferry Rd., Shelter Island Heights, NY 11965 (☎ 516/749-2041), is located in a historic home surrounded by pretty gardens complete with a gazebo. It's operated by Herbert, who studied hotel management in Switzerland, and Yvonne, who used to be a psychological nurse. The parlor/dining room where guests take breakfast looks out over the gardens. The breakfast features fresh juices, fruits, and choices of omelets, French toast, or similar fare. The inn is comfortably and eclectically furnished with a grand piano topped with a calabash from Ghana, Oriental rugs, and gilt-framed paintings. The six guest rooms are comfortable, decorated with a mélange of patterns and colors. Some have canopied beds, some have refrigerators, and some share baths. All have a TV and air-conditioning. *Rates* (including breakfast): Summer, weekends (2-night or 3-night minimum stay) $185 to $235, weekdays $105 to $135; spring/fall, $105 to $135.

SHELTER ISLAND DINING

The best dining is found at the **Ram's Head Inn** (see "Shelter Island Lodging," above). Recommendable dining establishments are hard to find, and locals swear by the simple roadside fish/shellfish stands and bars like **Chips**, on Route 114 (☎ 516/749-8926). A step leads down from the fish market into the dining area furnished with plain wooden tables. The choice of fish is wide—dolphin, mako, swordfish, flounder, weakfish, and tilefish, as well as lobster, all priced from a low of $11 to $22 (for a twin lobster). *Hours:* Summer, daily 5 to 9:30pm; winter, Thursday to Sunday 5 to 9:30pm.

Other possible lunch spots? The deck overlooking the pond at **The Dory**, Bridge Street (☎ 516/749-8871). Here you can secure sandwiches, salads, and fish and meat dishes for lunch and steaks and seafood at dinner. *Hours:* Summer, daily noon to 3pm and 6 to 10pm; spring and fall, Thursday to Tuesday noon to 3pm and 6 to 10pm. Closed mid-December to mid-April.

Or try the terrace/restaurant at the **Chequit Inn** (see "Shelter Island Lodging," above), a secluded spot set behind a privet hedge and dotted with hydrangea from which you can glimpse blue waters and sailing craft through the trees.

Shelter Island
Special & Recreational Activities

Beaches: Beach permits can be obtained from the Town Hall, Ferry Road (☎ 516/749-0291).

Bicycling: Piccozzi's Service Station, Bridge Street (☎ 516/749-0045), rents bikes for $18 to $22 a day; at **Coecles Harbor Marina** (☎ 516/749-0700) they charge $16 a day for a basic bike with a few speeds .

Fishing: Charter fishing trips (limit of four passengers) are offered aboard **Quality Time** with Captain Bob Hand. Call ☎ 516/725-2314.

Golf: The **Shelter Island Country Club**, 26 Sunnyside Ave. (☎ 516/749-8841), has a nine-hole course for which the greens fees are $12.

Hiking: The **Mashomack Preserve**, 79 S. Ferry Rd. (Route 114), is open Thursday to Tuesday and has 15 miles of hiking trails. Guided walks are given, but you need to reserve ahead (☎ 516/749-1001).

Kayaking: Two-hour tours are given by **Shelter Island Kayak Tours,** P.O. Box 360, Shelter Island, NY 11964 (☎ 516/749-1990). They leave in early morning and early evening and cost $45 per person.

Picnicking: Head for the beaches, picking up supplies at **George's IGA Market** or **Fedi Market** (open until 8pm). The **Island Food Center** has barbecued chickens, ducks, and sandwiches to go.

The North Fork & North Shore

Greenport ◆ *Orient Point* ◆ *Southold* ◆ *Cutchogue* ◆ *Mattituck* ◆
Setauket ◆ *Port Jefferson* ◆ *Smithtown* ◆ *St. James* ◆ *Northport* ◆
Centerport ◆ *Cold Spring Harbor* ◆ *Huntington*

Distance in miles: Cold Spring Harbor, 37; Northport, 46; Stony Brook, 58; Greenport, 102; Orient, 107

Estimated driving time: 45 minutes to 2 hours

◄O►◄O►◄O►◄O►◄O►

Driving: Take the Long Island Expressway (LIE) to the last exit (no. 73) and then take Route 25/County Road 48 east for towns on the North Fork. Take the LIE to Walt Whitman Road for Huntington and Cold Spring Harbor; take the LIE to Deer Park Avenue for Northport and Centerport or to Nicolls Road for Stony Brook. If you drive to Sag Harbor, you can take the ferry to Shelter Island and from there to Greenport.

Bus: Sunrise Express (☎ 516/477-1200) provides rapid service to North Fork towns—the last stop is Greenport.

Train: The Long Island Rail Road (☎ 718/217-5477) stops at Cold Spring Harbor, Huntington, Green Lawn (for Centerport), Northport, Smithtown, St. James, Stony Brook, and Port Jefferson. On the North Fork it stops at Mattituck, Cutchogue, Southold, and Greenport.

Further Information: For more about New York in general, contact the **Division of Tourism,** New York State Department of Commerce, One Commerce Plaza, Albany, NY 12245 (☎ 518/474-4116).

For general information about Long Island, contact the **Long Island Convention and Visitor's Bureau,** 350 Vanderbilt Pkwy., Suite 103, Hauppauge, NY 11788 (☎ 516/951-3440).

For specific information about the North Fork, contact the **North Fork Visitor Information Center,** North Fork Promotion Council, P.O. Box 1865, Southold, NY 11971; the **Greater Port Jefferson Chamber of Commerce,** 118 W. Broadway, Port Jefferson, NY 11777 (☎ 516/473-1414); the **Three Village Chamber of Commerce** (☎ 516/689-8838) for Stony Brook information; and the **Huntington Township Chamber of Commerce,** 151 W. Carver St., Huntington, NY 11743 (☎ 516/423-6100).

◄O►◄O►◄O►◄O►◄O►

Events & Festivals to Plan Your Trip Around

June: Strawberry Festival, Mattituck.

August: Long Island Barrel Tasting is *the* wine and food event when the Merlots and Chardonnays are uncorked and the wineries showcase their wines. Call ☎ 516/369-5887.

September: Labor Day Craft Show, Greenport.

October: The Maritime Festival at Greenport draws crowds to see the tall ships and to watch whale and sailboat races, plus parades, fireworks, and rescue demonstrations by the Coast Guard.

The North and South Forks of New York's Long Island are like two siblings: one is gentle and retiring; the other is brash and flamboyant. The **South Fork** is the famous one—home to "Hollywood East" and renowned for its surf-pounded Atlantic shores and its social whirl when more than 200,000 summer visitors participate in the action. The **North Fork** offers the more contemplative and smaller-scale pleasures of rural windmill-laced landscapes, quiet bays and coves, and historic villages. Abundant traces remain of an earlier way of life, when fishermen went on and off the bay in search of oysters, scallops, and clams; and farmers tilled the soil and shipped their produce, livestock, and salt hay to Manhattan.

The North Fork landscape consists of a lovely, crazy-quilt of ponds and marshlands, hills, and wooded strands, plus acres of vines, all among a string of unassuming country towns. At the very eastern tip of the fork lies **Orient,** whose main street has a post office, a general store, a church, and one or two residences. West from Orient there's the old whaling port of **Greenport,** whose narrow streets boast antiques stores and art galleries; **Cutchogue,** with its historic central Green; and many others, all enfolded into Southold Township. All offer beaches and opportunities for water-oriented pastimes as well as hiking, bicycling, and the pleasures of wine tasting and dining on succulent lobster and other seafood.

Riverhead is where the two forks of Long Island part company. When you turn off Route 25 onto Northville Avenue, which will bring you to Sound Avenue, you enter a world far removed from the neon and strip development to the south. The road winds past sod farms, where brilliant green swards stretch into the distance under the great wheels of their irrigation systems, past Christmas tree nurseries, orchards, and fields that in summer are bursting with strawberries and raspberries and in fall are stippled with orange pumpkins. In summer and fall, farm stands abound and flatbed trucks at the side of the road are piled high with fruits, flowers, and vegetables. Driving this road is a wonderful way to start your North Fork weekend of wine tasting, birding, beachcombing, or walking or just plain contemplating the beautiful bounty of the landscape and the bay. Even though farming and fishing are still serious pursuits, it's wine that's making the North Fork famous once again.

To the west of Riverhead lies the so-called **Historic Triangle**, centered on the picturesque 19th-century town of Stony Brook, site of an exquisite museum collection and close to Old Field Point, bustling touristy Port Jefferson, and (to the west) St. James, which still possesses a wonderful old country store. This area is great for exploring, where the wealthy still live along hedgerowed roads. From St. James it's only a short distance to the charms of Northport and Cold Spring Harbor, both old whaling towns. Sandwiched in between is Centerport, site of the Vanderbilt Mansion and Observatory Planetarium.

GREENPORT & ORIENT POINT

GREENPORT ATTRACTIONS

Greenport is relatively modern in a way, having been incorporated in 1838, even though it was settled in 1682. It still has a salty flavor, especially in the off-season. In the early to mid–19th century it was a whaling port rivaling Sag Harbor and an important link on the shipping route between New York and Boston. Back then, Stirling Creek was a busy port where whaling ships were being outfitted or loaded with cargo bound for Boston or for the West Indies. Vessels of all sorts—schooners, barkentines, minesweepers—were built here from 1830 to 1950. Legend also insists that Greenport was a major rumrunning entrepôt.

To get a sense of the rich history of the port stop at the **East End Seaport Museum** at the Ferry Dock on Third Street (☎ 516/477-2100). Depending on the schedule, you could learn about the extraordinary area lighthouses, like the Bug Light that stands at Long Beach Bar in Orient, or the role sailing yachts and crews played in U-boat patrol during World War II. See also the oyster dredger, the Beebe lifeboat, and pieces salvaged from the *Ohio,* which sits at the bottom of Greenport's harbor. *Hours:* May to mid-October, Thursday to Sunday 11am to 6pm; July and August, also on Wednesday. Closed rest of the year.

Shopping

Stop in at **Preston's,** a real seafarer's store. Browse the handful of antiques stores and galleries including **Island Artists Gallery** at 429 Main St. (☎ 516/477-3070), a cooperative gallery that features the works of more than 25 local artists (open daily noon to 5pm).

ORIENT ATTRACTIONS

From Greenport it's only 5 or 6 miles to Orient and Orient Point, which hangs by the thread of a causeway. Look for the outline of the striking **Bug Light Lighthouse** at Long Beach Point between East Marion and Orient. It was originally built in 1870 and survived until 1963 when it was destroyed by an arsonist. What you see today is a reconstruction. Orient was originally called Oysterponds—oysters were plentiful before a 1938 hurricane destroyed the industry. Orient is a delightful village of weathered, shingled homes and was at one time a popular honeymoon destination.

The **Oysterponds Historical Society,** Village Lane in Orient (☎ 516/ 323-2480), maintains several museum buildings and a slave burial ground. The Village House, for example, displays an interesting parlor, dining room, and kitchen. Upstairs are portraits of local family ships' captains and toys, including an incredible locomotive built by Orrin F. Payne of Southold, who began it at age 11 in 1858 and finished it in 1881—a fine work of art. *Hours:* Mid-June to mid-September, Thursday, Saturday, and Sunday 2 to 5pm; at other times by appointment. *Admission:* $3 adults, 50¢ children ages 11 and under.

From the village, wander along the marsh-lined back roads along Hallocks Bay and then head out toward Orient Point to **Orient Beach State Park** (☎ 516/323-2440), a finger of land where the ocean meets marsh and wetland. Here, osprey can be seen gliding down onto their nests, swans floating on the salt marsh, and turtles basking in the sun. Facilities include a swimming beach and picnicking tables. Walk to the end of Long Beach for a close up of the Bug Light. At the tip of the park is a bird sanctuary.

GREENPORT LODGING

The North Fork is sadly lacking in attractive accommodations. The best place to stay in this area is the charming **Bartlett House,** 503 Front St., Greenport, NY 11944 (☎ 516/477-0371), built in 1908. It was restored in 1982 and is now owned by Bill and Diane May. The house has an elegant bone structure with handsome decorative elements—stained-glass windows, Corinthian columns, and a large porch facing Front Street. Step inside to an impressive Corinthian-columned living room with intricate molding and a classical-style fireplace. The 10 guest rooms (all with bath and air-conditioning) are up the handsome staircase. Room 2 is especially appealing, containing a working fireplace, an iron-and-brass bed, an oak dresser and rocker, and a marble-topped treadle table; the bathroom is huge. Other rooms feature similar furnishings. In the morning, homemade muffins, fruit cobblers, or freshly squeezed fruit juices are spread out buffet-style. The inn is within walking distance of the village and the Shelter Island Ferry. *Rates* (including breakfast): Memorial Day to October 31, $100 to $130 double; off-season, $90 to $130.

Although the white-pillared mansion bearing the name **Townsend Manor Inn,** 714 Main St., Greenport, NY 11944 (☎ 516/477-2000), looks gracious and full of character (it was built in 1835), the varied accommodations, decorated in "late motel" style, are very plain and basic. Many have white candlewick bedspreads and Scandinavian-style furniture; each has a TV, a phone, and air-conditioning. The setting is pleasant enough, with the secluded grounds abutting the Stirling Basin, so that many yachtsmen find the place convenient for docking and staying overnight. There's a cocktail lounge/ dining room serving a selection of meats and seafood, from veal parmigiana and steaks to grilled or broiled swordfish, flounder, and fisherman's platters. Prices run $14 to $18 ($24 for the fisherman's platter). There's also an attractive grass-bordered outdoor pool. *Rates:* June 26 to Labor Day, weekends $125 to $150 double, from $160 apartment; May 30 to June 25 and Labor Day to October 12, $85 to $105 double, from $115 apartment; April to May 29 and October 10 to November 26, $80 to $95 double; from $105 apartment; November 27 to early April, $75 to $80 double, $90 apartment.

Midweek the rates are discounted about 25%. *Dining hours:* Summer, Wednesday to Monday noon to 2:30pm, Wednesday to Thursday 5 to 9:30pm, Friday to Saturday 5 to 10pm, Sunday noon to 9:30pm; spring and fall, Wednesday to Monday noon to 2:30pm, Wednesday to Friday 5 to 9pm, Saturday 5 to 9:30pm, and Sunday noon to 9pm.

Silver Sands, Silvermere Road (P.O. Box 285), Greenport, NY 11944 (☎ 516/477-0011; fax 516/477-0922), off Route 25, is a motel in a quiet location overlooking the bay with a landscaped backyard for sitting and contemplating the vista. In fact, the motel has its own beach and nature preserve that shelters osprey. All the air-conditioned rooms have a color TV, a phone, a refrigerator, a coffeemaker, and access to the beach. A heated outdoor pool and waterskiing and sailing lessons are available. *Rates* (including continental breakfast): Mid-June to mid-September, $135 to $220 double; mid-September to mid-June, $115 to $125 double. Special packages offered off-season.

The **Sound View Inn**, Route 48 (P.O. Box 68), Greenport, NY 11944 (☎ 516/477-1910), right on the bay, is a down-home kind of place. Accommodations are in two-story motel-style buildings where all rooms face the sound, each with two double beds, a bath, a sundeck, air-conditioning, a TV, a phone, and a refrigerator. Some have full kitchens; others are two-room suites with a bedroom and living room; still others have two bedrooms. The furniture is typical Scandinavian-style motel or light-oak modern. Other facilities include a dining room, a lounge/piano bar, four tennis courts, an outdoor heated pool, and a private beach. *Rates:* Mid-June to mid-September, $115 to $155 double, from $170 suite; early May to mid-June and mid-September to late October, $95 to $130 double, from $145 suite; late October to early May, $80 to $115 double, from $130 suite.

On the highway but set well back from the road with attractive grounds, shade trees, and flowers in front, is the **Drossos Motel**, Main Road, Greenport, NY 11944 (☎ 516/477-1339). Each room has a TV, air-conditioning, and kitchen facilities. Facilities include miniature golf and a snack bar. *Rates:* Mid-June to mid-September, $105 to 130 double; mid-September to December and April to mid-June, from $75 double. Closed January to March.

GREENPORT DINING

Aldo's, 105 Front St. (☎ 516/477-1699), is famous for its breads and pastries and is perhaps the most charming and best place to dine in Greenport. The menu is very limited, and you'll need to bring your own wine. You might find a fish of the day, steak au poivre, and chicken paillard, priced from $17 to $22. Antiqued walls, classical accents, and decorative majolica pieces create a warm Italian atmosphere. *Hours:* Summer, daily 6pm to closing; rest of the year, Friday to Sunday 6pm to closing.

The **Porto Bello**, Manhasset Avenue, at Stirling Harbor (☎ 516/477-1717), has a lovely setting overlooking Stirling Harbor toward Greenport that is perfect for romantic summer dining—you gaze past the bobbing masts to the shady bank opposite, where a steepled church is etched against the sky. The decor is restful and simple—cane-seated ladderbacks, stucco arches, a stone hearth, and a pleasant bar that takes advantage of the view. The food is traditional Italian all the way. Pasta dishes range from linguine with clam sauce to a house specialty like fettuccine alla Farma, made with chicken, mushrooms, sun-dried tomatoes, and broccoli in a Marsala sauce. Veal and seafood dishes are predictable favorites, too—veal piccata, Marsala, and parmigiana or scampi in garlic white wine. Prices range from $15 to $19. Desserts are typically cheesecake, cannoli, and tiramisu. To reach the Porto Bello, take Main Street out of Greenport toward Orient, then turn right. Take Manhasset Avenue to Stirling Harbor. *Hours:* June to August, Sunday to Thursday 5 to 9pm, Friday and Saturday 5 to 10pm; at other times, Thursday, Sunday, and Monday, 5 to 9pm, Friday and Saturday 5 to 10pm. Closed Tuesday and Wednesday September to May.

Claudio's, 111 Main St. (☎ 516/477-0627), the local favorite for fish, has been purveying food at the dock since 1870. It's a typical waterfront restaurant that serves fresh fish and steaks, priced from $16 to $30, the latter for lobster tail and New York steak. In summer, on the wharf outside, the clam bar offers a variety of steamers, burgers, and chowders from $6 to $11. *Hours:* In season, daily 11:30am to closing; off-season, Wednesday to Monday 11:30am to closing. Closed January to March.

At **Bootleggers** in Sterling Square, on Main Street and Bay Avenue (☎ 516/477-0012), you can dine out on a brick patio or inside in a pubby atmosphere. On the menu is usually a fish of the day that might be cooked with lemon and capers, or in a Creole style with tomatoes, peppers, and onions; as well as such meat dishes as New York shell steak with whiskey-peppercorn butter or any of several other ways. Prices range from $13 to $17. On Sunday a jazz trio plays from 3 to 7pm. *Hours:* In season, daily 11:30am to 10pm; off-season, Wednesday to Saturday 11:30am to 10pm.

Another dining possibility is the **Rhumbline,** 34 to 36 Front St. (☎ 516/477-8697), a pleasantly nautical dining room serving seafood and steaks from $12 to $19. *Hours:* Daily 11:30am to 3pm and 5 to 9pm.

For a spot of afternoon tea, drop into the **Greenport Tea Company,** 119A Main St. (☎ 516/477-8744), a charming tearoom that also sells teapots and other accoutrements for serving and enhancing the tea ritual. For $19 for two you can sample a full tea, consisting of scones and sandwiches and pastries accompanied by a pot of properly brewed tea.

Greenport & Orient Point
Special & Recreational Activities

Berry Picking: Raspberries, strawberries, and pumpkins can be picked at **Wickham Fruit Farm,** one of the oldest single family farms in the nation (Route 25, Cutchogue; ☎ 516/734-6441; Monday to Saturday). **Lathams** at Orient is another famous farm stand, plus there are many farms along Sound Avenue.

Fishing: Flounder, bluefish, cod, striped bass, mackerel, and tuna are all available, depending on the season. Numerous party boats operate from Orient by the Sea Marina on Main Road: *Prime Time III* (☎ 516/323-2618); *Shinnecock Star* (☎ 516/728-4563); *SunDowner* (☎ 516/765-2227); *Wandera* (☎ 516/765-3445); and *Nancy Ami* (☎ 516/477-2337). A day trip averages $45. The *Peconic Star II* (☎ 516/289-6899) is based in Greenport.

Golf: The **Island's End Club**, Greenport, on Route 25 (☎ 516/477-0777), offers a scenic course along the bluffs overlooking the sound. Greens fees are $29 weekdays and $33 weekends.

Horseback Riding: Zimmer Farm, Main Road, Orient (☎ 516/323-1317), offers 1-hour trail rides for $40 per person. Open April to Labor Day only.

Swimming: Orient Point State Park. Open year-round.

Tennis: The **Sound View Motel's** courts are open to the public (☎ 516/477-1910). The charge is $12 an hour for doubles, $8 for singles. On Route 48, the **Brick Cove Marina**, Sage Boulevard (☎ 516/477-0830), has courts renting for $10 per hour.

SOUTHOLD, CUTCHOGUE, MATTITUCK & JAMESPORT

SOUTHOLD ATTRACTIONS

Going west from Greenport will bring you to Southold. Southold likes to challenge Southampton, on the South Fork, for the title of first settlement on the East End, but no one is really sure who deserves the title. Both were settled around 1640, and Southold's **Old First Church** on Main Street was founded in that year, although the stately building that you see today was built in 1803. Wander through the adjacent burial ground, which is one of the oldest on the island.

The **Indian Museum,** on Bayview Road (☎ 516/765-5577), houses one of the most complete collections of Native American artifacts on Long Island—Algonquin pottery, spear and arrow heads dating back 10,000 years, a variety of tools from knifes and hoe blades to gouges and drills, plus jewelry, toys, pipes, and other items. Much of the material was dug up by local farmers. The collection contains 300,000 to 400,000 artifacts, but only a handful are on display. *Hours:* July to August, Saturday to Sunday 1:30 to 4:30pm. *Admission:* Free.

The **Historical Society Museum,** on Route 25A (☎ 516/765-5500), has a diverse collection of buildings and collections relating to local history. The buildings range from a 1750s colonial home to an 1897 Victorian, and vary in function from the hat shop of famous turn-of-the-century milliner Frank Smith to an old privy. The Thomas Currie Bell landscapes and portraits are notable, as is the clothes collection. Demonstrations are given in the print and blacksmith shops. *Hours:* July to Labor Day, Wednesday and Saturday to Sunday 2 to 5pm. *Admission:* Free.

For great views of Long Island Sound, detour to **Horton's Point Lighthouse**, Lighthouse Road, Southold (☎ 516/765-2101).

CUTCHOGUE ATTRACTIONS

Cutchogue has a Native American name meaning "the greatest or principal place," which refers to the food bounty that the Native American tribes enjoyed here before the arrival of the white settlers.

The village clusters around a pretty green that has three historic homes standing on it. The gem of the three is referred to as **Old House** (☎ 516/734-7122, or 516/734-7113 for the historical society). The 1649 shingled frame house with leaded casement windows was built for wealthy English merchant John Budd. It boasts a great chimney and stairs that arch over the closets below. The **Wickham Farmhouse** (ca. 1740) and **Old School House Museum** (ca. 1840) are also on the green. The first belonged to the Wickham family, one of the oldest on Long Island, having arrived shortly after the original settlers in 1640. They were Tories and lost much of their land after the American Revolution. The second is Cutchogue's first district school, built in 1840. *Hours:* July to August, Saturday to Monday 1 to 4pm; Memorial Day to June and September, Saturday to Sunday 1 to 4pm. *Admission:* $1.50.

While you're in Cutchogue drop by the **George Braun Oyster Company**, Main Road, Cutchogue (☎ 516/734-6700), to purchase some oysters, clams, scallops, or lobster. Also in Cutchogue, **Wickham Fruit Farm**, Route 25 (☎ 516/734-6441), is a great place to stop for really choice fruits and vegetables. In season, you can pick your own. *Hours:* Monday to Saturday 9am to 6pm.

It's worth turning at the traffic light in Cutchogue south to New Suffolk, which opens to Robins Island and Great Peconic Bay. Savor the grand Victorian homes and the Victorian-style schoolhouse before you reach the waterfront, where you can linger at one of the cafes at the tip of the peninsula overlooking Cutchogue Harbor. New Suffolk was a center for oystering and scalloping at the turn of the century. It was also home to the John P. Holland Torpedo Boat Company, which developed the first modern submarine for the U.S. Navy in 1899 (the company moved to Groton in 1905). From New Suffolk there are great views of Robins Island in the Great Peconic Bay.

MATTITUCK ATTRACTIONS

Mattituck is considered a second-generation village because it was settled in 1662. Among its charms are the general store located in the Octagon House (1856) and the old Presbyterian Church, which was established in 1715. Mattituck is famous for its berry farms, which line Sound Avenue with many locally famous names like Levin's, Young's, and Briermere. The last, at 79 Sound Ave. Route 48, Riverhead (☎ 516/722-3931), is legendary for its delicious fruit pies. The farm's secret, of course, is using fresh fruit from the farm, in such enticing combinations as strawberry-rhubarb, raspberry-peach, and blackberry-apple. It's open daily except in January and February, when it's open weekends only.

SOUTHOLD DINING

For seafood that's well and imaginatively prepared, try **Ross' North Fork Restaurant,** North Road (Route 48; ☎ 516/765-2111). Chef/owner John Ross uses local, fresh ingredients. On the menu, which lists a dozen or so entrees, you might find tuna with red wine sauce, swordfish with white wine and capers, or fresh sea scallops with olive oil and lime. The meat dishes are also well prepared, like the grilled fillet of pork with apple, pear, and ginger chutney, or Long Island duck with plum sauce. Prices run from $18 to $22. To start, select any of the shellfish dishes or the hearty clam chowder. The ambience is simple, but elegant. *Hours:* Spring, summer, and fall, Tuesday

The Wineries

While farming and fishing are still important to the North Fork of Long Island, the true gold is being mined from grapevines, which appreciate the sandy soil and the temperate climate of this bay-bathed spit of land. Pioneers Alex and Louisa Hargrave planted the first vines in Cutchogue back in 1973, and today, only 25 years later, there are more than 20 wineries lining County Road 48 and Route 25, most along Route 25 between Cutchogue and Southold.

Although *Wine Spectator* announced in 1988 that Long Island wines had arrived, the region really came into its own in 1993–1995 when the weather helped produce wines that belong on the table with their French and California counterparts. About 1,800 acres are planted with grapes, and the region produces about 250,000 cases of wine per year. The climate is very similar to Bordeaux, so the wines are more in the austere and lean French style than the California wines.

The area has become the premier wine-producing region of New York. If you travel west along routes 25 and 48, you'll come to a series of wineries. They are listed below in the order you'll come to them.

In Southold, **Corey Creek Vineyards,** Box 921 (☎ 516/323-1224), has a large wooden deck overlooking the vineyards at its ultra-modern tasting room, which opened in 1997. In Peconic, along Route 25, you'll find **Osprey's Dominion,** Main Road (☎ 516/765-6188); **Lenz Winery** (☎ 516/734-6010); and **Pindar Vineyards** (☎ 516/734-6200).

In Cutchogue, still along Route 25, are the following: **Bedell Cellars,** Main Road (☎ 516/734-7537); **Pugliese,** Main Road (☎ 516/734-4057); and **Peconic Bay Vineyards** (☎ 516/734-7361). **Hargrave** (☎ 516/734-5111), the oldest winery, has the oldest vines and produces some of the finest wines. It also has the most Frenchified atmosphere, with a baronial-style tasting room furnished with an elegant, boardroom-type table and Chippendale chairs. **Gristina** (☎ 516/734-7089) has a tasting room overlooking the vineyards, with wooden chairs along a deck; and **Pellegrini Vineyards,** 23005 Main Rd. (☎ 516/734-4111), produces a wonderful elixir, called *Finale,* an extraordinary dessert wine.

Other vineyards are **Laurel Lake Vineyards,** Main Road, Laurel (☎ 516/734-6010); **Macari Vineyards,** Bergen Avenue, Mattituck (☎ 516/298-0100); **Jamesport Vineyards,** Route 25, Jamesport (☎ 516/722-5256); **Paumanok Vineyards,** Route 25, Aquebogue (☎ 516/722-8800); and **Palmer Vineyards,** Sound Avenue, Aquebogue (☎ 516/722-WINE).

Most of the wineries offer self-guided tours and tastings. Most are open from 10am or 11am to 5pm daily in season, weekends only in winter. Additional information about new wineries and other news about the wine country is available from the **Long Island Wine Council** (☎ 516/369-5887).

to Saturday noon to 2:30pm and 5 to 9pm, Sunday noon to 9pm. Closed Tuesday and Wednesday in winter, and January to mid-February.

The **Seafood Barge,** Route 25, at Port of Egypt Marina (☎ 516/765-3010), overlooking the marina and Peconic Bay toward Shelter Island, offers ultra-fresh well-prepared seafood that's a far cry from the old fried-fish days of yore, although fried shrimp and fried scallops are still available. Today you're likely to find grilled salmon served with a cucumber and tomato mint ragoût, oven-roasted yellowtail snapper with grilled vegetable caponata, plus such meat dishes as grilled pork tenderloin in wild mushroom bourbon sauce. Pasta dishes round out the menu. Appetizers are given a creative twist, too, like the crab cakes served on fresh cilantro-mint vinaigrette, or the fried calamari accompanied by a roasted red pepper aïoli. Prices range $14 to $26. The wine list concentrates on local wines. *Hours:* Summer, daily noon to 3pm and 5 to 10pm; rest of the year, Thursday to Friday 5 to 9pm, Saturday 1 to 10pm, and Sunday 1 to 9pm.

For classic continental cuisine in a very pretty atmosphere there's **Coeur des Vignes,** 57225 Main Rd. (☎ 516/765-2656), in a white clapboard house surrounded by flowering shrubs. Here you can enjoy scampi served over tagliatelle, filet mignon with béarnaise sauce, Dover sole meunière, and other such dishes. Prices range from $17 to $34. The appetizers are also classics— frogs' legs sautéed in tomato, garlic, and herb butter; escargots in parsley, garlic butter, and white wine; and French onion soup. *Hours:* Summer, Saturday and Sunday noon to 2pm, Wednesday to Monday 5 to 9 or 10pm; winter, Thursday to Sunday 5 to 9pm, although you're advised to call ahead. Closed February.

CUTCHOGUE LODGING

Aliano's Beachcomber, 3800 Duck Pond Rd. (at the foot of Depot Lane; P.O. Box 947), Cutchogue, NY 11935 (☎ 516/734-6370), offers 60 large rooms, all with a refrigerator and color TV, some with a kitchenette with full-size stove and refrigerator. Added bonuses are the 800-foot private beach on the Sound, outdoor pool, and bocce court. *Rates:* Memorial Day to October 15, $125 to $145 double; April to Memorial Day and October 16 to 31, slightly less. Closed November to March.

CUTCHOGUE DINING

The **Fisherman's Rest,** Route 25 (☎ 516/734-5155), is a down-home spot for steamers, lobster, and other seafood mixed with some Italian specialties, all priced from $8 to $17. For lobster lovers, there's the best treat of all—a 1¼-pounder for $15 and a 1½ pounder for $17. *Hours:* Summer, Tuesday to Thursday 3:30 to 9pm, Friday 3:30 to 10pm, Saturday 11:30am to 9pm; rest of the year, Tuesday to Thursday 3:30 to 8pm, Friday 3:30 to 9pm, Saturday 11:30am to 8pm.

NEW SUFFOLK DINING

Legends, 835 First St. (☎ 734-5123), is a popular sports bar–restaurant, and the ambience of the dining room continues the theme with a crew boat suspended from the ceiling and the occasional saddle or baseball bat as a decorative accent. The bar offers more than 200 beers. The fare in the dining room is honest and reasonably priced—barbecued ribs, flounder stuffed with crabmeat and served with lemon-butter sauce, stuffed shrimp, and grilled chicken breast with portobello mushrooms. Prices range from $12 to $19. In summer, there's music on weekends and live comedy on Thursday. *Hours:* Sunday to Friday noon to 9pm, Saturday noon to 10pm with a late-night menu until 11pm weekdays and until midnight Friday and Saturday.

JAMESPORT DINING

Jamesport Country Kitchen, Main Road, Jamesport (☎ 516/722-3537), is a casual and cozy dining room where you can settle in behind the lace curtains at the plain wood tables and enjoy a fine meal served by a friendly staff. The ingredients used in the cuisine are super-fresh, and it makes a difference in the simple dishes that are served, from the shrimp and filet mignon brochettes marinated in a sesame sauce, to the tuna steak with mango salsa, and the local duck served with a wonderful relish of pear, walnut, and cranberry. Prices range from $12 to $17. To start, the soups are equally good and the lobster cakes are delicious. Desserts are simple, too—fresh blueberry tart with vanilla ice cream, apple crisp, or white chocolate cheesecake. *Hours:* Monday and Wednesday to Sunday 11:30am to 4:30pm; Sunday, Monday, and Wednesday to Thursday 4:30 to 9pm, Friday and Saturday 4:30 to 9:30pm.

Southold, Cutchogue & Mattituck Area
Special & Recreational Activities

Beaches: The main beaches have lifeguards and other facilities. *New Suffolk:* **New Suffolk Beach** on Jackson Street. *Southold:* **Kenny's Beach** at the end of Kenny's Road, **McCabe's Beach** on North Sea Road, and the **Town Beach** on North Road (Route 48), which is the most popular. Parking at all these beaches is by permit only. For additional information, call ☎ 516/765-1800.

Boating: Strong's, Camp Mineola Road, Mattituck (☎ 516/298-4770), rents small runabout motorboats from $200 a day. Sunfish can be rented for $50 per day at **Capt. Marty's,** First Street at King Street, New Suffolk (☎ 516/734-6852).

Fishing: Capt. Marty's, First Street at King Street, New Suffolk (☎ 516/734-6852), rents boats, tackle, and bait for $75 per day.

Hiking: For nature rambles there are 34 acres at **Goldsmith's Inlet** and another 37 acres to explore at **Inlet Point,** good birding terrain, where naturalists lead guided walks.

THE NORTH SHORE'S HISTORIC TRIANGLE

The so-called Historic Triangle area stretches from Stony Brook and Setauket all the way west via Smithtown to St. James and Northport, to Huntington and

Cold Spring Harbor. It's an area worth exploring on any weekend. There's even a historic old inn to stay at right in Stony Brook.

STONY BROOK
Stony Brook Attractions

Stony Brook is a beautifully restored 19th-century shipping and fishing village, complete with mill pond, gristmill, rock garden, brook, and harbor.

The **Museums at Stony Brook,** Route 25A (☎ 516/751-0066), are made up of a superb museum complex of four major collections devoted to history, art, period buildings, and carriages. The carriage collection is internationally renowned. Its 250 vehicles include cabriolets, grand Victorias (by manufacturers like Abbot-Downing, Studebaker, Brewster, and Million Guiet), royal coaches, and a brilliantly painted ornate Gypsy wagon said to have belonged to Queen Phoebe, a Gypsy woman who lived on Long Island in the early 1900s.

The art collection contains most of the works by William Sidney Mount (1807–68), a major figure in 19th-century American art who was noted for his paintings of everyday life and his sympathetic depiction of African Americans. Other highlights include 15 exquisite miniature period rooms, a fine costume collection, and carved decoys. Period buildings on the site also include a one-room schoolhouse, blacksmith shop, and barn. *Hours:* July to January, Monday to Saturday 10am to 5pm, Sunday noon to 5pm; rest of the year, Wednesday to Saturday 10am to 5pm, Sunday noon to 5pm. *Admission:* $4 adults, $3 seniors, $2 children ages 6 to 18.

The **Stony Brook Mill,** Grist Mill Road (☎ 516/751-2244), is one of the few fully operational 18th-century mills whose millstones are original. Kids love to feed the ducks on the pond afterward. *Hours:* June to September, Wednesday to Friday 11am to 4:30pm, Saturday to Sunday noon to 4:30pm; spring and fall, Saturday to Sunday noon to 4:30pm. Closed January to March. *Admission:* $1 adults, 50¢ children ages 11 and under.

Stony Brook Lodging & Dining

At the center of this classic 19th-century village stands the delightful **Three Village Inn,** 150 Main St., Stony Brook, NY 11790 (☎ 516/751-0555). Sloping, creaky floors, rooms tucked under the eaves, iron door latches, and costumed and bonneted waitresses add color and character to this hostelry that was once (1751) the home of shipbuilder Jonas Smith and later the site of the Presbyterian Church's retreat and conference, the Stony Brook Assembly. There are a total of 26 rooms. Rooms in the main building (all with private baths, TVs, telephones, and air-conditioning) are furnished with comfy, country-style antiques set against floral wallpapers and exposed beams. A series of cottages house pleasant, modern, superior-grade motel rooms, some opening onto lawns facing the harbor. The parlor is more classically furnished, with wing chairs, Martha Washington chairs, clubfoot tables, and a handsome writing desk, all placed to take full advantage of the large fireplace.

The dining room specializes in traditional American cuisine—prime rib, Yankee pot roast, Long Island duckling, medallions of veal with wild mushrooms and chestnuts, and lobster—that's plain and good. Prices for complete dinners including appetizer, salad, dessert, and coffee range from

$26 to $34. Brunch is a good bet here, too. On Friday, Saturday, and Sunday people gather around the piano for a jovial song session. In summer the patio is a lovely place to sit out under the shade trees surrounded by flowers.

Rates: Weekends $129 single, $149 double. *Dining hours:* Sunday to Thursday 7am to 11am, noon to 4pm, 5 to 9pm; Friday to Saturday until 10pm. Closed Christmas.

A more colorful summer setting would be hard to find than the one at the **Country House Restaurant,** at Main Street and Route 25A (☎ 516/751-3332). Fresh flowers adorn the three bright dining rooms, each painted variously green, blue, and lilac and pink. Lemons and oranges garlanded with ivy form the centerpiece on the Good Luck Penny bar, flanked in summer by dishes of strawberries or peanuts and cheese puffs. On weekends a pianist entertains. The menu varies according to the season and might feature pan-seared sea bass with leeks and lobster sauce, poached salmon with dill sauce, and fillet of beef with garlic wine sauce. Prices range from $16 to $24. Brunch is prix fixe at $17 and offers a variety of fare, from steak and barbecue shrimp to quiche and other egg dishes. *Hours:* Sunday to Thursday noon to 3pm and 5 to 9pm, Friday noon to 3pm and 5 to 10pm, Saturday 5 to 10pm.

SETAUKET & PORT JEFFERSON
Area Attractions

From Stony Brook, take Route 25A into Setauket, turning off for a detour to the **Old Field Lighthouse,** where you can get an inspiring view all the way along the sound. There are a couple of old houses for history or architecture buffs to visit.

The **Thompson House,** on North Country Road (☎ 516/692-4664), dating to the early 1700s, displays a collection of early Long Island furniture, including the distinctive double-paneled blanket chest, the Dutch-influenced kas, several rural chair types, and a 1797 clock made by Nathaniel Dominy IV of East Hampton. There's also a colonial herb garden to view. *Hours:* May to mid-October, Friday to Sunday 1 to 5pm. *Admission:* $1.50 adults, $1 seniors and children ages 7 to 14.

The 18th-century **Sherwood-Jayne House,** Old Post Road, Setauket (☎ 516/692-4664), located in a bucolic setting, is also filled with a varied collection of furniture and objects. The hand-painted frescoes in the east parlor and bedroom are fine examples of Early American wall decoration. *Hours:* Memorial Day to mid-October, by appointment only. *Admission:* $1.50 adults, $1 seniors and children ages 7 to 14.

From here it's a short run into Port Jefferson, docking point for the Bridgeport, Connecticut, **ferry,** which during the summer deposits hundreds of day-trippers who swarm into the dockside restaurants, boutiques, and antiques stores.

You may want to visit the **Mather House Museum,** 115 Prospect St. (☎ 516/473-2665), a complex of buildings and exhibits featuring costumes, shell craft, Native American art, ship models, and much more. *Hours:* Memorial Day to June, Saturday and Sunday 1 to 4pm; July and August, Tuesday, Wednesday, Saturday, and Sunday 1 to 4pm; *Admission:* $2.

Port Jefferson Lodging & Dining

Danford's Inn, at Bayles Dock, 25 E. Broadway, Port Jefferson, NY 11777 (☎ 516/928-5200), occupies a prime waterfront spot with views of the prettier side of the harbor. The lobby is accented with mallard and pheasant trophies and hunting paraphernalia. Tucked into an area created by a bay window is a TV and couch for guests' convenience. Accommodations are in several two- or three-story buildings connected by a brick walkway bordered by stores that make a pleasant shopping area. Many of the 80 rooms overlook the water, and all are quite large and furnished with good-quality antique reproductions; the baths contain the full list of amenities. Two buildings in particular have extremely large rooms, with beds decorated in a special draped effect, desks with Queen Anne chairs, armoires, and sitting areas furnished with a couch and armchairs. The design layout of rooms in another building make them suitable for families or two couples traveling together; they contain two double beds and there's a bath in between.

The restaurant serves continental cuisine—duckling with orange sauce, pistachio- and horseradish-crusted salmon with caramelized red onion marmalade, and veal Oscar. Prices range from $17 to $26. Buffet brunch and buffet dinner are available on Sunday. On weekends there's dancing in the sail loft.

Rates: $159 to $350 (the higher price for suites). Special packages are available. *Dining hours:* Sunday to Thursday 7am to midnight, Friday and Saturday 7am to 1am; Sunday 8:30am to noon.

Port Jefferson & Setauket Dining

Metropolis Bistro, 316 Main St., East Setauket (☎ 516/751-2200), has won top ranking for serving well-prepared, reasonably priced modern bistro fare. It offers an up-to-the-minute menu featuring everything from pasta and pizza to hand rolls, and about 10 or so entrees. The pizzas are made with such ingredients as sweet sausage, roasted peppers, scallions, sun-dried tomatoes, and Gorgonzola; one of the hand rolls combines fried oysters, cheddar cheese, bacon, lettuce, tomato, and a basil tartare sauce. Among the pastas there might be penne with shrimp, sun-dried tomatoes, cannellini beans, and broccoli rabe cooked in a herb and garlic broth. The fish dishes, like Moroccan spiced tuna and grilled Chilean sea bass in mustard sauce, are well prepared. Prices range from $6 to $9 for pizza and hand rolls and from $9 to $18 for pasta and entrees. The artworks on the walls complement the art on the plate. On Friday and Saturday at 11:30pm there's piano/jazz entertainment. *Hours:* Daily 11:30am to 11pm. On Friday and Saturday a limited late-night menu is available from 11:30pm.

Costa de España, 9 Traders Cove (☎ 516/331-5363), has a small bar, tables with red cloths, a pleasant warm atmosphere, and fine Spanish food. The emphasis is on seafood—paella valenciana con langosta (with sausage, chicken, and lobster), or seafood combination dishes in a variety of sauces, from green and garlic to hot and egg. There's also such meat dishes as veal in almond sauce, and a special chicken with onions, mushrooms, wine, and tomato sauce. Prices run $13 to $22. *Hours:* Monday to Thursday noon to 3pm and 5 to 10pm, Friday to Saturday noon to 3pm and 5 to 11pm, Sunday 1 to 10pm.

Printer's Devil, Wynne Lane (☎ 516/928-7171), is a pubby local favorite decked out in typical oak, stained glass, and plants. Chicken parmigiana, filet mignon and other steaks, pasta dishes, and burgers typify the fare, priced from $7 to $22. *Hours:* Monday to Thursday 11:30am to 11pm, Friday to Saturday 11:30am to 1am, Sunday 11am to 3pm and 4 to 11pm.

SMITHTOWN & ST. JAMES
Area Attractions
If you head west on Route 25A from Stony Brook you'll pass **Wicks Farm Stand**, famous not only for fresh produce but also for their imaginative Halloween display that kids love. Turn left at Moriches Road and head for the **St. James General Store** (☎ 516/862-8333), established in 1857. The porch is lined with baskets of all sorts, a big old teddy bear, and a cigar store Indian. The interior offers all kinds of old-fashioned favorites—sugarcanes and candies, jams, preserves, cookie jars, quilts, spices, and craft items, all displayed on the original counters, shelves, or cases. In winter the place is warmed by an old potbellied stove.

From here, Moriches Road north takes you through Nissequogue, a land mass that separates Stony Brook Harbor from the Nissequogue River. Follow Moriches Road until it loops around into Nissequogue Road, which leads into River Road. All through here you'll be driving along winding, tree-shaded lanes bursting with rhododendron and mountain laurel, which in early summer shield the grand houses from the prying eyes of the passing motorist.

Getting back on Route 25A brings you into Smithtown, one of the nation's fastest-growing townships. It has several historic landmarks: The **Caleb Smith House**, on Route 25A (☎ 516/265-6768; open Monday to Friday 8am to 4pm, Saturday noon to 4pm; admission by donation), is the home of the historical society. The **Epenetus Smith Tavern**, Middle Country Road (☎ 516/724-3091; open only on Heritage Day, usually the second Sunday in September), is where memories of mirth and mead are preserved in the one-room bar, as is the lifestyle of an earlier era in pictures, sea chests, tea caddies, and rockers.

Smithtown Area Dining
Unfortunately, there are no attractive country inns (the closest is Stony Brook's Three Village Inn), but there are plenty of fine dining establishments.

Smithtown Haus, 65 E. Main St., Smithtown (☎ 516/979-9113), offers good German fare in a warm wooden room with a large bar: sauerbraten, bratwurst and sauerkraut, jaegerschnitzel with mushrooms in cream sauce, sole almondine, and filet mignon, from $13 to $20. *Hours:* Tuesday to Friday noon to 3pm and 5 to 9pm, Saturday 5 to 11pm, Sunday noon to 9pm.

Fine-quality Italian cuisine draws crowds to **Casa Rustica**, 175 W. Main St., Smithtown (☎ 516/265-9265). From the cozy, fire-warmed bar a ramp leads into the stucco-and-timbered country dining room. Start with carpaccio with radicchio and Parmesan dressed with a pink sauce, or a delicious seafood salad of calamari, scungilli, octopus, mussels, and shrimp. There are several pastas, like meat-filled agnolotti; risotto with calamari, shrimp, mussels, and scallops; along with such richly flavored dishes as baby rack of lamb in a barolo sauce, or liver with caramelized apples and onions with a touch of balsamic vinegar. Prices run $17 to $25. *Hours:* Monday to Thursday noon to

3pm and 5 to 10pm, Friday noon to 3pm and 5 to 11pm, Saturday 5 to 11pm, Sunday 2 to 9pm.

Mario's, 644 Vanderbilt Motor Pkwy., Hauppauge (☎ 516/273-9407), features an extensive menu offering chicken breast Marsala, veal with artichokes and mushrooms, saltimbocca, red snapper with spinach, and such pastas as cannelloni, manicotti, and linguine alla vongole. The decor is rich: gilt pictures, chandeliers, banquettes, and chairs covered in floral fabric. Prices run from $13 to $25. *Hours:* Monday to Thursday noon to 2:30pm and 5 to 9:30pm, Friday noon to 2:30pm and 5:30 to 10:30pm, Saturday 5:30 to 10:30pm, Sunday 3 to 9:30pm.

Mirabelle, 404 North Country Rd., St. James (☎ 516/584-5999), serves the best food in the area and has a rather spare modern decor that relies on color—pale peach with gray trim, red banquettes—for effect. The menu changes seasonally, but may feature pistachio-crusted pompano stuffed with lobster and wild mushrooms and served with golden beets and roasted onion sauce, roast loin of venison served with a chutney of exotic fruits, and grilled duck breast followed by confit leg. Prices run $21 to $32. Begin with dill-marinated salmon that is baked and served with cucumber, or with the richly flavored fricassee of wild mushrooms. The natural finish for the meal is a soufflé. *Hours:* Tuesday to Thursday noon to 2pm and 6 to 10pm, Friday noon to 2pm and 6 to 11pm, Saturday 6 to 11pm, Sunday 5 to 9pm.

The North Shore
Special & Recreational Activities

Boating: *Port Jefferson:* **Craftis Fishing,** Barnum Avenue (☎ 516/473-2288), rents small fishing boats for $65 a day.

Swimming/Picnicking: *Port Jefferson:* **West Meadow Beach,** West Meadow. *Smithtown to St. James:* For fishing, ice-skating, rowboats, camping, and hiking, **Blydenburgh Park** (☎ 516/853-4966) has 588 acres that are all yours. The **Nissequogue River State Park** is great for hiking. A permit is required.

Tennis: There are courts at **SUNY at Stony Brook.**

CONNECTICUT

The Litchfield Hills

New Milford ◆ *Bull's Bridge* ◆ *Kent* ◆ *Cornwall Bridge* ◆
West Cornwall ◆ *Sharon* ◆ *Dover Plains, N.Y.* ◆ *Amenia, N.Y.* ◆
Lakeville ◆ *Salisbury* ◆ *Norfolk* ◆ *Riverton* ◆ *Litchfield* ◆
Lake Waramaug ◆ *New Preston* ◆ *Woodbury* ◆ *Washington*

Distance in miles: Woodbury or Litchfield, 99; Sharon, 111; Winsted, 117
Estimated driving time: 2 hours to Litchfield, 2 hours to Winsted

◄◦►◄◦►◄◦►◄◦►◄◦►

Driving: Take the Henry Hudson Parkway north to the Sawmill River Parkway, take Route 684 north to Brewster, and then get on I-84 east to Danbury (Exit 7). Take Route 7 north to New Milford and then Route 202 east to Litchfield.

For the Salisbury area, take the Taconic Parkway to Route 44 all the way into Salisbury, or take I-684 to Route 22 north and then to Route 44.

For Winsted, take I-84 to the Waterbury exit and pick up Route 8 north.

Bus: Bonanza (☎ 800/556-3815) travels to New Milford, Kent, Southbury, Gaylordsville, and Sheffield.

Train: The closest destinations by train are Brewster, Danbury, and Waterbury East (via Metro-North's Harlem line). Call ☎ 212/532-4900.

Further Information: For more about the area's events and festivals and about Connecticut in general, call or write **Connecticut State Tourism**, 505 Hudson St., Hartford, CT 06106 (☎ 800/282-6863 or 860/270-8081).

For specific information about the Litchfield area, contact the **Litchfield Hills Travel Council**, P.O. Box 968, Litchfield, CT 06759 (☎ 860/567-4506).

◄◦►◄◦►◄◦►◄◦►◄◦►

One weekend or several spent exploring the northwest corner of Connecticut, the so-called Litchfield Hills, will take you along roads bordered by hedgerows dotted with colorful wildflowers, past sagging old russet barns, through forests and fields, and over rolling hills to the classic New England town of **Litchfield** and the lesser-known but picturesque hamlets of **Cornwall, Sharon,** and **Salisbury.** All are perfect in their quiet, unassuming way, hence their appeal to their many wealthy residents, like Henry Kissinger, Tom Brokaw,

The Litchfield Hills

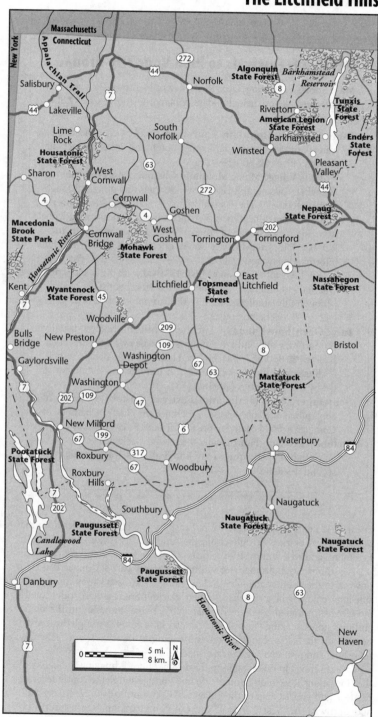

Events & Festivals to Plan Your Trip Around

May: Sports car racing, Lime Rock (begins Memorial Day weekend and continues on major holidays until mid-October). Call ☎ 860/435-2571.

June: Winsted Mountain Laurel Festival, with a parade, a waterskiing exhibition, and other entertainments. Contact the mayor's office (☎ 860/379-2713).

    Falls Village Music Mountain Chamber concerts, with the Shanghai, Cassatt, and Leontovich quartets and others (through mid-September). The festival offers 16 string quartet concerts plus a jazz series, as well as preconcert performances by students from Mannes College of Music. Write Music Mountain Inc., P.O. Box 738, Lakeville, CT 06039 or call ☎ 860/824-7126 for information and reservations.

    Yale's **Norfolk Chamber Music Festival,** with the Tokyo String Quartet and others, at the Ellen Battell Stoeckel Estate, Norfolk (through July). Call ☎ 860/436-3690 for information or ☎ 860/542-3000 for the box office.

July: Open house tour of Litchfield's historic homes, usually the Saturday after July 4. Confirm the dates with the historical society (☎ 860/567-4501) or the Litchfield Hills Travel Council.

    Sharon Audubon Festival, with lectures and nature walks led by top authorities (late July).

September: Chrysanthemum Festival, Bristol (last week of September, first of October). Contact the Bristol Chamber of Commerce, 55 N. Main St., Bristol, CT 06010 (☎ 860/584-4718).

October: Riverton Fair (usually the second weekend).

    Salisbury Antiques Fair and Fall Festival (usually the second weekend).

Oscar de la Renta, and Philip Roth. In Salisbury you're only 4 miles from the Massachusetts border, 12 miles from the southern Berkshire town of South Egremont, and well within striking distance of Tanglewood and Lenox.

    The prime reason, though, for visiting this pretty part of Connecticut is to unwind in the countryside—by cycling along back roads, stopping at roadside inns, enjoying historic villages where gracious houses stand under stately old trees surrounded by perfectly manicured lawns, browsing in the many antiques stores, seeking out craft and country fairs, hiking through the forests, boating on the lakes, canoeing on and fishing in the rivers, and generally refreshing and resuscitating the tarnished urban spirit.

    You can travel in one long loop from New Milford, hugging the banks of the Housatonic River along Route 7, to Bull's Bridge and Kent. Continue along Route 7 and you'll come to the villages of Cornwall Bridge, West Cornwall, and Cornwall. At West Cornwall you can either continue farther north on

Route 7 to Falls Village, the center of canoeing on the Housatonic, or detour west to Sharon, the auto-racing track at Lime Rock, Salisbury, and Lakeville before rejoining Route 7 and then turning off east along Route 44 to Norfolk. From Norfolk it's only 10 miles or so to Riverton, home of the Hitchcock chair factory, and Winsted, site of a renowned spring mountain laurel festival. Another 10 miles brings you to Torrington, only a stone's throw along Route 202 from Litchfield. From Litchfield you can take Route 202 past Bantam and New Preston, with a detour to Lake Waramaug, and return eventually to New Milford. You can drive a shorter loop by starting in Southbury and taking Route 67 to Roxbury, then Route 199 to Washington and Washington Depot, before returning along Route 47 to Southbury via Woodbury. This makes for a particularly fine antiquing weekend.

THE LITCHFIELD HILLS & THE HOUSATONIC RIVER

EXPLORING THE HOUSATONIC FROM NEW MILFORD TO THE CORNWALLS

If you appreciate arts, crafts, and cuisine, you'll want to stop in New Milford at the **Silo** on Upland Road, off Route 202 (☎ 860/355-0300), which is owned by Ruth and Skitch Henderson of Boston Pops fame. Here in a wonderful old barn you'll find a first-rate gallery featuring some fine local arts and crafts; a store selling kitchenware, china, and gourmet foodstuffs; and a cooking school where you can take weekend classes. *Hours:* Daily 10am to 5pm.

Return to New Milford and take Route 7 north through Gaylordsville to **Bull's Bridge,** which dates back to the American Revolution and is one of only two covered bridges in the state open to automobile traffic. From here it's only 3 miles to Kent, where there are several fine antiques shops, boutiques, and several art galleries. The **Kent Antiques Center,** in Kent Station Square on Main Street (☎ 860/927-3313), has 12 dealers. The **Paris–New York– Kent Gallery,** also in Kent Station Square (☎ 860/927-3357), has a solid reputation as a fine-arts gallery and is open Friday to Sunday. It was established in 1984 by Jacques Kaplan, who began by exhibiting work by Max Ernst and Georges Seurat; other galleries have opened in its wake like the **Heron American Craft Gallery** and the **Bachelier-Cardonsky Gallery.**

Kent's role as an art center though goes back to the early 20th century when George Laurence Nelson had his home and studio in Flanders (now part of Kent). His oils, watercolors, and lithographs, including his notable flower studies, can be seen at Seven Hearths (1756) which houses the **Kent Historical Society,** Route 7 (no phone, open weekends only July and August).

On Route 7, a mile north of Kent, is the **Sloane Stanley Museum** (☎ 860/ 927-3849), which has an extensive collection of Early American tools amassed by the late artist/writer Eric Sloane to commemorate "the early American's ingenuity, craftsmanship, and reverence for wood." Mauls, froes, drawknives, lathes, chisels, scythes, and axes are displayed as objects of great beauty that were used to build sturdy beautiful homes and barns, fences, bridges, tables, and chairs in an age when humans went from wooden cradle to wooden coffin. Sloane's cluttered Warren studio has also been faithfully re-created, and some of his paintings are on view in a special gallery. His most familiar work adorns the Smithsonian's National Air and Space Museum in Washington, D.C. *Hours:* Late May to October, Wednesday to Sunday 10am to 4pm. *Admission:* $3 adults, $1.50 seniors and children ages 6 to 17.

Slightly farther north, **Kent Falls State Park** is well known for its 200-foot waterfall, which is especially lovely in spring. Take the short, steep trail to the head of the falls.

About 10 miles north of Kent you'll reach Cornwall Bridge, home of the famous **Cornwall Bridge Pottery** (☎ 860/672-6545), renowned for stoneware (open Thursday to Sunday only). Continue north, passing by Housatonic Meadows State Park, into the village of West Cornwall. Before your reach the village, you can sign up for a canoeing adventure with **Clarke Outdoors** (see "The Litchfield Hills Area: Special & Recreational Activities," below). West Cornwall is well known for its fine craftspeople, but it is best known for its **covered bridge,** built in 1837 of native oak; it's on Route 128 (off Route 7 north, 5 miles north of Cornwall Bridge). This is a scenic spot; the bridge spans the rapids below.

West Cornwall has two excellent craft stores worth browsing on Main Street (Route 128): **Cornwall Bridge Pottery Store** (☎ 860/672-6545) and **Ian Ingersoll Cabinetmakers** (☎ 860/672-6334), which specializes in reproduction furniture in the Shaker tradition. If you're a book lover, walk up the hill to the wonderful antiquarian bookstore **Barbara Farnsworth** (☎ 860/672-6571), a large two-story building that contains well-cataloged collections that include outstanding art, horticulture, and illustrated titles in particular.

Continue north along Route 7 into Falls Village, but before you reach the town, detour along Route 112 to the **car-racing track** at Lime Rock. The stretch of the river around Falls Village was once heavily industrialized, and the mills and factories (most significantly the Ames Iron Works) turned Falls Village into a boomtown in the early 1800s. The hydroelectric plant still functions today. From Falls Village take Route 126 north to Route 44 and continue on Route 44 until it links with Route 7. From here Route 7 crosses the border into Massachusetts to Sheffield and Great Barrington (see "The Central Berkshires & Pioneer Valley," later in this book).

At Cornwall Bridge, you can turn off along routes 4 and 41 to Sharon, a charming old town noted for its large, gracious homes. It's hard to believe that both Sharon and Salisbury were once referred to as the arsenals of the Revolution because of the iron furnaces that turned out much of the patriots' cannons and cannonballs. Little remains of this industrial era when charcoal mounds dotted the woods, although you can visit a relevant museum in Lakeville (see below).

At the **Sharon Historical Society,** 18 Main St., Route 41 (☎ 860/364-5688), you can view objects relating to local history including paintings by Ammi Phillips. It's open mid-June to Columbus Day Friday to Sunday and in winter Tuesday and Wednesday to Friday. Sharon is also notable for the **Sharon Playhouse,** 49 Amenia Rd. (☎ 860/364-6066), which stages a series of musicals in July and August.

From Sharon, pick up Route 41 north through Lakeville, home of the **Hotchkiss School,** and also the **Holley House and Salisbury Cannon Museum** on Route 44. Knives and cutlery were manufactured at the Holley factory from 1844 to about 1920. The knives were individually ground and ranged in size from tiny to large grafting knives used in hybridizing fruit trees. You can tour the Holley family residence and see a collection of Holley knives, plus portraits by such famous itinerant artists as Erastus Salisbury Field and Ammi Phillips. It's open mid-June to mid-October.

Continue on Route 41 into Salisbury. This picturesque village is the site of a busy flea market in late September and also of a large antiques fair in the fall, when the foliage is at its peak. From Salisbury take Route 44 back to Route 7.

NEW MILFORD LODGING & DINING

The mid-18th-century **Homestead Inn,** 5 Elm St., New Milford, CT 06776 (☎ 860/354-4080), is at the center of town facing the village green. The main building's eight rooms are traditionally furnished with chintz wallpapers, dried-flower wreaths, and other country touches. Another six clean and comfortable rooms are located in a motel-style building. Guests may use the living room and front porches to relax. *Rates* (including continental breakfast buffet): $98 to $110 double in the main house, $85 to $93 double in the motel building.

Adrienne, 218 Kent Rd. (Route 7), New Milford, CT 06776 (☎ 860/354-6001), provides elegant dining in an 18th-century home. The cuisine is up to the minute and is inspired by several different traditions. For example, you might find among the dozen entrees an Indonesian curried stew of chicken and potatoes combined with coconut milk and steamed broccoli, or roast venison with natural jus. There will always be a vegetarian dish like portobello mushrooms layered with grilled and roasted vegetables, tomato, orange sauce, and crisp potatoes; plus a steak offering like the filet mignon served with a spinach hollandaise. Prices range from $14 to $24. The appetizers are equally enticing. Try the grilled polenta with Gorgonzola, walnuts, and sage oil; or the crab cakes served on a cucumber yogurt sauce. To finish, there's the beautifully presented bittersweet chocolate terrine with caramelized pears and raspberry coulis, or the amazing rice pudding with raisins and hazelnuts that is served in a chocolate tulip. *Hours:* Tuesday to Saturday 5:30pm to closing; Sunday brunch in fall/winter.

BULL'S BRIDGE & KENT LODGING & DINING

The British and the American flags fly outside the white clapboard house with green shutters named the **Chaucer House,** 88 N. Mountain St., Kent, CT 06757 (☎ 860/927-4858). It's conveniently located on the main street, a short stroll from the Kent galleries and stores. British owners Alan and Brenda Hodgson welcome guests warmly into their home, where they offer three rooms (all with bath). A full breakfast is served. *Rates* (including breakfast): $79 to $97 double.

Named after Jacob and Mary Bull, who established the first inn here during the American Revolution, the **Bull's Bridge Inn,** 333 Kent Rd., on Route 7 between Kent and Bull's Bridge (☎ 860/927-1617), is a local favorite. Folks gather at the bar separating the two simple dining rooms, and there's a small patio with an awning for summer dining. The menu offers typical continental/American dishes like blackened swordfish or salmon, grilled maple-mustard chicken, and meat loaf with mashed potatoes. Prices range from $11 to $17. Bull's Bridge is also known for its Sunday brunch. *Hours:* Monday to Thursday 5 to 9:30pm, Friday to Saturday 5 to 10pm, Sunday 4 to 9pm.

Owner Dolph Traymon's piano artistry alone makes the **Fife 'n' Drum,** Route 7, Kent (☎ 860/927-3509), worth a trip. Dolph, a Juilliard graduate who used to play for Peggy Lee and the late Frank Sinatra, plays nightly. Some would say the very popular taproom is also worth the trip. The food rates highly, too. Barn siding, red brick, and country scenes establish the tone in the still quite formal dining room where several of the dishes are flambéed tableside. Duckling with a brandied sauce, steak au poivre, and Châteaubriand are classic favorites, along with veal, fish, and chicken dishes like the herb-crusted chicken breast in a lemon, caper, and white wine sauce. Prices run $15 to $23. The luncheon menu changes daily. The brunch menu changes weekly and along with eggs Benedict offers roast leg of lamb, chicken au poivre, and similar fare. *Hours:* Monday and Wednesday to Thursday 11:30am to 3pm and 5:30 to 9:30pm, Friday 11:30am to 3pm and 5:30 to 10pm, Saturday 11:30am to 3pm and 5:30 to 10:30pm, Sunday 11:30am to 9pm.

CORNWALL BRIDGE & WEST CORNWALL LODGING & DINING

The **Cornwall Inn,** Route 7, Cornwall Bridge (☎ 860/672-6884), is a roadside hostelry offering five guest rooms (three with bath) that have wide-plank floors and country antique furnishings. Eight plainer rooms are in an adjacent building. Some have TVs. Guests have access to a sitting room and an outdoor pool. *Rates* (including breakfast): Weekends $95 to $110 double, weekdays $60 to $85 double.

The view from the sunroom and the flagstone terrace is reason enough to stay at **Hilltop Haven,** 175 Dibble Hill Rd., West Cornwall, CT 06796 (☎ 860/672-6871), but there are others—notably the 63 surrounding acres and the setting on a bluff above the Housatonic River with views of the Berkshire foothills, the Taconic Mountains, and the distant Catskills. Book lovers will appreciate the library with its fieldstone fireplace, soaring cathedral ceiling, oriental rugs, floor-to-ceiling glass bookcases, and Victorian furnishings. Additional relaxing space can be found in the music room, which has a baby grand piano, French tile fireplace, and more oriental rugs. There are only two guest rooms (both with private baths), each furnished with a double bed, armchairs, a writing desk, coffeemaker, and phone. Breakfast, featuring such favorites as Grand Marnier French toast, is served in the sunroom, the library, or on the terrace. *Rates* (including breakfast): $140 double.

WEST CORNWALL DINING

The **Brookside Bistro,** on Route 128 in West Cornwall (☎ 860/672-6601), has a serene location overlooking a fast-flowing brook. In summer the deck is the preferred dining area; at other times diners sit on burgundy or dusty-pink banquettes at butcher-block tables in a light, modern room. The menu changes frequently, but always features French classics. For example, there might be full-flavored coq au vin, rib-eye steak with béarnaise sauce, and mussels poached in a broth of white wine and shallots and served with garlic mayonnaise. Prices range from $14 to $18. Appetizers might include brie en croûte with leek sauce; or eggplant terrine rolled and stuffed with goat cheese, spinach, and roasted red pepper. Similar classics are offered at lunch—daube Provençale; a delicious stew made with beef, bacon, onions, mushrooms, tomato, and garlic; or poached salmon with mustard sauce; roast chicken; and several charcuterie salads. *Hours:* Wednesday to Sunday noon to 2pm and 6 to 9pm. Closed for 3 weeks in March.

SHARON LODGING

The 1890 **Colonial Bed & Breakfast**, Route 41 (P.O. Box 25), Sharon, CT 06069 (☎ 860/364-0436), is an elegant center-hall colonial home set on 5 acres. The innkeeper was formerly a flight attendant, and the comfortable living room is filled with objets d'art she acquired all over the world—Japanese screens, Indian buddhas, Etruscan pieces, and so on. The three guest rooms (all with bath) are spacious and eclectically furnished with a mixture of pieces. One has a private entrance and offers a kitchenette with a hot plate, sink, and microwave. The suite with twin beds and a sitting room is pleasant, too. *Rates* (including breakfast): Summer, $119 double weekends, $95 double weekdays; rest of the year, $105 double weekends, $85 double weekdays.

JUST ACROSS THE BORDER IN NEW YORK
Lodging & Dining in Dover Plains, N.Y.

Across the state border, the **Old Drovers Inn**, on East Duncan Hill Road, 3 miles south of Dover Plains off Route 22 (☎ 914/832-9311), is loaded with atmosphere acquired over the last 250 years. The stairs leading to the four guest rooms creak, as do the floors, and the ceilings are low. The upstairs library offers three walls of books, plus some comfy chairs in front of the wood-molded fireplace. Two other sitting rooms are available, both with fireplaces—one formally furnished in Empire style with a striking bull's-eye mirror. The guest rooms (three with wood-burning fireplaces) are variously furnished. One has a sleigh bed; another contains cannonball beds, wing chairs for fireside dozing, candlestand tables, and wainscoting. The Meeting Room has a unique barrel-shaped ceiling and is furnished with two antique beds, a fireplace, a desk, and wing chairs.

The Tap Room, with its crackling fire, heavy wood beams, stone walls, and attractive old banquettes, is one of the region's most appealing dining rooms. Pewter and china adorn the space; copper pans, scoops, and strainers grace the brick fireplace. The tables are set with candles, pewter, and burgundy cloths. The bill of fare is written on a chalkboard, and although it changes daily, it's likely to offer the following for dinner: browned turkey hash with mustard sauce, broiled double-cut rack of lamb chops served with a tangy tomato chutney, pan-seared scallops with red wine and garlic jus, and cowboy steak with caramelized onions. Appetizers might include lobster-and-corn chowder, vegetable terrine with tomato vinaigrette, and cheddar-cheese soup, an Old Drovers specialty that actually tastes very good. The excellent wine list features more than 200 selections. Dinner prices run $17 to $35; luncheon fare is similar, but priced from $11.75 to $18.75. The outdoor patio is lovely in summer.

Rates: $160 to $240 double weekdays including continental breakfast; $330 to $405 double weekends including breakfast and dinner for two. *Dining hours:* Friday to Sunday noon to 3pm; Monday, Tuesday, and Thursday 5:30 to 9pm, Friday 5:30 to 10pm, and Sunday 3 to 8:30pm.

A Special Retreat & Fine Dining in Amenia, N.Y.

For a truly inspirational weekend retreat, head to **Troutbeck**, Leedsville Road, Amenia, NY 12501 (☎ 914/373-9681; www.troutbeck.com). Acres of flower- and shrub-filled gardens surround this lovely ivy-covered Tudoresque country house. It once belonged to Myron B. Benton, a poet/naturalist friend of Ralph Waldo Emerson, naturalist John Burroughs, and Henry David Thoreau; it was a gathering place for 1920s literati and liberals. A brook courses through the gardens, and along its banks daffodils, blue grape hyacinths, and crimson, gold, and purple tulips blossom in spring, with lilacs and apple blossoms adding their fragrant scent and colors. Beyond the gardens are over 400 wooded acres.

During the week the property is used for conferences, but on weekends it's open as a country resort. There are 42 accommodations (19 in the main house, 18 in the Farmhouse, 5 in the Garden House); 37 have baths and 9 have fireplaces. Many have porches and feature canopied beds; each is individually decorated with antique reproductions. Some are furnished in an Early American style; in the main house the style is more European. There are also six handsome rooms with whirlpool tubs located above the ballroom. The house is filled with gorgeous authentic antiques. Entrance-parlor floors are covered with oriental runners and rugs, Chinese porcelain lamps harmonize with a handsome French partner's desk, while richly upholstered French chairs, Queen Anne chairs, and a carved sideboard all blend perfectly. Beamed ceilings, leaded windows, and fresh flowers underline the very English atmosphere. For quiet conversation there's a luxurious sitting room with a grand player-piano and fireplace, plus an adjacent bar with a fireplace. There are tennis courts, indoor and outdoor pools, 13,000 books, and videotapes for guest entertainment.

The dining rooms overlook a pond populated with white ducks. The menu changes weekly, but a weekend menu might begin with salmon pastrami with fresh corn cakes, crème fraîche, and chive oil; or grilled asparagus with balsamic vinegar and Parmesan crisps. There might be nine or so dishes— Dunham brook trout roasted on a cedar plank, filet mignon with a red wine reduction, or rack of lamb with tapenade. Prices range from $15 to $25. Among the desserts may be a luscious lemon tart, chocolate ganache torte, or a selection of sorbets and gelato. An open bar is included for inn guests, and wine is served during meals. In good weather, lunches are served poolside.

Rates: Friday 5pm to Sunday 2pm, $650 to $1,075 per couple (including six meals with drinks). One night only, $360 to $620 per couple (including three meals with drinks).

A visit to the **Cascade Mountain Winery & Restaurant**, Flint Hill Road, Amenia (☎ 914/373-9021), is a delightful experience. It's out in the country, surrounded by meadows and fields, and in summer the deck is a lovely place to enjoy lunch or an early dinner. Cascade Mountain is one of the leading Hudson Valley wineries, making a good Seyval blanc as well as Beaujolais-style reds and late-harvest dessert wine. The lunch menu offers a good balance between salads and light and heavier dishes. There might be a fine smoked-trout plate, or pâté plus local Coach Farm and Hollow Road cheeses, or house-smoked baby-back barbecued ribs with Dijon potato salad. The dinner menu changes weekly. It's likely to feature four or so main dishes, like roast leg of lamb with natural jus and horseradish, or grilled salmon with lemon-caper beurre blanc. The terrine of Hudson Valley foie gras with lavender vignoles reduction and sautéed ramps makes a luxurious beginning. To finish, select the rich frozen sabayon with blackberries, or fresh apple crisp, also enhanced by sabayon. Prices are $9 to $15 at lunch and $22 to $30 at dinner. Free tours and tastings are given at the winery on weekends. It's located off Route 22 north of Amenia. *Winery Tours:* Daily 11am to 5pm. *Dining hours:* Daily noon to 3pm, and Saturday 6 to 9pm.

LAKEVILLE LODGING & DINING

Set on 12 acres, the **Wake Robin Inn**, Route 41, Sharon Rd., Lakeville, CT 06039 (☎ 860/435-2515), is located in an imposing 1896 building that originally served as a school. With its classical portico and balustraded terrace, it's quite impressive. The most attractive accommodations are the 24 rooms in this main building. They are equipped with private baths, TVs, and telephones and are furnished with a mixture of eclectic pieces, from sleigh beds to oak dressers. There are also 15 rooms in a motel-style addition that have private baths (no TVs or phones). *Rates:* $110 to $170 double; $220 suite.

Although the exterior of the **Interlaken Inn**, 74 Interlaken Rd. (west of Route 41 on Route 112), Lakeville, CT 06039 (☎ 860/435-9878), screams "modern convention complex," the 80 rooms will win you over with their plush comforts, especially the 7 duplex town-house suites at the back of the property, each with a full kitchen, a living room with fireplace, a sleeping loft containing two double beds, two baths, and access to a tree-shaded deck. The Victorian House's 11 old-world rooms have brass beds and antiques, while the 55 deluxe rooms have a pleasant contemporary look. And six rooms, with Queen Anne reproductions, are in a fine English Tudor–style house. All rooms have air-conditioning, private baths, and cable TV/VCRs.

The Interlaken is set on 30 beautifully kept acres between two lakes. You can lounge by the heated outdoor pool or on the shore of Lake Wononscopumic, where canoes, paddleboats, and rowboats are available. Two tennis courts, a nine-hole golf course plus pitch-and-putt facility, a games room with table tennis and billiards, and a fitness center with racquetball courts complete the facilities. A variety of massage treatments is available at the fitness center.

The Vineyard is a contemporary-style dining room serving modern American cuisine—oven-roasted halibut on a bed of sweet onions with pine nuts, chili peppers, tomato, and lemon; pork medallions in a pomegranate sweet and sour sauce; and breast of chicken stuffed with cheese and fresh asparagus and topped with sun-dried tomato sauce. Prices range from $15 to $23. Appetizers range from traditional items like mussels steamed in white wine, leeks, and saffron to such Greek-style dishes as hummus and marinated stuffed grape leaves. Save room for the chocolate decadence, a rich chocolate-mousse cake layered with raspberry confit and chocolate cream and served with raspberry sauce, or the Interlaken torte, a walnut-and-maple cake soaked in rum and served with crème Chantilly. There's also a deck for summer dining. Brunch ($16 per person) is buffet style, offering prime rib, ham, smoked salmon, salads, canapés, and much more. The Circuit Lounge, overlooking the pool and cocktail lounge, doubles as a luncheon spot; it's filled with "auto art," which should appeal to Lime Rock visitors. On weekend nights bands entertain here.

Rates: Deluxe rooms and Victorian House, weekends $159 to $199 double, weekdays $109 to $139 double; town-house suite, $285 for two. Rates reduced about 20% in winter. *Dining hours:* Monday to Thursday 7 to 10am, 11:30am to 2:30pm, and 5:30 to 9pm; Friday 7 to 10am, 11:30am to 2:30pm, and 5:30 to 10pm; Saturday 7 to 10:30am, 11:30am to 2:30pm, and 5:30 to 10pm; Sunday 7:30 to 10am, 11am to 2pm, and 5:30 to 9pm.

LAKEVILLE DINING

The **Woodland Restaurant**, Route 41 (☎ 860/435-0578), is an airy plant-filled restaurant. In one of the six large booths you can dine at lunchtime on a Woodlands specialty of a muffin with mushrooms, onions, and tomatoes. You can eat more substantially at dinner with such items as chicken breast sautéed with lemon, capers, and pine nuts; salmon crusted with pistachio nuts and served with lemon-champagne beurre blanc; and balsamic-glazed pork chops with grilled eggplant and risotto cakes. Dishes are priced from $14 to $20. Chalkboard specials emphasize such seafood dishes as Cajun-blackened tuna, but might also offer barbecued ribs and several pasta dishes. *Hours:* Tuesday to Thursday 11:30am to 2:30pm and 5:30 to 9pm, Friday 11:30am to 2:30pm and 5:30 to 10pm, Saturday 11:30am to 2pm and 5:30 to 10pm, Sunday 5:30 to 8:30pm. Closed Sunday and Monday, 2 weeks following Labor Day, and 2 weeks in March.

SALISBURY LODGING & DINING

The **Ragamont Inn**, Main Street, Salisbury, CT 06068 (☎ 860/435-2372), has offered solace and sustenance to passing travelers for the last 180 years, and today people are still sitting happily under the green-and-white-striped awning or are cozily ensconced in the plank-floored dining room warmed by a blazing fire. The nine guest rooms are unique and very fairly priced—a suite with a fireplace and low-beamed ceiling rents for only $110. Room 6 is particularly attractive, thanks to the cast-iron stove, pine floor, shield-back chairs, and an old desk that give it character.

The dining room is known for the many Swiss-inspired dishes of chef/owner Rolf Schenkel—sauerbraten, Wienerschnitzel, and jaegerschnitzel (with white wine and mushrooms), along with fine fresh scrod, salmon, swordfish, and other seafood. Main courses range from $16 to $21. The linzertorte and peach-custard pie are dessert favorites, while at brunch raclette and beef burgundy add some interest to the typical eggs Benedict and waffles menu.

Rates: May to November 1, $100 to $130 double. *Dining hours:* Wednesday to Thursday 5:30 to 9pm, Friday to Saturday 6 to 10pm, Sunday 5 to 9pm.

Under Mountain Inn, 482 Under Mountain Rd. (Route 41), Salisbury, CT 06068 (☎ 860/435-0242; fax 860/435-2379), is 5 miles out of Salisbury in a secluded 1732 white clapboard farmhouse that stands on 3 acres. Peter and Marged Higginson offer seven rooms (all with bath) that provide a charming, serene home away from home. They'll most likely contain a large canopied or four-poster bed, a couple of Williamsburg blue wing chairs, and a fine cherry highboy placed on wide-plank floors that are softened by hook rugs. Early American wallpapers add character. The downstairs parlors are comfortable, and among the Early American furnishings you'll find an antique Welsh cupboard that Marged's grandfather made. The Union Jack flies outside, and the *Manchester Guardian* is available, along with numerous books about Britain and a video collection of more than 100 British films.

There are three intimate dining rooms with fireplaces. A limited menu featuring four entrees is offered to guests. It might include roast goose, chicken tarragon, roast leg of lamb, and fish du jour. For British expatriates or Anglophiles there's also steak-and-kidney pie and bangers and mash, and Marged provides a "proper" cup of tea from a pot kept warm under a tea cozy. For dessert there's authentic sherry trifle or lemon curd tart and home-baked pies. Main courses are priced from $12 to $18. Note that the dining room is open to the public by reservation on Friday and Saturday only.

Rates: MAP (2-night package that includes two dinners and two breakfasts) $350 to $400 double. Special discounted weekday packages are also available. From November 1 to September 30 (except holidays) Wednesday is free when you stay Monday and Tuesday. *Dining hours:* Friday and Saturday 6 to 8pm by reservation.

At the center of Salisbury, the lovely **White Hart Inn,** on the Green, Salisbury, CT 06068 (☎ 860/435-0030), is more than 200 years old. Its 26 rooms are prettily decorated in chintz with antique reproductions (each has a bath, a TV, a phone, and air-conditioning). The front porch is the quintessential place to catch the quiet stirring of a New England village.

The inn is famous for the well-prepared and beautifully presented cuisine served in the American Grill, a comfortable dining room that has a glamorous glow in the evening. Start with the grilled pancetta-wrapped shrimp served with bruschetta and Tuscan bean puree, or the slow roasted beef with chèvre and red wine–walnut vinaigrette. Among the main courses might be grilled salmon with an Asian barbecue sauce, grilled lamb in a Pinot Noir sauce, or medallions of pork with a Calvados sauce. There are also several steaks on the menu served in a variety of ways, plus a very popular signature dish—tuna towers, served with a soy ginger sauce. Prices range from $17 to $26. The tavern with a double fireplace is also a popular spot for lunch (sandwiches, salads, pizza, and such light entrees as chicken pot pie or cold poached salmon). The Garden Room is the breakfast spot for delicious blueberry pancakes or French toast made with challah bread as well as traditional egg dishes. Sunday brunch offers an even more lavish selection of dishes including burritos with scrambled eggs, salsa, sour cream, and hash browns. Prices range from $4 to $13.

Rates: April to October, weekends $135 to $205 double, weekdays $115 to $180 double; November to April, $95 to $165 double. *Dining hours:* Garden Room, Monday to Saturday 7 to 10am, Monday to Friday 11:30am to 2:30pm and all day Saturday and Sunday; Tavern, Monday to Friday 11:30am to 2:30pm, Saturday and Sunday 11:30am to 5pm, Sunday to Thursday 5 to 9:30pm and Friday and Saturday 5 to 10:30pm; American Grill, Sunday 8am to 1pm and 5:30 to 10pm, Friday and Saturday 5:30 to 10pm.

EAST TO NORFOLK, RIVERTON & WINSTED

NORFOLK ATTRACTIONS

From Salisbury, you can take Route 44 all the way to Norfolk, which in mid-June and July hosts **Yale's Norfolk Chamber Music Festival** (☎ 860/542-3000), featuring, among others, the Tokyo String Quartet at the Ellen Battell Stoeckel Estate.

To get a sense of this quintessential New England village, walk around the Green, noting the **Eldridge Fountain**, designed by Stanford White; the tall-steepled **Church of Christ** (ca. 1814), next to the **White House** (home of the Yale Summer School of Music and Art); the Richardson-style **library** (ca. 1888); and the **Historical Society Museum**, featuring a small collection of Connecticut clocks and other local historical artifacts.

Norfolk also has some offbeat attractions. For example, you might like to call ahead and make an appointment to visit **harpsichord maker** Carl Dudash's studio (☎ 860/542-5753). At **Hillside Gardens**, Litchfield Road, Norfolk (☎ 860/542-5345), you can purchase some herbaceous perennials and view the gardens of Mary Ann and Frederick McGourty, who are well known in horticultural circles. The **Horse and Carriage Livery** (☎ 860/542-6085) is another interesting stop, where you can sign up for a horse-drawn carriage ride in summer and a sleigh ride in winter. The charge for a 40-minute to an hour-long ride is $75 for two people.

Norfolk also boasts three state parks for hiking and picnicking: **Haystack Mountain** (from Norfolk, follow Route 44 west and take Route 272 north for a mile to the entrance), **Campbell Falls State Park** (another 6 miles along Route 272), and **Dennis Hill State Park** (take Route 272 south). Haystack Mountain and Dennis Hill have at their summits stone monuments affording grand views.

RIVERTON ATTRACTIONS

Back on Route 44, either you can proceed into Winsted, the self-proclaimed mountain laurel capital, then double back on Route 20 to Riverton, or you can drive directly to Riverton by cutting off on one of the back roads.

Riverton was once called "Hitchcocksville" after the famous and familiar **Hitchcock chairs**, emblazoned with bronze stencils of flowers, fruits, acanthus, and horns of plenty. They were made here on the banks of the Farmington River from 1826, when Lambert Hitchcock established his factory, until 1992 when the factory relocated to New Hartford. You can still purchase the chairs here in the factory store (☎ 860/379-4826). *Hours:* Monday to Saturday 10am to 5pm, Sunday noon to 5pm.

Nearby, **People's State Forest**, Route 44, Barkhamsted, is a must during fall, as is the area around Winsted in spring, when this town throws a big **Mountain Laurel Festival**. The best place to view the blossoms is at Indian Lookout, off Route 4 in Torrington, halfway to Litchfield.

NORFOLK LODGING & DINING

The **Mountain View Inn**, Route 272, Norfolk, CT 06058 (☎ 860/542-6991; fax 860/542-5689; www.mvinn.com), occupies a restored 1875 Victorian.

The oak staircase leads to 10 rooms (8 with bath). They are furnished with brass or four-poster beds, fainting couches, rockers, and other eclectic, Victorian-style pieces. Guests are served a full American breakfast featuring such dishes as omelets and waffles. On Friday and Saturday, from May through October, the inn is open for dinner; among the specialties offered are steaks, the catch of the day, bourbon bacon scallops, and roast duck with a savory fruit sauce, all priced from $14 to $21. Guests can relax on the porch overlooking a corner of the 5-acre grounds and walk to the chamber music concerts at the Yale Summer School. There's also a sitting room with cozy hearth for those frosty winter days. *Rates* (including breakfast): $85 to $100 double without bath, $100 to $145 double with bath.

The **Blackberry River Inn,** Route 44, Norfolk, CT 06058 (☎ 860/542-5100), contains 20 rooms (4 with wood-burning fireplaces) furnished with chintz and maple pieces in a country style. The rooms in the main inn have a fireplace, and the suites have either a fireplace or a Jacuzzi. Double fireplaces warm the public areas in the lounge/parlors, and guests can use the cherry-paneled library. There are 27 acres to enjoy, particularly in winter on cross-country skis. An outdoor pool and a tennis court complete the facilities. *Rates* (including breakfast): $110 to $210 double. Closed in March.

Manor House, the Inn at Norfolk, 69 Maple Avenue , Norfolk, CT 06058 (☎ 860/542-5690; fax 860/542-5690; www.manorhouse-norfolk.com), is indeed as grand as it sounds. A late Victorian building with tall Elizabethan chimneys and lattice windows, it was built in 1898 by architect Charles Spofford, who helped design, of all things, the London Underground. He was the son of Ainsworth Rand Spofford, a Cincinnati publisher who served in President Abraham Lincoln's administration. Charles was friendly with Louis Comfort Tiffany, who gave the windows that adorn the library and living room as a housewarming gift. Fine architectural details can be found throughout the house—a classical stucco frieze in the living room depicting Day being led by Night across the Sky, an Italianate green-tile fireplace in the dining room, a cherry-paneled staircase, and geometric patterns everywhere.

Mannequins dressed in antique costumes are scattered about, reflecting the inspiration of Diane Tremblay, who runs the place with her husband, Henry. Both love catering to their guests, providing information about the area, and preparing breakfast, which is served in a formal dining room at a large table surrounded by shield-back chairs. A sideboard and silver service add to the gracious atmosphere. Orange waffles, scrambled eggs with chives, blueberry pancakes, and poached eggs with lemon butter and chive sauce might be breakfast choices; these are accompanied by homemade breads, honey from beehives on the property, or raspberries from their own raspberry canes.

Nine individually decorated rooms, two with wood-burning fireplaces, two with gas fireplaces, and two with whirlpools are available. The large Spofford Room has a carved-wood fireplace, a private balcony, and a variety of furnishings—canopied bed, rocker, chest of drawers, dressing table, and cane-backed sofa. The Lincoln Room also has a fireplace; a sleigh bed with a half canopy and a Récamier sofa are two of the more characterful pieces. La Chambre is a small, charming room furnished with a brass-and-iron bed and lilac wing chairs. The most expensive room, the Victorian, has a gas fireplace and a double whirlpool tub that is set under a large skylight. Additional amenities include games (board games, Trivial Pursuit) that can be played in an airy conservatory-style room and chairs and tables set out in the yard for relaxing. *Rates* (including breakfast): $100 to $235 double.

George Schumaker has created luxurious and romantic surroundings at **Greenwoods Gate**, 105 Greenwoods Rd. East, Norfolk, CT 06058 (☎ 860/542-5439), making it a perfect place to relax. The parlor of this 1797 center-hall colonial home is richly furnished with oriental carpeting, pale-lemon wing chairs, a drop-leaf cherry table, a needlepointed French-style chair, and a grand piano; the focal point is the fireplace. The breakfast room contains a round table and a breakfront, among other fine objects. The coziest room is undoubtedly the wood-paneled country-style kitchen, decorated with wicker baskets and a cookie-cutter collection. Breakfasts featuring such dishes as omelets with cream cheese and strawberries, Grand Marnier French toast, and an open-face frittata with spinach, onions, and feta cheese are prepared. A deck off the kitchen furnished with white wicker makes an ideal breakfast spot.

All six guest rooms have fresh flowers, starched and ironed sheets, and fragrance and other amenities in the bathrooms. The E. J. Truscott Suite, off the kitchen, is very romantic: A Belgian lace coverlet and pillows grace the brass-and-iron bed, while an Empire chest, porcelain lamps, a marble bedside table, and a dollhouse filled with charming miniatures are set against China blue wallpaper. The Lucy Phelps Room is small, but prettily turned out in green and rose. The Levi Thompson Suite is a spectacular and private accommodation. Here you'll find a whirlpool bath and a split of champagne. A small foyer leads into a bilevel pink-and-blue room, the lower half serving as a sitting room. Upstairs, the cherry-wood bed sits under a brilliant stained-glass window. It's like being in your own dollhouse. *Rates* (including breakfast): $85 (Lucy Phelps Room) to $245 (Levi Thompson Suite) for two people. Mid-November to May, rooms are discounted 10%.

RIVERTON LODGING & DINING

The **Old Riverton Inn**, Route 20 (P.O. Box 6), Riverton, CT 06065 (☎ 860/379-8678), overlooks the west branch of the Farmington River. This old inn has been quenching the thirsty, feeding the hungry, and soothing the tired since 1796—the uneven floors and small doorways testify to its age. The 12 homey rooms, several with fireplaces, are all comfortably, if not stylishly, decorated. Room 3, for instance, has a bed with a chenille bedspread, a chest, and an adjustable wooden floor lamp, while its bath has a claw-foot tub/shower. Another room contains wicker chairs and a spinning wheel. A couple of rooms have spindle four-poster beds with canopies.

Traditional fare is served in the low-beamed dining room—good seafood and steaks, plus such specialties as veal Marsala, baked stuffed pork chop with applesauce, and chicken with black cherry sauce. Prices range from $13 to $21. *Rates* (including breakfast): $95 to $190 double. *Dining hours:* Wednesday to Friday noon to 2:30pm and 5 to 8:30pm, Saturday noon to 2:30pm and 5 to 9pm, Sunday 11am to 2pm and 5 to 8pm.

LITCHFIELD

LITCHFIELD ATTRACTIONS

Graceful, tree-lined streets, 18th-century residences, and the much-photographed Congregational church at the east end of the Village Green make Litchfield a fine example of a colonial revival village. Although many of the homes were built in the late 18th century, many have been drastically altered from their original appearance. In fact, many were "colonialized" during the late 19th and early 20th centuries. Begin your explorations by picking up a map at the historical society (see below) or at the information booth at the west end of the Green (summer only). Once a year, in July, Litchfield's historic homes are opened to the public (see "Events & Festivals to Plan Your Trip Around," above).

Try to spend some time at the **Litchfield Historical Society, Library, and Museum,** on the corner of South Street and the Green (☎ 860/567-4501). View the permanent display of portraits by Ralph Earl, including one of Mariann Wolcott, whose father, Oliver, was a town luminary and a signer of the Declaration of Independence. A lady of great determination, if her portrait is anything to go by, she undoubtedly helped mold the bullets cast from the statue of George III that had been brought from New York for that purpose during the American Revolution. Other exhibits explore the town's history through local furniture, decorative arts, textiles, and photographs. *Hours:* Mid-April to mid-November, Tuesday to Saturday 11am to 5pm, Sunday 1 to 5pm. *Admission* (including Tapping Reeve House and Law School, below): $5 adults, $3 seniors and students, free for children ages 15 and under.

From the historical society, a walk down South Street will bring you to the **Samuel Seymour House** (third down on the right), now the Episcopal rectory, but once John C. Calhoun's lodging place while he attended law school.

Tapping Reeve's Law School (☎ 860/567-4501), is located in the two buildings next door. Tapping Reeve was a Princeton graduate who moved to Litchfield in 1773, bringing his frail wife, Sally, sister of Aaron Burr. Burr was Reeve's first law student. On the tour of the house you can see the parlor Reeve used initially as a classroom and several rooms filled with the usual period antiques. What's most interesting is the wonderfully detailed inventory of his 1824 estate, which lists, among other things, "60 pounds of butter (not good) @ 10¢—$6; 160 pounds of ham and shoulders @ 6¢ a pound—$9.60," and "dwelling house and homestead . . . $3,600."

In the law school building next door, to which he later moved, you can view portraits of the many famous men who were trained at this first law school, including two vice presidents, Aaron Burr and John C. Calhoun; three Supreme Court justices; six cabinet members; artist George Catlin; and more than 100 congressmen. Reeve transformed the way lawyers were trained by introducing a fixed curriculum, oral exams, and "moot court," all of which are familiar to contemporary law students. The school's curriculum and rules and the events in the personal lives of Judge Reeve and his partner, Judge Gould, make for interesting reading. A new exhibit really helps visitors experience what life was like between 1784 and 1833, when the law school was operating. You'll be given a "passport" upon entering the exhibit that contains information about an actual student; you'll also see a video that dramatizes the life of several students and listen to snippets of lectures. *Hours:* Mid-May to mid-October, Tuesday to Saturday 11am to 5pm, Sunday 1 to 5pm. *Admission:* $5 adults, $3 students and seniors, free for children ages 12 and under.

Across from the law school you can see **Oliver Wolcott's house,** to which the equestrian statue of George III was dragged all the way from Manhattan's Bowling Green after it had been pulled down by New York's Sons of Liberty. Here, it was melted down into bullets by the redoubtable ladies of Litchfield. Mr. Wolcott was, of course, a signer of the Declaration of Independence, a member of the Continental Congress, and governor of Connecticut from 1796. During his lifetime he entertained George Washington, the Marquis de Lafayette, and Alexander Hamilton at this house, which is still in the Wolcott family.

If you continue south to where the road divides and take the right fork, you'll come to another famous son's house, that of **Ethan Allen,** the Revolutionary War hero who captured Fort Ticonderoga with his Green Mountain Boys.

Heading in the other direction up North Street from the Green will bring you to the **home of Benjamin Talmadge** (1775), George Washington's aide, past the site of **Miss Pierce's School,** the first American institution of higher education for women, founded in 1792. Young women from the school continued to take their daily walks under the elms to the tune of a flute and flageolet until 1855. Just beyond Prospect Street, on the left side, is the site of the **Beecher homestead,** where Henry Ward Beecher and his sister, Harriet Beecher Stowe, were born. Ahead, in the middle of the fork, stands the **house of Alexander Catlin,** uncle to the more famous George, and a member of the Wolcott, Talmadge group that formed the Litchfield China Trading Company.

Within a few miles of the village are several interesting spots: The **White Memorial Foundation,** west of Litchfield on Route 202 (☎ 860/567-0857), established in 1913, is a lovely place to stroll, whatever the season. It borders much of the shore of Bantam Lake. Within this 4,000-acre wildlife sanctuary are 35 miles of hiking, cross-country skiing, and horseback-riding trails; several picnic areas; and a museum (☎ 860/567-0857; open Monday to Saturday 9am to 5pm, Sunday noon to 5pm) dedicated to conservation and ecology. This museum includes various exhibits relating the history of the property and documenting the natural life found in the various habitats. The Holbrook Bird Observatory overlooks an area specially landscaped to attract a variety of birds in all seasons. Field trips are offered on Saturday, and there's camping at two campgrounds.

SHOPPING

In Litchfield, you can also browse through the interesting shops and boutiques clustered along **West Street** facing the Green and along **Cobble Court** at South and East streets. **White Flower Farm** (☎ 860/567-8789), just south of Litchfield, is a 200-acre retail and mail-order plant nursery you might enjoy, either for shopping or for just viewing the colorful displays in the 8-acre garden and the greenhouse (especially beautiful in July, when the begonias bloom).

On the way to Lake Waramaug, stop in New Preston and browse the handful of stores here. Book lovers will want to seek out **Ray Boas,** 6 Church St.

(☎ 860/868-9596), located across the creek by New Preston falls. It occupies an old barn that is filled with thousands of great books, which are well cataloged. Specialties include decorative arts and Americana. On Main Street, **Del Mediterraneo** (☎ 860/868-8070) has brilliantly colored and crafted ceramics and pottery from Spain. Also don't miss the **Garden House** (☎ 860/868-6790), which sells French, English, and American antique furnishings for the garden including statuary, urns, birdbaths, and fountains.

WINERIES

Two miles east of Litchfield, the **Haight Vineyard**, 29 Chestnut Hill Rd. (☎ 860/567-4045), off Route 118, was established in 1978. Today it offers walks through the vineyards, fermentation and aging areas, and the usual tastings. Wines are also sold by the glass and the bottle in the veranda wine bar. *Hours:* Monday to Saturday 10:30am to 5pm, Sunday noon to 5pm.

Out at Lake Waramaug, the **Hopkins Vineyard** (☎ 860/868-7954) occupies a 19th-century barn in an idyllic spot overlooking the lake and offers self-guided tours and some fine wines for tasting. The vineyard shop is stocked with gourmet foods and home, garden, and wine accessories. *Tours:* Saturday and Sunday at 2pm (charge $1). *Hours:* March to December, Monday to Saturday 10am to 5pm, Sunday 11am to 5pm; January to February, Friday to Saturday 10am to 5pm, Sunday 11am to 5pm.

LITCHFIELD LODGING & DINING

Litchfield itself has no truly special places to stay, except for the **Tollgate Hill Inn**, P.O. Box 1339, Litchfield, CT 06759 (☎ 860/567-4545), 3 miles north of the Village Green. Innkeepers Fritz and Anne Zivic have meticulously restored this fine 225-year-old colonial home, retaining those small details—like the original iron latches and hinges and the salmon milk-paint in the bar—that give the place a special feel.

They've furnished their 15 rooms and 5 suites with locally made reproductions of antique cherry candle stands, Shaker tables, quilt stands, and a butler's bar and added extra-special elements like goose-down comforters and choice Hinson wallpapers. All rooms have baths, air-conditioning, TVs, and phones. The two front rooms have fireplaces and canopied four-posters. The suites have fireplaces, TV/VCRs, bar/refrigerators, and canopied beds. Each room is known by its predominating color: peach, red, green, brown, lavender, or blue. Guests enjoy breakfast—freshly squeezed fruit juice, croissants, banana or blueberry bread with sweet butter—in their rooms, served on fine china arranged on a wicker tray.

The dining rooms consist of a small formal room with a corner cupboard and an oriental carpet, a low-ceilinged tavern room, and a very large "ballroom" overlooked by a real fiddler's loft. Each has a welcoming fire in winter. The seasonal menus offer new American cuisine—cinnamon-walnut crusted mahimahi with a zested orange glaze; grilled loin of pork with sun-dried tomatoes and a light tomato cream basil sauce; roasted duck with lime marmalade and apple compote; and a traditional shellfish pie made with shrimp, scallops, lobster, and crab in cream sauce under puff pastry. Prices range from $18 to $24. The Sunday buffet brunch featuring made-to-order omelets and a full spread of food is a popular place to rendezvous (it's priced at $12.95).

Rates (including continental breakfast): Mid-May to January 1 and all weekends, $120 to $150 double, from $185 suite; rest of the year, $100 to $125 double, $160 suite. *Dining hours:* Monday and Wednesday to Friday noon to 3pm and 5:30 to 9pm, Saturday noon to 3pm and 5:30 to 10pm, Sunday 11am to 2pm and 5 to 8pm.

LITCHFIELD DINING

The best dining is to be found at the Tollgate Hill Inn (above) and the restaurants around Lake Waramaug, most notably the Hopkins and Boulders Inns (below).

In Litchfield itself, though, is the outstanding **West Street Grill**, West Street, On the Green (☎ 860/567-3885), a study in black. Black-and-white-striped banquettes, black-framed mirrors, and black Windsor chairs create the sleek ambience. The food is rated as some of the best in the state. The menu changes seasonally, but there's always a broad range of tempting appetizers. The Thai-style shrimp are served with spiced cilantro sauce, and the nori-wrapped salmon is served with pickled ginger, wasabi, and ponzu sauce. Among the main courses are several pastas—like the flavorful linguine limoncello, which combines lemon juice, anchovy paste, garlic, red chili flakes, and kalamata olives. Other dishes are pan-seared dulce-crusted cod fillet in a malted vinegar and shallot reduction, and grilled marinated leg of lamb with white beans and a morel mushroom jus. Prices range from $19 to $24. *Hours:* Monday to Thursday 11:30am to 3pm and 5:30 to 9:30pm, Friday 11:30am to 2:30pm and 5:30 to 10pm, Saturday 11:30am to 4pm and 5:30 to 10pm, Sunday 11:30am to 4pm.

Grappa Restaurant and Trattoria, 26 Commons Dr., Litchfield (☎ 860/567-1616), is West Street Grill's inexpensive sister restaurant. Here you can secure some good wood-grilled pizzas. The basic pizzas are $5.50 for a 12-inch to $10 for a 16-inch pie. You can also select about 10 additional toppings—roasted garlic, black olives, shiitake mushrooms, hot sausage, and more for an additional small charge. Besides the pizzas, the menu offers a few starters like grilled portobello mushroom with warm goat cheese and balsamic vinaigrette, grilled calamari with a mustard seed vinaigrette, and baba ghanoush. *Hours:* Sunday, Wednesday, and Thursday 5 to 9:30pm, Friday and Saturday 5 to 10pm

The **County Seat on the Green**, 3 West St. (☎ 860/567-8069), is a favorite summer gathering spot at the corner of South Street. It offers a broadly appealing menu combining light fare like the classic Philadelphia steak and cheese or chicken quesadilla with heartier entrees that might include bourbon barbecued pork or roasted salmon with lemon-wine butter sauce. Prices range from $8 to $16. It's casual and comfortable at all hours. Note it's BYOB. *Hours:* Daily from 7am to midnight on weekends.

Opposite the Green, **Spinell's Litchfield Food Company**, West Street (☎ 860/567-3113), prepares spectacular box lunches and picnics. You can select from their 20 or so sandwiches and dozens of breads, cheeses, pâtes, and salads (pasta, rice, marinated vegetables, you name it). You might then walk out with a hamper containing smoked salmon, marinated portobello mushrooms, chicken breast stuffed with cheese and herbs, artichoke hearts in vinaigrette, a baguette or two, chocolate-mousse balls rolled in hazelnuts, and fresh seasonal fruit. A box lunch for one costs $7 to $15. *Hours:* Monday to Saturday 8am to 7pm, Sunday 8am to 6pm.

NEARBY LODGING & DINING
Lake Waramaug Lodging

Choice accommodations lie about a 15-minute drive west of Litchfield around Lake Waramaug, a summer resort area settled in the 1890s.

The **Boulders Inn**, Route 45, New Preston, CT 06777 (☎ 860/868-0541), is the premier accommodation on the lake. It offers a private beach for swimming, canoes, Sunfish, bicycles, a tennis court, and hiking trail up Pinnacle Mountain. As the name suggests, the main 1895 building is fashioned out of huge fieldstone boulders, plus granite lintels and shingles. It contains six individually decorated rooms and suites (all with bath and air-conditioning). Several have sunny window seats overlooking the lake, and all are furnished with antiques—sleigh beds, candlestand side tables, blanket chests, and the like. The comfortable living room furnished with sofas and wing chairs and the recently renovated library with well-stocked bookcases give great lake views. Four contemporary cottages, housing eight rooms, are nicely tucked away on the wooded hillside for ample privacy. Each has a porch, wood stove, or built-in fireplace, with a picture window facing the lake; several have double whirlpool baths. There are also three rooms in the carriage house, all with wood-burning fireplaces.

The inn's stone-walled dining room has a good reputation for serving innovative cuisine. The menu and specials change frequently, but sample appetizers might include Hudson Valley foie gras on frisée with blackberry compote; or duck quesadilla with goat cheese, grilled tomatillo salsa, and jalapeño crème fraîche. Entrees might include sesame-seared ahi tuna on wasabi-whipped potatoes with oriental vegetables and mango puree; pan-seared salmon on chive potato cakes with dill essence; or crisp-skinned duck breast on black beans, roasted vegetables, and corn salad with orange peppercorn sauce. Prices range from $18 to $24. A full breakfast of fresh fruit, pastries, eggs, pancakes, or omelets, and afternoon tea are also served. Guests can choose bed-and-breakfast only or MAP; most opt for the latter because it's only an additional $25 per person for a full dinner.

Rates (including breakfast and dinner): Memorial Day to November 1, $260 to $310 double ($25 per person weekend surcharge); winter rates are $50 less. B&B $50 less year-round. *Dining hours:* Summer, daily 6 to 8 or 9pm.

On the more remote west side of the lake, **The Birches Inn**, 233 West Shore Rd., New Preston, CT 06777 (☎ 860/868-1735), has been causing a stir with the cuisine offered in the dining room. The chef was trained in France, but the fare, which is meticulously prepared, is a fusion in inspiration. The menu is limited, offering about eight main courses plus daily specials. Among the entrees you might find grilled pork loin in a Calvados reduction, or steamed New Zealand mussels in a yellow coconut curry broth, and lo mein noodles with black tiger shrimp in a peanut saté sauce. Prices range from $16 to $19. Large picture windows overlook the lake, filling the room with light. To start try the grilled shrimp with a sweet chili and peanut crust served with ponzu sauce and wasabi aïoli, or the unusual roasted garlic custard—it succeeds in combining garlic into a custard with a sweet balsamic caramel flavor and then adding a portobello mushroom and some baby arugula. Desserts are also enticing, from the lime crème brûlée to the ultra-rich chocolate marquise, or the seasonal fruit tarts. There are more than a dozen wines available by the glass. The warm ambience is created by the coral palette and the addition of ficus, palms, and other plants. An open-air deck is a favorite spot in summer.

The eight rooms have been redecorated and furnished with an eclectic mix of furnishings from French-style armchairs to American antique dressers. They are equipped with air-conditioning, private baths, cable TVs, and phones; some are right down on the water in the boathouse. It's the dining room though that draws the crowds.

Rates (including continental breakfast and wine and cheese in the evening): May to October, weekends $185 to 310, midweek $135 to $235; November to April, weekends $160 to $235, midweek $105 to $160. *Dining hours:* Wednesday to Monday 5:30 to 9pm.

The **Hopkins Inn,** 22 Hopkins Rd., New Preston, CT 06777 (☎ 860/868-7295), is known primarily for its romantic location and dining room (open April to December only). When you dine here under the spreading chestnut tree, on a terrace overlooking the lake, watching the sun go down and the sky fill with stars, waited on by young women dressed in colorful dirndls, you'll swear you're dining by the Danube. The Swiss and many Austrian favorites on the menu will only help confirm the impression—backhendl with lingonberries, Wienerschnitzel, and rahmschnitzel. Other sample dishes include scallops in garlic butter, loin lamb chops, pork fillet in a Calvados sauce, plus steaks. Prices range from $17 to $20. The desserts are classics like pear belle Hélène and crème caramel, plus sundaes and parfaits. Luncheon and mid-afternoon menus are also served. Traditional breakfasts are also offered along with a dish called Tiroler Grosti, which is eggs over easy served on delicious rösti potatoes with bacon. Make sure you have dining reservations, especially on Friday and Saturday. The back tavern room is remarkable for its folk-painted bar and huge, rough-hewn beams.

The lemon-yellow house, built in 1847 as a summer home, offers 11 rooms and 2 apartments, available from late March to December. The apartments and nine of the rooms have private baths or showers. None contains a TV or phone; the furnishings are adequate in their homey, old-fashioned way. If you're lucky, you'll get a room with a brass bed or an Eastlake-style sofa.

Rates: $87 double with bath and lake view, $82 double with private bath, $78 double with lake view only; $94 per night for apartment. *Dining hours:* May to October, daily 8:30 to 9:30am, Tuesday to Saturday noon to 2pm; rest of the year, Tuesday to Thursday 6 to 9pm, Friday 6 to 10pm, Saturday 5:30 to 10pm, and Sunday 12:30 to 8:30pm.

New Preston Dining

Le Bon Coin, Route 202 (☎ 860/868-7763), is a typical French restaurant located in a small house occupying a very isolated spot. The decor is simple—country paneling, lace curtains, and paintings of typical French scenes—but the food is good and there's always a variety of enticing specials. Start with the assortment of smoked fish or the pork-and-duckling pâté flavored with cognac and port. Choose from among steak au poivre;

shrimp sautéed with tomatoes, parsley, and garlic; lamb sautéed with eggplant, peppers, tomatoes, and fresh herbs; or chicken breast with wild mushrooms. Crêpes Suzette or crème caramel makes a perfect conclusion. Prices run $16 to $24. *Hours:* Monday and Thursday to Saturday noon to 2pm and 6 to 9pm, Sunday 5 to 9pm (from 1pm in late September to Columbus Day).

In summer people are drawn to the pretty garden terrace at **Oliva,** Route 45, New Preston (☎ 860/868-1787). Here they can enjoy some fine Italian and Mediterranean fare. The daily changing menu offers a variety of choices, from pizza and sandwiches to five or so pasta and main dishes. For example, you might like a wonderful focaccia pizza made with onions, tomato, rosemary, and Gorgonzola; or a sandwich made with roasted squash, prosciutto, tomato, ricotta, and basil. Among the main dishes there might be farfalle with shallots, thyme, mixed wild mushrooms, and cream; or roasted chicken with pancetta, rosemary, white wine, and tomato. Prices range from $7 to $15. It's BYOB. *Hours:* Thursday to Sunday noon to 2:30pm, Wednesday to Sunday 5pm to closing.

SOUTHBURY, WOODBURY, WASHINGTON & ROXBURY

EXPLORING THE AREA

Start in Southbury, at the junction of Route 6 and I-84, and follow Route 6 east, passing Southbury Plaza. Take your first left at the set of lights to Heritage Village, a condominium complex that also shelters the "**Bazaar,**" with 25 specialty shops, two art galleries, three restaurants, and a resort—all under one roof.

Retrace your route and continue on Route 6 east toward Woodbury, driving along the "**Grand Army Highway of the Republic,**" so named because of its rich history as a major thoroughfare, used by Washington, Lafayette, and Rochambeau. For a side trip you can take Route 64 east off Route 6 to the **Whittemore Sanctuary,** especially recommended for birders, and to **Lake Quassapaug** in Middlebury, a large natural lake open to the public for swimming and boating. A family amusement park, **Quassy,** is also on the shoreline.

Going back on Route 6 east, you'll come to Woodbury, dubbed the antiques capital of Connecticut. There are close to 40 really fine **specialist antiques shops** to browse and shop—featuring everything from Early American furniture and paintings to country French, 18th-century English, oriental and Navajo rugs, and art deco.

The two historic points of interest in Woodbury are the Herd House and the Glebe House, within 1,500 yards of each other on Hollow Road (off Route 6 in the center of town). The **Herd House** is, in fact, two houses that have been joined (one ca. 1680, the other ca. 1720). It's furnished with period pieces and features a well-stocked herb garden. The **Glebe House** (☎ 203/263-2855) dates from the 1700s. Today the house contains period furniture and displays documents tracing the development of the Episcopal church. The garden is also notable for having been designed by the great English gardener Gertrude Jekyll. *Hours:* April to November, Wednesday to Sunday 1 to 4pm. *Admission:* $4.

From Woodbury, continue on Route 6 north to the junction of Route 61, taking it to **Bethlehem.** The best time to visit is around Christmas, when a special celebration features holiday arts and crafts, hayrides, festive music, a minifestival of lights, and, of course, a post office, where thousands of letters get the Bethlehem Christmas stamp. In August a horse show is held at the Bethlehem Fairgrounds, followed by a country fair in September.

From Bethlehem continue north on Route 61 to Route 109 and turn left to Lakeside, where you can visit one of the area's most fascinating art studios, **Lorenz Studios,** Route 109 (☎ 860/567-4280), the workplace of master glass blower and sculptor Larry LiVolsi. Roam through the outdoor sculpture garden and watch Larry working. He fashions often massive glass and metal sculptures, some of which are abstract and some of which are functional, like the tables made of swirls of colored glass. Browse in the gallery that displays LiVolsi's work along with paintings by Stephanie Kafka. *Hours:* Thursday to Monday 10am to 5pm. In spring, fall, and winter call ahead to make sure that someone is there.

From Lakeside Route 109 will take you to Washington Depot, home to the **Hickory Stick Bookshop** (☎ 860/868-0525), which is worth stopping at for new and secondhand books; it's a civilized place that even provides wing chairs for leisurely browsing.

From Washington Depot take Route 47 south to **Washington,** a picturesque town, much of whose charm derives from its setting on top of a hill. The heart of town lies on the Green around the Congregational church, built on the site of the original 1742 meeting house. Facing the Green are lovely 18th-century residences and a small post office housed in a white-clapboard colonial building that it shares with the country drugstore. The **Gunn Historical Museum and Library,** On the Green (☎ 860/868-7756), is located in a 1781 colonial house. It's named after Frederick Gunn, an abolitionist and temperance man, who founded the local Gunnery School. It's a fascinating local collection that is well worth visiting. The collections— clothing and glass negatives of historic photographs, works by artist-naturalist William Hamilton Gibson (brother of the creator of the Gibson girls), plus dolls, furniture, thimbles, and other local family heirlooms—cover the history of Washington from the late 18th to the 20th centuries. One hidden gem that should not be missed is the ceiling in the library, which was painted by H. Siddons Mowbray, who painted even grander murals at New York's University Club and the Pierpont Morgan Library.

From Washington follow Route 199 to the **Institute for American Indian Studies** (☎ 860/868-0518). It traces local Native American history through displays of artifacts. Cases contain exhibits taken from a local paleo-Indian site—bone harpoons, adzes and net sinkers, semilunar knives, and soapstone vessels. Artifacts from the Woodland period include luminescent turtle-shell bowls, copper and shell beads, and hand-thrown decorated pots. Kaolin pipes, beaded moccasins, and metal axes represent the later contact period, from 1550 to 1700. Probably the most interesting display, particularly for children, is the reconstruction of a longhouse made by Onondaga Indians and filled with everyday utensils and artifacts. The immense, 12,000-year-old mastodon skeleton found at the Pope Estate in Farmington in 1913 will also impress the kids—the beast stood 9 feet tall at the shoulder, had a 13-foot-long tail, and weighed 10 tons. You can also walk a 20-minute trail along which trees and plants are marked, tracing the evolution of the natural habitat from 12,000 years ago to today, and then view a simulated archaeological site and a replicated Algonkian village. *Hours:* Monday to Saturday 10am to 5pm, Sunday noon to 5pm. Closed major holidays. *Admission:* $4 adults, $3.50 seniors, $2 children ages 6 to 16.

Continue on Route 199 into the quiet, scenic village of Roxbury, which celebrates **Old Roxbury Days** on the last weekend in July with a fiddling contest, a chicken barbecue, an antique car display, arts and crafts, and more. From Roxbury, Route 317 leads back to Woodbury.

WOODBURY LODGING & DINING

The **Curtis House,** Main Street (U.S. 6), Woodbury, CT 06798 (☎ 203/263-2101), claims to be the state's oldest inn, opened by Anthony Stoddard in 1754. The venerable clapboard Federal house with black shutters and 12-on-12 windows is crowned by tall brick chimneys. The signs outside in front of the inn were made by writer and artist Wallace Nutting. An elegant portico surmounted by a balcony leads into the center hall. Past the grandfather clock, a creaking staircase leads to 14 air-conditioned guest rooms (all with canopied beds); 8 have private baths. In the carriage house are four more air-conditioned rooms with baths. In Room 22 in the main house you'll find beds with white canopies and coverlets, standing on painted floorboards; a chest of drawers, a side chair, and a metal closet complete the furnishings. Other rooms are similar. Some rooms have TVs; none have phones.

The ground-floor public rooms boast great character. The ceilings and door frames are low, the floors uneven, and the furnishings comfortably old. The ticking of the wall clock adds to the homey feel. In the parlor you can curl up in a wing chair or on a sofa and watch TV or read the magazines scattered on a table.

The dining room, decorated in colonial cranberry, has a similar air. The fare is typical New England—roast stuffed turkey, broiled bluefish, Yankee pot roast, and roast leg of lamb (weekends only), priced from $14 to $20. There's also an English-style pub in which lighter fare—salads, sandwiches, and dishes like turkey pot pie and broiled scallops—is served. Prices range from $5 to $8. On Friday and Saturday evenings people enjoy dancing here with a DJ.

Rates: $40 to $50 double without bath, $65 to $134 double with bath. *Dining hours:* Monday to Thursday 5 to 8:30pm, Friday to Saturday noon to 2pm and 5 to 9pm, Sunday noon to 8pm. Closed Christmas.

Carole Peck's Good News Cafe, 694 Main St. South (Route 6; ☎ 203/266-4663), is the domain of Ms. Peck, well-known chef and author of *The Buffet Book.* She provides some flavorful contemporary American and global cuisine with a definite healthy twist. Many of the ingredients are local and organic, and several main dishes will always be vegetarian like the trio of stuffed eggplant, tomato, and Vidalia onions. Start with the signature crispy onion bundle served with a fresh-tasting homemade ketchup or the warm crab taco with cheddar and smoked pepper tomatillo relish. Among the salads you'll find such inventive dishes as grilled apricots with marinated Vidalia onions and basil on arugula with a blueberry vinaigrette. Entrees range from sizzling wok-seared shrimp with green beans, peas, olives, potatoes, and garlic aïoli; to paprika-spiced tuna in a tomatillo gazpacho sauce; or Egg and I Farm pork chops stuffed with sausage and mozzarella. Prices range from $17 to $23. Close to a dozen desserts are offered. There's always a fresh fruit tart of the day plus such delicious dishes as dark chocolate pudding with cherries and toasted coconut marshmallow, or fresh peach upside-down cake with black currant sauce and crème fraîche. *Hours:* Wednesday to Monday 11:30am to 2:30pm and 5 to 10pm.

WASHINGTON & WASHINGTON DEPOT LODGING & DINING

Such a pretty and venerable town as Washington warrants an old-fashioned luxury inn like the **Mayflower Inn,** 118 Woodbury Rd. (Route 47), Washington, CT 06793 (☎ 860/868-9466). Cross the bridge by the pond inhabited by two swans and take the winding, tree-lined drive that leads to the house on the crest of the hill. It's set on 28 acres graced with splendid rhododendrons and maple trees and landscaped with rose gardens, wildflower cutting gardens, and knot gardens of boxwood and red barberry. Current owners Adriana and Robert Mnuchin, who exhibit fine taste and a superb eye for color and decoration, have spent millions in reconstructing the place and have successfully turned it into a captivating five-star Relais & Châteaux property. Of the 17 rooms and 8 suites, 15 are in the clapboard Mayflower Building, with a striking gambrel roof. Each has been individually decorated with the very best—luxurious fabrics, Frette linens and bathrobes, positively plush upholstery, exquisite antiques, and 18th- and 19th-century art. All have spacious marble baths with brass-and-Limoges fittings. Other features include fireplaces, stocked minibars, TVs in cabinets, down comforters, four-poster canopied beds, and walls papered in Regency stripes or Empire petit fleur.

The public areas are certainly as lavish, if not more so. The parlor is very inviting with its swag curtains, gilt-framed landscapes, and fine English antiques. The sumptuously paneled library is extraordinary and offers a large book collection that can be read sitting in the leather armchairs or on the cushioned window seat. The porch is beguiling, too, with its white wicker rockers overlooking the south lawn and Shakespeare garden, where a bust of the playwright is surrounded by flowers and shrubs that bear markers carrying lines from the Bard. To reach the other accommodations in the Speedwell and Standish buildings you'll pass the well-tended Terrace Gardens. Facilities include a state-of-the-art fitness club open daily, offering facials, shiatsu, aromatherapy, reflexology, and massages; an attractively landscaped heated outdoor pool with pool house; a tennis court; hiking trails; and a games room.

The cuisine in the dining room is also stellar, emphasizing fresh local ingredients. Start with the house smoked salmon accompanied by lahvosh (Middle Eastern bread) that's baked on the premises, or with a salad of chilled asparagus and grilled portobello mushroom with shaved Parmesan and Dijon vinaigrette. The eight or so main courses are prepared with organic ingredients whenever possible and cooked in a contemporary American style to concentrate the flavors. You might enjoy a pan-seared yellowtail snapper with sea scallop in a Merlot reduction, or charbroiled veal chop and wild mushroom ragoût, or a roasted free-range chicken brimming with flavor and natural jus. Prices range from $18 to $32. Desserts range from ice creams and sorbets to a lemon tart with strawberry coulis. The tables are set with Limoges china, crystal, and silver. The room's centerpiece is a magnificent floral and produce display. Orchids are everywhere throughout the house. The adjoining piano bar is a convivial place for cocktails and late-night conversation.

Rates: $260 to $425 double; $440 to $640 suite. *Dining hours*: Daily 7:30 to 10:30am, noon to 2pm and 6 to 9pm.

For lunch, many people head to Washington Depot to **The Pantry,** Titus Square (☎ 860/868-0258). It serves some of the best soups, salads, and sandwiches around, plus you can browse through gourmet foods, gifts, and culinary accessories. The chalkboard menu might offer a broccoli-leek or chicken-corn chowder, which can be followed by kedgeree or a more traditional Reuben sandwich. The desserts are excellent—like linzertorte and lemon cake. Afternoon tea is also served. Take out or eat in. *Hours:* Tuesday to Saturday 10am to 6pm.

THE AREA AFTER DARK

A good bet for evening entertainment is the **Bantam Cinema** in the town of the same name (a few miles southwest of Litchfield), which shows the latest Hollywood movies along with foreign and art films. During the summer there are **chamber music concerts** provided by the Armstrong Chamber Concerts of Washington Depot (☎ 860/868-0522). In Litchfield on selected summer and fall weekends, music, dance, and theater performances are arranged by **Litchfield Performing Arts** at the First Congregational Church and other venues in and around the village.

The Litchfield Hills Area
Special & Recreational Activities

Antiquing: Stores abound in Kent, Litchfield, New Preston, Salisbury, and Woodbury. **Woodbury's Main Street** in particular is lined with stores selling really fine English, American, and French antiques. If you cross the border into Massachusetts on routes 7 and 7A around Sheffield and Ashley Falls, you'll discover another good hunting ground. Most of the stores stock high-quality pieces at similarly high prices.

Auto Racing: Lime Rock Park, routes 7 and 112 (☎ 860/435-2571), hosts some of the largest spectator events in the Northeast and is home to the Skip Barber Racing and Driving Schools.

Bicycling: The **Cycle Loft,** 25 Litchfield Commons, Litchfield (☎ 860/567-1713), rents bikes for $12 a day. It also sponsors group rides.

Boating: O'Hara's Landing Marina, 254 Twin Lakes Rd., Salisbury (☎ 860/824-7583), offers rowboats, canoes, pontoon, and motorboats for rent.

Camping: White Memorial Foundation, on Route 202 west of Litchfield (☎ 860/567-0089), has several camping areas, open mid-May to October; the most popular is at Point Folly, a peninsula extending into Bantam Lake that's convenient for swimming and fishing.

Lake Waramaug State Park, New Preston, CT 06777 (☎ 860/868-0220), has 77 sites, open from mid-May to last weekend in September. **Macedonia Brook State Park,** Kent, CT 06757 (☎ 860/927-3238 or 860/927-4100 for camping), offers 82 sites near a brook in the Appalachian Trail area. Open from late April to late September. Sons of Liberty Cornwall Bridge, CT 06754 (☎ 860/672-6772), has 93 sites (some nicely situated near the river). Open from late April to December 31.

Hemlock Hill Resort Campground, Hemlock Hill Road(P.O. Box 828), Litchfield, CT 06759 (☎ 860/567-2267), offers 120 wooded sites, two outdoor pools, and other facilities. Open until mid-October. The charge is $20 a night for tent camping, $29 a night for a trailer.

Canoeing: Clarke Outdoors, Route 7 (P.O. Box 163), West Cornwall, CT 06796 (☎ 860/672-6365), has canoes, kayaks, and rafts for rent and provides shuttle service back to your starting point on the Housatonic River. The approximate charge per day is $50 to $55.

Country Fairs: Contact **Connecticut State Tourism,** 505 Hudson St., Hartford, CT 06106 (☎ 800/282-6863 or 860/270-8081), for information on these fun-filled celebrations with contests, auctions, entertainments, and demonstrations.

Fishing: *Barkhamsted:* **West Hill Pond,** off Route 44. *Cornwall:* **Housatonic Meadows State Park,** Route 7, Cornwall Bridge. *Litchfield:* **Lake Waramaug State Park,** Route 45; **Mount Tom State Park,** Route 202. *Salisbury:* **East Twin Lake,** off Route 44. *Sharon:* **Mudge Pond,** off Route 4.

Those who wish to learn fly-fishing should contact **Housatonic Anglers,** 484 Rte 7 (P.O. Box 282), West Cornwall, CT 06796 (☎ 860/672-4457), which offers 3-day schools for novices and half- and full-day guided trips.

Fruit Picking: *Washington Depot:* **Hallock Orchards,** Calhoun Street (☎ 860/868-2863), for apples, peaches, and more.

Golf: *Litchfield:* **Stonybrook Golf Club,** Milton Road (☎ 860/567-9977), has nine holes for which the charge is $17 on weekends

Hiking: *Cornwall:* **Mohawk Mountain,** from Route 4. *Kent:* **Kent Falls State Park,** Route 7. *Litchfield:* **White Memorial Foundation,** Route 202; **Mount Tom State Park,** a few miles west of Bantam on Route 202. *Norfolk:* **Haystack Mountain State Park** on Route 272 north and **Dennis Hill State Park** on Route 272 south are both spectacular. *Salisbury:* **Bear Mountain,** from Route 41. *Washington:* **Steep Rock Nature Reserve** has some lovely hiking trails beside the Shepaug River.

For detailed hiking trail information, write to the **Connecticut Forest and Park Trail Association,** 16 Meriden Rd., Rockfall, CT 06481 (☎ 860/346-2372), or the **Office of State Parks,** 79 Elm St., Hartford, CT 06106-5127 (☎ 860/424-3200). The Appalachian Trail cuts through the region.

Horseback Riding: *Litchfield:* **Lee's Riding Stable, Inc.,** 57 E. Litchfield Rd. (off Route 118; ☎ 860/567-0785), offers trail riding for $22 per person. The ride is about an hour long. *Millerton:* **Western Riding Stables,** Sawchuk

Road, Millerton NY (☎ 518/789-4848), offers terrific trail rides and pack trips. The trail rides range from 1½ hours to half and full days. Two- to five-day pack trips include camping gear and meals. Special moonlight trips are given during the week of the full moon in November.

Ice-skating: On **Lake Waramaug** or at **Mount Tom State Park.**

Mountain Laurel Viewing: From mid- to late June at **Indian Lookout,** Torrington.

Picnicking: You can always dine **on the Green** in Litchfield. More secluded spots are to be found at the **White Memorial Foundation, Lake Waramaug State Park, Kent Falls State Park,** or **Mount Tom.** Pick up supplies at **Spinel's Litchfield Food Company,** a gourmet takeout just off the Green.

Skiing: *Cornwall:* **Mohawk Mountain,** 46 Great Hollow Rd. (off Route 4), Cornwall, CT 06753 (☎ 860/672-6100), has a vertical drop of 640 feet, five lifts, and a 95% snowmaking capacity. There are 23 trails and 5 chairlifts (including a triple). Lift rates are $29 per day for adults.

Cross-country skiing can be enjoyed at *Kent:* **Macedonia Brook State Park,** off Route 341. *Litchfield:* **White Memorial Foundation** and **Mount Tom State Park,** on Route 202 just west of Bantam. *New Preston:* Around **Lake Waramaug.**

The Wilderness Shop, Route 202, 85 West St., Litchfield (☎ 860/ 567-5905), rents cross-country skis, snowshoes, and camping equipment.

State Parks: *Barkhamsted:* **People's State Forest,** Route 44, has hiking trails, picnicking, fishing, and cross-country skiing. *Cornwall:* **Mohawk Mountain State Park,** off Route 4, Cornwall-Goshen-Litchfield, offers picnicking and downhill and cross-country skiing. *Cornwall Bridge:* **Housatonic Meadows State Park,** on Route 7 a mile north of town, has camping, fishing, picnicking, and hiking on the Appalachian Trail. *Kent:* **Kent Falls State Park,** Route 7, is picturesque for picnicking; **Macedonia Brook State Park,** off Route 341, has excellent hiking, fishing, picnicking, and cross-country skiing. *Norfolk:* **Haystack Mountain State Park,** on Route 272 north, and **Dennis Hill State Park,** on Route 272 south, have hiking and picnicking. *Washington:* **Mount Tom State Park,** Route 202, Morris-Washington-Litchfield, offers hiking, picnicking, stocked fishing, swimming, and cross-country skiing; **Lake Waramaug,** on Route 475, 5 miles north of New Preston, has swimming, camping, fishing, and picnicking facilities. For information, write the **Office of State Parks,** 79 Elm St., Hartford, CT 06106-5127 (☎ 860/424-3200).

Swimming: *Kent:* **Macedonia Brook State Park,** off Route 341. *Litchfield-Bantam:* **Mount Tom State Park,** off Route 202. *New Preston:* **Lake Waramaug State Park.**

Essex, the Connecticut River Valley & Hartford

Middletown ◆ *Chester* ◆ *Deep River* ◆ *Hadlyme* ◆ *Old Lyme* ◆
Old Saybrook ◆ *Westbrook* ◆ *Madison* ◆ *Essex* ◆ *Ivoryton* ◆
Centerbrook ◆ *Haddam* ◆ *East Haddam* ◆ *Moodus* ◆
Hartford ◆ *Old Wethersfield* ◆ *Avon* ◆ *Farmington*

Distance in miles: Middletown, 101; Essex, 110; Hartford, 113; Old Saybrook, 113

Estimated driving time: 2 hours

◆◇◆◇◆◇◆◇◆◇◆

Driving: Take I-95 north to Route 9 going to Essex. For Middletown, take the Merritt Parkway to I-91, then pick up Route 66 east.

Bus: Peter Pan (☎ 800/343-9999) travels to Middletown and Hartford.

Train: Amtrak travels to Old Saybrook and Hartford. For information, call ☎ 800/872-7245.

Further Information: For more about the area's events and festivals and about Connecticut in general, call or write **Connecticut State Tourism**, 505 Hudson St., Hartford, CT 06106 (☎ 800/282-6863 or 860/270-8081).

For specific information about the area (except Old Lyme), contact the **Connecticut River Valley and Shoreline Visitors Council**, 393 Main St., Middletown, CT 06457 (☎ 860/347-0028; fax 860/704-2340; www.cttourism.org).

For Hartford, Farmington, and West Hartford contact the **Greater Hartford Convention and Visitors Bureau**, One Civic Center Plaza, Hartford, CT 06103 (☎ 860/728-6789).

◆◇◆◇◆◇◆◇◆◇◆

Today you can stand at the lower reaches of the Connecticut River and survey a scene that has changed very little since Dutch explorer Adrian Block first sailed up the river in 1614. The towns you'll encounter along its banks—**Old Lyme, Hadlyme,** and **East Haddam** on the east bank and **Old Saybrook, Essex, Deep River, Chester, Haddam,** and **Middletown** on the west—are all (except perhaps Middletown) unscarred by the industrial mills and

Events & Festivals to Plan Your Trip Around

June: **Essex Shad Festival.** Call ☎ 860/347-0028.

Rose Festival, Hartford. Call ☎ 860/728-6789.

July: **River Festival,** Hartford—music, boat races, fireworks (July 4). Call ☎ 860/728-6789.

Niantic Lions Lobster Festival, East Lyme—seafood, arts and crafts (July 4).

The Deep River Muster of Fife and Drum. Contact Deep River Town Hall at ☎ 860/526-6024 (usually the third weekend).

September: **Berlin Fair,** about 10 miles south of Wethersfield. It has all kinds of arts and crafts, bakery, photography, needlework, livestock, and other exhibits, along with country events like horse and oxen draws, frog jumps, nail-driving contests, and cornhusking bees (usually the last weekend). Call ☎ 860/347-0028.

The Durham Fair, largest in the state. Call ☎ 860/349-3625 (usually the last weekend).

Chrysanthemum Festival, Bristol (last week of September and first in October).

October: **Apple Harvest,** Southington, about 14 miles from Hartford—a parade, arts and crafts, and apple-related fare (early October). Contact the Southington Chamber of Commerce (☎ 860/628-8036).

Head of Connecticut Regatta, Middletown (usually Columbus Day weekend).

November: **Wesleyan Potters Exhibit and Sale,** Middletown (through December).

December: **Festival of Lights,** Hartford, when Constitution Plaza is ablaze with 250,000 Christmas lights (the day after Thanksgiving to New Year's Day). Call ☎ 860/728-6789.

Torchlight Parade, muster, and carol sing, Old Saybrook (usually the second Saturday).

---

manufacturing plants that marred so many other New England river towns. Lacking waterfalls (and therefore water power), they were able to avoid the destiny that created such industrial towns as Holyoke and Springfield. They are entrancing old towns that have retained their 18th- and 19th-century serenity.

No wonder the Native Americans called this river the Quinnehtukqut ("long tidal river")—its waters, abundant with salmon and shad, flow 400 miles from Québec to the New Hampshire border all the way south to Long Island Sound. At one time salmon was so plentiful it was fed to servants, and shad was reserved for animals. Although the Dutch discovered the river, it was John Winthrop Jr. who came from the Massachusetts Bay Colony to establish a new colony at the behest of certain English Puritans and Cromwellian followers. This new colony flourished largely because of the abundant harvest in the river and the trade that the waterway encouraged. **Ivoryton**, for example, was named because it was the final destination for shiploads and cartloads of ivory brought from the East to this small town, where the Pratt Read factory continues to turn out piano and organ keys (albeit no longer ivory ones). **Essex** grew into a major shipbuilding town where the first U.S. Navy boat, the 24-gun *Oliver Cromwell,* was constructed during the American Revolution. This was not forgotten by the British—they took vengeance during the War of 1812, when they bribed a local youth to help them navigate the treacherous sandbars at the river's narrow neck, and then proceeded to shell the town and destroy 28 ships, or $160,000 worth of American shipping.

Today, anchored in that same harbor are all shapes and sizes of yachts and pleasure craft. Their bronzed crews, sporting Topsiders and crewnecks, can be found winding down after a day's sail over a pint of ale or a drink in the old taproom at the area's finest hostelry, the Griswold Inn (see below).

Farther upriver, **East Haddam** was a shipbuilding town that turned out many of the great schooners that sailed downriver and then to points all around the world. One of the shipbuilders, William Goodspeed, was a hotel owner and theater lover who wanted to attract people to the area. So he built the **Goodspeed Theater,** a six-story gingerbread extravaganza in East Haddam (the theater is on the top floor, and his offices and a general store are below). For years, people traveling upriver stopped to attend a show. Sometimes whole Broadway shows were transported to Goodspeed's theater, which thrived from 1876 until the 1920s, when river travel was eclipsed by the railroad and, more important, the automobile. Goodspeed's opera house became a state garage and warehouse; threatened with demolition in the 1950s, it was narrowly rescued from the wrecker's ball. Now audiences can once again enjoy entertaining evenings in this Victorian gem, currently dedicated to preserving the legacy of American musical theater.

Close by, on the southernmost hill of the so-called Seven Hills, William Gillette was so moved by the beauty of the wooded bluffs and the river that one evening, on a return journey from Long Island, he canceled his plans for constructing a summer mansion at Greenport and built his idiosyncratic **Gillette Castle** here.

During the late 19th century it was common to see a huge sidewheeler churning up the river from New York City to **Hartford** on a 140-mile journey that, with luck, might take 18 hours. Such steamer passenger service continued until 1931, when it finally succumbed to the motor car and the railroad, which had come to the valley in 1871. Today you can take a nostalgic ride aboard one of the old-style locomotives that used to steam alongside the river. As the era of sail and steam gave way to the age of the automobile, the river towns slumbered, stuck in an epoch when the tall masts of schooners and the smokestacks of steamers jammed the river, and life flowed at a gentler pace.

That's why the whole area makes a wonderfully refreshing, magical place to retreat for a weekend. You can ramble through these pristine old towns, browse in antiques stores, wander down streets lined with colonial homes, and stop in at comfortable country inns. Experience the nostalgic thrill of

Connecticut

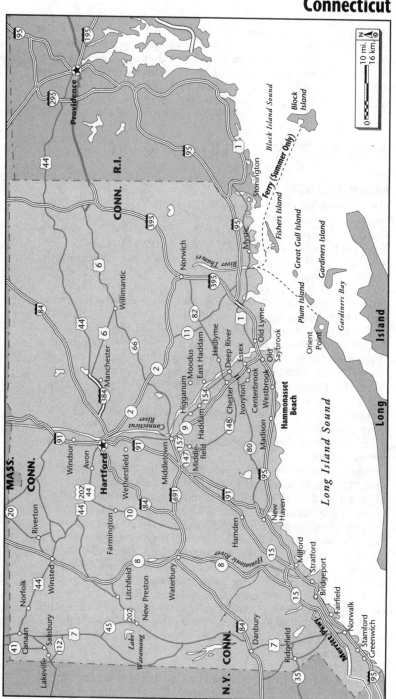

climbing aboard the big steam locomotive that runs from Essex to Chester, or cruise the river aboard all kinds of vessels. Canoe, swim, fish, go fruit picking, cross-country skiing, skating on the lakes, and enjoy an evening at the Goodspeed Theater or stop in at art galleries and craft shops. Or just revel in the countryside, shoreline, and riverbanks that Childe Hassam loved to paint. You'll return home totally rejuvenated—if you return at all.

MIDDLETOWN, CHESTER & DEEP RIVER

AREA ATTRACTIONS

Home to **Wesleyan University's** appealing campus, Middletown offers varied cultural events—concerts, theater, and art shows, many staged at the university's Center for the Arts; call ☎ 860/347-9411, ext. 2807, for a schedule. The **Wesleyan Potters Craft Center,** 350 S. Main St. (☎ 860/347-5925), is also here. The best time to visit is during the annual sale, from Thanksgiving to mid-December, when all kinds of crafts are on display. The center also operates a gallery that is open Tuesday to Saturday from 11am to 5pm.

Wander around the old campus and note what's going on at the riverside **Harbor Park,** the location for many special events, including the culmination of the **Head of Connecticut Regatta** on Columbus Day weekend. Cruises also operate daily from here from early June to Labor Day (weekends only in October). In fall there's a 4-hour cruise down the river on weekends, from Harbor Park to Gillette Castle, for foliage viewing. Cruise prices range from $6 to $18. For information, contact Deep River Navigation Company, P.O. Box 382, Deep River, CT 06417 (☎ 860/526-4954).

To the west of Middletown is the small town of **Durham,** an old farming community that has changed little since the 19th century; here you can recapture the era at the annual **Durham Fair,** the largest and one of the most popular in the state.

Southwest of Middletown, Middlefield offers the **Powder Ridge Skiing Area** (☎ 860/349-3454) and **Lyman Orchards,** at the junction of routes 147 and 157 (☎ 860/349-1793), a real treat at apple-blossom time or at fall harvest. The orchard's 25,000 trees (60% apples) are spread over 300 acres, and you can pick apples, strawberries, raspberries, pumpkins, and peaches. The farm, owned by the Lyman family since 1741, possesses a fascinating history and occupies some of the most scenic land in the valley. The farm store, Greenfield's, has all kinds of goodies: pies, breads, and cookies from ovens right on the premises; raw honey; varieties of squash and melon I'd never seen—in other words, a mass of farm-fresh produce all at very good prices. Events are often scheduled during summer and fall weekends. The store is open daily from 8am to 6pm. The golf course here, part of the farm and quite spectacularly designed by Robert Trent Jones, has eight water holes on the front nine.

From Middletown you can head south toward Chester. Along the way, take some time to detour to **The Sundial Herb Garden** in Higganum (☎ 860/345-4290), ideally for afternoon tea, which is served usually on Sundays (reservations required). It's a delightful place out in the woods. Ragna Tischler

Goddard will welcome you to her lovely barn store and tearoom either before or after you tour the gardens. If you have time, she will give you a short history course on the development of garden design from its origins in the Middle East. Garden design, as she explains it, is simply the architecture of the earth, and a garden is really a series of three-dimensional outer rooms that provide different experiences of light and shade, enclosure and vista. There are three gardens—a knot garden, an 18th-century garden, and a topiary garden that is very integral to the house. The gardens are delightfully small scale and yet manage to present a variety of experiences: A viewer can enjoy long vistas that extend down a pathway and through an arched trellis to a focal point like a statue; or go from the open, light-filled knot garden through a cool dark arbor of spaliered pear trees to the light-filled fountain garden, and then back into the shade of a 100-year-old grape arbor. If you have come for tea you will be treated to a full tea of cucumber sandwiches, English scones with lemon curd, clotted cream and jam, tea cake, fresh fruit tartlette, and a pot of tea chosen from 20 flavors available. The cost is $14.95 ($8.95 for just scones and tea). The store offers some very high quality teas as well as Yixing and other style teapots, tea strainers, and tea caddies. Ms. Goddard also stocks herbal and health products and a few gourmet items like stem ginger from Australia and tupelo honey from Georgia. Mail order is available. *Note:* No jeans, shorts, or sports outfits are allowed in the tearoom. *Hours:* Gardens and shop open Saturday and Sunday 10am to 5pm from mid-May to mid-October. Closed holidays. From the day after Thanksgiving to December 24 open daily 10am to 5pm. *Admission:* $1. To reach the gardens take Brault Hill Road off Route 81.

Chester is a pretty village worth strolling around and browsing. Look for **Ceramica,** which sells brilliant Italian majolica; **Souleiado,** offering luxurious table linens and other fine table accessories; the **Nillson Spring Street Gallery,** featuring fine art; and **One of A Kind,** an antiques store. Then head for the cross-river ferry (in operation since 1769, April to November only), which will take you across the river to Hadlyme and Gillette Castle.

MIDDLETOWN DINING

Harbor Park, 80 Harbor Dr. (☎ 860/347-9999), is designed to make you feel as though you're aboard a ship, with its sailcloth-canvas partitions attached to the staircase railings and neon-lighted mast at the center of the multilevel restaurant/lounge. On the ground floor is a large lounge that gives astounding views of the river, as do the two dining levels above. The menu is extensive. Specialties include a clambake consisting of a 1-pound lobster, steamers, littlenecks, and an ear of corn served in a pewter pot—plus steaks, fresh seafood (pine nut–crusted scrod served with lemon-caper-garlic sauce, beer-battered shrimp), and more. Prices range from $14 to $23. Sunday offers a 25-item buffet brunch and made-to-order omelets and waffles. *Hours:* Sunday to Thursday 11:30am to 2:30pm and 5 to 9pm, Friday to Saturday 11:30am to 2:30pm and 5 to 11pm.

CHESTER LODGING & DINING

A truly idyllic retreat on 12 acres surrounded by state forest, the **Inn at Chester,** 318 W. Main St., Chester, CT 06412 (☎ 860/526-9541), was created by building onto a colonial farmhouse. In the process, the old and the new have been harmoniously combined to create a hospitable, gracious, but modern inn. Owner Deborah L. Moore is a remarkable, energetic woman who pays attention to every detail and really cares about making her guests comfortable. Get her talking on her previous career.

The 42 spacious rooms are decorated elegantly with Eldred Wheeler reproductions. The most formal have a Chippendale-style chest and desk; the less formal have more country-style pieces—hoopback Windsor chairs, clubfoot tables, and porcelain or brass lamps. In all rooms (except three in the main house) the TV is tucked in a cabinet; phones, hair dryers, and air-conditioning complete the appointments. Amenities include laundry/valet service. Extra touches are fresh flowers and in-room massage.

The old barn that was moved here houses the delightful **Post and Beam** restaurant, which offers excellent New American cuisine. Start with the flavorful wild-mushroom gâteau made with layers of mushrooms and potatoes, the spicy shrimp with a pineapple and mango salsa, or one of the extra-special soups, like the vichyssoise garnished with truffles and chives. Among the eight or so main courses ($17 to $28) might be salmon fillet served over spinach with a roasted corn coulis, rack of lamb with Provençal sauce, or crispy duck breast served with a plum and lavender sauce. For a perfect ending select the orange crème brûlée or the crushed-chocolate soufflé with cappuccino mousse. A lighter, less pricey menu is served in the tavern.

Guests may retire downstairs to either the well-equipped fitness room or the pool room and library (some wonderful volumes, too) warmed by a fire on winter nights. From spring to early fall the grounds resemble an English garden redolent with lilacs, roses, hollyhocks, and many other flowering plants and shrubs. For outdoor exercise there's a tennis court, bikes, and miles of nature trails in the adjacent state forest. Nearby Cedar Lake is good for swimming or ice-skating.

Rates (including continental breakfast): $115 to $195 double, suite $225. *Dining hours:* Monday to Saturday 11:30am to 2pm and 5:30 to 9pm, Sunday 11:30am to 2:30pm and 4 to 8:30pm.

CHESTER DINING

As close as you'll get to a French country bistro, the **Restaurant du Village**, 59 Main St. (☎ 860/526-5301), is always gaily bedecked with plants and flowers placed in window boxes and along the small alley that leads to the entrance. Inside, you'll find two small rooms: One is a cozy lounge/dining area with a terra-cotta bar; the other is an intimate dining room. The menu changes frequently, but the cuisine is always imaginative. At the time of my visit, appetizers included a house-smoked trout served with walnut bread and horseradish sauce; veal-and-pork terrine studded with pistachios and served with cranberry chutney; snails sautéed with wild mushrooms in a garlic, parsley, and white wine sauce served in puff pastry snail shells; or an inspired gâteau aubergine—thinly sliced eggplant grilled and combined with layers of sautéed spinach and roasted red peppers, served with a tomato concassé. There were about six main dishes, among them duck roasted with orange and lemon wedges and served with balsamic vinegar sauce, and medallions of filet mignon served with a cognac and green peppercorn sauce. Game is often featured and there's always fresh fish, like the delicious roast monkfish with bacon and roast garlic cloves served with crème fraîche and Spanish sherry–wine vinegar sauce. Prices range from $23 to $26. For dessert, you'll be lucky if the special gâteau is featured—a chocolate génoise filled with orange liqueur–scented chocolate mousse and raspberry jam, covered in Belgian chocolate ganache. *Hours:* Wednesday to Saturday 5:30 to 10pm and Sunday 5 to 9pm.

A covered bridge over the Pattaconk Creek leads to the **Chart House,** Route 9, Exit 6 (☎ 860/526-9898). Located in a restored brush factory, it offers cozy dining and a pleasant lounge with oak furnishings and plush sofas. The menu features steaks (filet mignon with Cabernet sauce or sirloin in teriyaki sauce), as well as such dishes as herb-crusted chicken served with a Pommery mustard sauce, and delicious ginger citrus shrimp served with a jicama salad. Prices range from $17 to $31. *Hours:* Monday to Thursday 5 to 9pm, Friday to Saturday 5 to 10pm, Sunday 4 to 9pm.

Fiddler's Seafood, 4 Water St. (☎ 860/526-3210), is a plain and simple restaurant decked out in Wedgwood blue and furnished with bentwood chairs set at tables spread with white tablecloths. Nautical lithographs decorate the walls. A variety of fish is offered, depending on availability—swordfish, baked or stuffed sole, clams, shrimp casino (sautéed with green pepper, pimiento, and bacon in a sherry-butter sauce), lobster, and bouillabaisse. Prices range from $13 to $20. The fresh fish selections change daily, and you can choose to have it prepared in a variety of ways—mesquite-grilled, poached, Cajun-spiced, broiled, baked, or pan-sautéed. A few meat dishes are also available. *Hours:* Tuesday to Thursday 11:30am to 2pm and 5:30 to 9pm, Friday to Saturday 11:30am to 2pm and 5:30 to 10pm, Sunday 4 to 9pm.

The **Mad Hatter,** Main Street (☎ 860/526-2156), is so named because the baker who prepares the cuisine here loves to wear hats. It has an original ambience. You can sit in one of the trolley-seat booths and dine off marble-top tables. Contemporary art hangs on the walls and drapes are used in French style to soften the look of the single room. Among the baker's best are the eight or so kinds of bread she bakes—sourdough, double raisin, and a wonderful bittersweet Belgian chocolate. It's a great breakfast spot, where you can savor the wonderful brioche or succulent French toast made with challah or whole-wheat bread. Light lunches are also available. Start with a soup like carrot-ginger and follow with Tuscan white-bean salad or any of the singular sandwiches including a savory combination of onion jam and goat cheese on multigrain bread. On Friday and Saturday a three-course dinner ($20) is served, featuring such dishes as Provençal lamb chops with mashed potatoes and ratatouille, or tuna steak with tapenade and caponata, plus several pasta dishes. *Hours:* Saturday and Sunday 8:30 to noon, Wednesday to Saturday noon to 3pm, Friday and Saturday 5:30 to 9pm.

DEEP RIVER LODGING

An obvious love of life and an incredible amount of energy are reflected in **Riverwind,** Main Street, Deep River, CT 06417 (☎ 860/526-2014). The proud owner of this engaging bed-and-breakfast is Barbara Barlow, who hails from Smithfield, Virginia, where she taught learning-disabled children for many years. Her current life evolved from her part-time work as a restoration specialist. When she was asked to restore a house in Connecticut, she fell in love with the area, opened an antiques store, and then set about renovating this 1850 beige clapboard house. She's done a wonderful job, filling it with unique personal collectibles and furnishings. As her father was a hog farmer, Barbara has a definite fondness for pigs, so all kinds of references appear throughout the house—tiny wooden toys, weather vanes, and other "pig" art, not to mention Smithfield hams hanging in the kitchen.

In the parlor and breakfast room antiques abound—decoys, a sleigh, a collection of arrowheads Barbara personally unearthed from Virginia soil, a basket filled with large cones, an old quilt draped over a wooden field rake and tacked above the fireplace, a blanket chest serving as a coffee table. A filling breakfast is served at a harvest table in front of the fire in winter.

The eight guest rooms are upstairs. Each room is different, but all feature colorful old quilts and floor stenciling. The Smithfield Room's centerpiece is a maple rope bed (converted, of course) covered with a red, white, and blue quilt that inspires the decor. Personal accents include a miniature doll's chest that belonged to Barbara's grandmother and the *Oxford Book of English Verse* tucked into the bedside table. In Zelda's two-room suite you'll find a majestic carved oak bed, hall tree, and an old Virginia hotel washstand and rocker, all set against a deep green decor. The sitting room also has an antique brass daybed, and the bath is most entertaining (check out the 1862 wall plaque). The Havlow Room is named after her family farm and features pine furnishings and charming cornhusk dolls representing the travelers on the Yellow Brick Road. Most spectacular is the Champagne and Roses Room, featuring a mahogany pencil-post canopied bed and rose-colored wingbacks, as well as a Japanese steeping tub in the bathroom and a private balcony.

For guests' leisure there are eight common rooms (four with fireplaces), including a 12-foot-wide stone cooking hearth in the keeping room. In the front parlor there's a piano, which Dave Brubeck played when he stayed here. There's also a games room with board games and a porch furnished with wicker. For breakfast you can expect—what else?—Smithfield ham with pig-shaped biscuits, or baked French toast, coffee cake, fruit compote, and fresh fruit. In the backyard are hibachis for guests' use. Feel free to pour yourself a welcome glass of sherry from the decanter in the living room.

Rates (including breakfast): $105 to $175 double.

HADLYME & GILLETTE CASTLE

Just off Route 82 rise the towers of the 24-room Rhenish fantasy called **Gillette Castle** (☎ 860/526-2336), where actor William Gillette and his 15 cats lived from 1919 to 1937. Constructed of granite and hand-hewn timbers, the house will amaze you with its eccentric mechanical devices that Gillette invented—huge, cantilevered wooden locks on the massive entrance doors, wooden light switches, a dining table and desk chair that slide on metal runners, a cocktail cabinet rigged with several locks, and mirrors placed strategically to view who was breaking into the liquor cabinet or who was at the front door (so he could decide whether he was home). Here he entertained his friends—most notably with his outdoor miniature railroad, which ran down from "Grand Central Terminal," along the river's bluffs, and across a fragile bridge strung between two massive outcroppings of rock.

In the upstairs rooms, among Gillette's personal memorabilia are photographs depicting this stunningly handsome man as he appeared in *Dream Maker, Secret Service,* and *Private Secretary,* and in his most famous role as Sherlock Holmes. His scrapbooks, theater reviews, letters, and notes that he wrote to neighboring children are fascinating, as are his watercolors and oils. The whole place is capped by a magnificent view from the terrace and the tower (you can climb it only if you visit in the off-season).

So attached was Gillette to his idiosyncratic creation that in his will he stated that "this 122-acre property should not pass to any blithering saphead who has no conception of where he is or with what surrounded." After his death, it became a state park in 1944, and it now encompasses more than 200 acres.

Hours: Memorial Day to Columbus Day, daily 10am to 5pm; Columbus Day to the last weekend before Christmas, Saturday to Sunday 10am to 4pm. *Admission:* $4 adults, $2 children ages 6 to 11.

OLD LYME

AREA ATTRACTIONS

Miss Florence Griswold was the mentor, patron, and friend of many of America's great turn-of-the-century painters—Childe Hassam, Henry Ward Ranger, Willard Metcalf, Charles Ebert, Carleton and Guy Wiggins—who painted the surrounding landscapes when they spent their summers boarding at her Georgian mansion in Old Lyme between 1900 and 1915. Her home is now, appropriately, the **Florence Griswold Museum,** 96 Lyme St. (☎ 860/434-5542). The artists painted the house's door panels and overmantels with Connecticut scenes as a gift to their landlady, and today these treasured examples of the American impressionist movement are displayed on the lower floor. Also on view is the Chadwick studio, a turn-of-the-century artist's studio on the grounds. *Hours:* June to December, Tuesday to Saturday 10am to 5pm, Sunday 1 to 5pm; January to May, Wednesday to Sunday 1 to 5pm. *Admission:* $4 adults, $3 seniors, free for children ages 11 and under.

Across the street these same artists built a museum/gallery for their summer exhibits. It's still a prestigious summer gallery, now also home to the **Lyme Art Association,** 70 Lyme St. (☎ 860/434-7802), which sponsors several shows a year. *Hours:* May to mid-October, Tuesday to Saturday noon to 5pm, Sunday 1 to 5pm. *Admission:* Donation requested.

Elizabeth Tashjian is an attraction in herself (she's been on the *Tonight Show* and several other talk shows) at her very own **Nut Museum,** 303 Ferry Rd. (☎ 860/434-7636). In her 19th-century mansion, so nutty is she about nuts that she has gathered and displays all kinds of paintings, sculptures, nutcrackers, and "nutty" artifacts. *Hours:* May to October, Wednesday and Saturday to Sunday 1 to 5pm. *Admission:* $3 and one nut of any variety.

OLD LYME LODGING & DINING

Canopied beds, lace curtains, and colorful quilts add charm and elegance to most of the rooms at the **Bee and Thistle Inn,** 100 Lyme St., Old Lyme, CT

06371 (☎ 860/434-1667), an attractive 1756 residence set back from the road on 5 acres of tree-shaded gardens along the Lieutenant River (where you can sit peacefully in the garden watching the river flow). The 11 guest rooms (all with bath) include a twin with pine furnishings and oriental rugs and a large two-room family suite—one room containing a double bed, a single, and a couch-bed; the other, a single. Fires light up the parlors in winter, making the wing chairs and comfy sofas all the more inviting.

Breakfast, lunch, and dinner are served either by the fireside in the pretty dining room or on the two adjacent terra-cotta-tile terraces. Freshly squeezed juices, fresh fruits, omelets or strawberry crêpes, kippers, and homemade muffins make for a satisfying breakfast delivered to your room or served on the sun porches or in front of the fire. The dining room's menus change seasonally. The sophisticated and finely prepared food is far from traditional New England fare. At dinner, you might find sesame-encrusted salmon served in a carrot and ginger broth, roasted pork loin served on a rosemary-scented peach coulis with a savory corn pudding, or grilled free-range chicken breast marinated with lemon and sage and served with shiitake mushrooms. Prices range from $20 to $29. Try the house specialty dessert, called a pecan diamond, which is swathed in caramel sauce. The luncheon is also very appealing.

Rates: $85 to $165 double. *Dining hours:* Monday and Wednesday to Saturday 8 to 10am, 11:30am to 2pm, and 6 to 10pm; Sunday 8 to 10am, 11am to 2pm (brunch), and 5:30 to 10pm.

Across the street, a different ambience prevails at the **Old Lyme Inn,** 85 Lyme St. (P.O. Box 787), Old Lyme, CT 06371 (☎ 860/434-2600), an impressive 1850s farmhouse/mansion with a tree-shaded lawn and a porch. Large tapestries cover the walls of the high-ceilinged Empire-style dining room, handsomely decorated in royal blue. Polished silver and fine stemware are placed on white-clothed tables along with a single rose. Well known for its cuisine, the inn's restaurant has been awarded three stars by the *New York Times*. A few of its tempting dishes are salmon grilled with a coconut-cilantro butter, grilled medallions of veal served with double-smoked bacon, cipollini onions over a tarragon shallot sauce, or grilled duck with a sweet-and-sour plum sauce. Prices range from $21 to $28. For appetizers, there are close to a dozen seafood, shellfish, and meat dishes to choose from, including delicious Maine shrimp fritters flavored with scallions, cilantro, jalapeños, and red pepper and served with a chipotle-lime aïoli. If the raspberry cheesecake japonaise is featured, order it: layers of meringue and chocolate topped with fresh raspberries—who could possibly resist?

A lighter and less expensive menu is served in the handsome Victorian Grill Room, where there's also jazz guitar on Friday and Saturday evenings. In the front hall, note the paintings and stenciling done by Gigi Horr-Liverant depicting local scenes, as well as the many paintings and watercolors found throughout. All were collected by innkeeper Diana Atwood-Johnson, who continues the local tradition in her appreciation of art and artists.

The antique curly maple staircase leads to 13 guest rooms (all with bath), each furnished individually with ornate mirrors, old chests, and cannonball or canopied beds covered with candlewick spreads. All have air-conditioning, TVs, radios, and phones, and you'll also find some extra touches, like witch hazel made in nearby Essex and mints on your pillow. There's also a lounge with fireplace where guests can relax.

Rates (including continental breakfast): $130 to $160 weekends and $99 to $140 weekdays double. Closed the first 2 weeks of January and Christmas Eve. *Dining hours:* Monday to Saturday noon to 2pm and 6 to 9pm, Sunday 11am to 3pm and 4 to 9pm.

FROM OLD SAYBROOK TO MADISON

AREA ATTRACTIONS

From Old Lyme drive down to Old Saybrook and then head out along Route 154 to Saybrook Point, marked by two lighthouses—the inner one more often photographed than the outer. Loop around from Saybrook Point across South Cove, past the select community of Fenwick—which counts Katharine Hepburn among its residents—and through Westbrook, a typical beachfront community with shingled homes (here, Frankie's serves dependable shore dinners, and Bill's Seafood accepts the bathing-suit crowd), all the way out to Hammonasset State Park in Madison. By the way, they say if you can see across the sound to Long Island as you go, it's going to rain within 72 hours.

You'll pass through Clinton, home to the **Chamard Vineyards,** 115 Cow Hill Rd. (☎ 203/664-0299), which was established by Bill Chaney, who was the head of Tiffany in 1983. It's open year-round for tastings and tours. The heart of the vineyard is the attractive fieldstone building housing the cellars and a luxurious tasting room. It's a very attractive place to visit, and they produce some fine Chardonnay as well as Cabernet, Merlot, and Pinot Noir. To reach the vineyard take Walnut Hill Road off Route 81. *Hours:* Wednesday to Saturday 11am to 4pm.

Madison is an attractive town and has some stores worth browsing, including a great bookstore, **R. J. Julia,** 768 Boston Post Rd., where particular books are flagged with a personal recommendation from staff members, and a variety of readings and other events are sponsored. In the back you can sink into one of the cushioned banquettes of the cafe and linger over coffee and pastry.

OLD SAYBROOK LODGING

The **Saybrook Point Inn and Spa,** 2 Bridge St., Old Saybrook, CT 06475 (☎ 860/395-2000), is a stylish modern complex at the mouth of the Connecticut River overlooking Long Island Sound. The 62 rooms and 7 suites, most with a water views, are each comfortably furnished with antique Chippendale and Queen Anne reproductions and reveal that extra attention to detail that makes all the difference—an Italian tile bath with a hair dryer and extra towels for the pool, a desk with a phone with data ports for computers and fax, a sitting area and a fireplace, a refrigerator, and a wet bar. Each suite features a living/dining area, a Jacuzzi tub, a separate shower, and bathrobes. The most dramatic accommodation of all, though, is in the lighthouse at the end of the dock at the mouth of the river and the sound. The light streams into this suite from all sides. It features a bedroom, sitting room, kitchen, and a small bathroom with a pump-assisted toilet. The furnishings are suitably light with plenty of wicker. It's the waterfront view and the romance of staying under a lighthouse lamp that resonates.

The facilities are extensive—an indoor and outdoor pool with attractive deck, a fully equipped fitness center, and a spa offering facials, massage, and body treatments including Swedish body treatment, aromatherapy, acupressure, and more. Bicycles are available for rent and the marina offers 120 slips. The Terra Mar Grille looks out on the water, and guests can enjoy some excellent northern Italian and modern American cuisine. You might start with wild mushroom and roasted shallot torte, then follow with a choice from nine or so entrees—shrimp and scallops over capellini, rosemary-crusted rack of lamb with morel demi-glace, or pan-roasted chicken breast stuffed under the skin with spinach, shiitake mushrooms, and herbed cheese. Prices range from $15 to $26.

Rates: Memorial Day to October, $189 to $305 double, from $345 suites. *Dining hours:* Lunch, Sunday to Friday 11:30am to 2pm, Saturday noon to 2:30pm; dinner, Sunday to Thursday 6 to 9pm, Friday and Saturday 6 to 10pm.

The **Deacon Timothy Pratt House**, 325 Main St., Old Saybrook, CT 06475 (☎ 860/395-1229), stands well back from the road on 1½ acres. It's a handsome 1746 house owned by friendly Shelley Nobile. There are three guest rooms with wood-burning fireplaces. The largest is the honeymoon suite, furnished with a four-poster; the sitting area also has a daybed. The Sunrise room features strawberry-colored plank floors and a canopied bed covered with a pretty handmade quilt; it has a whirlpool tub in the bathroom. Guests gather around the hearth in the parlor, a bright and sunny place, thanks to the triple bay window. The heart of the house is the kitchen, which has a large fireplace with beehive oven. Shelley cooks up such dishes as eggs Benedict and heart-shaped pancakes for service at the large table in the dining room, where candles flicker and classical music plays. *Rates:* $105 to $160.

The **Sandpiper Motor Inn**, 1750 Boston Post Rd. (U.S. 1), Old Saybrook, CT 06475 (☎ 860/399-7973; fax 860/399-7387), is a modern accommodation offering 45 fully equipped rooms (air-conditioning, phone, TV) decked out in pastels, with floral quilts on the bed and light-oak furnishings. Some of the rooms also have refrigerators and wet bars. There's a fenced-in outdoor pool. Local beach passes are provided to guests. *Rates* (including continental breakfast): $105 to $145 (the higher price for rooms with couch and wet bar). Prices reduced in winter.

OLD SAYBROOK DINING

Aleia's, 1687 Boston Post Rd., Old Saybrook (☎ 860/399-5050), occupies a beautiful, restored 19th-century schoolhouse and offers some of the best dining in the area. It's under the expert supervision of chef Kimberly Snow, who prepares fine Italian cuisine. The appetizers are so varied and appealing that it's hard to choose among them. There's a fine seared yellowfin tuna roll served with wasabi, or luscious portobello mushrooms combined with marinated goat cheese and roasted red peppers and served with peppered breadsticks. You can follow with any of the six pastas—from the simple cappellini seasoned in an oven-roasted tomato-basil sauce to the rich cappellini in a lobster-and-shellfish bouillabaisse with saffron and fresh vegetables—or any one of the entrees. There might be a heart-warming roast chicken with aromatic herbs and a garlic sauce, or an ultra-flavorful seared veal chop with a wild-mushroom sauce accompanied by artichokes, caramelized onions, and potato ragoût. Prices range from $14 to $25. The adjacent bar is comfortable and offers entertainment on weekends. *Hours:* Sunday and Tuesday to Thursday 5:30 to 9pm, Friday and Saturday 5:30 to 10pm.

Wine and Roses, 150 Main St. (☎ 860/388-9646), is popular with the locals who appreciate the consistently good contemporary American cuisine. The setting is simple. Breuer cane chairs are arranged at tables set with cloths and glass tops. The menu mixes traditional and contemporary cuisine and offers a range of pastas, meats, and seafood. The filet mignon au poivre is made with a rich combination of crushed black peppercorns, brandy, cream, and mustard. The classic veal piccata is given an added frisson by the addition of capers and shallots as well as lemon, garlic, and white wine. There are always a great choice of daily specials like salmon with strawberries, blueberries, cassis, and raspberry vinegar; or striped bass with corn cakes and a mint and orange pesto sauce; or duck with mango and roasted red pepper salsa; and several more. Prices range from $12 to $20. About eight wines are available by the glass. *Hours:* Tuesday to Saturday 11:30am to 2:30pm, Tuesday to Sunday 5:30 to 9:30pm.

Little Siam, 1745 Boston Post Rd. (☎ 860/399-8848), offers decent Thai cuisine in an attractive setting. The dining room is warmed by a fire on cold evenings; you can also choose to eat in the bar. All the familiar Thai favorites are on the menu. To start with, enjoy a plate of the crispy appetizers—vegetable spring rolls, corn fritters, and pork dumplings. Some main courses are better than others—the duck in tamarind sauce, shrimp in garlic sauce, and the curries are good. The prices range from $8 to $14. *Hours:* Tuesday to Saturday 11:30am to 2:30pm and Tuesday to Sunday 5 to 10pm.

The Dock, at Saybrook Point (☎ 860/388-4665), takes full advantage of its water view and vista across the mouth of the Connecticut River to Great Island. Watch the barges and other craft slipping by or the anchored yachts bobbing dockside while you dine on well-prepared seafood—haddock, swordfish, scampi, scallops, sole, and lobster (one of the prime attractions), all cooked in a variety of ways—along with the usual steaks and chicken teriyaki for the uninitiated seafood diner. Prices run $12 to $28. You'll find the place bursting on weekend nights, sometimes with a 2-hour wait. In that case, retire to the bar and listen to the music—a piano-and-drums combo the night I stopped by. In winter a fire in the fieldstone fireplace will warm your cockles. Start with a sampler of the chowders or choice morsels from the raw bar, then move on to the seafood. If the halibut special in dill sauce is available, I highly recommend it.

The nightly entertainment varies from jazz to a pianist/vocalist. *Hours:* Monday to Thursday 11:30am to 9pm, Friday to Sunday 11:30am to 10pm. Closed Monday and Tuesday in winter.

A 1950s drive-in on Route 1, **Johnny Ads,** 910 Boston Post Rd. (☎ 860/388-4032), is a shoreline institution—famous for its foot-long hot dogs, lobster rolls, and broiled seafood. It's enjoyed by the bathing-suit crowd, and some of the local dignitaries enjoy it, too, as did the late Governor

Ella Grasso, who popped in when she summered in East Lyme. *Hours:* Daily from 11am.

For casual dining, try the popular **Saybrook Fish House,** 99 Essex Rd. (☎ 860/388-4836), where among the nautical regalia of nets and lanterns you can obtain fresh fish broiled in a white-wine and butter sauce, and a wide choice of shellfish—from shrimp, lobster, and scampi to oysters and little necks. Reservations are only taken for parties of five or more, so expect to wait on Saturday nights (maximum of about 2 hours). There are always some appetizers at the bar if you're really famished. Complete dinners are priced from $14 to $21. *Hours:* Monday to Thursday 11:45am to 4pm and 4:30 to 9:30pm, Friday 11:45am to 4pm and 4:30 to 10pm, Saturday 11:45am to 3:30pm and 4 to 10pm, Sunday noon to 9pm.

For a change of cuisine, there's also **Luigi's,** 670 Boston Post Rd. (☎ 860/388-9190), an informal spot that offers pizza and sandwiches along with more substantial fare like scampi, mussels marinara, veal parmigiana, spaghetti with clam sauce, and one or two steaks. Prices range from $10 to $16. *Hours:* Summer, Tuesday to Saturday 11am to 11pm; fall, Sunday to Thursday 11am to 9pm, Friday to Saturday 11am to 10pm. Closed 2 weeks in January.

WESTBROOK LODGING & DINING

Lee and Vern Mattin fell in love with their **Captain Stannard House,** 138 S. Main St., Westbrook, CT 06498 (☎ 860/399-4634). It's quite understandable, for the house is a beauty with its peaked gables, central cupola, and fan window over the entrance. The original building dates back to about 1860, when it was built by sea captain Stannard, who owned and commanded several ships that sailed mostly to the Far East. He also owned the legendary *Savannah,* which was used in the Mexican War.

The eight air-conditioned rooms are unpretentious and pleasant, incorporating such nice touches as fresh flowers, clock radios, and books and magazines as well as liquid soap and air freshener in the bath. Each room is different. The Captain's Quarters has a four-poster canopy with a pretty, pale-blue lacy trim; the walls have stenciled borders, and a rocker offers comfortable seating. Guests have use of two spacious common areas—a large sitting room with fireplace and pool table and a library that is equipped with a stereo and a TV. A full candlelit breakfast is served at separate tables in the bright dining room complete with a fireplace and baby grand piano. Persuade Vern to entertain you with the songs that he has written. He's obviously headed for another career.

Lee and Vern have traveled a lot during their careers and are mindful of business travelers' needs, so they offer an office with a phone available and will fulfill any special requests. Downstairs is a fridge for your use. Beach passes are available for the local strand, only an 8-minute walk away. In summer you can use the bicycles; play croquet, darts, or billiards; or simply relax on the back deck and lawn. There's also an antiques shop on the premises.

Rates (including full breakfast): May to October, $135 to $150 (slightly less at other times).

The **Water's Edge Inn and Resort,** 1525 Boston Post Rd., Westbrook, CT 06498 (☎ 860/399-5901), stands on a bluff overlooking the sound. In this large modern condo/resort complex, accommodations are in 68 villa blocks surrounding a central cobblestone building. These contain two-bedroom units; those on the second floor have balconies. The rooms are typically modern, with TVs, phones, and traditional reproduction furnishings.

The dining room, which looks out on the water, has an excellent reputation; it serves a wide range of dishes—from salmon with steamed escarole and sun-dried tomatoes, to grilled New York strip steak accompanied by port and horseradish demi-glace. Prices range from $12 for pastas to $24 for a classic veal Oscar. The brunch is renowned—including breads, fruit, cheese, salads, a raw bar, and desserts, plus three hot entrees and several stations serving omelets, roasts, and pasta. Dining on the terrace in summer is particularly pleasant. Facilities include an indoor and an outdoor pool, a well-equipped fitness center with a spa for massage and facials, and two tennis courts. Paddleboats, sailboats, and windsurfers are available at the beach.

Rates: Summer $195 to $300; spring, fall, and winter, $145 to $310. *Dining hours:* Daily 11:30am to 2pm, Sunday to Thursday 5:30 to 8:30pm, Friday and Saturday 5:30 to 10pm.

Interested in local color, lots of people, and food at reasonable prices? Then a table at **Bill's Seafood**, 548 Boston Post Rd. (Route 1), Westbrook (☎ 860/399-7224), will suit you just fine. Sit out on the deck and watch the craft maneuver under the bridge into the marina while you feast on crab-and-lobster rolls, clams, fish, or whatever is scrawled on the chalkboard. The fried clams are the proclaimed popular favorite. Inside, the dining room is strictly Formica-topped tables in a barroom. Real seafarers flock here. On Friday and Saturday there's New Orleans–style jazz entertainment. *Hours:* Sunday to Thursday 11am to 9pm, Friday to Saturday 11am to 10pm.

You'll cross over an old wisteria-covered footbridge to reach the **Captain Dibbell House**, 21 Commerce St., Clinton, CT 06413 (☎ 860/669-1646; fax 860/669-2300), an 1866 Victorian building. Four rooms are offered here, all furnished with antiques and country accents. The Garden Room's wicker bed sports a ring quilt and walls stenciled with flowers. In the Captain's Room the brass bed is swagged with fabric and dotted with cushions. Furnishings include a handsome blanket chest and a sitting area. A breakfast of muffins, coffee cake, or sweet rolls is served in the dining room, the garden gazebo, or your room. Throughout the house owners Ellis and Helen display the local art they've collected as well as articles they've hand-woven themselves. Fresh flowers and bathrobes in the rooms are nice extras, and so is the chocolate on the pillow in the evening. Guests have the added conveniences of a refrigerator stocked with beverages; bicycles; beach chairs, umbrellas, and beach towels; and transport from the airport, train, bus, or marina. *Rates:* $95 to $115 double. Closed January to March.

A BEACHFRONT LODGING IN MADISON

The **Madison Beach Hotel**, 94 W. Wharf Rd., Madison, CT 06443 (☎ 203/245-1404), is a true seaside place, with a certain Victorian flavor. From the parking lot, climb the few steps into the weathered-gray, balconied building. The dunes and the sound spread before you, dotted with rocky outcroppings and an occasional brilliant-colored windsurfer's sail. Turn into the lobby and sink into a cushioned wicker rocker or step out onto the veranda and breathe deeply from the shore air.

The 35 simple seaside accommodations have individual heating and air-conditioning, TVs, and phones. Second- and third-floor rooms have balconies; they're simply furnished with hardy seaside furniture. The baths feature pine floors.

The Wharf Dining Room is attached to the hotel and shares the marvelous view of the sound on two sides. Fresh flowers grace the bar; rattan furniture and silk flower arrangements give a tropical air to the room. Dinner-menu prices range from $13 for Boston baked scrod to $17 for surf and turf. There are always steaks and prime rib. Salads, sandwiches, and burgers make up the lunch menu. Upstairs, the Crow's Nest sports nautical rigging and decor, a central bar from which to view the ocean scene, and, even better, an outside balcony table. Before you leave, check out the guest register dating from 1920—you might recognize some of the names. *Rates:* Mid-May to September, $105 to $140 double, from $160 to $235 suite; rest of the year, rates are lower. Closed January 2 to February. *Dining hours:* Daily 11:30am to 2:30pm and 5:30 to 9pm.

Even though the **Tidewater Inn**, 949 Boston Post Rd., Madison, CT 06443 (☎ 203/245-8457), is on Route 1 it's set on a knoll well back from the road. It's a very comfortable place to stay. It offers nine rooms (two with wood-burning fireplaces), all with private baths, TVs, air-conditioning, and phones (for outgoing calls). You'll find a lot of Chinese/oriental accents throughout the house. In the Madison suite, for example, there's a Chinese display cabinet and several pieces of art along with the handsome four-poster dressed in lacy linens, a wing chair, and love seat. All of the rooms are attractive, and the parlor is very inviting, too. Beams and fireplace help, but the furnishings add another level of comfort—plush sofa, leather wingbacks, several oriental rugs, and lots of decorative accents, from a rose bowl to porcelain lamps. Breakfast is served at a long table at one end of the parlor. It will probably consist of a dish like coconut French toast, plus fruits and breads. The spacious gardens slope down to a creek where there are several seating arrangements for guests who want to enjoy quiet conversation. *Rates:* Summer, $110 to $170; winter, $100 to $150.

ESSEX

ESSEX ATTRACTIONS

The town of Essex itself is an attraction, with its quiet tree-lined streets bordered by fine old **colonial houses**, many of them shipbuilders' and sea captains' homes that have survived from when Essex was a great shipbuilding town. Take some time to walk the streets, browse in the stores, pop into the Griswold Inn (see below), and explore the harbor area at the foot of Main Street, where the 1878 **steamboat dock** has been restored. It now houses the **Connecticut River Museum** (☎ 860/767-8269), displaying models, tools, paintings, and instruments relating to the river's history and that era when a 230-ton sidewheeler was a common sight en route from Hartford to New York City. The museum also includes a replica of the first U.S. submarine, the 1775 *Turtle. Hours:* Tuesday to Sunday 10am to 5pm. *Admission:* $4 adults, $3 seniors, $2 children ages 6 to 12.

The **Valley Railroad,** Railroad Avenue (☎ 860/767-0103), came to the valley in 1871, and today you can take a nostalgic trip aboard an old steam locomotive from Essex to Chester. The train roars down the tracks, smoke hissing and billowing and whistle blasting its arrival. The engineer stokes the roaring orange-red fire in the firebox before slowly pulling out at the "all aboard" signal. You can ride either in the 1915 passenger cars or in the 1927 Pullman parlor car, seated on plush, ruby-red swivel armchairs while you listen to the old radio's background music from the 1920s and 1930s. The train uses 3 tons of coal and 3,000 gallons of water on its rhythmic journey past the tidal wetlands, where wild rice and bull reeds sway, and along the riverbank to Chester and back to Deep River.

The trip can be combined with a **cruise up the river,** past Gillette Castle (see above) and the Goodspeed Opera House (see below); you will hear the lore and tales of the river and even picnic aboard. At Deep River, those taking the riverboat cruise debark. The whole trip (rail and river combined) takes about 2½ hours. Although it's beautiful at any time of year, summer and fall are particularly spectacular; so is December, when Santa Claus boards the train on weekends.

Hours: Different schedules prevail in spring, summer, and fall, and there's a special Santa schedule. Call for information. *Admission:* Train only, $10 adults, $5 children ages 3 to 11; train and cruise, $15 adults and $7.50 children ages 3 to 11; $3 extra to ride in the parlor car.

ESSEX LODGING & DINING

Affectionately known as "the Gris," the **Griswold Inn,** 36 Main St., Essex, CT 06426 (☎ 860/767-1776; fax 860/767-0481), is the kind of place that inspires genuine love and loyalty from visitors and residents alike. In this lovely 1776 inn the food is good and fairly priced, and the atmosphere is extremely congenial and unpretentious. People enjoy themselves, and you're likely to engage the people at the next table in conversation. The tavern is always festive, as is the crowd that frequents it—a mixture of locals and sailors and yachting crews in summer. An old popcorn machine dispenses in the corner, a cast-iron stove warms the place, and a small Christmas tree sparkles year-round. There's entertainment and impromptu dancing every night. Especially popular are Friday night's banjo entertainment and Monday night's sea chanteys. The dining rooms behind and off the tavern display museum-quality collections of marine art—Currier and Ives shipping prints, many related to the days when Essex turned out the fastest clippers on the ocean; marine oil paintings by Antonio Jacobsen; and artifacts from the steamboat era. The largest dining room is, in fact, a covered bridge. Fires blaze in each dining room in winter.

A traditional treat is the Gris's Sunday Hunt Breakfast (a modest $13), when you can help yourself to unlimited servings of eggs, bacon, ham, sausage, grits, fried potatoes, chicken, pasta dishes, creamed chipped beef, smelts, and whatever else is offered. At dinner the menu has fine fresh fish dishes like the hazelnut-crusted rainbow trout served with Frangelico butter sauce, and such traditional items as a mixed grill of sausages accompanied by sauerkraut and German potato salad, or prime rib, priced from $14 to $22. Save some room for the mud-slide pie for dessert.

The 30 accommodations are found up the creaky stairs, along the low uneven corridors, where the rooms are quaint and old-fashioned, with exposed beams, hooked rugs, old armoires, and marble-topped vanities. All have baths, air-conditioning, and phones; some even have water views. House guests help themselves to fresh fruit and toasted muffins served with fine jams and marmalades in the library in the morning. In summer you must reserve several months in advance, especially on weekends.

Rates (including continental breakfast): $100 to $1,255 double, from $145 suite. *Dining hours:* Monday to Thursday 11:45am to 3pm and 5:30 to 9pm, Friday 11:45am to 3pm and 5:30 to 10pm, Saturday 11:30am to 3pm and 5 to 10pm, Sunday 11am to 2:30pm (Hunt Breakfast) and 4:30 to 9pm.

ESSEX DINING

The Black Seal, 29 Main St. (☎ 860/767-0233), is a cozy, casual, convivial bar/restaurant with a distinctly nautical flavor. In the Sail Loft bar oars stretch from one end of the ceiling to the other; the dining room sports an upturned scull, ships' lanterns and models, and even a rack of navigational charts. Pretty floral cloths cover the tables. Though famous for its sautéed shrimp, scallops, calamari, and crabmeat in a red clam sauce served over pasta, the Black Seal also features salads, sandwiches, pizza, and steaks. Prices range from $7 to $17. *Hours:* Monday to Thursday 11:30am to 3:30pm and 5 to 9:30pm, Friday 11:30am to 3:30pm and 5 to 10pm, Saturday 11:30am to 4pm and 5 to 10pm, Sunday 11:30am to 4pm and 5 to 9pm.

Oliver's Taverne, Plains Road, Route 153 (☎ 860/767-2633), offers good-value burgers and sandwiches, all under $9. A good place for lunch, it's also a popular nighttime spot and is great for beer lovers, since it stocks beers from all over the world. *Hours:* Daily 11:30am to 10pm.

IVORYTON

IVORYTON LODGING & DINING

The **Copper Beech Inn**, 46 Main St., Ivoryton, CT 06442 (☎ 888/809-2056 or 860/767-0330; www.copperbeechinn.com), has been voted the most popular restaurant in the state for a decade or more, but it's much more than just a restaurant. It's a handsome inn set on 7 wooded acres. Once the residence of an ivory importer, it was built in the 1880s as an elegant country residence, complete with carriage barn and terraced gardens. The inn takes its name from the massive, beautiful copper beech that stands at the entrance to the property.

A formal dinner (with silver service) is served in three lovely dining rooms, each furnished in a different period style. The wood paneling, the Chinese porcelain collection, and other fine accents provide an elegant atmosphere. The menu, which changes seasonally, usually features about a dozen items plus daily specials. Among the entrees you might find roasted saddle of lamb served with a pistachio-lamb glaze and a ragoût of wild mushrooms; fillet of salmon stuffed with arugula and shiitake mushrooms, poached and served with a saffron-scented white wine and butter sauce; or the grilled breast of free-range chicken lightly coated with chopped pecans and served with a sauce of brown chicken glaze, honey, and black pepper. Prices range from $23 to $28. Favorite appetizers include the salad of chilled, poached lobster, fresh mango, and diced red onion, dressed with a mango vinaigrette; seared fresh duck foie gras served with morel mushrooms and a glaze of duck stock and Armagnac; or the pastry filled with artichoke hearts, spinach, and goat cheese. To accompany the meal, the wine list offers a wide selection of choices.

The desserts are also special, whether it's the gâteau—layers of hazelnut rum cake with lemon curd filling and a warm lemon sauce—or the mango and coconut sorbets served with grilled pineapple. If you wish to dine here, you'll need to reserve well in advance, especially for a weekend. Just off the inn's front parlor is a plant-filled conservatory overlooking the gardens and the venerable tree that gives the inn its name. Here you can enjoy a quiet drink.

There are also 13 elegantly decorated accommodations, 4 in the main house and 9 in the carriage house, all with baths and air-conditioning. The carriage-house rooms have whirlpool tubs, TVs, and French doors leading onto private decks. Some are furnished with canopied four-posters, and the second-floor rooms are made even more appealing by the exposed beams and cathedral ceiling.

Rates (including buffet breakfast): $120 to $190 double. *Dining hours:* Tuesday to Saturday 5:30 to 9pm, Sunday 1 to 9pm. Closed Tuesday January to March. Closed also December 24, December 25, January 1, and the first week in January.

CENTERBROOK DINING

In neighboring Centerbrook, **Steve's Centerbrook Cafe**, 78 Main St. (☎ 860/767-1277), has a reputation for being "brilliant but inconsistent." Under the control of young, French-inspired chef Steven Wilkinson, the restaurant turns out fine classic French cuisine priced from $14 to $19. To start, the crab and coconut soup is richly flavored, while the grilled tiger shrimp with avocado and a sweet chili dressing stimulates the appetite. Follow with a pasta dish like wild-mushroom ravioli with haricots verts and prosciutto with a light cream sauce, a grilled or sautéed dish like medallions of pork tenderloin with fresh peaches and a ginger and apricot brandy sauce, or a classic dish like rack of lamb with grilled portobello mushrooms and a delicious Merlot-rosemary sauce.

During the day people stop by the cafe's pâtisserie for desserts like Sacher torte and blueberry cheesecake. But the pièce de résistance—for which Wilkinson is famous—is a marjolaine, an almond-hazelnut torte layered with crème fraîche and bittersweet Belgian chocolate (which you can enjoy as dessert after dinner). An extensive fine wine list is available.

The ambience varies from room to room. The front porch room is airy and furnished with rattan chairs. In the two other rooms, chintz wallpapers, a Federal-style fireplace, and chair rails impart a more formal atmosphere.

Hours: Tuesday to Sunday 5:30 to 9pm.

HADDAM, EAST HADDAM & MOODUS

AREA ATTRACTIONS

East Haddam is the home of the gorgeously intricate Victorian **Goodspeed Opera House,** 1 Goodspeed Plaza (☎ 860/873-8668). Built in 1876 by wealthy entrepreneur/shipbuilder William Goodspeed, it thrived as a theater until the 1920s, when traffic and life passed it by. The theater, atop the six-floor building, has been beautifully restored and is dedicated to the preservation of the American musical. Around it a small village of antiques, crafts (especially good ones), and gift stores has grown up. *Tours:* June to mid-October, Monday 1 to 3pm and Saturday 11am to 1:30pm. *Admission:* $2 adults, $1 children ages 11 and under.

Just across the river you can see the **cruise boats** that sail from Haddam and across the sound to the ports of Sag Harbor and Greenport on Long Island's east end. A cruise gives you about 3 hours to explore before returning. On some dinner cruises there's Dixieland entertainment; on others you can help solve a murder mystery. For schedules and information, contact Camelot Cruises, 1 Marine Park, Haddam, CT 06438 (☎ 860/345-8591). *Sailings:* Usually late June to Labor Day, daily.

Shopping Along the way, just outside East Haddam on Route 82, you may want to stop at the Christmas Shoppe (☎ 860/873-9352), where 'tis the season year-round. *Hours:* Memorial Day to December 24, daily 10am to 5pm; January to May, Wednesday to Sunday 10am to 5pm.

EAST HADDAM LODGING & DINING

At night the 1826 Victorian mansion known as the **Inn at Goodspeed's Landing to Gelston House,** 8 Main St. (P.O. Box 262), East Haddam, CT 06423 (☎ 860/873-1411), across from the Goodspeed Opera House, takes on a particular romance with its riverside setting, luminous interior, and summer garden strung with twinkling lights. The dining room's pink tablecloths, green napkins, and low lighting make it positively romantic; when it's filled with pretheater diners, the atmosphere is positively charged with anticipation.

Your meal might begin with a portobello mushroom stuffed with lobster and crabmeat, or chilled shrimp with a wasabi cocktail sauce. Among the main courses, choices run to grilled salmon with roasted fennel and red onion rémoulade; lobster risotto flavored with mussels, butternut squash, chives, sage, and saffron; and filet mignon with blue cheese butter. Prices range from 19 to $26. Sunday brunch is worth coming for. In addition to the usual egg specialties (frittata with asparagus, tomatoes, scallions, and Asiago or eggs Benedict), you can enjoy such dishes as roast pork loin with a port wine glaze and grilled salmon with artichoke dill pesto. If you have to wait for a table, there's an elegant mirrored bar lit by gilt sconces and emerald-green Waterford crystal chandeliers. The beer garden is open daily.

Upstairs are six extremely large guest rooms (three doubles and three suites). Some have river views through floor-to-ceiling Palladian windows (Room 21, for instance). Drop-leaf side tables, colored engravings of landscapes hanging above a sleigh bed, an Empire-style table nestled against two period side chairs, a secretary complete with a set of Kipling and other books, ceramic table lamps, and beige wall-to-wall carpeting bestow a special quality on the rooms. Gilchrist & Soames soaps, talc, shoe shine, and shampoo in the bath add to one's sense of well-being.

Rates: $110 to $135 double, $250 suite. *Dining hours:* Summer, Wednesday to Saturday 11:30am to 2:30pm and 5 to 9pm, Sunday 11am to 2:30pm and 4 to 7pm. Call for winter hours.

Only a few hundred yards from the Goodspeed Opera House, the **Bishopsgate Inn**, Goodspeed Landing, East Haddam, CT 06423 (☎ 860/873-1677; fax 860/873-3898), is owned by the Kagel family, who have created a cozy yet elegant atmosphere by filling it with their many books, collectibles, and family antiques. In this 1818 home are six guest rooms (four with fireplaces, and a suite with a sauna and private deck), all furnished with Empire-style and pine country pieces. A full breakfast is served in the dining room, and dinner can also be arranged in advance. Guests can choose from five or so three-course menus. The least expensive (at $22.50) offers salad to start and a vegetarian main course like wild mushroom ravioli with steamed asparagus and lemon butter, plus a lemon mousse torte. The most expensive ($35) might feature a salad followed by pork medallions in mustard cream sauce accompanied by Swedish potatoes and vegetables, plus a similar dessert. *Rates* (including breakfast): $105 to $160 double.

A MOODUS RESORT

In the quiet countryside just east of East Haddam are several resorts, if that's your style. The most famous is the **Sunrise Resort**, P.O. Box 415, Moodus, CT 06469 (☎ 800/225-9033 or 860/873-8681; fax 860/873-8681; www.sunriseresort.com), a 56-acre property set on 500 acres run by the Johnson family.

This won't be everyone's idea of a weekend retreat, but it's great fun for families. In season there's around-the-clock entertainment. Facilities include a large outdoor pool, miniature golf, scuba lessons, art lessons, four tennis courts, an exercise room, a sauna, a whirlpool, canoes, rowboats, and more, all designed to keep the whole family occupied. After-dark entertainments are provided, too—movies, magicians, poolside bands, and saloon-style piano playing. Several theme weekends are offered, like Traditional Jazz and Bluegrass.

The 160 guest rooms are in fairly modern two-floor motel units, older cabins back in the woods, or refurbished cabins at the river's edge. On the Salmon River, a tributary of the Connecticut River, you'll find a quiet oasis where an early morning breakfast is served every Tuesday as the sun rises behind the trees. There's no bar, but setups are provided for those interested, and wine or champagne is served at special events or celebrations. For a $20-per-person fee you can use the inn's facilities for the day and also enjoy one meal. *Rates* (AP): $80 to $100 double.

THE AREA AFTER DARK
Theater

The **Goodspeed Opera House**, 1 Goodspeed Plaza, East Haddam (☎ 860/873-8668), is dedicated to preserving the works of America's musical greats—Irving Berlin, Jerome Kern, Cole Porter—and introducing new works of musical theater. It was, for example, the birthplace of such Broadway successes as *Annie* and *Man of La Mancha*. It produces three musicals per season, which runs from mid-April to early December. Tickets are $20 to $45.

Goodspeed has a second stage in nearby Chester at the **Norma Terris Theatre** that is dedicated to the development of new musicals. Three are produced each summer (from early May to late November). For information call ☎ 860/873-8668.

The **Ivoryton Playhouse**, Main Street, Ivoryton (☎ 860/767-8348), offers professional summer stock by the River Rep and community-oriented events.

The **National Theater of the Deaf**, a professional ensemble of deaf and hearing actors, spends most of its time touring internationally, but presents a summer storytelling series on the grounds of its home at The Meeting House, Goose Hill Road, Chester (☎ 860/526-4971). The free performances are held every Sunday in June.

Evening Cruises

Evening cruises are operated on the river from June to Labor Day. For information, contact the **New England Steamboat Lines**, Marine Park, Haddam, CT 06438 (☎ 860/345-4507). Evening lighthouse cruises operate from Saybrook Point daily mid-June through Labor Day. Jambalaya cruises leave from Charter Oak landing in Hartford, June through September on Thursday and Friday nights. Both are operated by the **Deep River Navigation Company**, River Street, Deep River, CT 06417 (☎ 860/526-4954).

Other Entertainment

The **Griswold Inn**, Main Street, Essex (☎ 860/767-1776), always has some good musical entertainment on hand—Dixieland, sea chanteys, banjo, and the like—and people dance on Friday and Saturday nights. **Oliver's Taverne** (see above) is a popular drinking spot. For quieter entertainment, just take a stroll around Essex or Chester or down by the water by the light of the moon or setting sun.

The Connecticut River Valley
Special & Recreational Activities

Antiquing: There are four or five interesting stores for browsing in Essex and one or two in Chester, including a store that specializes in making lamps of all kinds patterned after old designs. Other shops are dotted around the area.

Bicycling: Rentals are available at **Village Provisions**, 6 Main St., in Essex (☎ 860/767-7376), for $25 per day.

Camping: The area boasts several choice spots, including some special camping reserved for canoeists where the only access is by canoe—making for a genuine camping experience. These campsites are available by reservation only between May 1 and September 30. Write or call Manager, **Gillette Castle State Park**, East Haddam, CT 06423 (☎ 860/526-2336), at least 3 weeks in advance of your chosen dates. Such camping exists at

Hurd State Park, East Hampton; **Gillette Castle State Park**, Hadlyme; and **Selden Neck State Park**, Lyme.

Camping with shore access can be found at either **Hammonasset State Park**, P.O. Box 271, Madison, CT 06443 (☎ 203/245-1817), where 560 sites are available near the 2-mile sandy beach; or at **Rocky Neck State Park**, P.O. Box 676, Niantic, CT 06357 (☎ 860/739-5471), with 160 sites.

For wilderness camping try **Devil's Hopyard State Park**, East Haddam, CT 06423 (☎ 860/873-8566), 5 miles south of Colchester on Route 82. Many legends have been attached to its name. Some say that it was named after a man named Dibble who grew hops and whose name became corrupted to "devil." Others say that the locals, mystified by the perfectly cylindrical potholes at the base of Chapman's Falls, concocted a story that the devil had passed the falls and accidentally got his tail wet, which made him so angry that he burned holes in the stones with his hooves as he bounded away.

For detailed information on state parks, call ☎ 860/566-2304.

Canoeing: Downriver Canoes on Route 154 in Haddam (☎ 860/345-8355) rents canoes for $30 a day, but they do not recommend going on the river on weekends when paddling traffic is heavy. Instead they can direct you to suitable lakes.

Fishing: Bashan Lake, off Route 82 in East Haddam; **Moodus Reservoir**, with access 2 miles east of Moodus and a mile southeast of Route 149. Brook trout can be found in the **Eight Mile River** in Devil's Hopyard.

Fruit Picking: *Middlefield:* **Lyman Orchards**, at the junction of routes 147 and 157 (☎ 860/349-1566), for apples, raspberries, sweet corn, tomatoes, squash, pumpkins.

Golf: At **Lyman Meadow Golf Club**, Route 157 (☎ 860/349-8055), greens fees are $47 or $59; the 18-hole par 54 **Cedar Ridge Golf Course**, Drabik Road, East Lyme (☎ 860/691-4568), charges $21.

Hiking: Plenty of local state parks have trails—**Hurd, Gillette Castle, Selden Neck, Chatfield Hollow,** and **Devil's Hopyard State Park**, East Haddam, CT 06423 (☎ 860/873-8566), 5 miles south of Colchester on Route 82. The last has 15 miles of trails. The main feature of the park is Chapman Falls, which drops 60 feet over a series of stone steps on the Eight Mill River. For detailed information, contact the **Connecticut Forest and Park Association**, 16 Meriden Rd., Rockfall, CT 06481 (☎ 860/346-2372).

Picnicking: The **banks of the Connecticut River** itself afford plenty of picnicking opportunities. At **Hurd State Park** you'll have to climb down to the river. Pick up supplies in Middletown or East Haddam. Five miles south of Colchester, **Devil's Hopyard** also has a hemlock shaded picnicking area. Farther south, **Gillette State Park** makes a beautiful picnic setting. Pick up supplies in Chester and take the ferry across the river to the park. **Haddam Meadows State Park** offers picnicking beside the river in a largely unwooded area filled with goldenrod and wildflowers. Stop in East Haddam for supplies.

For shore picnics, head for **Rocky Neck** or **Hammonasset State Park**. Pick up supplies in Old Lyme and Clinton, respectively.

Skiing: Downhill at Powder Ridge, Middlefield, CT 06455 (☎ 860/349-3454), off Route 147, provides five slopes, five chairlifts, and 15 trails.

State Parks: For information, contact **the Department of Environmental Protection,** State Parks Division, 79 Elm St., Hartford, CT 06106-5127 (☎ 860/424-3200).

Swimming: Shore swimming at **Rocky Neck State Park,** East Lyme (☎ 860/739-5471), with a boardwalk and so on ($12 weekend parking); also at **Harvey's Beach,** Old Saybrook; in Chester at **Cedar Lake.** Some of the resorts in Moodus open their facilities for the day for a moderate fee: for example, **Sunrise** (☎ 860/873-8681).

Tennis: Check with the local chambers of commerce for high school locations.

HARTFORD & ENVIRONS

If you were to continue up the Connecticut River by boat from Middletown, you'd soon reach Hartford. On land it's only a short drive up Route 9 and I-91 into this city, which—believe it or not—has several American cultural gems. State capital and world-famous insurance center, Hartford might not be a bucolic dream weekend destination, but it's worth visiting while you're in the area because it has several exceptional attractions.

For me the most thrilling experience is a visit to Mark Twain's bulky, convoluted mansion and the smaller, simpler home of Harriet Beecher Stowe that stands only 100 yards away from Twain's. These authors were two of the many notable residents of Nook Farm, a brilliant intellectual community that thrived here in the mid- to late 1800s. Just around the corner in West Hartford, you can visit the home of the indefatigable compiler of the American dictionary, Noah Webster. Downtown Hartford boasts the first public art museum established in the United States, the very fine Wadsworth Atheneum, and some first-rate architecture, including buildings by Henry Hobson Richardson. Here you'll also find Charles Bulfinch's first commission, the Old State House. Nearby, in the lovely village of Farmington, you can view a collection of works by Édouard Manet and other impressionist artists; a 10-minute drive south of Hartford is the historic village of Wethersfield.

HARTFORD ATTRACTIONS

The **Wadsworth Atheneum,** 600 Main St. (☎ 860/278-2670), sits across from Carl André's controversial *Stone Field* (36 boulders, seemingly thrown down haphazardly, commissioned in 1975 for $87,000). The Wadsworth is a delight. It's a perfect size for the museum-goer, housed in five buildings around a sculpture court and filled with an impressive selection of art—works by Monet, Renoir, Boudin and a group of interesting American primitives, including a lovely Asa Ames polychromed wood statue of a child with a lamb, two galleries of large 19th-century Hudson River landscapes by Thomas Cole and Frederic Church, and several works by Henry Tanner. Modern art by Sol Lewitt, Duane Hanson, and Joseph Cornell fills the Hilles Gallery. Other highlights include the Wallace Nutting collection of "Pilgrim Century" American furniture and decorative arts, the Amistad Foundation's collection

Hartford

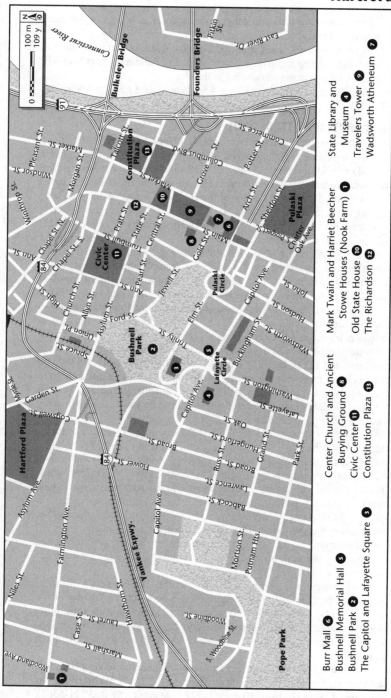

Burr Mall **6**
Bushnell Memorial Hall **5**
Bushnell Park **2**
The Capitol and Lafayette Square **3**

Center Church and Ancient
Burying Ground **8**
Civic Center **11**
Constitution Plaza **13**

Mark Twain and Harriet Beecher
Stowe Houses (Nook Farm) **1**
Old State House **10**
The Richardson **12**

State Library and
Museum **4**
Travelers Tower **9**
Wadsworth Atheneum **7**

of African American art, and other collections of silver, Early American furniture, and porcelain.

On your way out, don't miss Alexander Calder's massive *Stegosaurus,* between the Atheneum and the adjacent Municipal Building in Burr Mall. The Museum Café is also the place to eat in the city.

Hours: Tuesday to Sunday 11am to 5pm. *Admission:* $7 adults, $5 seniors, $3 children ages 6 to 17; free for everyone Thursday.

WEST HARTFORD ATTRACTIONS

An important cultural-intellectual community, **Nook Farm,** 77 Forest St., off Farmington Avenue (take Exit 46 off I-84), West Hartford, was settled in the last half of the 19th century by interrelated families and friends. Among them were such celebrities as Isabella Beecher Hooker, women's rights leader; Charles Dudley Warner, author and editor of the *Hartford Courant;* William Gillette, playwright and actor; and authors Mark Twain and Harriet Beecher Stowe.

Painted his favorite turkey red, **Mark Twain's house** (☎ 860/493-6411) is large, grand, and rather ungainly compared to the smaller Beecher house across the way. Once inside, you'll discover more quirks incorporated into the house by the ornery, eccentric humorist. For example, the telephone, which he abhorred, is located in a closet, and the etched windows in the top-floor study, where he wrote *Tom Sawyer, Huckleberry Finn,* and several other volumes, depict the activities Twain considered most important in life— smoking, drinking, and billiards. In the bedroom he placed the pillows at the foot of his bed so he could gaze at the ornately carved Venetian headboard, for which he'd paid a princely sum. Twain lived here with his wife, three daughters, and 11 cats from 1874 to 1881, when his debts (he'd lost $750,000 in two capital investment ventures) forced him to sell the house and go to Europe on a lecture tour. A visit to the house is particularly rewarding because it reflects Twain's whimsical personality and because you're able to actually enter the rooms instead of having to peer in from outside.

The **Beecher house** (☎ 860/525-9317), built in 1871, is more ordinary. Harriet moved here in 1873 and stayed until her death in 1896. The house still has many pieces of her furniture, paintings by her, and also the kitchen designed to her specifications as outlined in *The American Woman's Home,* which she co-authored with her sister. (They were the first to recommend that plants, instead of curtains, be hung in windows!) Whereas Twain's house contains a specific writing room (albeit filled with a full-size billiard table), the Beecher house has only a tiny desk where she supposedly wrote many of her 33 (yes, that's right) books. One gets the impression that she probably wrote on the run, wherever and whenever she could grab the time between her daily tasks.

Hours: Twain house, Memorial Day to Columbus Day, Monday to Saturday 9:30am to 4pm, Sunday 11am to 4pm; other months, closed Tuesday. Stowe house, Monday to Saturday 9:30am to 4pm, Sunday noon to 4pm; other months, closed Monday. *Admission:* Twain house, $9 adults, $8 seniors, $5 children ages 6 to 12; Stowe house, $6.50 adults, $6 seniors, $2.75 children ages 6 to 12.

From Nook Farm you can take Farmington Avenue west to West Hartford's Main Street, turning left down Main Street to the **Noah Webster House/ Museum of West Hartford History** at 227 S. Main St. (☎ 860/521-5362).

This 18th-century farmhouse was the birthplace of Noah Webster (1758–1843), patriot, schoolmaster, and lawyer who wrote *An American Dictionary of the English Language* (1828) and the *Blue Backed Speller* (1783), one of the nation's most famous schoolbooks. He helped establish the first copyright laws and was one of the founders of Amherst College. Webster lived here until he was 16 years old, when he left to attend Yale University. The house is furnished as it might have appeared in 1774 when he left, and it contains his memorabilia. Other exhibits document the history of West Hartford and the lives of its residents. Thirty pieces of Goodwin Pottery, which was made locally in the 19th century, are also on display. *Hours:* July 1 to August 31, Monday, Tuesday, Thursday, and Friday 10am to 4pm; Saturday and Sunday 1 to 4pm. September 1 to June 30, Thursday to Tuesday 1 to 4pm. Closed major holidays. *Admission:* $5 adults, $4 seniors, $1 children ages 6 to 12.

ATTRACTIONS IN & AROUND FARMINGTON

The **Hill-Stead Museum,** 35 Mountain Rd., Farmington (☎ 860/677-9064 or 860/677-4787), was once the home of self-made millionaire/steel magnate Alfred Atmore Pope, a pioneer collector of impressionist art. After his death his daughter, Theodate, preserved his collection in its original setting at the family home, which she had helped design for him at the age of 16—she was one of the first women in this country to qualify as an architect. A number of notable personages visited her at Hill-Stead: Painter Mary Cassatt loved to walk through these rooms, Henry James described the house in *The American Scene* as "apparently conceived—and with great felicity—on the lines of a magnificent Mount Vernon," Isadora Duncan danced in the gardens, and poet John Masefield contemplated the surrounding pastoral meadows. The Monets, Whistlers, and Manets are hung as if the house were still occupied, in rooms filled with majolica, Chinese porcelain, and other fine decorative objects and antiques. Hill-Stead still covers 150 acres of fields and woodlands. The grounds feature a reconstruction of the original Sunken Gardens designed by prominent landscape gardener Beatrix Farrand. *Hours:* April to October, Tuesday to Sunday 10am to 5pm; November to March, Tuesday to Sunday 11am to 4pm. By guided tour only; last tour given an hour before closing. *Admission:* $6 adults, $5 seniors, $3 children ages 6 to 12.

Only a 20-minute drive south of Farmington, the **New Britain Museum of Art,** 56 Lexington St. (☎ 860/229-0257), has a fine collection of American art, including works by Gilbert Stuart, William Jennys, Frederic Church, Albert Bierstadt, John Singer Sargent, Childe Hassam, and Charles Burchfield. They're displayed in a fine old residence. More modern works can be found in the new wing. *Hours:* Tuesday to Sunday 1 to 5pm. *Admission:* Donation requested.

EXPLORING OLD WETHERSFIELD

About 8 miles south of Hartford Old Wethersfield—the onion-raising capital of the colonies in the 18th century—is now a fascinating historic district where over 150 pre-1850 structures have been preserved. Barns, warehouses, and carriage houses have been transformed into shops selling everything from crafts and antiques to toys and gardening supplies.

If shopping is not your favorite pastime, two historic sites are worth visiting. The **Buttolph Williams House** (1692), at Broad and Marsh streets (☎ 860/529-0460), shelters an outstanding collection of pewter, Delft, fabrics, and furniture and displays a fine 17th-century kitchen filled with wooden plates and salvers, wrought-iron utensils, and a rare semicircular settle. The Greate Hall Chamber has a very fine 17th-century New England oak chest and several examples of flame-stitch embroidery.

The **Webb-Deane-Stevens Museum,** 211 Main St. (☎ 860/529-0612), consists of three 18th-century homes. The Webb home was used for Washington's conference with Rochambeau to plot the strategy that led to the defeat of the British at Yorktown. In 1916 photographer Wallace Nutting purchased the house and commissioned the striking murals in the front parlor depicting the story of the Battle of Yorktown. Each house reflects the individual lifestyle of its owner: merchant Silas Deane, who was America's first ambassador to France, and leatherworker Isaac Stevens. The decorative arts collections span the period from 1640 to 1840. *Hours:* May to October, Wednesday to Monday 10am to 4pm; November to April, Saturday to Sunday 10am to 4pm (last tours at 3pm). *Admission* (for three-house tour, plus the Buttolph Williams house): $8 adults, $7 seniors, $4 students ages 12 to 18, $2 children ages 6 to 11.

For more information on other local historic houses, call the **Wethersfield Historical Society** at ☎ 860/529-7656.

AREA LODGING & DINING

Hartford has no really outstanding lodging choices, but the major hotels do offer weekend packages. For additional B&Bs to those below, contact **Nutmeg Bed and Breakfast Agency,** P.O. Box 1117, West Hartford, CT 06127 (☎ 800/727-7592 or 860/236-6698). Call for a directory to B&Bs throughout the state. Rates for these B&Bs range from $95 to $260 double.

The nicest accommodations in Hartford are at the **Goodwin Hotel,** 1 Hayne's St. (☎ 860/246-7500), an apartment building that's been converted into a full-service hotel. The 124 extra-large rooms are handsomely decorated with modern sleigh beds and other reproductions. Other amenities include a phone with computer jack, a well-lit desk, and a phone and hair dryer in the bath. The restaurant, Pierpont's, is very popular locally and occupies a lovely room of glazed mahogany and mirrors. There's also a piano bar/lounge. Facilities include a fitness room. *Rates:* Weekdays $210 to $287 double, weekends $99 to $169 double (higher prices are for suites).

Fetching accommodations can be found at the **Babcock Tavern and B&B,** 484 Mile Hill Rd. (at Cedar Swamp), in Tolland (☎ 860/875-1239), where the innkeepers have been collecting antiques for more than 40 years. There are three guest rooms: The East Room features a brass bed and Shaker settle among its furnishings. The Ballroom, the largest, is the most appealing; it contains a canopied bed, a rocker, and such decorative pieces as a cradle and wash stand. Breakfast is served by candlelight to the strains of Mozart at pine tables. To get there, take I-84 to Exit 67. Then make a right onto Route 31. *Rates* (including breakfast): $80 to $95 double.

The **Tolland Inn,** On the Green, Tolland (☎ 860/872-0800), has seven rooms (all with bath) furnished variously with maple or brass beds, Mission-style rockers, and other pieces (some even crafted by the owner). The most expensive room has a fireplace and spa tub for two. *Rates* (including breakfast): $75 to $140 double.

For a serene luncheon setting, the **Museum Café,** 600 Main St. (☎ 860/728-5989), is at the Wadsworth Atheneum. The interior has a minimalist black-and-gray look, accented by one or two large Chinese urns, but in summer the restaurant moves out into the courtyard. The menu is short and simple. Among the entrees you might find grilled mahimahi with a scallion-ginger aïoli, along with caramelized onions, crimini mushrooms, and potato salad; or a wrap filled with gravlax, red peppers, tomato, scallions, and napa cabbage and spread with maple hoisin sauce. Desserts are somewhat predictable—carrot cake, ice cream, and lemon mousse cake. Prices range from $8 to $10. *Hours:* Tuesday to Saturday 11:30am to 2pm, Sunday 11:30am to 2:30pm (brunch).

AVON DINING

The Forge Room at the 1757 **Avon Old Farms Inn**, routes 44 and 10 in Avon (☎ 860/677-2818), is especially inviting, particularly in winter, when a blazing fire casts a warm glow over the stone floors and the blacksmith's tools adorning the walls. The tables have been artfully arranged, leaving the actual horse stalls intact. The menu consists of traditional old favorites like baked stuffed shrimp and prime rib, plus new American dishes. Among the latter you might find cumin-crusted salmon with a cilantro-lemon cream, or rack of lamb with mango and fresh mint barbecue sauce. Prices range from $15 to $27. The brunch is a huge $16 buffet spread. The tavern offers a lighter, less expensive menu. *Hours:* Monday to Saturday 11:30am to 5:30pm, Sunday 10am to 2:30pm; Monday to Thursday 5:30 to 9:30pm, Fri 5:30 to 10pm, Saturday 5:30 to 10:30pm, Sunday 5:30 to 8:30pm.

FARMINGTON DINING

In **Apricots**, 1593 Farmington Ave. (☎ 860/673-5903), crowds gather downstairs in the pub with piano entertainment. Upstairs are two dining rooms, one with a river view. The menu changes weekly, but here are some recent possibilities: rack of lamb with a mint pesto, grilled swordfish in a sweet basil and lemon beurre blanc, grilled herb and garlic marinated breast of chicken with a wild mushroom risotto, and a superb halibut in a blood-orange vinaigrette. Among the appetizers you might enjoy a chilled seafood salad made with lobster, shrimp, crab, and squid. Entree prices run $18 to $26. A lighter pub menu is also available. Brunch includes traditional egg dishes with items like fish or a pasta du jour and a seafood crêpe. *Hours:* Monday to Saturday 11:30am to 2:30pm and 6 to 9:30pm, Sunday 11:30am to 2:30pm (brunch) and 6 to 9pm.

Mystic & the Connecticut Shoreline

*Mystic ◆ Stonington ◆ North Stonington ◆ Stonington Village ◆
Watch Hill ◆ Ledyard ◆ Noank ◆ Shelter Harbor, R.I. ◆
Groton ◆ New London ◆ Norwich*

Distance in miles: New London, 121; Mystic, 130; Norwich, 138; Westerly, R.I., 147

Estimated driving time: 2 to 3 hours

◄o►◄o►◄o►◄o►◄o►

Driving: Take the FDR Drive to the New England Thruway (I-95).

Bus: Greyhound (☎ 800/231-2222) travels to New London. Greyhound also travels directly to the casinos at Ledyard.

Train: Amtrak travels to New London, Mystic, and Westerly. For information, call ☎ 800/872-7245.

Further Information: For more about the area's events and festivals and about Connecticut in general, call or write **Connecticut State Tourism**, 505 Hudson St., Hartford, CT 06106 (☎ 800/282-6863 or 860/270-8081).

For specific information about the area, contact **Connecticut's Mystic and More**, 470 Bank St. (P.O. Box 89), New London, CT 06320 (☎ 860/444-2206); the **Mystic Chamber of Commerce**, 28 Cottrell St. (P.O. Box 143), Mystic, CT 06355 (☎ 860/572-9578); the **Mystic and Shoreline Visitor Information Center**, Olde Mistick Village, CT 06355 (☎ 860/536-1641); the **Eastern Connecticut Chamber of Commerce**, One Thames Plaza, Suite 211, Norwich, CT 06360 (☎ 860/887-1647); or the **Norwich Tourism Commission**, 69 Main St., Norwich, CT 06360 (☎ 860/886-4683).

◄o►◄o►◄o►◄o►◄o►

If you've ever felt the call of the sea or the desire to "mess around in boats," then you'll be strongly attracted to Mystic and the Connecticut shoreline. You'll be in direct contact with the sea and the heritage of the seafarers that went out from these whaling and shipbuilding towns to risk their lives on the world's oceans.

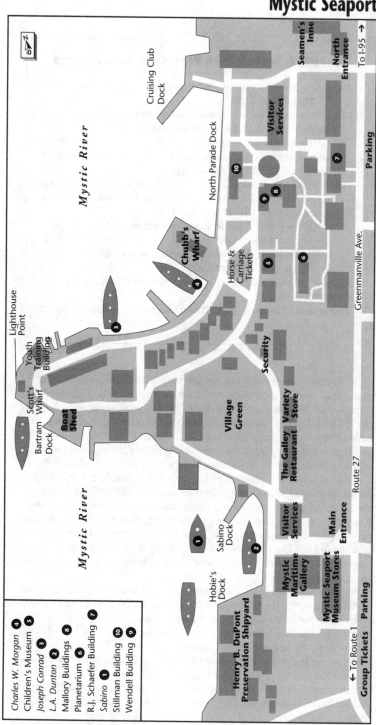

Mystic Seaport

Charles W. Morgan **4**
Children's Museum **5**
Joseph Conrad **3**
L.A. Dunton **2**
Mallory Buildings **8**
Planetarium **6**
R.J. Schaefer Building **7**
Sabino **1**
Stillman Building **10**
Wendell Building **9**

Lighthouse Point
Youth Training Building
Scott's Wharf
Bartram Dock
Boat Shed
Chubb's Wharf
Cruising Club Dock
North Parade Dock
Horse & Carriage Tickets
Seamen's Inne
North Entrance
To I-95 →
Visitor Services
Parking
Greenmanville Ave.
Security
Village Green
The Galley Restaurant
Variety Store
Route 27
Visitor Services
Main Entrance
Mystic Maritime Gallery
Mystic Seaport Museum Stores
Hobie's Dock
Sabino Dock
Henry B. DuPont Preservation Shipyard
← To Route 1
Group Tickets
Parking

Mystic River

Events & Festivals to Plan Your Trip Around

May: Sea Music Festival, Mystic Seaport (usually mid-May). Call ☎ 860/444-2206.

June: Rose/Arts Festival, Norwich—featuring entertainment, arts and crafts, and the Big Rose Parade (usually mid- to late June).

    Windjammer Weekend, Mystic Seaport—when schooners and sail-training vessels gather before the race to Newport (mid-June). Call ☎ 860/536-1641.

July: Blessing of the Fleet, Stonington Harbor—a mass, procession, and blessing in the Portuguese tradition (usually the second Sunday). Call ☎ 860/536-1641.

    Antique and Classic Boat Rendezvous, Mystic Seaport, complete with flotilla (usually late July). Call ☎ 860/536-1641.

    Coast Guard Day, New London and Mystic Seaport (usually the last Saturday). Call ☎ 860/536-1641.

August: Mystic Outdoor Art Festival (second weekend). Call ☎ 860/444-2206.

December: Lantern Light/Yuletide Tours, Mystic Seaport

In Mystic, besides the two prime attractions—the seaport and the aquarium—you can experience the life on the river that cuts through downtown Mystic. You can even spend one or both of your weekend days sailing out of Mystic harbor aboard a replica of the tall-masted schooners that used to embark from here to sail around the world. Across the harbor in Stonington, an unspoiled old whaling town that still maintains a fishing fleet, the streets are lined with clapboard sea captains' homes, many now owned by celebrities. Stonington is also the place to go for some fine romantic dining. North of Mystic and Stonington, you can take trips along the backroads to a cider mill, a vineyard, or the historic Denison Homestead, with its scenic nature reserve. And for those who've caught the gambling bug, there's the largest-grossing casino in the nation operated by the Mohegans at Ledyard. At Groton, you can tour the first nuclear submarine, the *Nautilus,* and the World War II submarine, the *U.S.S. Croaker,* a sober reminder of how far and how fast technology has come since the 1940s.

Various boat trips leave from here, including interesting oceanographic expeditions. Across the other side of the Thames River's mouth, New London holds some surprises. If you drove through, you'd think it was just another rather ugly industrial town, but it possesses one of the East Coast's finest arboretums, an engaging small museum, a special dollhouse and doll museum, the impressive Coast Guard Academy, and the summer home of one of America's greatest playwrights, Eugene O'Neill. Only 30 minutes up the Thames from New London lies Norwich, an old town that has a fascinating art and sculpture museum, the Slater Memorial, a lovely restored lodging place with full spa treatments, and a Native American museum nearby.

Besides all these attractions, the area affords wonderful opportunities for fishing, sailing, windsurfing, hiking, and swimming. Plus, you can explore a coastline dotted with state parks, like Harkness and Bluff Point, and lined with fine beaches, from New London's Ocean Beach (with a boardwalk and an amusement park) to the more rugged and natural beaches of Rhode Island.

MYSTIC, STONINGTON & LEDYARD

MYSTIC SEAPORT

There's always something happening at this 17-acre replica of a 19th-century seafaring village on Route 27 (☎ 860/572-0711). Mystic Seaport is the largest marine museum in the United States, built appropriately enough on the site of the George Greenman and Company shipyard, which constructed such vessels as the *David Crockett* (its average speed on 25 voyages around Cape Horn to San Francisco was never equaled).

For today's seafarers, the coal-fired steamboat *Sabino* (1908) chugs out from the dock every hour, daily from May to mid-October, for a 30-minute trip down the Mystic River. At Christmas, lantern-light tours and caroling add to the holiday festivities of a 19th-century village; sea chantey and other music festivals are put on in summer. As you stroll through the village you'll hear the clanking and hammering of the many craftspeople and artisans still demonstrating and practicing nautical trades—barrel making, sail making, figurehead carving, and shipsmithing. In the stores alongside them you can view the products and learn how they work. In the clock maker's store, for instance, you may even learn how to work an astrolabe. Hearth-cooking demonstrations go on in Buckingham House, while the many special demonstrations of seafaring skills range from sail setting and furling aboard the square-rigged *Joseph Conrad* (1882) to whaleboat rowing.

By the way, the whaling film is extremely informative and will give you some idea of how hair-raising a "Nantucket sleigh ride" can be and just how short-lived but vital the whale industry was in the mid-1800s. Another informative show (a small fee is charged), at the planetarium, concerns celestial navigation.

You may want to begin in the Stillman Building, which contains an exhibit tracing the history of the last wooden whaler afloat, the *Charles W. Morgan*, and illuminating New England's fishing and shipping history. Don't miss the beautiful and moving scrimshaw that's displayed on the upper floor or the dramatic (and sometimes alarming or amusing) figureheads in the Wendell Building across the way.

Although the museum actually owns about 480 craft—smacks, sloops, sandbaggers, and even something called a New Haven sharpie—there are three main ships to go aboard: the last survivor of America's once-vast fleet of wooden whalers, the *Charles W. Morgan* (whose 37 voyages between 1841 and 1921 yielded 54,483 barrels of oil and 152,934 pounds of whalebone); the 1921 *L. A. Dunton* (a fishing schooner that went regularly to the Grand Banks and whose lower deck and hold give you a good idea of the arduous task a fisherman faced living in such cramped quarters for so long at sea); and the square-rigged *Joseph Conrad* (1882).

The seaport was used as a location in the recent Steven Spielberg film *Amistad*. In 1998 the museum began building a replica of the schooner *Amistad* using the same materials and methods as would have been used for the original. The 80-foot, $3.1 million schooner is expected to be completed in 2000.

The museum suggests that you spend at least 4 hours here, but you could easily spend a full day. In summer you'll find many crowds, so get here early; the nicest time to visit (as usual) is in spring or fall, when everything seems less frantic. Fast food is available at the Galley; full-service meals at the Seamen's Inne, whose tavern section is the coziest and most appealing, but where only good luck and timing will ensure a seat.

Hours: Exhibit buildings and ships, daily 10am to 4pm year-round; grounds, daily 9am to 5pm. *Admission:* $16 adults, $8 children ages 6 to 12.

MYSTIC MARINELIFE AQUARIUM

This magnificent facility at 55 Coogan Blvd., Exit 90 off I-95 (☎ 860/572-5955), is just finishing a $52 million expansion that will add an Institute for Exploration that will be headed by deep-water archaeologist and *Titanic* discoverer, Dr. Robert D. Ballard. When the institute opens in spring 1999, visitors will be able to experience a simulated descent to 3,000 feet beneath the ocean's surface and to visit a replica of a control room aboard a research vessel used for discovering and exploring shipwrecks. The expansion also includes renovation of the main building and the Dolphin Theater, as well as a new outdoor Beluga whale display, scheduled to open in 1999.

The aquarium houses 6,000 marine life specimens representing 200 species. On your visit, try to attend one of the hourly training sessions given in the Dolphin Theater, where the natural talents of bottlenose dolphins and whales never cease to amaze and delight audiences. Dolphins leap 20 feet in the air, performing triple spirals, even walking on their tails and sweeping through the water, propelled by the 8 horsepower in their tails to reach speeds of 50 to 60 miles per hour. You'll also view the white Beluga whale cavorting with his trainer. Among the outdoor exhibits, don't miss Seal Island, a 2½-acre exhibit with four species of seals and sea lions, including the rarely seen Steller's sea lions.

Feeding time is always fun, and each creature has its own finicky habits— this one wants only tails, another only heads, and so on. Back in the Ocean Planet Pavilion you can visit four themed galleries of marine life. The most impressive is the 30,000-gallon tank that is the centerpiece of the Coral Reef gallery. This tank, which can be viewed from below and above, contains distinctive bonnethead sharks; rays; and butterfly, goat, and trigger fish plus other species. Another gallery explores shoreline habitats from the salt marsh to the mangrove swamp. The Upwelling Zones gallery focuses on the deep ocean and displays such marine life as sea nettle jellyfish with 3- and 4-foot-long tentacles. It's a fascinating world. Visitors will also want to browse in the new gift shop, which has some good educational books, toys, and games.

Hours: Daily 9am to 5pm (to 6pm in summer). Closed New Year's Day, Thanksgiving, and Christmas. *Admission:* $13 adults, $12 seniors, $8 children ages 3 to 12.

CRUISING FROM MYSTIC

Recapture the aura of the days when Mystic was filled with whalers and schooners lying cheek by jowl against smacks and packet sloops. You can do so by cruising aboard the *Mystic Whaler,* a windjammer schooner that sails on regular 3-hour trips, and 1-, 2-, 3-, or 5-day voyages on Long Island and Block Island sounds; it calls at Sag Harbor, Block Island, Newport, and other ports. The sails leave from 7 Holmes St., Mystic. For information, contact **Mystic Whaler Cruises**, P.O. Box 189, Mystic, CT 06355 (☎ 860/536-4218). Prices are about $70 for a 1-day sail (including lunch). The schooner *Argia*, a replica of a 19th-century windjammer, offers morning, afternoon, and evening sails, leaving from Steamboat Wharf in downtown Mystic from May to the end of October. Costs are about $30 per person. Contact **Voyager Cruises**, Steamboat Wharf, Mystic, CT 06355 (☎ 860/536-0416).

DOWNTOWN MYSTIC, OLD MYSTIC & ENVIRONS

After visiting the seaport, take a walk down Gravel and High streets, past the many **historic houses** outlined in the Mystic Chamber of Commerce's walking tour. Each has a tale attached. For example, Matilda Appleman lived at 27 Gravel St., where she conducted seances and sheltered slaves traveling the Underground Railroad.

You may also want to explore downtown Mystic at the river's mouth, where the **bascule drawbridge** joins the two municipalities of Stonington and Groton. Actually, there's no such political entity as Mystic. This downtown area was developed when shipbuilding became big business in the mid- to late 1800s.

Shopping

In the downtown area, drop in and browse the crafts, fashion, book, gift, and antiques stores here, including **Factory Square. Olde Mistick Village**, at the junction of I-95 and Route 27 (☎ 860/536-4941), is a quaint shopping complex designed to look like a New England village of around 1720. The shops are usually open Monday to Saturday from 10am to 6pm and Sunday from noon to 5pm with extended summer and holiday season hours.

NEARBY ATTRACTIONS

From Old Mystic, you can drive out to **Clyde's Cider Mill**, North Stonington Road (☎ 860/536-3354), and watch the apples being pressed for cider as they have been since the mill was established in 1881. It operates from mid-September to Thanksgiving, daily from 9am to 5pm.

Stonington Vineyards, east on Taugwonk Road (☎ 860/535-1222), is one of the few wineries that are located in this area. It produces annually more than 7,000 cases of wine that are distributed locally. *Tours:* Daily at 2pm; in winter call ahead to confirm.

Looping back toward Stonington, you can stop at the **Denison Homestead and Nature Center** on Pequotsepos Road (☎ 860/536-9248). Since 1722, the homestead has belonged to five generations of Denisons, one of Connecticut's first families, and the house is interesting because each room has been furnished to reflect the five different periods. Trails crisscross the 125-acre sanctuary (☎ 860/536-1216). *Hours:* Homestead, May 20 to October 15, Wednesday to Monday 1 to 5pm; Nature Center, year-round, Monday to

Saturday 9am to 5pm and Sunday 1 to 5pm. *Admission:* Homestead, $3 adults, $1 children ages 2 to 16; Nature Center, $4 adults, $2 children ages 6 to 16.

STONINGTON VILLAGE & WATCH HILL

In the dining section I'll describe two restaurants where you might want to dine, but before you do, take some time to discover this old whaling village. Edgar Allan Poe loved to visit this town, and Stephen Vincent Benet and James MacNeill Whistler both had residences. Today many a celebrity chooses to hide away here, as did the late poet James Merrill. Narrow streets lined with old sea captains' homes and Victorian residences cluster on a peninsula running between Stonington Harbor on one side and the Pawcatuck River and Fisher's Island Sound on the other.

Stroll down Water Street (plenty of good antiquing) to the 1840 **Stonington Light** (☎ 860/535-1440) that now houses a collection of whaling and fishing artifacts, toys, Stonington firearms, and stoneware. *Hours:* May to October, Tuesday to Sunday 10am to 5pm. *Admission:* $4 adults, $3 seniors, $2 children ages 6 to 12.

From Stonington, it's only a short drive to **Watch Hill**, a quiet, gracious shore enclave that possesses a number of rambling Victorian hotels, like the Ocean House, which have seen better days. The town is not too crowded. While you're here don't miss the carousel. Also stop at the Book and Tackle Shop, stacked with piles of old and new books and a good selection of historic postcards; have an ice cream across the street; walk to the Watch Hill Lighthouse; or just sit out on the Harbour House's deck and check out the scene.

For a casual meal head for the old-fashioned and fun **Olympia Tea Room** at 74 Bay St. (☎ 401/348-8211), which offers pasta and seafood accompanied by wine and beer served from the old-fashioned art deco soda fountain/bar. Dishes might include linguine marinara, chicken in a basket, shepherd's pie, sandwiches, plus a selection of seafood. Prices range from $6 to $18. It's a great place for breakfast, too, when you can secure some great omelets (lobster and scallion or jack cheese and salsa) plus French toast made with Portuguese bread. *Hours:* Easter to late October, daily 8am to 9pm, and to 10pm weekends.

NORTH TO LEDYARD

The village of Ledyard became famous when the Mashantucket Indians opened their first casino in 1992 (see below for details). The tribe has made an equally big impression with the opening in 1998 of the $193 million, state-of-the-art **Mashantucket Pequot Museum and Research Center**, 110 Pequot Trail, 1½ miles from Foxwoods Resort Casino (☎ 860/396-6800). The museum aims to tell the story of the survival and rebirth of the Mashantucket Pequots, tracing their history from the last Ice Age to the present. It does so with the help of dioramas, interactive displays, video, film, and simulation. Visitors begin by taking an escalator through a simulated glacier, complete with the sounds of cracking ice and the feel of icy air. Highlights from this early prehistoric era include a dramatic diorama of a caribou hunt. Four seasonal dioramas depict the way of life of the Woodland Indians. Aspects of daily life—the making of clothes, canoes, and wigwams; hunting, fishing, and raising food; and the creation and use of wampum—are explored in several films and video programs throughout the museum. The heart of the museum is a re-creation of a 17th-century Pequot village, populated by 51 life-sized figures showing the rituals of life in summer. Visitors carry an audio wand that explains the sights and sounds of the village. Several exhibits deal with the arrival of the Europeans and the impact on Native American life. A 30-minute film, *Witness,* dramatizes the Pequot War (1636–38) and massacre of the Pequots at Mystic Fort when 700 members of the tribe were killed in less than an hour by a small force of English soldiers and their Narragansett allies. The remainder of the exhibits trace the story from 1675 to the 1970s when the remnants of the tribe lived on the reservation. A replica of a typical farmstead house, circa 1780, contrasts with a mobile home from the 1970s, complete with outdoor shower and dented kettle on the stove.

Bringing the People Home is a short film that explains how the tribe rebuilt their nation. In 1970, only two elderly half-sisters lived on the reservation. One of them, Elizabeth George Plouffe, heard a rumor that the state was planning to take the reservation over. She summoned her family members home, and a couple of hundred members of the tribe returned to fight for tribal recognition. Finally achieved in 1983, recognition did not end the struggle for survival. Tribal members tried agriculture, hog raising, and maple sugaring—but it was bingo that was to ensure not only the tribe's survival but their enrichment.

There is a gallery for temporary exhibits and a research library capable of holding 150,000 volumes. Facilities include a restaurant and gift shop. A shuttle operates from the casino/hotels to the museum. *Hours:* Daily 10am to 7pm. *Admission:* $10 adults, $8 seniors, $6 children ages 6 to 15.

MYSTIC & LEDYARD LODGING & DINING

The House of 1833, 72 N. Stonington Rd., Mystic, CT 06355 (☎ 860/536-6325), is an elegant Greek Revival home on 3 acres that shelter an attractively landscaped pool and a tennis court. A grand circular staircase with a lovely mural of Old Mystic leads to five very prettily decorated rooms, all with private baths (two have whirlpool tubs). They are furnished with a combination of antiques and reproductions. The favorite is probably the Veranda Room, which has an old-fashioned lady-slipper tub to one side of the wood-burning fireplace. The room opens to its own veranda and features a white-pine bed draped with sheer curtains. The Cupola Room, richly decorated in plum and gold, is also charming. It is at the top of the house with stairs leading up to the cupola, which has been turned into a tiny sitting area. A rice cherry four-poster, dramatically swathed in fabric, dominates the room, which also features a woodstove. The first-floor Peach Room has a canopied bed, a fireplace, and a double whirlpool tub and separate shower in the bathroom. The small private porch is an extra special feature. On the first floor is a double parlor; one end is formally decorated and features a Belgian marble fireplace, and the other serves as a music room, with a baby grand piano and a pump organ. A lavish breakfast is served in the formal dining room while innkeeper Matt entertains at the piano. The cuisine is superb, especially the French toast. *Rates:* $105 to $235.

The Inn at Mystic, Route 1, Mystic, CT 06355 (☎ 860/536-9604), was formerly called the Mystic Motor Inn, and it still looks very much like a classy motor inn. However, it now also offers accommodations in the "Inn and

Gatehouse," an imposing colonial revival mansion, with a classical pediment supported by Corinthian columns, that stands on a hill at the back of the property. The mansion's ground-floor formal dining room and parlor, with exquisite 17th-century pine paneling and a carved mantel decorated with Delft tiles, are open to guests and are used for weddings and parties. Upstairs, the 10 guest rooms are lavishly furnished with canopied beds, antique sofas, and porcelain lamps; 4 rooms even have whirlpool baths that you can stand in and still look out over the harbor.

Besides the new inn, the place has some other outstanding attributes: the view of the harbor and 13 acres of landscaped grounds sloping down to the river. Rooms in the motor inn are furnished with antique reproductions of Federal-style mirrors and desks, brass lamps, and full- or half-canopied beds. TVs are tucked away in cabinets. The East Wing rooms, built in 1978, are even more luxurious, with fireplaces, wing chairs, handsome highboys, baths with Jacuzzi tubs and bidets, and sliding doors that lead to a balcony. All the rooms have air-conditioning, TVs, telephones, unstocked refrigerators, and hair dryers.

The inn's **Flood Tide Restaurant** has a good reputation. In an attractive country dining room, updated American-continental fare is served. You'll find such dishes as roast duck with blackberry Grand Marnier glaze; grilled salmon topped with whole raspberries and port wine; or grilled veal medallions served with sun-dried tomato, roasted garlic, and wild mushroom jus; plus such classics as beef Wellington and Châteaubriand, all well prepared and nicely presented. The tasty appetizers include cured salmon with fresh dill; grilled portobello mushroom filled with sautéed leeks, and escargot tossed in shallot–red wine sauce. Prices run $17 to $30. Special dessert treats are the bananas Foster and chocolate fondue. It's also a good spot for breakfast and luncheon. The restaurant is open year-round, and so are the wine bar and piano lounge. Additional facilities include a heated outdoor pool, tennis court, and canoes and rowboats for rent.

Rates: Summer, weekends $170 to $250 double in the motor inn, $250 to $285 double in the Mansion and Gatehouse, midweek $125 to $170 and $170 to $225; spring/fall, weekends $170 to $250 in the motor inn, $235 to $285 in the Mansion, midweek $95 to $155 and $135 to $235; winter, weekends $105 to $245 double in the motor inn, $235 to $270 double in the Inn and Gatehouse, midweek $85 to $150 and $135 to $195. Special packages are available. *Dining hours:* Monday to Thursday 7 to 10:30am, 11:30am to 2:30pm, and 5:30 to 9:30pm; Friday 7 to 10:30am, 11:30am to 2:30pm, and 5:30 to 10pm; Saturday 7 to 10:30am and 5:30 to 10pm; Sunday 7 to 10:30am, 11am to 3pm (brunch), and 5:30 to 9:30pm.

The **Steamboat Inn,** 73 Steamboat Wharf, Mystic, CT 06355 (☎ 860/536-8300), is down on the riverfront, so you can look out your window and see the sailboats. There are 10 delightfully decorated rooms, each with whirlpool bath, TV, phone, and air-conditioning; six have wood-burning fireplaces. The Ariadne room features a canopied bed and the additional luxury of a fireplace and a love seat for lounging. The Summer Girl is decorated in pine and pastels. The Mystic has great water views from two windows. A continental breakfast is served in a sunny room with black-and-white flooring and glass-topped tables. *Rates* (including breakfast): Summer and fall weekends, $200 to $285 double (slightly less other seasons).

The **Whaler's Inn**, 20 E. Main St., Mystic, CT 06355 (☎ 800/243-2588 or 860/536-1506; fax 860/572-1250; www.visitmystic.com), occupies a super-convenient downtown location. In the older section of this 41-room establishment designed around a motor court, the rooms tend to be small, with one double bed, but they're attractively furnished with four-posters and wingback chairs and sport rich color schemes like Chinese red and forest green. The eight rooms in the 1865 House are more floral/pastel in design. All rooms have baths, TVs, and phones. The inn also has a cafe, restaurant, and bagel shop. For those traveling by train to Mystic, the inn is only 4 blocks from the railroad station. *Rates:* Early May to Labor Day, weekends $119 to $155 double, weekdays $109 to $139; late March to early May and Labor Day to late November, weekends $109 to $149, weekdays $95 to $129; late November to late March, weekends $95 to $115, weekdays $79 to $105. Special packages available.

The **Mystic Hilton**, 20 Coogan Blvd., Mystic, CT 06355 (☎ 860/572-0731; fax 860/572-0328), has 187 rooms (all with air-conditioning, TVs, telephones, and hair dryers), an indoor/outdoor pool, a restaurant, and a lounge. It's full-service all the way, with room service from 6:30am to midnight, concierge, laundry/valet, business services, and complimentary newspaper, plus a courtesy limo to the train station and airport. It's a good choice for families because they offer kids' activities every weekend, and daily in July and August. *Rates:* Weekends $159 to $215 double.

Stonecroft, 515 Pumpkin Hill Rd., Ledyard, CT 06339 (☎ 860/572-0771; fax 860/572-9161), is a lovely accommodation and restaurant. It's located in a 1740 house that sits on several acres. There are four warm and inviting guest rooms in the house. The Buttery on the ground floor is the oldest, and some might feel the most characterful, with its gunstock beams and original door latches. It's furnished with a white-iron and brass bed covered with a patchwork quilt. The Stonecroft is the most luxurious. It boasts a wonderful wraparound mural, a wood-burning fireplace, and is furnished with tiger maple reproductions including a canopied pencil-post bed. Two other rooms have fireplaces. An additional four rooms and two suites are being installed in the Grange, a converted post-and-beam barn that also houses the restaurant. Each will have a gas fireplace, double whirlpool tub and separate shower, and fine furnishings. The restaurant is decorated in the style of an English country manor. French doors open onto a landscaped stone terrace with grapevine pergola and outdoor seating. In addition to the magic of the landscape and the pond, the innkeepers also offer accommodations with breakfast aboard their antique wooden vessel, the *Zephirine*. Massage is also available during the winter months. *Rates:* $140 to $180 in the house, $190 to $209 in the Grange, $210 double on the boat.

MYSTIC DINING

BeeBees, 33 W. Main St. (☎ 860/536-4577), is a favorite breakfast spot.

For picnic food, go to **2 Sisters Deli**, 4 Pearl St. (☎ 860/536-1244), for sandwiches and other luncheon fare. In West Mystic, **Grossman's** fish and cheese market, 401 Noank Rd. (☎ 860/536-1674), is open Monday 10am to 6pm, Tuesday to Saturday from 9am to 6pm, and Sunday from 10am to 5pm. And **Mystic Market**, 375 Noank Rd. (☎ 860/536-1500), is a deli/bakery that makes picnics to go.

The **Captain Daniel Packer Inne**, 32 Water St. (☎ 860/536-3555), has a very attractive ambience, especially in the downstairs low-beamed tavern, made even cozier by the fire. The upstairs dining room is traditional—Windsor chairs and polished wood tables, lit by hurricane lamps. The food is also traditional. Start with little necks, escargots, or stuffed portobello mushrooms before moving on to such dishes as roast duckling with a sweet apple cider sauce, sea scallops prepared with a Thai red curry, and filet mignon served with a garlic espagnole sauce. Prices range from $13 to $19. At lunch, burgers, pasta, pizza, and such dishes as grilled salmon with basil and red wine vinaigrette are available for $6 to $10. *Hours:* Monday to Saturday 11am to 4pm and 5 to 10pm, Sunday 11am to 10pm.

J. P. Daniels, Route 184, Old Mystic (☎ 860/572-9564), is a favorite romantic dining spot housed in a historic barn with a raftered ceiling high enough to hang a sleigh and a carriage. It has made its mark by offering a full range of tapas to start, which are priced from $5 to $8 each. They change frequently, but you might find sliced pork with a tangy mojo sauce, German sausage sampler (bratwurst, knockwurst, and bockwurst), lobster crêpes, and more. The main menu offers several pasta choices, plus such specialties as Long Island duck stuffed with seasonal fresh fruits and served with a sauce finished with apricot brandy and filet mignon with béarnaise sauce. Prices run $10 to $20. The desserts are classics like peach Melba and chocolate mousse. *Hours:* Monday to Thursday 5 to 9pm, Friday to Saturday 5 to 9:30pm, Sunday 11am to 2pm.

In Olde Misticke Village, the well-liked **Steak Loft** (☎ 860/536-2661), set in a pretty, barnlike building decorated with plenty of farm gadgets, purveys (surprise) steaks, seafood, and combinations thereof—sirloin, teriyaki, tenderloin, stuffed shrimp, and baked cod—priced from $12 to $23. *Hours:* Daily 11:30am to 2:30pm and 4:30 to 9:30pm; lounge, daily 11:30am to 11pm.

The **S & P Oyster Company**, 1 Holmes St. (☎ 860/536-2674), occupies a great vantage point from which to view the life of the river and the boats passing under the rare bascule bridge right in downtown Mystic. The menu offers an assortment of steaks and seafood, including steak teriyaki, lobster Alfredo, fish-and-chips, stuffed sole, and a variety of oysters. Prices range from $11 to $22. At lunch, burgers and sandwiches are the primary fare. *Hours:* Monday to Thursday 11:30am to 10pm, Friday to Saturday 11:30am to 11pm, Sunday noon to 10pm.

OLD MYSTIC LODGING & DINING

In Old Mystic, 2 miles from the coast, Ruth Keyes is the innkeeper of two lovingly restored buildings: the Crary Homestead, a 1770 colonial farmhouse, and the atmospheric Haley Tavern (1740). They stand on 7 acres and have been transformed into a secluded retreat named the **Red Brook Inn**, 10 Welles Rd. (P.O. Box 237), Old Mystic, CT 06372 (☎ 860/572-0349).

Throughout the houses Ruth has stenciled the wide-plank floors and furnished the rooms with authentic colonial antiques and fabrics. There are nine rooms available, six with working fireplaces. The favorites are in the atmospheric Tavern building with its low doors, creaking floors, original latches and windows, and authentic taproom. The Ross Haley Chamber features a 1790 high four-poster mahogany canopied bed embellished with fabric made in 1815. The crocheted canopy in the Mary Virginia Chamber is also over 100 years old. The solid-walnut cannonball bed in the Henry Haley Room sports a states quilt crafted in Michigan depicting all the state flowers. The three rooms (all with fireplaces) in the homestead are less formal and have more of country feel, with four-posters, quilts, old blanket chests, antique rockers, and cherry side tables. In the West Room there's an unusual so-called Mammy bench rocker, an ingenious early timesaver.

Down in the parlor guests can gather around the fire for a game of chess or backgammon and admire Ruth's glass collection, which includes many whale-oil lamps. The keeping room, however, is her pride and joy, containing a wide colonial hearth, with all the accoutrements for hearthside cooking. Ruth has mastered this art, and on winter weekends in November and December she serves special colonial hearthside dinners consisting of spit-roasted meats and vegetables cooked over the fire. The room is lit only by candlelight or natural light, and the breakfast is served on fine china at Early American wood tables. Most likely it will be apple, zucchini, or banana-nut bread; fresh peaches, grapefruit, or other seasonal fruit; muffins; walnut waffles or blueberry pancakes; and some unusual corn sticks. The 7-acre grounds ensure tranquillity and are ideal for picnicking or playing croquet.

Rates: $125 to $200 double. November and December, special 2-night packages (with dinner cooked over the open hearth) from $400.

FOXWOODS CASINO & LEDYARD LODGING

Foxwoods Resort and Casino, Route 2 (P.O. Box 410), Ledyard, CT 06339 (☎ 800/752-9244 or 860/312-3000), is the largest and most profitable casino in the nation—a status it has attained in an amazingly short time. The original bingo hall opened in 1986 and was followed by the first casino in February 1992. In 6 short years it has grown into a major complex with three hotels, 24 restaurants/lounges and food courts, 40-plus retail outlets (including some selling surprisingly good quality Native American jewelry and artifacts), a spa/fitness center, and an entertainment complex that attracts on average 50,000 to 60,000 people per day. Today, the casinos hold nearly 6,000 slot machines (including $5 to $100 machines), and more than 360 table games, including 75 in a room devoted to poker. The bingo hall seats more than 3,000. In addition, there's a very plush and comfortable racebook area that seats 200 and has 12 betting windows. Patrons can enjoy racing at tracks around the nation, with the races simulcast on a 15-foot, high-resolution screen. Foxwoods also offers a smoke-free casino and a smoke-free bingo area. If you're not bent on winning your fortune, go look at the many stunning sculptures by Allan Houser that are found in the lobbies of the two hotels and throughout the casino complex.

Of the three hotels in the complex, the most luxurious is the Grand Pequot Tower, which has 829 very spacious rooms. They are well furnished in a modern style, featuring good beds, custom-made armoires, and such extra touches as automatic lights and large marble bathrooms equipped with double vanities, phones, and hair dryers. The grand lobby is lit by a 60-foot-wide glass dome and is faced in marble and lace wood imported from Australia. The Great Cedar has 312 typically modern rooms. There is 24-hour room service and concierge, an indoor pool, and a health club/spa. The third hotel, the Two Trees Inn, is a three-story building in Mashantucket, just across from the casino. It has a more rustic, countrified air and offers 280 rooms, casual dining, an indoor pool, and an exercise facility. There's a 24-hour complimentary casino shuttle operated from the hotel for guests.

Dining facilities range from Cedars Steakhouse, Al Dente (serving northern and southern Italian cuisine), Han Garden (Chinese), and Fox Harbour (seafood), to the Bistro, which serves gourmet pizzas, pasta, and grilled dishes, as well as cafes, delis, fast food, and the popular Festival Buffet. Among the entertainment facilities are several special-effects theaters: Turbo Ride has seats that move in sync with the on-screen action; Cinedrome 360 features a 360° screen and converts at night into a fantastic dance club; while Cinetropolis offers the ultimate in virtual reality, allowing groups of six to journey beneath the ocean to save the eggs of the Loch Ness monster. There's also headline entertainment in the Fox Theatre, which opened with Frank Sinatra. Guest artists have included Donna Summer, Aretha Franklin, Liza Minnelli, Bill Cosby, and many more. Boxing events have also been held here. The biggest event of the year is Schemitzun, the Feast of Green Corn and Dance, which brings thousands of Native Americans to Foxwood to compete for cash prizes in dance and drum competitions and to demonstrate crafts and culture. It's usually held for 4 days in mid-September.

Rates (depending on the season): Grand Pequot, $150 to $300 double; Great Cedar, $160 to $220 double; Two Trees Inn, $110 to $170 double.

In sharp contrast, the **Applewood Farms Inn,** 528 Colonel Ledyard Hwy., Ledyard, CT 06339 (☎ 860/536-2022; fax 860/536-6015), is away from the hubbub in an 1826 center-chimney farmhouse on 33 acres. Fronted by stone walls and fences and still affording peaceful vistas, it offers five guest rooms full of character, four with fireplaces. All have air-conditioning and hair dryers. The Lillian Room contains a canopied bed and Laura Ashley decor. Stenciling enhances the Benadam Room, along with an antique bed covered with white eyelet linens. There are three common rooms, two with fireplaces, where guests can relax. Other facilities include a hot tub and chip-and-putt golf course. A full breakfast is served. *Rates* (including breakfast): $125 to $300 double.

STONINGTON & NORTH STONINGTON LODGING & DINING

Just east of Mystic lies the charming unspoiled whaling town of Stonington, which offers one simple accommodation. At **Lasbury's Guesthouse,** 41 Orchard St., Stonington, CT 06378 (☎ 860/535-2681), the owners rent three rooms: one with bath and two in a separate cottage sharing a bath. *Rates:* Summer, $100 double.

North Stonington stretches inland and here you'll find **Randall's Ordinary,** Route 2 (P.O. Box 243), North Stonington, CT 06359 (☎ 860/599-4540), that delivers an authentic and fun colonial dining experience in an atmospheric 18th-century home, a National Landmark built in 1685. Set on 27 acres, it consists of a complex of buildings that include a magnificent huge barn that was moved from New York State and attached to a silo. Both are now used for accommodations. The rooms in the barn are large and feature plank floors and high ceilings supported by strong beams. They're furnished with hoop-canopied beds, pine pieces, and Hitchcock rockers (all have TVs and phones). The most extraordinary room is the suite in the silo, with a Jacuzzi loft, a skylit sitting area, a gas-fired fireplace, and an Adirondack-style bed.

The rooms in Randall's Ordinary all have fireplaces and are more colonial in scale. They are authentically decorated and furnished with wingbacks and other antiques (they have no TVs or phones). Meals are served here by staff dressed in period attire. At dinner ($30 per person) you can watch the meal being cooked—over the fire in huge pots, on the spit, or in the oven. It will usually begin with a soup like butternut squash and follow with a choice of three dishes, say, roast leg of lamb, sautéed scallops, or roast goose with wild rice stuffing. Dessert may be a bread pudding or Vermont gingerbread. À la carte menus are offered at breakfast and lunch. Try the homemade sausages or the huge "ordinary" breakfast of griddle cakes, scrambled eggs, bacon, sausage, and fried apples and potatoes. Lunch brings assorted regional favorites—cod cakes, Nantucket scallops, and grilled venison sausage skewered with peppers, onions, and mushrooms. Prices range from $7 to $9.

Rates: $140 double, $205 silo suite. *Dining hours:* Monday to Friday 7 to 11am, noon to 2pm, Saturday to Sunday noon to 3pm, and one dinner seating at 7pm; Saturday 7 to 11am, noon to 3pm, and dinner seatings at 5 and 7:30pm.

Antiques and Accommodations, 32 Main St., North Stonington, CT 06359 (☎ 860/535-1736; fax 860/535-2613), is a delightful place, surrounded by lovely gardens. The house was built in 1860. Throughout you'll find wonderful antiques and collections assembled largely from England by innkeepers Tom and Ann Gray. There are three guest rooms, each with private bath. Timothy's room has a fine mahogany canopied bed, a charming miniature wing chair, plus two Martha Washington chairs, elegant bedside tables, and porcelain lamps. Susan's Room is especially bright because it has windows on three sides. The 1820 house set in the garden contains a two-bedroom and a three-bedroom suite plus full eat-in kitchen. The rooms and sitting rooms are very comfortably and attractively furnished with antiques. Expect to find hooped canopied beds, wing chairs, Empire chests, Hitchcock chairs, and other elegant pieces. Tom produces a candlelit four-course breakfast, turning out such delicious dishes as chilled cantaloupe soup, or a Stilton and aquavit omelet with dill rémoulade. It is served at a sumptuous table set with the finest crystal and silver. In summer it may also be served outside on the flower-filled stone patio. *Rates:* $139 to $209 double, suites from $209.

STONINGTON DINING

From Mystic, you may well prefer, as many locals do, to pop over to Stonington, where you have two fine choices.

The tiny, atmospheric **Water Street Cafe**, 142 Water St. (☎ 860/535-2122), is a welcoming spot with glowing red walls covered with paintings and artifacts. A local artsy crowd gathers here for some really terrific food. The fish dishes are particularly good, like the roasted salmon in a mushroom crust, or the delicious roasted monkfish and shrimp in a fennel and saffron broth. For a real treat try the braised sea bass in a wild mushroom Cabernet sauce. The meat dishes are also very fine, especially the roasted duck with green peppercorn–port reduction. Prices range from $16 to $20. Among the dozen or so appetizers some of the more tempting are the warm duck salad with asparagus and sesame orange dressing; and potato gâteau with goat cheese, pancetta, and tomato. Note that the restaurant may be relocating somewhere in the area. If it moves, don't miss out. *Hours:* Wednesday to Monday 11:30am to 2:30pm, daily 5 to 10pm.

Just up the street, **Noah's**, 115 Water St. (☎ 860/535-3925), is unpretentious and comfortable, yet still pretty at night. One dining room features comfortable casual booths; the other has tables. Both display works by local artists. Noah's is frequented by a local crowd that enjoys the moderately priced ($6 to $19) limited seasonal menu, which features everything from hamburger and quiche of the day to broiled flounder, steaks, and chargrilled breast of chicken. This menu is always supplemented by an array of daily specials. For example, you might find chargrilled shrimp with tropical fruit chutney, broiled halibut with mustard sauce, or Cuban-style roast pork. At lunch you can secure salads, pastas, burgers, sandwiches, and seafood dishes, all for under $9. It's great for breakfast, too, when you can enjoy real Irish-syle oatmeal and eggs, omelets, and pancakes. *Hours:* Tuesday to Thursday 7 to 11am, 11:30am to 2:30pm, and 6 to 9pm; Friday to Saturday 7 to 11am, 11:30am to 2:30pm, and 6 to 9:30pm; Sunday 7am to noon, 12:15 to 2:30pm, and 6 to 9pm.

Off Water Street, **Skipper's Dock** (☎ 860/535-8544) offers dockside dining in a plain setting. The menu offers eight to ten fresh fish that can be prepared with sun-dried tomato basil vinaigrette, honey-mustard sauce, or other combinations. There's also fish chowder and fisherman's stew Portuguese and lobsters and a clambake, of course. Prices run $12 to $20. *Hours:* Summer, daily 11:30am to 10pm. Closed from Columbus Day to early April.

NOANK LODGING

Noank is on a small peninsula about 2 miles from Mystic, also a former a whaling town, but far less opulent than Stonington on the opposite side of the harbor. Stonington residents were ship captains and ship owners; Noank's were whalers, plain and simple.

The **Palmer Inn,** 25 Church St., Noank, CT 06340 (☎ 860/572-9000), is a 16-room mansion built in 1907 for a member of the famous Palmer shipbuilding family. Its exterior is impressive, with a semicircular 30-foot-high columned portico; equally impressive is the interior, with its high ceilings supported by wood columns, among other architectural details. I especially like the sunrise-sunset stained-glass fan windows that change colors throughout the day.

Patricia White has restored the place, furnishing the six rooms (all with baths, one with a fireplace) in a Victorian manner. One room possesses a king-size wicker bed, a couch, a chair, and a side table, all of wicker. A favorite room is the dusky-rose master suite (with fireplace), where the walls are covered in French turn-of-the-century-design wallpapers, and the windows have lace curtains. One room has access to the semicircular balcony above the portico, offering a view past the church steeple to the water. Among the furnishings in the brass room are a brass bed and an oak dresser; the bath retains the old claw-foot tub and pedestal sink. The oak suite contains Eastlake oak pieces and has a little balcony and stained-glass windows. All rooms boast amenities like designer linens, plush towels, Crabtree & Evelyn soap, shampoo, and hair dryers. The guests gather in the large parlor around the fireplace or at the table at breakfast. In the smaller parlor, a comfortable sofa, wing chairs, and board games are the attractions.

At breakfast you'll find fresh fruits, home-baked items, and entertaining conversation, helped along by Pat, a former clinical psychologist who thrives on meeting and chatting with guests and seems to have hotelkeeping in her blood. She'll even show you, on those long winter nights, how to make a pomander. *Rates* (including breakfast): $130 to $225 double.

NOANK DINING

For summer luncheon or an early evening dinner, you can't beat **Abbott's Lobster in the Rough**, 117 Pearl St. (☎ 860/536-7719), where you can sit at one of the picnic tables commandeering a view of Fisher's Sound and enjoy some of the most succulent lobster anywhere. The lobster pound sits at the western tip of Mystic harbor at the edge of the sound, and the view only adds to the flavor of the lobster. You'll wait while your order of lobster, crab, mussels, clams, or steamers is cooked in the large steamers behind the counter, and then take it outside to the colorful picnic tables under a tent where you can watch the fishing boats and other craft and listen to the halyards clinking against the masts. Prices are very reasonable—$14 for a 1¼-pound lobster served with coleslaw, drawn butter, and chips; $33 for a 2- to 3-pounder. Lobster roll is $7 to $10. Before you leave, tour the holding facility, where they keep up to 22,000 pounds of these delicious crustaceans. Bring your own wine or beer. To get here, take Route 1 to Route 215 into Noank and turn down Pearl Street. *Hours:* May to Labor Day, daily noon to 9pm; Labor Day to Columbus Day, Friday to Sunday only noon to 7pm.

At the **Sea Horse Restaurant**, 65 Marsh Rd. (☎ 860/536-1670), a simple local tavern-style spot, you can obtain really fresh fish at reasonable prices—broiled flounder; fisherman's platter of fried clams, shrimp, scallops, and fish; and surf and turf—from $9 to $17. At luncheon there's fish-and-chips and sandwiches for under $9. *Hours:* Sunday to Thursday 11am to 9pm, Friday to Saturday 11am to 10pm.

The Fisherman, 937 Groton Long Point Rd. (☎ 860/536-1717), also serves good, fresh seafood even in winter, when a fire warms the hearth and a pianist entertains. The wide choice of fresh seafood—scrod, sole amandine, swordfish, stuffed shrimp—is supplemented by steaks, pasta dishes, and (weekends only) prime rib. Prices run $14 to $23. *Hours:* Monday to Thursday 11:30am to 3pm and 4:30 to 9:30pm, Friday to Saturday 11:30am to 3pm and 4:30 to 10pm, Sunday 11:30am to 9pm.

SHELTER HARBOR, R.I., LODGING

From Mystic-Stonington, if you take Route 1 or the more scenic Route 1A, which rejoins Route 1 beyond Westerly, you'll reach Shelter Harbor, a tiny community originally laid out as a musician's retreat, where the streets are named after composers like Bach and Verdi.

You can stay at the **Shelter Harbor Inn**, 10 Wagner Rd. (off Route 1), Westerly, RI 02891 (☎ 401/322-8883; fax 401/322-7907), a restored 19th-century farmhouse that was established in 1911 as the center for the adjacent music colony. Today it's a comfortable, unpretentious country inn where the sun porch/bar is a popular gathering place on weekend nights. The two small parlors offer the comforts of leather armchairs, a stove, and plenty of reading material. In the dining room, where floral wallpaper, pine cabinets, and wainscoting impart a country air, the menu might offer pistachio-crusted tuna, sautéed veal with double tomato relish, and filet mignon along with daily specials. Entrees run $15 to $20. Breakfast (7:30 to 10:30am) offers create-your-own omelets, banana-walnut French toast, granola, and other items. Prices average $6 or $7.

There are nine guest rooms in the house, three with fireplaces, and ten recently decorated rooms in the barn. In the Coach House are four additional rooms with fireplaces. Some rooms have private decks, and all have access to a third-floor deck with panoramic views and a hot tub. All have air-conditioning, TVs, and telephones.

While you're here, try your hand at paddle tennis on the two lighted courts or play a round on the professional croquet court. The inn also provides access to a 2-mile stretch of beach a short drive away in Weekapaug.

Rates (including breakfast): Mid-June–Labor Day, $112 to $152 double; May to mid-June and Labor Day to October, Friday and Saturday $112 to $152 double, Sunday to Thursday $102 to $136 double; November to April, Friday and Saturday $102 to $136 double, Sunday to Thursday $92 to $116 double. *Dining hours:* Daily 7:30 to 10:30am, Monday to Saturday 11:30am to 3pm and 5 to 10pm, Sunday 11:30am to 10pm.

GROTON & NEW LONDON

GROTON ATTRACTIONS

Shipbuilding continues to this day in Groton, where the nation's largest submarine producer, the General Dynamics Corporation, is located. Here the six-story-high Trident submarines are being built, each costing $1 billion and taking 4 to 5 years to complete.

The highlight of any visit is a tour of the $7.9 million **Historic Ship Nautilus and the Submarine Force Museum,** off Route 12 at the Naval Submarine Base (☎ 800/343-0079 or 860/449-3174); take Exit 86 off I-95. The displays in the museum building relate the history of submarine development, from the legend of Alexander the Great's descent in a glass barrel (as depicted in a medieval manuscript) to Sir Edmund Halley's 1690 "diving tub." On one wall there's a 50-foot-long scale model of a World War II fleet boat showing everything detailed to 1 inch. Video stations show films of loading missiles, a day in the life of a submariner, and so on. In earlier models, like the *U.S.S. Gato,* the men can be seen running around in shorts because of the heat (this was before air-conditioning). A whole wall of models shows all classes of submarines ever built, from the *Holland* to the modern *Seawolf,* clearly depicting a steady process of streamlining. You can also use periscopes to sight trucks speeding along I-95.

The tour of the *Nautilus* itself is most fascinating. Only 75 people are allowed aboard at one time, so get there early or be prepared to wait, often on a windy footbridge/gangplank. The *Nautilus* was the first nuclear-powered submarine. It broke records by cruising deeper (700 feet), faster (24 knots), and for longer periods (287 hours, covering 4,039 miles in one stretch) than any other. It carried 116 sailors and officers in highly confined quarters where every space-saving device was used—fold-away sinks and narrow bunks that doubled as storage boxes, for instance. Visitors carry electronic wands that activate commentaries about each area—navigation center, control room, sonar room, attack center, radio room, and the 10-foot-long by 2-foot-wide galley. The 1950s pinups were donated by the original crew. *Hours:* Mid-May to October 31, Tuesday 1 to 5pm, Wednesday to Monday 9am to 5pm; November 1 to mid-May, Wednesday to Monday 9am to 4pm. Closed

Thanksgiving, December 25, January 1, the first week in May, and the last week in October. *Admission:* Free.

Head up the hill to **Fort Griswold**, Monument Street (☎ 860/445-1729), which was attacked by a British force led by Benedict Arnold on September 6, 1781. When the American officer surrendered and handed over his sword, it was turned against him and he fell to his death. A massacre followed. Today the park provides glorious views of the Thames River and Fisher's Island and stays open from 8am to sunset daily. A museum (☎ 860/449-6877) tells the story. *Hours:* Memorial Day to Labor Day, daily 10am to 5pm; Labor Day to Columbus Day, weekends 10am to 5pm. *Admission:* Free.

CRUISES FROM GROTON

Project Oceanography, Avery Point, Groton, sponsors enormously interesting 2-hour trips led by expert guides aboard an Enviro-Lab. You'll learn how to use oceanographic instruments, pull in a trawl net filled with fish, and how lobsters are caught. For information, call ☎ 800/364-8472 or 860/445-9007. The boat departs from the Avery Point Campus of the University of Connecticut. *Hours:* Open mid-June through Labor Day only. *Admission:* $17.50 adults, $12.50 children under age 12.

NEW LONDON ATTRACTIONS

The U.S. Coast Guard Academy, Mohegan Avenue and Route 32 (☎ 860/444-8270), has made its home here since 1910. At the visitor's pavilion you can view a slide program that will introduce you to cadet life and visit the museum to see the nautical models, paintings, and memorabilia. Dress parades are held in spring and fall (usually on Friday; call for dates), and you can also go aboard the 295-foot square-rigged training barque *Eagle* on Sunday in spring and fall from 1 to 4pm. On this cutter cadets receive under-sail training handling more than 20,000 square feet of sail and over 20 miles of rigging. More than 200 ropes must be coordinated during a major ship maneuver, and the cadets must learn the name and function of each. *Hours:* Visitor's pavilion, May to October, daily 10am to 5pm.

Two other attractions are almost next door to each other. The **Connecticut Arboretum,** Williams Street (☎ 860/439-5020), on the Connecticut College campus, is one of the East's finest small (415 acres) preserves with many miles of self-guided trails.

The **Lyman Allyn Art Museum,** 625 Williams St. (☎ 860/443-2545), is a richly rewarding small museum. The period furniture collection on the ground floor is especially well diagrammed and described so that, in effect, any visitor can trace the hallmarks of each period from Jacobean through Queen Anne, Chippendale, Hepplewhite, and Empire to early Victorian. Glass (including Tiffany), china, and clocks are also on display. Downstairs has special appeal to children, for it contains an outstanding collection of dollhouses, doll furniture, toys, and dolls. Upstairs, a series of small galleries displays Greek terra-cottas, art and artifacts from various cultures, and impressionist paintings. The Chinese galleries are especially strong. Check out the sculpture gardens, which exhibit works by Sol LeWitt, Carol Krieger Davidson, Robert Taplin, and others. The gallery is also known for staging some stimulating temporary exhibits. *Hours:* Museum, Tuesday to Saturday 10am to 5pm, and Sunday 1 to 5pm. *Admission:* $4 adults, $3 seniors and students, free for children ages 6 and under.

New London was a great whaling port, second only to New Bedford in its heyday. To get a sense of its history, pick up a map at the **Southeastern Connecticut Chamber of Commerce**, 1 Whale Oil Row (☎ 860/443-8332), and walk around. Explore Huntington Street, Captain's Walk, and Whale Oil Row. Continue on Whale Oil Row to Washington Street, then take the first right onto Starr—a whole street lined with 21 restored 19th-century homes once belonging to whaling folk.

Take a left onto O'Neill Drive, then a right onto Pearl Street to view the **New London Custom House** (1833) on Bank Street (☎ 860/442-7848). It was customary for the Customs officer to climb up into the attic and onto the roof to scan the harbor and check that no whaling ships had avoided paying duty. Inside, maritime artifacts are displayed. *Hours:* By appointment only.

Shaw-Perkins Mansion, 11 Blinman St., New London (☎ 860/443-1209), is named after Nathaniel Shaw Sr. and Jr., who were both sea captains and co-owners of a mercantile business. They and their business played a major role during the American Revolution, outfitting vessels, providing supplies and ammunition, caring for the wounded, and keeping the harbor of New London open. In effect, they functioned as the naval office of the colony. *Hours:* Wednesday to Friday 1 to 4pm, Saturday 10am to 4pm. *Admission:* $4 adults, $3 seniors, $2 students, $1 children ages 12 and under.

Playwright Eugene O'Neill spent much of his boyhood in New London at the **Monte Cristo Cottage**, 325 Pequot Ave. (☎ 860/443-0051), a gray-and-white frame house in which his family summered from 1884 to 1920. It was named after the play *The Count of Monte Cristo* that paid his father $50,000 a year. When the family came here, the area was a popular summer resort. From here, O'Neill went to sea, returning about 1912 to work as a cub reporter on the *New London Telegraph*. The cottage was the setting for his tragic play *Long Day's Journey into Night* (a Pulitzer Prize winner) and his comic *Ah, Wilderness!* For O'Neill fans, and for anyone who empathizes with the tragedy of his family, this house has tremendous emotional impact; don't miss the 15-minute introductory film—one of the best of its kind that I've ever seen, dramatically portraying the tragic family. *Hours:* Memorial Day to Labor Day, Tuesday to Saturday 10am to 5pm and Sunday 1 to 5pm; other times, by appointment. *Admission:* $4.

Nearby, the **Eugene O'Neill Theater Center**, 305 Great Neck Rd., Waterford (☎ 860/443-5378), has been established on grounds that sweep down to the sound. This is a must for any theater lover, especially during the Playwrights' Conference from early July to early August, when a dozen or so plays selected from nearly 2,000 are developed in staged readings. Some may go on to Broadway success, as did *Agnes of God* and *Nine*. In August musical theater and cabaret are featured in a similar fashion, and a puppetry conference is held in June. At each of these sessions public performances are given. To secure information about dates call the number above as early as May. At other times you may catch a workshop in session, as I did when students were practicing their fencing for those swashbuckling period roles.

GROTON LODGING

Following the coastline west from Mystic will bring you to Groton Long Point, where the houses cluster along the shore. The only accommodation to be found among the many residences is the **Shore Inn**, 54 E. Shore Rd., Groton Long Point, CT 06340 (☎ 860/536-1180), facing out across the sound to

Fisher's Island. The seven accommodations are pleasant, but modest—typical seashore accommodations. *Rates:* (including continental breakfast): April to November, $125 to $135 double.

NEW LONDON LODGING & DINING

A grand fountain plays in front of the entrance to the **Lighthouse Inn,** 6 Guthrie Place, New London, CT 06320 (☎ 860/443-8411), a rambling old refurbished resort hotel built in 1902. The ground-floor public rooms filled with Eastlake and other Victoriana are elegant with their 15-foot-high ceilings. Swagged curtains cover the windows, and the cocktail lounge with a fireplace even has a chintz ceiling. The dining room looks out onto the sound.

The 27 rooms in the main building all have a bath. Some are huge, especially those with bay windows. Each room has been decorated with different chintz wallpaper and cream swag drapes, plus fetching furnishings like hooped canopy beds draped with a crochet or similar canopy. One room retains Mr. Guthrie's built-in shirt-and-sock closet complete with stepladder. The third-floor rooms, with sloping ceilings, are particularly appealing. There are 24 more accommodations, in the carriage house and other buildings on the estate. Some of the rooms have whirlpool tubs.

On Saturday there's dining and dancing to a four-piece orchestra. The dining room offers typical continental/American cuisine—veal Florentine with a mushroom–sun-dried tomato beurre blanc, pan-seared scrod in a pink peppercorn beurre blanc, and grilled tenderloin with a roasted plum tomato sauce—priced from $16 to $23.

Rates: $150 to $265 double in the main house, $110 to $160 double in the carriage house (highest price is for the waterfront suite with a whirlpool bath).

The **Queen Anne Inn,** 265 Williams St., New London, CT 06320 (☎ 860/447-2600), is a downtown bed-and-breakfast set in an intricately decorated Victorian with a witch's-cap tower and an ornate frieze on its peaked gable. Two parlors, both with fireplace, are comfortably furnished for guests' use, and in summer the rockers on the porch are favorite lounging places. Guests enjoy the hot tub, too.

The ten air-conditioned rooms (eight with bath) are variously and quite beautifully furnished. The Captain's Room has a working oak fireplace and a brass bed among its comforts. There's also a lovely bridal room featuring a private balcony and fireplace and furnished with a brass canopied bed and deep-blue swag drapes. The most expensive room boasts a brass king-size bed, plus living / dining area and kitchen. A full breakfast with such treats as Southwestern quiche or apple baked French toast is served along with afternoon tea. *Rates* (including breakfast and afternoon tea): $99 to $195 double.

The **Inn at Harbor Hill Marina,** 60 Grand St. (P.O. Box 452), Niantic, CT 06357 (☎ 860/739-0331), has a splendid waterfront location overlooking a marina on the Niantic River and Long Island Sound. It has a wonderfully fresh and light ambience. There are eight guest rooms—some with private waterfront balconies. All have private baths and water views and are decorated in a modern, upbeat way. The walls are painted in different colors, from lemon yellow to plain white; the floors covered with hard-wearing carpet; the beds are brass or iron, combined with wicker or cane furnishings; and there are a couple of wall lamps for reading. A continental breakfast is served at a long table in the Bayview Room, which is aptly named. This room is also where the guests gather in the evenings to watch the large screen TV. Guests can relax on the porch or enjoy a picnic on the patio. The inn caters to boaters and also has sea kayaks available. Picnic tables and several grills are situated on the waterfront lawn. *Rates:* May to November, weekends $135 to $160, midweek $120 to $145; December to April, weekends $115 to $135, midweek $95 to $115.

Timothy's, 181 Bank St., New London, CT 06320 (☎ 860/437-0526), is the place to dine in New London and for good reason. The cuisine is excellent, produced by a chef who has many years of experience, even though this is his first restaurant. You can watch him work in the glassed-in kitchen at the back. The menu is limited to six or so entrees, supplemented with daily specials. You might find grilled salmon flavored with a yellow tomato, caper, and fines herbes fumet; or grilled tournedos of beef seared and flavored with a brandy-roasted shallot, mixed peppercorn, and sun-dried tomato demi-glace. There are always a few pasta dishes, like the sautéed shrimp and scallops with angel hair pasta flavored with a sauce of roasted pepper, yellow tomato, opal basil vinegar, garlic, and oregano. Prices range from $15 to $25. Desserts are expertly prepared, too, whether it's the white-chocolate ganache tart, which has a crust coated in chocolate and a layer of raspberry puree topped with a dense white ganache. The dining room occupies a store front. It's light and airy and decorated with cooking accoutrements and food products displayed in glass cases. *Hours:* Tuesday to Friday 11:30am to 2:30pm; Tuesday to Thursday 5:30 to 9pm, Friday to Saturday 5:30 to 10pm.

NORWICH

From Groton and New London, the River Thames flows northward to Norwich, about a 30-minute drive away.

NORWICH ATTRACTIONS

The primary attraction for visitors in the Norwich area is the **Mohegan Sun Casino,** Mohegan Sun Boulevard, Uncasvillle (☎ 888-226-7711), which contrasts starkly with its Pequot rival. The Mohegan Sun incorporates Native American designs, motifs, materials, and seasonal themes. It's circular in design and uses logs and such decorative accents as faux animal skins to create a less extravagant, down-home country feel in contrast to the glitzy aura of Foxwoods. It's the third-largest casino in the country and offers gamblers 180 table games, close to 3,000 slot machines, and high-stakes bingo. The complex has a full range of 20 food and beverage outlets, offering everything from steaks and seafood to Italian, Chinese, deli, and fast foods. Live entertainment (The Four Tops, The Temptations, José Feliciano) takes the stage in the Wolf Den. Facilities include Kids Quest, where youngsters from age 6 weeks to 12 years can enjoy supervised play.

Nearby Norwich has other attractions, too. The outstanding discovery in Norwich, besides the handsome Victorian homes (for me at least), was the **Slater Memorial Museum,** Norwich Free Academy, 108 Crescent St. (☎ 860/887-2506). Stephen Earle's romanesque building is a magnificent treasure in itself. The main galleries, filled with plaster casts of famous Greek and

Renaissance sculptures, are amazing for their beauty, number, and rarity, for they'd be impossible to secure today; and the other collections are also very fine. There are wonderful temple carvings in the Eastern collection; exquisite ceramics, baskets, beadwork, and masks among the Native American artifacts; and some choice American primitives and some entrancing watercolors by George Henry Clements (1854–1935) in the art collections. And these are just the highlights. *Hours:* July to August, Tuesday to Sunday 1 to 4pm; September to June, Monday to Friday 9am to 4pm, Saturday to Sunday 1 to 4pm. Closed holidays. *Admission:* $2 adults, free for children ages 11 and under.

Representative of the time when Norwich was the 12th-largest city in the colonies, the **Leffingwell House**, 348 Washington St. (☎ 860/889-9440), is a fine example of a 1675 colonial that opened as a public house in 1701 and served as an important stage stop between Boston and New London. The rooms are full of interest, and the commentary is always lively. *Hours:* Summer, Tuesday to Sunday 1 to 4pm; winter, Saturday to Sunday by appointment only. *Admission:* $5 adults, $3 seniors, $1 children under age 12.

While you're in Norwich, take a drive around the village and explore the **Norwichtown Historic District,** an area around the Green where over 50 pre-1800 homes are concentrated, one of them the home of a signer of the Declaration of Independence, Samuel Huntington. Visit also **Yantic Falls**, off Sachem Street, off Route 2, known locally as Indian Leap because of the legend that during the last great battle between the Narragansetts and Mohegans in 1643, one band of Narragansetts was forced to plunge into the falls and was killed. The **Indian Burial Grounds** on Sachem Street is the resting place of Uncas, the Mohegan chief who gave the land for settlement.

Another highlight is the 350-acre **Mohegan Park**, Mohegan Avenue, off routes 2 and 32, offering swimming and picnicking, and a beautiful rose garden where 2,500 bushes bloom from May to November. The best time to visit is late June.

Downtown Norwich also possesses many historic buildings of architectural interest. Pick up a walking tour map at the Norwich Tourism Office, 69 Main St. (☎ 860/886-4683), and explore.

A NEARBY NATIVE AMERICAN MUSEUM

A visit to the **Tantaquidgeon Indian Museum**, Route 32, Uncasville (☎ 860/848-9145), is a unique experience. It's a very personal collection begun in 1931 by the late John Tantaquidgeon and his son, the late Chief Harold Tantaquidgeon, direct descendants of Uncas, chief of the Mohegan Nation. Until his death, Harold operated the museum along with his sister Gladys, who was born in 1899. Although Gladys is close to 100, she still occasionally visits the museum—if you're lucky, she will greet you and explain some aspect of the Mohegan culture. She is considered a medicine woman and guardian of Mohegan tribal culture who received the knowledge from women she calls "grandmothers," who were among the last fluent speakers of the Mohegan-Pequot language. Today she is the oldest living Mohegan, and she and her sister played major roles in the federal recognition of the Mohegans granted in 1994.

At the museum the artifacts tell some of the local Native American story. Photographs capture all the Mohegan descendants of Occum, a legendary figure in Native American history. He attended school locally and traveled to

England soliciting funds, greatly impressing the earl of Dartmouth, whose donations helped found Dartmouth College. Among the artifacts are roach or crest-type headdresses of deer hair, food bowls made only of sugar maple or applewood, Ralph Sturges sculptures, a birch-bark Penobscot canoe, exquisitely crafted straw baskets (including Makawisaug, tiny baskets that were used to put out a little cornbread or meat for the little people in the forest), and many other historical objects. There are also models showing the Green Corn Festival (last celebrated here in 1938) and depicting typical village scenes.

Another room, devoted to Plains and West Coast Indians, is filled with Navajo, Seminole, Hopi, and Tlingit artifacts, including a dramatic wolf kachina doll and a majestic Cree headdress. *Hours:* May to October, Tuesday to Sunday 10am to 3pm. *Admission:* Donation requested.

NORWICH LODGING

The Norwich Inn, Route 32, Norwich, CT 06360 (☎ 800/892-5692 or 860/886-2401), is a particularly appealing landmark that has been restored to its former elegance, with a dash of tropical and plantation-style largesse. Built in 1929, the inn originally drew such celebrities as George Bernard Shaw, Charles Laughton, and Frank Sinatra before it fell into decay. Now the place exudes elegance and romance. The 75 guest rooms are all designed in warm shades of cinnamon, sand, and Nantucket blue and have such added touches as ruffled curtains, pretty linens, dried-flower wreaths, quaint stepstools for the four-poster beds, and ceiling fans. Chintz-covered armchairs and sofas, country-print wallpapers, pine armoires, and brass fittings and old tubs in the baths create a comfortable country air. They also contain TVs, phones, and Gilchrist & Soames soaps and toiletries.

In summer you can sip a frosty mint julep in the peach-colored sunroom, or on a snowy evening you can relax by the fire in the Prince of Wales bar. For dining you have a choice of the outdoor deck overlooking the Norwich golf course or the elegant Prince of Wales dining room that offers fine cuisine along with great spa cuisine. Although the menu changes daily, you may find caramelized Chilean sea bass served with spaghetti squash, tomato chutney, and a splash of veal glaze; or roasted rack of lamb in a rosemary demi-glace; or grilled chicken breast in a roasted garlic vinaigrette. The spa menu offers four or so entrees like a steamed red snapper in a chickpea–miso-lemongrass bouillon or grilled filet mignon in a rich consommé. Prices range from $17 to $25. The spa desserts concentrate on fruit flavors in contrast to the regular menu, which features bread pudding with vanilla sauce or bourbon-pecan torte. There's a good brunch served, too.

The spa has recently been expanded and totally renovated with a separate hydrotherapy area; many additional massage, wrap, and facial rooms; two Vichy showers; and much larger locker rooms for both men and women. Treatments are carefully designed to each individual's needs. Among the spa facilities are a full range of exercise machines, along with fitness classes that range from aerobics to yoga and stress management. Beauty treatments are also offered. In addition, golf and tennis are available.

Rates: May to October, weekends $160 to $255 double, weekdays $140 to $235 double; winter, weekends $145 to $240 double, weekdays $125 to $220 double. Standard spa package (room, three meals per day, full spa treatments), from $335 per person per night based on double occupancy. *Dining hours:* Monday to Thursday 7 to 10am, noon to 2pm, and 6 to 9pm; Friday 7 to 10am, noon to 2pm, and 6 to 10:30pm; Saturday 7 to 10:30am, noon to 3pm, and 6 to 10:30pm; Sunday 7 to 10:30am and noon to 3pm.

Less expensive accommodations can be found at the **Ramada Norwich**, 10 Laura Blvd., Norwich, CT 06360 (☎ 860/889-5201). Each room has a TV, telephone, coffeemaker, ironing board, and hair dryer. Extra facilities include an indoor pool. *Rates:* Monday to Friday, $65 to $95 double, Saturday to Sunday, $89 to 159 double.

The Mystic Area
Special & Recreational Activities

Antiquing: Several stores are worth visiting in Stonington, also one or two in downtown Mystic.

Beaches: Ocean Beach, Ocean Ave., New London (☎ 860/447-3031), offers a sandy beach complete with boardwalk, concessions, and an amusement park featuring a fun triple water slide and an outdoor pool. This is New London's most crowded playground.

Most people head east toward the beach at **Watch Hill**, Rhode Island. There's also **Misquamicut,** the honky-tonk beach of Rhode Island. **Harkness State Park** and **Bluff Point State Park** both possess quieter ways to enjoy the shoreline.

Bicycling: Mystic Cycle Center, 42 Williams Ave., Route 1 (☎ 860/572-7433), rents 10-speeds, mountain bikes, and tandems. Rates start at $15 per day.

Boating: Shaffer's Boat Livery, Mason's Island Road, Mystic (☎ 860/536-8713), has 16-foot cruising boats for rent from $58 for the day. In Noank, **Coastline Yacht Club** (☎ 860/536-2689) has sailboats starting at 30 feet, which rent for $325 a day; **Wild Bill's Tackle Shop** (☎ 860/536-6648) rents fishing skiffs for $50 a day. **Spicer's Marina** in Groton (☎ 860/449-1162) rents small fishing boats with 9-hp engines for $50 a day.

Fishing: *Groton:* The largest party-fishing boat, the *HelCat II,* sails from the HelCat dock, 181 Thames St. (☎ 860/535-2066 or 860/445-5991), charging $7 for a trip from 7am to 3pm plus $5 for tackle. *New London:* The party boat *Captain Bob II* sails from New London's City Dock (☎ 860/442-1777). *Waterford:* Try **Captain John's Sport Fishing Center,** 15 First St. (☎ 860/443-7259), which charges $28, plus $5 for tackle. Leave at 6am or 1pm. *Noank:* **Mijoy,** 12 River St. (☎ 860/443-0663), sails year-round from the Noank Shipyard in Noank or Marster's Dock in New London; prices start at $28.

Several lakes in North Stonington also offer good freshwater fishing: try **Billings Lake** (north from Route 2 on Cossaduck Road) or **Wyassup Lake** (off Route 2 about 4 miles north of North Stonington).

Fruit Picking: *East Lyme:* **The Yankee Farmer,** 441 Old Post Rd. (☎ 860/739-5209), for apples, blueberries, raspberries, strawberries, and tomatoes.

Gaming: See "Foxwoods Casino & Ledyard Lodging," above.

Golf: *Groton:* **Shennecossett Municipal**, Plant Street (☎ 860/445-0262) is an 18-hole par-71 course that can be played for $25 weekdays, $30 weekends. *Ledyard:* Foxwoods Resort owns two golf courses: **Foxwoods Golf and Country Club** at Boulder Hills (☎ 401/539-4653), which is an 18-hole, par-70, 6,004-yard course, and **Foxwoods Executive Golf Club** at Lindhbrook (☎ 401/539-8700), a smaller par-54, 3,100-yard course. *Norwich:* **Norwich Municipal**, 685 New London Turnpike (☎ 860/889-6973) charges $26 weekdays, $30 weekends to play the 18-hole par-71 course. *Stonington:* **Pequot Golf Club**, Wheeler Road (☎ 860/535-1898), charges $22 weekdays and $27 weekends to play the 18-hole par-70 course; **Elmridge-Pawcatuck Golf Club**, 229 Elmridge Rd. in Pawcatuck, has an 18- and 9-hole course (☎ 860/599-2248). The charge for the 18 holes is $29 weekdays, $31 weekends.

Hiking: Ideal spots for walking are the **Connecticut Arboretum**, Williams Street, New London (☎ 860/447-1911); **Bluff Point State Park**, in Groton; and also the **coastline from Watch Hill out to Napatree Point**.

Picnicking: For shore picnicking, my first choice would be **Harkness State Park**, where you can spread your feast out and dine looking across the sound before going down to explore the beach (no swimming). Take Route 1 out of New London to Route 213. There's an adjacent special facility for the disabled with wooden ramps that run out onto and along the beach. **Rocky Neck State Park** is similar. **Fort Griswold** makes an ideal spot overlooking the Thames River and Fisher's Island. Or you might head for **Bluff Point and Coastal Reserve**, Groton, a 100-acre nature reserve. In Norwich, **Mohegan Park** is the place.

State Parks: *Groton:* **Bluff Point Coastal Reserve**, Depot Road, for great hiking, fishing, and picnicking; **Haley Farms State Park**, Route 215, Brook Street, has nature trails, hiking, and biking paths. *Waterford:* **Harkness Memorial State Park**, Route 213 (☎ 860/443-5725), has picnicking and fishing, plus a shoreline for walking (no bathing).

Tennis: *East Lyme:* **Lyme Racquet Club**, 22 Colton St. (☎ 860/739-6281), charges $32 per hour, including a $5 guest fee. *Mystic:* For local high school courts, call the **Mystic Visitor Information Bureau** (☎ 860/536-1641). The **Inn at Mystic** also has a court.

RHODE ISLAND

Block Island

Old Harbor ◆ New Harbor

Distance in miles: 167

Estimated driving time: Allow 3¾ to 4½ hours to reach the Point Judith ferry (you must be there 30 minutes ahead of departure).

◄o►◄o►◄o►◄o►◄o►

Driving: Take I-95 to Exit 92 to Route 78, which will lead onto Route 1. Take Route 1 to Route 108, which runs down the Point to Galilee/Point Judith.

By Plane: New England Airlines (☎ 800/243-2460 or 401/596-2460) flies from Westerly and Providence, RI; Action Airlines (☎ 800/243-8623 or 203/448-1646) flies (charter only) in summer from East Hampton, LaGuardia, and Groton airports.

Train: Amtrak (☎ 800/872-7245) service is available to New London (with easy connection to the Point Judith ferry); Westerly (with connecting taxi service to the airport); or Kingston (with cab connection to the Point Judith ferry).

Ferry: Interstate Navigation Co., Galilee State Pier, Point Judith, RI 02882 (☎ 401/783-4613), runs ferries year-round, eight trips per day in season. The round-trip cost is $16.30 for adults, $8.20 for children, and $52.60 for a car. The trip takes about 60 minutes. The company also operates ferries from Newport and Providence, Rhode Island, and from New London, Connecticut. Nelseco Navigation Co., P.O. Box 482, New London, CT 06320 (☎ 860/442-7891), operates one ferry daily in season (with an additional 7:15pm trip on Friday). The round-trip cost is $16.80 for adults, $8.20 for children, and $52.60 for a car. The trip takes about 2 hours. Advance reservations are needed. Other ferries leave from Montauk, New York. For information call *The Viking* (☎ 516/668-5700) or *The Jigger III* (☎ 516/668-2214).

Further Information: For more about Block Island, contact the **Block Island Chamber of Commerce**, Drawer D, Block Island, RI 02807 (☎ 800/383-BIRI or 401/466-2982).

◄o►◄o►◄o►◄o►◄o►

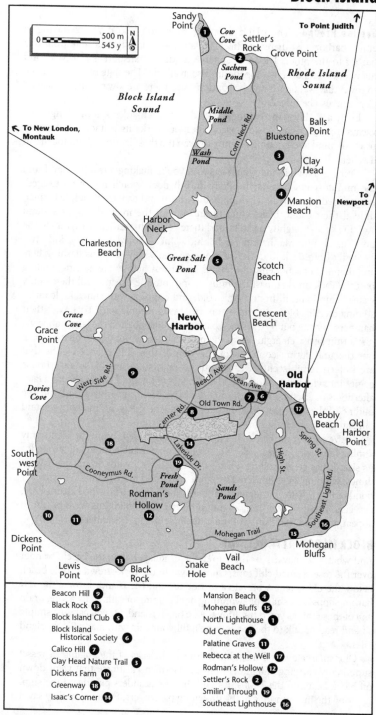

Block Island

To Point Judith

Sandy Point

Cow Cove

Settler's Rock

Grove Point

Sachem Pond

Rhode Island Sound

Block Island Sound

Middle Pond

Balls Point

Bluestone

Clay Head

To New London, Montauk

Wash Pond

Corn Neck Rd.

Mansion Beach

To Newport

Harbor Neck

Charleston Beach

Great Salt Pond

Scotch Beach

Grace Cove

New Harbor

Crescent Beach

Grace Point

West Side Rd.

Dories Cove

Beach Ave.

Ocean Ave.

Old Harbor

Old Town Rd.

Pebbly Beach

Old Harbor Point

Center Rd.

Spring St.

Southwest Point

Cooneymus Rd.

Lakeside Dr.

Fresh Pond

Sands Pond

High St.

Southeast Light Rd.

Rodman's Hollow

Dickens Point

Mohegan Trail

Mohegan Bluffs

Lewis Point

Black Rock

Snake Hole

Vail Beach

Beacon Hill 9	Mansion Beach 4
Black Rock 13	Mohegan Bluffs 15
Block Island Club 5	North Lighthouse 1
Block Island Historical Society 6	Old Center 8
Calico Hill 7	Palatine Graves 11
Clay Head Nature Trail 3	Rebecca at the Well 17
Dickens Farm 10	Rodman's Hollow 12
Greenway 18	Settler's Rock 2
Isaac's Corner 14	Smilin' Through 19
	Southeast Lighthouse 16

Getting Around The island is only 7 miles long, so if you're staying in either harbor area there's no need for a car—it's less than a mile from one harbor to the other. The most suitable mode of transport is a bicycle, and many outfits rent them. Mopeds are also available. The state beach is so close to town that walking is another option. And there are always taxis available. Cars can also be rented.

Even a 2-day trip to Block Island will seem like a long, langorous vacation as the island's slow-paced lifestyle works its miracle of restoring peace of mind and granting serenity to even the most jaundiced, frantic urban dweller.

Going to Block Island, you'll feel as if you're making a real journey. From the minute you arrive at the Point Judith dock, you'll notice an excited, exaggerated sense of anticipation. Gulls wheel and caw overhead, fishermen unload their catch, boats chug in and out of the inlet, the houses stand swaying ever so slightly on stilts, and there's a rough-and-ready rhythm to the port that leaves Manhattan far behind. Once aboard the ferry, kids run excitedly from deck to deck, their orange and yellow oilskins flashing here and there. Then, suddenly, the ship is under way and you're moving, pulling past the rock breaker, past the houses, and into the ocean, until there's only water behind and in front—gray, cold, and dappled with snowlike foam or shining metallic blue, depending on the season. People settle back with their hampers or hang out by the snack bar until on the horizon the island appears, just a thin sliver, emerging from the mist as often as not. First you can make out the undulating contours of the island, then the clay red cliffs that are indeed reminiscent of those other famous cousins. A solitary house comes into view, then another and another, and finally, if you're aboard a late-afternoon or evening ferry, the lights of the harbor sparkle ahead and the outline of the Victorian buildings appears as the gongs on the buoys sound out across the water.

You've arrived on Block Island, a largely unspoiled, beautiful island only 7 miles long and 3 miles wide, which offers an incredible variety of terrain for its size. It has gently rolling hillsides sprinkled with wildflowers, windswept dunes, winding lanes bordered by stone walls, and more than 200 freshwater ponds colored with abundant water lilies. You'll find no fast-food chains here, few cars, and hardly a traffic light, although condominiums have begun to appear, much to the dismay of the independent native islanders.

BLOCK ISLAND ATTRACTIONS

And what, you may ask, is there to do here? Relax, loll on the beach, wander over the rose-scented cliff tops, climb down to the rock-strewn pebble beach below the cliffs, rent a bicycle and ride around the island, browse the few harbor shops, go fishing or swimming or clamming or sailing, fly a kite, or do any of those things you'd traditionally do on an island. Or you can just simply sit and read or talk to the locals, who'll fill your ears with many Block Island tales.

One such tale you'll most likely hear is the saga of the *Palatine,* a vessel supposedly carrying emigrants from the German Palatinate that went down off Block Island in the 1700s. It's said that the islanders plundered the ship, ignoring the imprecations of the drowning passengers. Even today, they say, a ghostly light can be seen seeming to burn at sea, a haunting remembrance of that shameful day.

If you'd like to learn more of the island's legends and lore, pick up a copy of Livermore's *History of Block Island,* available at several stores on the island. Also stop by the **Historical Society Museum,** at the corner of Old Town Road and Ocean Avenue (☎ 401/466-2481), to view the period rooms and other local memorabilia. *Hours:* In season, daily 10am to 5pm.

Block Island was originally inhabited by a tribe of Native Americans who called it Manisses, or "Isle of the Little God." In 1524, on his way to what he hoped was Asia, Italian explorer Giovanni da Verrazano spied the island and named it Claudia, after the wife of François I of France, under whose flag he sailed. Before the name took hold, along cruised Dutch navigator Adrian Block, who charted the island's location in 1614. It came to be called Block Island in his honor. In 1661 the island was sold to 16 settlers from the Massachusetts Bay Colony. To view the spot where they landed, take Dodge Street from the Old Harbor to Corn Neck Road—this will lead you out past Crescent Beach northward to the area known as **The Maze,** a nature lover's delight with over 11 miles of trails that emerge on the cliff tops. From here it's only a few minutes' drive to **Settler's Rock,** where the first settlers' names are found on the monument marking their landing place. From here you can view the abandoned **North Light** at Sandy Point, built in 1867, and now housing a maritime museum.

At the center of the pork chop–shaped island lies the **Great Salt Pond,** on which the New Harbor is located, a fully protected basin for docking pleasure boats. One or two restaurants and lodging places are also located here. If you continue out along Ocean Avenue instead of turning right at Corn Neck Road, you'll eventually come to **New Harbor.** Turn left at the harbor, and the road will bring you to the island cemetery high on a hill. The decorated tombstones here stand witness to the local families and their members who contributed to the island's 300 years of history.

Nearby, **Redman's Hollow** is one of five wildlife refuges on the island, a great natural ravine, located off Cooneymus Road. Many paths wind their way down to a point below sea level where you can spend a leisurely afternoon observing the area's wildlife.

The most spectacular area, however, is the **Mohegan Bluffs,** clay cliffs extending 5 miles at the southernmost tip of the island, reached via Spring Street and Southeast Light Road. Here legend has it that the native tribe routed and starved out the invading Mohegan Indians and pushed them off the bluffs into the sea. Several dirt paths lead to the sea and a view from 200 feet up out over the Atlantic and down to the rocky shoreline. Stairs lead down at one place, or you can climb down on your own. Off to the left is the **Southeast Light,** a quaint brick structure built in 1874. The lens cost $10,000 then—today it would cost more like $7 million. It still warns seafarers of the treacherous shoreline.

BLOCK ISLAND LODGING

You'll need to make reservations well in advance, especially for July, August, and all holiday weekends. Be aware, too, that if you're planning to fly in and the weather is bad enough that your flight is grounded, most hotels will expect you to catch the ferry over. Otherwise you'll forfeit the charge for your room for that night. So make sure to check reservation and cancellation policies carefully.

The Top Choices

The island's two most sophisticated accommodations are the 1661 Inn and the Hotel Manisses, both owned by the Abrams family and each quite different.

The **1661 Inn,** Spring Street, Block Island, RI 02807 (☎ 401/466-2421 or 401/466-2063), has a colonial charm and looks out to the Atlantic Ocean across a pond frequented by regal swans—in short, it has a marvelous location that's only a 5-minute walk from Old Harbor. The inn is named in honor of the year Block Island was settled by courageous colonists from New England. Each of the nine guest rooms (all with bath) is named for one of the original settlers and is furnished individually, many with decks overlooking the ocean. In the Staples Room, even the Jacuzzi has a view; it also has an extra-large deck. The Simon Ray Room has cathedral ceilings and a brass canopied bed. The Ackurs Room has two brass beds, a kitchenette, and windows on two sides with great views.

In the guest house across the yard are 10 rooms (6 with bath). The upstairs rooms are furnished in country style with oak beds, marble-topped dressers, and lace curtains. The ground-floor rooms are more contemporary, although they also contain wicker love seats and chairs. Each room has a deck with an ocean view. Adjacent to the 1661 Inn, the Nicholas Ball Cottage is a replica of St. Anne's by the Sea Episcopal Church, which was destroyed in the 1938 hurricane. It contains three luxurious suites (each with a fireplace, Jacuzzi, and tiled bath), furnished with Victorian cottage pieces or similar. Two are very attractive duplexes.

There's a comfortable parlor in both the guest house and the main inn. A buffet breakfast—fresh fruit, cereals, waffles, hash, eggs and potatoes, bluefish, sausages, muffins, and smoked fish—is served either in a pretty chintz dining room at tables set with pink linens or out on the ocean-view deck.

Rates (including breakfast): Summer, weekends $165 to $345 double, weekdays $165 to $345 double; spring and fall, weekends $110 to $240 double, weekdays $95 to $210 double; winter, weekends $70 to $190 double, weekdays $70 to $170 double. *Open:* Inn, April to October; guest house and Nicholas Ball Cottage, year-round.

The **Hotel Manisses,** Spring Street, Block Island, RI 02807 (☎ 401/466-2421 or 401/466-2063), is a gracious, turreted, clapboard Victorian decked out in period style. On the ground floor is a comfortable wicker-furnished parlor where you'll find board games and some fascinating old volumes—*Historians' History of the World,* Bulwer Lytton's novels, and the like. There's also the small Top Shelf Bar, where guests can enjoy cocktails or flaming coffees.

The hallways leading to the 17 rooms (each with bath and phone, some with Jacuzzi and refrigerator) are lined with a variety of Victorian portraits and pre-Raphaelite pictures. A decanter of brandy and a dish of hard candy are placed in each room. The ground-floor Chelsea Room has a Jacuzzi, a high-backed oak bed, wicker chairs and table, and a marble-topped dresser. The Prince Augusta Room has similar marble-topped furnishings, along with a deep-well dresser and a Mme Récamier couch. The Pocahontas Room has its own deck. The William Frederick Room contains an assortment of Victoriana, including a chair with a fold-out footstool, a wedding-cake table, and a Stickley-style chair.

Breakfast is served at the 1661 Inn (above). The dining room is one of the best, if not *the* best, on the island. Bamboo chairs give it a tropical air. For those who prefer to sit outside, the sliding glass doors lead out onto a deck set with tables sporting umbrellas, overlooking the fragrant garden with a fountain.

At dinner, start with pepper-crusted tuna, a clam-filled chowder, or Alsatian tart. Follow with one of the dozen or so entrees—steaks, baked stuffed lobster, scallops with fines herbes, bouillabaisse, duck au poivre, or basil chicken sautéed with pine nuts, fresh basil, and tomato. Many of the vegetables and herbs come fresh from the large garden behind the inn. Prices run from $18 to $30. Dessert might be fresh strawberries, apple pie, chocolate layer cake with raspberry filling, or something similar. Guests who stay here can also enjoy the fascinating menagerie that grazes in the fields behind the house— llamas, Sicilian donkeys, Highland cattle, Indian runner ducks, and pygmy and fainting goats.

Rates (including breakfast): See rates for the 1661 Inn above. *Dining hours:* Mid-May to Columbus Day, daily 6pm to closing; check at other times of the year. For dinner reservations, call ☎ 401/466-2836.

Other Choices

The **Atlantic Inn,** High Street, Block Island, RI 02807 (☎ 800/224-7422 or 401/ 466-5883; fax 401/466-5678; e-mail: Atlantic Inn@BIRI.com), is an atmospheric old Victorian inn set splendidly on a bluff with views of Old Harbor and the ocean at its feet. It dates to 1879. Shores, hills, and ponds are spread out to view from the wraparound porch, and sunrises and sunsets, too. There are 21 rooms, all with baths, telephones, and wall-to-wall Wilton carpeting. The rooms are variously furnished. For example, Room 3 has a high oak bed with a floral comforter, a side table, a dresser, and an armoire. Third-floor rooms have knee walls (low walls under a gable or mansard roof) and shuttered windows, plus assorted oak, marble-topped, and Mission furniture.

From late April to October, a bountiful buffet breakfast of fruit, breads, pastries, and cereals is served to guests. Dinner is served in the dining room at tables set with white cloths; candlelight, classical music, and often spectacular sunsets make it a romantic spot. If you have to wait for a table, the bar is attractively furnished with a camelback sofa and Stickley chairs. The restaurant is one of the best on the island. It offers a four-course $40 prix-fixe menu with plenty of appetizers and entrees to choose from. It changes weekly. Dinner might start with such choices as grilled quail salad or bourbon-glazed lobster (the last served with a wonderful mixture of papaya, mango, and chopped peanuts), followed by such entrees as beef tenderloin with wild mushrooms or grilled mahimahi with pistachio couscous, and conclude with a raspberry Napoleon or blackberry flan. This can be accompanied by a selection from the modest, moderately priced wine list. Other facilities include a croquet court, two tennis courts (there are only four on the island), a horseshoe pit, and 6 acres of well-tended gardens and lawns from which to view the ocean.

Rates (including continental breakfast): April to June, $110 to $175 double; July, $125 to $225; August, $245; September and October, $110 to $225. Closed November to March.

Tucked away behind the Atlantic Inn on 20 acres of farmland, the **Rose Farm Inn,** Roslyn Road (P.O. Box E), Block Island, RI 02807 (☎ 401/466-2034; fax 401/466-2053), is located in two buildings. The first is an 1897 farmhouse offering ten rooms (eight with bath) that are sparkling clean and variously furnished. Some have carved four-posters, others high-back Victorian beds, and still others iron-and-brass beds. These are combined with oak dressers and rockers and other antique country pieces. Room 9 is a favorite, with a four-poster canopied bed, nautical wallpaper, a ship's-wheel mirror, and watercolors of seafaring vessels. There's a deck on the south side of the farmhouse furnished with chaise longues for sunning. There's also a TV lounge and such conveniences as an ice machine, a refrigerator, and a coffeemaker. All rooms have telephones. The newer building contains nine rooms, all with baths. The first-floor rooms have double, the second floor single whirlpool baths. The upstairs rooms also have appealing sitting areas tucked under the large dormer. They're furnished in similar Victorian style.

The breakfast room gets the morning sun and is welcoming with its tables set with blue cloths and pine Windsor chairs and its many hanging plants. Fruit, cereals, and breads are served. Bicycles are available.

Rates (including breakfast): Summer, $100 to $205 double; spring and fall, weekends $100 to $205 double, weekdays $85 to $160 double. Closed November to April.

Right down on Old Harbor and Crescent Beach, the **Surf Hotel,** Block Island, RI 02807 (☎ 401/466-2241), has a marvelous view of Crescent Beach and is a typical example of what Block Island's hostelries were like before the island was discovered by the modern urban tourist. Each of the 47 rooms (3 with bath) has floral wallpaper, lace curtains, a bed, a dresser, and a rocker. There's a sink in every room, plus an overhead fan. A kitchen is available with a communal refrigerator. The dining room is great fun, its tin walls hung with a pretty china collection; the tables sport blue cloths, and the room has a view of the ocean, of course. A light buffet breakfast is offered here. There's also a comfortably cluttered Victorian sitting area decked out in red with a splendid wood-burning stove from Kalamazoo, a variety of seating, a giant chess set (each piece is 8 inches high), and assorted other games, plus a TV and a grand piano. Wood rockers line the porches overlooking the harbor, street, and beach.

Rates: Late June to Labor Day, $100 to $110 double without bath, $130 to $150 double with bath; late May (excluding Memorial Day weekend) to late June and Labor Day to Columbus Day, $85 to $95 double without bath, $115 to $135 double with bath; 6-night minimum stay July and August. Closed mid-October to Memorial Day.

Just down the street from the Surf Hotel, the **Blue Dory Inn,** Dodge Street, Block Island, RI 02807 (☎ 401/466-5891), is a small, attractive accommodation. Past the entry porch hung with flower baskets you'll find a ground-floor parlor with a TV and Stickley furnishings. The main inn has 10 rooms with bath, some with high-backed oak beds, others with brass beds, and all with a variety of Stickley and oak furnishings and floral fabrics. The rooms are nicely decorated in a comfortable, feminine style using rose-patterned and other

Waverly fabrics, fringed lamps, down comforters and ruffles on the beds, plenty of pillows, fresh flowers, and potpourri. The top-floor rooms have skylights. A continental breakfast—fresh fruit, cinnamon rolls, croissants—is served at tables set with fresh flowers in a pretty room. There are also several cottages available. The Cottage contains a two-story suite that sleeps four and features a whirlpool tub; the Doll House has one room for romantics, the Tea House contains an efficiency and has its own porch overlooking the sea, and the Sherman Cottage is a three-bedroom contemporary. The Waverly Cottage contains three suites, each with a private deck. One has a full kitchen. Behind the main inn is a small patio with access to the beach, which is less than 100 feet away. Farther out on the island the Blue Dory also rents the four-bedroom, two-bath Harmony Cottage, which has a stone fireplace and is furnished with pine and other comfortable pieces. All in all, it's a charming accommodation.

Rates (including breakfast): Mid-June to mid-September and weekends Memorial Day to Columbus Day, $165 to $235 double, cottages $175 to $400, suites $285 to $450; spring and fall, $95 to $175 double, cottages $120 to $310, suites $200 to $230; winter, $75 to $105 double, suites $160.

Across the street, the **Gables Inn,** Dodge Street (P.O. Box 516), Block Island, RI 02807 (☎ 401/466-2213 or 401/466-7721), offers a variety of accommodations. There are 13 rooms (4 with bath) in the main inn, each decorated with chintz wallpaper and featuring an oak or an iron-and-brass bed. On the ground floor is a TV room and a sitting room with wicker armchairs. On the ground floor of Gables II are several paneled apartments, each with a fully equipped kitchen and dining area. These have immediate access to the lawn picnic tables and a barbecue. Guests also have access to an ice machine and refrigerator. *Rates* (including continental breakfast): Summer, $85 to $145 double without bath, $120 to $155 double with bath; spring and fall, $60 to $130 double without bath, $85 to $145 double with bath; apartment from $730 per week. Closed December to mid-April.

The Adrian, P.O. Box 340, Block Island, RI 02807 (☎ 401/466-2693), is located in an old sea captain's house that was built in 1880 and is now on the National Register of Historic Places. It stands on a knoll with a broad porch overlooking the Old Harbor. There are 10 extremely nice rooms with baths. Each is furnished individually with rockers and armoires, occasional wicker or Mission pieces, and high-back Victorian beds. The charming guest cottage has two twins and makes for a private retreat. Guests can enjoy lounging on the 3 acres of grounds, complete with a gazebo, or on the wraparound porch. Set on a bluff, the property offers panoramic views of the ocean and Old Harbor. It's close to town, but far enough away for guests to avoid the summer hordes of day-trippers. A continental breakfast and afternoon tea is served. *Rates* (including continental breakfast): Summer, weekends $135 to $185 double, $275 cottage; early June and September 15 to Columbus Day, $95 to $145, $95 to $145 cottage. Closed Columbus Day to May.

The **Old Town Inn,** a little way from Old Harbor at the junction of Old Town Road and Center Road (P.O. Box 351), Block Island, RI 02807 (☎ 401/466-5958, or 617/237-6751 November to April), is a B&B operated by the Gunter family, who hail from England. The inn incorporates two houses, the older dating from the mid–19th century, when it served as a merchant's residence. The East Wing was added in 1981. Six rooms are found in each, all neat, clean, and nicely, if simply, furnished with maple beds and chests set against chintz wallpaper. In the newer building the rooms are larger and have full baths. Monica serves a light buffet breakfast of fresh fruit and pastries. The inn is surrounded by 4 acres of lawn. *Rates* (including breakfast): Memorial Day to Labor Day, $100 double without bath, $110 to $145 double with bath; Labor Day to Columbus Day, $95 double without bath, $105 to $135 double with bath.

Midway between Old and New Harbor on a hill overlooking the Great Salt Pond, **The Barrington**, Beach and Ocean avenues (P.O. Box 90), Block Island, RI 02807 (☎ 401/466-5510), built in 1886, is operated by friendly Joan and Howard Ballard. There are six rooms in the house (all with bath) and two housekeeping apartments in an adjacent barn. Each of the three rooms on the second floor has a private deck and fine water views; third-floor rooms also have water views. Each room is simply furnished with country pieces and chintz wallpaper. Room 5 has a brass bed and a wicker rocker. The apartments have two bedrooms, a fully equipped kitchen, and a living room. On the ground floor is a large room overlooking the garden with a private porch—very cool in summer. Guests have two comfy sitting rooms with a TV/VCR and a selection of books and games. A breakfast of fresh fruit, muffins, and cereal is served in the dining room or on the deck out back with a view of the ponds. Out front are a lawn and shade trees. *Rates* (including breakfast): Mid-June to Labor Day and Memorial Day weekend, $120 to $168 double; May to mid-June (excluding Memorial Day) and Labor Day to October, $70 to $130 double; April and early to mid-November, $65 to $85 double.

The **Seacrest Inn**, 207 High St., Block Island, RI 02807 (☎ 401/466-2882), is an attractive, well-maintained accommodation conveniently located a short walk from the ferry landing. The 17 rooms (all with bath) are sparkling clean. Each contains a maple or brass bed, a side table, a dresser, and a wicker chair or rocker, all set against beige wallpaper; three rooms have brass beds. The grounds are prettily landscaped, with a latticework gazebo hung with flower baskets. Kids enjoy the play area. Umbrella-shaded tables are placed on the lawn. Coffee, juice, and danishes are provided in the mornings. Bicycles are available for rent. *Rates* (including breakfast): Mid-June to mid-September and holidays and weekends, $115 to $170 double; early May to mid-June and mid-September to mid-October, $75 to $135 double.

The next two hotels are island classics. The **Spring House**, Spring Street, Block Island, RI 02807 (☎ 401/466-5844), is the largest and oldest on the island, built in 1852. The striking white clapboard building crowned with a mansard and cupola is on a hilltop overlooking the ocean and "The Village." Wicker chairs line the wraparound porch, which overlooks the ocean and swan pond. Many famous guests have stayed here, from Ulysses S. Grant to Mark Twain and Billy Joel. The large lobby has a stone fireplace and flows into the ballroom/living room, which has 12-foot-high ceilings and is lit by 7-foot-tall windows. The 49 studios, rooms, and suites (17 in a separate building), are elegantly furnished in Victorian style with four-posters, wing chairs, and Eastlake and other reproductions. All have private baths and are equipped with telephones. The dining room is decked out in pink and forest green. Cocktails and afternoon tea can be enjoyed in Victoria's parlor, which has a long oak bar, while the sunroom with its wicker seating is a wonderful place to curl up with a book. The hotel stands on 15 acres dotted with Adirondack chairs and benches. Facilities include croquet, volleyball, and horseshoes. *Rates* (including continental breakfast): Mid-June to Labor Day and holiday weekends, $159 to $325 double; May to late May and mid-October to late October, $109 to $235 double; late May to mid-June and Labor Day to early October, $129 to $255 double. Closed November to April.

The **Harborside Inn,** overlooking the ferry dock at Old Harbor (P.O. Box F), Block Island, RI 02807 (☎ 401/466-5504, 401/466-2693 at the Gazebo), has 36 rooms, all with private baths. They are prettily decorated with beige and blue-striped wallpaper, color-coordinated carpets and spreads, and rattan furnishings. The quietest rooms are found at the Gazebo, about 300 yards from the inn. The Harborside outdoor dining terrace is a popular summer gathering place. *Rates:* May to mid-June, $79 to $129; mid-June to July, $99 to $209; August to Labor Day, $149 to $219; Labor Day to mid-October, $89 to $169.

If you're looking for a room with a TV and a phone, then the **National Hotel,** Old Harbor (P.O. Box 189), Block Island, RI 02807 (☎ 800/225-2449 or 401/466-2901; fax 401/466-5948; e-mail: BSGM97A@prodigy.com), is for you. It has 45 modern rooms located in a historic clapboard building dating to 1888 that has a gabled mansard roof with cupola and a long front porch overlooking the harbor. It also offers a series of shops, a dining room, bar, and regular live rock entertainment on the porch. *Rates:* Mid-June to September 1, weekends $169 to $219 double, weekdays $99 to $199 double; early May to mid-June and September to October, weekends $99 to $169 double, weekdays $89 to $129 double.

BLOCK ISLAND DINING
Breakfast & Lunch

Certainly you ought to take one breakfast at the **Surf Hotel,** served from 7:30 to 11am (see above).

Down on the Old Harbor, **Ernie's,** Water Street (☎ 401/466-2473), is another breakfast favorite, a coffee shop–style place from which you can watch ferries docking while eating eggs, omelets, or pancakes. *Hours:* mid-May to mid-October, daily 6:30am to noon.

If your hotel doesn't provide breakfast, pick up a delicious croissant or pastry at **Aldo's Bakery,** Weldon's Way (☎ 401/466-2198), just behind the Old Harbor on Main Street. Breakfast is also served, weekends only, at the **Harborside Inn,** right on Old Harbor.

The best choice for lunch is to pack yourself a picnic and take it to the bluffs or the beach. You can assemble the fixings at the Old Harbor supermarket.

The **Taffy Tent Cafe,** at the Empire Theatre, offers light lunch fare, plus delicious homemade ice cream. There are art galleries on the premises, too.

Also on the harbor, **Finn's** (☎ 401/466-2473) has burgers, sandwiches, fried clams, scallops, lobster, and clam rolls for $4 to $15. Nearby, **Ballard's,** 46 Water Street (☎ 401/466-2231), offers a variety of sandwiches and snacks, priced from $4, plus seafood, pasta, and other Italian dishes.

At lunch the **Harborside Inn,** at the ferry landing (☎ 401/466-5504), offers a variety of sandwiches and burgers, plus fish dishes like lobster roll, fried clams, baked scrod, and broiled scallops, priced from $7 to $13. Try the famous clam chowder that has won the island chowder cookoff on several occasions. At dinner, the menu offers about ten main courses ranging from potato-crusted salmon served with tarragon beurre blanc and scallops Provençale, to pecan chicken in a mustard-cream sauce, and filet mignon stuffed with roasted red pepper, mozzarella, and lobster meat. Dine inside amid the nautical rigging or outside under the umbrellas. *Hours:* Summer 7:30am to 10pm; shoulder season 11am to 10pm.

Dinner

For the three top choices for dinner—the **Hotel Manisses** (☎ 401/466-2836), **Atlantic Inn** (☎ 401/466-5883), and **Spring House** (☎ 401/466-5844)— see "Block Island Lodging," above.

Another top choice is **Winfields**, Corn Neck Road (☎ 401/466-5856), a pretty beamed candlelit restaurant where the tables have fresh wildflowers on the sparkling-white cloths. The menu offers about 10 or so entrees, which might include a pasta dish like penne primavera, plus several fish items like grilled tuna baked with an orange hoisin glaze and topped with fresh mango salsa. The ingredients are fresh and often organic. For example, you might find pan-seared statler breasts of chicken with tomatoes, artichoke hearts, sun-dried tomatoes, basil, lemon, and white wine. If the honey mustard–crusted rack of lamb with a rosemary and black currant demi-glace is on the menu, try it. Prices run $16 to $27. Start with any one of several shellfish dishes like the jumbo shrimp with pineapple and macadamia nuts or the delicious lobster quesadilla, and finish with the white-chocolate mousse with Chambord sauce or whatever is available that particular day. *Hours:* In season only, daily 6 to 10pm.

BLOCK ISLAND AFTER DARK

There isn't too much to do after dark except watch the sunset, curl up with a book or a loved one, and enjoy a fine dinner. But there is the **Empire Theatre and Cafe at Old Harbor** (☎ 401/466-2555). It's a wonderful vintage theater dating to 1882 that has been completely refurbished. It features first-run films, preceded by entertainment provided by a pianist. A variety of live events happen here, ranging from swing bands to stand-up comics and live theater. Another cinema, the **Oceanwest Theatre** (☎ 401/466-2971), is at New Harbor. It shows current releases.

Captain Nick's, Ocean Avenue (☎ 401/466-5670), has nightly dancing— a brick fireplace is the band's backdrop. So, too, does the **Yellow Kittens Tavern**, Corn Neck Road (☎ 401/466-5855 or 401/466-5856), but only in summer; though open year-round, in winter it functions as a bar with no dancing. There's usually some entertainment given at the **National Hotel** on Old Harbor.

Block Island
Special & Recreational Activities

Beaches: Block Island State Beach and **Crescent Beach** are the popular sandy beaches. For a secluded (but pebble) beach, try the **base of Mohegan**

Bluffs or the **west side of the island.** There are plenty of small sandy coves you can discover on your own.

Bicycling: Bikes and mopeds can be rented at **Aldo's,** behind the Harborside Hotel (☎ 401/466-5011); **Island Moped and Bike,** P.O. Box 280 (☎ 401/466-2700); and the **Old Harbor Bike Shop,** P.O. Box 338 (☎ 401/466-2029). Bikes can also be rented from the **Seacrest Inn,** 207 High St. (☎ 401/466-2882).

Birding: Block Island is on the Atlantic flyway and in spring and fall birders come to the island to watch the migrating birds. This is the third-largest migratory center in the United States, and as many as 150 species have been sighted.

Boating: Rowboat rentals for $12.50 a day are available from **Twin Maples** (☎ 401/466-5547). You can attach your own motor to these fiberglass boats. Jet boat rentals are available from **Block Island Parasail,** P.O. Box 216 (☎ 401/466-2474).

Camping: This is *illegal* on Block Island.

Canoeing/Kayaking: Oceans and Ponds, The Orvis Store, Ocean Avenue (☎ 401/466-5131), rents canoes and kayaks as well as surf rods for fishing.

Fishing: Many boats are available for charter, like those at **Captain John's Charter Fishing** (☎ 401/466-2526). You'll need a license to go shellfishing. If licenses are available, they can be obtained at the police station.

Beach fishing is popular. For bait and tackle, try **Twin Maples** (☎ 401/466-5547) or **Ocean and Ponds** (☎ 401/466-5131) (see above).

Horseback Riding: Rustic Rides Farm, West Side Road (☎ 401/466-5060), offers guided trail rides.

Mopeds: See "Bicycling," above.

Parasailing: Go to **Block Island Parasail,** P.O. Box 216 (☎ 401/466-2474).

Tennis: There are two courts at the **Atlantic Inn** (see above).

Newport

Downtown ◆ Bellevue Avenue & Ocean Avenue

Distance in miles: 183
Estimated driving time: 3¼ hours

◄◊►◄◊►◄◊►◄◊►◄◊►

Driving: Take I-95 to the Newport Bridge.

Bus: Greyhound (☎ 800/231-2222) travels to Providence, where you can change to a local Rhode Island bus into Newport.

Train: Amtrak (☎ 800/872-7245) services Providence along the Northeast Corridor.

Further Information: For more information about Rhode Island in general, write or call **Rhode Island Department of Economic Development,** Tourism Division, 1 W. Exchange St., Providence, RI 02903 (☎ 401/277-2601).

For specific Newport information, contact the **Newport County Convention and Visitor's Bureau,** 23 America's Cup Ave., Newport, RI 02840 (☎ 800/976-5122 or 401/849-8098), or the **Newport County Chamber of Commerce,** 45 Valley Rd., Middletown, RI 02842 (☎ 401/847-1600).

◄◊►◄◊►◄◊►◄◊►◄◊►

When Giovanni da Verrazano first discovered Aquidneck Island, he named it Rhodes because the quality of the light reminded him of that mysterious Greek island. Today, when one approaches the town from the west across the high-arching bridges, one is awestruck by the beauty of the bay, especially on a sunny day, when white, blue, and red sails—hundreds of them—bobbing on the water make kaleidoscopic patterns on the deep-blue background of the ocean, adrift as if in a romantic, dreamy idyll.

To visitors Newport offers the perspective of an island, the excitement of a port, and world-class events—a wonderful blend of contemporary and past delights. The town represents two great eras of American history. Downtown reflects the original, boisterous 17th-century mercantile community, and the mansions on Bellevue Avenue show the extravagance and outrageous fantasy and spectacle of the Gilded Age. It's a wonderful place to be.

Newport

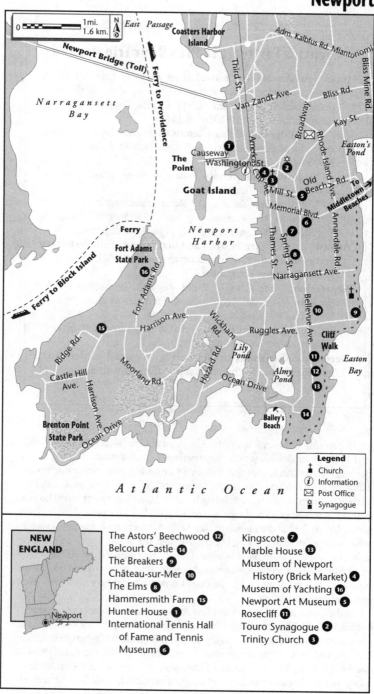

Events & Festivals to Plan Your Trip Around

July: Newport Music Festival. Two weeks of chamber music concerts, performed morning, noon, and night in the city's grand houses. Contact the Newport Music Festival, Box 3300, Newport RI 02840 (☎ 401/846-1133).

The **Miller Hall of Fame Tennis Championships.** For tickets and information, contact the Tennis Hall of Fame (☎ 401/849-3990).

Virginia Slims Tennis Tournament on grass courts at Newport Casino, Tennis Hall of Fame.

The Museum of Yachting's **12 Meter Regatta** features the yachts that raced in the America's Cup from 1958 to 1983, including Ted Turner's *Courageous.* Usually held weekend of July 4.

August: The **JVC Jazz Festival and Ben & Jerry Folk Festival** in Fort Adams State Park. For information call ☎ 401/847-3700.

The **Wooden Boat Show.**

September: The **Classic Yacht Regatta,** sponsored by the Museum of Yachting, concludes the summer in grand style on Labor Day weekend.

The **Outdoor Art Festival** (usually early September) makes a colorful splash on Bowen's Wharf.

December: Christmas in Newport with wassail parties, Bach and Handel in the churches, and topped off with a reading of

In summer it swarms with life. The wharves are filled with sleek yachts and millions of dollars worth of powerboats, clinking and rocking in the harbor, their bronzed captains and crews crowding into harborside restaurants, bars, and stores, eyeing and vetting each other as they go. Behind the harbor, the narrow streets are lined with stately 18th-century clapboard houses, painted in muted grays and sage greens, which add character and grace to the scene. Up on the hill the mansions stand empty, except for busloads of visitors who come to stare at the gilt, the marble, and the lavish rooms where great balls once were held. In these opulent, gilded surroundings, the 400 members of fashionable society once cavorted—daughters were pledged to dukes, insults were hurled, and even the dogs sat down to dinners of stewed liver, rice, and fricassee of bones.

In the beginning, Newport was first and foremost a colonial town, a mecca for ambitious 17th-century merchants, who risked their money, chances, and sometimes their lives, by engaging in the triangular trade between Africa, Europe, and the Caribbean, carrying slaves, molasses, rum, and sugar, defying the British and taking advantage of European wars to increase their share of world trade. They were fiercely independent people who had fled the narrow-mindedness of Massachusetts, and their ranks included dissidents of every sort—Methodists, Quakers, Jews, and all manner of those who chafed under the restrictions of British rule. They were the first to declare their independence, an act that brought a contingent of Redcoats into their city and led to its occupation and destruction during the American Revolution. When the French arrived in July 1780, 300 buildings had been wantonly destroyed, and they found a beleaguered town that continued to languish for many years thereafter.

Newport's reputation as a resort began in the mid-1800s, when many southern planters discovered its pleasant climate and sought refuge from malaria and the oppressive southern heat. They spent their summers here in pleasant cottages like Kingscote. Soon, Julia Ward Howe's literary set and the moneyed folk from New York and Philadelphia followed. The last group built "cottages" on a palatial scale, imitating the aristocracy of Europe and vying with each other in their extravagance and display. William K. Vanderbilt spent $11 million on the Marble House, a residence that he used only 2 months of the year.

Society flocked to Newport and spent their days languidly among luxurious surroundings. Breakfasts were followed by tennis or riding. Lunches were taken aboard yachts. Lavish dinners and balls followed afternoons of polo. The "cottages" that they used for the season have been preserved and now stand as witnesses to this era of incredible wealth, ostentation, fantasy, and spectacle.

Society also brought to the island the two sports that are still synonymous with Newport today—yachting and tennis. The America's Cup Challenge was moved from New York to Newport in 1930, and the cup remained here until 1983, when it was carried off by the Australians—only to be returned triumphantly to the United States in 1987. The U.S. National Tennis Championships were held at the Newport Casino from 1881 until they moved to Forest Hills, New York; if you like, you can play on those hallowed grass courts.

Mansions, extravagant hostesses, melodramatic scenes, colonial tales of freebooting merchants and pirates, ships and yachts, elegant pastimes—Newport has it all—chic, beauty, history, romance, the ocean, and the nerve to remain a prestigious East Coast resort, a role bestowed on it by the generations that have gone before.

THE MANSIONS

Plan to see only two or three mansions in a day. Tours last 1 hour, and you'll soon be exhausted. On weekends you'll want to get there early because the crowds and busloads of people can be horrendous. I would see Kingscote (1839), an example of the earlier cottages that preceded the Gilded Age, and the Chateau-Sur-Mer (1852), both of which have an added charm because they still seem lived in. The more extravagant era of the 1890s can be captured at The Breakers, Marble House, The Elms, or Rosecliff.

Kingscote (1839), Bellevue Avenue, was built by Richard Upjohn for George Noble Jones of Savannah, Georgia, and later was acquired by William Henry King, a China trader, after whom it is named. The house is furnished with fine oriental export pieces. Most dramatic is the dining room, added in 1881 and designed by Stanford White. Light shimmers over the opalescent Tiffany brick tiles that surround the Siena marble fireplace at one end of the room, while an intricate spindle-work screen encloses the other. The paneling is mahogany, while the ceilings and upper walls are of cork. The tour is intimate and interesting.

Chateau-Sur-Mer, Bellevue Avenue, was originally built in 1852 and transformed by Richard Morris Hunt into a grand chateau 20 years later. Owner William Shepard Wetmore, another China trader, entertained lavishly. At one of these affairs, held for George Peabody of London in 1857 and attended by 3,000 guests from both sides of the Atlantic, Wetmore served woodcocks, plovers, and snipes among the entrees, plus confections that were molded in the shapes of Washington and Lafayette. The house may appear austere and somber to some, with its granite exterior; extensive use of Eastlake ash paneling in the entrance hall, staircase, and morning room; and heavy butternut furnishings in the bedrooms. Note the extravagantly carved Italianate overmantel in the dining room depicting Bacchus.

The Breakers (1895), Ochre Point Avenue, was built for Cornelius Vanderbilt II and is the most lavish and Italianate of the cottages. It contains 70 rooms (33 were used for the 40-strong army of servants). The most striking attributes are the beautiful multicolored (rose to gray-green) marbles used throughout; the arched double loggia with mosaic ceilings, which provides dramatic ocean vistas; the music room, which was constructed in Europe and shipped here for reassembly; faucets that deliver salt and fresh water in the bathrooms; a two-story kitchen, sealed off so that none of the odors escaped; and a billiard room of gray-green marble, yellow alabaster, and mahogany. The house was used only 2 months of the year.

Rosecliff (1902), Bellevue Avenue, was the chosen setting for scenes in the films *The Great Gatsby* and *The Betsy,* and it certainly does have a romantic aura with its heart-shaped staircase, well-tended rose garden, and fountains. Theresa Fair Oelrichs was one of the three top hostesses of Newport, daughter of James Graham Fair, who struck the Comstock Lode. She was a stickler for perfect cleanliness and was even known to scrub the floor herself if it did not meet her standards. Designed by McKim, Mead, and White after the Grand Trianon, it contains the largest ballroom in Newport, where Tessie staged such extravagant balls as the White Ball, at which all the flowers and decorations were white, the guests were also all in white, while several white-sailed ships floated on the ocean to complete the effect.

Marble House (1892), Bellevue Avenue, was where Alva Belmont held court while she was the wife of William K. Vanderbilt. A dashing woman, she was the first of her set to bicycle in bloomers, to own a car of her own, to cut her hair at the shoulders, and to divorce (she remarried to O. H. P. Belmont). The $11 million cottage was modeled after the Petit Trianon by Richard Morris Hunt and contains the most ornate, gilt-encrusted ballroom you'll ever see, where daughter Consuelo debuted and became engaged to the ninth duke of Marlborough in 1895. The dining room is furnished with bronze chairs that weighed so much they required a servant's help whenever a guest wanted to sit or rise. The Chinese Teahouse was added in 1913 by Alva, who also had a tiny railroad constructed to ferry the footmen bearing tea from the main house. Later, she was one of the first to open the house to the public to raise funds for the suffragettes.

The Elms (1901), Bellevue Avenue, was built for coal magnate Edward J. Berwind by a relatively unknown Philadelphia architect, Horace Trumbauer, who adapted the design of the Chateau d'Asnieres, near Paris, creating a low-key, classically symmetrical mansion. The grounds, dotted with bronze statuary, gazebos, and fountains and planted with an amazing variety of trees, shrubs, and colorful sunken gardens, are the most remarkable aspect of the house.

Hours: In summer, May to October 31, all mansions are open daily from 10am to 5pm and sometimes later in the evenings. In winter you'd do well to check ahead. Usually only Marble House, The Elms, and Chateau-Sur-Mer are open on weekends from 10am to 4pm. The Elms, Chateau-Sur-Mer, and The Breakers are decorated for the holiday season. In April, The Breakers, Marble House, and Rosecliff are open daily 10am to 5pm; the others, on weekends only. For information, contact the **Preservation Society of Newport County**, 424 Bellevue Ave., Newport, RI 02840 (☎ 401/847-1000).

Admission: Your best bet is to purchase a strip ticket good for two ($14 adults/$5.50 children ages 6 to 11), three ($19/$7.50), four ($24/$9.50), five ($27/$10.50), six ($30/$11), seven ($33/$13), or eight ($35.50/$14). **Hunter House**, a colonial house (1748), and **Green Animals**, a topiary garden with 80 sculptured trees in Portsmouth, are included in this combination ticket. Individual admissions range from $8 at nine of the mansions to $10 at The Breakers (plus $3.50 for The Breakers stable).

OTHER MANSIONS

Two other small mansions operated by the Preservation Society are also open to visitors. **Chepstow** is an Italianate villa that was built as a summer home for Edmund Schermerhorn, a cousin of Mrs. William Astor Jr. It was later transferred to a member of New York's prominent Morris family; today it is worth visiting to see the American paintings by Fitz Hugh Lane and Granville Perkins, plus the furnishings (including a walnut Queen Anne chair that belonged to William Penn). *Hours:* By appointment only, Friday and Saturday until October.

Another house, the **Isaac Bell House** on Bellevue Avenue, is currently being restored and affords visitors an opportunity to see how a complex restoration is undertaken. It was built for a New York cotton broker by McKim, Mead, and White between 1881 and 1883 in a shingle style featuring multiple towers, chimneys, porches, and columns. *Hours:* Friday and Saturday only.

In addition to the mansions maintained by the Preservation Society, there are several others that are open to the public.

Belcourt Castle, Bellevue Avenue (☎ 401/846-0669), was built for Oliver H. P. Belmont and Alva, former wife of William K. Vanderbilt. It was designed in 1891 by Richard Morris Hunt in the style of Louis XIII's palace at Versailles. The most dramatic displays here are the 23-karat-gold coronation coach, the armor collection, and the stained-glass windows in the grand Gothic hall. Costumed guides lead the way through the house, and ghost tours are given on Wednesday and Thursday in season. *Hours:* Memorial Day to mid-October, daily 9am to 5pm; February to March, weekends and holidays 10am to 4pm; April to May, daily 10am to 5pm; November to January, weekends and by appointment. Closed Thanksgiving, Christmas. *Admission:* $7.50 adults, $4 for children ages 6 to 12.

Beechwood (1855), Bellevue Avenue (☎ 401/846-3772), was the home of William B. Astor, where his wife (the former Caroline Schermerhorn) held court as the doyenne of Newport society. With the help of a southern gentleman, Ward McAllister, she devised the famous "Four Hundred," a list of 213 families and individuals whose lineage could be traced back at least three generations. It was also the number of guests who could comfortably fit into the ballroom of her New York residence. So resplendent were her gowns and jewels that McAllister once remarked that she resembled a spectacular chandelier. Here at Beechwood you'll find no roped-off rooms or historic lectures, but a re-creation of the lifestyle that the Astors brought to Newport in the 1890s, re-enacted every day by the Beechwood Theater Company. *Hours:* Mid-May through November, daily 10am to 5pm, Friday to Sunday 10am to 4pm, except during Christmas, when hours vary. Closed January. *Admission:* $8.75 adults, $6.75 children ages 6 to 13.

Hammersmith Farm, Ocean Drive (☎ 401/846-7346), was the summer cottage of John W. Auchincloss and family, where the daughter of Mrs. Hugh Auchincloss, Jacqueline Bouvier, and John F. Kennedy held their wedding feast. It's a beautiful seaside retreat, and the tour tells charming details of the time spent here by the Kennedy family. The gardens are also worth exploring. *Hours:* April to mid-November, daily 10 am to 5pm. *Admission:* $8 adults, $3 children ages 6 to 12. *Note:* At press time Hammersmith Farm is up for sale, so you should call first to see if it's still open to the public.

COLONIAL-ERA ATTRACTIONS

Walking tours of Historic Newport are offered by the Historical Society (☎ 401/846-0813) on Thursday, Friday, and Saturday at 10am and 3pm, mid-May through October, at a cost of $7. They leave from the Museum of Newport History at Touro and Thames streets. Cliff walks are also offered.

Downtown, **Washington Square** is the center of colonial Newport. At the west end is the **Brick Market** (1762), which is now occupied by the **Museum of Newport History** (☎ 401/841-8770). At the other end is the **Old Colony House**, dating from 1739, which was used by the Rhode Island General Assembly until 1900. From the balcony here, Rhode Island issued its own Declaration of Independence on May 4, 1776. This act of defiance brought the wrath of the British Redcoats down on the city; when they occupied it during the American Revolution, they left it in ruins. Today you can only view the building's exterior. The interior is closed while work is done to bring it up to the fire code. The museum, which tells the city's story, is open year-round. *Hours:* April to December, Monday and Wednesday to Saturday 10am to 5pm, Sunday 1 to 5pm; in winter, Friday and Saturday 10am to 5pm and Sunday 1 to 4pm. *Admission:* $5 adults, $4 seniors, $3 children ages 6 to 16.

An independent town founded by dissidents from Massachusetts in 1639, Newport attracted a great number of diverse religious groups, and their houses of worship can still be seen. Most famous is probably the **Touro Synagogue**, 72 Touro St. (☎ 401/847-4794), built in 1759 (although the first member of the community arrived in the 1650s). *Hours:* July 4 to Labor Day, Sunday to Friday 10am to 4pm; Memorial Day to July 4 and Labor Day to Columbus Day, Sunday 11am to 3pm and Monday to Friday 1 to 3pm; in winter, Sunday 1 to 3pm, and by appointment Monday to Friday at 2pm.

A little way down Broadway from the synagogue stands the oldest house in Newport, the **Wyman Wanton-Lyman-Hazard House** (☎ 401/846-0813), which was built in the 1690s and is authentically furnished for the period. It also has an interesting colonial garden. *Hours:* June 1 to Labor Day, Friday to Sunday noon to 5pm. *Admission:* $3 for adults.

Back on Touro Street at no. 82, the **Newport Historical Society** (☎ 401/846-0813) has changing exhibits of furniture, colonial silver, toys, dolls, and other decorative arts. The **Seventh Day Baptist Meeting House** (1729) is also part of the museum. *Hours:* In summer, Wednesday to Saturday 9:30am to 4:30pm (until noon only on Saturdays). *Admission:* Free.

A few blocks away in Queen Anne Square, you can see the spire of the 1726 **Trinity Church** (☎ 401/846-0660), inspired by the work of Christopher Wren and also by the Old Boston Church. The bells ring quite beautiful changes. *Hours:* May to June, Monday to Friday 10am to 1pm; June to October, daily 10am to 1pm; after the second service on Sunday only in winter.

From here, the whole area between Spring Street and Bellevue Avenue, Touro Street and Mill Street, is known as **Historic Hill,** and it's well worth wandering around to view the old clapboard buildings of this once-thriving seaport community.

The other historic area, **The Point,** is down along Washington Street on the harborfront, where the **Hunter House** is located at 54 Washington St. (☎ 401/847-1000), a Tory residence that survived the occupation by the British, served as the headquarters for Admiral de Ternay when the French naval forces arrived in July 1780, and is worth visiting today to see the Townsend Goddard furniture and the floor-to-ceiling pine paneling. *Hours:* April, Saturday and Sunday 10am to 5pm; May to October, daily 10am to 5pm. *Admission:* $8 for adults, $3.50 for children ages 6 to 11.

OTHER NEWPORT ATTRACTIONS

Two absolute musts after (or even before) the mansions: Drive or cycle **Ocean Drive,** stopping for a picnic at Brenton Point State Park, and walk along the back of the mansions on the 3-mile **Cliff Walk** (which stubbornly remains a public thoroughfare) to see the rocky coastline to full advantage. Downtown, you'll want to explore the many dining, shopping, yachting, and people attractions at such harborside complexes as **Bowen's** and **Bannister's Wharves.**

The **International Hall of Tennis Fame,** located in the Newport Casino at 194 Bellevue Ave. (☎ 401/846-4567), exhibits trophies, art, videos, and memorabilia. The casino building, designed by Stanford White, was commissioned by James Gordon Bennett Jr., publisher of the *New York Herald,* after a good friend of his was thrown out of the Bellevue Men's Club for riding a horse through the building. With its horseshoe piazza, turreted porches, and breezy verandas, the casino instantly became the place to be seen and became the focal point of society, where people came to play and watch croquet, court tennis, cards, and billiards and to attend many special events. The U.S. Championships were played on the casino courts from 1881 until they moved to Forest Hills. *Hours:* Daily 9:30am to 5pm. *Admission:* $8 adults, $6 seniors, $4 children ages 6 to 18.

Newport Art Museum, 76 Bellevue Ave. (☎ 401/848-8200), puts on a variety of exhibits by artists associated with Newport. The shows range from the works of artists who painted in and around Newport in the 19th century to avant-garde, virtual-reality pieces, and photographs. The exhibits are staged in the Griswold House (1862), which was designed by Richard Morris Hunt and in the Cushing Gallery. *Hours:* Summer, Monday, Tuesday, and Thursday to Saturday 10am to 5pm, Sunday noon to 5pm; winter, closes at 4pm. *Admission:* Adults $4, seniors $3, free for children ages 5 and under.

Sailing enthusiasts will want to visit the **Museum of Yachting** in Fort Adams State Park on Ocean Drive (☎ 401/847-1018), which offers a gallery of small craft, an exhibit about the history of yachting in Newport and the America's Cup, and a slide show of 12-meter craft. *Hours:* May to October, daily 10am to 5pm. *Admission:* Adults $3, seniors $2.50, children $1.

Military buffs will want to visit the **Naval War College Museum**, Coasters Harbor Island (☎ 401/841-4052), which traces the history of naval warfare and the history of the naval presence in the Narragansett Bay region. *Hours:* Year-round, Monday to Friday 10am to 4pm; June to September, also Saturday and Sunday noon to 4pm. Closed holidays. *Admission:* Free.

NEWPORT LODGING

Castle Hill Inn and Resort, Ocean Drive, Newport, RI 02840 (☎ 401/849-3800), has to be the most picturesque Newport accommodation, offering a commanding view of Narragansett Bay, Newport Harbor, and the ocean. It's a prime vantage point from which to watch the sailing and fishing craft in the bay. In summer you can dine outside on the terrace, at the top of the grassy bluff that sweeps down to the water, or in the dining rooms where the fresh, innovative American cuisine will surprise and please everyone's palate. You won't forget an appetizer like the pan-seared foie gras served atop triangles of French toast with bourbon-flavored peach ginger jam, or the Grand Marnier–marinated oysters pan-fried in a cornmeal crust. Main dishes run from the traditional and wonderful soft-shell crabs or lobster Thermidor, to chicken with a rich bourbon gravy, or grilled sirloin and Cajun andouille sausage served with mashed Yukon golds flavored with blue cheese. Prices range from $18 to $28. Brunch dishes are just as thrilling—ranging from poached eggs and hash made with sausage, onion, and sweet pepper to a crispy salmon paillard served with whipped sweet potatoes.

The inn was built in 1874 by Alexander Agassiz, son of naturalist Louis Agassiz, and many an illustrious person has stayed here. The accommodation in the turret was inspirational for author Thornton Wilder, who wrote that he could "see the beacons of six lighthouses and hear the booming and chiming of as many buoys." The 10 rooms are all different in size and shape. Some have exquisite paneling, and some are oddly shaped, with dormer windows. Some, like Rooms 1 and 2, are undistinguished. Room 4, though, is beautifully paneled and sports a bold floral-and-bird-patterned wallpaper. Room 8 is tucked under the eaves and has wicker furniture. Harbor House rooms have such extras as whirlpool tubs, fireplaces, and French doors leading to a semiprivate deck with great views of the bay. There are also some rustic, unheated efficiencies available rented by the week.

Rates: Mid-June to mid-September, weekends $260, midweek $235; May to mid-June and mid-September to mid-November, weekends $260, midweek $175; mid-November to early May, weekends $175 to $205, midweek $135 to $145. The efficiencies rent for $900 to $1,100 a week.

Dining hours: Friday to Saturday and Monday noon to 3:30pm; Wednesday, Friday, and Saturday 6 to 10pm; Sunday 11:30am to 3:30pm.

Sanford-Covell Villa Marina, 72 Washington St. (☎ 401/847-0206), is a spectacular place with a marvelous view of the harbor. The house, which was built for Milton Sanford, a New York City industrialist, was completed in 1870 before the Newport mansions were built. It was designed by William Emerson, cousin of Ralph Waldo Emerson, in stick style. Step inside and you'll be transported to an earlier, more elegant era. In the soaring foyer (which retains the original gas lamps) stands a peacock, a bust of Sanford, and a grandfather clock, among other period furnishings. The walls are brilliantly painted and decorated with "pouncing," a technique that pounds the paint into the walls, creating a blistered but brilliant effect. There are only four rooms. My favorite is the Kate Field room up on the third floor. It has a window seat and a deck overlooking the water, a fine selection of books in the built-in bookcases, rocking chair, and a nonworking fireplace. Dolls, a blackboard, and the oak-slat paneling add more charm. It shares a bathroom that has a claw-foot tub, pull-chain toilet, and two marble sinks. The Cuvalier Room faces the Newport Bridge and has plenty of character, too, thanks to the coffered ceiling, old books, model ship on the mantel, tiny parasol, and an authentic Windsor chair. The Play Room is remarkable for a little balcony that extends out over the central lobby, a stained-glass window, and its contents, which include many antique toys and the diaries of William King Covell from 1919 to 1972. The most spectacular is the Covell Room, which has a working fireplace, French-style furniture, and a large sitting room filled with antiques, oriental carpeting, books, and TV.

Throughout the house there are fine decorative objects to admire including many clocks and dolls. A continental breakfast is served in the handsome dining room with its converted oil chandelier. The parlor features two baby grand pianos, two fireplaces, and plenty of comfortable seating. Complimentary sherry is served in the evening. In summer the most glorious feature of the house is the broad porch furnished with wicker and the heated saltwater pool below it. Beyond stretches the entrance to Newport Harbor. This is a magnificent nostalgic retreat.

Rates: Summer, $135 to $235; winter, $85 to $160.

The latest lodging with distinct cachet is **Vanderbilt Hall,** 41 Mary St. (☎ 888/826-4255; fax 401/846-0701). It's located in the Historic Hill District in a former boy's club that was built in 1909 by Alfred Gwynne Vanderbilt. The building has retained the lavish woodwork and detailing. There are 50 rooms, all furnished with handsome antique reproductions, fine wallpapers, and fabrics. Heated towel racks and makeup mirrors are among the additional room amenities; in the 10 executive studies spiral stairs lead to loft rooms featuring office equipment. Guests enjoy the spacious common areas as well as the pretty conservatory and outdoor terrace. The tiger-oak paneled dining room offers super cuisine, including a $50 five-course prix-fixe dinner that might feature a fish course of blue crab and lime sausage with a scallion and tomato salad followed by a breast of Guinea fowl in a Madeira sauce. More casual dining is offered in the orangery. Facilities include a fitness room, a clubby billiards room, and an indoor pool. *Rates:* Summer, $220 to $420; off-season, $200 to $320. Special packages available.

The Ivy Lodge, 12 Clay St. (☎ 401/849-6865), is a gorgeous place to stay. Architecturally the shingled house is extraordinary, with gables, chimneys, and a curving veranda. Step inside the front door and an impressive entrance/hallway rises in front of you. The woodwork is glorious. An oak staircase zigzags its way to the third floor landing, directing your eye to the stained-glass ceiling that glows above. There are eight rooms, seven with private bath. Each is handsomely decorated in different colors with brass beds, wing chairs, wicker, and some painted pieces. Room 1 has a spectacular highback Victorian bed. The Turret Room is among the most charming, offering a coral-colored sitting area with boudoir-style chairs and a bathroom with pull-chain toilet. Another favorite is the Under the Staircase room, which boasts a mahogany sleigh bed, a fireplace with the original Delft tiles, a large bay window, and a double Jacuzzi in the bathroom. The public areas are lavishly decorated. A breakfast buffet is served at the long table that seats 14 in a paneled room with floor-to-ceiling windows lit by a striking silk floral chandelier. There's a small sitting area off the lobby and a larger sitting room furnished with a baby grand piano, comfortable sofas, and chairs arranged around the central fireplace. A favorite spot in summer is in the swing seat on the wide porch overlooking the colorful gardens complete with fountain. *Rates:* April 1 to October 31, $145 to $185; November 1 to March 31, $100 to $140.

Cliffside Inn, 2 Seaview Ave., Newport, RI 02840 (☎ 401/847-1811), would be my other choice Newport accommodation, even though it's located out toward Middletown. The lovely Victorian residence was originally built in 1880 by a governor of Maryland and later occupied by the family of artist Beatrice Pastorius Turner. The 15 rooms (12 with fireplace and double whirlpools) have all been personally and authentically furnished with great flair. In your room you might find a large four-poster spread with eyelet linens and pillowcases or a cannonball bed dressed with a floral design comforter. The Governor's Suite offers lavish comforts—king-size four-poster, two-sided fireplace, whirlpool bath, antique Victorian birdcage shower, and double-pedestal sink. Miss Beatrice's Room features a Lincoln bed, Eastlake chairs, and marble-top tables as well as a black marble fireplace and an appealing window seat in the bay window. The bathroom contains whirlpool bath and double-headed shower. Several third-floor rooms have skylights. The bilevel Garden Suite has two fireplaces, a double whirlpool bath, and a private patio. All rooms have air-conditioning and TV; some have VCR.

The day begins with coffee and juice delivered to your room and ends with turndown accompanied by a homemade pastry. A full breakfast is served in a parlor crammed with Victorian couches, love seats, and objets d'art. The innkeepers employ a pastry chef who prepares the splendid afternoon tea that has been ranked up there with the Ritz's. The porch is a favorite gathering place, arrayed with turquoise wicker chairs on canvas-painted flooring.

Rates: $195 to $295 rooms, $295 to $360 suites.

Elm Tree Cottage, 336 Gibbs Ave. (☎ 401/849-1610), is a lovely, romantic accommodation located away from the waterfront. What makes the bed-and-breakfast special are the innkeepers, Priscilla and Tom Malone, who have decorated their 1882 home with flair and style and who welcome their guests with warmth. The house is situated on an acre of landscaped property 2 blocks from the beach. Each of the six rooms (all with private bath) has been individually decorated in a rich tapestry of fabrics and wallpapers. The Windsor suite is the largest and most elaborate. It contains a carved French Louis XV bed with a partial crown canopy, a fireplace with a gilt mirror above, and a ceramic French clock on the mantel, plus a sofa and a French side chair. The bathroom is spectacular, too, with its vanity dressing table with fabric skirting and the sink, which stands on gleaming crystal legs. The Harriman is more masculine with striped wallpaper with heraldic borders and paisley purple quilt and hunting prints. The bathroom is mirrored, and there's even a cushion in the deep tub. A former owner of the house was the heiress to a Pennsylvania Railroad fortune, and the bar that she installed is still here, studded with hundreds of 1921 silver dollars. Other public spaces are comfortably and lavishly furnished. The sunroom is filled with wicker. The living room, with grand and upright pianos, offers a variety of seating—camelback sofas and wingbacks—and is accented with putti and a mirror that was rescued from a mansion. In winter there's a view of First Beach from the property. A full breakfast (pear-stuffed crêpes, orange waffles) is served in the elegant dining room. Afternoon hors d'oeuvres and iced tea or hot chocolate are served. The pergola and the statuary add panache to the gardens, too. *Rates:* $145 to $220, $235 to $360 suite.

The **Francis Malbone House,** 392 Thames St. (☎ 401/846-0392), is right downtown on the waterfront, but it manages to retain a quiet air, thanks to a serene landscaped garden in the back where Adirondack chairs are set under the trees and on the flagstone patio. The house itself is supremely stylish with dentil moldings, wainscoting, and glorious scallop-shell corner cupboards. It was built in 1760 for shipping merchant Francis Malbone and designed by the architect responsible for both Touro Synagogue and the Redwood Library. The nine rooms are decorated in colonial colors like Wedgwood blue or slate gray and elegantly furnished with colonial reproductions—rice four-posters, oriental rugs, highboys, pier mirrors, and Martha Washingtons in front of the fireplace. Seven have working fireplaces. The curtains are swagged, and in some rooms there are inviting window seats under the casement windows. The Counting House suite behind the main house offers a bedroom, living room, and dining room, plus a Jacuzzi in the bathroom. The staff is extremely helpful and friendly. There are two parlors for guests to use, plus a library, which has a TV and some good books to read. The sumptuous breakfasts—peach granola pancakes, Belgian waffles, for example—are graciously served in a colonial-style formal dining room at a lace-covered table lit by candlelight. A great place to stay. *Rates:* May 1 to October 31, $185 to $265, $305 to $365 suite; November 1 to April 30, $155 to $205, $235 to $285 suite.

One of the friendliest and most attractive places to stay—and also very conveniently located—is the **Admiral Benbow Inn,** 93 Pelham St., Newport, RI 02840 (☎ 401/846-4256), built in 1855. The vibrant innkeeper, Maggie, has a wonderful way of tending to guests and a genuine enthusiasm for what she's doing. The 15 rooms in this handsome Victorian home, all with private bath, are large and comfortable. For example, the room I stayed in contained brass twin beds, dresser, wing chair, and couch. Curtains at the Palladian-style bay windows were cinched back; an old-fashioned gas lamp and chandelier provided light. Above the fireplace hung oriental prints, all reminiscent of an earlier era. Other rooms are furnished variously with fishnet canopy beds, satin eiders, and a mixture of antiques and reproductions. Room 2 has a kitchenette, and Room 12 has its very own large deck for sunning with a view of the harbor. The room itself is small, but it's furnished with oak dresser, brass bed, side table, and Mission rocker; it's comfortable enough. Room 9 has a handsome hooped canopy. Some rooms have air-conditioning—ask.

Breakfast is served downstairs in the basement, decked out with colorful kites serving as wall hangings. Muffins, cinnamon-raisin toast, cereals, and fresh fruit are spread out for you to help yourself. Guests gather here in the evenings if they want to watch TV or warm themselves in front of the wood stove. A collection of old barometers is on display and also for purchase.

Rates: May 1 to October 31, $120 to $235; November 1 to April 30, $80 to $155.

At the **Brinley Victorian**, 23 Brinley St., Newport, RI 02840 (☎ 401/849-7645), there are 17 rooms, 13 with private bath. It's a large, rambling place occupying two houses (joined by a breezeway), situated a little distance from the immediate downtown area. It possesses much character, and each of the rooms is carefully and personally furnished with extra touches like fresh flowers and magazines. On the ground floor, Room 5 has a stucco fireplace, plus a double-poster bed set with Laura Ashley pillows and coverlets. In Room 4 a cherry bed is matched with a handsome Mme Récamier sofa against a beige chintz wallpaper. My favorite room is Room 17, featuring a high oak bed, Eastlake chairs, and a brick colonial fireplace. Room 12 sports striped floral pink-and-brown wallpaper, oak furnishings, and two brass beds. The iron bed in Room 13 is covered with a pink, lace-trimmed coverlet. The second house also has a comfortable parlor furnished with books and marble fireplace. Room 6 has a large double bed set in the bay window and a single; other furnishings include a wicker sofa, kneehole dresser, and armoire. Third-floor rooms with knee walls are smaller and attractively furnished with oak and wicker. There's a fridge on each floor for guests' use.

A breakfast of fresh baked goods is served in the Victorian-style parlor filled with a love seat and an Empire-style sofa set in front of the fireplace. Windows are covered with cream swag drapes. In summer, breakfast is served in the brick courtyard. There's also an information/library area where guests can peruse books and menus of local restaurants or enjoy an assortment of games. Both houses have porches with swings and wicker furnishings.

Rates: May 1 to October 31, $115 to $160 double with private bath, $100 to $125 with shared bath; November to April, $95 and $79, respectively.

Melville House, 39 Clarke St., Newport, RI 02840 (☎ 401/847-0640), is a charming 1750s shingled home, located on one of the quieter streets in the downtown historic area. It's run by two enthusiastic innkeepers, Vincent DeRico and David Horan. In the country parlor you'll find comfortable wing chairs and rockers set in front of an old pine fireplace, home to a basket of cones and gleaming copper tea kettles. Breakfast—buttermilk biscuits, Rhode Island johnny cakes, stuffed French toast, and so on—is served at polished wood tables in a sunny room adjacent to the parlor. There are seven rooms (five with private bath, the rest sharing). Flowers and fruit are placed in every room, and each is nicely decorated in a colonial style. Ceilings are low, and all of the rooms have character. In the winter a romantic fireplace suite is available, and guests who stay in this room are welcomed with champagne and are served breakfast in bed. Games and books are available in the corridor leading to the rooms. Afternoon tea is served (hot soup on cold days), and complimentary sherry is available when guests gather to chat in the evenings. A hospitable, warm, and friendly place. *Rates:* May 1 to October 31, $120 to $155; November to April, $95 to $135; fireplace suite $185.

The **Inntowne**, at Mary and Thames streets, Newport, RI 02840 (☎ 401/846-9200), very conveniently located in the historic section, takes a contemporary approach to the interior of its two colonial-style buildings. The place is very nicely kept. There are 24 rooms, all with air-conditioning and telephones. And they are all clean as a whistle and prettily decorated, often with matching floral prints on walls and curtains. By far the most interesting accommodations to me are in the Mary Street House—the Rathskeller in particular, named because of the rounded pine door frames and doors, brick, and tile. It has a mirrored bedroom, a cozy sitting room with a couch and armchairs, and a full kitchen. It costs $250 in season. Other rooms in this house are also very attractively furnished with antique reproductions and often with coordinated wallpaper and bedspreads. An expanded continental breakfast of freshly squeezed juice, quiche and ham, baked muffins, rolls, and beverage is served in the pretty dining room with polished wood table and ladderback chairs. Afternoon tea is also served. *Rates:* $105 to $195 double.

If you stay at **Rhode Island House**, 77 Rhode Island Ave., Newport, RI 002840 (☎ 401/848-7787), you'll be treated to some fine breakfast cuisine prepared by the Paris-trained chef/innkeeper Michael Dupre, who was for many years the private chef to Mrs. Hugh D. Auchincloss at Hammersmith Farm. In addition, you'll be staying in a lovely shingle-style house where the first-floor sitting rooms and the five guest rooms have been elegantly and comfortably furnished. The largest room has a whirlpool tub in the bathroom in addition to bath and shower. The Hunter Room has an equestrian theme and is decorated with Ralph Lauren fabrics. The Garden Room is also appealing. Breakfast brings such dishes as eggs Florentine or gingerbread griddle cakes to a table set with fine linens, silver, and crystal. In winter you can attend a Culinary Escape weekend, when Michael gives cooking lessons. *Rates:* Summer, $195 to $235; winter, $185 to $215.

Wayside, Bellevue Avenue, Newport, RI 02840 (☎ 401/847-0302), was built by Elisha Dyer, one of the "400" and cotillion dancemaster for the Astors and Vanderbilts. It's certainly imposing and lavish. In the entrance hall a large, molded stucco fireplace is carved with cherubs and a coat of arms that includes the fleur-de-lys. A staircase of quarter-cut oak leads to the huge rooms. In fact, some of the rooms are so large that they seem a trifle bare. All have small TVs. Room 1 has a double canopy bed along with a single bed, both covered with candlewick spreads. A wicker chaise longue, wicker table, and drawers are among the furnishings in this room hung with blue-rose wallpaper. Broken scroll–decorated doors lead into the ground-floor room, which was formerly the library. Even though there's an oriental-style bed, couch, love seat, armchair, and oriental chest, there's still masses of space. This room, decorated in bold blue floral wallpaper, also contains a handsome carved stucco fireplace. Coffee and pastries are put out in the morning for guests to help themselves. Facilities include an in-ground pool. For what you get, rates are reasonable. *Rates:* May 1 to October 31, $150 to 1$60 double; off-season, $95 to $115 double.

Admiral Farragut Inn, 31 Clarke St. (☎ 401/846-4256), is located in an authentic colonial, but it has been decorated in a fresh and entertaining way, which is clear from the minute you enter the hallway boasting a large mural depicting a heron. There are ten rooms, all with private bath and telephone. The rooms are charmingly decorated. For example, the atmospheric low-ceilinged Admiral's Quarters contains a Shaker four-poster, fireplace made of Dutch tiles, and walls that are sponge-painted to resemble pale-green marble. The bathroom has a lovely ceramic tile sink with decorative floral motif. In other rooms you might find oak or pine furnishings and wingchairs and other nice pieces. The Ensigns Quarters on the third floor has a skylight, wooden beams, enchanting sloping ceiling, and small fireplace. In the Marquis Quarters one of the inn's most beguiling pieces can be found—a gray-and-red folk art chair depicting two cats. A continental breakfast is served in the dining room at a long harvest table. *Rates:* May 1 to October 31, $95 to $185; November 1 to April 30, $75 to $135.

Admiral Fitzroy Inn, 398 Thames St. (phone number same as the Farragut), is in the heart of the waterfront district. A redbrick building dating to 1890, it is named after the admiral who developed the barometer, and several modern versions decorate the front hallway and are for sale. There are 18 rooms, all with private bath, cable TV, refrigerator, coffeemaker, and hair dryer. Each room is hand-painted in a different way. You'll likely find a sleigh or iron-and-brass bed combined with different furnishings and color schemes. In Room 1, for example, the walls are painted moss-gray-green, and a large Eastlake dresser dating to 1853 is among the furnishings. Room 9 is particularly airy and bright and has roses and orchids hand-painted on the walls. In Room 10 the walls are adorned with a marvelous apricot tree. Rooms on the top floor have skylights and a view of the harbor from their private decks. A continental breakfast is served in the basement breakfast room. There's also a functional sitting room in the basement with TV and VCR. *Rates:* May 1 to October 31, $135 to $235; November 1 to April 30, $95 to $175.

Victorian Ladies Inn, 63 Memorial Blvd. (☎ 401/849-9960), occupies a large Victorian home with steep dormer roof. There are nine rooms, all with private bath, air-conditioning, and TV. Some have telephone. The rooms are attractively furnished with a variety of antiques—carved Victorian, Shaker canopy, or iron-and-brass beds combined with love seats and Queen Anne chairs or oak pieces. Room moods are created by dramatic use of color—forest green in one combined with silver-gray fabrics or burgundy, rose, and jade in another. Guests have access to a comfortable sitting room with fireplace; a full breakfast is served in the dining room. *Rates:* $105 to $205. Closed January.

Hydrangea House, 16 Bellevue Ave. (☎ 401/846-4435), is a small, attractive bed-and-breakfast occupying an 1876 house. It offers six rooms, all with private bath. Each is very attractively and tastefully furnished. The Rose Dutchess is gussied up with tasseled window treatments, candy-stripe wallpaper, and wall-to-wall rose carpeting. Joshua Reynolds prints from the 1790s adorn the walls. My favorite, even though it's the smallest, is La Petite Rouge with its lush, plum-red walls, hand-painted Edwardian chest of drawers, fireplace, and French cartoons. The Hydrangea Suite is the most lavish, with fine paneling, plush fabrics, and oriental rugs, plus a double whirlpool bath. There's a deck on the back of the house where breakfast (freshly squeezed juice and home-baked breads, plus raspberry pancakes or seasoned scrambled eggs) is served in summer. Otherwise it's served in the downstairs gallery, where you can enjoy a full breakfast and look at the collection of works by local artists. Afternoon tea is also served, and you'll get chocolate chip cookie at the end of the day. A sundeck on the third floor also offers barbecue facilities. *Rates:* May 1 to October 31, $110 to $175, suite $290; November to April, $85 to $135, suite $205.

Stella Maris Inn, 91 Washington St. (☎ 401/849-2862), was given its name by the Sisters of Cluny who occupied it in the 1920 when it was a convent. This stone mansion built in 1853, stands down in the Point. There are eight rooms, all with private bath. Several, like the Lady Gregory Room, have marble fireplaces. This room also contains a Victorian bed, marble-top side tables, and a camelback sofa among its furnishings. The bathroom has delightful porthole windows. Most rooms are large enough to have small sitting areas. The window seat offers a fine view of the bay in the J. M. Synge Room, which is furnished with a wicker bedroom suite and two wingbacks. There's a comfortable parlor with TV. In the dining room, in addition to the table and Chippendale chairs, there's a Yamaha baby grand piano. A continental breakfast is served here or out on the wide porch, which affords a peek of the harbor between the houses across the street. *Rates:* May 1 to October 31, weekends $135 to $205, weekdays $120 to $135; otherwise weekends $105 to $135, weekdays $85 to $105.

Cliff Walk Manor, 82 Memorial Blvd., Newport, RI 02840 (☎ 401/847-1300), is located out of town a little way (about a 10-minute walk) en route to Middletown, right on Eastons Beach. It was built in 1855, and as a consequence the rooms are large and the ceilings lofty. It was originally owned by the Chanlers, relatives of the Astors. Many of the 22 rooms overlook the ocean toward Middletown. So does the terrace adjacent to the restaurant/bar. Rooms have wall-to-wall carpeting, marble-top dressers and side tables, rockers, and often Renaissance Revival–style beds with Marseilles coverlets. Some have Jacuzzis, and all are air-conditioned and have TV. *Rates:* Weekends $165 to $310, midweek $150 to $285.

Pilgrim House Inn, 123 Spring St., Newport, RI 02840 (☎ 401/846-0040), a gray clapboard with a steep mansard located in Newport's historic area, functions as a simple bed-and-breakfast guest house. There are 11 rooms, 3 with shared bath. They are unpretentious and simply furnished with assorted furnishings—chintz wallpapers, ruffle-trimmed curtains, painted drawers, and occasional pieces of wicker. You'll find a plant in each room. At breakfast, muffins, fruit, coffee, and juice are served either inside or out on the rooftop deck, with a view of the harbor. Native Rhode Islanders, the Messerlians will help you plan your local sightseeing and activities. *Rates:* $75 to $165 double in season.

If you're looking for modern accommodations in the historic area, then the **Mill Street Inn,** 75 Mill St., Newport, RI 02840 (☎ 401/849-9500), may be for you. It's a converted redbrick mill in which there are 23 suites available, including 8 two-story "town houses" as they're called, featuring a downstairs sitting room and an upstairs bedroom with a sliding door that leads to a deck with a view across the rooftops to the harbor. Facilities include TV and telephone. Furnishings are strictly modern Scandinavian. The living room has a bar area and fridge, pullout sofa, TV, telephone, and track lighting. All rooms have air-conditioning. Guests have use of the large communal roof deck for sunning and relaxing. The one-level units have bar/fridge, pullout sofa, and other amenities. A continental breakfast is served at tables set with pretty pink tablecloths in a room with rough-hewn stone walls. Tea is also served in the afternoon. *Rates:* Summer, $165 to $265; off-season, $135 to $165.

The **Doubletree Islander Inn,** Goat Island, Newport, RI 02840 (☎ 401/849-2600), surrounded by water, is reached by a causeway. There are incredible views of the harbor in all directions. Parking is available (which is extremely important in this town), and you're only a 5-minute drive or 15-minute walk away from the center of town. The accommodations are spacious and modern. Double sinks are an added convenience. Touch-tone phone and cable TV are standard facilities. There are two dining rooms, a lounge-entertainment room, an indoor pool and outdoor saltwater pool, and tennis courts. *Rates:* January to mid-April, $109 to $184; mid-April to mid-June, $169 to $259; mid-June to late September, $209 to $309; late September to mid-November, $179 to $269; mid-November to December, $119 to $174.

Harborside Inn, Christie's Landing, Newport, RI 02840 (☎ 401/846-6600), is a modern accommodation with 14 rooms right in the center of the seaport action. They are furnished with modern pine furnishings (workbench-style). Suites have a skylit loft bedroom reached by a ship's ladder (in a water-view suite) or by a regular staircase (in land-side accommodations). Rooms are beamed, beds are covered with Tattersall-style comforters, and amenities include telephones, TVs, air-conditioning, refrigerators, and full baths. Water-view rooms and suites have small decks. There's a breakfast and sitting-room area furnished with director's chairs overlooking the dock and harbor. Help yourself to continental-style items at breakfast, hors d'oeuvres, and tea in the afternoons (in winter only). Parking is available. *Rates:* July to mid-September, weekends $265 to $295, midweek $165 to $195; spring/fall, weekends $165 to $205, midweek $95 to $145; winter, weekends $75 to $115, midweek $65 to $95.

Covell House, 43 Farewell St., Newport, RI 02840 (☎ 401/847-8872), has five rooms, all with private baths, in a beige clapboard colonial with a pretty front porch and attractive breakfast room and pleasant gardens, too. *Rates:* Summer, $120 to $140; off-season, $85 to $90.

The **Jenkins Guest House,** 206 S. Rhode Island Ave., Newport, RI 02840 (☎ 401/847-6801), is an authentic European-style guest house. In this house the Jenkinses raised their eight children, and today they open two homey rooms to guests. A continental breakfast is put out in the morning. Sally understands that some folks want their freedom and others want convivial conversation, and she respects your wishes. Guests tend to gather in the kitchen or on the back deck overlooking the garden for their morning coffee. It's a relaxed, casual place. Sally and Dave, who have lived all their lives in Newport, will regale you with tales of the town and its history and give you the rundown on what's going on. *Rates:* $75 double. *Hours:* In season only.

NEWPORT DINING

The **Black Pearl**, Bannister's Wharf (☎ 401/846-5264), is one of Newport's leading restaurants. The tavern is a cozy gathering place; the patio is great for a meal or drink and a sea breeze, and the intimate Commodore Room, decorated in forest green with brass accents and polished wood, is known for its classic French cuisine. Prices range from $18 to $25 for such dishes as paillard of chicken with lemon butter, sautéed duck with green-olive sauce, medallions of veal with morels and sauce champagne, filet mignon au poivre, and more. Among the desserts there might be cheesecake, home-made ice creams, and profiteroles. To start, lobster mousse and escargots are a fine choice. In the tavern prices range from $9 to $20. The chowders are so good I've seen people ask for several large bowls in the tavern, where the menu also includes burgers, omelets, and daily specials like bluefish with lemon caper butter. *Hours:* Daily 11:30am to 3pm and 6 to 11pm (10pm in winter). Jackets are required in the dining room.

Away from the bustle of the wharves, another of my favorites is the **White Horse Tavern,** at Marlborough and Farewell streets (☎ 401/849-3600), an old 1673 tavern that has a series of dining rooms with romantic ambience. The food is superb and ranges from traditional European to contemporary American. For example, you may start with either the iced shellfish (littlenecks, oysters, and shrimp) or the sauté of wild mushrooms served in puff pastry with a Madeira and herb reduction. Follow with the sautéed lobster with a cream sauce, baked salmon with chive butter sauce, the tournedos of beef served over a morel and porcini reduction, or rack of lamb served with a mint and lingonberry jus. Prices range from $23 to $33. Similar finely prepared dishes are offered at lunch and Sunday brunch. *Hours:* Wednesday to Monday noon to 2:30pm, Sunday to Thursday 6 to 9:30pm, Friday and Saturday 6 to 10pm. Jackets are required in the evening.

The **Clarke Cook House,** Bannister's Wharf (☎ 401/849-2900), for my money, is one of Newport's finest dining places. Located in an old colonial building are two dining rooms: The formal room, where black-tie waiters provide attentive service is delightfully colonial, with solid posts and beams, plank floors, and tables set with brass candlesticks. The Candy Store Cafe is more like a tavern/bar despite the marble tables. Here, models of ship's hulls and wood-framed pictures of sailing ships are the major decoration.

At dinner, start with ravioli of lobster and wild mushrooms with morels or gravlax on a crisp potato galette with crème fraîche and oscietra caviar. Follow with a selection from such dishes as tuna steak with sweet-and-sour sherry vinegar glaze, rack of lamb with minted tarragon glaze, or filet mignon with a balsamic port sauce. Prices run $24 to $30. Finish with crème caramel or Locke Ober's famous Indian pudding. The cafe menu offers lighter dishes—pastas, pizzas, and a variety of wood-grilled dishes—burgers, fish, and pork tenderloin with ancho chile and plum chutney, priced from $7 to $18.

Brunch offers an interesting array of egg dishes, plus such dishes as nachos with salsa, guacamole, and cheese; grilled shrimp and Cajun sausage en brochette; angel hair pasta Bolognese; codfish cakes served with baked beans; Mexican pizza (delicious, served on a taco shell); or Irish lamb-and-stout stew. Save room for a delicious dessert, especially the Snowball in Hell—chocolate roulade, vanilla ice cream, and hot fudge sauce with a sprinkling of coconut served in an iced wine glass coated with chocolate.

Hours: Saturday and Sunday 11:30am to 3pm; Wednesday to Sunday 6 to 10:30pm. The cafe is open 11:30am to 10:30pm on weekdays, until 11pm on weekends.

La Petite Auberge, 19 Charles St. (☎ 401/849-6669), is considered by many to be among the city's top three restaurants. The service is gracious, the ambience romantic, and the food good, although not as memorable as the prices might suggest. The menu is very much traditional French. Among the appetizers, you might start with a lobster bisque, goose liver pâté, or escargots bourguignonnes. Main courses, priced from $21 to $33, range from seafood—lobster tails with truffles, trout with hazelnuts—to meats, including tournedos Rossini, and filet mignon au poivre, Châteaubriand béarnaise, and saddle of lamb with garlic sauce. For dessert there are similar classics—crêpes Suzette, banana flambé, peach Melba, and strawberries Romanoff. Tables are set with lovely lace tablecloths, lanterns, and fresh flowers. A classical music background, low lighting by wall sconces, and a handsome fireplace complete the romantic atmosphere. *Hours:* Monday to Saturday 6 to 10pm, Sunday 5 to 9pm.

Some exciting cuisine can be found at **Yesterday's Ale House Bar and The Place,** 28 Washington Sq. (☎ 401/847-0116). It may not look like the domain of fine food, but it certainly is. On one side there's a popular wine bar; on the other is the restaurant, with both booth and table seating. Among the ten or so entrees there might be a maple-glazed duck with chipotle-cherry barbecue sauce, lamb loin in a pecan crust with a balsamic vinegar sauce, and pan-seared Chilean sea bass served on a port wine reduction. Appetizers are similarly inspired—mussels with sake and lime, or chiles relleno with black-bean venison. Prices range from $18 to $28. Those who appreciate wine will enjoy the opportunity to taste several wines from a so-called "flight" containing four 3-ounce glasses of different wines. Absolutely your first dinner stop. *Hours:* Sunday to Thursday 11:30am to 10pm, Friday and Saturday 11:30am to 11pm; summer, Tuesday to Sunday 5:30 to 10pm; winter, Wednesday to Saturday 5:30 to 10pm.

At **Elizabeth's,** Brown and Howard Wharf (☎ 401/846-6862), Broadway show tunes set the pace, and old and new movies add to the fun, although don't be surprised if the hostess, Elizabeth Burley (a former film producer), launches into song, too. The food is as theatrical as the ambience. You'll be served huge platters for two piled high with such treats as shrimp and piselli (shrimp sautéed with garlic and oil and topped with pesto sauce), plus pasta of the day; roasted hot herb sausage; and mushrooms, peppers, and onions. There's also the vegetable of the day, accompanied by piselli sauce and olives. Or there's the barbecue feast, which brings chicken, spare ribs with sweet potato pie, beans, apples, mushroom hot dog sausage, corn bread, and several vegetables. Prices range from $30 to $40 for the platters. The decor is charmingly eccentric and theatrical with assorted chairs and tables covered in exotic fabrics. Great deck in summer, too. Bring your own wine. *Hours:* Summer, daily 5:30 to 10pm; winter, Wednesday to Saturday 5:30 to 10pm. Usually closed January and February.

Puerini's, 24 Memorial Blvd. W. (☎ 401/847-5506), is a delightful, small Italian restaurant with a cozy ambience. The two dining rooms—upstairs and downstairs—contain tables spread with black plastic cloths covered with butcher paper. The walls are decorated with evocative photographs of Italy. The food is good and reasonably priced, too. Start with the sweet roasted peppers in oil and garlic with provolone, or the delicious portobello mushrooms sliced and sautéed with spinach, zucchini, roasted red peppers, pignoli nuts, and a touch of balsamic vinegar. Follow with a pasta like the ravioli stuffed with ricotta and Parmesan with pesto sauce, or one of the fine chicken dishes, Marsala or Fiorentina (with spinach). Prices range from $12 to $15. Beer and wine are available. *Hours:* Tuesday to Thursday 5 to 9pm, Friday and Saturday 5 to 10pm.

Muriel's, Spring and Touro streets (☎ 401/849-7780), is fun for breakfast, lunch, or dinner. Walls are covered with Maxfield Parrish posters, tables sport floral and lace-trimmed tablecloths under glass, and ficus trees set off the jade-colored walls. For breakfast choose the huevos rancheros or the French toast in spiced butter with walnuts and syrup. At lunch salads, pasta, sandwiches, omelets, and entrees under $10 are offered. At dinner the room is transformed by candlelight. The extensive seasonal menu might offer everything from vegetable stir-fry and lasagna to chicken Bombay with bananas, raisin, and walnuts; shrimp Louisiana; and grilled porterhouse with caramelized onions. Prices range from $10 to $17. My favorite dessert is the chocolate bread pudding with vanilla ice cream, chocolate sauce, and walnuts. Beer and wine are available. *Hours:* Year-round, Monday to Saturday 8am to 3pm, Sunday 9am to 3pm; weekends and in season, daily 5pm to closing.

Scales and Shells, 527 Thames St. (☎ 401/846-3474), is the quintessential waterfront fish restaurant. Up front is an open kitchen, and here chefs cook the produce of the sea. The choices are many. You can start with the cherrystones, littlenecks, and oysters on the half shell; the calamari; or grilled shrimp. Follow with lobster fra diavolo, or any one of close to 20 mesquite-grilled fishes— swordfish, salmon, tuna, bluefish, red snapper, mahimahi, and so on. Prices range from $15 to $20 (market price for the lobster). Although there's litte decor to speak of, the crowds create a charged atmosphere. The second-floor dining room, known as Upscales, offers more intimate dining with the same great seafood. *Hours:* Summer, Monday to Thursday 5 to 10pm, Friday to Saturday 5 to 11pm, Sunday 4 to 10pm; winter, Sunday to Thursday 5 to 9pm, Friday to Saturday 5 to 10pm. January to May closed Monday. Upscales is open May to September, Sunday to Thursday 6 to 10pm and Friday and Saturday 6 to 11pm. No credit cards accepted.

Christie's, Christie's Landing (☎ 401/847-5400), is home to the powerboat crowd and is also a hangout for local politicos who like to drink and dine on steaks and seafood priced from $18 to $28. There's veal Oscar, salmon, lobster (stuffed, broiled, or served with tenderloin), swordfish, bouillabaisse, scallops, scrod, sole, and so on; also a clam boil of lobster, steamers, corn, potatoes, and onions; plus steaks and lamb chops. The dining room is large and crowded, and a warm atmosphere prevails. In winter it's warmed by the large stone hearth. The long bar, separated from the dining room, is usually filled with locals anxiously watching the outcome of one of the Boston team's games. Luncheon brings salads, sole, seafood pie, scrod, and other dishes for $6 to $10. Many famous folks' faces line the entryway here. *Hours:* Daily 11:30am to 3pm, and Sunday to Thursday 5 to 9pm, Friday and Saturday 5 to 10pm.

The yachting crowd and the locals favor the **Mooring**, on Sayer's Wharf (☎ 401/846-2260), off America's Cup Avenue, which has a multilevel deck right over the water and a large outdoor bar. The menu features steaks, lobsters, and fresh fish priced from $12 to $25. Favorite dishes are the seafood stew (lobster, shrimp, scallops, mussels, and fish poached in cream with aromatics and herbs), baked stuffed jumbo shrimp, and crabmeat baked en casserole. The chowders are famous; sandwiches and salads are also available. *Hours:* Daily 11:30am to 10pm.

The Pier, Howard Wharf (☎ 401/847-3645), is another Newport tradition, for steaks, seafood, and lobster served in half a dozen or so ways. Prices range $13 to $20. In summer there's nightly entertainment and dancing on weekends. *Hours:* Daily 11:30am to 10pm (in winter, lunches on weekends only).

Canfield House, 5 Memorial Blvd. (☎ 401/847-0416), is a popular restaurant among Newporters. It has been recently restored to its earlier splendor: The barrel-vaulted room with its ornately carved wood ceiling and solid-oak wainscoting now positively glows. If you have to wait for a table, take refuge in front of the huge fire in the bar. The food is inspired by a mixture of traditions, from Italian to Asian. Among the selections you'll find eight or so pastas—pappardelle with pancetta, chicken, littlenecks, onion, and spinach in a white-wine chicken broth, for example. Main dishes include sesame-crusted tuna served with wasabi butter sauce, or a bouillabaisse, plus grilled tenderloin in a Merlot-thyme demi-glace, or pork tenderloin with a pecan-honey glaze. Prices run $19 to $24. *Hours:* In season, daily 4:30 to 10pm; off-season, Tuesday to Thursday 5 to 9pm and Friday to Saturday until 10pm.

Le Bistro, Bannister's Wharf (☎ 401/849-7778), offers classic bistro fare including a worthy steak and frites, plus some really fine seafood dishes. Try the sea scallops with sherry vinegar sauce, broiled mahimahi with champagne sauce, or steamed lobster. To start, try the charcuterie selection of sausages and prosciutto or the escargots bourguignonne. Prices run $15 to $27. The dining room is comfortable country French. At lunch there are omelets, sandwiches, and salads; although, if you wish, the kitchen will prepare dinner items. *Hours:* Daily 11:30am to 11pm.

Breakfast, Brunch & Lunch Spots in Newport

A fine way to spend Sunday morning is to spend it looking out from the terrace at **Inn at Castle Hill**, Ocean Drive, while you enjoy a good brunch. Other great brunch/breakfast places include **Muriel's** (☎ 401/849-7780); the **White Horse Tavern** (☎ 401/849-3600); the **Clarke Cook House** (☎ 401/849-2900); **The Pier**, Howard Wharf (☎ 401/847-3645); and the **Mooring**, on Sayer's Wharf (☎ 401/846-2260). For a more casual but delicious experience, head for **La Boulangerie Obelix**, 382 Spring St. (☎ 401/846-3377), and purchase one of their croissants or breads. It's also a good luncheon spot, serving up creative sandwiches on their terrific breads— chicken-mango salad or prosciutto with Asiago cheese, for example.

You'll probably want to have a waterside lunch on the piers at the places I've already described, or at the Inn at Castle Hill, and enjoy the watery vista while you dine at the places I've already described. Or you can try such casual spots as the **Brick Alley Pub and Restaurant,** at 140 Thames St. (☎ 401/849-6334), which attracts a young, friendly crowd to the bar and the tables for an incredible assortment of reasonably priced good food. The menu spreads over several pages, and the inspiration for the cuisine comes from several continents, offering fish, sandwiches, salads, nachos, and all kinds of items priced from $7 to $20. *Hours:* Sunday to Thursday 11:30am to 9pm; until 11pm on weekends.

Music Hall Cafe, 250 Thames St. (☎ 401/848-2330), is another fun place for lunch. Decorated in brilliant Southwestern colors—sand, jade, and coral—with buffalo skulls and a kiva ladder hanging from the trompe l'oeil painted wall, it offers cuisine to match. In addition to some standard Mexican dishes you'll find blackened salmon with guava-ginger sauce and jerk-spiced chicken. Prices range from $9 to $18 for main dinner courses, less for luncheon items. *Hours:* Daily noon to 3pm, Sunday to Thursday 5 to 9pm, Friday and Saturday until 10pm.

Salas', 345 Thames St. (☎ 401/846-8772), is a cheery, noisy, bustling place. Here you can enjoy a clambake with a 1-pound lobster, clams, sausage, fish, corn on the cob, onions, potatoes, and clam broth, washed down with beer served in pitchers and wine from jugs. There are plenty of other seafood dishes, too—stuffed shrimp, baked scallops, cod, or sole. Salas' is also famous for serving pasta by the quarter, half, and full pound, accompanied by your choice of sauce—red clam or oil and anchovy, for example. Prices range from $9 to $14 (clambakes and lobsters at market prices) and pastas from $3.75 to $14, depending on the size of the serving.

Down at First Beach, **Flo's Clam Shack,** 4 Wave Ave. in Middletown (☎ 401/847-8141), is a counter operation that offers plenty of ocean goodies—clam and lobster rolls, stuffed quahogs, clam cakes, chowder, and calamari. Prices range from $$5 to $10.

NEWPORT AFTER DARK

For the most current information, ask at the Convention and Visitor's Bureau for their nightlife paper. Sunday-afternoon jam sessions are held at the **Newport Harbor Hotel** on America's Cup Avenue (☎ 401/847-9000).

Christie's of Newport (☎ 401/847-5400) and the **Clarke Cooke House,** Bannister's Wharf (☎ 401/849-2900), offer bands and dancing on weekends.

For light entertainment, the **Newport Playhouse and Cabaret Restaurant,** 102 Connell Hwy. (☎ 401/848-7529), mounts a variety of productions year-round. Most tend to be comedies. A buffet dinner is served before the play, and afterward you can return to the dining room for a cabaret performance.

In season, an exciting evening can be spent at the **Newport Jai Alai,** 150 Admiral Kalbfus Rd. (☎ 401/849-5000), watching the fast-paced Basque game of jai alai and wagering on the teams. The facility also offers simulcast horse racing and more than 400 video-lottery machines featuring blackjack, poker, and other games with payoffs up to $6,000.

Newport
Special & Recreational Activities

Antiquing: There are plenty of stores in Newport, although they're most concentrated along **Franklin Street** between Thames and Spring.

Beaches: Bailey's Beach, at Ocean Drive and Bellevue Avenue, is where the "400" park in their monogrammed parking spaces to frolic in private. **Gooseberry Beach** (☎ 401/847-3958) on Ocean Drive is attractive and open for a parking fee of $12 or so. **Fort Adams State Park,** Ocean Drive, also has a beach with a lifeguard. Other beaches are **Newport Beach,** at the eastern end of Memorial Boulevard; **Second Beach** (☎ 401/846-6273) in Middletown, on Sachuest Beach Road; and **Third Beach** (no phone) is around the corner at the mouth of the Sakonnet River.

Biking: Rentals are available at **Ten Speed Spokes,** 18 Elm St. (☎ 401/847-5609). Daily charges average $25. *Hours:* April through October, daily; off-season Monday to Saturday.

Cruises: Oldport Marine Services, Sayer's Wharf (☎ 401/847-9109), offers harbor cruises mid-May to mid-October. **Classic Cruises** (☎ 401/847-0299) offers cruises on vintage powerboats and also aboard a 72-foot reproduction of a 19th-century schooner. Cost is $15 to $20 per person.

Viking Tours, 184 Thames St. (☎ 401/847-6921), runs cruises of the harbor from their Goat Island dock six times daily in season. From mid-May to Columbus day, a 1-hour narrated cruise to Jamestown is offered, costing $8.50 for adults, $3 for children ages 4 to 11.

Golf: In Portsmouth, a 10-minute drive from Newport, you can choose from two courses: **Green Valley** (☎ 401/847-9543) and **Montup** (☎ 401/683-9882).

Hiking: The **Cliff Walk** is a marvelous coastal experience, from the end of Newport Beach to Bellevue and Coggeshall Avenues. **Norman Bird Sanctuary,** 583 Third Beach Rd. (☎ 401/846-2577), has 7¼ miles of hiking trails to marsh, ridge, and pond. *Hours:* Tuesday to Sunday 9am to 5pm; admission $4 for adults, $1 for children.

Horseback Riding: Newport Equestrian Center, 287 Third Beach Rd. (☎ 401/848-5440), offers both beach and trail rides. The 2-hour beach ride goes to two beaches and costs $65. Another trail takes riders around the island. Rides by reservation only.

Picnicking: Brenton Point State Park and **Fort Adams State Park** are pleasant spots.

Polo: Take along a picnic and watch the game, played during late August and early September at **Glen Farm,** off Route 114 in Portsmouth.

Sailing: Newport Sailing School (☎ 401/848-2266) gives lessons and offers 1- and 2-hour sails for $18 and $25. Many companies also charter sailboats for half or full days. **America's Cup Charters** (☎ 401/846-9886) offers evening sails for roughly $50 per person. **Seascope Systems** (☎ 401/847-0299) charters 12-meter sailboats.

State Parks: Brenton Point State Park (☎ 401/846-8240) is mainly a parking area off Ocean Drive with access to a fishing pier and rocky inlets. **Fort Adams State Park** has swimming and picnicking.

Swimming: The pools at the **YMCA**, 792 Valley Rd. (☎ 401/847-9200), and also at **Howard Johnson's**, 351 W. Main Rd., Middletown (☎ 401/849-2000), are open to the public for a small charge ($7 to $10). Or you can head for the beaches mentioned above.

Tennis: The big thrill is to play on the courts at the **Casino Indoor Racquet Club**, 194 Bellevue Ave. (☎ 401/849-4777), for which the charge is $25 per hour, or on the grass courts at the **Tennis Hall of Fame** (☎ 401/849-3990), which will cost about $35 per person per 1½ hours. You can also watch or try to play the forerunner of tennis, "court tennis" (☎ 401/849-6672) at the Tennis Hall of Fame ($30 per person per hour).

Windsurfing: Island Sports, 86 Aquidneck Ave. (☎ 401/846-4421), offers rentals for $50 a day at Third Beach. They also rent kayaks and surfboards.

MASSACHUSETTS

The Central Berkshires & the Pioneer Valley

The Berkshires: Lenox ◆ Lee ◆ South Lee ◆ Stockbridge ◆
West Stockbridge ◆ South Egremont ◆ North Egremont ◆
Hillsdale, N.Y. ◆ Great Barrington ◆ Sheffield ◆ Hartsfield ◆
New Marlborough ◆ Sandisfield ◆ Pittsfield ◆ Dalton ◆
Hancock ◆ Jiminy Peak ◆ Williamstown ◆ Mount Greylock
◆ North Adams ◆ Adams

The Pioneer Valley: Deerfield ◆ Northfield ◆ Amherst
◆ Northampton ◆ South Hadley ◆ Springfield ◆ Northfield

Distance in miles: Pittsfield, 137; Great Barrington, 164; Williamstown, 158; Springfield, 92; Deerfield, 114

Estimated driving time: 1½ to 2¾ hours

◆◇◆◇◆◇◆◇◆◇◆

Driving: For Great Barrington, Lenox, Lee, and the Egremonts, take Exit 2 off the Mass Pike. Route 7 north will take you to Williamstown.

For Deerfield, take the Mass Pike to I-91 north to the Deerfield Exit.

Bus: Bonanza (☎ 800/556-3815) travels to Great Barrington, Lee, Lenox, Stockbridge, Pittsfield, and Williamstown. **Peter Pan** (☎ 800/343-9999) also services these towns, plus Springfield and Deerfield.

Train: Amtrak services Springfield and Pittsfield from Boston. Call ☎ 800/872-7245.

Further Information: Massachusetts in general: **Massachusetts Office of Travel and Tourism,** 100 Cambridge St., Boston, MA 02202 (☎ 800/447-6277 or 617/727-3201).

For specific information about the area: **Berkshire Visitors Bureau,** Berkshire Common Plaza Level, Dept. MA, Pittsfield, MA 01201 (☎ 413/443-9186); **Stockbridge Chamber of Commerce,** P.O. Box 224, Stockbridge, MA 01262; **Lenox Chamber of Commerce,** P.O. Box 646, Lenox, MA 01240 (☎ 800/25LENOX or 413/637-3646); **Southern Berkshire Chamber of Commerce,** 362 Main St., Great Barrington, MA 01230 (☎ 413/528-1510).

Events & Festivals to Plan Your Trip Around

End of June through Labor Day: Summer festivals.

    Jacob's Pillow Dance Festival. Call ☎ 413/243-0745 for tickets.

    Williamstown Theatre Festival. Call ☎ 413/597-3400 for tickets.

    Berkshire Theatre Festival, Stockbridge. Call ☎ 413/298-5576 after June 1, 413/298-5536 at other times.

    Tanglewood. For tickets, which go on sale in early April, call ☎ 800/274-8499. Call ☎ 413/637-1666 for information, or write to Boston Symphony Orchestra, Symphony Hall, Boston, MA 02115 (☎ 617/266-1492).

July: Aston Magna Festival, Great Barrington (☎ 800/875-7156 or 413/528-3595), features 17th- and 18th-century works performed on original instruments at various locations on weekends.

September: Josh Billings Race combines a 26-mile cycle trip from Great Barrington to the Stockbridge Bowl, two laps by canoe around the lake, and a 6-mile run to Tanglewood (usually mid-September).

    That same weekend the **Lenox Tub Parade** celebrates an earlier tradition. Horse-drawn carriages or "tubs" decorated with the harvest of the season parade through the streets, recalling the way the "cottagers" used to say their good-byes before heading back to the city.

September/October: South Mountain Chamber Concerts, South Mountain, Box 23, Pittsfield, MA 01201 (☎ 413/442-2106).

October: Harvest Festival at the Berkshire Botanical Garden in Stockbridge. Call ☎ 413/298-3926.

December: The **Annual Holiday House Tour** gives visitors the opportunity to view privately owned historic properties that are not usually open to the public.

For Deerfield area information: **Pioneer Valley Convention and Visitors Bureau,** 56 Dwight St., Springfield, MA 01103 (☎ 413/787-1548); **Mohawk Trail Association,** P.O. Box 7, Dept. MA, North Adams, MA 01347 (☎ 413/664-6256).

THE BERKSHIRES

It would take a lot of weekends to "do" the Berkshires because the events and attractions are so many and so varied. First, of course, there are all those outstanding cultural events—Tanglewood, the Williamstown Theatre Festival, the South Mountain concerts, the Jacob's Pillow Dance Festival—that bring people flocking to this scenic area of lakes and wooded hills. There's also the history of the region, which yields all kinds of attractions—some literary or artistic, like the homes of Herman Melville, Edith Wharton, Nathaniel Hawthorne, William Cullen Bryant, Daniel Chester French, and Norman Rockwell. Others are from a more worldly past, like the sumptuous mansions that line the streets and dot the countryside around Lenox and Stockbridge—Blantyre, Bellefontaine, Wheatleigh, and Naumkeag. And last, but far from least, there is the landscape—mounts Greylock, Everett, and Monument, and the forests that surround them, with all kinds of opportunities for hiking, skiing, blueberry picking, bird watching, picnicking, and just plain basking in the beauty of it all. In short, it's a rich area to mine for many weekends or longer stays.

Early Days The first settlers of the Berkshires were the Mahkeenac Indians. Driven by the Iroquois from the Hudson Valley, the Mahkeenacs found the lush streams, lakes, and wooded hills around Stockbridge and Great Barrington to be bountiful hunting and fishing grounds. As pioneers moved west from the Massachusetts Bay Colony, they, too, entered into the area, establishing thriving farming and trading communities—the first at Sheffield in 1733 and the second at Stockbridge in 1735. Some of the settlers attempted to convert the Mahkeenacs to Christianity, as did the Reverend John Sergeant, whose Mission House can still be seen today in Stockbridge. During the American Revolution, Berkshire County supported the patriots' cause, and, indeed, as early as 1774 the townsfolk of Great Barrington showed their resistance to British rule by refusing to allow royal judges to sit in court. The domestic turmoil that followed the American Revolution was also experienced here—in 1787, Daniel Shay led his famous farmers' rebellion against the Articles of Confederation, an event recalled today by a marker on Route 23 in South Egremont, where he supposedly surrendered to Colonel John Ashley of Sheffield. Soon after the American Revolution the Shakers arrived. This community of pacifist celibates who dedicated their lives to hard work established their City of Peace in 1790 at Hancock, and it is a fascinating place to visit today.

A Wealthy Playground Less simple folk soon followed. First to arrive was Boston financier Samuel Gray Ward, who persuaded his friends, the Higginsons, to join him. Such figures as Nathaniel Hawthorne, Herman Melville, Henry Wadsworth Longfellow, and James Russell Lowell soon followed. But these early comers were folks of modest means compared to the super-rich people who followed. Largely attracted by the stories written by these authors about the Berkshires, they turned the area into a playground for the wealthy. These people represented the great fortunes that had been made from steel, milling, railroads, and other industries in the 19th century, and they looked for places to vacation and display their wealth. They built ever more lavish and ostentatious mansions and mock palaces in imitation of the European aristocracy. Those who liked the ocean summered at resorts such as Newport, Cape May, and Bar Harbor, while the Berkshires and Saratoga Springs attracted

The Berkshires

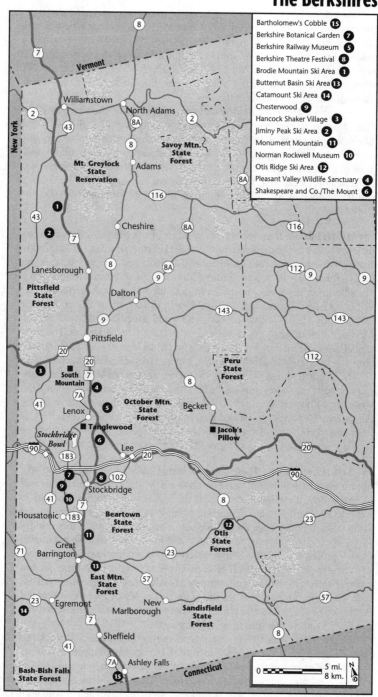

Bartholomew's Cobble **15**
Berkshire Botanical Garden **7**
Berkshire Railway Museum **5**
Berkshire Theatre Festival **8**
Brodie Mountain Ski Area **1**
Butternut Basin Ski Area **13**
Catamount Ski Area **14**
Chesterwood **9**
Hancock Shaker Village **3**
Jiminy Peak Ski Area **2**
Monument Mountain **11**
Norman Rockwell Museum **10**
Otis Ridge Ski Area **12**
Pleasant Valley Wildlife Sanctuary **4**
Shakespeare and Co./The Mount **6**

Vermont

New York

Williamstown

North Adams

Savoy Mtn.
State
Forest

Mt. Greylock
State
Reservation

Adams

Cheshire

Lanesborough

Pittsfield
State
Forest

Dalton

Pittsfield

South
Mountain

Peru
State
Forest

Lenox

October Mtn.
State
Forest

Becket

Tanglewood

Jacob's
Pillow

Stockbridge
Bowl

Lee

Stockbridge

Housatonic

Beartown
State
Forest

Great
Barrington

Otis
State
Forest

East Mtn.
State
Forest

Egremont

New
Marlborough

Sandisfield
State
Forest

Sheffield

Bash-Bish Falls
State Forest

Ashley Falls

Connecticut

0   5 mi.
    8 km.

N

277

those who preferred the mountains. Edith Wharton, tired of Newport and marriage, built her $40,000 mansion here in 1901. She used to drive the dusty roads in her large automobile, with her frequent visitor, Henry James, often at her side. Harley Procter (of Procter & Gamble) built a "cottage" in Lenox, and other industrialists like George Westinghouse, the Vanderbilts, and Andrew Carnegie established estates in the area.

From about 1880 to 1900 the Berkshires experienced their heyday. After that, their popularity declined with the advent, among other things, of the automobile and later of the airplane, both of which afforded increased mobility to the younger generation. The mansions stood empty and unused, and most of them were sold and converted into schools, camps, or guest houses. Bellefontaine, for example, which had been copied from Louis XV's Petit Trianon and reputedly cost $1 million to build in 1899, sold for a mere $70,000 in 1946.

The Creative Arts   Despite the wealthy influx, the Berkshires always retained their image as a creative arts colony. Nathaniel Hawthorne wrote his *Tanglewood Tales* looking out over Lake Mahkeenac (the Stockbridge Bowl). In 1850 he met Herman Melville at a Monument Mountain picnic, and after that, they visited each other often. Melville even dedicated *Moby-Dick* to Hawthorne. William Cullen Bryant, editor of the *New York Post*, jurist Oliver Wendell Holmes, poet Henry Wadsworth Longfellow, and James Russell Lowell are just a few of the writers and intellectuals associated with the Berkshires. The artist Daniel Chester French built his Chesterwood in 1898, and Norman Rockwell, chronicler of America's small-town life, came to the Berkshires much later.

The artistic tradition of the area was further entrenched with the establishment of major cultural events like the Berkshire Music Festival, founded in 1936 when Serge Koussevitzky conducted the first concert at Tanglewood; the Jacob's Pillow Dance Festival, established by Ted Shawn and Ruth St. Denis 5 years later; and the Berkshire Theatre Festival, which helped establish the careers of such legendary actors as James Cagney, Ethel Barrymore, and Katharine Hepburn.

The Berkshires Today   These summer events still draw enormous crowds, but no matter what time of year you choose to visit the Berkshires, they will always delight. In winter they present the idyllic winter scenes captured in Norman Rockwell's famous seasonal illustration of Stockbridge. There's skiing at Catamount, Jiminy Peak, Brodie, Berkshire East, and Butternut; cross-country skiing everywhere; skating on the lakes; and hot toddies and blazing fires in quaint, old-fashioned inns to help you recover from outdoor exertions. Whether you come to ski or nod by the fireside in winter, to wander amid the mountain laurel in spring, to view the fantastic palette of the trees in fall, or to spread out your blanket and picnic under the stars at Tanglewood to the sounds of Beethoven or Mozart, you'll experience a deep thrill and contentment that will leave you wanting to return time and time again.

You'll probably want to visit several times during the summer, once to attend some of the cultural events, again to visit all the attractions clustered around Stockbridge or farther north in Hancock and Williamstown, and still again to hike, fish, or canoe in the mountains and lakes. Therefore, I have not arranged this chapter around a single typical weekend but rather have tried to outline all the possibilities that each town and area offers. It's up to you to choose.

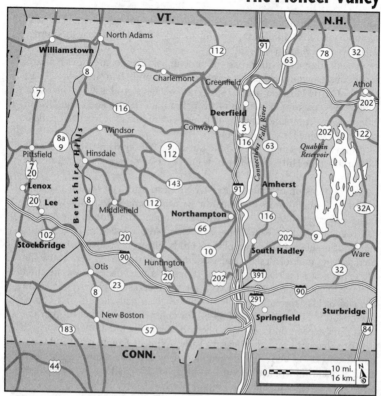

LENOX

Today, you can stay in many of the old mansions that were once the summer retreats for such industrial magnates as Harley Procter, George Westinghouse, and Andrew Carnegie, who were drawn to the Berkshires' unspoiled beauty, and the tidy farms and streets of Lenox in particular.

Besides these wonderful mansions, the main attraction for visitors is, of course, the **Berkshire Music Festival at Tanglewood,** just outside Lenox, overlooking the lovely Stockbridge Bowl, which inspired Hawthorne to write his *Tanglewood Tales.* Although the festival may have lost some of its earlier seriousness and serenity, it still attracts dedicated listeners to its shaded lawns and large music shed, and it is still a very pleasant way to spend some of your time in the Berkshires. (For detailed information, see "Festivals in the Berkshires," below.)

Adjacent to Tanglewood, visit the **Frelinghuysen Morris House and Studio,** 92 Hawthorne St. (☎ 413/637-0166), the Bauhaus-inspired summer home of abstract artists Suzy Frelinghuysen and George L. K. Morris, who also collected modern art. Morris co-designed the house with architect John Butler Swann. He painted the frescoes in the living room, and Suzy painted those in the dining room. Their paintings are on display along with works by Juan Gris, Pablo Picasso, and Georges Braque. On the grounds stands the massive sculpture *The Mountain* by Gaston Lachaise. *Hours:* July to August, Thursday to Sunday 10am to 4pm; June, September, and October, Thursday to Saturday 10am to 4pm. *Admission:* $7.50.

A walk around the village past the rambling old clapboard houses is always a pleasure. On your way, at the corner of Walker and Main streets you'll pass the old **Curtis Hotel,** a noted 19th-century stage stop that welcomed such illustrious guests as Chester Alan Arthur, Franklin Delano Roosevelt, Dwight Eisenhower, Jenny Lind, and Serge Koussevitzky. Today, it has been remodeled into a home for retired people.

From here be sure to walk to the top of the hill on Main Street to see the **"Church on the Hill,"** a very fine New England Congregational church erected in 1805.

At the junction of routes 7 and 7A, you can tour **The Mount** (☎ 413/637-1899), an impressive mansion with a dramatic widow's walk, an octagonal cupola, and a terrace with balustrade. The Mount was built in 1901–2. Modeled on Belton House, a 17th-century estate in Lincolnshire, England, it shows how accomplished Edith Wharton was when it came to architecture, interior design, and gardening. Wharton lived here while she wrote her novel *The House of Mirth* (1905); this is also where she was inspired to write *Ethan Frome* (1911), which is set in the Berkshire countryside. From the end of May through October, tours are given daily from 9am to 2pm. Admission is $6 for adults and $4.50 for children ages 13 to 18. After the tours, Shakespeare and Company offers theater at the Mount.

For a change of pace, the **Pleasant Valley Wildlife Sanctuary,** West Mountain Road (☎ 413/637-0320), maintained by the Massachusetts Audubon Society, offers miles of nature trails. Admission is $3 for adults, $2 for children ages 3 to 12. It's located just off Route 7 north of Lenox.

Lenox Lodging

Although there are plenty of wonderful accommodations within a 30-minute drive of Tanglewood (which I'll describe later), Lenox is the closest place to stay, and the village is full of notable hostelries. You'll have to book well in advance, pay ahead, and probably stay a minimum of 2 or 3 nights. Tanglewood operates an **accommodations hot line** providing rooms in local homes. Call the festival number: ☎ 413/637-1600.

The true connoisseur stays house party–style at **Blantyre,** 16 Blantyre Rd., Lenox, MA 01240 (☎ 413/637-3556 after May 1, 413/298-3806 off-season), built in 1902 for Robert Paterson, the president of W. J. Sloane, director of a Manhattan Bank, and a friend of Carnegie. Costing $135,000 ($300,000 if you add in the furnishings), it was the most expensive and lavish villa in the Berkshires (The Mount cost only $40,000). It was modeled after his wife's Scottish ancestral home.

In its heyday, when the summer set walked to and from each other's houses attended by maids with lanterns, it was the scene of tea parties, games, charades, and formal balls and dinners. Thereafter it experienced a checkered, but nevertheless fascinating history. In 1925 it, along with 250 acres, was sold for a mere $25,000; it served briefly as a country club before being bought by D. W. Griffith, who dreamed of turning it into an East Coast studio, but died before he could do so. Various owners tried to make something of it until finally Senator and Mrs. Fitzpatrick, the inspiration behind the Red Lion in Stockbridge, bought it and created this luxurious accommodation.

So magnificent—veritably museum quality—are the furnishings that the proprietors have had to close the house to uninvited visitors because too many appeared to gawk at the splendor. In the main hall, lit by shimmering chandeliers, Elizabethan and Jacobean pieces and oriental vases are arrayed before the ornately carved fireplace. The similarly furnished music room also features a priceless Coromandel screen and a grand piano. There are four rooms and four suites in the main house and 12 additional, beautifully appointed rooms in the carriage house, out by the open-air swimming pool.

The suites are spectacular. The Cranwell has a dramatic four-poster, and the various furnishings are all beautiful, genuine antiques—ormolu mirrors, inlaid tables, porcelain lamps, and couches and chairs covered with fine fabrics. The ceilings are at least 14 feet high, with elegant moldings. A pink fireplace, gilt-framed portraits, a pencil poster with a dusky-rose eiderdown, a silver brush set on a mahogany desk, and even a bathroom with crystal light fixtures and a marble sink are just a few of the highlights of the Laurel Suite. All bathrooms contain shampoo, conditioner, lotions, bath salts, and Crabtree & Evelyn soaps.

Note that there are only 20 accommodations, so you may well be unable to secure a room without reserving at least a year ahead. Please don't harass the staff—this is simply a fact that is beyond their control.

In the paneled dining room, hung with rich tapestries, guests sit at a long Tudor refectory table bearing a lace tablecloth and impressive table settings of crystal and fine china. Here a $70-per-person, three-course dinner is served. Among the seven or eight entrees you might find pan-seared halibut with littleneck clams served with chervil and brown butter vinaigrette; sautéed lobster with chanterelles, haricots vert, and lemon verbena; or roast rack of lamb with zucchini, eggplant, pistou, and red wine. For breakfast the conservatory makes a beautifully bright setting. Other facilities include the previously mentioned swimming pool and four tennis courts.

Rates: Late June to Labor Day and late September to late October, main suites $525 to $700, rooms $325 to $500, carriage house rooms $300, suites $375, cottages from $430. Rates are slightly less at other times. A 2-day minimum stay is required on weekends and in July, August, and October.

Canyon Ranch, 165 Kemble St., Lenox, MA (☎ 413/637-4100), is, of course, the outpost of the famous Tucson establishment of the same name. It's the place to go to restore your health and well-being and to learn ways to relieve stress and lead a more healthful life. The setting will certainly help to restore some lost vitality, for it occupies the marble-and-brick mansion, Bellefontaine, which is surrounded by 120 acres of woodland. It consists of the Mansion, the Spa, and the 120-room inn, all connected by covered glass walkways. The Mansion houses the elegant dining room, the medical and behavioral consultation areas, and the beautiful library with ornately carved marble fireplace, Palladian windows, carved ceiling, and floor-to-ceiling bookcases. The spa offers every conceivable form of exercise and body therapy—exercise rooms, indoor and outdoor tennis, racquetball and squash, indoor and outdoor pools, and a suspended indoor running track. There are, in fact, 30 fitness classes each day. Treatments include mud and salt, herbal and aroma wraps, a variety of massages and facials, and other salon services. On hand is a professional staff to assist you in developing a healthful diet and exercise regimen with the techniques ranging from biofeedback to hypnotherapy. In the dining room the menu lists nutritional information, and, besides eating healthfully here, guests can learn how to continue the habit at home. *Rates:* $440 per person per night. In summer, 3-night weekend packages, including a series of health services packages, start at $1,470.

Overlooking a lake, **Wheatleigh,** West Hawthorne Street (P.O. Box 824), Lenox, MA 01240 (☎ 413/637-0610), the magnificent former home of the countess de Heredia, has 22 acres of lawn and gardens. Modeled after a 16th-century Italian palazzo, it was built on the site of the Gideon Smith tavern; he was a Tory who was hanged for his British loyalties. The gravel driveway ends in a circular courtyard with a central marble fountain standing in front of the wrought-iron and glass canopy. Inside, the most striking features of the great entry hall are the huge white marble fireplace, sculpted with Cupids and flowers, and the grand staircase, also of marble.

Upstairs are 11 very spacious rooms and four smaller accommodations, each possessing its own mood. They all have extremely high ceilings, marble fireplaces, and large, old-fashioned bathrooms. Some have canopied beds, and the furnishings are a combination of English and French antiques. The rooms in the rear have lovely views of the lake. All have air-conditioning, telephones, and TV/VCRs. The house also has a unique accommodation in the former aviary—a duplex that Leonard Bernstein always chose to stay in when he was conducting at Tanglewood.

The restaurant at Wheatleigh is also a gem, with swag drapes, Chippendale chairs, fine table settings, and unique Dalton wall plaques. The $68 fixed-price menu is supplemented by both low-fat, vegetarian menus, and a *menu degustation.* You will find two main dishes like sautéed halibut with fresh saltwater shrimp and loin of lamb with garlic flan and rosemary-infused jus. Breakfast offers an interesting array of egg dishes, including poached eggs and Mornay sauce served on an English muffin.

On the 22-acre grounds landscaped by Frederick Law Olmsted are a serene rock garden, a pool surrounded by fragrant pine and conifers, and a tennis court. In winter the grounds have cross-country skiing.

Rates: $185 to $435. *Dining hours:* Daily 8 to 10:30am, 6 to 9pm.

The beautiful residence now known as the **Gateways Inn,** 71 Walker St., Lenox, MA 01240 (☎ 413/637-2532), was once Harley Procter's mansion (of Procter & Gamble). Wrought-iron gates mark the entrance to the drive that leads to the classical, white-columned portico; a balustrade runs along the top of the front facade. Inside, a sweeping staircase leads to 12 large elegant accommodations (1 suite), 3 with fireplaces, all furnished with large Victorian pieces, most often of mahogany. Some feature canopied beds, others sleigh beds. The bathroom in the Victorian room contains the oversize tub that was custom-made for Mr. Procter. All rooms have telephones, TVs, air-conditioning, and private baths; many feature old-fashioned pedestal sinks.

The Gateways is known for excellent cuisine, served in elegant surroundings. On the seasonal menu you might find such entrees as a delicately flavored rack of lamb Provençale, penne alla arrabbiata (one of a dozen pastas), veal Marsala, or a grilled pavé of salmon finished with an olive sauce. Prices range from $18 to $25. The restaurant is especially noted for its desserts: apfelstrudel, luscious Black Forest torte, and strawberries Gateways—fresh strawberries with kirschwasser, whipped cream, and melba sauce, all blended together into one super taste treat.

Note: If you stay at the Gateways, you can use the pool, bicycles, and tennis court at the Haus Andreas, nearby in Lee, under the same management.

Rates (including continental breakfast): June to October, Thursday to Sunday $215 to $250, Monday to Wednesday $130 to $170; November to May, Thursday to Sunday $170 to $185, Monday to Wednesday $120 to $135. *Dining hours:* Summer, daily 5:30 to 9pm. Closed Tuesday in winter.

Idyllically situated diagonally across from the west entrance to Tanglewood, the **Apple Tree Inn,** 334 West St. (P.O. Box 699), Lenox, MA 01240 (☎ 413/ 637-1477), does in fact stand on 22 acres in the midst of a fragrant apple orchard bordering the 750-acre Pleasant Valley bird sanctuary. The rooms in the 110-year-old house with its dormers and classical portico offer spectacular views over the Stockbridge Bowl and daisy-dappled fields to the hills beyond. There are 11 rooms and 2 suites in the main house. Room 4 has eyelet lace pillowcases on the bed, attractive Schumacher flower-and-bird wallpaper, ruffled curtains, and an inviting window seat. Room 2, or the Blue Room, affords a large pineapple bed with a stepstool, two armchairs, a small ormolu mirror placed over a chest, and lace-curtained French doors that lead to a private terrace with a magnificent view. Room 3 is where Leontyne Price used to stay, a pretty country room of celery and pink hues, with a brass bed, marble-top side tables, and a fireplace. Rooms 5 and 6 have skylights, and the suite (no. 8) has books and records as well as a fireplace, a TV, and other amenities. Third-floor rooms come in odd, interesting shapes. Brass beds, quilts, wing chairs, and braided rugs continue the country theme. A newer guest lodge has 20 rooms, which are motel-style, but still pleasant, clean, and tasteful; some people prefer them because they're closer to the pool. All of the accommodations are air-conditioned and have private baths.

The pool is spectacularly located and reached via a trellised walkway covered in roses and clematises. It has a flagstone apron, which is bordered by flower beds of roses, poppies, stocks, and more. From here there's a marvelous view over the valley to distant hills. There's also a clay tennis court for tennis enthusiasts, plus cross-country ski trails and miles of hiking.

For guests' comfort, there's a parlor furnished with plush couches and armchairs, small chess and backgammon tables, and a piano where you might be lucky enough to find one of the featured Tanglewood artists "rehearsing."

There are two dining rooms. The Tavern, the former billiards room, with a large brick fireplace, and oak beams and paneling, serves late-night snacks in summer and full meals in winter. It's ideal for dessert and coffee after a concert. The circular Gazebo is lighter in ambience, furnished in dusky rose with white bentwood chairs. The tented ceiling is strung with tiny lights. In summer you can dine to the symphonic melodies wafting on the evening breezes from Tanglewood. There's also a deck for outdoor dining, brightened by colored umbrellas and by some of the 350 varieties of roses that the innkeeper cultivates. The food is continental/American—shrimp Dijon, duckling with cherry sauce, veal saltimbocca, and filet mignon with rosemary sauce. Several pasta dishes are also available. Desserts include profiteroles, pie of the day, and seasonal fruits. Brunch varies. Dinner prices range from $12 to $23.

Rates: Summer (late June to Labor Day and from October 1 to 24), $140 to $310, the lower price for room with shared bath; mid-April to late June and early September to October 1 and New Year's (shoulder season), $105 to $250; winter, $65 to $175. Reduced midweek rates are offered during shoulder and winter seasons. *Dining hours:* Thursday to Sunday 5:30 to 9pm (daily 5 to 9:30pm during the Tanglewood season); Sunday brunch 10:30am to 2pm year-round.

The **Birchwood Inn,** 7 Hubbard St., Lenox, MA 01240 (☎ 413/637-2600), is a tastefully decorated and impeccably run accommodation. Set halfway up the hill, across from the "Church on the Hill," it was originally built in 1776 by Isreal Dewey. Later it became a veterans' home before being converted into a stunning inn. There are 12 very distinctively decorated guest rooms (all with telephones, ten with private baths) with antique reproductions and beautiful wallpapers. Three rooms have four-poster canopied beds. Downstairs, the sunken living room is especially charming with its inviting window seats, gilt mirrors, and bookcases filled with interesting volumes; a smaller den makes a cozy stopping place for late-night conversation before retiring. Additional accommodations, consisting of one-bedroom efficiency apartments, are located in the carriage house. *Rates* (including continental breakfast): July and August, $100 to $210; October, $70 to $160; winter, $70 to $150.

Across the street from the Birchwood Inn, **Whistler's Inn,** 5 Greenwood St., Lenox, MA 01240 (☎ 413/637-0975), is named after the second owner of the house, artist James Whistler's nephew. There's a charming air about this French/English Tudor mansion built in 1820 with its mansard roof and lattice windows, approached via a lovely lych-gate. On the ground floor the music room has a grand piano and a marvelous library, complete with comfortable wing chairs and a marble fireplace; the formal dining room has a large table and Chippendale chairs seating eight. Upstairs, there are 11 rooms, all with private baths (most with air-conditioning). Six rooms have dormer windows and sloping ceilings, and painted chests; there are two doubles with brass beds and three others with cannonball or pineapple bedsteads. The two master bedrooms, which have fireplaces and couches, are particularly welcoming. On sunny days you can take a light breakfast of muffins and coffee or tea out on the back veranda overlooking the 7 acres of gardens. *Rates:* June 16 to October 31, weekends $100 to $235, midweek $90 to $190; otherwise weekends $90 to $170, midweek $80 to $150.

Garden Gables, 141 Main St., P.O. Box 52, Lenox, MA 02140 (☎ 413/637-0193), is a delightful accommodation surrounded by 5 acres of beautiful gardens. The original house was built in 1780, but extensions were added in 1909. The Canadian owners are extremely relaxed and friendly. The 18 rooms all have air-conditioning and telephones; some have cable TV/VCRs. All are comfortably furnished in an unpretentious manner and have chintz or floral wallpapers. You might discover a maple bed, a maple dresser combined with a brass bed, or, as in room 15, a brick fireplace, a Shaker pencil four-poster, and wing chairs. Room 15 also has a large bathroom with whirlpool tub and a small porch. Room 9 is a favorite with its rose quilt and solid, carved four-poster. It, too, has a deck furnished with wicker and also a Jacuzzi bathtub and separate shower. There are two large and tastefully decorated sitting rooms for guests' use. One features a copper-hooded fireplace and is furnished with a Steinway grand piano, comfortable slip-covered chairs and couches, plenty of books, and some fine art on the walls. Fresh flowers are found throughout the house—a romantic touch. Fine crystal, candles, and Sheraton-style chairs set the scene in the dining room, where a full breakfast is served buffet-style— croissants, muffins, bagels, fruit, yogurt, cereal, and a hot dish like smoked salmon quiche. Facilities include a 72-foot-long outdoor pool. *Rates:* Summer, weekends $140 to $235; slightly less at other times.

Peggy and Richard Houdek, who migrated from California where he was an arts administrator and music critic and she was managing editor of *Performing Arts* magazine, naturally sought a culturally rich area to which to relocate as innkeepers. They found an 1804 landmark building, **Walker House**, 64 Walker St., Lenox, MA 01240 (☎ 413/637-1271), only minutes from Tanglewood. Being music lovers, they have decorated all eight of the spacious rooms (all with private baths, five with working fireplaces) in honor of a particular composer. In the somber-colored ground-floor Beethoven Room, which has a fireplace, are portraits and a bust of the genius himself; upstairs there's a lighter, sunnier Chopin Room, a brilliant-blue Tchaikovsky Room, a summery green-and-white Verdi Room, and three other rooms named after Handel, Puccini, and Mozart, and an intimate room honoring Debussy. Downstairs, there's a large parlor with a grand piano, a cozy hearth, plenty of reading material, and some astonishingly healthy plants. Equally beautiful plants share the long, wide veranda with the comfortable wicker furniture. Breakfast conversation flows easily at the tables, and fast friendships are sometimes made. Cards and addresses are exchanged over a morning repast of fresh juice or baked fruit, Peggy's home-baked muffins, cereal, hard-boiled eggs, and plenty of piping-hot, freshly ground coffee. And then, of course, the special delight of a stay here is the sound of glorious classical music that usually fills the house throughout the day. On cold winter nights films, operas, and sports are shown on the 7-foot-screen TV. There are also 3 acres of wooded grounds for guests to explore. This is a no-smoking inn. *Rates:* Late June to Labor Day, weekends $120 to $200 (Thursday to Sunday), midweek $90 to $130 (Monday to Wednesday); Labor Day to mid-September and November 1 to late June, weekends $90 to $130, midweek $80 to $100; mid-September to October 31, weekends $120 to $170, midweek $80 to $130.

Seven Hills Country Inn and Restaurant, 40 Plunkett St., Lenox, MA 01240 (☎ 413/637-0060), is a lavish, gracious resort. The public rooms are extravagantly furnished; the 27 acres include two tennis courts, a large pool, and very well-kept landscaped gardens. Some of the service personnel are selected from the major music schools—Juilliard, Mannes, Manhattan, and Peabody—and when they're not waiting tables, they perform. The nightclub is most elegant, with its softly lit, mauve-pink tented ceiling and plush sofas, and features a variety of Broadway and jazz artists such as Natalie Lamb and Ed Linderman on weekends. On Monday, Tuesday, and Wednesday local artists perform.

The whole place is built on a grand scale. The so-called living room is more like a baronial hall, with floor-to-ceiling gilt mirrors, intricately carved and needlepointed Charles II chairs, a central double fireplace of carved wood on one side and wedding cake stucco on the other, ornamented with cherubs and gryphons. Other features include another grand piano, handsome carved sideboards, and dragon-decorated chairs. Window seats look out over the wide balustered flagstone terrace set with umbrella tables and marble benches. The balustrade supports a series of sculpted marble lions. Gravel paths lead between carved pillars and vine arbors down to the pool. The gardens are filled with peonies, shrubs, and trees.

Every Monday and Tuesday there are concerts in the Music Room, and although the management doesn't like to publicize particular names, many famous artists have performed here. Folk and square dancing are also enjoyed once a week during the summer and the Emmy Award–winning "News in Revue" performs 6 nights a week.

The 52 rooms are located in either the main building or in motel-style units. A carved, paneled staircase decorated with two compelling landscapes leads to what, to me, are the nicest rooms. Room 1 has a fireplace, a large mahogany bed and chest, and a Williamsburg cane eagle chair, all set on a slate-blue carpet against similarly colored walls, ball-fringe curtains, and eyelet lace linens. Room 3 also has a fireplace and a small balcony. Room 7 possesses a high Victorian bird's-eye maple bed and marble-top dresser coupled with bold floral-and-bird wallpaper. It, too, has a fireplace.

The 100-seat restaurant offers contemporary continental cuisine, for example, muscovy duck breast braised in balsamic vinegar and ruby-red grapes, topped with porcini mushrooms; or breast of chicken stuffed with sun-dried tomatoes in a sauce of port wine and sage, topped with grilled portobello. Main courses are priced from $19 to $27. The carved-walnut Italian chairs, the oriental-style Van Luit wallpaper, and the bronze and porcelain chandelier make an elegant setting for the food.

For additional entertainment there's a library with TV and a small lounge with a grand piano and a wood fireplace. Seven Hills is definitely an experience. It's a chance to taste the opulent way of life that used to exist in the Berkshires, but with a refreshing lack of excessive pretense.

Rates (including breakfast): Summer/fall, $114 to $260; off-season, $94 to $160. MAP is also offered.

Cliffwood Inn, 25 Cliffwood St., Lenox, MA 01240 (☎ 413/637-3330), occupies a large mansion set back from the road only 2 blocks from the center of town. An impressive semicircular drive leads to the oval portico supported by classical Ionic columns. The detailing of this building designed by Arthur Rotch—carved shell and urn moldings above the windows, some of which are oval—is quite fine and certainly worthy to be the summer home of Edward Livingston, American ambassador to France, for whom it was built in 1889. The entry hall is lit by an Italian alabaster statue of a woman on a marble column holding an illuminated globe. To the right there's a favorite little corner anchored by a fireplace with window seats.

It's filled with the antiques and antique reproductions collected by owners Joy and Scottie Farrelly, who are also dealers in Eldred Wheeler's fine-quality colonial reproductions. Floor-to-ceiling gilded mirrors and a handsome marble fireplace add to the grand atmosphere of the living room. French doors lead to a wide back veranda where baskets of begonias hang and rockers overlook the pool and gazebo. The oval dining room features a magnificent, 400-year-old sideboard and is lit by a Venetian chandelier. Here or on the veranda, a continental breakfast of fresh fruit, muffins, and breads is served. There are seven guest rooms, all with baths and air-conditioning, six with working fireplaces. Each is named after a Farrelly ancestor. The Jacob Gross Jr. Room has a four-poster canopied bed and easy chairs in front of the fireplace. Facilities include an indoor swimming pool and spa.

The owners also offer guests a computerized, up-to-date calendar of cultural events, chairs and cushions for the lawn at Tanglewood, and easy access to the concert venue just down the street by a less heavily trafficked entrance. Foreign visitors will appreciate the owners' knowledge of French, Spanish, and Italian.

Rates: July to August and foliage season, $133 to $223; November to mid-May, $88 to $151.

Amadeus House, 15 Cliffwood St., Lenox, MA 01240 (☎ 800/205-4770 or 413/637-4770), is owned and operated by John Felton and his wife, Marty Gottron, two journalists who share their love of music and their huge collection of compact discs with their guests. The inn is located on a quiet street a short walk from town. It is a welcome sight with its wraparound porch, inviting old rockers, and brilliant geraniums. Eight rooms are available in summer and fall, five from November to April. The rooms are comfortable and not overly decorated. Each is named after a composer. The most appealing room is Mozart, on the first floor with a private porch and wood stove. The third-floor apartment (Beethoven Suite) has two bedrooms, plus a full kitchen and a small bathroom with double shower. A full breakfast of fresh fruit, muffins, and a dish like apple waffles is served along with afternoon refreshments. *Rates:* Late June to Labor Day, weekends $100 to $165 double, $235 suite, midweek $80 to $120 double, $170 suite; mid-May to late June and September to October, weekends $90 to $140 double, $200 suite, midweek $75 to $110 double, $150 suite; November to mid-May, weekends $85 to $125 double, $155 suite, midweek $75 to $100 double, $110 suite.

The **Village Inn,** 16 Church St., P.O. Box 1810, Lenox, MA 01240 (☎ 800/253-0917 or 413/637-0020), is the one place where you can stop for a formal English Devonshire cream tea, consisting of homemade scones and preserves, plus desserts accompanied by a pot of fine tea of your choice. It is served in the dining room from 3 to 4:30pm. At this friendly, comfortable place, run by Clifford Rudisill and Ray Wilson, there are rooms to satisfy every pocketbook. The public areas are perhaps the most lavishly appointed, furnished with family antiques. The reception desk, which doubles as a small bar, faces the small parlor, where armchairs near the hearth are ideal for chatting over a glass of sherry. Across the hall there's a larger parlor with a grand piano and antique furnishings. There's also a separate TV room. Over the years the innkeepers have furnished the 32 comfortable rooms, all with private baths, telephones, and air-conditioning, in an eclectic and unpretentious way. The standard and superior rooms are a little more "furnished," whereas the economy rooms contain homey, old-fashioned pieces. Some have canopied beds. The Dining Room has an excellent reputation for value. Menu selections might include pan-seared swordfish drizzled with a cucumber-yogurt sauce on a bed of couscous, black Angus sirloin with a wild mushroom sauce, or roast chicken with a pineapple-mango salsa, priced from $12 to $19. There's also a downstairs tavern for after-concert snacks.

Rates: Summer, $100 to $220; fall, $90 to $185; winter, $80 to $175; spring, $65 to $145. In winter and spring 30% discount midweek. Three-night minimum stay weekends in July, August, and holidays. *Dining hours:* Summer and fall, Tuesday to Sunday 5:30 to 9pm; breakfast and tea served daily in summer, weekends only the rest of the year.

Brook Farm Inn, 15 Hawthorne St., Lenox, MA 01240 (☎ 413/637-3013), just down the hill from Lenox center occupies a century-old house. What makes this place special is the keen pleasure innkeepers Anne and Joe Miller take in literature and music. One wall of the living room is devoted to books, many of them poetry, and the strains of all kinds of music—Mozart, light opera, or Broadway musicals—waft through the house. A poem of the day starts each morning, and Joe reads poetry during Saturday afternoon tea. There are 12 rooms, all with private baths, 6 with fireplaces. Room 2 features a canopied bed, wing chairs, and the romance of a fireplace and small balcony. The coziest, if not the grandest, rooms are tucked under the eaves. One is decked out in deep purple and mauve, lit by a skylight from above. Furnishings might include a brass bed, Hitchcock rocker, cottage dresser, and similar country pieces. Out back, guests can relax in the hammock or enjoy the pool. A full breakfast is served buffet-style, and on Sunday mornings breakfast is accompanied by a quartet from the Tanglewood Institute. *Rates:* $100 to $210 double; less in midweek and spring/fall.

If you prefer modern accommodations with all the razzmatazz of TVs, phones, bars, and lounges, then there are plenty around, like the **Berkshire Quality Inn,** 390 Pittsfield/Lenox Rd. (Route 7), Lenox, MA 01240 (☎ 413/637-4244), which has an outdoor pool and tennis courts; or the **Susse Chalet,** routes 7 and 20, Lenox, MA 01240 (☎ 413/637-3560), which also has a pool. *Rates:* $65 to $169 double, depending on the season.

LENOX DINING

Besides the outstanding restaurants at the establishments already mentioned, there are several other fine dining options.

Lenox 218, 218 Main St. (Route 7A; ☎ 413/637-4218), is very modern. The upfront bar is boldly decorated with black-and-white tile with a purple scaffold-like sculpture above the bar itself. The two dining rooms are dramatically designed in black, featuring Milan-style chairs, walls accented with Japanese prints, and tables set with gray tablecloths and black napkins. The cuisine ranges from nutty chicken, which is prepared with almonds, sesame, and sunflower seeds; to roast duck with raspberry chambord sauce; and scrod Florentine served on a bed of spinach and flavored subtly with pesto. There are also half a dozen simple pasta dishes. Prices range from $13 to $22. For an appetizer, I recommend the roasted garlic soup or the polenta with tomato and basil sauce. The menu is supplemented by daily specials. The shrimp cocktail is very tangy with its horseradish and chili sauce accompaniment. Desserts tend to be popular favorites—pies, shortcakes, and hot fudge sundaes. Light snacks are available in the bar. *Hours:* Daily 11:30am to 2:30pm and 5 to 10pm.

The **Pillars Carriage House,** Route 20, New Lebanon (☎ 518/794-8007), has two dining rooms. One is modestly decorated with tables set with forest-green tablecloths and captain's chairs; the other is slightly more formal. There's also a bar area warmed in winter by a fire. The cuisine is modern American with a menu that offers such traditional favorites as rack of lamb, filet mignon with a mushroom sauce, veal Oscar, and fillet of sole Nantua, which is baked with lobster, butter and cream, and garnished with lobster meat and Hollandaise. Prices range from $15 to $24. *Hours:* Tuesday to Saturday 5 to 10pm, Sunday 4 to 9pm. Closed December 31 for 6 weeks.

Antonio's Restaurant, 15 Franklin St. (☎ 413/637-9894), is a comfortable, casual, California-style place that sports a miscellaneous collection of postcards, banknotes, business cards, and buttons covering one entire wall in the front. Here you can tuck into oversize portions of Italian specialties—paglia e fieno (with peas and prosciutto), linguine with clam sauce, veal Marsala, shrimp primavera, or chicken bianco sautéed in white wine with garlic, pimientos, scallions, and capers in a brown sauce. Prices range from $12 to $18. *Hours:* Monday to Saturday 4 to 10pm; off-season closes a little earlier.

The **Church Street Cafe,** 69 Church St. (☎ 413/637-2745), is a local favorite for soups, salads, burgers, and pasta dishes, all priced under $10 and served in a pleasant light-wood-and-plants atmosphere. For dinner there's always a fresh fish and pasta of the day, plus six or so entrees like pan-roasted chicken breast with pancetta, wild mushrooms, and a potato chestnut cake; crab cakes with a dilled tartar sauce; or rustic beef stew with wild mushrooms, caramelized carrots, shallots, and mashed potatoes. Prices range from $15 to $19. *Hours:* Summer, daily 11:30am to 2pm and 5:30 to 9pm; spring/fall, Monday to Saturday 11:30am to 2pm, Monday to Thursday from 5:30 to 8:30pm, Friday and Saturday 5:30 to 9pm. Closed Sunday and Monday in winter.

Just across the street, the **Cafe Lucia,** 90 Church St. (☎ 413/637-2640), is a fine lunch choice, serving soups, sandwiches, and salads, including caponata, an eggplant-and-tomato salad garnished with hard-boiled eggs, black olives, tomato, basil, and mozzarella. Egg dishes like zucchini frittata (made from eggs, cheese with mushrooms, and zucchini), pâté plate, and chilled mussels in white wine complete the selections. Pasta and good Italian dishes like osso buco, wild rabbit ragoût, veal, and fish of the day are served at dinner, priced from $13 to $29. There's a pleasant outdoor patio under an awning. *Hours:* Summer/fall, Tuesday to Sunday 5:30 to 10pm; winter/spring, Tuesday to Saturday 5:30 to 9:30pm. Closed Sunday in winter/spring and Monday all year.

Cheesecake Charlie's, 60 Main St.(☎ 413/637-3411), serves breakfast from 8 to 11am, but the prime attraction is the 13 flavors of cheesecake plus daily specials. If you order in advance, you can choose from over 50 flavors.

Picnic Supplies

Obviously you'd expect to find many picnic suppliers in Lenox for all those bountiful Tanglewood spreads. Here are two of them.

Crosby's, 62 Church St. (☎ 413/637-3396), offers gourmet food to go. There are two different picnics a week to choose from and also a full range of deli and salad items. *Hours:* Summer, Sunday to Wednesday 10am to 6pm, Thursday to Saturday to 8pm; winter, Sunday 11am to 3pm, Thursday to Saturday 11am to 5pm. Closed for several weeks in February and March.

Special desserts can be found at **Suchele Bakers,** 27 Housatonic St. (☎ 413/637-0939). *Hours:* July and August, daily 7am to 6pm, Sunday until 12:30pm; other months, Tuesday to Saturday 7am to 4pm.

LEE

Although Lee has lived largely in the shadow of Lenox as a down-to-earth town, somewhat careless of its beauty, it has shown much greater interest in preserving its past recently, as you'll see from the descriptions of accommodations below. Still, the main attraction here is the superb Jacob's Pillow Dance Festival just east of Lee in Becket.

LEE/SOUTH LEE LODGING & DINING

Devonfield, 85 Stockbridge Rd. (R.R. 1, Box 605B), Lee, MA 01238 (☎ 413/243-3298), is a 200-year-old mansion with a lovely pastoral view. Originally built by an American Revolution soldier, it was modernized by George Westinghouse Jr. and was briefly, in 1942, the residence of Queen Wilhelmina of The Netherlands, her daughter, Princess Juliana, and her granddaughters, Beatrix (now the queen) and Irene. The public areas include a large, comfortable living room, a good reading area with a fireplace, and a TV room. Although all of the ten rooms (four with fireplace, five with TV) are furnished differently, you might find an intricately carved mahogany bed or a marble-top chest in yours. The penthouse suite features a Jacuzzi and so does the guest house/cottage, which also has a fireplace and kitchenette among its attractions. It's a lovely, quiet place; it has a pool, bicycles for guest use, and a tennis court. *Rates* (including full breakfast): Summer/fall, weekends $165 to $270, midweek $120 to $200; winter/spring, weekends $110 to $200, midweek $80 to $165 (lower prices are for rooms with shared baths). In July and August a minimum stay of 3 nights is required.

The **Federal House Inn**, Route 102, South Lee, MA 01260 (☎ 413/243-1824), offers lavish settings and furnishings in the public areas of this classically proportioned, restored Federal house. The dining rooms have been a smash hit on the Tanglewood dining scene for years. Two elegant rooms, each with only about seven tables, are the setting for some classic continental cuisine—fillet of salmon baked in a potato crust with herbed beurre blanc, roast tenderloin of pork with a balsamic glaze on caramelized onions and pureed potatoes, and roast duckling with fresh pear chutney sautéed with wild rice pancakes and preserved currant- and English-mustard sauce. Start with the delicious house smoked trout with warm cornmeal blinis, fresh grated horseradish sauce, red onions, chive oil, and leeks; or the galantine of goose breast, dried apricots, and figs, with lingonberry sauce. Prices run from $17 to $24. In summer, a special $38 four-course prix-fixe is served.

Upstairs, there are ten rooms, all with private baths and air-conditioning. They are furnished in country style with chintz wallpapers and rugs on wide-plank floors. A couple have canopied beds.

Rates: In season, $195; off-season $175. *Dining hours:* July and August, daily 5:30pm to closing; winter, Thursday to Sunday 5:30pm to closing.

If you stay at the **Historic Merrell Inn**, Main Street (Route 102), South Lee, MA 01260 (☎ 800/243-1794 or 413/243-1794), just down the street, you'll be overnighting in a truly historic hostelry. Among its authentic features is the original 1817 circular birdcage bar (no longer in use). Now listed in the National Register of Historic Places, this brick Federal building (1794) with double balcony was bought in 1980 by Faith and Charles Reynolds, two former teachers who have carefully restored it according to architectural and historical records. It looks as much like a stagecoach stop as it ever did, from the small entry hall featuring a tall case clock, Federal mirror, and candlesticks, to the old tavern room with fireplace, pewter, and appropriate period furniture. The original iron latches have been retained throughout the house. Upstairs, the nine rooms—all with private baths, air-conditioning, and telephones—have been exquisitely decorated with colonial-period furnishings, most with canopied beds. Guests have use of a TV room, but best of all is the gazebo down by the river for relaxing on a summer afternoon. Swimming is available at Benedict Pond in Beartown Mountain State Park, only 10 minutes' drive away. *Rates* (including full breakfast): Mid-June to October 31, weekends $145 to $175 double, midweek $100 to $125; November 1 to mid-June, weekends $85 to $125 double, midweek $80 to $115.

Chambery Inn, 199 Main St., Lee, MA 01238 (☎ 800-537-4321), is an unusual accommodation. It occupies a former school, and the people who converted it had the wit to retain the blackboards, which provide a wonderful outlet for a variety of commentary. As you can imagine, the six rooms are extra-large (about 500 square feet) and have very high ceilings. Each is a suite, possessing a sitting area with a fireplace and a king canopied or queen bed. All rooms have TVs and telephones and a whirlpool baths. Furnishings are comfortable. Floors are covered with thick pile carpets, windows are draped with lace curtains, and you might find an elegant peer mirror in your room. Chippendale-style tables, desks, and sofas complete the picture. The largest room, Le Lycee, has five huge windows looking out onto the street. The bed is covered in a Ralph Lauren Indian design coverlet, and there's a glass table with a capital as its base. Le Aubusson is decorated with tapestries, as you would expect, and also contains a handsome rolltop desk. There's also a well-equipped room for those with disabilities. *Rates:* Summer and fall, weekends $135 to $260, midweek $109 to $145; mid-June to July 1 and September, weekends $135 to $230, midweek $85 to $160; mid-October to mid-June, weekends $135 to $230, midweek $85 to $160.

The **Morgan House Inn,** 33 Main St., Lee, MA 01238 (☎ 888/243-0188 or 413/243-0181), is not a well-seasoned rural New England inn for the well-heeled traveler. Instead, it's a historic coaching inn standing on the main street of Lee. Built in 1817 as a private residence, it was converted into a stagecoach inn in 1853 and received such renowned visitors as Ulysses S. Grant and George Bernard Shaw, whose carefully preserved signatures can be seen on the wall by the reception desk. The 11 rooms are furnished in a country style. In the tavern bar, you'll find locals as well as travelers. The low-ceilinged tavern dining room is unpretentious, warm, and comfortable with polished wood tables and paneling. It offers contemporary American cuisine featuring such dishes as pistachio-crusted swordfish with candied ginger and lime beurre blanc or hazelnut-crusted rack of lamb with tomato-mint chutney. For an appetizer try the lobster, scallop, and sweet potato cakes with roasted red pepper sauce. Prices range from $13 to $24. It's also a convenient popular lunch spot, where prices and quality are hard to beat for such dishes as chicken and mushrooms in a popover or pasta primavera, plus salads and sandwiches priced from $5 to $10. The paintings that grace the walls are works of owner Lenora Bowen. *Rates:* June to October, weekends $100 to $170, midweek $90 to $115; November to May, weekends $75 to $110, midweek $65 to $90. *Dining hours:* Monday to Saturday 11:30am to 2:30pm, Monday to Thursday 5 to 9pm, Friday and Saturday 5 to 9:30pm, Sunday noon to 9pm (brunch 10:30am to 2:30pm).

Sullivan Station (☎ 413/243-2082), housed in a converted railway station, is a good Saturday luncheon spot and also convenient at the beginning or end of the scenic ride that leaves from here. The menu features a daily pasta, fish, and quiche special, plus sandwiches, burgers, and barbecue ribs priced from $5 to $7. At dinner the menu features such traditional favorites as baked scrod with lemon butter, veal parmigiana, and chicken amandine (from $13 to $17). *Hours:* Summer, daily 11:30am to 9:30pm; rest of the year until May 1, Wednesday to Sunday only.

STOCKBRIDGE

The name most often associated with Stockbridge is that of Norman Rockwell. His pictures and magazine covers captured the essence of life in an earlier, more innocent America. Born in New York City in 1894, Rockwell moved to Stockbridge in 1953, and he remained here until he died in 1978. He is buried in the Stockbridge cemetery. In his life he produced more than 4,000 pictures, many of them covers for the *Saturday Evening Post* and *McCall's,* and here at the **Norman Rockwell Museum,** Route 183 (☎ 413/298-4100), you can see a lot of them. You may well see his first *Saturday Evening Post* cover (it appeared in 1916) of the schoolboy pushing a baby carriage, or one of my favorites, a family seen heading off for a day trip or vacation, children hanging out the window in their excitement, grandma sitting under her hat like a solemn stooge, and the same family returning, children downcast and grandma still stolid, stern, and unmoved. *Hours:* May to October, daily 10am to 5pm; November to April, weekdays 11am to 4pm, weekends 10am to 5pm. Rockwell's studio is open also May to October. Closed major winter holidays. *Admission:* $9 adults, $2 children ages 6 to 18.

Along Main Street, stop in at the **Mission House,** (☎ 413/298-3239), built in 1739 and home of the Reverend John Sergeant, first missionary to the Stockbridge Indians, who was followed by the first great writer to live in the Berkshires, the fire-and-brimstone preacher Jonathan Edwards, who played such a great role in the Great Awakening. The house has a fine collection of furnishings, and the garden is also interesting, displaying plants only from that period. *Hours:* Memorial Day to Columbus Day, daily 10am to 5pm (last tour 4:15pm), Sunday and holidays, 11am to 3:30pm. *Admission:* $5 adults, $2.50 children ages 6 to 12.

Across the street from the Red Lion, **St. Paul's Episcopal Church** has some famous associations—McKim was the architect, the baptistery was created by Auguste St. Gaudens, one of the nave windows is by Tiffany, and the chancel window is by LaFarge.

Farther along Main Street you'll come to the **Children's Chimes,** erected on the site of the original mission church by David Dudley Field, as a memorial to his grandchildren. They are played every evening at sunset from "apple blossom time until frost."

The modest **cottage** where Hawthorne wrote *Tanglewood Tales* can also be seen on Hawthorne Street near Tanglewood. Of the view (still unchanged) across the Stockbridge Bowl, he wrote: "I cannot write in the presence of that view."

The marvelous house on Prospect Hill, **Naumkeag** (☎ 413/298-3239) was designed by Stanford White in 1886 for Joseph H. Choate, President McKinley's ambassador to the Court of St. James. The 26 sumptuous rooms and the formal gardens with fountains and Chinese pagodas provide a good insight into the opulent lifestyle of the time. *Hours:* Memorial Day to Columbus Day, daily 10am to 5pm (last tour 4:15pm). *Admission:* $7 for both the house and the garden, $5 for the garden only, $2.50 for children ages 6 to 12.

A must in Stockbridge is a visit to the **Berkshire Botanical Garden,** routes 102 and 183 (☎ 413/298-3926), a glorious place in any season. From spring to early fall the spectacular 15 acres display an array of annuals and perennials—delphiniums, clematises, azaleas—plus such flowering shrubs and trees as rhododendron and dogwood, roses of all hues, and ornamental and other herbs. Specialty collections include crabapples, primroses, and day lilies; there's also a shady pond garden and woodland trail. The greenhouses with permanent collections are open through the winter. The gift shop offers interesting garden-related items. *Hours:* May to October, 10am to 5pm. *Admission:* $5 adults, $4 seniors, free for children under age 12.

Daniel Chester French referred to his summer home, **Chesterwood,** off Route 183 (☎ 413/298-3579), as "heaven," and certainly the view of Monument Mountain, both from the house and from his radiant 23-foot-high studio, does warrant such a description. The skylit studio, where he worked from 1898 to 1931, is most remarkable for the floor-to-ceiling double doors through which he rolled his sculptures on a small railroad trestle out into the daylight to examine them. One can also imagine his taking a break to entertain guests in the adjoining reception area furnished with fireplace, library, and piano. The studio contains sketches, plaster casts, and bronze models of his sculpture, including his seated Lincoln. From the house and studio, you can wander through the gardens. In the barn there are sketches and working models of many of his other famous works—*Brooklyn and Manhattan,* formerly at the entrance to the Manhattan Bridge, *Alma Mater* at Columbia University, and the *Minuteman* at the Concord North Bridge. Chesterwood is about 2 miles west of Stockbridge. Take Route 102 west to Route 183; turn left and drive for about a mile and follow the signs. *Hours:* May 1 to October 31, daily 10am to 5pm. *Admission:* $7 adults, $3.50 children ages 13 to 18, $1.50 for children ages 6 to 12.

Stockbridge is the home of the respected **Berkshire Theatre Festival,** which takes place from June to August. For details, see "Festivals in the Berkshires," below.

Stockbridge Lodging & Dining

The large country inn, the **Red Lion,** Main Street, Stockbridge, MA 01262 (☎ 413/298-5545), whose porch faces the main street, has become a symbol of hospitality in Stockbridge and the Berkshires. Many vacationers come expressly to visit the Red Lion, flocking into the front parlor where the fires blaze and overflowing into the snug tavern or downstairs into the "Lion's Den" pub for a cocktail and nightly entertainment. The original structure, which served as a small tavern on the Albany-Hartford-Boston stage route in 1773, was destroyed by fire in 1896. A string of celebrities has bedded down here, among them Presidents McKinley, Teddy and Franklin Roosevelt, and Coolidge, and also William Cullen Bryant and Henry Wadsworth Longfellow.

At the Red Lion you'll be living amid the charm of Staffordshire china, colonial pewter, and 18th-century furniture. There are 111 air-conditioned guest rooms, including 26 suites. Most are in the main inn, but some are located in seven smaller guest houses nearby. Each room is individually decorated in a country style. In summer the courtyard, colorfully decorated with impatiens and other flowers, makes a lovely dining spot. A swimming pool, and fitness room (massage therapist available) complete the facilities.

The dining room specializes in seasonal New England favorites— herb-and-mustard-crusted prime rib served with a Stilton popover, roast turkey with a sage cornbread dressing, or New England bluepoint oyster stew— ranging from $18 to $24. Two remarkable features of the Red Lion are the friendly personnel and the quality of the food, both of which are sustained, even when 1,200 people are served per day (200 at breakfast, 500 at lunch, and 500 at night). At a recent meal the caramelized sea scallops were perfectly tender, and complemented well by the accompanying bacon- and thyme-flavored kraut. Crystal chandeliers, ornate gilt mirrors, willow-pattern china, damask tablecloths, and a posy of fresh flowers on each table set an elegant tone.

Rates: Mid-April to late October, $125 to $175, $97 room with shared bath, $195 to $365 suites; late October to mid-April, $97 to $140, $82 with shared bath, $177 to $335 suites. *Dining hours:* Breakfast, Monday to Friday 7 to 10am, Saturday and Sunday 8 to 10am; lunch, Monday to Saturday noon to 2:30pm; dinner, Monday to Thursday 6 to 9pm, Friday and Saturday to 9:30 p.m., Sunday noon to 9pm. Jacket and tie for men required at dinner; no jeans permitted.

A discreet wooden sign hangs out front of the **Inn at Stockbridge**, Route 7, Box 618, Stockbridge, MA 01262 (☎ 413/298-3337). Step onto the classical portico and into the plushly furnished parlor-hall graced with a grand piano and comfortable wing chairs set around the hearth. Although the 12 rooms (all with private bath, air-conditioning, and telephone) are not as lavishly decorated with antiques, they are all very prettily furnished with antique reproductions. The Chinese Room has Asian accents in the wallpaper and accessories, and the Rose Room sports cabbage rose wallpaper and an antique English armoire. The Terrace Room has a private terrace and whirlpool tub under a skylight in the bathroom. A separate building contains four specially themed junior suites, each with fireplace, canopied bed, whirlpool tub, and TV/VCR. They are decorated to reflect Provence, Kashmir, St. Andrews, and "Out of Africa." Hosts Alice and Len Schiller also serve a full breakfast on fine china. Alice turns out some extraordinary fare—fresh fruit cup, cheese-and-ham soufflé, cinnamon coffee cake, and a very special brew. Sunday breakfasts are extra-special, consisting of a mimosa followed by eggs Benedict and banana bread. At the back of the house, the garden's lilacs and other flowering shrubs provide a welcome retreat. So does the pool. *Rates:* July to October 31, weekends $205 to $270, midweek $185 to $230; November to June, weekends $180 to $215, midweek $150 to $200.

Set on a quiet back road not far from Stockbridge, the **Williamsville Inn,** Route 41, West Stockbridge, MA 01266 (☎ 413/274-6118), has all the pleasures of an English country inn. It has the physical makings of a delightful accommodation: a small and cozy 1797 farmhouse with wide-plank floors, fireplaces throughout the public areas, comfortable wing chairs, and antiques. There are 16 rooms, two with fireplaces, some with four-posters, country furniture, and private bathrooms. There's also a pool and tennis court.

The four dining rooms offer modern American cuisine. Try such dishes as salmon basil roulade with pesto sauce served with corn pudding, tenderloin of beef with red-wine sauce and portobello mushrooms, or roasted breast of duck with peaches and balsamic glaze. Prices range from $15 to $23. For dessert, try the chocolate truffle cake, hazelnut daquoise, or the varied pies and tarts. The inn has become popular for its Sunday night storytelling and dinner series, which is given during the winter season. *Rates:* July to October, $130 to $195; November to June, $115 to $170. A 3-night minimum is required on summer weekends. *Dining hours:* July to October, Wednesday to Monday 5 to 9pm; November to June, Thursday to Sunday 6 to 9pm.

Roeder House, Route 183, Stockbridge, MA (☎ 413/298-4015), is a lovely accommodation occupying a Federal-colonial–style house that was built in 1856 and is surrounded by 4 acres of well-tended gardens. Owners Diane and Vernon Reuss have hung numerous Audubon prints throughout the house. There are six rooms, all with private baths and all furnished with antiques in fine taste and fetching colors. The Red Bird Room sports Lambeth wallpaper with a peafowl design, a luxurious silk fabric on the wingback chairs, while the bed is covered with a handmade log cabin quilt. Ben's Room contains a four-poster with a crocheted canopy. There's also a room on the ground floor that boasts a hoop canopy with Laura Ashley linens, a Chinese rug, and wingbacks with iron floor lamps well placed for comfortable reading. A bell will summon you to a breakfast table set with crystal and fine English china and lit by candlelight. The fare might include blueberry coffeecake, fruit compote, a frittata, peach juice, and hazelnut coffee. Guests may use the well-designed and landscaped pool and enjoy the screened-in porch and the trellised gardens. *Rates:* Summer, weekends $205 to $215 double; spring/fall, $185 to $205; less in winter.

Other Stockbridge dining choices include **Main Street Market Cafe,** on Main Street (☎ 413/298-0220), which serves great breakfasts, a wide variety of luncheon items—soups, salads, sandwiches, grilled vegetables, hummus, and pretty much whatever you want to select in the market. You can eat in the comfortable, cheery cafe or assemble a picnic. Dinner is served on Thursday and Friday nights by reservation only. *Hours:* Daily 7:30am to 7pm (later on Thursday and Friday).

WEST STOCKBRIDGE

West Stockbridge has been touted as the in-the-know place in the Berkshires because of the many potters, painters, glassmakers, and other artisans who have been attracted to this area. If you want to learn about the work of some of the area's more important artisans and where it can be found, pick up the pamphlet "The Art of West Stockbridge," available in display racks through-out the area.

The **Berkshire Center for Contemporary Glass**, 6 Harris St. (☎ 413/232-4666), is a new enterprise in a new building that contains both a show-room and a large work area. Classes and workshops are scheduled. It's located in the heart of the village. *Hours:* May to October, daily 10am to 10pm; November to April, 10am to 6pm.

The town has a number of artificially old shops and boutiques, but there's really little else here except for a couple of good restaurants.

WEST STOCKBRIDGE DINING

The story of Luy Nguyen and his wife, Trai Thi Duong, is very moving. They first went to Hartford when they came to this country before being invited to West Stockbridge, to open the **Truc Orient Express**, Harris Street (☎ 413/232-4204). Their photograph album, which is proudly displayed, tells the story of their family—how their young son was separated from them for 6 years after they escaped from Vietnam; they were reunited when Senator Ted Kennedy came to their assistance. Try the crab-and-asparagus soup first, then choose among such main dishes as shrimp with straw mushrooms, sweet-and-sour chicken, or a delicious duck with lemongrass, all priced from $12 to $17 at dinner. The atmosphere is extremely pleasant, with bamboo chairs and wicker-based, glass-top Parsons tables set on tile floors in a light and airy space. *Hours:* Daily 11:30am to 3pm; Sunday to Thursday 5 to 9pm, Friday to Saturday 5 to 10pm. Closed Tuesday in winter.

La Bruschetta, West Stockbridge (☎ 413/232-7141), offers a fresh approach to the ingredients in their up-to-the-minute Italian cuisine. It's hard to choose among the appetizers, most of which lean toward vegetarian tastes. The grilled radicchio is enhanced with smoked pancetta with Rawson Brook chèvre, sun-dried tomatoes, and oil and balsamic vinegar; while the delicious timbale of wild mushrooms is served with a fresh tomato herb coulis. These can be followed by one of several pastas—orecchiette with grilled shrimp, oven-roasted tomatoes, beet greens, garlic, and basil, for example—or one of the secondi piatti like the double center-cut pork chop served with apple leek compote and a cider pepper glaze, or the poached salmon with fresh fennel, grilled potatoes, Prince Edward Island mussels, and fall greens. Prices range from $16 to $20. *Hours:* Thursday to Tuesday 6 to 9pm.

WEST STOCKBRIDGE AFTER DARK

Shaker Mill Tavern, on Albany Road (routes 102 and 41) in West Stockbridge (☎ 413/232-4369), attracts a young crowd. A deck cafe is open in summer, and jazz, Latin, and comedy entertainment are offered Thursday through Sunday nights. There's a huge roster of international beers on sale. *Hours:* Memorial Day to Columbus Day, daily. Closed Wednesday at other times.

THE EGREMONT AREA

South Egremont is a lovely, quiet village worth stopping in to browse through the several antiques stores, bookshops, and the old-fashioned general store.

Located on Route 23, it is surrounded by some dramatic scenery and provides access to Mount Everett and BashBish Falls. Other great antiques hunting grounds are also nearby in Ashley Falls and Sheffield, along routes 7 and 7A. If you continue west along Route 23 you'll come to Catamount, crossing the border into New York, where there are a couple of renowned restaurants.

SOUTH EGREMONT LODGING & DINING

The **Egremont Inn,** Old Sheffield Road (P.O. Box 418), South Egremont, MA 01258 (☎ 413/528-2111), is a charming old place originally built in 1780 with a wraparound veranda. Inside, the tavern is especially alluring, with a curved brick fireplace, low ceilings, and colonial-style furnishings. The dining room offers new American cuisine. Prices range from $15.50 for a boneless chicken breast stuffed with prosciutto, spinach, and fontina to herb-crusted rack of lamb with braised Brussels sprouts. Other appealing dishes might include seared salmon fillet with lemongrass beurre blanc, or breast of duck with a Cabernet reduction. The tavern menu offers burgers, pasta, and salads. Facilities include a pool and two tennis courts. None of the 21 rooms has telephone or TV, but all have private baths. Live jazz or similar in the tavern on Saturdays. *Rates:* Spring/summer/fall, weekends $110 to $175, midweek $100 to $130; winter, weekends $105 to $145, midweek $90 to $120. Special packages available. *Dining hours:* Wednesday to Sunday 5:30 to 9:30pm.

At the **Weathervane Inn,** Route 23 (P.O. Box 388), South Egremont, MA 01258 (☎ 413/528-9580), seasonal potted flowers bloom on the side porch of this attractive white clapboard house with black shutters, into which you'll be welcomed by the Murphy family. There are ten rooms, all with private baths. Room 6 is tucked over the kitchen under the eaves, giving it an interesting shape and feel. It's large enough to accommodate two brass beds, a marble-top dresser adorned with a dried-flower arrangement, a maple side table, a desk, and an armchair. All rooms have electric blankets and air-conditioning; at night you'll find a miniature nightcap—amaretto, perhaps. Breakfast is served in a skylit room decorated with Hitchcock chairs and tables that overlook the back lawn. You'll most likely dive into Irish soda bread; freshly squeezed juice; eggs of your choice with home fries, sausage, or bacon; and toast. Afternoon tea is also served. Adjacent to the dining room is a sitting area with a small service bar in the corner. There's also a lounge with TV, books, and games. The outdoor pool has a good deck for sunning. *Rates:* Late June to early September, weekends (3 nights only) $475 for two, midweek $105 to $160 per night double; early September to mid-June, weekends $135 to $160, midweek $125 to $145.

A large white clapboard house, where you can sit on the porch and look over toward the lush greens of the Egremont Country Club, the **Windflower Inn,** Route 23 (Egremont Star Route, Box 25), Great Barrington, MA 01230 (☎ 413/528-2720), offers warm hospitality in antique-style surroundings. There are 13 rooms, all with private baths, some with fireplaces. Each is decorated in a Laura Ashley country style. There's an outdoor pool. Golf and tennis facilities are conveniently located across the road. *Rates* (including full breakfast): $110 to $180.

DINING IN AND AROUND SOUTH EGREMONT

For breakfast and an experience that probably recalls your childhood if you're over age 25, head for the **Gaslight Store** (☎ 413/528-0870) in South Egremont. Here a few tables have been placed in the center of an old-fashioned general store that sells everything from aspirin to salami, newspapers to candy, complete with real wooden counters, scratched and burnished with use.

The **Old Mill**, Route 23, South Egremont (☎ 413/528-1421), is famed for its picturesque setting overlooking a small brook, and it has an excellent local reputation for consistently fine meals. The ambience is romantically country. The room is lit by a Shaker-style chandelier and little copper lanterns on the tables that make the white linens and wide-board floors glow. The menu offers a diverse range of bistro-style dishes. There will likely be pan-roasted cod wonderfully enriched with a roasted tomato vinaigrette, or New York steak with truffle butter and fries, along with several daily specials. Prices range from $16 to $23. To start, I'd select either the caramelized onion tart with greens or the garlicky pan-roasted shrimp. Among the desserts, my favorites are the profiteroles, but you might prefer crème brûlée, apple walnut tart, or peach melba. *Hours:* June to October, Sunday to Thursday 5 to 9:30pm, Friday to Saturday 5 to 10:30pm. Closed Mondays November to May.

Farther along Route 23 you'll come to **John Andrew's**, South Egremont (☎ 413/528-3469), which is a refreshing change from the traditional, cozy, New England–style restaurants that abound in the Berkshires. White tablecloths, the original black chairs from the Copacabana, and track lighting provide an art deco ambience. Among the appealing appetizers are the grilled shrimp with avocado; mango with lime, chiles, and cilantro; and the whole roasted garlic with peasant bread, goat cheese, sun-dried tomatoes, and black olives. The main courses are made with the freshest of ingredients, and free-range poultry is used. You might find grilled yellowfin tuna with lemongrass, ginger, cilantro, scented coconut milk, and baby bok choy; loin of elk with a cracked peppercorn sauce accompanied by Black Mission fig compote and hazelnut Indian pudding; or grilled leg of lamb with red wine and roast garlic jus. Prices range from $15 to $24. Desserts change daily. Cocktails or meals can be taken on the pleasant deck out back. *Hours:* July to August, daily from 5pm. Closed Wednesday in winter.

NORTH EGREMONT LODGING & DINING

Some locals recommended the dining room at the **Elm Court Inn**, Route 71, North Egremont, MA 01252 (☎ 413/528-0325), more highly than any other in the immediate area. Floral curtains, a fireplace, polished wood tables with place mats and a sprig of fresh flowers complete the decor. There's also a small, cozy bar with a brick hearth. Dishes might include olive-crusted salmon served with roasted garlic and tomato coulis, grilled duck breast with green peppercorns and lingonberry sauce, and rack of lamb Provençale. The chef trained in Zurich and certain dishes, like the veal à la suisse are accompanied by those delicious rösti potatoes. Prices range from $19 to $26.

The three simply furnished rooms (one with private bath) feature chenille bedspreads, chintz curtains, painted chests, and braided rugs. Room 4 is the nicest, in my opinion, with its corner cupboard, small captain's desk, and blue-and-white braided rug and burgundy curtains, and a sink with a marble surround.

Rates: $65 to $75. Rates do not include breakfast. *Dining hours:* Wednesday to Saturday 5 to 9pm, Sunday 4 to 8:30pm.

LODGING & DINING IN HILLSDALE, N.Y.

Across the border in New York is the **Swiss Hutte**, Route 23, Hillsdale, NY 12529 (☎ 518/325-3333), a beautifully kept accommodation at the base of Catamount that also offers some of the finest cuisine in the area. The expertly groomed grounds include a swimming pool, gardens with roses and herbaceous borders, a pond, and two tennis courts. In the restaurant, aglow with red lanterns, the specialties are Wienerschnitzel topped with brown caper butter, and continental dishes like duck à l'orange or rack of lamb with a red-wine glaze. Desserts are delicious—try the hazelnut torte or the raspberry cream pie. Prices run $19 to $24, including dessert and beverage.

Rooms are motel-style, but they have been attractively decorated, and all have air-conditioning, TVs, telephones, and coffeemakers.

Rates: In summer, MAP $110 per person double (3-night stay required on weekends); in winter, MAP $100 per person double (2-night minimum stay required on holiday weekends). *Dining hours:* Summer, daily noon to 2pm and 5:30 to 9pm; winter, Wednesday to Sunday only.

At **Aubergine**, on routes 23 and 22 (P.O. Box 387), Hillsdale, NY 12529 (☎ 518/325-3412), chef-owner David Lawson and his wife have furnished this 1783 brick Dutch colonial home with many of their own antique heirlooms. Interesting features of the inn include three splendid Palladian windows, a corner cupboard of museum quality, and eight fireplaces, all but one with the original mantelpieces. The ground floor of the inn consists of a handsome center hallway, four dining rooms (each with its own fireplace), and a bi-level Victorian bar and lounge (ca. 1850), with an unusual curving stairway leading to the gallery level. The former executive chef at Blantyre, Chef Lawson's cuisine has won wide acclaim, and people go out of their way to dine here. The menu, which changes monthly and seasonally, is limited, in keeping with the chef's desire to use only the very freshest of ingredients. There might be a Brittany-style fish stew of cod, mussels, cockles, leeks, and toasted barley flavored with apple cider and a touch of cream; roast venison with red-wine jus with cranberries; or herb-and-mustard-crusted rack of lamb with rosemary lamb jus. Among the appetizers might be Hudson Valley foie gras with carrot and orange salad, brioche toast and Sauternes gelee, or Maine scallop cakes with shiitakes, scallions, and bean sprouts with a warm ponzu vinaigrette. For dessert order the Grand Marnier soufflé or the chocolate hazelnut cake with pistachio sauce. The wine cellar concentrates on fine French and American wines, but the diner can also sample such local wines as Millbrook's Chardonnay. Prices run $19 to $24.

There are four accommodations, each decorated in a particular color scheme. Those on the second floor share a bath; the Lavender and Coral rooms on the third floor have private baths. The furnishings are antique reproductions—candle stands, pine chests, and Windsor rocking chairs.

Rates: $95 to $120 double. *Dining hours:* Wednesday to Sunday 5:30pm to closing.

GREAT BARRINGTON & SHEFFIELD

This is the largest town in the southern Berkshires, a major crossroads and commercial center. Just outside town, you may want to explore the **Albert Schweitzer Center**, 50 Hurlburt Rd. (☎ 413/528-3124), where you'll be greeted by this quotation: "The meaning of maturity which we should develop in ourselves is that we should strive always to become simpler, kinder, more honest, more truthful, more peace-loving, more gentle, and more compassionate." You can wander along Philosopher's Walk, by the brook, or in the universal children's garden. Lecture and concert series are given through the summer at this special haven. *Hours:* The grounds are open June to August, Tuesday to Saturday 10am to 4pm, Sunday noon to 4pm; September, November, and March to May, Thursday to Saturday 10am to 4pm; December to February, by appointment only.

SHOPPING

Inveterate shoppers and browsers will stop at **Jenifer House,** on Stockbridge Road, about a mile north of Route 23 on Route 7 (☎ 413/528-1500). This complex houses two antiques centers (with about 150 dealers), an art and print gallery, and a microbrewery. *Hours:* Monday to Saturday 9am to 5:30pm, Sunday 10 am to 5pm.

A NEARBY ATTRACTION

From Great Barrington take Route 23 east to Monterey and the turnoff north to Tyringham. Here you can visit the magical gingerbread house **Santarella,** 75 Main Rd. (☎ 413/243-3260), which was the studio of Sir Henry Hudson Kitson. Kitson is most famous for his sculpture of the *Minuteman* at Lexington and the *Pilgrim Maiden* at Plymouth, but this building is a sculpture in itself. He built it in the early 1930s (he was in his 70s) and worked here until his death in 1947. It's remarkably imaginative. The swirling, rolling roof that is meant to resemble the rolling hills of the Berkshires in the fall took 3 years to make. It looks as if it's been thatched, even though it's made of shingles. Kitson laid out exotic gardens on the property, including a pond filled with 2,000 goldfish. In his later years he became a recluse and was seen only occasionally, wearing his beret, silk cravat, and old-fashioned Victorian clothes. The studio and gardens have been lovingly restored and now serve as a museum, art gallery, and sculpture garden. The gallery shows an eclectic mix of art by several regional artists; the studio-museum is devoted to Kitson and shows many of his plaster models—Robert Burns, Edward Everett Hale, and Lord Nelon among them—plus personal memorabilia, including proof that the model for the *Minuteman*—the ultimate courageous American—was in fact an Englishman. A pathway leads from the studio down to the lily pond past a series of 28 sculptures. It's an inspiring place to visit. *Hours:* May to October, daily 10am to 4:30pm. *Admission:* $4 adults.

GREAT BARRINGTON LODGINGS

Little John Manor, One Newsboy Monument Lane, Great Barrington, MA 01230 (☎ 413/528-2882), is certainly one of Great Barrington's most secluded bed-and-breakfasts. I missed it several times. It's on Route 23, but tucked on a quiet loop, behind the statue of the Newspaper Boy, a gift presented to Great

Barrington by Colonel William L. Brown, publisher of the *New York Daily News* in 1895. Owners Paul and Herb have four rooms sharing two baths. They've run resorts before, and their experience shows. The four rooms are immaculately kept and pleasingly decorated in harmonious colors. The twin, for example, has rose carpeting, Wedgwood-blue curtains, and a colorful floral bedspread. Fresh flowers stand on a chest. A small double features a bed with eyelet pillow cases and dust ruffle and white eiderdown, set off by an oak dresser, bishop's chair, and Japanese prints. The living room is comfortably cluttered. Couches, rockers, and other chairs cluster around the white-brick fireplace and the TV.

In the morning a full English breakfast is served in the dining room. Tea, coffee, and juice are placed on the sideboard, and piping-hot scrambled or fried eggs, ham, English sausages, mushrooms, broiled tomatoes, and potatoes in jackets emerge from the kitchen. English muffins or crumpets can be spread with homemade jams and marmalade. An afternoon tea of scones, Scottish oatcakes, banana bread, and fruit butters is either served in the lounge or taken out to the porch or the benches scattered through the garden.

A hutch in the dining room is filled with oils and vinegars, which Paul makes from the 55 to 60 varieties of herbs that he cultivates in the garden. You'll smell the aroma of everything from marjoram and horseradish to Egyptian onion. In summer the borders are also blooming with peonies, lilies, roses, and other flowers.

Rates: Memorial Day through October, $90 to $110 double with fireplace; November to Memorial Day, $80 to $95.

At **Green Meadows,** 117 Division St., Great Barrington, MA 01230 (☎ 413/528-3897), owners Frank Gioia and Susie Kaufman have created a self-contained bed-and-breakfast wing by converting several rooms at the back of an 1880 Victorian farmhouse, which stands on 6 acres looking out over the fields. All four rooms have private baths and air-conditioning and are pretty and sparkling. The ground-floor room contains a brass bed with a navy blue floral comforter, and an oak dresser and side table, all set against pink walls. Rooms upstairs are similar, with wide pine floors—the colors of rose and celery predominate in the decor. Breakfast is satisfying, likely to begin with berries or melon followed by an omelet or French toast with local maple syrup. *Rates:* $90 to $100.

Irv and Jamie Yost, owners of the **Turning Point Inn,** Route 23 at Lake Buel Road (R.D. 2, Box 140), Great Barrington, MA 01230 (☎ 413/528-4777), really bring the personal touch to their business by sending guests hand-written notes with their brochures. They have restored an old stagecoach stop right near Butternut (east of Great Barrington) and offer six rooms, two with shared bath. There are a couple of parlors to relax in, and the whole place has a distinct home-away-from-home feeling. There's also a two-bedroom housekeeping cottage available for $210 a night. The full breakfast consists of eggs (with dishes like pancakes), cereal, breads, fruit, and more. *Rates:* $95 to $115 double.

Seekonk Pines, 142 Seekonk Cross Rd., Route 23, Great Barrington, MA 01230 (☎ 413/528-4192), a little farther west along Route 23, represents great value in this area. Innkeepers Bruce, Roberta, and Rita Lefkowitz bring their own personalities and ideas to this homey accommodation filled with their antiques and collectibles. The house was built between 1830 and 1832 as a farmhouse and remained in the same family for three generations. One of the previous owners was a friend of Thomas Edison, and Edison's portrait hangs in the entrance hall. There are six rooms, all with private baths and all named after previous owners. In the largest, the Harry G. Treadwell, the lace canopied bed is covered by a colorful quilt, Chinese paintings adorn the walls, and a chest of drawers, side tables, a blanket chest, and two comfortable chairs complete the furnishings. Quilts are found in every room and stenciling appears in many.

The dining-room table supported a vase of purple Canterbury bells when I visited. A breakfast of fresh fruit, homemade muffins, and a hot entree is served, along with juice and coffee or tea. The garden is quite lovely—filled with foxgloves, lupines, sweet williams, and pansies. There's an outdoor pool secluded by a private hedge and fence, and for indoor entertainment, a TV/VCR, books, and games are available in the living room. Bikes are also available.

Rates: Memorial Day to October, $110 to $145; in winter, $90 to $125.

GREAT BARRINGTON DINING

Castle Street Cafe, 10 Castle St. (☎ 413/528-5244), occupies a large, high-ceilinged storefront where the brick walls are accented with pieces of art portraying food ingredients in all their wondrous colors and shapes. There's a small bar in back, and jazz is usually playing quietly in the background. The cuisine is carefully prepared and uses locally grown and produced products. The flavor of the grilled breast of chicken is set off with a wild mushroom sauce, the cedar-planked salmon with maple glaze is wonderfully moist, and the rack of lamb has a fine garlic rosemary sauce. For the less hungry there's a simple burger served with straw potatoes as well as a couple of pasta dishes. Among the desserts the chocolate mousse cake rates high. There is a good, reasonably priced wine list. *Hours:* Sunday, Monday, Wednesday, and Thursday 5 to 9pm, Friday and Saturday 5 to 10pm.

Martin's, 49 Railroad St. (☎ 413/528-5455), offers good, healthful cuisine. You'll find such items as veggie burgers, scrambled tofu (which really does substitute for eggs), apple pancakes, and omelets made with hot peppers, salsa, and cheese. The tables are plain wood, and the nice thing is that they serve breakfast all day. *Hours:* Daily 6am to 3pm.

La Tomate, 293 Main St., Great Barrington (☎ 413/528-8020), will introduce you to Provençal cuisine, which is lighter than traditional French cuisine and uses olive oil rather than butter as the cooking medium. The limited menu emphasizes fish and shellfish. There might be a wonderful grilled salmon with wild mushroom risotto, or a trio of salmon, sole, and scrod braised in a lemon beurre blanc. On the meat side, there might be roasted half chicken brushed with olive oil and garlic, or veal scaloppine with caramelized apples and calvados sauce. There are also several delicious pasta dishes, the most characteristic being the penne Provençal made with tomatoes, basil, black olives, garlic, capers, olive oil, and a dash of red-wine vinegar. To start there's a classic caramelized onion tart or roasted goat cheese with mushrooms, thyme, and garlic; or mussels in white wine, tomatoes, and garlic. Prices range from $16 to $22. Finish with crème brûlée, chocolate mousse, or any one of the delicious tarts. *Hours:* Tuesday to Thursday, and Sunday 5 to 9pm, Friday and Saturday 5 to 10:30pm.

20 Railroad Street, whose name describes its address, (☎ 413/528-9345), is a classic tavern-restaurant possessing a 28-foot-long Victorian carved mahogany bar and oak booths. The menu is broad, ranging from Philly steaks and tuna melts and burgers to a hot turkey platter, pasta with seafood and sun-dried tomatoes, and grilled sirloin, priced from $7 to $14. The brunch menu provides good value and offers cooked-to-order choices among omelets, French toast, quiche, and other egg dishes, plus selections from the regular menu. *Hours:* Daily 11:30am to 11pm.

Daily Bread Bakery, 278 Main St. (☎ 413/528-9610), has tempting breads, cookies, and pies made of seasonal fresh fruits. Delicious and fun, they "contain no refined sugar unless marked." *Hours:* Monday 8am to 1pm, Tuesday and Wednesday 8am to 3pm, Thursday to Saturday 8am to 4pm.

LODGING IN SHEFFIELD

From the minute you see **Ivanhoe Country House,** Under Mountain Road (Route 41), Sheffield, MA 01257 (☎ 413/229-2143), you'll be struck by how neat and trim the white clapboard house with black shutters is kept (the lawns and flowers are neat, too). The oldest part of the house dates to 1780. Dick and Carole Maghery have nine rooms, all with private baths. There are two rooms on the first floor: One large room has a fireplace and a porch that accommodates a private Ping-Pong table along with wicker furnishings; the room itself contains a bed with a white eiderdown, an armoire, and a bathroom with claw-foot tub. Rag rugs made by a local woman are found throughout. The Sunrise Room has a country painted bed and rust-and-blue chintz wallpaper. The Lakeview Room (which does indeed have a view) is decorated in dusky rose. The Willow Room has a sleigh bed, a Windsor rocker, and other appealing pieces. There's also a two-bedroom unit with a kitchenette and a porch that is very private—ideal for families or two couples. Both bedrooms have a fireplace and brass bed.

The living room is comfortably large and welcoming, with Victorian sofas, chestnut paneling, a brick fireplace, wing chairs, and plenty of books and magazines spread out on top of an early piano as well as a TV. French doors lead onto a brick terrace with umbrella tables. Begonias and other flowers brighten the gardens. You'll probably meet the four golden retrievers (Dick and Carole used to raise them). The pool is beautifully located on the crest of a hill, where chaise longues are lined up for sun worshipers. From the grounds there's a serene view of Berkshire Lake. A continental breakfast is served or will be delivered to your room.

Rates: May through October, weekends $119 to $125, midweek $100 to $110; winter, $70 to $90. The two-bedroom unit for four with private bath costs $195 in summer, $145 in winter.

Staveleigh House, South Main Street, Sheffield, MA 01257 (☎ 413/229-2129), is a private home set back from Route 7 that is operated by two widows, Dorothy Marosy and Marion Whitman. Many of the quilts on the beds or the walls, including the large one on the staircase wall, were crafted by Marion, and the rugs were hooked by Dorothy. Plants brighten the rooms, too, and the landing is inhabited by teddy bears. There are five rooms (three upstairs and two downstairs), two with private bath. The most charming one features a dresser (with mirror), rocker, and chaise longue, all made of wicker, and plank-wood floors; a quilt hangs over the bed rail. In the bathroom the floor has been decorated with sponge painting. Another favorite, on the ground floor, has a private entrance at the back. It's radiantly decorated in yellow and white and has maple furnishings. In the living room the name Staveleigh is carved above the grate, although neither owner knows the exact provenance. The center hall walls have been opened so that the living room flows into the dining room. Here on a table spread with a lace tablecloth, a full breakfast is served—juice, fresh fruit, a hot dish like puffed oven pancakes, and home-made muffins and jams. Afternoon tea is also served. The room is personal-ized by a cobalt-blue glass collection and a display case containing a glass candlestick collection. *Rates:* $115 with private bath, $105 with shared bath.

When Ronald and Judith Timm had the task of furnishing **Centuryhurst**, Main Street (Route 7), Sheffield, MA 01257 (☎ 413/229-8131), they had the distinct advantage of owning and operating the antiques store located in the barn behind the main house. It's no surprise, then, that the four rooms sharing two baths are furnished with early-19th-century American pieces; many also feature clocks collected by Ron. You'll find tiger maple cannonball beds, grain-painted dressers and blanket chests, mirrors with reverse-painted glass, and many other decorative pieces. The house was built in 1800 and still has its original hardware, unique keystone archways, and an unusually large fireplace with beehive oven. There are two large sitting rooms, both with fireplaces overlooking the 3 acres of landscaped grounds. Guests can relax in the old New England rockers on the porch, too. Clock mavens will love the store, which also specializes in Wedgwood and offers two floors of American country furniture. *Rates:* $66 to $88.

The **Stagecoach Hill Inn**, Route 41, Sheffield, MA 01257 (☎ 413/229-8585), exudes history. It's a rambling old brick building on 160 acres that dates back originally to 1794. By 1802 there was a barn on the property, which is now the dark, beamed MacDougall's Tavern. The bar is decorated with car badges and other auto insignia—the place is frequented by many Lime Rock drivers and fans. It's made cozy by the double-brick hearth tiled on one side with Delft. Oil lamps hang from the beams. There's even a comfortable raised section with couches and TV. The brick building was constructed in 1820 and the smaller building in back was erected in the mid-1800s as a poorhouse. The place has since functioned variously as a summer house, guest house, and, since 1946, as an inn. The previous owners were English, and certain traces of their influence remain. A sign invites lords, ladies, and gentlemen to follow the pointer past the tavern into the dining rooms. A varied menu is offered at dinner—featuring, for example, rack of lamb with rosemary Merlot demi-glace, fillet of salmon with roasted red pepper coulis, game hen with Cabernet-braised vegetables, and steak-and-mushroom pie. Prices range from $10 to $24. To start try the portobello mushrooms with greens drizzled with balsamic vinaigrette, or the corn and crabmeat wontons with green chile sauce. Pub fare is available in the tavern daily except Wednesday.

The 11 rooms—most with private baths and all with air-conditioning and telephones—are located in the main house and cottage annex. They are furnished with an eclectic mix of antiques and antique reproductions. The nicest rooms, to my mind, are in the addition out back. Room 5, for instance, has a rope four-poster covered with a red-blue old quilt, a side table draped with a floor-length tablecloth, wing chairs, a dresser, and chest. Room 4 is even brighter, thanks to the fantail light. Facilities also include an outdoor pool.

Rates: Summer/fall, $85 to $155; winter/spring, $65 to $135. Lower prices are for shared bath. *Dining hours:* Sunday to Tuesday and Thursday 5:30 to 9:30pm, Friday and Saturday 5:30 to 10:30pm.

The **Ramblewood Inn,** Under Mountain Road (P.O. Box 729), Sheffield, MA 01257 (☎ 413/229-3363), is located in an unusually spacious log house tucked away in the pine woods. Rooms all have private tiled baths. Each is attractively furnished with pine beds, polished pine-wood floors, ruffled curtains, and pinkish-gray wall-to-wall carpet. The ground-floor room has a high, cathedral-style ceiling and light-filled atrium. One room has a private deck adorned with flower-filled tubs. Upstairs rooms are also prettily and variously decorated, with one wall sporting chintz wallpaper, cream-and-rust curtains at the windows, and a Hitchcock rocker. Quiche, blueberry pancakes, omelets, and sausage and eggs are likely breakfast dishes, along with home-baked items. Guests may use the canoe on the lake across the road. *Rates:* $100 to $135 double.

Orchard Shade, Maple Avenue, P.O. Box 669 (☎ 413/229-8463), is the name given to this beautiful 1840 house standing on 10 acres with well-tended gardens and a swimming pool. There are seven rooms sharing three baths. All are furnished tastefully with antiques. In one you might find, for example, an Empire-style chest and bull's-eye mirror, along with a camelback sofa and wicker chair. Another might have painted cottage-style furniture. The guest parlors with fireplaces are very comfortable and decorated with good rugs, interesting objects, family portraits, and a good selection of books, art, and sculpture. A breakfast of breads and pastries is served. *Rates:* $70 to $135.

HARTSVILLE DINING

The **Hillside Restaurant,** a few miles southeast of Great Barrington on Route 57 (off Route 23) in Hartsville (☎ 413/528-3123), is in an old farmhouse set on the crest of a hill with a beautiful Berkshire Valley view. It serves such continental-Italian specialties as veal francese or veal piccata, fillet of sole Oscar, and fettucine Alfredo, all priced from $15 to $22. Staffordshire china is used for service; the two dining rooms are warmed by fires in winter, while in summer there's a porch that takes full advantage of the view. *Hours:* Summer, Sunday noon to 2pm, Tuesday to Sunday 5 to 9pm; winter, Sunday noon to 2pm, Wednesday to Sunday 5 to 9pm.

NEW MARLBOROUGH/SANDISFIELD LODGING & DINING

At the **Old Inn on the Green and Gedney Farm,** Route 57, New Marlborough, MA 01230 (☎ 413/229-3131), the Old Inn is set back behind a green in an 18th-century building with a classic double-porch facade. There are five rooms, all with private baths and air-conditioning. Each one is eclectically furnished in a decidedly country style. The rooms might contain iron-and-brass beds, desks, armoires, wing chairs, or perhaps a white-painted table and chair. Some rooms have access to the long front balcony. Gedney Farm is located a short distance down the road. The 16 accommodations here are in a magnificent turn-of-the-century Normandy-style barn, and the interior decoration is refreshingly different from the traditional New England inn. Rooms are painted in brilliant Southwestern colors. All have private baths, and some have granite fireplaces and tiled whirlpool baths.

At the Old Inn the four colonial-style dining rooms have fireplaces and are lit entirely by candlelight. Here a fixed-price dinner is served on Saturday. Dinner specialties vary from week to week, but a typical sample menu might begin with oyster and crab bisque, followed by a choice between seared Arctic char en croute with a roasted pomodoro sauce, or beef tenderloin with red-wine mushroom jus. The finale might bring lemon chiffon tart or caramel pear ice cream—a fine repast indeed and well worth the $48 price tag. During the week an à la carte menu is served in the dining rooms or on the canopied terrace by candlelight. Prices range from $18 to $23. You will always find a fish of the day as well as sea scallops in a tarragon-infused fumé, and loin of pork with roasted onion cider sauce. The wine list is extensive. Breakfast is served in the room with a refectory table.

Rates: Old Inn, $150 to $185 double; Gedney Farm, $185 to $215, suites from $235. *Dining hours:* Lunch on summer weekends. The Gallery at Gedney Farm features a variety of art shows during the year including an outdoor sculpture part in summer and fall.

The oldest section of the **New Boston Inn**, 101 N. Main St. (routes 8 and 57, Village of New Boston), Sandisfield, MA 01255 (☎ 413/258-4477), dates back to 1735. Today it serves as the taproom (open for guests only) of this zesty country inn. There are eight guest rooms, all with private baths. The floors are bleached wood, the decor soft florals. Room 4 is stenciled with a Tree of Life, done by a local artist. It also possesses a cottage-style Victorian suite and a striking turkey-red rush-seat chair and desk. The cove-ceilinged ballroom now serves as a place where guests gather to talk or to play billiards. According to local legend, Pearl Buck wrote *The Good Earth* here, Vladimir Horowitz played in the ballroom, and Anne Morrow Lindbergh wrote *Gift from the Sea* here. A full breakfast of bacon, sausage, and French toast is served. *Rates:* $105 double.

PITTSFIELD-DALTON & THE NORTHWESTERN CORNER

AREA ATTRACTIONS

Pittsfield and Dalton, with their more extensive commercial development, present a different face from the picturesque villages that have been explored thus far. Neither one is pretty, but they do possess several attractions.

Some of the displays in the **Berkshire Museum**, 39 South St. (☎ 413/443-7171), in the center of Pittsfield, will help you get to know the history of the area. There are some fine paintings from the Hudson River School. Other exhibits concentrate on ancient civilizations and nature (including an aquarium featuring local and other aquatic specimens). *Hours:* Tuesday to Saturday 10am to 5pm, Sunday 1 to 5pm; July and August, daily. Admission is $3 for adults,

$2 for seniors, $1 for children ages 12 to 18. Free Wednesday and Saturday 10am to noon.

Just south of Pittsfield lies **Arrowhead**, at 780 Holmes Rd., Pittsfield (☎ 413/442-1793), where Herman Melville lived from 1850 to 1863. As you stand in the room where he wrote *Moby-Dick, Pierre, The Confidence Man, Israel Potter,* and the *Piazza Tales,* you can imagine how often he must have contemplated the grim visage of Mount Greylock with despair, for his novels were failures in his time, and he was dogged by debt. Even sadder is that when he died, his wife threw out his books because she thought they were worthless. Three rooms are devoted to his life and works and other memorabilia. The house is also the headquarters of the Berkshire County Historical Society. *Hours:* Memorial Day to Labor Day, daily 10am to 5pm; Labor Day to October 31, Friday to Monday; November to May, by appointment. *Admission:* $5 adults, $4 children ages 6 to 16.

From Pittsfield you have access to a really fascinating attraction 5 miles along Route 20, best visited in good weather; don your boots and slickers on rainy days, for a visit involves a lot of outdoor walking. This is the **Hancock Shaker Village,** Route 20 (P.O. Box 898), Pittsfield, MA 01202 (☎ 413/443-0188). Allow at least 3 hours to tour this fascinating living museum dedicated to the Shakers, a communal religious sect that in 1790 established Hancock, the City of Peace, as the third of 18 Shaker communities settled in the United States.

Founded by Mother Ann Lee, the Shakers were dedicated to celibacy, simplicity, and equality. They were known for their excellence in agriculture and industry, and for their lively dance-worship, which gave the sect its name. Celibate, they took children and orphans into their community; the children were free to leave if they wanted to (many did). You can see the dorms where the men and women slept separately, their separate staircases, and the corridors where two narrow strips of carpet were placed—one for the women to walk on, the other for the men. In summer they rose at 4:30am (5am in winter) to begin their daily round of farming, craftsmaking, and cooking. You can tour 20 original Shaker buildings, and watch the old crafts being demonstrated along the way—cooking that follows Shaker recipes, furniture making, box making, weaving, sewing, spinning, and so on. There's also a Discovery Room where you can try your hand at spinning and weaving or try on Shaker-style clothing. The village also has a working farm with historic breeds of livestock and vegetable and herb gardens. In the museum shop fine crafts can be purchased—their famous wool cloaks, tables, chairs, candleholders, boxes, vinegars, and herbs. A delightful outing. To get there: Don't go to Hancock Village itself—the Shaker Village is separated by a mountain barrier. Coming from the north, take Route 7 south to Route 20 west. From the south, take Route 22 to Route 295 and then east to Route 41 north.

Hours: May 23 to October 18, 9:30am to 5pm daily. *Admission:* $13.50 for adults, $5.50 for children ages 6 to 17. April 1 to May 23 and October 18 to November 1, there are guided tours on the hour from 10am to 3pm. Tours are $10 for adults and $5 for children ages 6 to 17.

The **South Mountain Chamber Concerts** are also given about 1 mile south of Pittsfield.

Due east of Pittsfield lies the other industrial town of Dalton, where you can explore part of its heritage at the **Crane Museum**, South Street (☎ 413/684-2600), located off Route 9, by viewing the exhibits that document the art of fine papermaking since 1801. Unfortunately, this one will have to be done on a weekday. *Hours:* June to mid-October, Monday to Friday 2 to 5pm.

From Dalton, take Route 9 east to West Cummington and continue on until you reach Route 112 south. Off this road you'll come upon the white clapboard Dutch gambrel-style house that was **home to poet William Cullen Bryant** (☎ 413/684-0148). It stands at the end of a maple line drive with fine views of the landscape—mountain, spruce, brook, and rock—that inspired the poetry that Bryant wrote as a young man before he turned to law and newspapering. He wrote his first major poem, "Thanatopsis," in the upstairs bedroom of this house. Although this boyhood home was later sold, Bryant was able to repurchase it and use it from 1865 to his death in 1878 as a country retreat from his labors as editor of the *New York Evening Post*. Today what makes the house unusual is that it stands in its original 195-acre setting. You can see the poet's cradle and 23 rooms containing memorabilia and the furnishings of three generations of the Bryant family. *Hours:* Late June to Labor Day, Friday to Sunday 1 to 5pm; Friday and Saturday only until Columbus Day. Closed Columbus Day to late June. Admission $7 adults, $2 children.

PITTSFIELD-DALTON LODGING

The **White Horse Inn**, 378 South St. (routes 7 and 20), Pittsfield, MA 01201 (☎ 413/442-2512), is a beige clapboard home with cream shutters and an elegant portico supported by classical pillars. All eight rooms have private baths, TVs, and telephones. They are neat and clean, and furnished with oak desks, beds, and dressers. The breakfast room overlooks the lawn and trees in back. Fresh flowers adorn the glass-topped tables. An ample continental breakfast of fruit, cereal, homemade muffins, and quiche is served here. *Rates:* July to Labor Day, $120 to $180 double; off-season, $100 to $145 double.

The **Dalton House**, 955 Main St., Dalton, MA 01226 (☎ 413/684-3854), will always have seasonal flowers in bloom, for owners Gary and Bernice Turetsky are enthusiastic gardeners. The main house was built by a Hessian soldier in 1810 and contains five comfortable rooms. The six rooms in the carriage house out back are especially nicely decorated to achieve a country look. All rooms have private baths, air-conditioning, and telephones. The public areas in the house itself are warm and cozy. The sitting room has a large fireplace and also contains a piano, and you can retire to the loft area above to play cards or watch TV, especially after a day's skiing. This is a popular spot with skiing groups. Breakfast is served buffet-style in the skylit, Shaker-style dining room. In summer, loungers and tables are placed out on the deck. There is a large pool for guests. *Rates* (including breakfast): July and August, $95 to $125; spring and fall, $78 to $95; winter, $60 to $80.

PITTSFIELD DINING

An entrance surrounded by Chianti bottles welcomes you to the homey **Giovanni's**, located on Route 7 just south of Pontoosuc Lake (☎ 413/443-2441). Tiffany-style lamps, a few hanging plants, and pictures of Venice set the scene for tasty Italian dishes. Typical appetizers—gnocchi, calamari fritti—are priced from $5. Pastas run from $10 for ravioli with meat or marinara sauce to $18 for a linguine with sea scallops and shrimp in a basil pesto sauce. Main courses encompass everything from veal Marsala and chicken cacciatore to Giovanni's sirloin finished with sautéed mushrooms and caramelized onions in a garlic sauce. In addition to the menu there are always daily specials. Prices range from $13 to $20. *Hours:* Monday to Saturday noon to 3pm, Monday to Thursday 4:30 to 9pm, Friday to Saturday 4:30 to 10pm, Sunday noon to 8pm.

LODGING & DINING OVER THE NEW YORK BORDER

The **Inn at Shaker Mill**, Cherry Lane (off Route 22), Canaan, NY 12029 (☎ 518/794-9345). Idyllically situated by a flowing brook and waterfall, this lovely 1824 stone gristmill affords peace and quiet. Here you can sit in the living room, actually listening to the water running over the rocks. The couches are modern and so are the wood stoves; Shaker stools serve as coffee tables. Ingram Paperny, who has lived here for 30 years, restored the mill, handcrafting most of the built-in furniture himself. Some people may find the 20 rooms austere, for the Shaker inspiration is strong. Rooms have wood side tables, chests, wide-board floors, and beams. The most appealing accommodation to my mind is a top-floor skylit apartment with wicker furnishings and a kitchen. There's a TV in the living room. The best pastimes are sitting out by the brook and looking across the fields dotted with cows or walking through the countryside. The prime reason for visiting the inn is the warm welcome given by Ingram, who relishes conversation and obviously has warm interest in and affection for his guests. Meals are obligatory on weekends during the summer season. *Rates:* B&B $45 to $70 per person (the lower price off-season). Add $20 to $25 per person for MAP. Bring your own wine.

The **Sedgwick Inn**, Route 22, Berlin, NY 12022 (☎ 518/658-2334; fax 518/658-3998), is an exquisite home filled with antiques personally collected by Robert and Edith Evans, who restored and opened this inn as "a retirement project" after long careers in psychology. Accommodations consist of four rooms, with private baths, and a two-room suite, plus six motel-style units. The one room I viewed contained two brass beds and a bird's-eye maple dresser. If the others reflect the quality of the public areas, they ought to be beautiful. The place is full of interesting artifacts. In the living room is a case filled with ivory pieces, figureheads, toby jugs, and other small collectibles and a number of stone sculptures, the work of Edith. A sofa, wing chairs, an oriental rug, and a fireplace ensure comfort. A Will Moses, given to the Evanses by the artist, graces the wall. A marvelous etched-glass door depicting peacocks—a great find—leads to the porch breakfast room that has a view of the garden out back and is fittingly furnished with white metal chairs and tables on a brick floor. The library offers magazines, books, and comfortable chairs. In the corner, the cupboard is filled with jewelry and small antique items for sale. In a separate building that once served as a Civil War recruiting station guests can enjoy a game of pool on the antique table. A gift shop and gallery are behind the inn. Wicker chairs line the front porch.

The Coach Room Tavern is a very popular restaurant, for which you'll certainly need a reservation on weekends. The kitchen is supervised by Edith. The menu changes weekly, but will feature five entrees and a vegetarian choice. There might be oven-poached haddock with a Creole pepper sauce, baked chicken with artichokes and sun-dried tomatoes, or chargrilled filet mignon.

Prices range from $13 to $22. The chef turns out many soups such as roasted eggplant and Vidalia onion. Edith is Viennese, and desserts are her specialty— frozen cappuccino mousse pie covered with a dark chocolate glaze, bananas Foster, or four-berry coupe flavored with Cointreau and served over vanilla ice cream. A pianist plays on Friday and Saturday evenings.

Rates: June to October, $105 to $115 double, suite $140, motel $88; November to May, $95 to 105 double, suite $120, motel $78. *Dining hours:* Wednesday to Saturday 11:30am to 2pm and 5 to 9pm, Sunday 1 to 8pm.

It's not surprising that the **Mill House Inn** (P.O. Box 1079, Hancock, MA 01237) on Route 43 in New York's Stephentown (☎ 518/733-5606), really does look like a Central European mountain chalet, for one of the owners, Romana Tallet, hails from Slovenia. She will welcome you into her cozy living room with its large, arched, stucco fireplace that throws out much-needed heat on winter days. The Tallets go to great lengths to ensure that everyone is content, and they are very well versed and forthcoming about the attractions of the area. There's a small games room, croquet is available, and there's a small swimming pool in back. All rooms have air-conditioning and private baths with continental-style showers; they're eclectically furnished, some with pine. In summer, breakfast is served on the terrace. The inn is only 10 minutes from Mount Greylock. *Rates:* $95 to $105 double, suites $115 to $150. Three-night minimum stay in July, August, and holiday weekends.

Les Pyrenees, off Route 295, in Canaan, NY (☎ 518/781-4451). Master chef Jean Petit has been attracting patrons to this secluded restaurant for 30 years. A stone stairway covered by a red, white, and blue awning leads to the restaurant; flowers bloom on either side. The front room is a low-lit bar. The dining room behind glows. Gilt portraits, many of family and friends, adorn the Chinese lacquer pink walls. The atmosphere is relaxed. Dishes are primarily French classics—chicken in Burgundy, poached halibut in white-wine-and-cream sauce, escalope de veau viennoise, poulet au champagne, or frogs' legs. They are priced from $12 to $27, the higher price for pheasant with pâté de foie gras and truffles. Among the desserts, the crème brûlée is extra-special. Cash or personal check only. *Hours:* Summer, Tuesday to Saturday 5 to 10pm, Sunday to 10pm; winter and spring, Friday to Saturday 5 to 10pm, Sunday 4 to 9pm.

HANCOCK/JIMINY PEAK LODGING & DINING

The **Hancock Inn,** Route 43, Hancock, MA 01237 (☎ 800/882-8859 or 413/738-5873), is a highly idiosyncratic kind of place—an expression of Ellen and Chester Gorski. A small cement path lined with irises and marigolds leads to the small porch/foyer filled with ferns and cane rockers. Open the door into the hall and you'll discover a very Victorian hallway. Stern Victorian portraits stare down from the walls; a Victorian-style couch and sideboard stand imperiously. To the right, a doorway surmounted with a semicircular stained-glass window leads into the dining room, where tables are set with white tablecloths and napkins, a sprig of fresh flowers, and glass candleholders. A large wall clock ticks away. Grapevine wreaths and cream ball-fringe curtains add a country touch. In winter it's warmed by a fire in the wood-burning stove. The food has been highly rated by the *Albany Times Union* critic. The menu is limited, featuring eight or so dishes—duckling braised in port wine with figs; filet mignon with shallots, red wine, and cognac; fish of the day; or chicken breast sautéed in a light apricot sauce. Prices run $16 to $20. Desserts are created by Ellen—homemade ice creams, white-chocolate mousse cheesecake, crème brûlée with strawberries. They'll be served on fine Depression glass of a harmonious color: cobalt blue, green, or burgundy. *Hours:* Friday to Sunday 5 to 10pm.

Eight rooms with private baths are very idiosyncratically styled, but not in a lushly decorated way. Room 1 has stenciled walls, a country pine dresser and bed, a side table, a wardrobe, a desk with a handful of old books, and a costumed doll in the corner. The bathroom has wainscoting, and the room has bold pink- and white-rose wallpaper. Other rooms might have an old country teardrop dresser, a bird's-eye maple or Jenny Lind bed, a comfortable chair such as an old carpet-chair rocker, or a rare Larkin desk. The place has great charm, and Ellen is a warm, entertaining hostess.

Rates: Late May to August and October, $80 double; September and November to early May, $60 double; $12 for additional person.

Jiminy Peak Inn and Mountain Resort, Corey Road, Hancock, MA 01237 (☎ 413/738-5500), is a well-designed, very attractive resort complex at the base of the mountain of the same name. All the accommodations are suites. Each is modern, containing a kitchen fully equipped with dishwasher, stove, fridge, and toaster; a living room with a couch that makes up into a queen-size bed, a TV hidden in a cabinet, plus comfortable seating and a service bar. A bathroom with two sinks (a vanity outside) and bedroom with brass bed and pine furnishings complete the layout. The six-on-six and eight-on-eight windows give each an old-fashioned air. The dining room, Founders Grill, has a full view of the mountain, while the bar area has a stone fireplace and comfy wing chairs to rest in après-ski. The food is typical American/continental fare—chicken Parmesan, chicken and seafood kebabs, prime rib, and baked scallops, priced from $10 to $20. The Founders Grill is open for lunch and dinner daily; breakfast depends on the season.

The list of facilities is long. There are six tennis courts and an outdoor pool from which you can see tree-covered mountains. Facing the mountain is another outdoor heated pool that's used year-round. Just off this pool area is a Jacuzzi and a fitness room with Universal equipment, sauna, and resident masseuse. The games room on the lower level (furnished with video games) is only one area that the kids enjoy. The Alpine slide is thrilling fun in the summer ($4 a ride, $13 for a five-ride book, or 1½ hours' worth for $9.75). There's also laser trap shooting available. The miniature golf here is beautifully landscaped, and each hole is a scale reproduction of a famous hole. Trout fishing is offered at the stocked pond. Patio and picnic tables stand outside the round house, which is the tavern in winter, a sandwich place in summer. The grounds are well kept—colorful window boxes and fences with rambling roses show that extra attention to detail that has made Jiminy Peak the prime skiing and summer resort in the Berkshires.

Rates: Winter, one-bedroom, weekends $309, midweek $149; two-bedroom, weekends $445, midweek $249; three-bedroom, weekends $499, midweek $295. These prices require a 2-night minimum stay and include ski lift tickets for two. Summer, weekends $229 to $335, midweek $109 to $225. *Dining hours:* Summer, Sunday to Thursday 5 to 9:30pm, Friday and Saturday 6 to 9pm; winter, Thursday to Sunday 6 to 9pm.

WILLIAMSTOWN

Originally established in 1753 as a plantation called West Hoosuck, it was renamed for Colonel Ephraim Williams in 1755. When he left an estate for founding a free school with the proviso that the township's name be changed to Williamstown, of course it was. And that's why **Williams College**, whose buildings are scattered along Main Street against a mountain backdrop, is here in this pretty town of rolling hills and dales. If you like, you can tour the college; ask at the Admissions Office in Hopkins Hall. The college's museum of art (☎ 413/597-2429) in Lawrence Hall on Main Street and the Hopkins Observatory are also worth visiting. But the outstanding attractions here are really the Clark Institute and the Williamstown Festival.

WILLIAMSTOWN ATTRACTIONS

The **Sterling and Francine Clark Art Institute**, 225 South St. (☎ 413/458-9545), houses a distinguished personal art collection purchased between 1912 and 1955. Most famous for a room of Renoirs and paintings by Monet, Degas, Pissarro, and other 19th-century French impressionists, the collection also contains some other fine works—Mary Cassatt pastels; Venetian scenes by John Singer Sargent; several Winslow Homers, including his *Undertow* (1886), a luminous picture of lifeguards pulling two girls from the waves; a Remington bronze; some glorious Corots; Turner's *Rockets and Blue Lights;* and two Berthe Morisots, along with representatives from many other schools and periods.

What makes the collection so remarkable is that Clark only bought what he liked—his taste was impeccable. His favorite work among them all was Renoir's *Onions* because he especially appreciated the artistry that could transform the mundane onion into a shimmering object of beauty. Part of the museum is set aside for special exhibits.

Hours: July 1 to Labor Day, daily 10am to 5pm; September to June, Tuesday to Sunday 10am to 5pm; open Memorial Day, Labor Day, and Columbus Day, but closed Thanksgiving, Christmas, and New Year's Day. *Admission:* Free.

The Adams Memorial Theatre (☎ 413/597-3400) is home to the **Williamstown Theatre Festival**, the premier summer theater in the Berkshires. Stars who have performed there include Richard Chamberlain, Blythe Danner, Richard Dreyfus, Roberta Maxwell, Christopher Reeve, Maria Tucci, and many others. See "Festivals in the Berkshires," below for information.

WILLIAMSTOWN LODGING & DINING

The **Orchards**, Route 2 East, Williamstown, MA 02167 (☎ 800/225-1517 or 413/458-9611), stands on the site of an old apple orchard. It's a tasteful modern lodging with plenty of atmosphere. The design is extremely pleasing, laid out as it is around a large, triangular garden with rockery and a goldfish pond. Here you can relax on the deck with its umbrella tables and enjoy cocktails or after-theater supper. Guests also appreciate the large living room, where a full afternoon tea of finger sandwiches and pastries is served. The fireplace is fashioned from Vermont marble with a mantel from England while oriental rugs grace the floors. Bookshelves span each side of the mantel, and the elegance is further underlined by the grand piano, large crystal chandelier, antique furnishings, and what will certainly be a bounteous bouquet of fresh flowers. A personal touch is revealed in the glass cases containing the owner's collections of antique silver teapots and of model soldiers ranging from a French Algerian cavalryman to a Norman knight.

The 47 extra-large rooms have been carefully designed and handsomely decorated in smoky blues and dusty pinks with wallpaper panel moldings. Fifteen rooms possess fireplaces. The marble-floored bathrooms are fully tiled and have the added convenience of double sinks, a separate tub and shower, as well as many extra touches like bathrobes and extra-fine amenities. The rooms feature solid-wood closet doors, telephones, TV in armoires, nightlights, refrigerators, and a bar with a basket of fruit and bottles of Perrier. There's also plenty of working and seating space. The so-called smaller rooms (hardly small) lack the separate tub and shower and the refrigerator. The Tennessee Williams Suite is huge, decked out in Wedgwood blue with a pencil four-poster without a canopy.

Plush dark-green walls, pastel-patterned banquettes, Queen Anne chairs, dusty-rose napkins and tablecloths, fresh flowers in stem vases, and fine china settings provide the appropriate backdrop for fine food in the dining room. Start with the smoked Scottish salmon served with mixed greens, asparagus, and curry olive oil dressing, or the house Caesar salad with cheese croutons. There will be about seven main courses to choose from—grilled swordfish with cilantro butter or honey, sesame-roasted duck breast with plum sauce, or tenderloin of beef with caramelized onions. Prices range from $24 to $28. Desserts are carefully prepared and so good it's hard to select just one. Still the vanilla crème brûlée with an orange confit is certainly up there.

Facilities include an outdoor pool and a well-equipped fitness room. The lounge draws a crowd and is particularly attractive in winter when a fire roars in the large stone fireplace. It's also well equipped with board and other games for those long, dark evenings and, of course, with comfortable lounge chairs.

Rates: Memorial Day to mid-November, $170 to $235; mid-November to May, $135 to $185. Special packages are available. *Dining hours:* Daily 7 to 10am, noon to 2pm; Sunday to Thursday 5:30 to 8:30pm, Friday and Saturday to 9pm.

River Bend Farm, 643 Simonds Rd. (Route 7), Williamstown, MA 01267 (☎ 413/458-3121), rewards guests with an authentic historic experience in a warm, hospitable atmosphere. The house was built in 1770, and when you stand in the taproom, it's as if time had stood still. The wood paneling, the iron door latches, and the cupboard filled with pewter all make it seem real. So does the paneled keeping room with its great hearth, numerous hutches, copper sink, and bunches of herbs hung up to dry. A breakfast of granola, breads, and fruit is served. There are four rooms, each furnished with appropriate antiques and accents like wrought-iron or Shaker-style tin lamps. The ground-floor room features Williamsburg blue paneling, and is furnished with a double bed, a blanket chest, a wing-back chair, and a maple chest. Oriental rugs embellish the plank floors in all the rooms. The grounds are entrancing, too. *Rates:* April to October only, $90 double.

Field Farm House, 554 Sloan Rd., Williamstown, MA 01267 (☎ 413/458-3135), is a refreshing surprise. It was formerly the home of art collector and Williams College librarian Lawrence Bloedel. Some of his collection can still be seen on the grounds and in the house, including a striking sculpture called *Sandy Seated in a Square* by Richard A. Miller. The house and the interior design is 1940s modern. Although Bloedel discussed the project with Frank Lloyd Wright, Ned Goodell was the original architect. The rooms have minimal furnishings because most of them are built-ins—dressers, drawers, closets. Where there are furnishings they're Danish modern, like the glass-top tables and the chairs found in the North Room. This room also features a fireplace with brilliant tiles painted with butterfly designs, and a small deck. The seamless carpet is original to the house and the pinch-pleat track curtains are designed to shut out all light. The Master Bedroom is a study in serenity—creamy white carpet, teak dresser, and a fireplace with tiles depicting bluebirds are the crucial elements, along with a huge deck which commands views of the mountains. The woodwork in the living room is stunning, and the cork parquet floor is certainly unique. Books and sculptures add interest to the room, and there are great views of the mountains, the beaver pond, and the grounds—all 296 acres. In summer guests may use the lovely kidney-shaped pool and the tennis court. There are marked trails for hiking in the summer and cross-country skiing in winter. An eye opener, this place certainly made me see Danish modern in a new light. To reach the property take Route 7 south to Route 43. Turn right onto Route 43 south and take an immediate right onto Sloan Road. Field Farm is 1 mile up on the right. *Rates:* $110 double.

WILLIAMSTOWN DINING

Two miles south of Williamstown on routes 2 and 7, **Le Jardin** (☎ 413/458-8032) serves excellent food in elegant surroundings. You may begin your meal with caviar, or less extravagantly with a fine homemade soup, and follow with one of the daily specials on the blackboard menu. Among the favorite dishes are duckling with a Bing cherry sauce, poached salmon with a Dijonnaise sauce, and a fine rack of lamb. Prices range from $15 to $24.

There are also six accommodations (four with fireplaces) available here in this lovely country-house atmosphere.

Rates: $80 to $100. *Hours:* July and August, Sunday to Friday 5 to 9pm, Saturday 5 to 10pm, Sunday 10:30 to 2pm; September to December and May and June, Sunday, Monday, and Wednesday to Friday 5 to 9pm, Saturday 5 to 10pm, Sunday 10:30am to 2pm. Closed January 1 to April 1.

The **Mill on the Floss,** Route 7, New Ashford (P.O. Box 718), Lanesboro, MA 01237 (☎ 413/458-9123), has country charm and serves some fine, if traditional, French cuisine. The limited menu offers such classics as chicken amandine, tournedos béarnaise, poached salmon hollandaise, and rack of lamb, all priced from $18.50 to $27. Start with the escargots with garlic butter or the crab cake with a piquant Dijon sauce. *Hours:* Tuesday to Sunday from 5pm.

A SIDE TRIP TO MOUNT GREYLOCK

While you're in the Berkshires, climb or drive to the summit of Mount Greylock and ascend the spiral stairway to the top of the tower. From here you have a 360° vista looking over 50 miles to the Catskills and over 100 miles to the distant Adirondacks.

You can even sojourn here at **Bascom Lodge,** P.O. Box 1800, Lanesboro, MA 01237 (☎ 413/443-0011 for advanced reservations; 413/743-1591 for current week), built in the 1930s to accommodate hikers. Lodgings are in four bunkrooms sleeping six to nine or in four private rooms sleeping two each. Note though that all share corridor baths. A family-style breakfast ($6) and dinner ($12) are served daily. Snacks and sandwiches are also available from a counter and can be eaten at the refectory tables. *Rates:* Rates are discounted for members of the Appalachian Mountain Club: August and weekends, bunk rooms $30 for nonmembers, $20 for members; at other times, $25 for nonmembers, $15 members. Private rooms are $65 per room for non-members, $55 for members. Open mid-May to late October.

ADAMS & NORTH ADAMS AREA

From Williamstown it's only a short drive to North Adams, gateway town to the Mohawk Trail, which leads out to Whitcomb Summit, where you can stop for a breakfast or a meal before traveling on through Florida and Charlemont, all the way to Shelburne Falls and eventually into the Pioneer Valley.

North Adams and Adams, a few miles to the south, were famous in the 19th century as manufacturing towns producing paper, textiles, and leather goods. You may want to stop at some of the mill outlets that offer discounted prices on clothing. Adams is also famous for being the birthplace of Susan B. Anthony, whose home is at 67 East Rd., a private residence that is not open to the public.

At **Western Gateway, Heritage State Park,** Furnace Street in North Adams (☎ 413/663-8059), start at the visitor center, where displays relate the story of how the remarkable 4¾-mile-long, $14 million railway tunnel was blasted and built through the mountains in 1875. It took 25 years to build, and claimed the lives or injured some 195 workers. No one was sure how to be certain that the two halves of the tunnel, dug from either side of the mountain, would meet, but when the final blast was set off, the total error in alignment was a mere ⁹⁄₁₆ inch! The story of the tunnel is told in movies, displays, and photographs. The tunnel helped fuel the town's growth, and fascinating photo exhibits reveal the course of this growth and the community's daily life and history. In 1898 North Adams was a thriving community of 25,000 that supported 500 businesses, including 58 grocery stores, 19 saloons, 17 barbers, 16 shoe stores, 11 cigar factories, 11 bicycle dealers, 9 blacksmiths, 8 hotels, 7 photographers, 5 florists, 5 undertakers, and 3 weekly and 2 daily news-papers. *Hours:* Daily from 10am to 5pm. Closed Thanksgiving, Christmas, New Year's Day, January 15 to 18, and Easter.

Afterward, browse in the many stores—a country bakery, country gift store, and ice-cream parlor, among others—each housed in restored 19th-century structures set around a cobbled courtyard.

Just outside the center of North Adams on Route 8 north there's a natural phenomenon worth visiting, the **Natural Bridge State Park** (☎ 413/663-6392). Rangers will point out and explain the outstanding features of the park. Among these are "glacial erratics," great striated glacial stones; a narrow, deep gorge (50 feet from top to floor) cut at the rate of ¹⁄₁₆ inch per year by the stream; botanically rare species like maidenhair ferns and horsetails; and a marble dam and stack of marble that still stands because the quarry workers needed it to retreat behind after they set their charges. The natural bridge was formed during the last glacial formations 13,000 years ago, although technically it's a 550-million-year-old marble formation created from shells that existed in the prehistoric ocean. Over millions of years, sand, silt, and mud changed into limestone and eventually into marble. From the 1800s to 1940 a marble quarry was operated here. Make sure you go down to the platform that gives the best view of the bridge. Stairways crisscross the huge rocks, making it easy. Such steps were not there for the intrepid youths who carved their names on the rocks. See if you can find the signature of J. S. Barnforth, dated 1740. It's said that Nathaniel Hawthorne carved his name here, but his signature has never been found. He did mention the bridge in his *Visitations. Hours:* Memorial Day to the fourth Sunday in October, 10am to 4pm. *Admission:* $2.

ADAMS/NORTH ADAMS LODGING & DINING

The **Freight Yard Pub** in the Heritage State Park, North Adams (☎ 413/663-6547), is popular for reasonably priced meals. Specials are written on a blackboard and may well include a dinner for two consisting of chicken cordon-bleu and fried clams or top sirloin and scallops. The regular menu offers fish-and-chips, sandwiches, burgers, pasta dishes, and fajitas, all priced from $6 to $12. The decor is typical modern pub—wood tables, brick fireplace, pine bar, and a popcorn machine. On weekends a DJ spins the music. *Hours:* Daily 11:30am to 11pm.

Festivals in the Berkshires

Classical Music: Tanglewood, West Street (Route 183), Lenox, MA 01240 (☎ 413/637-1600). Spread your picnic on the lawn on this 210-acre site overlooking the lovely Stockbridge Bowl. Fuchsias and begonias make the scene even lovelier in summer, when the festival runs for 9 weeks, from early July to the end of August. Get there 2 hours early if you want space near the Music Shed. Evening performances are given on Friday at 7 and 8:30pm, Saturday at 8:30pm, with matinees on Sunday at 2:30pm and open rehearsals on Saturday mornings. For information before June 15, call Symphony Hall in Boston (☎ 617/266-1492).

    South Mountain Concerts, P.O. Box 23, Pittsfield, MA 01202 (☎ 413/442-2106), features such chamber music greats as the Beaux Arts Trio and the Tokyo and Guarneri string quartets. Schedules vary, but concerts are usually held on Sunday afternoons from the end of August to mid-October, approximately every 2 weeks. Tickets run $20 to $25. Performances are given in a concert hall built in 1918 by the concert's founder, Mrs. Elizabeth Sprague Coolidge.

Dance: Jacob's Pillow, P.O. Box 287, Lee, MA 01238 (☎ 413/637-1322), is the superb 10-week dance festival founded by Ted Shawn and Ruth St. Denis in the 1930s when modern American dance was considered beyond avant garde. It's the oldest dance festival in America. Martha Graham created some of her earliest works here. More recently it has featured such greats as the Merce Cunningham Dance Company, the Mark Morris Dance Group, the Paul Taylor Dance Company, and the Trisha Brown Company. In addition, enjoy the Pillow Cafe and Pub and free showings on the Inside/Out stage prior to performances. Tickets range from $15 to $50. The festival runs from the end of June to Labor Day. Jacob's Pillow is located off Route 20 on George Carter Road in Becket, east of Lee. Call ☎ 413/243-0745 for tickets.

Theater: The Williamstown Theatre Festival, under the direction of producer Michael Ritchie, has established itself over the last 44 years as the premier summer theater in the Berkshires. The festival's Main Stage features classics by Williams, Brecht, Chekhov, Shaw, Ibsen, and others, performed by star-studded casts. On the Other Stage new works by Albert Innaurato, Edvardo Machado, Donald Margulies, and others are presented. For information, call ☎ 413/597-3400 or write to the festival at P.O. Box 517, Williamstown, MA 01267.

MacHaydn Theater, Route 203, Chatham, NY 12037 (☎ 518/392-9292). Here some of the best authentic summer stock can be found— refreshing, enthusiastic productions of *My Fair Lady, Sweet Charity,* and *Oklahoma!*

The **Berkshire Theatre Festival,** Main Street, Stockbridge, MA 01262 (☎ 413/298-5536 or 413/298-5576 after June 1 for the box office), offers a four-play season from the end of June to the end of August in a Stanford White–designed building constructed in 1886 as a casino. Such notables as Katharine Hepburn and James Cagney started their careers here.

Shakespeare and Company, The Mount, Plunkett Street (off Route 7), Lenox, MA 01240 (☎ 413/637-1199 or 413/637-3353 after May 10 for the box office). Bring a picnic before the outdoor performance at this dramatic mansion setting. The season runs from late May to the end of October.

The Berkshires
Special & Recreational Activities

Antiquing: South Egremont is an excellent hunting ground, and so is **Route 7 around Sheffield** and **Route 7A through Ashley Falls.** Other stores are dotted throughout the Berkshires.

Boating: *Lee:* **Laurel Lake,** on Route 20. *Pittsfield:* At **Pontoosuc Lake,** water-sports equipment is available for rent by the hour—motorboats cost $14.50 with a 10-h.p. engine, $23 for 50 h.p., and $32 for 75 h.p.; water skis are $7; canoes, $10; rowboats, $8; paddleboats, $9; Wave Runners rent for $40 per 20 minutes; and sailboats are available. For information, contact **U-Drive Boat Rentals,** 123 Burke Ave. in Pittsfield, or 1551 North St. (Route 7), at Pontoosuc Lake (☎ 413/442-7020). The **Ponterril YMCA,** in Pittsfield (☎ 413/499-0647), also has boats for rent at its Pontoosuc Lake facility. Canoes rent for $10 an hour, Sunfish for $20 an hour, and a sailboat with a mainsail and jib for $25 an hour. Call the marina at ☎ 413/499-0694.

Camping: *Lenox area:* **Woodland Hills Family Campground,** Austerlitz, NY 12017 (☎ 518/392-3557), offers camping convenient to Tanglewood at 160 sites with water, electricity, and sewer hookups, and a full range of facilities. *Hours:* From May 1 to Columbus Day. It charges $16 to $20.

North Egremont: **Prospect Lake Park,** Prospect Lake Road, North Egremont, MA 01252 (☎ 413/528-4158), only 6 miles from Great Barrington, is ideal for families because of the great number of facilities—boat rentals (paddleboats, canoes, and rowboats), tennis, lake fishing, and two swimming beaches. *Hours:* From mid-May to October. From $24.

Pittsfield-Dalton area: **Pittsfield State Forest,** Cascade Street (☎ 413/442-8992), has 31 sites at various locations throughout the park. In **Windsor State Forest,** River Road, Windsor (☎ 413/684-9760), there's camping in the scenic Windsor Jambs area.

Canoeing: The **Connecticut, Battenkill, Hoosic,** and **Upper Housatonic rivers** will provide some easy paddling. The more experienced will want to try the **Westfield** or **Deerfield rivers** after a good rain. For information, rentals, and sales contact **Berkshire Outfitters Canoe and Kayak Center,** Route 8, Cheshire Harbor, Adams, MA 01220 (☎ 413/743-5900); or **Riverrun/North,** Route 7, Sheffield, MA 01257 (☎ 413/528-1100).

Cross-Country Skiing: You can ski the trails on Mount Greylock Ski, and snowshoe rentals are available at **Berkshire Outfitters Canoe and Kayak Center,** Route 8, Cheshire Harbor, Adams, MA 01220 (☎ 413/743-5900). In Lenox, there's cross-country skiing in **Kennedy Park. Brodie Mountain,** Route 7, New Ashford, MA 01237 (☎ 413/443-4752), has 16 miles of trails and also offers snowboarding. Cross-country skiing is available at **Notchview** in Windsor. **Canterbury Farm,** Fred Snow Road, Becket, MA 01223 (☎ 413/623-8765), has 11 miles of ski trails plus rentals and instruction. It is really secluded, located on a dirt road off Route 8 about 1 mile south of Becket.

Fishing: *Lee:* **Laurel Lake** has a fishing ramp off Route 20. *Pittsfield:* **Pontoosuc Lake** has a ramp off Hancock Road near Route 7. **Onota Lake** is known for trophy-size bass and lake trout. *Stockbridge:* The **Stockbridge Bowl** has a ramp off Route 183.

Golf: Egremont Country Club, Route 23 (☎ 413/528-4222), has a course with 18 holes; near Lenox, **Cranwell Golf Course,** 55 Lee Rd. (☎ 413/637-2563), has an 18-hole par-71 course. **Pontoosuc Lake Country Club,** Ridge Avenue, Pittsfield (☎ 413/445-4217), has an 18-hole par-70 course. **Oak 'n' Spruce Resort,** South Lee (☎ 413/243-3500), has a 9-hole pitch-and-putt. **Taconic Golf Course,** Meacham Street, Williamstown (☎ 413/458-3997), has an 18-hole par-71 course; **Waubeeka Golf Links,** on routes 7 and 43 (☎ 413/458-5869), has an 18-hole par-72 course.

Hiking: There's plenty of mountain terrain hiking. Lanesboro is the gateway to **Mount Greylock.** A visitors' center is located on Rockwell Road, just off Route 7, although the most scenic route up the mountain is probably via Notch Road from North Adams. **Pleasant Valley Wildlife Sanctuary,** off Route 7 between Lenox and Pittsfield (☎ 413/637-0320), offers 7 miles of hiking trails. It's owned by the Massachusetts Audubon Society, which also operates a nature museum. **Berry Mountain** in the Pittsfield State Forest is great for blueberrying, viewing the azalea fields, picnicking, and camping, as well as just plain walking. Walk the path to the summit of 2,626-foot **Mount Everett** for fine views of New York, Massachusetts, Vermont, and Connecticut. Access is from Route 23 or 41 via South Egremont or from Route 22 via Copake Falls. Just south of Sheffield and west of Route 7, **Bartholomew's Cobble** gives prime views of the Housatonic.

Hike to the summit of **Monument Mountain** (1,642 feet), on Route 7 between Great Barrington and Stockbridge. **Hopkins Memorial Forest,** Bulkey Road off Route 7, has 25,000 acres on the slopes of the Taconic Mountains, a museum, and miles of trails, including self-guided nature trails. **Notchview** has 15 miles of hiking trails. For information about the **Appalachian Trail,** write to Pittsfield State Forest, Cascade Street, Pittsfield, MA 01201 (☎ 413/442-8992).

Horseback Riding: In Lenox, **Under Mountain Farm** (☎ 413/637-3365) offers 1-hour trail rides with an instructor for $45.

Picnicking: See the Lenox and Stockbridge dining sections for picnic suppliers. Tanglewood is not the only spot for picnicking; other places abound— **Berry Mountain** (in the Pittsfield State Forest), **Mount Everett** (reached from Route 23 or 41 via South Egremont), at the bottom of **Monument Mountain,** or **Mount Greylock,** and at **Windsor Jambs** in Windsor State Forest (☎ 413/684-0948).

Skiing: The Berkshires offer five skiing areas. Tallest and toughest of the five is **Berkshire East,** P.O. Box S, Charlemont, MA 01339 (☎ 413/339-6617), in a lovely setting on the Mohawk Trail. It has 34 trails served by one triple and three double chairlifts and a J lift. **Butternut,** Route 23, Great Barrington, MA 01230 (☎ 413/528-2000), has a vertical drop of 1,000 feet, 22 trails with dramatic views, and one poma and six chairlifts (one quad, one triple, four doubles) that can accommodate 10,000 skiers per hour, 98% snowmaking capacity, and a base lodge. The terrain is about 20% beginner and advanced and 60% intermediate. The cost is about $40 per day. There's also about 6 miles of cross-country trails. **Jiminy Peak,** Corey Road (off Route 7 or 43), Hancock, MA 01237 (☎ 413/738-5500), offers day and night skiing on close to 40 trails accessed by eight chairlifts and one tow. Also has a summer slide.

Catamount, Hillsdale, NY 12529 (☎ 518/325-3200 or 413/528-1262), offers fine skiing for beginners, intermediates, and experts on over 24 trails serviced by four double chairs and one J-bar. The steepest trail, dropping 500 feet over a 1,700-foot distance, is the Flipper Dipper. The mountain offers a 1,000-foot vertical drop and 96% snowmaking capacity. There's a modernized base lodge with cafeteria, cocktail lounge, and picture windows looking out onto the mountain. Also offered is a mountain coaster in summer. **Brodie Mountain,** Route 7, New Ashford, MA 01237 (☎ 413/443-4752), has 40 trails serviced by six lifts, including four double chairs and two tows. Day rates range from $24 adult to $39.

State Parks & Forests: East Mountain State Reservation, Route 7 (☎ 413/528-2000), has hiking and skiing at Butternut. **Mount Greylock State Reservation,** Rockwell Road (☎ 413/499-4263 or 413/499-4262), offers bicycling, camping, fishing, hiking, picnicking, cross-country skiing, and snowmobiling. **October Mountain State Forest,** Woodland Road (☎ 413/243-1778 or 413/243-9726), has bicycling, camping, fishing, hiking, horseback riding, cross-country skiing, and snowmobiling. **Beartown State Forest,** Blue Hill Road (☎ 413/528-0904), has bicycling, boating, camping, fishing, hiking, horseback riding, picnicking, skiing, snowmobiling, and swimming. **Mount Washington State Park and Mount Everett,** East Street (☎ 413/528-0330), offers BashBish Falls along with 15 wilderness camping sites, hiking, horseback riding, and snowmobiling. **Toland State Forest,** Route 23 (☎ 413/269-6002), has boating, fishing, hiking, cross-country skiing, and snowmobiling. **Pittsfield State Forest,** Cascade Street (☎ 413/442-8992), offers bicycling, boating, camping, fishing, hiking, picnicking, cross-country skiing, snowmobiling, and swimming. **Windsor State Forest,** River Road (☎ 413/684-9760), offers bicycling, camping, fishing, hiking, picnicking, cross-country skiing, swimming, and snowmobiling.

Swimming: Egremont Country Club (☎ 413/528-4222) has an outdoor pool. **Pittsfield State Forest** (☎ 413/442-8992) has a beach with lifeguards; **Pontoosuc Lake** has a free supervised beach. **Oak 'n' Spruce Resort** (☎ 413/243-3500) has outdoor and indoor pools; no children under age 16. At **Stockbridge Bowl** you can swim off West Street. **Sand Springs,** off Route 7 near the Vermont border, has a 50-by-70-foot mineral pool with year-round temperature of 74°. You can swim at the **Windsor Jambs.**

Tennis: Brodie Mountain, Route 7, New Ashford, MA 01237 (☎ 413/443-4752), has a racquet club featuring five indoor tennis and five racquetball courts. Prospect Lake Park, Prospect Lake, 3 miles west off Route 71, has two courts available. **Berkshire West Athletic Club,** Tamarack Road, Pittsfield (☎ 413/499-4600), has eight outdoor and five indoor courts ($15 admission plus $18 to $20 an hour). **Egremont Country Club** (☎ 413/528-4222) has four courts; **Oak 'n' Spruce Resort,** South Lee (☎ 413/243-3500) has two clay courts available. **Williams College** (☎ 413/597-3151) has 12 clay and 12 hard courts available.

ALONG THE MOHAWK TRAIL TO HISTORIC DEERFIELD

The Mohawk Trail (Route 2) follows an old Native American footpath through the mountains. The trail will take you through awesome scenery, with mountains and forests rising on either side, past the 900-pound bronze *Hail to the Sunrise* memorial to the Mohawk Indians. The route travels from summit to summit, around hairpin curves—you come first to Whitcomb Summit, the trail's highest point, where there's a place to stop and dine. At **Shelburne Falls** you can marvel at the glacial potholes in the riverbed, some as wide as 39 feet, and also view the old trolley-track bridge that is now abloom with all kinds of flowers. Incidentally, Linus Yale (of lock fame) was born here. Browse the handful of country stores before continuing along Route 2 to Greenfield. From Greenfield it's a short distance south down Route 5 to Deerfield.

HISTORIC DEERFIELD

To escape the harried, trying times of this century there's one place to hide, and that's Deerfield, a village that has managed to retain its 18th-century serenity, grace, and civility, thereby providing a real weekend haven to refresh and restore rushed and troubled 20th-century spirits.

When the Reverend William Bentley of Salem, Massachusetts, rode on horseback into Deerfield in the spring of 1782, he remarked, "The Street is one measured mile, running North and South . . . there is a gate at each end of the Street and about 60 houses in the Street in better style, than in any of the Towns I saw." Some 25 of the handsome houses on which Bentley remarked still stand on "The Street" in Deerfield.

Deerfield is in the north of the Pioneer Valley, whose low hills and fields embrace the Connecticut River as it runs south to the Atlantic Ocean. The valley is traversed by I-91 and Route 5 from south to north.

The **Pioneer Valley Tourist Information Center** (☎ 413/665-7333) is at the intersection of routes 5 and 10 in South Deerfield. There is also an information center at **Historic Deerfield** (☎ 413/774-5581).

DEERFIELD ATTRACTIONS

Let's return to **"The Street,"** with its rows of lovely 18th-century houses, one inn, and a church. The focal point of the village has remained the **church**, originally the parish of Sam Mather and John Shelburne, the latter killed by French and Indians in 1704. Walk by the church and you can see the rocks bearing memorial plaques in remembrance of the massacre and destruction of this fragile and then farthest-west outpost of colonial settlement. The inn, of course, was and is another focal point of the village, which I'll discuss later.

Thirteen museum houses dating from about 1720 to 1850 display more than 20,000 objects made or used in America from 1600 to 1900. These houses have indeed been preserved, but not in an artificial way. There are no cute costumed guides spouting canned commentaries. Instead, the guides are real, their lives and their roots are right here, and the history they tell us is in their bones, their blood, and their hearts. To see the key houses requires at least one day; a whole weekend would be preferable, just to immerse yourself in the 18th-century atmosphere. Head first for the **Hall Tavern Museum**, across from the Deerfield Inn, for maps, information, and an audiovisual introduction. For first-time visitors, the curator recommends the following highlights.

The **Allen House** (1720) is for collectors. It was the home of Mr. and Mrs. Henry Flynt, founders of the Deerfield Heritage Foundation, and displays their distinguished collections.

The **Fabric House** is a must for anyone interested in needlework, weaving, and the history and evolution of fabric design techniques. Examples of work include Marseilles, calamaricco, wood block–printed fabrics, 19th-century appliquéd quilts, and candlewicking, all of top museum quality. In addition, about 20 mannequins display 17th-, 18th-, and 19th-century costumes of various fabrics, including Spitalfields silk and hand-embroidered and hand-painted French silk.

The **Parker and Russell Silver Shop** in an adjacent farmhouse displays silver objects made from melted coins before 1800. A guide will explain the art of silversmithing and how the artisan uses a series of hammers (first metal, then wood and leather) to achieve a really smooth sheen. The collection includes Paul Revere spoons, and tankards, braziers, bowls, and Apostle spoons by various silversmiths—Dummer, Coney, Myers, de Lamerie, and others. In the middle of it all, you'll come across a charming corner dedicated to the cross-eyed hero of British democracy, John Wilkes, a passion of Mr. Flynt's, apparently. In the workshop you can see all the tools and instruments used to chase silver; the pewter collection and work room are also worth a visit.

The **Wells-Thorn House** is the oldest of the houses, having been built in 1717, only 13 years after the massacre, which no doubt explains why the wooden walls were built so thickly with few and very small windows, a form of construction that contributes to a distinctly barricaded feeling. Here in this house, though, you can almost enjoy a mini-course in furniture and design by stepping from the colonial through the Federal and Queen Anne periods to the Georgian section of the house, which was added 34 years later.

The **Asa Stebbins House** was Deerfield's first brick house. Built in 1799, it is a typical home for a rich farmer who sat in the state legislature. It contains some beautiful work by cabinetmaker Daniel Clay, Willard clocks, and a magnificent staircase enhanced by some stunning hand-painted French wallpaper.

At **Frary House** (1740) you'll have several interesting things pointed out to you—for example, the tea caddy that has a lock on it (not surprising, when tea was $50 a pound), a straw doll with a face like a death mask (originally made because the daughter had left to live with the Native Americans), and a demonstration of "Pop Goes the Weasel."

This house and the adjacent **Barnard Tavern** were bought and preserved by a fascinating woman, Alice Baker, with the aim "to rescue it and provide for mother and for dancing." She restored it in 1892 and held an annual costume ball in the upstairs ballroom with its fiddler's balcony. In the tavern you can see mud shoes for horses and clay pipes, which were rented to those who frequented the tavern. By the way, watch your p's and q's (pints and quarts).

And finally, there's the **Jonathan Ashley House**, which from 1732 to 1780 belonged to the parish minister, who was a stubborn Tory. The parishioners denied him firewood and even locked him out of his pulpit at one point.

Hours: The houses are open all year, except major winter holidays, Monday to Saturday 9:30am to 4:30 pm, Sunday 11am to 4:30pm. *Admission:* $5 for one house; $11 for a ticket good for a week. For information call ☎ 413/774-5581, or write Historic Deerfield, P.O. Box 321, Deerfield, MA 01342.

Memorial Hall Museum (☎ 413/774-6476) is appropriately named, for the collection displayed here constitutes both the Native American and Puritan heritage of the inhabitants of the Pocumtuck Valley. Here you can see the tomahawk-gashed doors from the Sheldon homestead, an eerie reminder of the 1704 massacre when Deerfield was an isolated frontier outpost. The photographs taken by the Allen sisters—two early glassplate-camera photographers who took up photography after they went deaf and could no longer teach—provide a fascinating, sometimes sentimental, sometimes very stylized, record of village life. You'll also find displays of the Society of Blue and White Needlework—part of the turn-of-the-century craft movement—plus locally made furniture, kitchenware, and musical instruments. *Hours:* May 1 to October 31, Monday to Friday 10am to 4:30 pm, Saturday and Sunday 12:30 to 4:30pm; April and November, by appointment only. *Admission:* $2.

DEERFIELD LODGING

At **The Deerfield Inn,** The Street, Deerfield, MA 01342 (☎ 413/774-5587), brass chandeliers and lanterns cast a warm glow over the polished, Georgian-style tables and Queen Anne chairs in the dining room. The dinner menu changes monthly, but it might feature such dishes as tuna with a Szechuan black-bean butter sauce, or pork rib eye with a Kentucky bourbon pepper-corn sauce. Prices range from $17 to $25.

There are 23 rooms—11 in the main house built in 1884, and 12 in the south wing, reached by a covered walkway. All rooms are furnished with reproductions and antiques. The common rooms are convivial and furnished with exquisite antiques and fabrics reproduced from patterns culled from the town's decorative arts collection. Along the halls of the main house you may find an elegant writing desk tucked into a little nook or a bookcase filled with books of plays and a variety of classics. *Rates:* $150 to $251 double. *Dining hours:* Daily 7:30 to 9am, noon to 2pm, 6 to 9pm.

A LODGING IN NEARBY NORTHFIELD

Northfield Country House, School Street (R.R. 1, Box 79A), Northfield, MA 01360 (☎ 413/498-2692), is a lovely, quiet retreat set on 16 acres. Innkeeper Andrea Dale, a longtime director of credit for Saks, stayed here and fell in love with the place so much that she was moved to say to the owners, "If you ever want to sell, keep me in mind." They did, and so Andrea became the proud owner of this handsome 1901 home built by a wealthy Boston shipbuilder as a weekend residence for use when he attended the revivalist meetings led by Reverend Moody in Northfield. Inside, rooms are large and luxuriously comfortable. The focal point of the living room is a large stone fireplace with a mantel supporting two bronze stag candlesticks. Beams and an oriental rug make it cozy; two couches and plush wing chairs provide restful seating. Musically inclined guests may play the grand piano, which stands in the bay window. A full breakfast of eggs, juice, fruit, and homemade muffins is served in the intricately carved cherry-paneled dining room. There are seven guest rooms available (sharing four bathrooms), all differently decorated, three with working fireplaces. My favorites are rooms 5 and 6. The latter is large, has a fireplace, and comes lavishly furnished with oriental carpet, an iron-and-brass bed sporting frilly linens, a chest of drawers supporting an ormolu mirror, a blanket chest at the foot of the bed, and a cozy love seat. Chintz wallpaper and a dried-flower wreath complete the country look. Room 5 contains several wicker pieces set against a dark-blue floral wallpaper and has the added charm of a small Palladian-style window. There are two large decks with sturdy stone pillars on which you can relax in cane-seated rockers. An outdoor pool completes the facilities. In winter excellent cross-country skiing is right there at the Northfield Recreation area, and in spring, magnolia and cherry trees blossom in the backyard. *Rates:* $60 to $100 double (highest price for rooms with fireplaces).

AMHERST, NORTHAMPTON & SPRINGFIELD

From Deerfield you can travel south along the Pioneer Valley to Springfield. On your way, you can explore the college towns of Amherst, Northampton, and South Hadley.

AMHERST ATTRACTIONS

Amherst's attractions include all those associated with old college towns and fine campuses, plus poet **Emily Dickinson's House** at 280 Main St. (☎ 413/542-8161), where she lived with her father and wrote close to 2,000 poems—only 7 were published during her lifetime. Her grandfather Samuel was a founder and benefactor of Amherst College, but his generosity led him into financial difficulties. His son Edward and his wife moved into the western half of the house, and here, on December 10, 1830, Emily was born. Although the house is primarily an Amherst College faculty residence, the rooms and halls open to the public do contain many Dickinson possessions, including several portraits. *Hours:* May 1 to October 1, Wednesday to Saturday. Reservations are necessary for the mandatory tours, given at 1:30, 2:15, 3, and 3:45pm; by appointment the rest of the year. *Admission:* $3. Emily's grave can also be visited in the **West Cemetery** on Triangle Street.

Amherst College (1821) occupies the area beside the town Green (which, by the way, is home to a farmer's market on Saturday mornings in the summer). The college is worth exploring for its architecture and to view the American paintings and decorative arts in the **Mead Art Museum** (☎ 413/542-2335), an impressive small museum. *Hours:* During the academic year, 10am to 4:30pm weekdays, 1 to 5pm on weekends; summer, Tuesday to Friday 1 to 4pm. Tours of the campus led by student guides are given on weekdays when school is in session. For information, call the public affairs office at ☎ 413/542-2321.

Compared to Amherst's intimate groves of academia, the **University of Massachusetts** is vast and largely a collection of high-rises. From the top of one of them, the Campus Center, you'll be rewarded with a view of the valley. The Fine Arts Building has a strange, haunting, futuristic effect: Great slabs of concrete and huge triangular supports dwarf the individual, creating an awesome landscape. Go over to the **art gallery** just to view the huge timber-like object caught by its sculptor in time and space as it seems to glide down the concrete steps. The university's art gallery also has a good collection of 20th-century American drawings, photographs, and prints. For information on campus tours, head for the information desk in the Campus Center, at the east end of the second-floor concourse (☎ 413/545-4237). Tours are usually given daily at 11am and 1:15pm (weekdays only in summer).

NORTHAMPTON ATTRACTIONS

Northampton is an attractive town with some fine architectural stock. At one end of the main street stands **Smith College,** the largest women's college in the country, founded in 1871 and built in a largely Gothic Revival and romanesque style.

The college's **art museum** (☎ 413/585-2770) is internationally recognized for its outstanding holdings in 19th- and early-20th-century art. The basis of the permanent collection are 19th-century French paintings including Gustave Courbet's *Preparation of Dead Girl,* wrongly identified previously (and somewhat ironically) as *Preparation of the Bride;* Degas's *The Daughter of Jephthah;* three lyrical canvases by Monet; and paintings by Renoir, Cézanne, Gauguin, Vuillard, Sisley, and Boudin. Nineteenth-century America is represented by Hudson River School landscapes, folk art, and paintings by such major artists as Bierstadt, Inness, Homer, Sargent, and Whistler. Thomas Eakins's late masterpiece *Portrait of Edith Mahon* and the *Mourning Picture* by regional artist Edwin Romanzo Elmer are signature works from the period. Visitors exploring this area for the first time will also want to see *View of the Connecticut River from Mount Holyoke* (1840). The 20th-century American holdings range from Charles Sheeler's *Rolling Power* to Frank Stella's 40-foot-long canvas *Damascus Gate (Variation III)* and recent work by Smith alumna Sandy Skoglund. Sculptures by Barye Rodin, Arp, Giacometti, Calder, and others complement the painting collection. The sculpture court is particularly serene. *Hours:* July and August, Tuesday to Sunday noon to 4pm; September to June, Tuesday 9:30am to 4pm, Sunday and Wednesday noon to 4pm, Thursday noon to 8pm, Friday and Saturday 9:30am to 4pm. Closed major holidays.

The college's **Botanic Garden** includes a campus-wide arboretum and the greenhouses of the Lyman Plant House. These 12 greenhouses display major botanical collections arranged according to climatic zones—Palm House, Temperate House, Succulent House, and so on. The Spring Bulb Show opens the first weekend in March, and the Chrysanthemum Show the first weekend in November. Other gardens around the campus include Capen Garden with its rose arches, the wildflower garden, a Japanese garden, and the Rock Garden. The plant house is open daily 8am to 4:15pm.

SOUTH HADLEY ATTRACTIONS

South Hadley is home to **Mount Holyoke College**, the nation's oldest women's college, founded in 1837. The campus, designed by Frederick Law Olmsted, is as one might expect, the most picturesque of all, landscaped with brooks and Dutch-style and Victorian buildings. The college's **art museum** is strong in oriental art. For a campus tour, call ☎ 413/538-2023.

SPRINGFIELD ATTRACTIONS

The main reason to visit Springfield is to see the enclave of museums that are clustered together around a tree-shaded quadrangle off Chestnut Street. The entrance is marked by Saint Gaudens's statue *The Puritan.*

The oldest building on the quad, the **George Walter Vincent Smith Art Museum**, 222 State St. (☎ 413/733-4214), an 1895 Renaissance Revival villa, houses the vast collections of its namesake and his wife Belle Townsley Smith. Avid collectors, the couple acquired an exotic array of Japanese arms and armor, screens, Noh masks, lacquers, textiles, and ceramics that is outstanding. Note the large wheel shrine (late 18th- and early-19th-century) made of keyaki wood and carved beautifully—each animal or natural element symbolizing an abstract characteristic like power or longevity. The Japan Decorative Arts Gallery displays exquisite objects—netsukes, Imari and other porcelains, glistening shun uri lacquer objects, okimono ivory figures, inro, tea ceremony implements, and a fantastic 19th-century hand-carved vase by Kyozo Ishiguro, depicting Buddha and his 500 disciples.

One of the largest collections of cloisonné in the Western world is displayed upstairs. The six processes of production are clearly illustrated and explained, and a variety of objects—vases, incense burners, ewers, bowls, birds, and animals—are on view. Most spectacular is an 18th-century covered vessel in the form of a temple drum decorated with the flowers of the four seasons—lotus, plum, peony, and chrysanthemum.

The museum's collection of 19th-century American art is quite strong, containing works by Albert Bierstadt, Samuel Colman, George Inness, Frederic Church, and the largest number of paintings by J. G. Brown in a public museum. I particularly enjoyed the watercolors by Alfred Thompson Bricher. Other galleries of note are the Sculpture Hall, housing plaster casts of classical and Renaissance sculptures, and a couple of rooms containing exquisite kilims and rugs from Anatolia and the Caucasus.

Hours: Thursday to Sunday noon to 4pm. *Admission* (to all four museums): $4 adults, $1 children ages 6 to 18.

The **Museum of Fine Arts,** 49 Chestnut St. (☎ 413/732-6092), is itself a fine example of art deco architecture. Inside the visitor is immediately struck by Erastus Salisbury Field's huge canvas *Historical Monument of the American Republic, 1867,* which dominates the ground-floor gallery. Other American works of note are Winslow Homer's watercolor *New Novel,* Fredric Church's *New England Scenery,* and significant works by Copley, Homer, Remington, and Sargent. The upstairs galleries exhibit such notable European artists as Chardin, Boucher, Corot, Boudin, Courbet, Millet, Rouault, and the impressionists. Among the less frequently viewed paintings are Gauguin's *Seascape in Britanny* and John Singer Sargent's *Glacier Streams—the Simplon.* The 20th-century gallery displays works by Bellows, Sheeler, O'Keeffe, and Lyonel Feininger. Modern sculptors are also represented—Alexander Calder, Richard Stankiewicz, and George Sugarman. In short, there's much to enjoy here. *Hours:* Thursday to Sunday noon to 4pm. Closed major holidays. *Admission:* $4 adults, $1 children ages 6 to 18.

The **Connecticut Valley Historical Museum,** 194 State St. (☎ 413/732-3080), preserves the history and traditions of the Connecticut River Valley. The artifacts and documents on display tell the story of the region from 1636 to the present. The exhibits provide an overview of Springfield's growth from a town with only 11,300 inhabitants in 1850 to one with 150,000 in 1930 only 80 years later. This rapid growth was fueled by the manufacture of all kinds of products—armaments during the Civil War, beer, soda, carriages, cigars, corsets, saddles, saws, and all other manner of goods. An entire gallery is devoted to Springfield's famous firearms industry. The story of the lives of Springfield's residents is told through photographs, correspondence, objects, advertisements, and portraits done by itinerant artists. The Genealogy and Local History Library contains the Ellis Island passenger records and more than 1.3 million archival documents, which attract researchers and family historians from around the country. *Hours:* Thursday to Sunday noon to 4pm. *Admission:* As above.

The **Springfield Science Museum,** 236 State St. (☎ 413/733-1194), contains 10 galleries, a planetarium, an aquarium, and an observatory. Kids will love the dinosaur hall, the Transparent Anatomical Mannekin (a life-size transparent woman that describes her physical systems and how they function), the hands-on exhibits in the Exploration Center, and the programs on the Native Americans, Africa, and so on. *Hours:* Thursday to Sunday noon to 4pm. Planetarium programs are given on Saturday and Sunday; the observatory is open one evening per month. Call for exact times.

AMHERST, NORTHAMPTON & SPRINGFIELD LODGING & DINING

Amherst's prime dining and lodging place is the **Lord Jeffery Inn**, 30 Boltwood Ave., Amherst, MA (☎ 413/253-2576), named after the town's hero of the French and Indian War, Lord Jeffery Amherst, and located in a handsome brick Georgian building facing the Common. Chestnuts, pine, and other shade trees give it a bucolic appearance, and so, too, does the lawn, as well as the begonias, petunias, and other flowers that bloom on the grounds. The 50 guest rooms are individually furnished with locally crafted furniture and feature telephone, air-conditioning, and TV. Some have working fireplaces; others have balconies that look down onto the garden courtyard. The sitting room has a walk-in fireplace and comfortable seating arrangements. The dining room offers formal dining in a colonial atmosphere created by the Windsor-style chairs and brass chandeliers. Dinner entrees ($14 to $20) might range from a vegetarian pasta to veal au poivre; from grilled swordfish with orange, lime, and lemon butter to duck breast served with blackberry coulis and pâté crouton. Boltwood's Tavern features traditional sandwiches and flatbreads spread with such combinations as clam, garlic, bacon, diced pepper, and goat cheese. *Rates:* $83 to $118 double; suites from $125.

A cafelike atmosphere prevails at **Judie's**, 51 N. Pleasant St., Amherst (☎ 413/253-3491). Dine on everything from lobster salad and seafood bisque to paella and Southwest sirloin (with bacon, provolone, and cilantro pesto sauce), from stuffed popovers and sandwiches to pasta dishes. Prices range from $7 to $15. The greenhouse-style dining room is enhanced by hand-painted impressionist tables and copies of famous paintings by Matisse, Degas, and Manet. The desserts are renowned. *Hours:* Sunday to Thursday 11:30am to 10pm, Friday to Saturday until 11pm.

The **Hotel Northampton**, 36 King St., Northampton, MA 01060 (☎ 413/584-3100), is a Georgian Revival building constructed in 1927. In the entranceway, display cases are filled with old wood dolls and other antique collectibles, while the lobby, with its square chestnut columns, is large. The 85 rooms are adequately furnished with wall-to-wall beige carpeting, Wedgwood-blue walls, bed, reproduction Chippendale desk, and a couple of armchairs. All have private bath, color TV, telephone, and air-conditioning. Suites feature Jacuzzis. Because of its age, the closets have good wood doors. Besides Wiggins Tavern, there's also a bar with an outdoor brick patio for summer cocktails. *Rates:* $80 to $155 double, suites from $220.

Wiggins Tavern, 36 King St., Northampton (☎ 413/584-3100), in the Hotel Northampton, is wonderfully atmospheric. It's not a tavern—it's two post-and-beam dining rooms, both with fireplaces. At night it glows golden, lit by oil-style lamps. The trestle-style wood tables are set with pewter platters and napkin rings, and the room is decorated (but not overly so) with farm implements, candles hanging from the beams, and ceramics in corner cupboards. The menu offers traditional favorites like the Yankee pot roast and chicken pot pie, several steaks, plus some more interesting seafood selections like the grilled swordfish with kiwi apple butter or the pan-seared salmon with pecan honey mustard sauce. Prices run $13 to $25. *Hours:* Wednesday to Saturday 5:30 to 10pm, Sunday 9:30am to 1:30pm and 4:30 to 9pm.

The **East Side Grill**, 19 Strong Ave., Northampton (☎ 413/586-3347), receives strong local recommendations. From the bar, which also serves as a raw bar, steps lead into the modern oak-and-brass dining room where food with a Cajun inspiration is served. For example, there's chicken Creole, barbecued shrimp, pasta jambalaya (shrimp, scallops, and broccoli in Creole sauce over spinach, tomato, and egg pasta), blackened prime rib and fish, plus steaks and a Cajun burger. The appetizers reflect the same style—gumbos, barbecued shrimp or shrimp rémoulade, and Louisiana fried oysters. Key lime pie, mud pie, and pecan pie are among the dessert attractions. At lunch it's soup, salad, sandwiches, and several items mentioned above. *Hours:* Monday to Saturday 11:30am to 3pm, Sunday to Thursday 5 to 10pm, Friday and Saturday to 11pm.

A traditional favorite, the **Student Prince and Fort**, Fort Street off Main, Springfield (☎ 413/734-7475), ladles out hearty German fare and 1-liter "boots" of beer from its bar festooned with an incredible collection of steins amassed on shelves and ledges everywhere. In my opinion, dining in the bar area is the most fun, tucked away on high-backed settles. There's also a dining room that's warmed in winter by a fire in its large brick hearth.

The menu is extensive—jaegerschnitzel (and several other schnitzels) with noodles, sauerbraten with potato dumplings and spiced red cabbage, zwiebelfleisch (an onion-gravy pot roast), broiled scrod, bratwurst with sauerkraut and potatoes, and filet mignon Rossini. Prices run $10 to $20. *Ein prositt* to this fine local spot. *Hours:* Monday to Saturday 11am to 11pm, Sunday noon to 10pm.

THE AREA AFTER DARK

Evening entertainment is centered on the campuses, where varied performances—ballet, jazz, classical music—are given. Call the universities for information. Also check the *Valley Advocate,* a free paper for event listings.

For a coffeehouse charged with youthful debate and aspiration, head for the **Iron Horse** at 20 Center St. in Northampton (☎ 413/584-0610), which offers 52 beers and a full schedule of evening entertainment, from the best local talent to nationally known folk, jazz, and blues artists. Purchase tickets for the concert at the Northampton Box Office.

Pioneer Valley/Mohawk Trail
Special & Recreational Activities

The **Northfield Mountain Recreation and Environmental Center**, 99 Millers Falls Rd., Northfield, MA 01360 (☎ 413/659-3714), offers a whole range of environmental and recreational programs and weekend workshops—birding and wildlife watching, nature photography, night experiences, organized hikes, and more, lasting a few hours or a whole day. Many other activities are available: camping, canoeing, and nature walking at **Barton Cove** (for reservations, call ☎ 413/659-3714 in pre-season, ☎ 413/863-9300 during the camping season); and picnicking along the eastern bank of the Connecticut River at Riverview picnic area. An interpretive river cruise is also given aboard the *Quinnetukut II* lasting 1½ hours (summer only; for reservations call ☎ 413/659-3714). This is also prime cross-country skiing territory (for a recorded snow report call ☎ 413/659-3713).

Bicycling: For rentals, repairs, and touring information, contact **Peloton Sports** in Northampton (☎ 413/584-1016), which charges $17 a day for a bike.

Boating: Canoes can be rented at the **Northfield Mountain Recreation Area**, Route 63 (R.R. 1, Box 377), Northfield, MA 01360 (☎ 413/659-3713). Also contact them for information about cruises on the Connecticut River.

Camping: The areas along the **Mohawk Trail** provide dramatic wilderness camping. The **Mohawk Trail State Forest Camping Area**, in Charlemont (☎ 413/339-5504), has 56 sites, plus swimming, fishing, hunting, hiking, cross-country skiing, boating, snowshoeing, and snowmobiling. **Mount Greylock State Reservations**, in Adams (☎ 413/449-4263), has 35 sites; and the **Savoy Mountain State Forest**, in Florida (☎ 413/663-8469), has 35 summer-only sites off Route 2, east of North Adams, plus log cabins available year-round. There's good camping in the **Stoney Ledge section** of Mount Greylock, and tent camping at **Barton Cove**, in Gill (☎ 413/863-9300 in season, 413/659-3714 off-season). Closed after Labor Day.

Also on Mount Greylock, from May 1 to November 1 lodging and meals are available at the summit at **Bascom Lodge** (☎ 413/743-1591). The Visitors Center (☎ 413/449-4262) is 2 miles from Route 7 on Rockwell Road.

Fishing: There's good fishing in the **Connecticut and Deerfield rivers** and at several lakes in the area. For information, call the Franklin County Chamber of Commerce (☎ 508/528-2800). Or you can write to the **Division of Fisheries and Wildlife**, 100 Cambridge St., Boston, MA 02022 (☎ 617/727-3151).

Golf: Golf courses are: **Crumpin' Fox Club**, Parmenter Road, Bernardston (☎ 413/648-9101); **Mohawk Meadows**, Greenfield (☎ 413/773-9047); and **Oak Ridge**, West Gill Road, Gill (☎ 413/863-9693).

Hiking: Great hiking is found in the **Mohawk Trail State Forest** in Charlemont, at **Mount Greylock**, and at **Erving State Forest**, east of Greenfield. There's also a trail along the Connecticut River in the **Northfield Recreation Area** (☎ 413/659-3713), and **Savoy Mountain State Forest**, east of North Adams (☎ 413/663-8469), also has trails.

Horseback Riding: The only stable that offers trail rides in the area is **Agawam Stables** in Agawam (☎ 413/786-1690).

Shopping: For information about crafts studios and galleries, of which there are many throughout the Pioneer Valley, write **Arts Extension Service**, Division of Continuing Education, University of Massachusetts, Amherst, MA 01003 (☎ 413/545-2360).

Skiing: In a lovely setting on the Mohawk Trail, **Berkshire East**, River Road (P.O. Box S), Charlemont, MA 01339 (☎ 413/339-6617), has 34 trails served by one triple and three double chairs and a J lift. A basic weekend costs $32.

The **Mount Tom Ski Area,** Route 5 (P.O. Box 1158), Holyoke, MA 01040 (☎ 413/536-0416), has downhill skiing on 17 slopes served by eight lifts. The lifts are also open in peak summer months from 10am to 10pm. In summer the Alpine slide and water slide provide the thrills.

There's also cross-country skiing at the **Northfield Mountain Recreation Area,** Route 63 (R.R. 1, Box 377), Northfield, MA 01360 (☎ 413/659-3713).

VERMONT
&
NEW HAMPSHIRE

Manchester & the Mountains

Bennington ◆ *Arlington* ◆ *Manchester* ◆ *Dorset* ◆
Bromley ◆ *Stratton Mountains*

Distance in miles: Bennington, 180; Manchester, 207
Estimated driving times: 3¼ to 3½ hours

◆◇◆◇◆◇◆◇◆

Driving: Take the New York State Thruway to Troy, then Route 7 into Bennington, or take I-684 to I-84 to I-91.

Bus: Greyhound/Trailways (☎ 800/231-2222) travels to Bennington and Manchester.

Train: Amtrak (☎ 800/872-7245) travels to Brattleboro.

Further Information: General: **Vermont Department of Travel and Tourism,** 134 State St., Montpelier, VT 05602 (☎ 802/828-3236); the **Vermont State Chamber of Commerce,** P.O. Box 37, Montpelier, VT 05602 (☎ 802/223-3443); the **Department of Forest, Parks, and Recreation,** 103 S. Main St., 10 South, Waterbury, VT 05670 (☎ 802/241-3655), for state park camping information.

For specific town information contact the **Bennington Chamber of Commerce,** Veterans Memorial Drive, Bennington, VT 05201 (☎ 802/447-3311); **Manchester and the Mountains Chamber of Commerce,** R.R. 2, Box 3451, 2 Main St., Manchester Center, VT 05255 (☎ 802/362-2100); **Dorset Chamber of Commerce,** P.O. Box 121, Dorset, VT 05251 (☎ 802/867-2450).

◆◇◆◇◆◇◆◇◆

Southern Vermont was home to Ethan Allen and his Green Mountain Boys, where they stalked the British and turned the tide to victory at the Battle of Bennington. Historic it may be, but today the area offers an incredible variety of both summer and winter activities. Surely, though, Vermont is her shining best in winter when the ski slopes at Stratton, Bromley, and Magic Mountain are dotted with colored parkas streaming down the trails, the inns and lodges are warmed by blazing hearths, and people return burnished from the slopes to enjoy an evening's entertainment. During the summer there's a variety of events and performances to watch at the Southern Vermont Arts Center, Hildene

Events & Festivals to Plan Your Trip Around

February/March: **Winter carnivals** are held at Bromley Mountain and at Stratton Mountain, featuring ice-skating, snow sculptures, fireworks, ski races, and more.

March/April: **U.S. Open Snowboarding Championships** at Stratton Mountain. Call ☎ 802/297-2200 for information.

May: **Bennington County Horse Show** at Hildene in Manchester. Call ☎ 802/362-1788 for information.

June: The **Dorset Theatre Festival** presents a series of plays from mid-June through Labor Day at the Dorset Playhouse, Dorset Village (☎ 802/867-2223, or ☎ 802/867-5777 for information).

   Vintage Car race up Mount Equinox over a 3,140-foot change in elevation. The record was set by John Meyer over the 5.2-mile course of 4 minutes, 8.8 seconds. Call ☎ 802/362-2100.

July: **Old-Fashioned Fourth,** a celebration complete with square dancing. **Vermont Symphony concert. Polo season** opens and continues every third weekend. **Hildene and Dorset Antiques shows.** Call ☎ 802/362-1788 or ☎ 802/867-2450.

   Stratton Summer Music Series, which includes the Vermont Symphony and jazz and blues groups in a series of concerts performed as the sun goes down over the mountains. Call ☎ 802/297-2200.

   Vermont Race for the Cure. This day is an emotional one for Manchester and local communities when people of all ages and from all walks of life celebrate the survival of those fighting breast cancer by running or walking in the race to raise money. Call ☎ 802/362-2100.

August: The **Acura Tennis Tournament** at Stratton. Call ☎ 800/787-2886 for information.

   Hildene Crafts Fair, which exhibits work by 250 craftspeople along with an array of Vermont food specialties. Call ☎ 802/362-1788.

September: **Stratton Arts Festival.** Call ☎ 802/297-2200 for information.

December: **Prelude to Christmas** is a series of celebrations with the signature event being a huge potluck supper at which whole communities donate the food. Appetizers are usually served at Hildene, main courses at the Equinox, and desserts and coffee followed by dancing at a local Congregational Church. Call ☎ 802/362-2100.

Meadowlands, and Stratton, as well as plenty of antiques stores and craft studios to visit, for here in this region (especially around Bennington) many of the 1960s generation settled down to practice their crafts. Fall brings an even greater glory, when the mountains are turned into great pyramids of color. There are also the quiet villages, perfectly groomed town greens, inviting inns,

Southern Vermont & New Hampshire

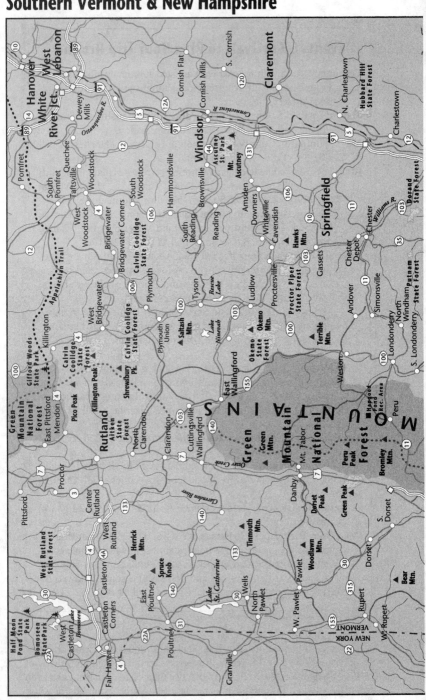

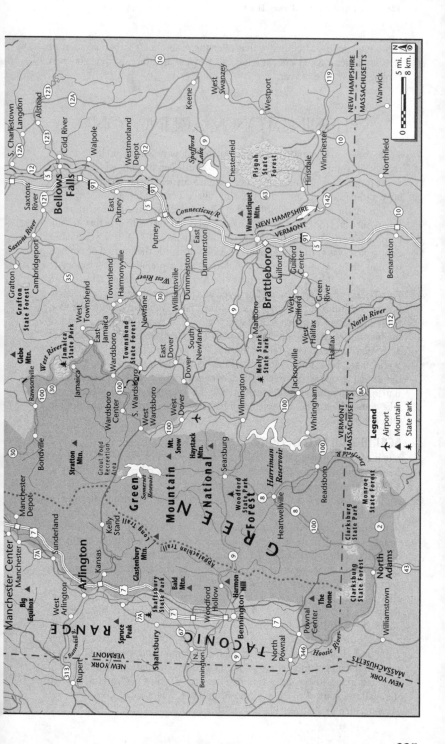

335

and white clapboard churches that offer the visitor the gentle relaxation of another, much quieter era. In short, it's a lovely area for any weekender to explore at any time of year.

BENNINGTON & ARLINGTON

There are several Benningtons—a commercial downtown, an old historic area west of downtown, and the tiny village of North Bennington, which is home to the progressive Bennington College, whose curriculum emphasizes the creative and performing arts and gives this village a certain hip air.

During the American Revolution era Bennington was the headquarters for Ethan Allen and the Green Mountain Boys, who, together with Benedict Arnold, captured Fort Ticonderoga from the British in 1775. A few years later Bennington was at the center of another famous battle that turned out to be a turning point in the American Revolution and a prelude to the victory at Saratoga. The British were pursuing the American army on its retreat from Fort Ticonderoga, but General Burgoyne was in desperate need of supplies, so he sent a column of Hessians under Colonel Baum north to capture the food and ammunition being stored in Bennington. The American forces heard of the plan, and General John Stark, a tough New Hampshire Indian fighter, and Seth Warner and the Green Mountain Boys intercepted the British at Walloomsac, New York, where they killed Baum and inflicted great losses on the British troops who retreated to Saratoga. The 306-foot-high **Bennington Battle Monument** is a fitting memorial to this historic event. An elevator will take you to the top for a marvelous three-state view. Open daily mid-April to October 31.

BENNINGTON ATTRACTIONS

Much of the history as well as the crafts of the area can be reviewed at the **Bennington Museum,** West Main Street (Route 9), Old Bennington (☎ 802/447-1571), which is filled with an assorted collection of glass, stoneware (including that of the famous Bennington potters), Early American paintings by Erastus Salisbury Field, furniture, military items, and other household wares from the 19th century. Most appealing of all, though, is the gallery devoted to Grandma Moses, or Anna Mary Robertson, a New York farm girl who turned her full attention to art at age 78 and achieved her first show at age 80 at the Gallerie St. Etienne, New York, in 1940. She became a legendary figure, who continued to paint until she died in 1961 at the age of 101, an inspiration to all aspiring artists for her late start and her untutored, natural gift. *Hours:* Daily 9am to 5pm. Closed Thanksgiving and major holidays. *Admission:* $5 adults, $4.50 students, free for children under age 12.

From the obelisk of the battle monument, you can stroll past gracious 18th- and 19th-century homes through Old Bennington, past the **Old First Church burial ground,** where some Hessians who fell in the battle are buried in a mass grave. Robert Frost is buried here, too. If you wish, you can pick up the **walking tour** of the area at the Bennington Chamber of Commerce, on Veterans Memorial Drive (Route 7 north).

The **Park-McCullough House** (☎ 802/442-5441) is an extremely well-kept Victorian mansion at the corner of West and Park streets in North Bennington. Besides the house itself, which is filled with period furnishings and personal effects, be sure to see the miniature "manor," used as a children's playhouse, and a cupola-topped carriage house, complete with century-old carriages. *Hours:* Late May through October, daily 10am to 4pm. *Admission:* $5 adults, $4 seniors, $3 students ages 12 to 18.

Bennington also has its own theater company, **The Oldcastle** (☎ 802/447-0564), which plays a summer season that mixes new and modern dramas. One of the best around.

Shopping

You may want to stop by **Williams Smokehouse**, 1001 E. Main St., Bennington (☎ 802/442-1000), and pick up some fine smoked hams or bacon (without nitrates) plus many other fresh Vermont products. Also visit **Bennington Potter's Yard** (☎ 802/447-7531), a shopping and gallery complex at School and Country streets where you'll find Bennington Pottery selling their new ceramics and seconds, plus **McCleod Woodwares**, selling all kinds of wood items from toys and pegs to cutting boards and salad bowls. The company makes the latter item for Williams-Sonoma, but you can purchase them here at a substantial discount. **Cinnamons** stocks kitchenware, and **Terra Sua** has assorted ethnic crafts.

ARLINGTON ATTRACTIONS

A short distance north of Bennington, Arlington has quite a history of its own. It was the seat of the first governorship under Thomas Chittenden, and it was here supposedly that the seal of the state was created by an officer on a mission to Chittenden. The officer drew the view of the mountain to the west of Arlington, and so it remains today. The resident chronicler of the village was Dorothy Canfield Fisher, who attracted other creative artists like her friend Carl Ruggles to the area.

To most visitors today, it is famous as Norman Rockwell's hometown from 1939 to 1953, and fans of his will want to visit the **Norman Rockwell Exhibition and Gift Shop**, on Route 7A (☎ 802/375-6423). Hundreds of *Saturday Evening Post* covers are on display in the gallery, which is hosted by former models and neighbors of Rockwell's. A 20-minute film is also shown. *Hours:* Summer, daily 9am to 5pm; winter, 10am to 4pm. *Admission:* $2 adults, free for children ages 6 and under.

Another artist who also lived in Arlington for a time was Rockwell Kent; many of his woodcuts were inspired by the landscape around Arlington.

BENNINGTON LODGING & DINING

South Shire Inn, 124 Elm St. Bennington, VT 05201 (☎ 802/447-3839), is on a quiet residential street, 1 block off Main. It's a handsome Victorian, dating to 1879, with a semicircular front porch. It possesses some handsome interiors, such as the mahogany-paneled sitting room with its mahogany lead-glass bookcases and the breakfast room, which has much intricate molding. There are nine rooms, five in the main house and four in the carriage house. All have telephones; some have fireplaces and charming window seats. Each is decorated differently. The Peach Room, for example, has a cottage-style carved bed in contrast to the Gold Room, where a handsome rice four-poster is the main feature. All four rooms in the Carriage House have Jacuzzi and fireplace and are furnished with four-posters, armoires, and other antique reproductions. The Sleigh Suite has a pine sleigh bed and side tables, plus a pine desk and dresser and a chaise longue all set under a cathedral ceiling with skylight. Breakfast is served at separate tables and will likely bring fresh fruit, muffins, and such entrees as apple sesame pancakes, eggs Benedict, and waffles. *Rates:* In season, $105 to $160; foliage season, $125 to $175; off-season, $90 to $140.

Molly Stark Inn, 1067 E. Main St., Bennington, VT 05201 (☎ 802/442-9631), occupies an 1890 Queen Anne–style Victorian with wraparound porch set on 1 carefully tended acre. Six rooms are available, decorated in country style with quilts and oak pieces, and claw-foot tubs in the bathroom. The most private accommodation is in the guest cottage, which contains a brass bed set in the loft, Jacuzzi, wet bar, woodstove, and many other creature comforts. Guests also may use the den and parlor, which is warmed in winter with a wood-burning stove. A hearty breakfast is served. *Rates:* $75 to $100 double, cottage $150.

The **Brasserie,** in Potter's Yard, 325 County St., Bennington (☎ 802/447-7922), has pleasant outdoor dining in summer and is a fine lunch or dinner spot year-round. At lunch, have the Yard Special, a platter of Danish pâté, French bread and butter, and a Boston lettuce salad. Or you can choose from a variety of salads, omelets, and sandwiches under $9. At dinner it's candlelit for romance, and the short menu proffers a spicy seafood puttanesca made with scallops, shrimp, clams, and halibut in broth spiced with tomatoes, olives, capers, and anchovies, along with lamb chops with an apple mint chutney, or steak au poivre. Prices range from $15 to $18. Turn off Main Street at Dunkin Donuts (at 460 Main). *Hours:* Summer, daily 11:30am to 8pm; winter, Sunday to Thursday 11:30am to 3pm.

Alldays & Onions, 519 Main St. (☎ 802/447-0043), is a casual place with plain wood tables and chairs. It's the place to come for breakfast or lunch. You can create your own sandwich using a variety of great fresh breads—pumpernickel, marble, sourdough—and assorted fillings that include corned beef and pastrami. In addition, there are soups, salads, quiches, and vegetarian specialties. At dinner the room takes on a more intimate ambience with candles and cloths on the tables. The food is well prepared and very reasonably priced. About ten entrees are offered, always including a fish, pasta, and beef or game dish of the evening. You might find roasted chicken breast with lingonberries or a rack of lamb with honey rosemary sauce. Prices range from $11 to $15. *Hours:* Monday to Saturday 7:30am to 5:30pm, Wednesday to Saturday 6 to 8:30pm.

The Publyck House, Route 7A, Harwood Hill (☎ 802/442-8301), is a remodeled barn that has been given an 18th-century decor and an indoor greenhouse. Good beef and seafood are the staples here, priced from $11 to $16. There might be grilled halibut with an herb butter, salmon with dill-hollandaise, and chicken teriyaki, as well as several steaks and surf-and-turf combinations. *Hours:* Monday to Thursday 5 to 9pm, Friday and Saturday 5 to 10pm, Sunday 4 to 9pm.

ARLINGTON LODGING & DINING

The **West Mountain Inn,** half a mile west of Arlington on Route 313, Arlington, VT 05250 (☎ 802/375-6516), is one of my favorite retreats for several reasons, but primarily for the spirit and character of its owners, Wesley and Mary Ann Carlson. Both love animals and tend to a menagerie of Netherland dwarf lop-eared rabbits, goats, and several llamas. The inn's 150-acre setting is lovely. Cornflowers, irises, and other flowers bloom. The house looks out onto Red Mountain, and the grounds are filled with hemlocks, pine, and maple. To get there, you'll have to cross the Battenkill and take a dirt road to the top of a hill. There are 14 rooms, plus a special one—as caring individuals, Mary Ann and Wesley have created on the ground floor Gwendolyn's Room, a really accessible room for persons with disabilities. Light switches and the bars in the closet are placed low; the bathroom is fully equipped, even with an open-style shower to accommodate a wheelchair. The room itself, with a brick fireplace, is one of the nicest. Each room is named after a favorite historical figure. The Robert Todd Lincoln Room has a carved oak, lace-canopied bed covered with a hand-loomed 1830 quilt—"snowflakes on evergreen," a special Vermont pattern. In the Daniel Webster Suite there are sleigh beds; Grandma Moses's small, pale-blue room has a fireplace, rocker, and, of course, her farm scenes; the Robert Frost Room has its own porch with wicker chairs overlooking the llama pasture; the Carl Ruggles Room, with fireplace and deck, features a carved high-backed oak bed, Stickley couch, and rope rug. The largest room of all is the Rockwell Kent Suite. It has a native-pine cathedral ceiling and loft bed, brick fireplace, a Native American rug as a wall hanging, and an eclectic mix of pine and Victorian furnishings. There are still other accommodations, including a Booker T. Washington Room with original pine paneling. In addition there are three millhouse suites with living room, kitchen, two bedrooms, and bath. Two have wood-burning stoves.

The dining room is basically for inn guests, who receive a six-course dinner that changes daily. It might feature veal Marsala and a chicken and a shrimp dish. The fireplace makes it cozy in winter, and the orchids and other plants give it a homey feel. Adjacent, there's a bar with Windsor-style bar stools and, oddly enough, a tank full of exotic tropical fish and plenty of books and magazines. Other popular gathering spots for guests are the games room, equipped with cribbage, backgammon, and other games; and the sitting room, warmed by a Franklin stove and offering plenty of couches, armchairs, and a piano for guests to entertain each other. In summer the enclosed flagstone porch set with cushioned bamboo chairs is a favorite lounging spot. At breakfast, eggs Benedict, omelets, and vanilla crêpes with butterscotch sauce are all likely choices.

Rates: Fall, $182 to $254 double; winter, $162 to $194 double; summer, $186 to $234 double; spring, $176 to $234 double. Mid-March to mid-June, special midweek rate $155 double.

Occupying a cream-colored Greek Revival building with rust-colored shutters, the **Arlington Inn,** Route 7A, Arlington, VT 05250 (☎ 802/375-6532), stands behind a row of stately maple trees. A marble path fringed with flowers and ferns leads to the central portico. Inside, the hallway, handsomely furnished with oriental carpet, carved Chippendales, and color engravings of London scenes dating back to 1848, is a refreshing change from colonial New England.

It's both an inn and a restaurant. In the main dining room, tables are elegantly covered in white and set with crystal candlesticks and gilt-rimmed china. There's a faintly Empire-style ambience created by a couple of classical urns and an ornate clock that stands on the fireplace mantel. A meal here might start with a strudel of pheasant in a cream sauce with sun-dried cranberries, or sauté of Maine crab cake with cilantro, orange, and green peppercorn beurre blanc. Among the main courses, priced from $17 to $22, might be pan-roasted breast of duck with port and currant game sauce or rack of lamb with garlic and cumin red wine sauce. A lighter menu is offered in the tavern. Breakfast offers eggs, bagels, omelets, and pancakes. If you have to wait for your table, relax in the Sylvester Deming Tavern while a pianist entertains (Friday and Saturday only) in this cozy, forest-green tavern decorated with stoneware and hunting prints. Don't miss the two huge (you'll see what I mean) Canadian rawhide rockers on the adjacent porch. There's also a greenhouse dining room that looks very summery with its green, peach, and pink color scheme and marble floor.

The accommodations are variously decorated in a 19th-century style; some have fireplaces. For example, the Pamela Suite features flounce pillow cases, valanced windows, a Mme Récamier sofa, and a marble Victorian dresser in one room. The Martin Chester Room contains a broken-scroll bed, needlepoint side chairs, camelback sofa, an armoire, a carved wood table, orange-and-green macaw and bird of paradise wallpaper, and a huge sideboard with turnip feet. The tongue-and-groove ceiling makes it very cozy and unusual. Some of the rooms are tucked under the eaves. Many of the bathrooms have claw-foot tubs; quilts, Victorian prints, and period pieces like a spinning wheel are found throughout the rooms. Guests have the use of the parlor (furnished Stickley-style), which is most comfortable in winter when the fire is lit. Active folks will like the tennis court out back.

Rates (including breakfast): July 1 to September 15, $90 to $170; September 16 to October 31, $100 to $195; November 1 to June 30, $80 to $160 (the higher price is for fireplace rooms). *Dining hours:* Summer, Tuesday to Sunday 5:30 to 9pm; winter, Tuesday to Saturday 5:30 to 9pm.

The **Inn on Covered Bridge Green**, Road 1, Box 3550, Arlington, VT 05250 (☎ 802/375-9489), has several things going for it. It was the home of Norman Rockwell, and it has a remote, picturesque location on the Battenkill. Views from the front porch are of the covered bridge and a small church etched against the mountains. Granite steps lead up to the entrance of this 1792 house with its historic outdoor brick smokehouse and 5 acres of grounds. There are five rooms in the inn and two cottages in the back, which Rockwell used as studios. Narrow doors lead into the rooms, which are furnished in typical country style with floral patterned wallpapers and braided rugs. The Bicentennial Room, for example, has a maple four-poster, a pine chest, two wicker chairs, and a fireplace. The bathroom has a whirlpool tub. The large studio cottage has two bedrooms and a kitchen and incorporates the room where Rockwell painted. The low-ceilinged parlor is a comfy room where people can browse through the books and maps, look at Rockwell's *Four Freedoms* paintings, or watch the large TV. A breakfast of French toast, eggs baked in tomato, or similar dishes is served at a communal table. Facilities include a tennis court. *Rates:* $120 to $155.

Bennington & Arlington
Special & Recreational Activities

Boating: Rental boats are available in **Woodford State Park,** east of Bennington on Route 9.

Canoeing: Battenkill Canoe, Box 65, Arlington on River Road (leading to West Arlington), off Route 313 (☎ 802/362-2800), will rent a canoe for $44 a day and pick you up at the end of the trip. They also offer interpretive nature trips on the river and guided day trips, plus many other longer trips in the Northeast and also father afield in places like Costa Rica.

Cross-Country Skiing: Prospect Ski Mountain Touring Center, Woodford, near Bennington, VT 05201 (☎ 802/442-2575), has 40km of trails.

Fishing: Woodford State Park has some great trout fishing.

Golf, Swimming and Tennis: Mount Anthony Country Club, Bank Street below the Battle Monument in Bennington (☎ 802/442-2617).

Horseback Riding: Valley View Horse and Tack Shop, Box 48A, Northwest Hill Road, Pownal, VT 05261 (☎ 802/823-4649), offers trail rides and such specialty rides as Haunted Halloween rides. Take Route 346 off Route 7.

THE MANCHESTER-DORSET VALLEY

A beautiful area bordered on each side by mountains and cut through by the famous Battenkill River, the region has much to offer visitors. **Manchester Village** has always attracted visitors—often wealthy ones—especially to its grand old hotel, the Equinox. People came in the mid–19th century to take Dr. Sprague's famous water cure, a phenomenon that hotel owner Frank Orvis capitalized on when he advertised that he had piped the precious water from the mountain and bottled it. (His ads appeared briefly in subway cars and on buses in New York City until a federal agency intervened.) Today people come to the area for various reasons: to attend events held at the Hildene Meadowlands and at the Southern Vermont Arts Center; to climb Mount Equinox; and to fish, cycle, ski, canoe, or just plain relax. The current winning pastime seems to be shopping the 125-plus outlets in and around Manchester.

Just 6 miles up Route 30, **Dorset** is a far more somnolent but well-endowed village that boasts the Dorset Playhouse (☎ 802/867-2223), where the **Dorset Theatre Festival** takes place from mid-June through Labor Day. Beyond are two villages that are much rougher around the edges—Pawlet and Danby, both of which have some appealing, worthwhile surprises.

MANCHESTER & DORSET AREA ATTRACTIONS

The prime sightseeing destination in the valley is **Hildene,** off Route 7A 2 miles south of Route 30 (☎ 802/362-1788), which was the home of Robert Todd Lincoln, the eldest son of Abraham Lincoln, who first discovered

Vermont in 1863 when he was brought by his mother to the Equinox House on a summer retreat. A visit begins in the carriage house, where a video show records the highlights of Robert Todd Lincoln's life—his birth in August 1843; his army service (he was present at Appomattox); his years as a partner in the Chicago law firm of Isham and Lincoln; and his appointments as secretary of war under President Garfield, as minister to the Court of St. James under President Harrison, and later as chairman of the board of the Pullman Palace Car Company; and finally his 1902 purchase of the 500 acres on which he built his Georgian Revival home overlooking the Battenkill Valley.

Hildene means "hill" and "valley." During Robert Lincoln's working and retirement years he and his family summered here. He was involved in local affairs until he died at Hildene in 1926. His widow summered at Hildene until her death in 1937. Later, it was occupied by various family members, including Robert Lincoln's granddaughter, Mary Lincoln Beckwith, until her death in 1975. Peggy Beckwith was a fascinating, outspoken woman who flew her own biplane, painted, sculpted, studied piano and guitar, and tried to operate the property as a working farm.

On the house tour you can view the room where Robert Todd died and his office, containing one of Abe Lincoln's stovepipe hats and all of the original furnishings. The original rolls are also played for visitors on the 1908 Aeolian player pipe organ. In the toy room, note the screen depicting fairy tales that Robert Todd Lincoln commissioned for his grandchildren, and be sure to go down to the garden terrace for the view of the Green Mountains on one side and the Taconics on the other. The restored formal garden, designed after a stained-glass window, contains 25 varieties of peonies (the best time to visit is in mid-June, when they're blooming). Stroll the nature trails, enjoy a picnic, or visit the kitchen/cutting garden as it is being restored.

Hours: Mid-May through October, daily 9:30am to 5:30pm (last tour begins at 4pm). *Admission:* $7.

Don't miss driving up **Mount Equinox Sky Line Drive** (☎ 802/362-1114) for the glorious views of the valley and the Green Mountains. Ekwanok means "where the top is," and quite a top it is, 3,816 feet in the air. It's said that Ethan Allan lived on the eastern slope, and it's believed that the settlers who lived on the southern and northern slopes built logging roads and climbed to Lookout Rock, where they carved their names. Frank Orvis built the first 4-mile-long wagon road in 1860 from Beartown Gap to Lookout Rock. There's a hotel on the summit, and a bar-restaurant that was built by Dr. J. G. Davidson, an organic chemist who founded Union Carbide and who was also an enthusiastic hiker. He acquired 8,000 acres here in 1939; when he and later his wife died, it was left to the Carthusian monastery located on the mountainside so that the whole mountain might be preserved for the public's enjoyment. It costs $6 per car and driver and $2 for each additional passenger, $1 for children ages 6 to 12.

The **Southern Vermont Art Center**, West Road, off Route 7A (P.O. Box 617), Manchester, NH 05254 (☎ 802/362-1405), is worth a visit for its setting alone. Here against a woods-and-meadow backdrop a Festival of the Arts is celebrated from early June to mid-October on the slopes of Mount Equinox. Paintings, sculpture, and photographs are displayed, and music, dance, and vocal performances given in the performance barn. *Hours:* Galleries and gardens are open in summer, Tuesday to Saturday 10am to 5pm, Sunday noon to 5pm; in winter, Monday to Saturday 10am to 4pm. Closed after Columbus Day to early December.

Even nonanglers and those who've only read Izaak Walton on fishing might find the **American Museum of Fly Fishing,** Route 7A at Seminary Avenue in Manchester (☎ 802/362-3300), interesting. Tying a fly to lure a fish is a very delicate art indeed, and an exotically colorful one. The traditional feathers used in Atlantic salmon flies, for example, include peacock, kingfisher, jay, heron, and macaw. Artificial flies are created in thousands of patterns that range from literal to impressionistic and gaudy in style. Here, the works of great fly tiers are displayed. The museum also shows 18th- and 19th-century fly rods, some 20 feet long, the earlier ones made from ash, hickory, lance-wood, and greenheart, and the later (mid–19th century and later) from bamboo. Today, of course, fiberglass, graphite, and boron are used, and these, too, are displayed. Exhibits also include the fly-fishing tackle of many famous Americans: Winslow Homer, Arnold Gingrich (founder of *Esquire* magazine), Dwight Eisenhower, Daniel Webster, and Ernest Hemingway. *Hours:* Daily 10am to 4pm. *Admission:* $3, free for students.

If you want to learn to fish yourself, contact the **Orvis Fly Fishing School** (☎ 800/548-9548), near Manchester, open April to October. A 2-day course will cost anywhere from $450 to $475 per person and will teach you the intricacies of tying flies, casting, and all the other skills of the sport. They offer a variety of packages including one for a parent and child and another for women only. Orvis also operates a shooting/hunting school. It's also fun to drop in and browse among the hunting and fishing gear at the **Orvis Company store** (☎ 802/362-3750) on Route 7. *Hours:* Daily 9am to 6pm.

SHOPPING IN THE AREA

Manchester Area   Many people come to Manchester just to shop the outlets. Along Route 7 you'll find several, including such famous brand names as Anne Klein, Bass, and Van Heusen. There are in fact about 125 such stores in the area—Cole Haan, Ralph Lauren, Liz Claiborne, Brooks Brothers, Giorgio Armani, and many more. Dexter Shoes (☎ 802/362-4810) is at routes 11 and 30, and the Hathaway Outlet (☎ 802/864-4828) is located in the Equinox Shops.

Stock up, too, on Vermont specialties—ham, cheese, and maple syrup—at **Harrington's** (☎ 802/362-2070) at the junction of routes 7, 11, and 30 (open daily 9am to 5pm). On Route 7A, **Coffee, Tea and Spice** has a wide selection of gourmet items. At **Mother Myrick's Confectionary and Ice Cream Parlor,** stop by to savor ice cream or fantastic pastries and cakes that you can enjoy out on the awning-shaded deck. The **Jelly Mill,** on Route 7A (☎ 802/362-3494), shelters a number of stores offering everything from handmade lamps to gourmet cookware, crafts, and foodstuffs (open daily 9am to 6pm). The **Woodcarver** is special here. The town also possesses two terrific bookstores—**Johnny Appleseed Bookshop** (☎ 802/362-2458) and the **Northshire Bookstore** (☎ 802/362-2200), both on Route 7A.

North on Route 7, the **Enchanted Doll House** (☎ 802/362-1327) welcomes all ages to its 12-room toy shop featuring all kinds of dolls, miniatures, stuffed animals, books, games, and creative toys. Open daily 9am to 5:30pm.

Dorset   In Dorset, on Route 30, the **J. K. Adams Company Factory Store** (☎ 802/362-2303) stocks a whole line of gourmet woodware—spice racks, knife racks, butcher block, and other home accessories (open daily 9am to 5:30pm). Dorset also has a very atmospheric country store called **Pelletiers Market**, where you can pick up a picnic lunch.

Pawlet   From Dorset you can continue up Route 30 to the less touristy and more authentic small village of Pawlet. Several interesting workshops, studios, and stores have been opened here. On School Street, stop into the potter **Marion Waldo McChesney studio** (☎ 802/325-3039) to see her whimsical ceramics that include a series of raku pieces that she calls "Roadkill," plus some lovely floaters and organic art nouveau–style polished ceramic sculptures. Across the street **Judy Sawyer Lake** (☎ 802/325-6308) makes lampshades using wallpapers with such fun motifs as sunflowers, cats, fish, and ladybugs as well as the more traditional cut-out-style shades, too. Don't miss stopping into **Mach's Market** (☎ 902/325-6113), where you can see the "river in the box."

Other artists working in the area who are worth stopping to see are **Rosalind Compain** (☎ 802/325-3231), who creates contemporary stone sculpture, and **Roy Egg**, who paints wild and whimsical canvases. Also contact the **Jay H. Connaway Studio** (☎ 802/325-3107) if you appreciate marine paintings created by this contemporary of Winslow Homer. By appointment only.

Danby   From Pawlet you can take Route 133 to Danby and then turn south back to Manchester. Danby is also sprucing up, and there are some artisans and galleries to visit here, too. **The Peel Gallery** (☎ 802/293-5230) on Route 7, 2 miles north of Danby, represents 50 artists and has launched some—Martin Carey, Betty Ann MacDonald, Yale Epstein—onto national recognition tracks. The gallery represents artists only on an exclusive in Vermont basis, and it's a great spot to capture the cultural pulse and just to browse even if you don't buy. Prices range from $35 to $30,000. Also in Danby **Robert Gasperetti** makes Shaker- and Craftsman-inspired furniture (☎ 802/293-5195); and the **Danby Marble Company**, Route 7 (☎ 802/293-5425), offers high-quality marble items from bookends to candlesticks, soap holders, and wine coolers.

AREA SKI RESORTS

Six miles east of Manchester, **Bromley Mountain**, Ski Resort, Route 11 (☎ 802/824-5522), offers winter skiing and summer fun, too, when you can fly down the Alpine Slide or the DeValkart dirt track, which you descend in a go-kart. Single rides on the Alpine Slide are $5.50 for adults and $4.50 children ages 7 to 12; $15 and $12, respectively, for three rides; $23 and $18 for five rides; and $42 and $33 for 10 rides. The go-kart ride is $6 single and $16 for three rides. The slides are open weekends only from late May to mid-June and then daily through early October. You can also take the chairlift to the summit for $5.50 and $4.50 children ages 7 to 12.

Before you reach Bromley there's a turnoff at Route 30 that will take you to the major ski resort of **Stratton**, Stratton Mountain, VT 05155 (☎ 800/ STRATTON or 802/297-2200). Even if you're not a skier, you may want to visit this resort that has been built to resemble a Tyrolean village and manages to achieve a charm in winter that almost makes you believe you're in the Tyrol.

Stratton is a full facility resort complete with a sports center that also offers tennis, badminton, swimming, and more. Accommodations include the Stratton Mountain Inn, Stratton Village Lodge, and Stratton Mountain Village as well as Liftline Lodge and the Birkenhaus. For reservations call ☎ 800/787-2886. There are plenty of shops and restaurants for browsing, and in summer it's fun to take the gondola up the mountain (open 9:30am to 4pm, $10 per ride). To get there, from Manchester take Route 11 east, and then Route 30 south to Bondville. The entrance to Stratton is located in the village center. Follow the Stratton Mountain Road for 4 miles.

MANCHESTER LODGING & DINING

Antiques lovers will adore the **1811 House,** Route 7A, Manchester Village, VT 05254 (☎ 802/362-1811), a salmon-and-beige clapboard structure situated in the center of Manchester. It was, in fact, built as a farmhouse in the 1770s. In 1811 the roof was raised and it was turned into a tavern. Later, Charles Isham and his wife, Mary Lincoln (President Lincoln's granddaughter), resided here until she died in 1939. Today it is run by Marnie and Bruce Duff, who both have Scottish ancestry.

The 14 rooms, all with private baths, are exquisitely furnished. The Robert Todd Lincoln Room contains a canopied pencil four-poster with a candlewick bedspread and a Federal-style slate-blue mantel and fireplace; chintz curtains hang at the pelmeted windows. Most of the rooms have desks, and all have comfy chairs for reading, plus such extra touches as clocks, makeup mirrors, and nightlights. In each, you'll find a personal touch—for example, in the Grace Hoyt Singer Room, a cross-stitched rug, a small glass case filled with china cats and birds, and a handsome porcelain figure on the chest of drawers; or the framed pressed flowers in the Franklin Orvis Room. The Henry Ethel Robinson Room possesses a great bathroom containing a claw-foot tub with a sunflower-size, old-fashioned shower-head. The Robinson room has a private balcony with a glorious view of the mountains. In the Hidden Room the 12-over-12 windows are original; so, too, are the beams in the Burr Room.

The tavern is very authentic. Pewter mugs hang from the old beams, horse brasses adorn the fireplace and bar, brass candlesticks stand on tables smoothed by long use, and Windsor chairs and barstools complete the scene. Guests can make a selection from a superb collection of 50 single-malt whiskies, including some very rare ones, and enjoy it in a crystal glass. A breakfast of fresh fruit, breads, and an entree like French toast with Canadian bacon or eggs Benedict, is elegantly served at the Duncan Phyfe table, set with fine silver and china. For relaxing, there are two homey sitting rooms. One has book-filled, built-in bookcases, a wooden chess set, and a TV for guests' pleasure. The basement also contains a games room with table tennis and a billiards table. The gardens (7 acres) are lovely and have been landscaped with a pond. In spring they burst into full color with flowering trees and azaleas, and later with lilacs, peonies, and perennial plants. From the lawn the view extends across the Equinox golf course to the Green Mountains beyond.

Rates (including breakfast): $180 to $230 double.

The owners of the **Inn at Manchester,** Route 7A (P.O. Box 41), Manchester, VT 05254 (☎ 802/362-1793), go out of their way to welcome their guests and inform them about the area. The 1880 house has 14 rooms and 4 suites. The Primrose Suite has a spacious bedroom furnished with a maple bed and a separate sitting room with a working fireplace. The Woodlilly Suite is dramatically decorated in Chinese red and features an iron-and-brass bed. The Garden Suite, furnished with country pine and oak, pretty comforters, frilled curtains, and chintz wallpaper, has a wood-burning fireplace.

There are also four rooms in the carriage house that offer mountain and meadow views. Columbine has a handsome carved-cherry bed with a Ralph Lauren blue and white comforter and matching drapes at the windows. The antique Tiffany-style floor lamp and a beautifully carved lion's-head chair immediately catch the eye. These rooms are large and will likely contain a brass bed, bold chintz wallpaper, Victorian-style mahogany chests, cherry side tables, and wing chairs.

The full country breakfasts are delicious. Stanley and Harriet whip up great apple-buttermilk pancakes with Vermont maple syrup, omelets, and homemade granola. Afternoon tea is also served.

Rates: $100 to $150 except foliage season and holidays, when rates are $120 to $175.

From the road you can't help noticing the celery-and-mauve splash of color from the hanging flower baskets that adorn the front porch of the **Village Country Inn**, Route 7A, Manchester, VT 05254 (☎ 802/362-1792). It's run by Anne and Jay Degen. Anne is the one who has the natural flair for interior decoration, amply demonstrated throughout the 1889 house. As a child she built her own dollhouses, making the furniture and picking out the fabrics; here she has created a magical romantic retreat filled with flowers and lace. Celery and mauve are the predominant colors in the large front parlor area, which offers an array of seating arrangements—a corner furnished with Stickley, a high-backed Victorian love seat, and a mauve camelback sofa—all set around a fieldstone fireplace in a room accented with a gilt mirror and a stained-glass door.

The 31 accommodations, all with private baths, are highly individual. Room 111 is large and features a carved-oak bed set under a tented effect of cream lace, a wicker chaise longue, oak dresser, lace-draped table, bold chintz wallpaper, and inviting window seats. Room 107 is a small country space furnished primarily with oak pieces. Other rooms might have a Laura Ashley decor, or a gray and lavender color scheme with a lacy swag above the bed. There are also a couple of garden rooms in the back by the pool. All rooms have fluffy towels and pretty eyelet linens.

In the dining room the lattice trellises, floral-green wallpaper, and pink and forest-green napery create a romantic, gardenlike effect. Even the fireplace is mauve. The menu is continental and changes seasonally. You may find medallions of veal with wild mushrooms, shallots, and Madeira; fish of the day grilled with oil, oregano, garlic, and lemon; breast of chicken sautéed with shiitake mushrooms, garlic, parsley, and lemon; or charcoal-broiled venison with caramelized onions and red wine sauce. To start, there might be roasted onion tart with Merlot-thyme sauce or a trio of smoked seafood with lemon-chive-horseradish sauce; and, to finish, a crème brûlée or pears poached in red wine. Prices run $16 to $24. A pianist entertains softly at the grand piano. There's also a comfortable tavern that opens onto a summer patio furnished with wrought-iron, celery-colored furniture set among fountains and flowers.

The gardens are brimming in spring with pink mountain laurel, golden coreopsis, and white Virginia spiderwort; the flowers make the outdoor pool an even more inviting place to relax. Anne also offers different weekend packages—including one called "A Blooming Affair," which includes a champagne picnic delivered to the garden's gazebo at a prearranged hour. Always inquire about her latest idea.

Rates: Summer/fall, MAP $150 to $285 double. Special rates apply in April, May, and November. No children.

You can't miss the purple-and-cream clapboard building that's called **The Reluctant Panther Inn,** Route 7A (P.O. Box 678), Manchester Village, VT 05254 (☎ 802/362-2568), known for its fine restaurant as well as its accommodations. The Greenhouse dining room seats 60 in a highly colorful, almost tropically inspired setting of plants, flagstone floor, and brilliant orange, yellow, and peach napery. The stone fireplace makes it cozy in winter, and in summer the marble terrace dotted with flowers, plants, silver birches, and stone ornaments with a view of Equinox Mountain makes a lovely spot for cocktails. Or you can enjoy drinks in the unusual bar. Green-leather low chairs on casters are set at Vermont marble tables; ceiling, paneling, and shutters are a brilliant purple; and in one corner a full bear trophy, teeth bared, stands ready to party, no matter what. A fire adds warmth in winter.

The menu, which changes daily, will offer a dozen or so entrees. Seafood is finely prepared—grilled or poached salmon with orange butter sauce or grilled trout finished with lemon, parsley, and almonds—and so are meat dishes such as flank steak marinated in dark beer and honey reduction or pan-seared duck breast with raspberry demi-glace. Prices range from $21 to $27. Among the appetizers try the raclette, a Swiss specialty of melted cheese, boiled potatoes, and pickles, or the delicious PEI mussels steamed with white wine and saffron.

There are 12 rooms in the main house, all with private bath, air-conditioning, color TV, and phone; 6 have working fireplaces. Each is dramatically and differently decorated. Half a bottle of wine is placed in each room for guests. The wallpapers are quite extraordinary: mushroom in Room A, purple poppies in Room C, Queen Anne's lace in Room E, for example. Room G is exceptionally attractive: Eyelet pillows grace the bed, which is covered with a light-purple comforter and adorned by a draped lace curtain effect. A fireplace, a dusky-rose carpet, marble-top table, and a bathroom with claw-foot tub and pedestal sink complete the effect. Room J is exceptionally large and possesses a Victorian oak bed and furniture in a matching style, while Room L contains a cherry Stickley bed, carved-oak Victorian chair, a chestnut armoire, and a black-walnut chest of drawers. There are also four suites in the adjacent Mary Porter House, which have whirlpools, fireplaces, and four-poster beds.

Rates: Summer/fall, MAP weekends $210 to $360; midweek $180 to $310; foliage (mid-September to late October) $245 to $385; winter/spring, MAP weekends $210 to $390; B&B only, midweek $120 to $290; MAP holidays $265 to $405. *Dining hours:* Daily 6 to 9pm; winter, Thursday to Monday 6 to 9pm.

The famous old resort, the **Equinox,** Route 7A, Manchester Village, VT 05254 (☎ 802/362-4700), once welcomed Mary Todd Lincoln and other dignitaries in its heyday. It has been restored to its former glory in partnership with the Guinness family. Although on the site of a prerevolutionary tavern, its life as a fashionable summer resort was really begun by the Orvis family in 1854. Behind the facade, with its stately columns and veranda stretching a full block along the marble sidewalk, you'll find a small lobby and a tavern/ restaurant.

Each of the 183 rooms has air-conditioning, TV, and telephone, and has been decorated in a light modern style using bleached pine, Audubon prints, and richly textured fabrics. The most luxurious rooms are located down the street in the Charles Orvis Inn, which dates to 1812, and was owned by Charles Orvis himself. It contains six two-bedroom and three one-bedroom suites. Each features a marble bathroom with Jacuzzi, cherry-paneled kitchen, and a handsome sitting and living room with gas fireplace. Amenities include CD/stereo, TV, and telephone. In true club style there's a bar and a luxurious billiards room for guests.

The most impressive public space is the main dining room, the Colonnade. Designed in 1913, this domed room with a semicircular series of Palladian windows provides splendid mountain views. The menu features about six expertly prepared entrees—poached lobster and mussels with saffron basil risotto; medallion of hickory-smoked beef tenderloin with Cabernet demi-glace; veal loin medallions with crabmeat custard, asparagus, fresh morels, and a cognac demi-glace. Prices range from $21 to $25. The Marsh Tavern is authentic and original dating back to 1769. Today it's furnished with Windsor chairs and polished wood tables and is open for breakfast, lunch, and dinner. The menu offers a variety of dishes like Yankee pot roast, shepherd's pie, and pan-seared trout in a Dijonnaise sauce. Prices range from $9 to $20.

What sets the inn apart from many other resorts is its British School of Falconry and its Land Rover Driving School. At the first you can don a glove and learn how to hunt with a magnificent Harris hawk; the second teaches you how to handle this beguiling vehicle over all kinds of terrain and under all conditions. Other facilities on the 1,100-acre property include two swimming pools (indoor/outdoor), three clay tennis courts, a fitness center and spa (with massages, wraps, and scrubs available), and the Gleneagles Golf Course, a recent update by Rees Jones of the original 1927 Walter Travis course.

You can dine at the Dormy Grill at the clubhouse, or outside under an awning and enjoy the glorious view. In winter there are 35km of cross-country ski trails, plus ice skating and snowshoeing, rentals available. Services include concierge, valet, and room service. While you're here you can also stroll across and down the street to the Equinox shops.

Rates: $179 to $319, suites from $479, Charles Orvis rooms $679 to $939. Special packages available. *Dining hours:* Tavern, daily 7am to 9:30pm; Colonnade, June to October, daily 6 to 9pm, November to May, Friday and Saturday 6 to 9:30pm.

The Inn at Ormsby Hill, R.R.2, Box 3264, Manchester Center, VT 05255 (☎ 802/362-1163), is a restored manor house standing on 2½ acres of landscaped grounds with lovely mountain views. Legend has it that Ethan Allen took refuge here from the English, and the innkeepers will happily show you the secret room in which he is said to have hidden. Spectacular hand-carved staircases and woodwork and other handsome architectural elements are found throughout the house, part of which dates back to 1764. The remainder was added in the 1800s by Isaac Isham. Guests enjoy two comfortable sitting rooms, both decorated in warm style using damask wallpapers and rich fabrics and rugs. There's also a splendid flagstone terrace with glorious mountain views. The ten rooms are all luxuriously decorated with antiques and original artwork. Nine have fireplaces and heart-shaped Jacuzzis. The Library Room has built-in bookcases with decorative dental molding and offers a rice four-poster; beamed tongue-and-groove ceilings add an extra glow. The other furnishings consist of an armoire, a rocker and wing chairs, and an old steamer trunk. Frances has the best view and is also elegantly decorated with a toile wallpaper and furnished with a richly upholstered chaise longue, love seat, and a burled maple chest. The Ethan Allen has a private entrance and sports a beautiful carved mahogany four-poster. In this accommodation one can sit in the Jacuzzi and enjoy the glow of the gas fireplace. The large size, jade-and-lemon decor, and the daylight brilliance of the dining room/conservatory will beguile you and so will the view beyond of Hildene and the Green Mountains. An excellent breakfast is served here with such relishing items as white-chocolate pound cake, bananas with cream and almonds, and bread-and-butter pudding with fresh fruit. On Friday evening a casual supper is served (linguine with shrimp and vegetables, say), but on Saturday there's a four-course, single-entree dinner. It might begin with a leek, bacon, and Stilton polenta with tomato sauce; continue with a tenderloin of pork with port and dried cranberries; and finish with a triple chocolate torte with white-chocolate sauce. The supper is $20 for two; the dinner $65 for two. Afternoon tea is also served. Delicious cookies are provided in the room, along with terry-cloth robes and turndown service. Guests also have access to a treasure chest of such amenities as toothpaste and other items that they might have forgotten to bring. The innkeepers pamper guests in every way possible. *Rates:* $125 to $245.

The **Seth Warner Inn**, Route 7A, P.O. Box 281, Manchester, VT 05255 (☎ 802/362-3830), is a more modest accommodation, but is very well kept and operated by a warm and welcoming host. It's set on 4 acres and has a lovely pond with resident ducks plus inviting gardens and lawns furnished with Adirondack chairs. All five rooms are attractively decorated with stenciling and braided rugs and are furnished with oak and wicker country pieces. The Seth Warner room has a four-poster with a crochet canopy, made up with a star quilt. Breakfast is served by candlelight at separate tables. It might be delicious, German-style pancakes or baked eggs. Chinese rugs and a sofa and wing chairs clustered around the mantel await in the sitting room, which has a small TV. Guests can play chess in the library nook. Afternoon tea and wine are served. This has to be one of the best values in the valley. *Rates:* Summer, $100; fall, $110; off-season, $95.

The **Equinox Mountain Inn**, Skyline Drive (☎ 802/362-1113), is the place to stay if you want the thrill of being at the summit of a mountain with glorious views. It's a great place for stargazing, and on clear nights owner Tim Cunningham takes a star finder down into the parking lot. In spring you might also spot cougar, bobcats, or bears. Don't expect fancy accommodations. The place was built in the 1940s, and the 18 rooms are plain and simple, furnished in maple motel style and equipped with TV. Some have small balconies. A large living room with stone fireplace is where guests gather around the piano or play games. There's also a lounge with the original circular bar and green vinyl stools; it opens at 4pm and folks gather to enjoy the views of Stratton, Bromley, Mount Mansfield, and other peaks. The original Thonnet chairs are still in the dining room, where a fine dinner is served. Among the favorite dishes on the current menu are the Mount Inn duck made with spring onions and ginger, and the veal sweetbreads served with a caper and wine sauce. To start, the duck livers sautéed with caramelized onions, mushrooms, bacon, and a hint of vermouth are something to write home about. A full breakfast of eggs, pancakes, and bacon is served. *Rates*: $100 to $150. *Dining hours*: Mid-May to the last weekend in October.

The **Chantecleer,** Route 7A, Manchester Center (☎ 802/362-1616), is considered the premier local restaurant. The fieldstone fireplace, rafters, and barn siding give a pretty country atmosphere to the room filled with captain's chairs and tables covered in pink cloths. The inspiration is distinctly Swiss. For example, you might find such specialties as veal tenderloin, which has been marinated in truffle oil, roasted, and then sliced and layered with truffle pâté and shallot confit, and finished with a Chardonnay velouté. It's served over wild mushroom mashed potatoes with a drizzle of balsamic-maple reduction. Other dishes are equally inspired and executed in high style, such as the filet mignon Grand Marnier or the superb whole Dover sole served with a choice of classic sauces. Don't overlook the delicious, Swiss-inspired accompaniments, whether it's rösti or spaetzle. Among the appetizers, the trademark dish is the escargots Chantecleer, which is simmered with garlic and wine as usual, but is then glazed with hazelnut-garlic butter with a hint of Pernod. Prices run from $21 to $28. Chantecleer is located about 4 miles north of Manchester on Route 7A. *Hours*: Wednesday to Monday 6 to 9pm, Sunday 11:30am to 2pm (winter only). Closed mid-April to mid-May and mid-November to mid-December.

Mistral's at Tollgate, Tollgate Road (☎ 802/362-1779), is definitely one place to plan for dinner on any weekend. It has a very pretty setting by a stream that you can hear cascading over and around the large boulders. Picture windows look out onto the scene. There are two small dining rooms and a bar with cushioned banquettes. The menu balances meat and fish, and there will likely be a fillet of salmon with black sesame seeds and warm honey-mustard vinaigrette, or roast duckling with Beaujolais wine and Bing cherries. Classic appetizers include a rich French onion soup, escargots bourguignonne, and delicious smoked salmon with blinis and horseradish cream sauce. Prices range from $19 to $26. *Hours*: Thursday to Tuesday 6pm to closing.

Bistro Henry, routes 11/30, Manchester (☎ 802/362-4982), is a fun, up-beat kind of place with a jazzy background. It's light and airy and furnished in a casual, welcoming style with French posters for decoration. Tables are set with white tablecloths. The food is fresh and memorable, and there's a well-rounded list of wines at reasonable prices. The duck prepared with a spiced green peppercorn sauce is a favorite, and so is the grilled orange shrimp sorrentina, flavored with orange, balsamic vinegar, and basil. Other dishes might include a roasted salmon with an almond crust and red pepper sauce, or a grilled veal chop with a flavorsome Pinot Noir sauce accompanied by roasted yams. Prices range from $14 to $19. To finish, there are any number of delights, from the mandarin Napoleon to the crème brûlée and banana strudel. The best of all is the flourless chocolate Chambord cake. *Hours*: Tuesday to Sunday from 6pm and for Sunday brunch from 9am to 1:30pm.

The **Black Swan,** Route 7A, Manchester (☎ 802/362-3807), offers some good country dining in its two small dining rooms, where tables are set with pink undercloths and windows are decorated with chintz fabrics. The cuisine is good. Specials enliven the menu, and you might find such appetizers as oriental spring rolls with plum sauce and grilled portobello mushrooms with onion marmalade or an avocado-and-tomato soup. Much of the fare is New England traditional—roast rack of lamb with mint jelly, apple-glazed pork chop, and fried chicken with pan gravy. Some dishes are more successful than others. In the salmon piccata, the sauce overwhelms the fish. Prices range from $13 to $22. Desserts run to apple pie and raspberry chocolate cheese-cake, which are presented on a tray for your selection. *Hours:* 5 to 8:30 or 9pm depending on the traffic. Closed Wednesday.

The **Perfect Wife**, Route 11/30, Manchester Center (☎ 802/362-2817), offers two dining options. Downstairs there are two dining rooms, one a plant-filled atrium and the other more formal with stone walls that are decorated with original art. In addition there's an upstairs tavern featuring about 50 bottled beers, plus many on tap. Many of the dishes have a mixture of flavors and cuisines. For example, you might find a classic garlic-basted grilled salmon with a tarragon-horseradish mayonnaise alongside a sesame-crusted tuna with a spicy Asian sauce. Or there could be pork chops slathered with barbecue sauce that is made with achiote paste, honey, and dark rum. Prices range from $13 to $17. Appetizers are similarly internationally inspired. The tavern serves a light menu of burgers and sandwiches. *Hours:* Tuesday to Sunday 5 to 10pm; the tavern is open later.

DORSET LODGING & DINING

Standing at the center of a quiet community, the **Dorset Inn**, on the Green, Dorset, VT 05251 (☎ 802/867-5500), is a genuine country inn. Ferns, lupins, and geraniums add a splash of color to the borders by the crazily paved marble paths and steps that lead into the white clapboard building. Operating as an inn since 1796, it has recently been extensively renovated. The upstairs accommodations and decor vary. Room 24 (with private bath) is invitingly arrayed with a brass bed, ruffled curtains, floral wallpaper, comfortable Martha Washingtons, and a chest of drawers. A cannonball-style bed dominates Room 26, while Room 28 offers a four-poster, a Martha Washington chair, and a view of the center Green. Third-floor rooms under the eaves are interestingly and cozily shaped.

Besides the lovely accommodations, the inn has an excellent reputation for its food—and it's well deserved. The same menu is served both in the tavern and the dining room and affords lots of choice—from simple turkey croquettes served with mashed potatoes to crispy duck confit served with plum chutney. Prices range from $10 to $20. Green paint, plank floors, plaid tablecloths, and white shutters provide the country dining atmosphere. The taproom is a cozy supper spot, especially in winter when a fire flickers. A broad selection of beers and a fine selection of wines are offered. Guests can also enjoy the two comfortable, stenciled parlors with fireplace, furnished with thick rugs, books, and such country objects as an old spinning wheel.

Rates: MAP $100 to $150 single, $130 to $235 double. *Dining hours:* Summer, daily 11:30am to 2pm and 5:30 to 9pm; winter, Wednesday to Sunday only.

The **Barrows House**, Dorset, VT 05251 (☎ 800/639-1620 or 802/867-4455), is a large rambling property on 11 acres that still retains a warm country feel. The 28 rooms and suites are dotted around the property in eight buildings as well as in the main house. The grounds are quite beautiful and fragrant, bursting with lupines, irises, cornflowers, tulips, honeysuckle, and lilacs and shaded by hemlocks, weeping willows, and silver birches.

There are eight rooms in the white clapboard, black-shuttered inn, originally built as a parsonage in 1804. Each is decorated in a simple country style with pine or oak furnishings, perhaps a four-poster, slip-covered chairs, and desk. Six similar rooms are in the Hemlock House. The Truffle House contains three double rooms and a large living room with a fireplace. The upstairs suite is attractive, the window seat and canopied four-poster making it especially so. The Schubert House holds one double room and two suites with fireplaces. The Stable suites are pleasantly rustic with plank floors, a pine hutch, and a Windsor chair among the furnishings. Each has a kitchenette and living room with TV. The Carriage House contains ideal accommodations for a family. All the accommodations are attractively furnished and very well kept.

The grounds are beautiful, and the outdoor pool is idyllically situated and surrounded by grass. A sauna is located in the stables, as is the bicycle and cross-country ski shop, at which equipment for both is available for rent. There are also two tennis courts.

In the dining room fresh flowers grace the tables along with atmospheric hurricane lamps. The whole room is fresh and gardenlike, but when you're sitting in the atrium, it's as if you're sitting in a garden. The Tap Room gleams with polished wood and fine books. Here people gather to chat, entertain at the piano, or play backgammon. The food is regional New England. At dinner you might find veal tenderloin with pancetta, tomatoes, and shiitake mushrooms; grilled swordfish on chipotle pepper and roasted corn puree; or rack of lamb with a three-mustard sauce. Among the appetizers don't miss the crab cakes Chesapeake-style. Prices range from $15 to $24.

Rates: MAP $210 to $270 double. B&B rates available. *Dining hours:* Daily 6 to 9pm.

The **Inn at West View Farm**, Route 30, Dorset, VT 05251 (☎ 802/867-5715), has enjoyed a fabled reputation for its Auberge dining room. Here, contemporary American cuisine is offered. Among the appetizers there might be escargots in garlic butter and white wine, baked Brie in phyllo with poached pears and a port sauce, and always a daily appetizer of the day. Among the 10 or so entrees try the sautéed sesame shrimp with sweet red pepper agnolotti, served with a ginger and apricot beurre blanc; the loin of pork served with fresh fruit salsa on wilted scallions and a semisweet puff crouton; or the herb crusted rack of lamb topped with a pear bourbon sauce served with jus. Prices range from $19 to $24. In the tavern you can enjoy such dishes as crab cakes, grilled bratwurst, or marinated rosemary chicken in a spiced tomato herb sauce priced from $10 to $14. For dessert there are homemade sorbets and ice creams, tarts, chocolate mousse, and crème caramel. Tables are arrayed with Villeroy and Boche table settings and hurricane-style lamps. Choice tables are set in the large bay window. If you have to wait, there's a small bar in which you can study the 1920s news photos from the *New York Times* that cover the walls.

There are also ten guest rooms available, all with private baths. The nicest, in my opinion, has a pineapple-style bed covered with a star quilt, a cane-seated rocker, chest, and side table. In the Carriage House the suite has two double rooms, one with a turned four-poster sans canopy.

Rates: MAP $165 to $210 double, B&B $95 to $150 double. *Dining hours:* Tuesday to Sunday 6 to 9pm, Friday and Saturday only in winter. Closed April and November to December 11.

Cornucopia of Dorset, Route 30, Box 307, Dorset, VT 05251 (☎ 802/867-5751), is an attractive bed-and-breakfast that offers guests those extra little services like a champagne welcome, a wake-up tray with coffee or tea and fresh flowers, evening turndown, and a library of VCR movies. There are four rooms, all with private baths, phones, and air-conditioning; plus a cottage suite, which has a skylit loft bedroom, a living room with a cathedral ceiling and fireplace, a fully equipped kitchen, and a private patio. All the rooms have sitting areas, and three have fireplaces. Most have canopied beds covered with down comforters in winter and quilts in summer. The ground floor offers a living room and study, both with fireplaces and a sunroom overlooking the grounds. A full breakfast is served. *Rates:* Weekends $135 to $165, weekdays $125 to $150; cottage weekends $235, weekdays $210.

LODGING & DINING NEAR STRATTON & BROMLEY MOUNTAINS

The **Windham Hill Inn,** West Townshend, VT 05359 (☎ 802/874-4080), takes some finding, but it's worth it for it's set on 150 lovely secluded woodland/mountain acres overlooking Rattle Snake Mountain and offers a peaceful garden filled with irises, roses, poppies, pansies, and a redolent fringe tree. There are 13 guest rooms in the restored 1825 farmhouse, and 8 more in the white barn annex. Each has a private bath and telephone; some have fireplace or stove. Most of the rooms have beds with candlewick spreads, country maple furnishings, and chintz wallpapers. My favorites are in the barn—a real barn that also hosts chamber music concerts. Most rooms here have high beamed ceilings and, best of all, decks that have gorgeous views; some are low-beamed, like Matilda's Room, but still with that glorious view and deck. Three new rooms at the "loft level" have extra-lavish appointments like fireplaces and sunken bathrooms with double soaking tubs or Jacuzzis. The cupola in Marion Goodfellow is a great reading nook.

Guests can choose among three sitting areas, two parlors, and an outside deck. Each has either a fireplace or wood-burning stove. In the small dining room where wall niches hold china displays, a five-course meal is served at oak tables covered with pink tablecloths. It might feature wild mushroom ravioli in a savory forestière bouillon to start, followed by five-onion soup with lentils and a salad of mesclun greens. Among the five or so main courses there might be pan-seared Arctic char served in a light Provençal broth flavored with Pernod, or breast of duck with wild berry-juniper sauce, along with a vegetarian and a pasta dish. Desserts are equally enticing and might bring chocolate–peanut butter mousse torte or an intensely flavored raspberry-cassis sorbet. A full country breakfast is also served.

In summer guests can enjoy swimming in the heated outdoor pool, playing tennis, or hiking the trails that lead to a brook with a swimming hole; in winter, the trails are for cross-country skiing.

Rates: MAP $255 to $335 double; add $50 during foliage season and Christmas week. The higher price is for rooms with whirlpool tub. Loft rooms are MAP $380 double; again add $50 during foliage season and Christmas week.

Manchester-Dorset Area
Special & Recreational Activities

Biking: **Stratton** has a mountain bike park. An all-day pass is $20.

Boating: **Emerald Lake State Park** is on Route 7 (☎ 802/362-1655); **Lake Shaftsbury State Park** is 10 miles north of Bennington (☎ 802/375-9978); the **Hapgood Pond Recreation Area** (☎ 802/362-2307) in Peru is about 6 miles from Manchester.

Camping: **Emerald Lake State Park**, Route 7 (☎ 802/362-1655) has campsites; **Hapgood Pond Recreation Area** in Peru, about 6 miles from Manchester (☎ 802/362-2307), has 28 sites.

Cross-Country Skiing: **Hildene Ski Touring Center** (☎ 802/362-1788) has 30 miles of trails. It's open daily from 9am to dusk if there's sufficient snow (usually from the third week in December to March 1). The **Viking Ski Touring Centre**, R.R.1, Box 70, Little Pond Road, Londonderry, VT 05148 (☎ 802/824-3933), has 25 miles of trails and also offers inn-to-inn tours and guided tours.

Fishing: The **Battenkill** is one of the East's great fishing rivers. See information above for the famous **Orvis Fly Fishing School** (☎ 800/548-9548).

Golf: The **Dorset Field Club** (☎ 802/867-5553) has a course, as does the **Equinox** (see above). The **Stratton Mountain Country Club** hosts the McCall's LPGA Classic Golf Tournament.

Horseback Riding: Stratton offers 1- and 2-hour trail riding at the **Sunday Bowl Ranch** for $30 to $55.

Skiing: **Bromley**, off Route 11 in Bromley, is a full-facility resort offering 39 trails serviced by 9 lifts. Slopeside accommodations are available at Bromley Village. For information call ☎ 802/824-5522 or write to P.O. Box 1130-B, Manchester Center, VT 05255.

    Stratton, Stratton Mountain, VT 05155 (☎ 802/297-2200), has 90 trails on 563 acres, serviced by 12 lifts including one high-speed 12-passenger gondola, one high-speed 6-passenger chair, and 4 quads. For snow conditions call ☎ 800/297-2211.

Swimming: **Emerald Lake State Park**, Route 7 (☎ 802/362-1655) and **Lake Shaftsbury State Park**, 10 miles north of Bennington (☎ 802/375-9978), have beaches. **Hapgood Pond Recreation Area** in Peru, about 6 miles from Manchester (☎ 802/362-2307), has a shallow swimming area.

Tennis: The **Stratton Tennis School**, site of the Acura Women's Tennis tournament during the summer, has 15 Har-Tru and Deco Turf II courts, 4 indoor courts, and 3 racquetball courts, plus other athletic facilities. Special packages including accommodations in a variety of room types are available. Call ☎ 800/787-2886 or 802/297-2200. From Manchester take Route 7 to Route 11 east to Route 30 south to Bondville. From the center of the village follow the Stratton Mountain Road to the resort. Courts are also available at the **Equinox**.

Wilmington, Mount Snow & the Southeast Corner

Brattleboro ◆ *Marlboro* ◆ *Newfane* ◆ *Grafton* ◆ *Chester* ◆
Saxtons River ◆ *Wilmington* ◆ *Mount Snow* ◆ *West Dover*

Distance in miles: Brattleboro, 194; Wilmington, 201; Mount Snow, 213; Newfane, 215; Saxtons River, 227; Grafton, 229

Estimated driving time: 3¾ to 4½ hours

◄○►◄○►◄○►◄○►◄○►

Driving: To Brattleboro take I-95 to I-91 north to Exit 1 or 2.

Train: Amtrak (☎ 800/872-7245) travels from New York to Brattleboro.

Further Information: On Vermont generally: **Vermont Department of Travel and Tourism**, 134 State St., Montpelier, VT 05602 (☎ 802/828-3236); **Vermont State Chamber of Commerce**, P.O. Box 37, Montpelier, VT 05602 (☎ 802/223-3443). For state park camping information: **Department of Forests, Parks and Recreation**, 103 S. Main St. (10 South), Waterbury, VT 05671 (☎ 802/241-3655).

For specific town information: **Brattleboro Chamber of Commerce**, 180 Main St., Brattleboro, VT 05301 (☎ 802/254-4565); **Grafton Information Center**, Grafton, VT 05146 (☎ 802/843-2255); **Chester Chamber of Commerce**, P.O. Box 623, Chester, VT 05143 (☎ 802/875-2939); **Ludlow Area Chamber of Commerce**, P.O. Box 333, Ludlow, VT 05149 (☎ 802/228-5830); **Londonderry Chamber of Commerce**, P.O. Box 58, Londonderry, VT 05148 (☎ 802/824-8178); **Mount Snow Valley Chamber of Commerce**, West Main Street (P.O. Box 3), Wilmington, VT 05363 (☎ 802/464-8092).

◄○►◄○►◄○►◄○►◄○►

This corner of Vermont has much to offer visitors. The major town of Brattleboro is still hip and friendly, a town where the 1960s lingers on in an updated form. Walk the streets and drop into the stores and galleries. Take a look at the restored Latchis Hotel and the movie theater next door—an art deco extravaganza where the ceiling is emblazoned with the zodiac. The town is at the confluence of the West and Connecticut rivers, making it an ideal location for canoeing and other outdoor pursuits.

Events & Festivals to Plan Your Trip Around

February/March: Brattleboro holds a large **carnival** with more than 50 events, including an ice fishing derby and a 70-meter ski jump. Call ☎ 802/254-4565.

March/April: Easter Weekend at Mount Snow, when a sunrise service is held at the summit along with a variety of other events, including parades and egg hunts. For information call ☎ 802/464-3333.

July: Art on the Mountain at Haystack Mountain, which is in its 35th year, displays the works of New England's finest artists and craftspeople. The show includes pottery, glass, quilts, watercolors, photographs, furniture, and jewelry, all of terrific quality. Don't miss it. Usually the third weekend.

July/August: Marlboro Music Festival. Weekend concerts from mid-July through mid-August at Marlboro College's Persons Auditorium. To book tickets call ☎ 802/254-2394 between June 15 and August 15, 215/569-4690 before June 15.

August: Vermont State Zucchini Festival in Ludlow celebrates this humble vegetable with competitions for the largest specimen grown, plus cooking contests, and a hill climb, golf tournament, and other events. Call ☎ 802/228-5830.

Four mountains are within a 45-minute drive—Mount Snow, Okemo, Stratton, and Bromley. The first is a major Vermont mountain, and is blessed with some wonderful inns and bed-and-breakfasts scattered through the Deerfield Valley. The anchor town here is Wilmington, which has been experiencing a minirenaissance in the last few years, sprouting interesting stores and galleries of its own.

Quiet, tiny villages sit in the valleys surrounded by forest—Marlboro, famous for its music festival, Newfane, Grafton, and Chester, each one worth some time, and each possessing some choice places to stay.

BRATTLEBORO & MARLBORO

Brattleboro is an old, historic industrial town, southeastern Vermont's major shopping and service center, and one of the state's larger cities. In its heyday it was full of Yankee vigor and was home to such men as Jacob Estey, who founded an internationally famous company that manufactured parlor organs; Peter Latchis, the movie theater mogul; and Jubilee Jim Fisk, partner of railroad baron Jay Gould, the man who defrauded hundreds of investors in his getrich-quick schemes. Fisk is buried in Brattleboro under a gaudy memorial depicting, among other things, semi-clad beauties clutching and stroking bags and bags of money. This edifice was created by another native son, Larkin

Mead, brother of William Rutherford Mead, a partner in McKim, Mead, and White. The town also went through a period, like Manchester, as a spa or water curing place. This enterprise was begun by a Dr. Wesselhoeft in 1845, who used the waters of the Whetstone Creek to attract many famous clients, including Harriet Beecher Stowe and Henry Wadsworth Longfellow.

Today, thanks to the generation of young urban pioneers who arrived here in the 1970s, Brattleboro has a casual, relaxed air. In fact the town is often referred to as the college town without a college. It's always been a magnet for artists and writers. Rudyard Kipling, who married Carrie Balestier, a Brattleboro girl, in 1892, stayed for a while in Dummeston at Naulakha, where he wrote his *Just So Stories* and *The Jungle Book*. Today there's a large concentration of painters, potters, writers, musicians, sculptors, and performers of all sorts tucked away in the surrounding hills—painters Wolf Kahn and David Utiger, comedy team Gould and Stearns, and many others.

BRATTLEBORO ATTRACTIONS

You can occasionally catch local regional exhibits along with national shows at the **Brattleboro Museum and Art Center**, Old Union Station (☎ 802/257-0124). It also contains a collection of Estey organs. *Hours:* May to November.

Shopping for Arts & Crafts

Other works by local artists can be seen at **Vermont Artisan Designs** at 115 Main St. (☎ 802/257-7044) and at the **Hays Gallery**, 103 Main St. (☎ 802/257-5181). Check out the other galleries and individual stores downtown for antiques, curios, folk art, and the rest.

Outside Brattleboro on the way to Wilmington, book lovers will want to stop at the **Bear Book Shop** off Route 9 (R.D. 4, Box 446), Brattleboro (☎ 802/464-2260), where you'll find 30,000 categorized books housed in a big old barn. The owner, John Greenberg, was at one time a professor of philosophy in Montreal. The store is open by chance or appointment during the warm weather.

Beyond the book barn is one of my favorite craft studios, the **Gallery in the Woods**, Butterfield Road (off Route 9, 1 mile east of Hogback Mountain; ☎ 802/464-5793), which is home to cabinetmaker and wood-carver Saturday Singh and potter Saturday Kaur Khalsa of Hawkwings Pottery. Their furniture is exquisite and the pottery is very original and strikingly glazed. Other artists and sculptors also display their works here. Another studio worth visiting is **Malcolm Wright**, on the Turnpike Road, in Marlboro (☎ 802/254-2168), who crafts wood-fired traditional, Japanese-style pieces.

MARLBORO ATTRACTIONS

Just 9 miles outside of Brattleboro, Marlboro is more a state of mind than an actual place, for when you arrive at the dot on the map you'll find only a church, a post office, a few houses, and an old inn next door to the church. This little village is home to the famous **Marlboro Music Festival**, founded in 1951 by Rudolf Serkin and others. Each summer dozens of the most talented musicians from the United States and abroad gather together for 7 weeks of intensive chamber music study and rehearsal. Weekend concerts are presented from mid-July through mid-August at Marlboro College's Persons Auditorium.

If you wish to attend the concerts, you must book tickets early. Write or call Marlboro Music, Box K, Marlboro, VT 05344 (☎ 802/254-2394 between June 15 and August 15; 215/569-4690 before June 15).

Naturalists will want to stop at the **Southern Vermont Natural History Museum**, Route 9, Marlboro (☎ 802/464-0048), to see the collection of 500 mounted birds arranged in more than 50 dioramas. The museum was started by local taxidermist Luman Ranger Nelson and affords an opportunity to observe species close up. *Hours:* Memorial Day to October 31, daily 9am to 5pm. Admission is $2 for adults, $1 for children under age 18.

While you're in Marlboro, take a drive to the top of Hogback Mountain for the spectacular 100-mile view. The **Skyline Restaurant**, Route 9 (☎ 802/464-5535), is at the summit and makes a great spot for a Vermont breakfast of waffles and real maple syrup. *Hours:* Monday and Tuesday 7:30am to 3pm, until 8 or 9pm on other days.

BRATTLEBORO & MARLBORO LODGING & DINING

You're best bet is to stay outside Brattleboro in Saxtons River, Chester, or Marlboro where you'll find attractive inns. In Brattleboro itself, with one major exception, the options are primarily motels.

If you want to be in town, then the **Latchis Hotel**, 50 Main St., Brattleboro VT 05301 (☎ 802/254-6300), is the place to stay. When it was built in 1938 it was the town's social center, with the largest ballroom in the state, a solarium cocktail lounge, and the Latchis Theatre, an extravagant, art deco movie palace. It's still owned by the Latchis family, and they have restored this historic landmark to its former chrome and terrazzo glory while keeping the original simplicity of the rooms. All have private baths, phones, TVs, refrigerators, and coffeemakers. The hotel dining room, the Latchis Grille, overlooks Whetstone Brook and serves an innovative American cuisine. Don't miss seeing a movie in the gem of a theater with its Greek murals and star-studded ceiling. *Rates:* $65 to $100.

The other gem close to town is **Naulakha**, ℅ The Landmark Trust, R.R. 1, Box 510, Brattleboro, VT 05301 (☎ 802/254-6868), where you can settle in for a week (the minimum stay). This is the home that Rudyard Kipling and his wife, Caroline Balestier, built shortly after they were married. On a hillside, it's a shingle-style home standing on a deep stone foundation. The Kiplings lived here for 4 years. The study is the heart and soul of the house. The views across the Connecticut River Valley to Mount Monadnock must have inspired Kipling, for he managed to write *The Jungle Book, Second Jungle Book, The Seven Seas, Captains Courageous,* and *The Day's Work* while he was here. The interior is surprisingly sleek and unfussy given its turn-of-the-century provenance. Many of the rooms have ash paneling and feature simple sturdy furniture. It can accommodate eight people (there are three bathrooms with original tub and shower fixtures). Facilities include a fully equipped kitchen. *Rates* (1-week minimum in summer, 3-night minimum at other times): June to October, £1,200 to £1,525 ($1,980 to $2,516) per week double; November and December, £186 ($307) per day or £900 ($1,485) per week; January to May, £169 ($279) per day or £799 ($1,318) per week.

The glorious old inn by the church in Marlboro is the **Whetstone**, Marlboro, VT 05344 (☎ 802/254-2500). Here Jean and Harry Boardman welcome guests into their living room, which is lined with interesting books, and houses a piano and a bar and a fireplace that is used on cold Vermont days. Built in 1786, this venerable building has nearly always flourished as a tavern. Many of the musicians performing at the Marlboro Festival stay here, so you'll enjoy interesting company. Rooms vary in decor and size, although most are furnished in keeping with the colonial atmosphere of the inn. Most have private bathrooms and all look out on meadows and forest. In winter, the inn is ideal for cross-country skiing, sledding, and snowshoeing.

Meals are served in what was originally the big kitchen in the back, with a fireplace large enough to accommodate a cooking crane. Full breakfasts are $7 to $9; complete dinners run $18 to $25. Although Jean will accommodate friends of yours at table, dining is really only for guests. In summer, dinner is served on concert nights—Wednesday to Saturday; in winter, only on Saturday. Dishes will be homemade, from the cheddar-cheese soup and roast leg of lamb or pork to the brandy Alexander pie.

Rates: $70 to $80 double without bath, $75 to $90 double with bath. Rates go up in July and August during the Music Festival, when priority is given to weekly rentals.

T.J. Buckley's, 132 Elliot St., Brattleboro (☎ 802/257-4922), is an unlikely local dining favorite—an old diner, now looking avant garde, that seats 16 people maximum. Michael Fuller, who runs it, is a creative cook. He prepares a different menu daily, consisting of four entrees made with local and often organic ingredients. You might find roasted chicken stuffed with Bûcheron with black truffles under the skin, served with flageolets and a caramelized cumice pear and parsnip-porcini sauce; or striped bass in a roasted lobster stock with carrots, celery, fresh horseradish, and rosemary, served with risotto; or shrimp and clams in two sauces (parsley pesto and sweet red pepper). The $25 price includes salad and rolls. Desserts are prepared daily. On weekends you'll need to reserve at least a week in advance. *Hours:* Late May to mid-February, Tuesday to Sunday 6pm to closing; mid-February to early May, Thursday to Sunday only.

Peter Havens, 32 Elliot, Brattleboro (☎ 802/257-3333), has also been gaining a reputation for carefully prepared cuisine. It's a tiny restaurant where original art by local artists adds warmth to the spare white walls of the dining room. The menu is short with a definite emphasis on seafood, which plays to the chef's particular strength. Try the scallops sautéed with fire-roasted red peppers, crabmeat, and light cream sauce; or the broiled salmon with smoked pesto butter. In both dishes the flavor of the seafood shines through. For meat dishes you might find filet mignon with a Roquefort walnut butter, or a duck breast roasted with a fresh fig and Merlot sauce. Prices range from $16 to $22. To start try the delicious smoked lemon-pepper trout. *Hours:* Tuesday to Saturday 6pm to closing. Closed 2 weeks in July, March, and November.

The other local spot is **Common Ground**, 25 Elliot St. (☎ 802/257-0855), where many of the craftspeople can be seen lingering over vegetarian and natural foods on the second-floor enclosed terrace in summer. Downstairs, the entryway and stairwell serve as the town's alternative bulletin board. It's strictly vegetarian, with such items as cashew burgers, lentil stew, lasagna, bean and cheese burritos, and stir fries made with vegetables plus tofu, tempeh, and seitan. Prices range from $4 to $10. *Hours:* Sunday 10:30am to 2:30pm and 5:30 to 9pm, Monday to Saturday 11:30am to 9pm.

NEWFANE, GRAFTON, CHESTER & SAXTONS RIVER

From Brattleboro it's only about 12 miles or so, following Route 30 and the West River, to **Newfane**, a quintessential Vermont village blessed with two fine inns and a steepled Congregational church clustered around a green with the Windham County Courthouse at the center. As you travel the route there are plenty of antiques shops for you to explore, and east of Newfane, Putney is a major center for crafts lovers.

If you continue farther along Route 30 you'll come to the Townshends and Windham, where you can turn off to Grafton, taking Route 121. From there, a 7-mile drive north along Route 35 will bring you to Chester, or you can continue along Route 121 for about 6 miles east to Saxtons River. Both are picture-book New England villages.

Grafton was settled in 1780 and grew throughout the 19th century. Farming, milling, and soapstone quarrying were the major occupations of the villagers, and in 1850 there were about 10,000 sheep grazing in the surrounding meadows. The town was on the Boston-Montreal stage route, and the Phelps Hotel (now the Old Tavern) serviced overnight travelers. Around the turn of the century the town declined as people were lured west or moved to the cities. By 1940 many of the buildings in the community were in a decrepit condition. It wasn't until the Windham Foundation was founded in 1963 that the serious work of restoration was undertaken. Today, you can stroll (or take a narrative tour in a horse and carriage) through the beautifully restored town.

Don't miss visiting the **Grafton Village Cheese Company,** half a mile south on Townshend Road (☎ 802/843-2221). They make their very own Covered Bridge cheddar; you can watch the process and take a few tangy samples home. *Hours:* June to October, 8:30am to 4pm weekdays, Saturday 10am to 4pm.

History buffs will want to stop at the **Grafton Historical Society Museum,** Main Street (☎ 802/843-2489), just down from the post office. Old photographs, memorabilia, historical objects, and genealogical books reflect the town's story. *Hours:* Memorial Day to Columbus Day, Saturday and Sunday 1:30 to 4pm.

Chester is a Victorian-style New England classic with a village green and a wide main street lined with handsome late-19th-century homes and commercial buildings. Among them are more than 20 pre–Civil War buildings faced in gleaming mica schist. Take a stroll along both sides of the street to view these remarkable buildings. Examples are the MacKenzie House, with its marble newel posts and ornamental metal roof crest, and the fanciful Eastlake–Queen Anne Sherwins House at Depot and Maple streets.

Stores to browse in are **Century House Interiors** (☎ 802/875-4872), the **Carpenter's Emporium** (☎ 802/875-3267), the **Vermont Country Store** (☎ 802/463-2224), **Vermont Stone Works** (☎ 802/875-4141), and the **Reed Gallery** (☎ 802/875-6225), which is tucked away off the main street.

Chester is a terminus for the Green Mountain Railroad's (☎ 802/463-3069) **Green Mountain Flyer,** which steams 26 miles round-trip from Bellows Falls. Trains operate in summer and during special holidays. Tickets cost $12 for adults, $10 for seniors and children ages 3 to 12, and $3 for children under age 3.

Saxtons River is more gritty. There's not an awful lot to do in any one of these towns, but that's the whole point—this is biking and rambling country, havens for those who just want to enjoy the bounty of the mountains and the backroads.

LODGING & DINING IN THE AREA

The **Four Columns Inn**, on the Common at 230 West St., Newfane, VT 05345 (☎ 802/365-7713), occupies an 1832 building fashioned after a Southern mansion, whose Greek Revival columns give this marvelous country inn its name. It's complete with trout pond and swimming pool, flower and herb gardens, and hiking trails. The dining room is exceptional as well as being appealing, with a large brick fireplace, old beams, and decorative kitchen and farm utensils. The cuisine is always exciting, incorporating American, Mediterranean, and Pacific Rim flavors and techniques. Among the appetizers, you may find quail rubbed with Thai spices; crunchy watercress and vegetable salad; or sautéed foie gras with leeks, Napa cabbage, and balsamic vinegar. Specialties include poached salmon with a spicy tamarind sesame sauce and shrimp wontons and aged Black Angus sirloin with a horseradish chervil sauce. Prices range from $21 to $27.

In the front building, there are nine rooms, and several more are in the renovated barn. All have private baths and are furnished in an elegant country style with quilts on the brass beds and chintz on the walls. Some have gas fireplaces, and deluxe rooms have Jacuzzis.

Rates: B&B, winter, spring, and summer, $120 to $205 double; fall, $150 to $235; MAP, fall foliage season, $220 to $305. *Dining hours:* Wednesday to Monday 6 to 9pm. Closed April.

Old Newfane Inn, Route 30, Newfane, VT 05345 (☎ 802/365-4427). Eric and Gundy Weindl run this typical New England inn with uneven floors, beamed ceilings, and flocked wallpaper. The dining room possesses a large brick fireplace and offers food that runs from fillet of sole amandine and frogs' legs Provençale to veal Marsala, duck à l'orange, and a variety of steaks. Desserts include the classic cherries jubilee, crêpes Suzette, and baked Alaska. Main dishes go for $16 to $26. The inn's 10 guest rooms are furnished with pleasant oak pieces. *Rates* (including continental breakfast): $115 to $155 double. Closed November to mid-December and April to mid-May. *Dining hours:* Tuesday to Sunday 6 to 9pm.

West River Lodge, R.R. 1 Box 693, Newfane, VT 05345 (☎ 802/365-7745), has a beautiful setting on 30 acres and possesses 1,200 feet along the West River. People come primarily for the English riding stables, which offer dressage instruction and other riding clinics. There are also other kinds of workshops—watercolor painting, for example. Innkeepers Jack and Gill Winner, former college biology teachers, gladly share their intimate knowledge of the area. The eight rooms (two with private bath) are simply furnished with half-posters and other country pieces. Guests gather around the hearth in the living room. A full breakfast is served in the pine-paneled dining room. Dinners are also available. Trail rides are offered at the stable for $20. *Rates:* B&B, $90 to 100 double; MAP, $130 to $140.

At the center of the idyllic, meticulously kept New England village of Grafton, the **Old Tavern**, Grafton, VT 05146 (☎ 802/843-2231 or 802/843-2245), is a town landmark dating from 1801. It occupies a main building as well as a number of historic homes in the village, and has a long and proud tradition dating back to 1788. Among the famous visitors who have stayed here are Henry David Thoreau, Ralph Waldo Emerson, Nathaniel Hawthorne, Teddy Roosevelt, and Rudyard Kipling. Today the tradition of attracting celebrities continues.

The main building contains 14 guest rooms, all with private baths, some with canopied beds. Behind it, in what was originally the livery stable, is a bar with an upstairs gallery, a slate fireplace, and beams and barn siding. Most of the accommodations in the beautifully furnished cottages—White Gates, Barrett House, Tuttle House—contain canopied beds, mahogany chests, comfortable armchairs, candle-stand tables, and sitting rooms ideally furnished for quiet reading. They have accents like broken-scroll mirrors and demi-lune tables set with a Staffordshire or similar vase filled with fresh flowers. A couple of the cottages are reserved primarily for families and are furnished appropriately. There are no telephones or TVs in any of the rooms. The place is filled with authentic antiques (and a few reproductions). A number of really tasteful antiques-filled guest houses, sleeping 7 to 16, with full kitchens are also available.

There are several choices of dining rooms: first a formal room, whose oak tables are set with place mats and Mottahedeh china; second, the pine room, with a beamed ceiling, fireplace, and Windsor chairs; and third, the garden room, with a brick floor, and flowers and plants in pots. The food in all is traditional New England fare—New England lobster pie, rack of lamb with a minted Madeira sauce, plus some lighter entrees like the salmon with a fresh yellow-pepper puree. To start, try the smoked rainbow trout with horseradish sauce or the classic escargots with garlic butter. To finish, there's a selection of parfaits, along with strawberry shortcake and white-chocolate mousse. Entree prices run from $18 to $26.

The Old Tavern is not the place to visit if you're looking for nightlife—come in search of peace and quiet, a comfortable chair, a good book, and a brandy in front of a crackling fire. The inn also offers 20 miles of cross-country ski trails, sleds and toboggans, and a natural swimming pond. Two tennis courts just down the street are free to guests. Platform tennis and a games room with billiards and Ping-Pong complete the facilities.

Rates: Rooms and cottages, $130 to $250 double per day, $525 to $730 per week. *Dining hours:* Monday to Saturday noon to 2pm, 6 to 9pm; Sunday 11:30am to 2pm, 6 to 9 pm. Closed April.

Chester House, 266 Main St. (☎ 802/875-2205), sits on the main street overlooking the green. This charming 1780 house is operated by Paul and Randy, who have renovated and furnished it with style. They are experienced innkeepers, having operated a similar place on Cape Cod. The rooms are furnished with antiques and decorated with stenciling. The largest room has a canopied bed and bathroom with a double Jacuzzi. Some rooms also have decorative fireplaces. A superb breakfast is served in summer outside on the side porch. It's exquisitely presented and will consist of fresh fruit and a delicious entree. *Rates:* $95 to $125.

The Inn at Long Last, Box 589, Chester, VT 05143 (☎ 802/875-2444), has welcoming public areas—a lobby with a stone fireplace and a library/bar, also with a flagstone hearth. The dining room features a contemporary

American menu with such main courses as grilled chicken breast with roasted red peppers and ginger salsa or roasted veal chop with Merlot and wild mushrooms. Prices range from $12 to $18. There are 26 rooms and 4 suites, all with private baths. They are plainly furnished with brass or Jenny Lind beds and painted furniture. The owners are sprucing them up, but it's a slow and arduous process. Facilities include two tennis courts and a garden that extends down to a fishing stream. *Rates:* B&B, $120 double; MAP $100 per person or $170 for two. Closed April and 10 days in mid-November. *Dining hours:* Monday to Saturday noon to 2pm, Sunday 11:30am to 2pm; daily 6 to 9pm.

What makes **Inn Victoria,** Box 788, On the Green, Chester, VT 05143 (☎ 800/732-4288), special is the innkeepers' dedication to afternoon tea. The inn was built in the 1850s and is furnished in Victorian style. Parlors have Empire-style couches and Victorian armchairs. There are nine rooms and suites, several with double Jacuzzis and gas fireplaces. The beds are high-back carved Victorians with plenty of pillows and cushions. A family loft accommodates six and has a full kitchen, a wood-burning fireplace, and a TV. The innkeepers set a lovely table with elegant bone china and lace place mats at breakfast and at afternoon tea. They also operate the Tea Pot Shoppe, and many a guest carries home one of their handsome international teapots. *Rates:* $105 to $170.

Halfway to Londonderry from Chester on Route 11 in Simonsville is **Rowell's Inn,** R.R. 1, Box 267D, Chester, VT 05143 (☎ 802/875-3658), a very beautiful and elegant inn. The 1820 brick building with double porches served originally as a coaching inn. Step through the front stained-glass doors and you'll find yourself in a lovely historic home with cherry and maple floors and a tin ceiling. The sitting room has lavish carpeting, a brick hearth flanked by bookcases, and a Remington sculpture. There's another sitting room and the dining room/bar that have such notable pieces as a medieval carved Portuguese chest and an Early American hutch sheltering a strutting cockrell. The tavern is warmed by an old wood stove inserted into the inglenook fireplace and is decorated with suitable scenes of debauchery. There are six rooms. None has a phone or TV, but all have been carefully decorated with choice pieces. In one you might find a canopied brass bed, an oak dresser, and a Victorian sofa in a setting of blue chintz. Room 5 occupies a barrel-vaulted space and has a bed with a tent treatment supported by the carved top of an armoire, along with another single sleigh bed. A full breakfast is included in the rates, and you can also enjoy a very fine five-course dinner. No credit cards are taken, and no children under age 12 are allowed. *Rates:* MAP $170 to $185.

At the heart of Saxtons River, you'll find the very Victorian **Inn at Saxtons River,** Main Street, Saxtons River, VT 05154 (☎ 802/869-2110), a friendly, idiosyncratic place where you can loll on the front porch or enjoy afternoon tea in the garden. It's not a precious, perfectly coiffed New England inn, but it has great character. Throughout the house are Southern pine door frames and woodwork. The 16 rooms are decorated in a handsome Victorian country style with antiques. At the end of the day guests gather in the Victorian pub, where there is piano entertainment Friday and Saturday night, or else around the hearth in the very comfortable lounge. There's also a TV/VCR room tucked away. The dining room has harvest tables and Windsor chairs. Food is updated traditional—pork medallions with an apple and juniper berry sauce, chicken Marengo over fettucine, roast duck with raspberry–red wine sauce, and scampi in lemon-garlic cream sauce. Prices range from $17 to $20. Appetizers are equally popular; try the smoked trout with Dijon-honey-dill mayonnaise or the steamed mussels in white wine shallots, garlic butter, and fresh herbs. *Rates:* $82 to $102 double ($112 in October). Closed in March and April for 5 weeks. *Dining hours:* Tuesday to Sunday 11:30am to 2pm; Sunday and Tuesday to Thursday 5 to 9pm, Friday and Saturday 5 to 10pm.

LUDLOW, LONDONDERRY, WESTON & LANDGROVE

From Chester Route 103 north will take you through Proctorsville, home of the **Joseph Cerniglia Winery,** Route 103 (☎ 802/226-7575), which has been producing wines for 10 years, to Ludlow, an old milling town that is right at the base of **Okemo Mountain,** the state's fastest growing resort. From Ludlow it's a short cruise down Route 100 to the little village of Weston, a charmer indeed with a famous summer theater, and—to catalog aficionados—the hometown of the Vermont Country Store.

The **Farrar-Mansur House** (☎ 802/824-4399) has some fine furniture, which has survived in remarkable condition. Among the highlights are silver items made by Bailey of Woodstock, a Rawson shelf clock made in Saxtons River, and paintings by folk artists Asahel Powers and Aaron Dean Fletcher. Murals in the parlor were painted by WPA artist Roy Williams in the 1930s. The house was built in 1797 and served as home and tavern to several generations of the Mansur family until it was donated to Weston in 1932. Next to the house, the **Old Mill Museum** displays collections of tinsmithing, woodworking, and agricultural tools. *Hours:* July to August, Wednesday to Sunday 1 to 4pm, and on fall weekends.

SHOPPING

Stop at the **Weston Bowl Mill and Annex** (☎ 802/824-6219) for some reasonably priced woodware; at the **Vitriesse Glass Gallery** (☎ 802/824-6634); and also at **Susan Sargent Designs** (☎ 802/824-3184), where exuberant designs are woven into colorful, unique pillows, rugs, and throws. **Todd Gallery** (☎ 802/824-5606) is the studio of watercolorist Robert E. Todd, who also shows works by other Vermont artists.

LODGING & DINING IN THE AREA

The Castle, Route 103 at Route 131 (P.O. Box 207), Proctorsville, VT 05153 (☎ 802/226-7222), occupies a unique turn-of-the-century mansion that was modeled on a Cotswold manor house. It's located on a hillside overlooking the Black River Valley with views of Okemo Mountain. It was built in 1904 for lumber-quarry baron and Vermont governor Allen M. Fletcher. The interior woodwork and detailing is extraordinary, from the elaborate stucco ceiling in the sitting room to the boiserie in the dining room. There are ten very spacious rooms, all with CD players; six have fireplaces and two have Jacuzzis. Even the smallest room (Room 9) is larger than most accommodations at other places, and it has a gorgeous fireplace. Each room is decorated in a different palette, from cran-apple red to moss green. Room 8 is predominantly deep blue and has a wood-burning fireplace. Room 4 is dramatic—it has a black Chinese Aubusson rug, a carved bed, and a red and gold brocade sofa. The largest room, Room 11, is 420 square feet and has been decorated in deep purple. A Chinese screen hangs on the wall above the bed. A full breakfast is served, as well as afternoon tea. You can either dine in the oak-paneled former billiards room or in the elegant smaller oval dining room, which has superb boiserie. The contemporary American cuisine has obvious Asian traces. On the menu you might find sautéed salmon with black-bean cakes and lemon-grass beurre blanc, or pork tenderloin with a pesto Marsala sauce. In fall and winter, expect to find game dishes like venison with juniper berries and red wine. Prices range from $15 to $24. A splendid conclusion to any meal would be the chocolate Grand Marnier torte. *Rates:* $160 to $210; MAP is an additional $60 per couple per night.

A trellis gate hung with fuchsias leads into the garden entrance of the **Three Clock Inn**, R.R. 1, Box 59, Middletown Road, South Londonderry, VT 05155 (☎ 802/824-6327). This secluded establishment is best known for its restaurant, which is very good indeed. The dining room has a warm ambience, and a glass-enclosed wine cellar plus a lounge with a fireplace. It offers a $35 three-course fixed-price menu. The updated French/continental cuisine features fresh local ingredients. You might find duck breast with a wild berry sauce, pistachio-crusted swordfish, or rack of venison with risotto galette. Prices range from $18 to $23. To start, there might be smoked salmon with buckwheat crêpes and horseradish cream or pâté maison. Desserts include classics like crème brûlée, hot apple tart, and profiteroles.

Upstairs, four rooms are available, including a small suite with two bedrooms. The largest has a canopied bed and a fireplace. The guests also can use a colonial-style living room, also with a fireplace. At breakfast the gracious proprietors will serve whatever you fancy.

Rates: $95 to $130 double. *Dining hours:* Tuesday to Sunday 5:30 to 8:30pm. Closed April and November.

THE AREA AFTER DARK

The **Weston Playhouse** (☎ 802/824-5288 in season; 802/824-8167 off-season), is the oldest professional theater in the state and one of the finest. It's a handsome Greek Revival theater in a lovely riverside setting with a downstairs restaurant and bar where you can secure a fine dinner before the show. Comedies and musicals are its stock in trade, and there's also after-hours cabaret.

Brattleboro & Southeastern Vermont
Special & Recreational Activities

Auctions: Contact the **Townshend Auction Gallery** for their schedule. They're located on Route 30 in Townshend (☎ 802/365-4388).

Biking: **Grafton Ponds Mountain Bike Center** at the Old Tavern (☎ 802/843-2400) has 30km of trails. Rentals available. Rentals are also available from the **Brattleborough Bike Shop** (☎ 802/254-8644).

For tour information, contact **Bike Vermont**, P.O. Box 207, Woodstock, VT 05091 (☎ 802/457-3553). It offers inn-to-inn bicycle touring from May through October, on weekend and 5-day trips. Or try **Vermont Bicycle Tours Worldwide Active Vacations**, P.O. Box 711, Bristol, VT 05443 (☎ 802/453-4811). They will also supply bikes. Note, too, that they also offer hiking holidays.

Camping: Two state parks in the area offer camping: **Fort Dummer** (☎ 802/254-2610) in Brattleboro; **Townshend** (☎ 802/365-7500) has 34 sites as well as trails up Bald Mountain for great views.

For information write to **Department of Forests, Parks and Recreation**, 103 South Main St. (10 South), Waterbury, VT 05671 (☎ 802/241-3655).

Canoeing: This can be done along the **Connecticut** and West rivers. Rentals available at **River Safari** (☎ 802/257-5008).

Cross-Country Skiing: This is great terrain for cross-country skiing, which is available at **Grafton Ponds Cross Country Ski Center** at the Old Tavern (☎ 802/843-2400) with 20 miles of trails. In Ludlow, **Fox Run**, 89 Fox Lane (☎ 802/228-8871), has 12 miles of trails. Rentals are available.

Fishing: For information, contact the **Vermont Fish and Wildlife Department**, Waterbury, VT 05676 (☎ 802/241-3700). Licenses are available by mail, but allow plenty of time for them to arrive. A useful guide to fishing and a booklet outlining state laws and regulations are also available.

Golf: **Tater Hill Country Club**, R.R. 1, Chester (☎ 802/875-2517), has an 18-hole course with some fine mountain views.

Hiking: Grafton Ponds Center offers some decent hiking.

Horseback Riding: English riding, including trail rides, are offered at the **West River Lodge. Jack's Horse Farm**, Westminster West Road in Putney (☎ 802/387-2782), also offers trail rides. In Proctorsville contact **Cavendish Trail Horse Rides**, 20 Mile Stream Rd. (☎ 802/226-7821). The average price is $25 per hour.

Ice-skating: There's a public rink in Brattleboro—the **Memorial Park Skating Rink** (☎ 802/257-2311).

Picnicking: Good picnicking sites are available in **Townshend State Park.**

Shopping for Crafts: Many craftspeople have settled in the area, and their works are displayed in many locations. At the **Marlboro Craft Studios,** Lucy Gratwick exhibits her hand-weaving (☎ 802/257-0181), the **Applewoods** their furniture and wood pieces (☎ 802/254-2908), and Malcolm Wright (☎ 802/254-2168) his wood-fired pottery. Call any of them to make an appointment.

Skiing: The star of the region is Okemo (☎ 802/228-4041), which has developed a reputation for challenging expert skiers since 50% of their 88 trails are considered "more difficult." It has a vertical drop of 2,150 feet, 485 acres with 95% snowmaking coverage, and 13 lifts, including 7 quads (2 high-speed). A 2-day lift ticket is $90.

Ascutney Mountain (☎ 802/484-7711) in Brownsville has great views from the top. It's much less challenging, with a vertical drop of 1,530 feet. There are 31 trails accessed by three triples and a double chair.

State Parks: For information, contact the **Department of Forests, Parks, and Recreation**, 103 S. Main St. (10 South), Waterbury, VT 05671 (☎ 802/241-3655).

Swimming: Try Newfane's **Townshend State Park.**
Tennis: There are municipal courts in Brattleboro. **Tater Hill Country Club** in Chester (☎ 802/875-2517) has two clay courts.

WILMINGTON, WEST DOVER & MOUNT SNOW

From Brattleboro it's only about a dozen or so miles to Wilmington, a small town that is undergoing a sort of renaissance. From here Route 100 begins its winding journey north through the Green Mountains to the first of Vermont's major ski areas, **Mount Snow,** Mount Snow, VT 05356 (☎ 802/464-3333), in West Dover. In summer take the chairlift to the summit for the four-state view. Beyond this resort the road continues on its way to the villages of Wardsboro, Jamaica, Londonderry, and Weston.

SHOPPING FOR ARTS & CRAFTS

In Wilmington, **Young and Constantin Gallery** is in the church (☎ 802/464-2515), which makes a perfect backdrop for some exquisite hand-blown glass art. Jewelry, ceramics, wood sculpture, and paintings and pastels are also on sale. Photographs, watercolors, and paintings are shown at **Roseate Creations,** 7 N. Main (☎ 802/464-1466). There are also several worthy antiques stores in town.

Around the corner on Route 9, **John McLeod** (☎ 802/464-3332) sells beautifully turned woodware and also offers fine crafts in the **Eclectic Eye** on the same premises. About 10 miles west of Wilmington on Route 9, book lovers will want to seek out **Austin's Antiquarian Books** (☎ 802/464-3727), which sells books, prints, and maps.

In Wardsboro don't miss **Anton of Vermont Fiber Art Gallery and Quilts,** where Judith Anton creates her richly colored Vermont quilts. Much of her inspiration comes from Japan, which she visits frequently. Call ☎ 802/896-6007 for location and availability of the artist.

WILMINGTON LODGING & DINING

For an ideal weekend, I'd head for the warm and idiosyncratic hospitality of Jim McGovern and Lois Nelson at the **Hermitage Inn,** Coldbrook Road, Wilmington, VT 05363 (☎ 802/464-3511). Jim certainly has his own way of doing things. He's a renegade Connecticut gent, who more than 25 years ago fled the South to the 24 acres he now owns. Here he can indulge his own particular hobbies and enthusiasms without too much interference.

From the minute you cross the bridge over the tiny stream onto the property, you know you're somewhere special. Off to the left stand a series of farm structures. After investigation, these turn out to be houses for the game birds—goose, pheasant, duck, and wild turkey—that Jim raises specifically for the table and for which his dining room is famous. He also has collected some 35 species of rare beauties that are worth far too much to put on any table—gold and silver pheasants, India blue peacocks, and New Zealand and Arctic snow geese, to name a few. Walk up toward the house at the top of the hill and you'll discover a whole run full of wild turkeys, an area where Jim and Lois raise English setters, and a sugar house where every spring 5,000 buckets of maple sap are turned into 700 gallons of pure maple syrup. The syrup is sold in the store, along with jams, jellies, and other McGovern favorites, notably decoys and fine wines. You can also rent ski equipment in the store to ski 25 miles of cross-country trails or the downhill slopes at Mount Snow. A clay tennis court and a trout pond complete the picture.

The inn itself dates back 100 years. Wide pine floors and chairs cozily placed in front of the hearth in the bar engender a convivial atmosphere conducive to conversation. Check out the gallery, where Jim has assembled a huge collection of Delacroix lithographs. In the dining rooms you'll enjoy some of the finest dining in the area, enhanced by really fine wines from Jim's virtuoso wine cellar (2,000 labels with many vintages over 30 years old). Start with mushrooms Hermitage, stuffed with caviar. I can heartily recommend the pheasant braised in white wine cream sauce. Prices range from $14 to $25.

In the newer wing, added by Jim in the mid-1980s, all of the 15 rooms have private baths, working fireplaces, and telephones, and are furnished individually, some in mahogany, some in honey oak. A typical large room contains a pineapple half-poster, a chest of drawers with a broken-scroll mirror, a Stickley love seat, and a comb-back Windsor chair. From most of the rooms there's a glorious view looking toward Haystack Mountain. Additional rooms are located a short distance down the road in Brookbound. Guests can use a pine living room with fieldstone fireplace, TV, and an upright piano. Brookbound rooms vary in size. The largest, Room 42, possesses a high carved-oak bed, a needlepointed Victorian rocker, a Stickley chair, a Chippendale side table, and a brick fireplace. Most have private baths.

This may not be the ultimate designer-stamped, glossy magazine–quality establishment, but it offers a deeply satisfying sense of honesty, character, and individuality. In winter you can enjoy the miles of ski trails; hunters appreciate the sporting clays and hunting preserve.

It's located 2 miles north of Wilmington; from Route 100, turn left at Coldbrook Road and continue for about 2 miles. Turn left at the sign marking the inn.

Rates: Spring and summer, MAP $230; fall and winter, MAP $260 double; winter in Brookbound, MAP $150 to $220 double; summer, B&B, $70 to $130. *Dining hours:* Daily 5 to 11pm.

You won't miss the **Nutmeg Inn,** Route 9, Wilmington, VT 05363 (☎ 802/464-3351), a Chinese-red clapboard house with a long front porch that always supports some colorful floral display—roses in summer and potted bronze, yellow, and orange mums in fall. The place is very lovingly cared for, and everything is spick and span at this comfortable, homey, 180-year-old farmhouse. The special warmth is most evident in the large living room in the carriage house, where guests gather either to read in front of the fire, play cards or games, or enjoy a drink at the "bring your own" bar. Out back there's a lawn where you can sit under the apple trees by the brook. Throughout the house pine furnishings add special coziness. Each of the 10 rooms, with private bath and air-conditioning (most with a fireplace), is decorated in country fashion with pine or oak pieces, tables draped with Laura Ashley prints, brass beds, or four-posters, and so on. There are also three two-room suites with fireplace, TV/VCR, and double Jacuzzi. There are two cozily furnished dining rooms—one containing a Norman Rockwell plate collection and the other, warmed by a wood stove, giving a hillside view.

Rates (including breakfast): Summer, $100 to $150, suites $165 to $198; fall, $120 to $170, suites $210 to $250; winter, $135 to $190, suites $205 to $235. These are weekend rates; weekday rates are $10 to $15 less.

Tall maples, manicured lawns, and a vegetable garden surround the white clapboard **Red Shutter Inn**, Route 9 (P.O. Box 84), Wilmington, VT 05363 (☎ 802/464-3768). The house on 5 acres was built in 1894 and inside there are five guest rooms, all with private bath, and most furnished in chintz country fashion. Deerfield is a corner room with a whirlpool tub. Chimney Hill is furnished in wicker, and Jenny's Room has a four-poster. The largest is a two-room suite with a fireplace, color TV, and private deck. In the carriage house behind the inn are three rooms plus a fireplace suite, which features a double whirlpool bath. The dining room, with a stone fireplace, is a welcoming retreat on a winter's night. In summer there's alfresco dining on the awning covered porch. Guests also enjoy the wood stove's warmth in the living room/pub. *Rates* (including breakfast): $110 to $130 double. *Dining hours:* Summer, Wednesday to Sunday 6 to 9pm; winter, Friday to Saturday only.

Set atop a hill with a great view of the Deerfield Valley, the **White House**, Route 9, Wilmington, VT 05363 (☎ 802/464-2135), was built as a private summer home in 1914 for a lumber baron and possesses a gracious Georgian-style portico and rows of dormers jutting from the roof line. As you might expect, the 16 rooms in the main inn are extra-large—all with private baths. Nine of the rooms have fireplaces, and two have double whirlpool tubs. Seven additional rooms are located in the Guest House, which has a common living room with a fireplace and cable TV. The public areas include large, antiques-filled sitting rooms, a dining room with rich mahogany paneling, and a bar, which was sunken so as not to impair the view of sunsets across the valley. An outside terrace also takes advantage of the vista. The grounds are delightful. Roses climb around a trellis by a garden fountain, creating a romantic arbor; there's an outdoor swimming pool as well. In winter, 27 miles of ski trails are available. There's also a spa with a small indoor pool, whirlpool, and sauna. The restaurant offers a selection of continental dishes—chicken Marsala, veal piccata, filet mignon with a bordelaise sauce, and salmon with a country glaze, priced from $18 to $22. *Rates:* $138 to $188 double, $150 to $205 on holidays. Guest House rooms are $118 double, $128 holidays. *Dining hours:* Daily 5:30 to 9pm; Sunday 11:30am to 2:30pm in addition.

Le Petit Chef, Route 100 (☎ 802/464-8437), is a local favorite for superb food served in homey country surroundings. Although the dishes change frequently, you might find rack of lamb, fillet of beef with a Merlot wine sauce and morels, veal chops marinated in balsamic vinegar, poisson Méditerrané (fish, clams, mussels, and shrimp poached in tomato broth with aromatic sea herbs), or venison with cranberry demi-glace and chutney; there's always a vegetarian dish. Desserts are tantalizing—especially the crunchy meringue pie (if it's available), chocolate torte, and any of the fresh fruit pies. Main-course prices run $21 to $27. *Hours:* Sunday and Monday, Wednesday and Thursday

6 to 9pm, Friday and Saturday 6 to 10pm. Closed Tuesday, mid-April to mid-May, and November until Thanksgiving.

MOUNT SNOW/WEST DOVER LODGING & DINING

Close to 100 lodges, inns, and motels are clustered near the ski area, and one or two of them are quite exquisite. I've already mentioned the Hermitage Inn. The other accommodation, the **Inn at Sawmill Farm**, Route 100 (P.O. Box 367), West Dover, VT 05356 (☎ 802/464-8131), created by Rodney Williams and his wife, Ione, from an old farmhouse and barn, has international renown and is a Relais & Chateaux property. It's famous for its classic dining room, the designer-perfect quality of its rooms and cottages, and the understated elegance of its grounds. The dining room positively glows with copper pots, fresh flowers, and fine crystal and china. Their son, Brill, creates the cuisine. At dinner there's a selection for every palate—pan-seared salmon with crispy skin and saffron sauce, breast of pheasant with forestière sauce, rack of lamb with mint sauce, or steak au poivre. Prices run from $27 to $35. Appetizers are equally tempting—coquille of crabmeat au gratin; delicious local trout with white wine, lemon, and capers; or sautéed chicken livers with bordelaise sauce, for example. The wine list offers 900 selections. Jackets are required for men after 6pm. The garden dining room has a sun atrium filled with huge ferns and hydrangeas. Pine hutches, Windsor chairs, and burgundy floral wallpaper complete the summer atmosphere. A pianist quietly entertains in the evening.

In winter the living room is especially welcoming, as guests gather around the large fireplace and settle into the couches and wing chairs. The upstairs gallery overlooking the living room contains games, chess, books, and a large TV. Tea is served at 4pm, classical music making the announcement. The ten guest rooms in the main inn are very large and individually decorated with antiques and bright chintzes, combined with cannonball, pencil-post, or similar beds. Some have balconies, and some have sitting areas. The prime accommodations, though, are in the cottages. For example, Farmhouse 2 is decorated in peach tones and possesses a full-canopied bed and fireplace, handsome china lamps, a desk tucked into the bay window, a candle-stand table, and floor-to-ceiling drapes. The Woodshed, Mill House, and Spring House offer rooms with fireplaces, sitting areas, and views of the beautifully landscaped grounds and ponds. All of the rooms are richly appointed with fine linens and fabrics, original artwork, and fresh flowers, plus such extra treats as Godiva chocolates at nightly turndown.

On the grounds are a swimming pool, a pond with canoes, a tennis court, and two trout ponds. The Mount Snow Golf Course is conveniently located up the road. No children under age 10 are allowed.

Rates: MAP, $370 to $480 double. Higher prices are for lodgings with fireplaces. Closed Easter to mid-May. *Dining hours:* Daily 6 to 9:30pm.

The **Deerhill Inn**, Valley View Road (P.O. Box 136), West Dover, VT 05356 (☎ 802/464-3100), is my personal favorite. It's tucked away off Route 100 and offers inspirational rooms, great food, serene gardens, and great views of the valley and Haystack Mountain. Thanks to owners Michael and Linda it also has a warm and wonderful feel. The 17 guest rooms, all with private baths, have been creatively decorated in different palettes, using the finest fabrics, linens, and other furnishings without making the rooms seem precious or too beautiful for comfort. One room, decked out in rose-lavender, features a four-poster with a canopy and a floral dust ruffle. It has French doors leading to a balcony overlooking the attractively landscaped pool. Room 4 has been sponge-painted sea blue. A picket-style headboard crowns the bed, which is made up with broad-striped blue linens. The walls, painted by the staff, depict shore and sailboat scenes, while the furnishings are light wicker. Another room has been dramatically decorated with a bamboo four-poster, a Korean armoire, side tables, and a chest. Still another room looks as if the stenciling of a trellis and potted plants is three-dimensional. A gentle, moss-green theme creates the serene atmosphere of Room B-3, which has all the comforts you could possibly seek—a beautifully dressed iron bed, a built-in TV, and books. Around the house and pool Linda has planted a gorgeous array of wonderful plants including many unique, scented flowers. Guests also have the use of a large upstairs sitting room complete with a brick fireplace, a variety of ultra-comfortable seating, plus a supply of books as well as a TV. Another, more formally furnished parlor downstairs serves as a waiting area for diners. A new swimming pool opened in the summer of 1998.

The inn offers a romantic dining experience. One dining room has a lovely mural of an English garden and a slate-and-brick hearth. Both offer a view of the valley that is equally lovely in winter or summer. The art that adorns the walls of both rooms is for sale. The menu is limited and changes seasonally, but it will likely feature some signature dishes like the five-layered veal (comprised of three layers of veal interspersed with a layer of caramelized onions, mushrooms, and artichokes, and a layer of mozzarella and tomatoes). Fish is emphasized; a favorite dish is the candy-stripe fish, made by alternating layers of white fish like bass with salmon fillet. Among the appetizers, the mussels and the shrimp K-Paul are the chief draws. As for dessert, if you don't select the homemade ice cream then opt for the white-chocolate-and-pumpkin cheesecake with caramel sauce. Prices range from $18 to $24. A full breakfast is served.

Rates: Weekends, B&B $120 to $185, MAP $190 to $255; midweek, B&B $105 to $170, MAP $175 to $240. Holiday rates, B&B $160 to $224, MAP $230 to $295. *Dining hours:* Sunday to Thursday 6 to 9pm, Friday and Saturday 6 to 9:30pm. Closed Wednesday off-season.

Doveberry Inn, P.O. Box 1736, Route 100, West Dover (☎ 802/464-5652), is a favorite valley dining room that also has eight rooms to rent, all with private baths and TVs. They are decorated in simple style with tartan walls; the bathrooms have copper counters. They're comfortable and represent good value. The dining room is decked out in tartan, too, and uses wine storage bins as decorative accents. The table scarves or runners are changed with each season: birds in spring and summer, maple leaf in fall, and red and green for Christmas. There are only eight or nine tables. The specialties include a wood-grilled veal chop served with a host of mushrooms, and fillet of salmon grilled and served over orzo with tomatoes, garlic, and mixed herbs. To start there's homemade gnocchi tossed with fresh sage, garlic, and Parmesan or a delicious Gorgonzola salad. Prices range from $18 to $28. Finish with a bittersweet chocolate crème brûlée or the peach Napoleon, which is made with peaches poached in Chianti and cinnamon and served with mascarpone cream. *Rates:* $85 to 160. *Dining hours:* Wednesday to Monday 6 to 9pm.

If you're looking for an Alpine-style ski lodge, there's the nicely kept **Kitzhof**, on Route 100 in West Dover, VT 05356 (☎ 802/464-8310), only half a mile from Mount Snow. Here, no two rooms are alike except in their comfort and cleanliness. Knotty-pine boards, logs, and a fieldstone fireplace impart a mountain coziness; a mahogany hot tub is an added luxury. There's a BYOB bar with set-ups and a full service restaurant. Facilities include a heated swimming pool. *Rates:* Summer, $68 double; fall, $90 double; winter, $75 double midweek or weekend package for $128 double. During the summer many bus tours stop here.

WEST DOVER/MOUNT SNOW DINING

Prime dining spots I've already mentioned are the Inn at Saw Mill Farm, the Deerhill Inn, and the Hermitage.

Two Tannery Road (☎ 802/464-2707) has a fine reputation locally. Its name comes from its location on the old site of two sawmills and a tannery. The original old frame building, with plank floors and a piano for impromptu entertainment, offers a comfortable, romantic, candlelit setting for dinner, while the high-ceilinged, barnlike extension is most inviting in summer, though it's warmed by a wood stove in winter. Specialties include veal Tannery, made with a Marsala sauce; chicken Roosevelt flavored with crumbled bacon, spinach, shallots, and a Madeira wine sauce; shrimp Provençale; and desserts like mud pie and baklava à la Nancy. Prices range from $18 to $25. Take the left fork off Route 100 about 2 miles north of West Dover. *Hours:* Sunday to Thursday 6 to 9:30pm, Friday and Saturday 6 to 10pm (Thursday to Sunday only in November and April).

THE AREA AFTER DARK

Evening activities in the winter are largely confined to having a drink in a cozy spot like the **Hermitage Inn** in Wilmington, and following it with dinner.

In Wilmington, check out what's happening at the **Memorial Hall Center for the Arts** on West Main Street. Recitals, chamber music concerts, and jazz are also given at the **Shield Inn**. During the summer, **Mount Snow Playhouse** (☎ 802/464-3333 or 802/295-7016) offers summer stock.

There is plenty of après-ski at the **main base lodge** at Mount Snow and at the **Snow Barn** on the access road. Other favorite spots in Wilmington include **Deacon's Den, Dover Bar & Grill,** and **The Pub.**

Wilmington & Mount Snow
Special & Recreational Activities

Biking: Mount Snow operates a mountain-bike park with a 100-mile trail network. Rentals are from $38 to $52 a day and instruction is available (☎ 800/245-SNOW). The all-day lift is $28 and trail access another $9. Rentals are also available at **Bonkers Boardroom,** Route 100, West Dover (☎ 802/464-2536) and the **Cupola Ski and Bike Shop,** Route 100, West Dover (☎ 802/464-8010).

For information on touring, contact **Bike Vermont,** P.O. Box 207, Woodstock, VT 05091 (☎ 802/457-3553). It offers inn-to-inn bicycle touring from May through October, on weekend and 5-day trips. Rentals are available. Or try **Vermont Bicycle Tours Worldwide Active Vacations**, P.O. Box 711, Bristol, VT 05443 (☎ 802/453-4811). They will also supply bikes. Note, too, that they also offer hiking holidays.

Boating: At Lake Whitingham you can rent a sailboat from **Green Mountain Flagship Co.**, 389 Rte. 9, Wilmington (☎ 802/464-2975). Also in **Woodford State Park.**

Camping: Two state parks in the area have campsites: **Molly Stark**, Route 9, Wilmington (☎ 802/464-5460), has 34 sites; **Woodford State Park**, Route 9, Woodford (☎ 802/447-7169), between Wilmington and Bennington, has 104 sites.

For information write to **Department of Forests, Parks and Recreation**, 103 S. Main St. (10 South), Waterbury, VT 05671 (☎ 802/241-3655).

Canoeing: At **Lake Whitingham**, also known as Harriman Reservoir, south of Wilmington, you can rent a canoe from **Green Mountain Flagship Co.**, 389 Rte. 9, Wilmington (☎ 802/464-2975). Rentals are also available at **Equipe Sports**, Mount Snow Access Road (☎ 802/464-2222).

Cross-Country Skiing: Mount Snow's cross-country centers are at the **Hermitage**, P.O. Box 457, Wilmington, VT 05363 (☎ 802/464-3511), with 30 miles of trails; **Sitzmark**, East Dover Road, Wilmington, VT 05363 (☎ 802/464-3384), with 25 miles of trails; and the **White House**, P.O. Box 757, Wilmington, VT 05363 (☎ 802/464-2135), with 28 miles of trails.

Fishing: There's freshwater fishing in Lake Whitingham and Lake Raponda for trout, bass, perch, salmon, and pickerel. For information, contact the **Vermont Fish and Wildlife Department**, Waterbury, VT 05676 (☎ 802/241-3700). Licenses are available by mail, but allow plenty of time for them to arrive. You can pick them up usually at general or tackle stores. A useful guide to fishing and a booklet outlining state laws and regulations are also available.

Golf: Mount Snow is also famous for its golf school and championship course (☎ 802/464-4184). **Haystack Golf Club**, R.R. 1 Box 173, Mann Road, Wilmington (☎ 802/464-8301), has a fine course, too. At the **Mount Snow Country Club** (☎ 802/464-3333) the fourth hole has been named one of the most beautiful in North America. There's also an 18-hole course at the **Sitzmark Lodge**, East Dover Road, Wilmington (☎ 802/464-3384). Mount Snow and several inns, including the Hermitage (see above), offer golf packages.

Hiking: Among the legendary mountain trails are the **Long Trail**, the **Molly Stark Trail**, and the **Appalachian Trail**. **Mount Snow** has a hiking center, and there are also trails in **Molly Stark** and **Woodford state parks**. **Haystack Mountain** has trails, too.

For detailed information and maps contact **Appalachian Trail Conference**, P.O. Box 236, Harpers Ferry, WV 25425. Long Trail information can be obtained from the **Green Mountain Club, Inc.**, R.R. 1 Box 650, Route 100, Waterbury Center, VT 05677 (☎ 802/244-7037). Information is also available from **Green Mountain Forest** at ☎ 802/362-2307.

Horseback Riding: Flames Stables, Wards Cove Road, Wilmington (☎ 802/464-8329), has trail rides for $25 an hour.

Llama Trekking: Green Mountain Expeditions offers llama trips around Lake Whitingham. Call ☎ 802/368-7147.

Picnicking: Good picnicking is available in the state parks: **Molly Stark** and **Woodford.**

Skiing: Only 9 miles north of Wilmington in West Dover, **Mount Snow** (☎ 802/464-3333) is one of the state's largest ski resorts and draws great crowds from the metropolitan areas of Boston, Hartford, and New York. The trails are myriad (130-plus), serviced by 24 lifts. There is good skiing for beginners and intermediates, and on the North Face, skiing for experts, with 85% snow-making capability. Lift passes are about $50 on weekends. Facilities include a nursery, bar, cafeteria at the summit, rentals, ski school, and 40 miles of cross-country trails.

Besides Mount Snow/Haystack, there's also more modest **Hogback** in Marlboro, VT 05344 (☎ 802/464-3942), which has 12 trails and 4 T-bars.

State Parks: For information, contact the **Department of Forests, Parks and Recreation,** 103 S. Main St. (10 South), Waterbury, VT 05671 (☎ 802/241-3655).

Swimming: There's a couple of beaches at **Lake Whitingham** at Mountain Mills, off Fairview Avenue, and at **Ward's Cover,** off Route 100. There's also a beach at **Lake Raponda,** north of Route 9 between Wilmington and Brattleboro. The **Deerhill Inn, Sitzmark Lodge,** the **White House,** and several other accommodations have swimming pools.

The Monadnock Region

Temple ◆ *Rindge* ◆ *Fitzwilliam* ◆ *Jaffrey* ◆ *Peterborough* ◆
Dublin ◆ *Chesterfield* ◆ *Walpole*

Distance in miles: Keene, 215; Jaffrey, 232; Peterborough, 239
Estimated driving time: 4 to 4¼ hours

◄o►◄o►◄o►◄o►◄o►

Driving: Take I-684 to I-84 to I-91 or I-95 to I-91 and take Exit 3 to Route 9 east into Keene. From Keene take Route 101 to Peterborough and routes 101 and 124 to Jaffrey.

Bus: Greyhound / Trailways (☎ 800/231-2222) services Keene.

Train: Amtrak travels daily to Brattleboro (☎ 800/872-7245), which is about 17 miles from Keene.

Further Information: Hillsborough Chamber of Commerce (☎ 603/464-5858); **Jaffrey Chamber of Commerce** (☎ 603/532 4549); **Monadnock Travel Council,** Keene (☎ 603/355-8155); **Peterborough Chamber of Commerce** (☎ 603/924-7234); **Rindge Chamber of Commerce** (☎ 603/899-6040).

◄o►◄o►◄o►◄o►◄o►

The solitary, 3,165-foot-high **Mount Monadnock,** called by the Native Americans "one that stands alone," dominates this "quiet corner" of New Hampshire. Many a literary figure has been moved by the beauty of the mountain and inspired by the surrounding landscape, as Ralph Waldo Emerson was when he wrote on a visit to the Halfway House on the slopes of the mountain:

> *Every morn I lift my head,*
> *See New England underspread*
> *South from St Lawrence to the Sound,*
> *From Katskill east to the sea-bound.*

On clear days you can still see a 150-mile panorama of the six New England states from the summit of this aerie citadel—north to the Presidential range and Mount Washington and west to mounts Tom and Greylock in the

Berkshires, and to Vermont's Green Mountains. Ever since Captain Samuel Ward made the first ascent of Grand Monadnock in 1725, it has drawn climbers, seekers, writers, artists, and poets to its barren crags. It's still a most-climbed mountain; if you want to climb it, the best access is from Monadnock State Park outside Jaffrey. Even if you don't climb it, you should take the road up to the summit to get a true impression of the beauty of this region and the somnolent towns that lie at is base.

THE VILLAGES BY THE MOUNTAIN

The hilltop town of **Temple** will return you to the 18th century. It's notable for its triangular common and the rows of historic buildings that face it. On one side is an old stagecoach inn that contains murals painted by itinerant artist, inventor, and journalist Rufus Porter. Stroll down into the graveyard on one side of the common, where the stones evoke memories of the past—among those resting here is the boy Frances Blood Moses, who was sent by General Washington on a spying mission to Nova Scotia, and Ebenezer Edwards, who fought at Concord Bridge. Temple was the location of the first glassmaking factory in New Hampshire, founded in 1780 by Robert Hewes, who employed Hessian mercenaries from the British army.

It seems that Grand Monadnock can be seen from every vantage point in the region. One of the best views is off Route 119 in **Rindge,** from the outdoor altar at the national **Cathedral of the Pines** (☎ 603/899-3300). The Cathedral was created by Dr. and Mrs. Douglas Sloane in memory of their son, who died in World War II. *Hours:* May through October, daily.

Other peaks thrust up around Grand Monadnock, including Little Monadnock, which looms above the picturesque village of **Fitzwilliam.** It's a classic New England village with a steepled church and Federal-style homes facing the small green. At one time it was a quarry town. To get a sense of local history, stop in at the small **Amos J. Blake House Museum** on the Common (☎ 603/585-7742), which has 13 rooms filled with collections of toys, early farming tools, glass, and pottery. The house itself dates to 1837. *Hours:* Memorial Day to October 1, weekends only.

If you visit Fitzwilliam in spring you'll want to stroll along the paths that wind through a mass of huge rhododendrons in nearby **Rhododendron State Park.**

Jaffrey Center is another pretty village and is home to Monadnock State Park. Pilgrims of a different stripe visit the Old Burying Ground behind the

The Monadnock Region

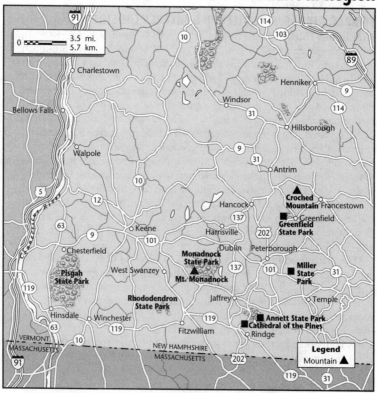

classic Jaffrey meetinghouse, where Willa Cather is buried. She is resting here, far from her Nebraska home, because she used to summer in Jaffrey at an inn where she wrote much of *My Antonia* (1918) and *One of Ours* (1922). If you wander around this old graveyard, you'll discover some other remarkable memorials, like the one created by artist Count Vigo Brandt Erickson to his infant daughter and his first wife, a Jaffrey native who loved to sit here and read. Amos Fortune is another celebrated local name, and he, too, is buried here. Amos was a slave who secured his freedom and amassed a substantial sum of money, some of which he left to a local school. It is said that he was an African prince and maintained great dignity of bearing and dress, always appearing at church in a fine black suit and top hat. Even so, he was not allowed to take communion, and it's somewhat ironic that he donated a communion plate to the church.

For additional insights into local history visit the **Jaffrey Historic District Melville Academy Museum**, Thorndike Pond Road, Jaffrey Center (☎ 603/532-7455). Local railroad magnate Jonas Melville financed the academy, which was founded in 1843. Subsequently, he lost his fortune and the school was closed in 1857. It now houses a fine small museum that has notable collections of Hannah Davis bandboxes among other objects. *Hours:* July and August, Saturday and Sunday. *Admission:* Free.

TEMPLE, RINDGE, FITZWILLIAM & JAFFREY LODGING

Ram in the Thicket, Maple Street, Wilton, NH 03449 (☎ 603/654-6440), reflects the entertaining, fun personality of the Reverend Andrew Tempelman and his wife, Priscilla. It's a delightful, white clapboard Victorian home, set on a little hill in a very quiet area. The rooms are all tastefully decorated with wicker, chintz, ruffled curtains, and brass-and-iron beds; some of the rooms have four-posters with canopies. The ground floor houses several small, intimate dining rooms, candlelit at night, which offer fine food to a classical music background. The menu might feature such dishes as chicken mulligatawny, chunks of chicken in a mildly spicy coconut milk sauce; or roasted pork wrapped in bacon and sprinkled with brown sugar. Prices range from $16 to $20. For summer dining there's a screened-in porch overlooking the garden. *Hours:* Wednesday, Thursday, and Sunday from 5:30 to 8:30pm, Friday and Saturday from 5:30 to 9:30pm. Whatever else you do, be sure to take a seat at the tiny bar and listen to the former reverend as he serves up a few bons mots along with an ounce or two of alcohol. *Rates:* $80 double with private bath, $65 double with shared bath.

The Birchwood Inn, Route 45, Temple, NH 03084 (☎ 603/878-3285), is an old brick coaching inn dating to 1800 that overlooks the green in Temple. The seven rooms (five with private baths) have been decorated in country style with quilts and chintz and oak. The innkeeper is a train buff and one room has been decorated with photographs of trains and reliefs of locomotives. The most notable historic room is the dining room, which has murals by Rufus Porter portraying a clipper ship scene. There's also an atmospheric tavern. The dishes are prepared daily and are listed on a blackboard—roast duck, filet mignon, and usually a chicken, veal, and fish dish. The tavern is filled with eye-catching objects from puzzles and games to china and model trains. *Rates:* $70 to $80.

The Amos A. Parker House, Route 119, P.O. Box 202, Fitzwilliam, NH 03447 (☎ 603/585-6540), is a lovely place to stay, not just for the richness of the accommodations and the historic home in which it's located, but also for the heavenly gardens that owner Freda B. Houpt has created over the years. Laced with fountains and ponds, the garden beds contain 1,500 plants and are completely entrancing; they alone are reason enough to stay here. The circa 1780 house itself is filled with character, especially the post-and-beam sitting room, which is thought to date to 1700. Throughout Freda has decorated with sumptuous personal collections. The most obvious are the oriental rugs, but there are eye-catching accents all around, including delightful flower stencils. There are two rooms and two suites (three with wood-burning fireplaces). One suite has a sitting room with a sofa, two wing chairs, a table, and Windsor chair; the bedroom has an iron-and-brass bed. One room has a striking four-poster with a lace canopy and toile bedspread and a wing chair upholstered with the same beautiful fabric. A full breakfast is served in a very handsome dining room that has a fireplace with a baking oven. Guests also have the pleasure of gathering in a gracious sitting room. *Rates:* $90 to $100.

Innkeepers Mike and Kaye Terpstra at the **Hannah Davis House,** Route 119, 186 Depot Rd., Fitzwillliam, NH 03447 (☎ 603/585-3344), extend a warm greeting to their guests. The 1820 home has fine architectural elements such as random-width pumpkin-pine floors and chair-rail wainscoting. There are three rooms and three suites, all nicely decorated (four with wood-burning fireplaces). Even though Hannah's Room is small, it accommodates an iron bed, oak chest, and wing chair with iron floor lamp. The Canopy Room, of course, has a canopied bed, while Chauncey has an iron-and-brass bed dressed with lace-trimmed linens and a striped ruffle. The most fetching room is actually above the garage. Here the ceilings are high and there's a sitting area with enough room for a table and four chairs. The bed is an antique cannonball, and the suite has its own private deck and entrance. A small TV/VCR is available in the inn's sitting room, and there's also an upright piano if guests want to entertain. The heart of the house is the large country kitchen. *Rates:* $70 to $145.

The **Fitzwilliam**, on the Common, Fitzwilliam, NH 03447 (☎ 603/585-9000), dating back to 1796, is almost as venerable as the John Hancock. Old family portraits and wedding certificates hang in the beamed dining room; an adjoining room displays the family's huge basket collection. For summer dining, the Country Dining Room overlooks the pool and garden and also exhibits some handsomely painted corner cupboards. The food is traditional—steaks, salmon with lemon hollandaise, roast duck, chicken Marsala—priced from $11 to $20. In the winter you'll likely find three fireplaces blazing, one in the dining room, another in the library (where there's also a TV), and another in the taproom. There are 25 guest rooms, 12 with private baths, all differently furnished in simple country fashion. For example, Room 5 has chintz wallpaper and stenciling and a sage-green painted chest, while Room 16 sports a pink gingham coverlet and curtains set against rose-colored wallpaper. *Rates:* $70 to $80 double. *Dining hours:* Daily 8 to 9:30am; Monday to Saturday noon to 2pm and 5:30 to 9pm, Sunday noon to 8pm.

Benjamin Prescott Inn, Route 124 East, Jaffrey, NH 03452 (☎ 603/532-6637), is in a Greek Revival home dating to 1853 that is surrounded by a 700-acre dairy farm. It has nine rooms, all attractively decorated with country furnishings. One room has a cottage-painted bed, drop-leaf side tables, an acorn dresser, and an Eastlake chair. Others might have brass beds or a marble-top dresser or Victorian chairs. The most luxurious accommodation is the third-floor suite, which has a skylit sitting area with French doors leading to a private balcony with pastoral views. It's equipped with a refrigerator, wet bar, and small TV. In the bedroom is a canopied bed, plus two beds ingeniously tucked under the eaves. Breakfast dishes run to temptations like peach French toast and multigrain waffles. While you're eating you can contemplate the collection of sand from around the world—begun by Barry's grandfather, it comes from 31 different countries and 30 states. There's a comfortable parlor for guests. *Rates:* $75 to $140.

RINDGE DINING

Lily's on the Pond, Route 202, Rindge (☎ 603/899-3322), has a warm country feel with its wagonwheel lamps and wood-burning stove. The food is good and reasonably priced and the variety of selections will satisfy everyone, whether you want burgers or sandwiches or more interesting fare like Cajun-style sirloin. My choice would be one of the many daily fish specials, for example, the red snapper with mushrooms, tomatoes, and garlic. Prices range from $10 to $15. There's an attractive post-and-beam tavern room, too. *Hours:* Tuesday to Saturday from 11:30am to 9pm, Sunday from 10am to 8pm.

HENNIKER, HILLSBOROUGH, ANTRIM, HANCOCK, PETERBOROUGH, DUBLIN & HARRISVILLE

Henniker is a pretty historic town nestled by the Contoocook River. It has a couple of appealing inns, and the stores along Main Street are worth browsing. Nearby **Hillsborough** is made up of four villages: Bridge Village, an old mill town on the banks of the Contoocook, is the commercial center; Hillsborough Center has a cluster of Early American homes arranged around a green; the upper village is the home of the Fuller Library; and the lower village is on Franklin Pierce Lake. Hillsborough was settled in 1748, and many of the original old homes can be seen still standing in Hillsborough Center. Visit **Gibson Pewter Workshop** (☎ 603/464-3410) just off the common, or attend one of the many auctions that are held under tents on the green during the summer. For information on the latter contact **Richard Withington,** 590 Center Rd. (☎ 603/464-3232).

The **Franklin Pierce Homestead Historic Site,** at routes 9 and 31, Hillsborough (☎ 603/478-3165), is the childhood home of Franklin Pierce, our rather bland 14th president. Built in 1804 by his father, General Benjamin Pierce, who was twice governor of New Hampshire, it reflects the atmosphere of wealth in which the young Franklin grew up. The rooms are spacious and have stenciled walls and fine imported wallpapers. Upstairs there is a ballroom where Benjamin drilled the local militia as well as entertained such figures as Daniel Webster. After serving terms as a congressman and senator, Franklin was nominated to run for the presidency at the Democratic Convention of 1852; he was elected largely because he supported the Fugitive Slave Law that won him the votes of the South. During his term, pre–Civil War social conflict intensified, and he did little to calm it. *Hours:* June and September to Columbus Day, Saturday 10am to 4pm and Sunday 1 to 4pm; July and August, Monday to Saturday 10am to 4pm and Sunday 1 to 4pm.

Hancock is another delightful village that was once an old mill town. Nearly every building on Main Street is in the National Register of Historic Places. The old clapboard and brick homes, four-room schoolhouse, town market, and classic steepled church evoke another, earlier era. If you're interested, stop in at the **Hancock Historical Society** (☎ 603/525-9379). *Hours:* July and August, Wednesday and Saturday; June and September, Saturday only; winter, Wednesday only. *Admission:* Free.

In this region, **Peterborough** is the biggest town and has the most to see. The redbrick buildings cluster along the banks of Goose Brook and the Contoocook River, which were both lined with mills back when this town was a center of Yankee ingenuity. It was settled largely by Scotch-Irish folk who left Londonderry, New Hampshire, because they could not eke out a living from the stubborn soil there.

Many an enterprising and successful inventor-entrepreneur set up business here or in the surrounding towns in the 19th century, and the factories turned out everything from textiles and paper to machinery and precision instruments. The Phoenix Mills operated from 1793 to 1908 and at one time employed 200 people; Goodell cutlery was made in nearby Antrim. Charles Wilder started making thermometers in North Peterborough and later sold his company to an instrument manufacturer in Troy, New York. These industries have long gone, but today the town is well known for the 40 or so special-interest magazines that are published in the town or nearby—from *CD Review* to *Byte Magazine,* which occupies the former site of the Phoenix factory. The biggest building in town at one time was the Guernsey Cattle Club, which kept the genealogical records of the nation's Guernsey herds until it moved out to Ohio.

The **Peterborough Historical Society,** 19 Grove St. (☎ 603/924-3235), has a whole floor of exhibits tracing town history and also some beautifully crafted New Hampshire furniture. They provide a walking tour map of the main buildings along Grove Street on request. *Hours:* July and August, daily 10am to 4pm; rest of the year, Monday to Friday 10am to 4pm.

Peterborough was the model for Thornton Wilder's *Our Town,* which he wrote while he was staying at the famous **MacDowell Colony,** 100 High St., Peterborough (☎ 603/924-3886), a retreat for artists, musicians, and writers on the northwestern edge of town. Just before composer Edward MacDowell died, he dreamed of establishing a place to which creative artists could retreat to write and paint in solitude surrounded by natural beauty. He died before he could realize his dream, but his wife, concert pianist Marian Nevins MacDowell, took on the task at the age of 50 and built the colony on the 450 wooded acres. Since then it has nurtured more than 4,500 artists—writers Stephen Vincent Benet, Edward Arlington Robinson, Willa Cather, James Baldwin, Alice Walker, Spalding Gray, Barbara Tuchman, Padraic Colum, Maxwell Bodenheim; composers Aaron Copland, Virgil Thomson, Leonard Bernstein, and Mrs. H. H. Beach; and artists Milton Avery and Jules Feiffer.

The artists work in the 32 studios on the property, where they are free to follow their own inspiration. They may be inspired—or discouraged, as the case may be—by the names of previous occupants of their studios displayed on the walls. The studios are for work only—the artists sleep elsewhere. Break-fast and dinner are taken at the red barn; lunch is delivered in a panier to the porch of each studio. Ask for the key to the Savidge Library if you want to see all the books and scores of those that have spent time here. It's an inviting space, lit by Palladian windows and furnished with oriental rugs, a fireplace, and wing chairs.

Other in-town entertainments include browsing and shopping, especially at Dock Square, where there are several galleries including a branch of the famous Sharon Arts Center (in nearby Sharon) plus **Haskell Russell Antiques,** and other interesting stores.

Four miles south of town the **Sharon Arts Center,** Route 123, Sharon (☎ 603/924-7256), operates two galleries exhibiting fine arts and crafts—pottery, jewelry, prints, furniture, textiles, glass, wood and metal sculptures—plus a reputable craft school, which offers a variety of lectures and workshops throughout the year in painting, weaving, jewelry, stained glass, sculpture, and pottery. *Hours:* Monday to Saturday 10am to 5pm, Sunday noon to 5pm.

From Peterborough, Route 101 will take you to the hill town of **Dublin,** which is the highest town in the region and offers great views of Monadnock and Dublin Lake. It has been a summer resort for more than 150 years, attracting a number of authors, musicians, artists, and executives. Among them were poet Amy Lowell, artist and naturalist Abbot Thayer, and artists George de Forest Brush and Joseph Lindon Smith. Today it's home to *Yankee Magazine*.

A side road off Route 101 will bring you to **Harrisville,** a classic mill village incorporated in 1870, huddled beside a pond. Unlike the other villages in the region, which were largely agricultural, this was at one time a thriving industrial enclave of mills, warehouses, and workers' housing, all made of brick. Today it's a National Historic Landmark (☎ 603/827-3722), in which the buildings have been restored and reused (more than 200 are landmarks). At the center stands a wool storage building that is now home to **Harrisville Designs,** a mecca for weavers, who come to take instructional courses and to purchase looms, yarn, or finished clothing. Stay a while and take in the setting of the old buildings standing in a wooded valley beside reed-rimmed Harrisville Pond and Goose Creek.

AREA LODGING

Colby Hill Inn, P.O. Box 778, Henniker, NH 03242 (☎ 603/428-3281), is a 1795 farmhouse charmer in an idyllic setting with 6 acres of beautiful gardens and a weathered barn. There are 16 rooms (10 in the main house and 6 in the carriage house). They are decorated in a country style. One might have a brass bed combined with an Empire chest and club chairs, all set against striped wallpaper with a decorative tassel border pattern. Another might contain a sleigh bed and a Victorian-style sofa against a cabbage rose–patterned wallpaper. Some have gas fireplaces. Carriage house rooms are a little smaller, but still attractive. There are two wonderful old barns on the property, one is 110 years old, the other 190. The pool, with a flagstone apron, is shaded by maples and has great views of tree-clad hills. The garden is shaded by honey-locust and black-and-white birch and has a fountain and colorful flower beds, too. The gazebo is a romantic place in the evening. Dinner is served daily and the food is well prepared. It features a traditional menu with such dishes as filet mignon with roasted garlic and shallot-peppercorn sauce, or chicken saltimbocca pie, which consists of chicken sautéed with mushrooms, red peppers, and prosciutto, baked under a pastry. The minted red wine sauce with rack of lamb is delicious, and the shrimp and fennel, flamed with Pernod, blends perfectly. Prices range from $16 to $24. *Rates:* $95 to $125. *Dining hours:* Monday to Saturday from 5:30 to 8:30pm, Sunday 4:30 to 7:30pm.

Meetinghouse Inn & Restaurant, 35 Flanders Rd., Henniker, NH 03242 (☎ 603/428-3228), is a charming accommodation made even more so by the trellis and gardens along the front, the hot tub, and an excellent restaurant. The post-and-beam dining room is a romantic, candlelit trysting place with cabbage-rose decor and an occasional cherub for good measure. If you are puzzled by the Ziploc bags of sand on one wall, they are equally sentimental in their way—the collection began 15 years ago when some local students returned from Bermuda with the first sample. The classically prepared food is great, and there's a full selection to choose from. Tenderloin of beef is served with a rich cassis sauce with blackberries and green onions, or you can order beef Wellington. On the seafood side the shrimp Alfredo is cooked in a blend of basil, wine, and cheese; while the plain broiled halibut is delicious. Prices range from $16 to $22. The rooms are also charming, with canopied oak or brass beds and wide-board floors. A full breakfast is served. *Rates:* $75 to $115. *Dining hours:* Wednesday to Sunday 5 to 9pm.

The Inn at Maplewood Farm, 447 Center Rd., Hillsborough (☎ 603/464-4242), is a beautifully situated landmark farmhouse on 14 acres that is operated by an engaging young couple, Jayme and Laura Simoes. There are four suites—two with sitting rooms and two with two bedrooms. Each is large and nicely furnished. One room has a canopy bed, marble-top side tables, and a wood-burning fireplace. Kilims and dhurries enhance the floors. In the barn room the floor has been painted to look like a rug and then furnished with a four-poster and oak pieces. In each room you'll find an old radio that plays old radio shows. Jayme is a passionate collector of old radios and enjoys sharing them with guests. In the parlor, where guests relax, Jayme has his collection of radios on display, and there's lots of reading material and comfortable places to sit. The breakfasts are superb, served in a light and airy dining room, where Laura displays her collection of teapots. Expect such dishes as peach soup followed by the lightest quiche you've ever tasted, or spinach wrap containing scrambled eggs and fresh salsa with stuffed pattypan. It's a serene place where you can sit on the front porch or at the tables by the apple orchard. *Rates:* May to October, $75 to $85 double. Closed November to April.

The **Hancock Inn**, Main Street, Hancock, NH 03449 (☎ 603/525-3318), is a seasoned inn, in continuous operation since 1789. The staircase creaks as you step up to the 11 guest rooms, all with private baths and all furnished with antique country pieces set against stenciled walls or striking murals. Room 16 has a pastoral scene painted by the famous itinerant painter Rufus Porter. Its furnishings include a pencil four-poster canopied bed matched with a painted blanket chest, maple dresser, rocker, and wing chair. Most of the wide-plank floors are covered with braided area rugs. The ground floor features an inviting tavern room that serves as a common room for guests. The dining room positively glows at night. It's sponge-painted in red with colonial blue trim and lit by tin wall sconces and candles on the tables. The fare is traditional New England: baked Boston scrod, Nantucket seafood casserole (scallops, shrimp, and lobster), filet mignon, chicken amandine, and lamb chop mixed grill. The specialty is Shaker cranberry pot roast that's so tender it just flakes onto the fork. Prices range from $16 to $22. *Rates:* $108 to $160 double. *Dining hours:* Monday to Saturday from 6pm to closing, Sunday from 5pm to closing.

The **Inn at Crotched Mountain**, Mountain Road (off Route 47), Francestown, NH 03043 (☎ 603/588-6840), a brick building covered with ivy, has a magnificent setting on a mountain side overlooking a valley and wooded hills—a surprising, delightful hideaway and a great place for skiers. The ceilings are low in parts of the 1822 building. There are 14 rooms, 8 with private baths. Room 9 is my favorite—it has a door that leads out to the pool and also offers a dramatic view. Three of the rooms have fireplaces, one has a wood stove, and all are nicely furnished with maple pieces, braided rugs, country style. Guests are free to use the comfortable living room, with wing chairs and a sofa around two fireplaces. The dining room is crisply turned out with white and red napery and maple Windsor chairs. There's also the cozy Winslow tavern, where you can snuggle up by the fireside at tables made from old wagon-wheel hubs. The menu features filet mignon with béarnaise, cranberry-port pot roast, and lamb chops with apple mint jelly, priced from $13 to $17. Facilities include a large swimming pool, two clay tennis courts, and 5½ miles of cross-country skiing trails. *Rates:* $80 to $90 double. Closed for 3 weeks in November. *Dining hours:* May to October, Friday to Saturday 6 to 8pm.

The **Greenfield Inn**, at routes 31 and 136, Greenfield, NH 03047 (☎ 603/547-6327), 10 minutes from Greenfield State Park, is run by friendly Victor and Barbara Mangini. The old Victorian house has a wraparound veranda leading onto a spacious deck overlooking Mount Monadnock. Guests have use of a hammock, a TV room, parlor, and a breakfast room, where a full buffet breakfast—ham and egg soufflé plus muffins and granola—is served to the strains of Mozart and his contemporaries. Photos of Bob Hope, a good friend of the couple, adorn the walls in a nook of the sitting room. The 12 rooms (9 with private bath) are attractively furnished with chintz wallpapers and oak and pine furnishings. The most alluring accommodation is the Honeymooner's Hideaway, which is tucked away under the house with stone foundation walls. In the Samson and Delilah Room, a brass bed covered with a rose-and-cream eiderdown shares space with a rocker, a table with a mirror, and a rush-seated stool. Fringed lamps, lace curtains, and other accents add a touch of romance to all the rooms. *Rates:* $59 to $109 double.

Harrisville Squires Inn, Keene Road, Harrisville, NH 03450 (☎ 603/827-3925), is located on a quiet, little-traveled road in a wooded valley in a mid-19th-century homestead. The owners, Pat and Doug McCarthy, have been hosting guests for the last 14 years. The house is set on 50 acres, with more than 6 miles of ski trails across 30 acres. Since Doug runs Monadnock bike touring, he's really familiar with all the back roads. There are five rooms, all furnished in a country style with iron-and-brass beds with quilts, wing and Windsor chairs, acorn chests, and wicker or oak furniture. Room 3 has a Jacuzzi, and the bedroom has been sponge-painted and furnished with a high-back cottage bed, a wicker rocker, and an oak dresser. The garden contains a tiny meditation garden by the pond-fountain. Breakfast is served in an attractive dining room where baskets hang from the beams and French doors lead out to a tree-shaded area with tables. Facilities include 30 acres of ski trails and the store, which sells dried flower arrangements, stained glass, and wooden bowls that Pat has made. *Rates:* $80 to $90.

PETERBOROUGH & DUBLIN DINING

Latacarta, 6 School St., Peterborough (☎ 603/924-6878), occupies an old movie theater. The restaurant decor is simple. Crisp white tablecloths and kitchen chairs are set against terra-cotta/peach-colored walls hung with choice Japanese kimonos. The food is prepared with spiritual consciousness and is primarily Japanese-inspired. You can begin with gyoza or nori rolls along with a sea chowder filled with fresh fish. Ginger chicken over linguine or salmon in a creamy dill sauce are among the main courses, but the signature dish is the Latacarta dinner—a stuffed artichoke steamed with garlic, tofu, and basil filling and served with zucchini and summer squash that has been simmered with soy sauce and sherry. Prices range from $16 to $19. *Hours:* Monday to Friday noon to 2pm, Monday to Thursday 5 to 8:30pm, Friday and Saturday 5 to 9pm.

Del Rossi's Trattoria, Route 137 at Route 101, Dublin (☎ 603/563-7195), is a fun place to dine, especially if you like bluegrass music. Some of the best bluegrass artists, like Kate Campbell, appear in the back room. The smaller dining rooms are more formal with their beamed ceilings, wide-board floors, and Windsor chairs. To start, try the polenta Gorgonzola, a perfect combination of flavors topped with a little marinara sauce. Or there's the very popular cream of garlic soup. Among the traditional Italian fare are a number of refreshing dishes—for example, try Butter's chicken, a Ligurian dish that features breast of chicken sautéed with pancetta, onion, mushroom, garlic, fresh sage, red pepper, and pine nuts, simmered with Chianti and tomato, and finished with a splash of balsamic vinegar. Another unusual dish is the Sicilian-style pork, which is breaded with a special mixture and finished with lemon. Prices range from $9 to $18. The owners operate a store upstairs that sells acoustic stringed instruments. Saturday night there is always entertainment.

Aesop's Tables, 12 Depot St., Peterborough (☎ 603/924-1612), occupies a corner of the Toadstool Bookstore. The main staples are sandwiches—turkey, egg, and BLTs, all under $5, plus soup, pastries, and breads. *Hours:* Monday to Saturday 7am to 5pm.

THE AREA AFTER DARK

The **New England Marionette Opera,** Main Street, Peterborough (☎ 603/924-4333), is a rare marionette theater devoted primarily to opera. Patrons climb up a narrow spiral staircase to the 135-seat theater, which has velvet and mahogany seats and a state-of-the-art sound system to see performances by 32-inch-tall personalities in full costume on elaborate sets. Tickets are $24 for adults; shorter children's shows are $14 for adults, $10 for children ages 11 and under.

A better-known company is the **Peterborough Players,** Hadley Road (☎ 603/924-7585), off Middle Hancock Road, which has provided summer theater since 1933 at the 125-acre Hadley Farm. Alumni of this venerable theater company include Avery Brooks, Jean Stapleton, and James Whitmore. On weekends tickets range from $21.50 to $24.50 for such productions as Shakespeare's *Romeo and Juliet,* Neil Simon's *Broadway Bound,* and A. R. Gurney's *Sylvia.*

ALONG THE CONNECTICUT RIVER FROM HINSDALE TO WALPOLE

Keene is the major town of the Monadnock region. Art lovers will want to visit the **Thorne-Sagendorph Art Gallery** at Keene State College, 229 Main St. (on Wyman Way; ☎ 603/358-2720). The collection focuses on local and regional artists and contains works by Alexander James, Richard Meryman, Joseph Lindon Smith, and Barry Faulkner. Contemporary artists featured include Robert Mapplethorpe, Vargian Bogosian, and Jules Olitski. From Keene it's easy to reach **Pisgah State Park** and the small towns that cluster around its perimeter from **West Swanzey** to **Winchester** via Route 10. From

Winchester Route 119 will bring you to the river town of **Hinsdale** and then north through the mountains to **Chesterfield** and eventually, via Route 12, to **Walpole.** Chocolate lovers make this little village a destination just to visit **Burdick Chocolates,** where they can select their own choices and have them put into the hallmark cigar box that is then tied with a bow and closed with a wax seal. They are absolutely wonderful chocolates. Or you can relax at one of the tables and enjoy a cappuccino or chocolate espresso and a pastry.

CHESTERFIELD & WALPOLE LODGING

The **Chesterfield Inn**, Route 9, P.O. Box 155, Chesterfield, NH 03443 (☎ 603/256-3211), is an exquisitely decorated lodging offering 13 guest rooms, all with private baths, telephones, and TVs (8 have fireplaces). Rooms in the new Johanna Wetherby building have private garden patios. Nine rooms in the restored 1787 farmhouse / carriage house have great character with their handsome beams and many fine antiques. Each room is tastefully decorated. In Room 14 you'll find a round Empire-style table, a scallop-shell secretary, attractive oak side tables, and wing chairs, all set against a pretty blue-and-rose floral wallpaper. Carved Victorian love seats, desks with decorative inlay, and drop-leaf tables are just some of the fetching antiques that are found throughout. A full breakfast is served. The dining room serves American/continental cuisine—duck with raspberry sauce, grilled gingered swordfish, lamb shanks with rosemary and zinfandel. Prices run $16 to $22. *Rates:* Summer, $135 to $160, $175 suites; winter, $135 to $185, $190 suites. *Dining hours:* Daily 5:30 to 9pm.

The **Josiah Bellows House,** Walpole, NH 03608 (☎ 603/756-4250), occupies a lovely 1813 house that has a back flagstone patio and gardens that offer views of wooded hills. It's a center-hall building with large rooms and some very distinctive interior details—Belgian blue tiles around the fireplace in the parlor and wood floors with patterned borders crafted from maple and cherry. The four rooms (two sharing a bath) are furnished with iron-and-brass beds, rugs spread over wide-board floors, and such pieces as marble-top dressers and Victorian button chairs. One room features a half-poster and an Empire chest. Breakfast is served at a lace-covered table in a room that is flooded with light from the Palladian-style windows. Guest have the use of two parlors furnished with a sofa and armchairs. *Rates:* $70 to $80.

AREA DINING

The best dining is to be found across the river in Bellows Falls, Vermont at **Leslie's.** There's a series of country dining rooms furnished with polished wood tables; in summer an outdoor dining area is open. Ingredients are fresh and the food is tasty and reasonably priced. There might be salmon in a Beaujolais cream sauce, or Boston scrod baked in wine and lemon, plus meat dishes like veal Marsala or roast duckling served with raspberry Chambord sauce. Prices range from $13 to $17. Service is casual. *Hours:* Wednesday to Friday 11:30am to 1:30pm; Wednesday to Monday 5:30 to 9pm.

Also on the Vermont side in Saxtons River, **Averill's,** Route 121 (☎ 802/869-2327), is a good choice. It has a tavern on one side and a more formal dining room on the other. The food is good, and you can expect to find such daily specials as salmon with a Caribbean sauce along with steaks and other items. The Cuban bread is a great start to the meal. *Hours:* Summer, Monday to Saturday 5:30 to 10pm; winter, Wednesday to Saturday 5 to 9pm.

Monadnock
Special & Recreational Activities

Biking: Although the terrain is somewhat hilly, it's a scenic region for biking. For information and tours contact **Monadnock Bicycle Touring Center** (☎ 603/827-3925); rentals are available at **Spokes and Slopes** (☎ 603/924-9961). Temple Mountain is the place for mountain biking.

Cross-Country Skiing: Several of the inns listed (like the Fitzwilliam) have facilities, or you can head into **Monadnock State Park** (☎ 603/532-8862), **Greenfield State Park** (☎ 603/547-3373), or to the facility at **Temple Mountain. Road's End Farm,** Jackson Hill Road, Chesterfield (☎ 603/363-4703), also has 32km of trails.

Fishing: Licenses are available from town clerks and sporting goods stores. Nonresidents can contact the **New Hampshire Fish and Game Department,** 34 Bridge St., Concord, NH 03301 (☎ 603/271-3421).

Golf: Bretwood Golf Course, East Surry Road, Keene (☎ 603/352-7626); **Keene Country Club,** R.R. 2, Box 264, Keene (☎ 603/352-9722); **Monadnock Country Club,** Peterborough (☎ 603/924-7769); and **Angus Lea** in Hillsborough (☎ 603/464-5404) are places to try.

Hiking: There are plenty of hiking trails at **Rhododendron State Park** and other reserves. **Grand Monadnock** itself is the most climbed mountain in the United States. A round-trip hike to the top up the popular **White Dot Trail,** which begins at the entrance to Monadnock State Park in Jaffrey, will take about 3 hours. For information about the five main trails, call **Monadnock State Park** at ☎ 603/532-8862.

At **Crotched Mountain** there are three trails to the summit. The sign-posted **Bennington Trail** starts 3 miles north of Greenfield on Route 31 and is probably the easiest to find. The **Francestown Trail** begins at the base of what was Crotched Mountain ski area. For additional information call the **New Hampshire Division of Forests and Lands** (☎ 603/271-2214).

Other trails and hikes include the **Monadnock-Sunapee Greenway Trail** and several in **Shieling State Forest.** From **Miller State Park** you can also hike to the summit of Pack Monadnock Mountain. For additional hiking, see "State Parks," below.

Skiing: Day and night Alpine, cross-country, and snowboarding can be enjoyed at **Temple Mountain,** off Route 101, Peterborough (☎ 603/924-6949), which has a quadruple chairlift, snowmaking capability, night skiing, and 35 miles of cross-country skiing.

State Parks: Rhododendron State Park, off Route 119, 2½ miles west of Fitzwilliam (☎ 603/532-8862), consists of 16 acres where you can stroll under these wild, majestic shrubs (some as tall as 20 feet). The park itself is 494 acres and offers fine views of Monadnock. Visit in July for the rhododendrons in bloom. **Annett State Park,** Cathedral Road, off Route 119, Rindge (☎ 603/532-8862), is a 1,336-acre park for hiking and picnicking. **Monadnock State Park,** off Route 124, 4 miles west of Jaffrey (☎ 603/532-8862), has 40 miles of trails. It provides the easiest access to the summit of Grand Monadnock. The park offers hiking, camping, and ski touring. **Fox State Forest,** School Street, Hillsborough, 2½ miles from

Hillsboro Center (☎ 603/464-3453), is a 1,432-acre forest with 20 miles of trails and roads. **Miller State Park,** off Route 101, 3 miles east of Peterborough (☎ 603/924-3672), provides access to the summit of Pack Monadnock Mountain (2,290 feet). Named after General James Miller, hero of the Battle of Lundy's Lane in the War of 1812 at Niagara, this park offers picnicking, hiking trails, and great views of the Green Mountains. **Pisgah State Park,** Chesterfield, Hinsdale, Winchester, off Route 63 or Route 119 (☎ 603/239-8153), affords 13,000 acres of wilderness for hiking, hunting, and fishing, and ski touring and snowmobiling in winter. **Greenfield State Park,** off Route 136 (☎ 603/547-3373 or 603/547-3497), shelters Otter Lake for swimming. Picnicking and camping are also available in this 400-acre park.

Tennis: Courts are available at the **Inn at Crotched Mountain** in Francestown (☎ 603/588-6840) and **Monadnock Country Club** in Peterborough (☎ 603/924-7769).

Wildlife Watching: Near Peterborough, **Wapack National Wildlife Refuge,** off Route 101 at Miller State Park, is a wilderness area of bog, rock, and swamp on Pack Monadnock Mountain. It's great for hawk spotting and other wildlife observation.

NEW JERSEY

Cape May

Downtown Area ◆ *Cape May Point*

Distance in miles: 150
Estimated driving time: 3 hours

Driving: Take the New Jersey Turnpike to the Garden State Parkway all the way to the end, which will bring you right into Cape May on Lafayette Street. Turn left on Madison and you'll be at the beaches.

Bus: New Jersey Transit (☎ 973/762-5100) operates daily express buses from the Port Authority Bus Terminal to Cape May. The trip takes 5 hours.

Further Information: For more about New Jersey in general, contact the **New Jersey Division of Travel and Tourism**, 20 W. State St. (P.O. Box 826), Trenton, NJ 08625-0826 (☎ 609/292-2470). For specific information about the Cape May area, contact the **Chamber of Commerce of Greater Cape May**, P.O. Box 556, Cape May, NJ 08204 (☎ 609/884-5508).

When you arrive in Cape May, you'll find yourself in a different world and a different era. Drive or walk through the streets to see lovely old Victorian homes painted white, sage green, pale blue, gray, or pink. Swing seats and rockers are on wraparound verandas; intricate towers, turrets, and cupolas rise from fish-scale mansard roofs and deep projecting bays—row after row, they line the streets running down to the promenade and the sea. What's even more exciting is that you can stay in them, for many have been restored by young, professional couples who've chosen Cape May as their refuge from the treadmill of corporate and urban life and now run these marvelous homes as guest houses. Here you can sleep on lace-trimmed pillows and sheets under antique quilts spread on brass or Renaissance Revival beds; wander through rooms filled with Mission-style furniture, Eastlake sofas, Empire-style couches, brilliant chandeliers, and ornate clocks and mirrors; or spend time rocking gently on the veranda, enjoying the cool sea breezes that waft in from the shore. During the day, cycle around town or out to Cape May Point to survey the lighthouse, the marshlands, and—best of all—the rolling dunes that back

Cape May

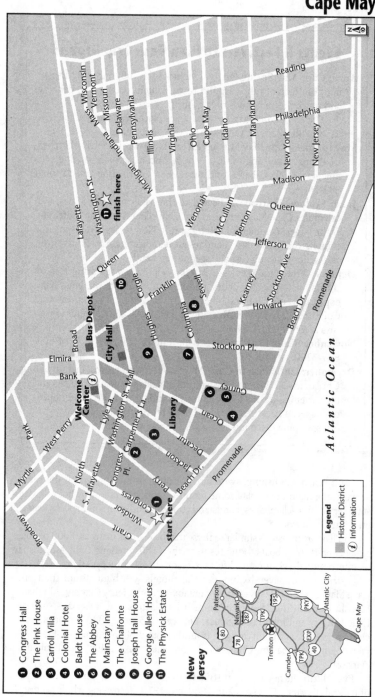

Legend
- Historic District
- (i) Information

1. Congress Hall
2. The Pink House
3. Carroll Villa
4. Colonial Hotel
5. Baldt House
6. The Abbey
7. Mainstay Inn
8. The Chalfonte
9. Joseph Hall House
10. George Allen House
11. The Physick Estate

New Jersey

Atlantic Ocean

Events & Festivals to Plan Your Trip Around

April: Cape May Spring Festival includes the Tulip Festival, display-ing hundreds of tulips around town, Dutch food, crafts, dancing, and music (usually mid- to late April).

    The Cape May Jazz Festival takes place in spring and fall. Call ☎ 609/884-7277 or 609/884-7200 for information.

May to June: Cape May Music Festival is a 4-week festival of orches-tral pops, jazz, tango music, opera, and a cappella singing plus bluegrass, folk, cabaret, and more. For information call ☎ 609/884-5404.

June: Seafood Festival, dedicated to the fishermen lost at sea, also celebrates Cape May's position as a Coast Guard training center and as the largest commercial fishing port in New Jersey. Events include exhibits, dramatic Coast Guard rescue demonstration on Friday night, and seafood tasting (usually second weekend).

October: Victorian Week—a 10-day celebration featuring fashion shows, historic house tours, antiques and craft shows, brass band concerts, vaudeville, and other appropriate entertainments (around Columbus Day weekend). Contact the Mid-Atlantic Center for the Arts at ☎ 609/884-5404.

November: Cape May Jazz Festival. Call ☎ 609/884-7277 or 609/884-7200.

December: Christmas in Cape May is filled with events, including a Christmas Candlelight house tour that visits ten historic homes and inns, evening wassail tours, craft fairs, and more. Many guest houses offer special packages then, and the stores along the Mall offer spe-cial shopping discounts along with festive wine and cheese.

the sand beach. Go fishing, swimming, birding, or boating; watch the catch arrive at the main dock; play some tennis or golf; and enjoy a whole slew of summer events—clambakes, bandstand concerts, and even some special events on winter holidays.

You'll enjoy pleasures similar to those that brought as many as 3,000 people a day aboard steamboats to the resort in the 1850s, making Cape May a spa of international acclaim. Its life as a resort began much earlier, in 1816, when the first of several Congress Hall hotels was built. From then on, Cape May received a steady stream of notable visitors: Henry Clay and Abraham Lincoln came in the 1840s, then much later actors and musicians such as Lillie Langtry and John Philip Sousa. Between 1850 and 1890 five presidents chose it as their temporary escape from the round of government—Franklin Pierce, James Buchanan, Ulysses S. Grant, Chester A. Arthur, and Benjamin Harrison.

Even during its heyday, from 1850 to 1913, Cape May experienced a series of natural disasters. Fire struck in 1869 and 1878, destroying whole sections of the town, including the 3,500-room Mount Vernon, which had been the biggest hotel in the world. Each time, the town was rebuilt in the same brack-eted Italianate style.

At the confluence of the Delaware River and the Atlantic, the town is ex-tremely vulnerable to storms. The major storm of 1962, which buried Cape May under sand and water, prompted many to think seriously about preserva-tion. This set the course that ensured the survival of the town's great Victorian legacy and rescued it from the doldrum days when it existed only as a military base and a commercial fishing port, visited only by a handful of loyal tourists who stayed at rather run-down rooming houses. Today Cape May is again playing the role of the grand resort, and it's a lovely place to experience the charm and grace of an intimate seaside resort that's escaped the ugly overlay of honky-tonk entertainment and gross modern development.

TOURS & TRANSPORTATION

Cape May is easy to walk around and great for bicycling. Rental bikes are available in town at **Village Bike Rentals** (☎ 609/884-8500) in the Acme parking lot, and at **Shields**, 11 Gurney St. (☎ 609/898-1818). From June to October, trolleys serve the whole area from 10am to 10pm daily.

The **Mid-Atlantic Center for the Arts**, 1048 Washington St. (☎ 609/884-5404; fax 609/884-0574), offers a variety of both trolley and walking tours. The trolley tours follow three different routes: around the east end, the west end, and along the beachfront. Moonlight trolley rides are offered from April to October, and Garden trolley tours between June and September. There's also a maritime heritage tour that visits the life-saving station and the U.S. Coast Guard training center, and a nighttime tour to the lighthouse. The charge for tours is $5.50 adults, $2.75 children ages 3 to 12; they leave daily April to December, and weekends only in January and February. The trolley tours leave from the information booth on the Washington Street Mall. (For other tours, starting locations can and do change, so call for the schedule.)

The 2-hour walking tours usually leave on Saturday mornings from the information booth on Washington Mall ($5 adults, $2.50 children ages 3 to 12). There are several other walking tours offered that combine visits to inns or gardens. Living History tours are given at the Emlen Physick estate and also at the lighthouse. Some tours even include afternoon tea or breakfast.

Gaslight tours of the Abbey and the Humphrey Hughes House plus a visit to the Goodman House, home of the Dollhouse and Miniature museum of Cape May, are given on Wednesday during summer ($12 adults, $6 children).

CAPE MAY ATTRACTIONS

Start at the **Welcome Center,** across from the bandstand at 405 Lafayette St. (☎ 609/884-9562). You'll find a hot-line phone center for conducting your own accommodations search if you've come without reservations. The staff is exceedingly friendly and helpful; coffee is available, as is plenty of written information about all kinds of events—concerts at the bandstand, foot races, quilt and decoy shows, barbecues, fish fries, clambakes, vintage movies, con-tests (kite flying, bike racing, and so on), and other summer frolics. During summer, information is also dispensed from the booth on the Washington Mall. *Hours:* May to October, daily 9am to 4pm.

Most people will want to spend much of their time at the **beach,** swim-ming, fishing, sailing, windsurfing, sunbathing, and enjoying other shore pastimes; but for those with an interest in history and architecture, Cape May offers a lot. First on the list, of course, are the 150 or so Victorian homes that still stand in the heart of town.

I recommend that one of the first things you do is take the 1- to 2-hour **walking tour** (see above), for you'll learn an incredible amount about architecture and the history of Cape May. The tours depart from the information booth on Washington Mall. If you prefer to ride, take one of the trolley tours.

STROLLING AROUND TOWN

Even if you don't take the walking tour, spend some time exploring the area between Congress and Franklin streets and from Beach Drive to Lafayette, where the greatest number of Victorian gems are concentrated.

Start at Beach Drive and Congress Street, where you'll find **Congress Hall,** an L-shaped three-story mansion screened by a multistory colonnade; this served as the summer White House for President Benjamin Harrison. Turn right on Congress Place past nos. 203, 207, and 209 onto Perry Street to see the much-photographed **Pink House** (1880) at no. 33, absolutely encrusted with gingerbread ornamentation. Cross Perry to Jackson Street, turn right, and stroll toward the sea past some beauties—the **Queen Victoria,** the **Carroll Villa** (now The Mad Batter), the **George Hildreth cottage** at no. 17, and the seven identical cottages commissioned in 1891 (they were considered unusual in their time because of their standardization).

Turn left on Beach Drive, pass the **Colonial Hotel** at Ocean Street (where Wallis Warfield, long before Edward VIII abdicated the throne of England for her, had a coming-out ball), and turn left at Gurney Street. Here you'll find a whole row of highly ornamental homes—the **Baldt House** at no. 26, the **1869 house,** the **Gingerbread House**—all culminating at the corner of Columbia Avenue in **The Abbey,** built by Stephen D. Button for wealthy Pennsylvania coal baron John B. McCreary, from 1869 to 1870. Turn right along Columbia Avenue, and at no. 635 you'll find the **Mainstay Inn,** originally designed to serve as a gambling house.

Take a detour down Howard Street to view the **Chalfonte** at no. 301, built in 1875 for Henry Sawyer, Cape May's Civil War hero, and then double back, turning right on Columbia Avenue and then left on Franklin Street, going up to Hughes Street, which is the oldest street in Cape May and still has the original gas lamps, stepping stones, and hitching posts that were used in the truly horse-powered era. There are some marvelous houses on this street, including the mauve-and-gray **White Dove cottage,** the 1868 **Joseph Hall House** with a lot of acroteria decoration, and many others with shark's-tooth and fish-scale tiles, witch's cap towers, intricate verge board carving, and more. Note, too, the **Albert Hughes House** (1838), which stands out because it's the only structure in a typical Federal style.

At Ocean Street, turn right and go over to Washington Avenue and take another right to the **George Allen House** at no. 720, an opulent bracketed mansion worthy of Newport. Continue down Washington to the Physick House (below) if you have the time and the energy.

The Physick House

In contrast to the fussily ornamental gingerbread style that flourished in Cape May stands the simplicity of Frank Furness's masterpiece, the **Physick House**

at 1048 Washington St. (☎ 609/884-5404), which is so much more rewarding to visit than most because you can actually go into the rooms and experience what it was like to live among the period furnishings, instead of having
to peer in from behind a set of ropes. A mentor of Louis Sullivan (who was in
turn a mentor of Frank Lloyd Wright), Furness turned away from the extravagant Italianate style and developed his own elaborate stick style, of which the
Physick House is a good example. Commissioned in 1878 to build a summer
home for Frances Ralston, Furness finished this 18-room mansion in 1881.
He designed both the exterior (note his trademarks—the inverted chimneys,
jerkin-head dormers, and oversize porch brackets) and the interior and even
some of the furniture, including a bedroom set that's classic in its simple geometric decoration.

Other highlights include several fireplaces easily identifiable as Furness's
by their geometric detailing and classic lines, unusual lincruster (a kind of
papier-mâché) wainscoting and ceilings in the hallway, a golden oak staircase
with linear grooving, a parlor with an Eastlake couch and a magnificent ceramic tureen that defies description, a William Morris print fabric in the dining room, and (a favorite with children) a kitchen filled with all kinds of early
gadgetry. The eccentric owner, Dr. Physick himself, had a curious life story.
Admission includes the Carriage House, now the home of the Cape May County
Art League, and an outbuilding containing a collection of antique tools.

Tours: Daily, call for times (weekends only in January). *Admission:* $7 adults,
$3.50 children ages 3 to 12.

ATTRACTIONS NEARBY

The **Cape May County Historical Society,** Route 9 (☎ 609/465-3535), possesses a collection of local memorabilia that includes period rooms, maritime
objects like the original flag from the *Merrimac,* and a children's room featuring toys, dolls, and needlework. Take Stone Harbor Boulevard off the Garden
State Parkway to Shore Road (Route 9). Turn right and travel north about
three-quarters of a mile. *Hours:* Summer, Tuesday to Saturday 9am to 3pm;
December to February, Saturday 10am to 3pm. *Admission:* $2.50 adults,
50¢ children ages 11 and under.

The **Wetlands Institute,** on Stone Harbor Boulevard in Stone Harbor
(☎ 609/368-1211), is a research facility with an aquarium and educational
displays that will interest naturalists. Visitors can follow the salt marsh trail,
walk out on the marsh boardwalk and the pier over the tidal creek, or climb
the observation tower for a panoramic view of the wetlands. The best time to
visit is at 10am, noon, or 2pm (Sunday at 11am and 1pm) when a film about
the salt marsh is shown and naturalists lead guided tours. *Hours:* Mid-May to
mid-October, Monday to Saturday 9:30am to 4:30pm, Sunday 10am to 4pm;
mid-October to mid-May, Tuesday to Saturday 9:30am to 4:30pm. *Admission:*
$5 adults, $2 children.

About 3 miles north of Cape May, **Cold Spring Village,** 731 Seashore Rd.
(☎ 609/898-2300), is a replica of a typical South Jersey farm village. Although
the buildings have been moved here from other places, the village has been
laid out with an eye to authenticity. It's worth spending some time wandering
through wooded areas from one building to another. All kinds of craft
and skills demonstrations—baking, basketry, tinsmithing, and more—are
given. The village also hosts a lot of weekend special events, like the Civil War

weekend when Union and Confederate regiments set up camp and re-create Civil War camp life with drills and training, medical practice, and battle and skirmish tactics based on the Suffolk campaign of April 1863.

To get there, the Garden State Parkway to Exit O, turn right on Route 109 to the traffic light, then follow the signs to the ferry until you reach the next light, which is Seashore Road. Turn right. *Hours:* Memorial Day to Labor Day, daily 10am to 4:30pm; after Labor Day to October, Saturday to Sunday 10am to 4:30pm. *Admission:* $5 adults, $4 seniors, $2 children ages 5 to 12.

A SIDE TRIP TO WHEATON VILLAGE

Only a 30-minute drive away in Millville, you may enjoy a visit to **Wheaton Village**, 1501 Glasstown Rd., between 10th and G streets (☎ 609/825-6800), a 60-acre museum/cultural center dedicated to American glass and regional crafts. In addition to the museum, where you can view all types of glass—from early bottles through art nouveau to modern—visitors can see demonstrations in the glass factory and pottery and wood-carving studios. It's worth the trip. *Hours:* April to December, daily 10am to 5pm. Closed Monday to Tuesday January to March. *Admission:* $6.50 adults, $5.50 seniors, $3.50 children ages 6 to 18.

CAPE MAY LODGING

Note: On weekends, most of the following accommodations require a 2- or 3-night minimum stay. Also, most of them (some exceptions) don't encourage children under age 12, not because they don't like kids, but simply because children are likely to find a weekend when they're asked to keep quiet a big bore. If you plan to visit during summer, make your reservations far in advance. Owners will usually provide complimentary beach tags.

A note on parking: In summer, parking is particularly difficult and you'd do well to leave your car at home and walk or cycle around. Some accommodations do provide free parking; others will charge for the privilege of parking on the property. Always check first.

The Guest Houses

The Cape May showpiece that's been featured so many times in magazines is the **Mainstay**, 635 Columbia Ave., Cape May, NJ 08204 (☎ 609/884-8690), a beauty designed by Stephen D. Button to serve as a gambling house. Passersby invariably stop to admire the architectural features of this grand inn—a pilastered cupola, 13-foot-tall Italianate windows flanked by shutters, and a wraparound porch supported by exquisitely fluted and turned columns encrusted with gingerbread. Depending on your taste in vacation lodgings you may find it too overwhelming and too perfect. Making this a particularly idyllic spot are the well-tended gardens spilling over in early spring and summer with roses, hydrangeas, irises, pinks, pansies, and tiger lilies, all set around a small fountain.

Devoted preservationists Tom and Sue Carroll have spent their time and energy restoring this place to its former magnificence. The public rooms, with 14-foot-high ceilings, ornate plaster moldings, and elaborate chandeliers, have been furnished with extravagant Victoriana—12-foot-high carved mirrors in the hall and a wrought-iron stove in the small front parlor. The drawing room boasts gilt-framed oils and colorful paintings on glass, richly patterned oriental rugs, damask-covered tufted chairs, and a grand piano standing against a long-case clock and a graceful wrought-iron floor lamp. Here you'll always find fresh-cut flowers on the marble-top table. In the dining room the formal table seats 12, and the tall windows are draped with lace, capped by a scarlet tasselled valance.

The six large guest rooms (each with bath) are furnished with thick pile carpets and beds with walnut Renaissance Revival headboards; one of the baths features a copper tub. Sue and Tom also have accommodations in "the cottage next door," another pleasant Victorian where there are six additional rooms, all similarly furnished. Across the road, the Officer's Quarters contains four luxurious suites, each with a large whirlpool tub, a kitchenette with mini-fridge, a TV/VCR, and a gas fireplace in the living room.

Guests are invited to enjoy a full breakfast on the porch in summer (strawberry crêpes, anyone?) or in the formal dining room at other times. Afternoon tea is served on the porch. *Note:* The public is invited to take a tour and afternoon tea at 4pm on Saturday, Sunday, Tuesday, and Thursday for $7.50 adults, $5 children.

Rates (including breakfast and afternoon tea): Memorial Day to mid-October and all weekends and holidays, $160 to $255 double in the inn and cottage, $225 to $300 in Officers' Quarters; October to mid-May, weekdays $105 to $195 double in the inn and cottage, $155 to $235 in Officers' Quarters. Three-night minimum stay required in summer. The inn is closed January 2 to mid-March; the Officer's Quarters are open year-round.

The other museumlike lodging is **The Abbey,** Columbia Avenue and Gurney Street, Cape May, NJ 08204 (☎ 609/884-4506). It was built for coal baron John B. McCreary in 1869. You can't miss its steep mansard roof and soaring 60-foot tower. Owners Jay and Marianne Schatze enjoy entertaining at breakfast and in the early evening, when guests gather in the drawing room to get to know one another over a glass of wine. Jay, in particular, is a real ham. In the morning he'll be setting the breakfast table with great panache wearing a hat (from his 100-plus collection). At breakfast he'll regale you with one tale or joke after another. Marianne is a creative designer and needlewoman who fashioned the lambrequins that cover the Gothic windows of the double parlor. It's elaborately furnished with high Victorian sofas, side chairs, and a huge Empire mirror over the mantel, where an ornate French clock from the same period stands.

It's hard to imagine that pigeons were inhabiting the upper floors when the Schatzes took over the house in late 1979. Now, upstairs you'll find a series of rooms, many with large armoires, floor-to-ceiling mirrors, Victorian sofas, walnut beds, and ornate gas fixtures. Even the smallest room is charming. In the morning, sunlight streams through the Gothic-style, ruby stained-glass windows, lighting up the white eyelet lace bedspread and scallop-edged pillows. All rooms have a bath, a small refrigerator, and air-conditioning or a fan. There are an additional seven rooms in The Cottage, an adjacent Second Empire–style home that was built in 1873 by George D. McCreary, son of John.

You can look forward to a luxurious breakfast served at a large formal table in the dining room, whose most exquisite piece is a sideboard carved with Indian heads, eagles, and wolflike creatures. Your gourmet breakfast will consist of juice, a choice of teas or coffee, an egg dish of some sort—perhaps quiche with wide noodles or a delicious concoction of poached eggs with onions and bacon in a cream sauce served over grits—plus muffins, jams, honey, and always a fresh fruit cup, sometimes laced with brandy. After breakfast Jay will take you up to the tower for a splendid view of the whole Cape May area. Afternoon refreshments are also served. *Note:* If you just want to see the splendid interior, tours followed by tea are given Monday, Wednesday, and Friday at 4pm from April through October.

Rates (including breakfast): April to December, $110 to $285 double. Free parking.

Several blocks farther from the beach, away from the central cluster of Victorian hostelries, stands the **Barnard-Good House,** 238 Perry St., Cape May, NJ 08204 (☎ 609/884-5381; fax 609/884-2871). This stunning purple clapboard house topped with a mansard roof is run by the effervescent Nancy Hawkins and her husband, Tom. Enter through the small picket gate, pass the white picket fence, and step up onto the porch with its intricate fretwork, further enlivened by one or two hanging ferns and a window box with colorful pansies. Although Nancy doesn't pretend to have furnished the house authentically, it does have a period charm and warmth. The dining room features what she calls a Turkish corner, with a tasselled brocade Victorian-style sofa beneath a tented effect. A foot-pedal organ, an old gas fire, heavy mirrors, and a Victorian glass dome filled with a silk flower arrangement add character to the front parlor.

Upstairs are three air-conditioned rooms and two suites (all with bath). The rooms are individually and eclectically furnished: One has a four-poster with lace curtains, another a brass bed with a candlewick spread, and another a delicate Empire-style dressing table created by Nancy herself. One of the most popular rooms has been dubbed the purple passion room because the iron-and-brass bedstead is extra-large, with a purple quilt, leaving room for only one white wicker chair, an oak chest, and a porcelain wash bowl; its bath is worth noting for its original zinc-coated copper tub, marble sink, and old-fashioned pull-chain toilet. Another favorite is the top-floor compact suite, decorated in white and pink with a small sitting room, complete with a fainting couch and a full bath.

Nancy is an extremely skilled cook who even relishes the challenge of catering to a special diet (if she's informed ahead). Her gourmet breakfast might consist of a chilled apple soup; pineapple, white grape, or lime juice (never standard grapefruit or orange); Swiss enchilada crêpes filled with celery, onions, chiles, and tomato sauce, topped with cheese, and served with assorted homemade breads; and dessert-like maple walnut and date cheesecake. Beach chairs, beach towels, and an outdoor shower are available.

Rates: April to November, $100 to $170 double. Free parking. *Note:* Allergy sufferers—no cats reside here.

For the last 16 years Joan Wells and her husband, Dane, have been creating a warm, homelike atmosphere at the **Queen Victoria,** 102 Ocean St., Cape May, NJ 08204 (☎ 609/884-8702; www.queenvictoria.com). It's in a trio of restored landmark buildings: One is a lovely sage-green 1881 Italianate building with striking corner bays, a curvaceous fish-scale mansard roof, and ornamental porch; the Prince Albert Hall is a Stick-style 1882 home in mustard yellow with signature green trim; and the Queen's Cottage across the street, is a Queen Anne painted in a historic shade of brown, complete with a porch and garden. On the ground floors of the first two are handsome dining rooms with the inn's signature wallpaper, designed by William Morris for Queen Victoria's Balmoral Castle. The parlors feature Mission and arts and crafts furniture, and here guests can sit and browse through one of the many art and architecture books that Joan collected when she was executive director of the Victorian Society. You'll really be welcomed as friends of the family, which includes daughter Elizabeth, whom you might find practicing her piano lesson at the Mission upright player piano. The parlor of the Prince Albert has a TV.

The 23 air-conditioned rooms and suites (all with baths, suites have TVs) are named either after legendary Victorians—Disraeli and Lillie Langtry are the smallest, for example—or after romantic places. Kew Garden and Hampton Court are suites with whirlpool tubs and TVs. The smallest rooms are on the third floor of the first house and have space only for a lowboy, a chair, and a brass-and-iron bed. Most rooms have ceiling fans, and all have colorful Mennonite quilts and fresh flowers.

In the morning, Joan will fortify you with a variety of egg casseroles or soufflés served buffet-style in both of the main dining rooms, along with home-made muffins, nut and fruit breads, the Queen's Oats, granola, and fresh fruit. Later in the day, a casual tea is served. The side porch is a sheltered spot for rocking (50 rockers available). Bicycles are available free, and Joan and Dane also provide a useful package of information on activities and entertainment available in the area. If you stay here, you'll also receive a regular newsletter, which keeps you in touch and makes you really feel like part of the family.

Rates (including breakfast): Mid-June to mid-September, $200 to $225 double, $255 to $290 suite; less in other months to lows of $130 to $165 double and $180 to $210 suite in January and February. Extra person, $25. Two-night minimum stay November to March; 3- and 4-night minimum in summer and during holidays.

The **Queen's Hotel,** 601 Columbia Ave., Cape May, NJ 08204 (☎ 609/884-8702; www.queenshotel.com), is also owned by Dane and Joan Wells (above). It was built in 1876 as a commercial structure with a pharmacy on the first floor and a gambling casino above. The second-floor rooms have very high ceilings and elegant plaster cornices and medallions reflecting their past use as casino rooms. The third-floor rooms are cozier, with sloping ceilings that follow the lines of the steep mansard roof. The nine rooms are well furnished with antiques, comfortable chairs, good reading lights, and handsome appointments. All have private baths, TVs, phones, hair dryers, air-conditioning, refrigerators, and coffeemakers. This is a "green hotel," practicing conservation by providing soap dispensers, recycling, and energy-conserving towel laundering services. No meals are included and the accommodations appeal more to those who value their privacy and appreciate modern conveniences. Guests do have the use of a guest pantry with ice, soda machine, and such amenities as ironing boards, shoe-shine kits, and data ports. *Rates:* Summer, weekends, $180 to $260 double; rest of the year, $120 to $220 double.

The **Wilbraham,** 133 Myrtle Ave., Cape May, NJ 08204 (☎ 609/884-2046), was built in 1840, but it was not until a millionaire steam-engine producer purchased it in 1900 that it acquired its grand dimensions. The architecture and the interiors are a feast for the eye. The wallpapers throughout the house will probably shock you—exotic in the extreme—and 12- to 15-foot-high Empire mirrors dominate the main parlor, along with a weird and whimsically painted chandelier. The house is stuffed with treasures of all sorts that would take several days to really examine.

The rooms have been elegantly furnished with antiques and wicker pieces. No matter what the season, guests enjoy the indoor pool and the enclosed, flower-filled porch. A full breakfast and afternoon tea is served.

Rates: $115 to $165; the two suites are $175 and $205.

The **Virginia Hotel and Ebbitt Room,** 25 Jackson St., Cape May, NJ 08204 (☎ 609/884-5700; fax 609/884-1236; www.virginiahotel.com; e-mail: Virginia@Jerseycape.com), was opened as a hotel in 1879. Today this Victorian with its lacy wood porches has been restored and turned into a small hotel with modern amenities and services. Each of the 24 rooms has a bath, a phone, a TV/VCR, and air-conditioning. Some have Jacuzzi tubs. The furnishings are not overwhelmingly Victorian. The polished wood beds are covered with down comforters and the furnishings are minimal—a white-painted chair and desk, a tall planter, and similar accents. What makes the hotel unusual by Cape May standards is that it offers room service, valet parking, and complimentary morning newspaper with your continental breakfast.

It also boasts the Ebbitt Room for fine dining and an innovative cuisine. Among the ten or so entrees you might find pan-seared yellowfin tuna in sesame-seed crust with crisp rice paper, hoisin, and wasabi; roast rack of lamb in a Merlot reduction; grilled sirloin with shallots, cilantro, ginger, soy, and sesame; or oven-roasted lobster and monkfish wrapped in wontons and served with stir-fried vegetables, wakame, and dual tabasco sauces. Among the appetizers, the jumbo lump crab raviolis with spinach and spiced carrot broth or the grilled portobello mushroom stuffed with prosciutto, sun-dried tomatoes, and mascarpone and served with roast garlic–basil vinaigrette hit the spot. Prices range from $22 to $28. Guests can relax in front of the hearth in the sitting room, on the spacious front porch, or in the rear garden.

Rates (including breakfast): Spring, weekends $160 to $260 double, weekdays $90 to $165 double; summer (until mid-October), weekends $190 to $305 double, weekdays $150 to $255 double; fall, weekends $170 to $260 double, weekdays $90 to $165 double; holiday season, weekends $190 to $285 double, weekdays $100 to $175 double; winter, weekends $140 to $220 double, weekdays $90 to $165 double. *Dining hours:* Daily 5:30pm to closing.

The **John F. Craig House,** 609 Columbia Ave., Cape May, NJ 08204 (☎ 609/884-0100; fax 609/898-1307), dates back to 1866, though parts of the house were built before 1850. It has had several rather flamboyant owners, but is named after John Fullerton Craig, a wealthy sugar broker and Philadelphian who summered here for many years at the turn of the century. It's a Carpenter Gothic house with 10-foot ceilings and floor-to-ceiling windows that open to expansive porches. The nine guest rooms (all with bath) and one suite are furnished with Eastlake and Renaissance Revival antiques and decorated with reproduction period wallpapers. Victorian linens and laces cover tables and dresser tops, and antique crocheted spreads grace the beds. The third-floor rooms are more casually decorated with floral-pattern carpets and wicker pieces. Guests enjoy the pillared living room with its fireplace, the book-lined library, and the formal dining room where an elaborate breakfast is served by candlelight. *Rates* (including breakfast): $95 to $175 double, $125 to $205 suite. Closed January and February.

The pretty lavender-and-cream **Captain Mey's Inn**, 202 Ocean St., Cape May, NJ 08204 (☎ 800/981-3702 or 609/884-7793), is named after the Dutch explorer and discoverer of Cape May, Captain Cornelius Mey. The Dutch motif is seen in the dining room's Delft-tile fireplace and the parlor's Delft collection. A lovely oak staircase leads to the nine guest rooms, all with private baths (including two Jacuzzis) and air-conditioning. Two rooms feature TVs, and three have refrigerators. Great care has been taken to provide each with an individual atmosphere, using a variety of styles and textures—Victorian bedroom suites, handmade quilts, and lace curtains among them. Throughout the house are several mannequins wearing Victorian dresses and lingerie from owner Kathleen Blinn's collection. A full breakfast of fresh fruit, breakfast meats, and homemade breads is served by candlelight—a charming, romantic way to start the day. It can also be enjoyed on the front porch, among wicker and hanging ferns. In late afternoons, guests gather for tea. *Rates* (including breakfast): $115 to $235 double. Free parking.

Some 100 rosebushes were planted around the property on which stands the **Victorian Rose**, 715 Columbia Ave., Cape May, NJ 08204 (☎ 609/884-2497), a blue-gray building made colorful by the cream-and-rust gingerbread fretwork. The rose theme is followed throughout on sheets, towels, wallpaper, and dining-room place settings. Lively owners Linda and Bob Mullock offer eight rooms. Number 3 in the front is their largest and comes with an oak sideboard, a king-size bed, a couch, wall-to-wall carpeting, and louvered doors that open into the bath with a claw-foot tub. The other rooms vary, but most feature high-back oak beds, oak dressers, candlewick spreads, and cane-seat chairs. Ceiling fans and sea breezes substitute for air-conditioning.

Linda and Bob are not interested in maintaining a perfectly authentic Victorian atmosphere; rather, they have a romance with the 1930s and 1940s, which explains the Glenn Miller–style sounds that waft through the house. Former nursery-school teacher Linda serves a light breakfast of fresh fruit, quiches, peach soufflé pancakes, or homemade sweet rolls and breads in the dining room, which contains a large sideboard purchased from the Boardman estate (Mr. Boardman supposedly built the boardwalk in Atlantic City).

At the back of the house is a pleasant cottage with a full kitchen and room enough to sleep five; it's available for weekly rental, but you'll need to call well ahead.

Rates (including breakfast): $100 to $165 double. Closed January to March.

In 1979 this classic 1872 home that had belonged to the Dannenbaums of Philadelphia until 1930 was converted from a simple tourist home into the **Brass Bed**, 719 Columbia Ave., Cape May, NJ 08204 (☎ 609/884-2302; fax 609/884-2296), a friendly B&B. Period perfection was not the goal, though the house is comfortably furnished with antique pieces: 19th-century brass beds, elegant wallpapers, and billowy lace curtains. During the restoration it was discovered that many pieces of furniture were original to the first owners and still had shipping tags attached to the backs—dated 1872! Collectibles like statuary and early photographs are on view, including a portrait that looks like a Victorian version of John himself. The parlor boasts an 1890s upright piano, a five-piece Renaissance Revival set of chairs and a settee, and a turn-of-the-century phonograph.

The innkeepers offer a relaxing, convivial atmosphere to guests, who have the choice of eight rooms (six with bath). Furnishings vary: In the room named in honor of the famous Congress Hall Hotel there's a brass bed, needlepoint chairs, a walnut armoire, and an oak dresser—furniture original to the house. The Stockton Room has a cozy air, achieved by the area rug, floral wallpaper, Eastlake settee, antique brass bed, and large walnut armoire. Third-floor rooms are tucked under the eaves, and one of them, the Mount Vernon, enjoys a private bath with a claw-foot tub. A full breakfast and afternoon refreshments are served year-round. Half the front veranda has been enclosed to make a comfortable sunroom that offers a variety of games, books, and puzzles. Guests really enjoy lolling in the hot tub in the back garden.

Rates: Early June to mid-September, $85 to $100 double without bath, $90 to $150 double with bath; mid-September to December, $85 to $100, and $90 to $155; January to April, $70 to $90 and $90 to $135; April to early June, $90 to $105 and $110 to $145.

The **Windward House** (1905), 24 Jackson St., Cape May, NJ 08204 (☎ 609/884-3368; fax 609/884-1575), boasts some really outstanding architectural details, especially stained glass (check out the stained-glass double doors leading to one of the guest rooms). It also has some very personal features in Sandy Miller's vintage clothing and accessories displayed on mannequins around the house and Owen's collection of German bisque bathing beauties and figurines. The parlor is accented with many eye-catching objects, including a blue glass collection assembled atop the window pelmets.

All eight rooms (with bath) are well furnished and equipped with refrigerators, ceiling fans, air-conditioning, hair dryers, and TVs. My favorite is the Summer Suite: It's tucked away behind the dining room on the first floor and has its own entrance; its bedroom has a carved Victorian bed that's complemented by marble-topped pieces, and its tiny sitting room features a cozy love seat, an armoire, and a small refrigerator. Room 5 is decked out in Rococo Revival splendor, with lemon peony wallpaper. Third-floor rooms like no. 7, the Wicker Room, are tucked under the eaves. In this room the iron-and-brass bed is draped with white lace, wicker chairs and a couch add a dash of comfort, and there's an adjoining single room that makes it ideal for a trio. Up here there's also a large deck at the back of the house from which there's a great ocean view. More seating is available on the ground-floor front porch set with wicker.

A full breakfast is served at the lace-clothed table in the dining room, in which there's still another collection—egg cups this time. The meal might feature poached peaches with white cheese mousse, ham and cheese bake, and pear ricotta coffee cake along with granola and other breads. This is one of Cape May's quirkily and appealingly personal accommodations.

Rates (including breakfast): Summer, $140 to $192 double, off-season, $100 to $165 double. Extra person $40.

The **Humphrey Hughes House**, 29 Ocean St., Cape May, NJ 08204 (☎ 609/884-4428), was built in 1903, a little later than many other homes in Cape May, and consequently the rooms are larger. The porch is really wide and expansive and has a fine ocean view. The seven rooms and four suites, all with baths, air-conditioning, TVs, and hair dryers, are well furnished with an eye for detail. One of my favorites is the Ocean View Room, featuring a Renaissance Revival carved bed made up with eyelet bed linen, a large armoire, side tables set with gas-style lamps, and a polished floor covered with oriental-style rugs. Other rooms are decorated in iron, brass, and wicker. A full breakfast is served at 9am. Tea, served at 4pm, consists of iced tea, cakes, pies, cheese, and crudités. A large, well-furnished parlor is available for guests. *Rates* (including breakfast): $145 to $255 double.

The owners of the **Sea Holly Inn,** 815 Stockton Ave., Cape May, NJ 08204 (☎ 609/884-6294; fax 609/884-5157; www.bbhost.com/seaholly), recently won an award for the quality of the restoration that they accomplished with alacrity, turning a neglected building into a Victorian beauty. The six rooms, all with air-conditioning, TVs, hair dryers, electric blankets, and baths, have been painstakingly decorated with Schumacher papers and fine fabrics and furnishings. Room 9, at the back of the house, has a bed covered with French blue satin and lace-trimmed pillows, with a brilliant, ruby-red upholstered Eastlake chair among the furnishings. Room 8 has a highly ornate iron bed covered with lace and satin, rose carpeting, and pretty chintz wallpaper. Room 2 houses a crested Victorian bed and mostly wicker furnishings set against gold chintz wallpaper.

A full breakfast is served, featuring such dishes as steamed sausage with apricot sauce or peach 'n' berry croissant and French toast. Afternoon tea and home-baked chocolate chip cookies are offered later in the day. Guests gather in the parlor on the camelback and wicker sofas or on the concrete porch's wicker rockers. A refrigerator is available for guests.

Rates: Late June to early September, $110 to $190; April to June and September to December, $105 to $180; February and March, $95 to 180

The **Sand Castles,** 829 Stockton Ave., Cape May, NJ 08204 (☎ 609/884-5451), a Carpenter Gothic cottage, has to be one of Cape May's best buys. It's operated by Bill and Jill Bianco, both corporate escapees, she from advertising and he from the auto industry. On the porch stand inviting rockers, and inside warm green, peach, and red tones in the parlors provide a very warm welcome, especially when there are fires in their fireplaces in winter. There are eight guest rooms (four with bath) and two suites with kitchens. Each of the rooms is charming, and many are under the eaves, which gives them interesting shapes. Room 3 contains an old brass bed and has an appealing "steeple"-pointed Gothic window. This same style of window is also found in Room 4, along with a highback oak bed covered with a Marseille-style bedspread, an oak dresser, and a side table. In the breakfast room, complete with ornate sideboard and gilded chairs, a complete breakfast is served. Afternoon tea is also served. *Rates* (including breakfast and afternoon tea): $79 to $120 double with shared bath, $120 to $145 double with private bath, $150 to $170 suite.

One of the famed Stephen D. Button houses (known as "The Seven Sisters"), the **Seventh Sister Guesthouse,** 10 Jackson St., Cape May, NJ 08204 (☎ 609/884-2280; fax 609/898-9899), is very different from the establishments discussed so far. Artist Joanne Echevarria, who shares the house with her husband, Bob Myers, has chosen to decorate with white-painted furniture and wicker so that the whole place positively blazes with light. It's also filled with examples of Joanne's art—abstract pastels, collages, and conceptual art. Not surprisingly, many of her guests are artists, photographers, or other like-minded visitors who need privacy and quiet to pursue their inspirational muse. Of the six rooms sharing two baths, four have ocean views. The back porch is great for idling, while the lawn at the side of the house makes a pleasant change from the beach, which is only 100 feet away. *Rates:* June to August, $105 to $160 double; May and September, $100 to $145 double; April and October, $95 to $135 double; November to March, $90 to $130 double. Children over age 7 are welcome.

Across town, Joanne's brother, Fred Echevarria and his wife, Joan, run the year-round **Gingerbread House**, 28 Gurney St., Cape May, NJ 08204 (☎ 609/884-0211; www.gingerbreadinn.com; e-mail: joaneche@algorithms.com). It was one of the Stockton Row cottages that surrounded the old Stockton Hotel, built in 1869 by railroad money and designed by Stephen D. Button. Here, Fred exhibits his talent for photography (note the striking pictures of Nova Scotia and Maine throughout the house) and for furniture making; you'll see in front of the fireplace in the parlor the coffee table he built to display their seashell collection. The house is furnished with Victorian-style sofas, lowboys with marble tops, and many other period furnishings. Among the six guest rooms (three with bath), the highest priced is large enough to accommodate two double beds and comes with a spacious private porch. A breakfast of fruits, cereal, and homemade breads, and afternoon tea is served. *Rates* (including breakfast): $110 to $230 double (discounts available off-season).

Geraniums were spilling out of the hanging baskets on the ocean-view porch when I last visited **Holly House**, 20 Jackson St., Cape May, NJ 08204 (☎ 609/884-7365), a sage-green boxlike house decorated with Chinese-red trim; this is also one of the seven cottages built by Stephen D. Button deliberately facing away from Jackson Street. It's a great budget choice that is conveniently located close to the beach in the center of town. Up the visually striking staircase, you'll find six guest rooms, all informally furnished, primarily with oak pieces—a desk, a cane-seated chair, a dresser, a double towel rack, and an iron bedstead—and kept very simple because Bruce and Corinne Minnix want to evoke the sense of a home away from home. The rooms share two bathrooms. The parlor has a platform rocker, a Victorian sofa, the original coal-burning fireplace, a Baldwin piano, and a comfortable spot to sit quietly and read as though you were settled in at your own cozy place. Breakfast is not included. *Rates:* Memorial Day to Columbus Day, $75 to $85 double; off-season, $55 to $60 double. Closed late October to early May.

The **Albert G. Stevens Inn**, 127 Myrtle Ave., Cape May, NJ 08204 (☎ 609/884-4717), is an impressive home built in 1898 for Dr. Albert G. Stevens, a homeopathic medical doctor who gave it as a wedding gift to his bride. A wonderful, turreted Queen Anne, it still has its original unusual floating staircase, suspended from the third floor. Prime Victorian pieces can be found throughout, like the parlor's late Empire couch and side chairs in front of the oak mantel. The seven rooms and two suites, all with private baths and air-conditioning, have a beautifully color-coordinated decor featuring exquisite individualized French wallpapers and wall-to-wall carpeting. Some rooms have Eastlake or iron-and-brass beds, while others feature Lincoln and even art deco bedroom sets. The Victorian Tower suite has the extra convenience of a small refrigerator. A hearty, three-course, Norwegian-style breakfast is served. Owners Curt and Diane Diviney-Rangen are cat lovers and they have established a special Cat's Garden that provides a safe haven, with water, food, and medical attention for Cape May's stray felines. Guests can enjoy afternoon tea in the gazebo on Thursday, Saturday, and Sunday (for a $3 to $6 charge that helps support the Cat's Garden) and relax in the hot tub. *Rates* (including breakfast): $75 to $165 double. Free parking.

Since it was built in 1876 by Civil War hero Colonel Henry Sawyer, the venerable 103-room **Chalfonte,** 301 Howard St., Cape May, NJ 08204 (☎ 609/884-8409; fax 609/884-4588; www.chalfonte.com), has drawn loyal families year after year to rock on its veranda, sample its Southern-style cuisine, and generally enjoy its simple charms. Two short blocks from the beach, this three-story building, screened by a two-story colonnade and crowned with a cupola and some fine gingerbread ornamentation, has been renovated by owners Anne Le Duc and Judy Bartella. It's the only real chance you'll have to experience the kind of hotel accommodations that used to keep Cape May so crowded in its heyday. Only 11 of the rooms have baths (most have sinks), and all (at least at the time of my visit) are furnished spartanly with iron bedsteads and marble-top dressers.

The dining room is famous for its $21 fixed-price Southern dinners, served along with a fish of the day and a vegetarian entree of the day. The dinner usually features one or two dishes like Southern fried chicken, Cajun grilled catfish, smothered pork chops, or crab cakes. The $8.50 breakfasts featuring bacon and eggs, kidney stew, French toast, sausages, spoonbread, biscuits, grits, fish, and other items are equally famous. On the ground floor are the King Edward Room bar, a writing room, a library, and a comfortable hall/ lounge with a fireplace and TV. In the Henry Sawyer Room there's a variety of entertainment provided—jazz, classical music, and theater. The hotel also hosts a popular weeklong Children's Festival. Workshops are also given in such subjects as watercolor painting and massage.

Rates (including breakfast and dinner): Weekends $130 to $198, midweek $110 to $165 (Sunday to Thursday). Higher prices are for rooms with baths and/or ocean views. Weekly rates and special packages available. On Work Weekends in May and October, you can stay for only $20 (bring your own sleeping bag or linens) and receive three meals a day for two days while you help spruce the place up.

The owners of **Alexander's Restaurant,** 653 Washington St., Cape May, NJ 08204 (☎ 609/884-2555; www.alexandersinn.com), rent four rooms to guests in a home built in 1883. Each room is decorated in Victorian style and features a TV, telephone, VCR, hair dryer, and unstocked refrigerator. In the Rose Room the brass bed with its pink satin eiderdown looks very inviting. The walls of the Green Room sport a wallpaper originally designed to celebrate the opening of the Suez Canal—a truly Victorian touch. Breakfast is served on the veranda or delivered to your room. Afternoon tea is served, too. *Rates* (including breakfast): June to mid-October, 3-night weekend package $435 to $555 double, weekdays $120 to $160 double; mid-October to June, 2-night weekend package $310 to $375 double, weekdays $120 to $160 double.

Built around 1896, the cream-and-rust **Duke of Windsor Inn**, 817 Washington St., Cape May, NJ 08204 (☎ 609/884-1355), with its quirky 45-foot conical tower (where two rooms are located), makes a lovely stopping place in a more secluded area, midway between the town and the harbor, within walking distance of the Physick Estate and the tennis club. On the first floor the tower has a well-used games and conversation room, just large enough to accommodate a wicker couch and two wicker armchairs. A double parlor with a corner fireplace, an ornate plaster ceiling, swag drapes, solid-oak accents, and a crystal chandelier is divided in two by an archway supported by two solid-wood colonial revival pillars. One half is used as a reading area and contains large bookcases; the other half is used as a sitting area, furnished with Victoriana. The back parlor adjoins the dining room, which possesses a lovely gilt-molded ceiling, several chandeliers, a reproduction of the wallpaper from Queen Victoria's throne room, and refurbished lincrusta on the walls. Here a full breakfast is served amid mirrored sideboards at one large table.

A staircase climbs past a brilliant stained-glass window to the ten air-conditioned guest rooms (two share a bath), all tastefully furnished. One room, for example, contains a Renaissance Revival bed set against gray-and-burgundy wallpaper; the carpet is rosy-red burgundy, the furnishings are oak, and the bath has a hand-painted porcelain sink. The most charming rooms are the tower rooms, which have space for only one brass bed, an Eastlake chair, and a dresser. Lace curtains and fringed lampshades or gas-style lamps are only some of the period effects used. The porch, with its upholstered rattan chairs, is a favorite musing spot. The full breakfast includes a hot entree, fruit, home-baked breads, juice, and coffee. An informal tea is also served.

Rates (including breakfast): February to December, $80 to $120 double without bath, $100 to $195 double with bath. Free parking.

Woodleigh House, 808 Washington St., Cape May, NJ 08204 (☎ 609/884-7123; fax 609/884-5174), in the same area as the Duke of Windsor, is run by a friendly couple (he's an elementary school principal and she's a teacher) and has a genuinely homelike atmosphere. In the comfortably modern sitting room you'll find a personal collection of Danish plates, and in the dining room is another colorful collection of glass and china. Here a continental breakfast is served, unless the weather is nice, in which case it's served on the porch. Each of the six guest rooms has a private bath and air-conditioning. One of the nicest is off the ground-floor kitchen; it's decorated with cherubs and furnished with a high-backed oak bed, a dresser, a rocker, and a washstand, on top of which are a pair of high-button boots! The two suites are equipped with TV/VCRs and coffeemakers. In the back there's a secluded small porch and brick patio and a small garden area where guests can barbecue. *Rates* (including breakfast): May to October, $120 to $195 double; November to April, $100 to $185. Closed January and February.

Carroll Villa, 19 Jackson St., Cape May, NJ 08204 (☎ 609/884-9619; fax 609/884-0264), is one of Cape May's more moderately priced accommodations. Its 21 rooms, all with private baths, air-conditioning, and phones, are attractively decorated with wall-to-wall carpeting, pretty drapes and fabrics, and a mixture of antiques and modern furnishings. Some feature high-Victorian cottage-style bedroom furnishings. The downstairs living room with a fireplace and TV is for guests only, as is the garden terrace out back. The accommodations are in the same building as the Mad Batter restaurant, and (depending on the location of your room) you might be disturbed by the kitchen staff in the early morning. If you're an early riser it won't matter a fig, but if you like to sleep in. . . . The breakfast is great and served on the front porch, in the dining room, or on the garden terrace. *Rates:* Late May to late September, $110 to $175 double; mid-March to late May and late September to early January, $90 to $170; early January to early March, $76 to $137.

The **Manor House,** 612 Hughes St., Cape May, NJ 08204 (☎ 609/884-4710), boasts some fine architectural features, like oak door frames with geometric decoration and stained glass. There are nine rooms (seven with bath). Several are on the small side, but all are prettily decorated with chintz/floral wallpapers, and such accents as floor lamps with fringed lampshades. Room 6 has a whirlpool tub and separate shower plus a sitting room. Most of the beds are made up with colorful quilts. Room 8 has a cross-stitch quilt on a brass bed, cranberry-colored chintz wallpaper, a chaise longue, a chest, and a Windsor chair. In Room 4 there's a lovely star quilt. Amenities include hair dryers, irons and ironing boards, and bathrobes. In refreshing contrast to the country decor, the walls throughout are adorned with bright, contemporary art. Guests may use the parlor with plenty of classic books on hand; the wraparound veranda is also a favorite spot. An added advantage is the location on one of the town's less trafficked streets. A four-course breakfast is served at 8:30 and 9:30am on lace-covered oak tables. It might include fresh fruit, a cinnamon sour-cream coffeecake or Mary's signature sticky buns, lemon-ricotta pancakes, and sausage, plus freshly squeezed juice. *Rates* (including breakfast): $94 to $197 double, $157 to $227 suite.

You can't miss the **Inn at 22 Jackson,** 22 Jackson St., Cape May, NJ 08204 (☎ 609/884-2226), an 1899 house with a blue, purple, and white exterior and double porches. There are four suites available, each with a bath, a wet bar with microwave, a small refrigerator, coffeemaker, cable TV/VCR, and air-conditioning. My favorite is the two-bedroom turret suite, on the third floor with an ocean view and a private deck. A two-bedroom cottage is also available. The furnishings may include a cottage-style Victorian bed and antiques, plus the innkeepers' eclectic collections of novelties—like the bawdy ladies, painted dishes, and toys and games found in the public areas. There's even an 1880 pump organ to play if you're so inclined. In summer the verandas are lined with rockers for afternoons when you just want to relax and breathe the salt air. Innkeepers Barbara Carmichael and Chip Masemore take pride in their buffet breakfasts. Afternoon tea is also served. *Rates* (including breakfast): $105 to $185 suite for two, $145 to $340 turret suite and cottage.

At **Poor Richard's Inn,** 17 Jackson St., Cape May, NJ 08204 (☎ 609/884-3536), artists Richard and Harriet Samuelson attract a younger crowd to their casual home, where the furnishings are more eclectic than most, a trifle faded, and less "picture-perfect" than those at many of the other guest houses. They aim to provide unpretentious, comfortable surroundings at moderate prices. Richard and Harriet are also one of the few innkeepers who'll accept children (they have a couple of their own). The house itself is quite magnificent, built in 1882 for a man named George Hildreth, with a wonderfully steep fish-scale mansard roof, deep projecting bays, and an unusual hexagonal porch. There are ten rooms, all with air-conditioning; two have tub-showers, and seven have showers only. The two top-floor rooms are pleasantly furnished with wicker rockers, a painted country bed, a Mission rocker, or an oak dresser. Other rooms mix painted cottage beds with oak and pine, really old patchwork quilts, hooked rugs, and other Victoriana. There are also two apartments with kitchens available. Throughout the house hang Harriet's collages, which I wanted to purchase on the spot—they're stimulating, weirdly affecting visions. A continental breakfast of bagels, breads, pastries, cereal, and fresh fruit is included in the price. *Rates:* July to August and weekends Memorial Day to September, $65 to $80 double without bath, $100 to $145 double with bath; March to June and September to December, $55 to $75 double without bath, $85 to $130 double with bath. Apartments rented by the week only, $625 to $850. No parking.

The **Mooring Guest House,** 801 Stockton Ave., Cape May, NJ 08204 (☎ 609/884-5425; fax 609/884-1357; www.themooring.com; e-mail: info@themooring.com), offers 12 rooms (7 with showers and 5 with baths), most with air-conditioning and all furnished in Victorian style, but not stiflingly so. One of the most appealing is Room 10, the largest, which boasts an intricately carved high-backed cherry bed, an acorn chest with a marble top, and French doors that lead directly to the front porch with an ocean view. Other rooms are pleasantly furnished with mixtures of wicker, white iron, and oak. The halls are extremely wide—a reminder of earlier days when steamer trunks needed accommodating. A full breakfast (Mexican frittata or cream cheese–stuffed French toast, for example) is served at tables for two in the spacious dining room. Afternoon tea is also offered to guests. *Rates* (including breakfast): April to January 1, $85 to $185 double. Closed January 2 to March 31.

The **Twin Gables Guest House,** 731 Columbia Ave., Cape May, NJ (☎ 609/884-7332), is run by friendly Regina and Harry McCaren. The 1879 house is one of the few houses (if not the only one) to possess a screened-in porch with wicker rockers and hanging plants. Guests gather in the comfy parlor on the sofa, around the old pump organ, or on the window seats. The four rooms (all with baths) are homey. Room 2 has chintz wallpaper, an Eastlake bed, a teardrop dresser, an armoire, and marble side tables. Room 3 has a gold bed coverlet and carpet matched with yellow wallpaper. At breakfast there's always fresh fruit, home-baked breads, and an entree such as banana-stuffed French toast. Afternoon tea is served. Guests can enjoy the back garden with a small goldfish pond and waterfall. Open year-round. *Rates* (including breakfast): $95 to $140; lower rates for weekdays and off-season.

Other Accommodations

Cape May also has a goodly number of modern, resort-style hotels/motels, many located on the seafront.

The **Marquis de Lafayette,** 501 Beach Dr. (between Ocean and Decatur), Cape May, NJ 08204 (☎ 800/257-0432 or 609/884-3431 in New Jersey), is one of the largest. It has rooms and suites that can accommodate as many as six people. Facilities include pool, deck, and patio, plus two restaurants. *Rates:* Memorial Day to Labor Day weekends, $179 to $329 double, $339 to $369 suites; weekdays, $119 to $189 and $199 to $229. Rates are slightly reduced after Labor Day with steeper discounts January 1 to Memorial Day. Special packages are available.

CAPE MAY DINING

In season, reservations are a must; on weekends you'd do best to reserve ahead if you don't want to be disappointed. Most of the restaurants lack liquor licenses. For the largest liquor selection and the best prices, go to **Colliers** on Jackson Street, the big green place across from the bandstand. It's open on Sunday.

The best breakfasts, as you'll have gathered from the previous section, can be found at your guest house. If you're not staying at such an accommodation, don't despair; simply head for **The Mad Batter,** 19 Jackson St. (☎ 609/ 884-5970), for a choice selection of omelets, pancakes, French toast with fresh-fruit sauce, and all kinds of egg dishes including such delights as rösti potatoes combined with eggs and Gruyère cheese, or a frittata incorporating langostino tails, spinach, potatoes, tomatoes, black olives and provolone, priced from $7 to $9. You can dine either out under the yellow-striped awning at white pedestal tables or inside. At lunch there are sandwiches, burgers, pasta dishes, and salads, plus many exciting chalkboard specials, from $8 to $11. And at Harry's Juice and Java Bar you can also sample freshly squeezed fruit and vegetable juices and cappuccinos and lattes, which can be accompanied by finger foods.

The dinner menu offers imaginative dishes, many inspired by different cuisines. Choices might include grilled salmon served with a red pepper, mushroom, and caper sauce finished with pepper vodka; or sweet and spicy cilantro chicken made with apples, sweet onions, and a blend of Cuban-style spices served with fried plantains and rice. Prices range from $14 to $22. Save some room for dessert, especially the key lime tart or chocolate-chip cheesecake. By the way, you're dining in another of Cape May's Victorian beauties, built in 1882 complete with a cupola.

Hours: Weekends only, November to April 1, serving breakfast Friday to Sunday and dinner Friday to Saturday; May 1 to October 31, daily 8am to 2:30pm and 5:30 to 9:30pm.

For a top gourmet restaurant, number one has to be **Alexander's,** 653 Washington St. (☎ 609/884-2555). Lace doilies, roses on the table, and coffee served from a silver coffeepot on a swing add a dash of romance to tables set in the Victorian manner—the silverware placed face down. Dinner is served in four intimate, candlelit rooms decorated with gilt-framed pictures. The food is exciting, never dull. The menu changes daily, but specials always include a fish of the day, like swordfish au poivre or salmon Dijon. Other entrees might be duckling with grape blueberry glaze, rabbit poached with onions and finished with Portuguese chocolate-burgundy sauce, and rack of lamb with béarnaise. Prices range from $25 to $40. To start, I recommend the soup du jour (perhaps cream of crab and wild mushroom) or the well-textured sausage-nut strudel (almonds, walnuts, pecans, cream cheese, and sausage wrapped in flaky pastry). The desserts will undoubtedly include chocolate profiteroles and their very special brandy Alexander pie, flavored with brandy and crème de cacao in a graham-cracker crust.

The tuxedoed service is impeccable, even a little too much so: The bread appears in a silver basket, the cream comes in a Victorian-style silver jug with a lid carved in the shape of a lion's head, and the maître d' sports tails. The porch, bedecked with ferns and lace curtains, is a favorite spot for a brunch that's more lavish than most. Juice and a plate of seasonal fruit precede such main courses as Belgian waffles, omelets, and eggs Alexander. Dessert and coffee follow. Brunch runs $17. Four guest rooms are available here (see "Cape May Lodging," above).

Hours: Memorial Day to late October, Monday and Wednesday to Saturday from 6pm to 9pm, Sunday 10am to 1pm (brunch) and from 6 to 9pm; November to Memorial Day, weekends only.

A longtime favorite on the Cape May scene is the pretty **Washington Inn,** 801 Washington St. (☎ 609/884-5697), set in a large, rambling house. It contains a screened-in side porch overlooking the colorful garden for summer dining, a pleasant piano bar with comfortable sofas and brocade Victorian chairs, and a front porch with wicker furniture for cocktails. The dining room is made especially attractive by an attached greenhouse filled with a brilliant show of orchids. Among the nine or so entrees you might find a dish called the Jewel of Provence, a sauté of shrimp and scallops tossed with tomatoes, garlic, and white wine served over linguine; Cajun-dusted chicken topped with corn salsa and shrimp and served in a Cajun butter sauce; or a 14-ounce sirloin steak with a horseradish butter and jus. Prices range from $20 to $32. Fresh, homemade pies like apple-walnut and strawberry, plus such mouth-watering delights as blackberry mousse, are added attractions. There's an excellent wine list, plus at least 15 by the glass. *Hours:* Mid-May to October, daily 5 to 9pm; mid-March to mid-May and November to Christmas, Thursday to Sunday 5 to 9pm. Closed January to mid-February.

Dining at the **Lobster House,** on Fisherman's Wharf (☎ 609/884-8296), is an old Cape May tradition. The dining rooms are large and lack any spectacular decor, but people come for the steamed lobster or the popular schooner dinner, consisting of a 1-pound lobster, cherrystone clams, scallops, shrimp, and mussels served in a large kettle. Other selections depend on the seasonal catch—bluefish, soft-shell crab, tuna, mako, and other bounties of the sea. Entrees include salad, potato, vegetable, and coffee or tea and start at $17, rising to $40 for the lobster tails.

This restaurant grosses millions in sales a year, and on most nights, especially weekends, expect a 2-hour wait. Names are announced over a loudspeaker and somehow the people get fed. My favorite reason for going to the Lobster House, though, is to have a drink aboard the schooner *America.* Arrive about 5pm and take a waterside seat; enjoy a cocktail while watching the families of ducks paddling back and forth, boatmen training their retrievers, seagulls casting moving shadows on the surface of the water, large vessels gliding into port, and the sun going down. You can order a clambake, crab sticks, steamed shrimp or crab, barbecued clams, and other such dishes.

At the fresh seafood market, you can pick up a lobster to take home or take out clams, scallops, or fresh fried fish with french fries onto the dock and watch the sun set while you enjoy a good meal for a fraction of the restaurant price. Get there early because the market usually closes about 6pm.

Hours: Monday to Saturday noon to 3pm and 5 to 10pm, Sunday 4 to 10pm.

If you desperately want seafood, but don't want to wait at the Lobster House (the food might even be a fraction better here), you can always go across the street to the **Anchorage Inn** (☎ 609/898-1174), at the foot of the canal bridge. The decor is nautical, the tables are set with red gingham, and there's usually entertainment on weekends. At lunch I had a delicious crab soup, full of crab in a tomato-based stock. The clam chowder was equally well stocked with clams and potatoes and used far less than the usual amount of cornstarch. Dinner prices run $17 to $24 for shrimp, flounder, swordfish, sautéed crabmeat, fried or broiled scallops, baked crab Imperial, and some meat dishes. Real seafood fans will want the clambake feast for two—lobster and all kinds of steamed shellfish accompanied by potato and vegetable, for $44. Luncheon prices are about half those at dinner. *Hours:* Mid-May to mid-September, daily 5 to 10pm; mid-September to mid-October, Friday and Saturday 5 to 10pm.

Cucina Rosa, 301 Washington Mall (☎ 609/898-9800), serves typical Italian cuisine—veal parmigiana and piccata, shrimp oreganata, and swordfish with lemon butter. Among the pasta specialties opt for the cannelloni or the delicious linguine with clam sauce. Prices range from $11 to $19. Cheesecake, cannoli, and tartufo make up the dessert list. *Hours:* February to December, Sunday to Thursday 5 to 9pm, Friday and Saturday 5 to 10pm.

Dinner Only

410 Bank Street (that's the address, too) (☎ 609/884-2127), is Cape May's top-rated restaurant and certainly deserves praise for bringing the Cajun, Creole, and Caribbean cuisine to this waterfront town raised on seafood and prime rib. The specialties include a fine Bayou oyster stew and a Jamaican steak that sizzles with one of the kitchen's Caribbean sauces. About six fish are offered every night and can be grilled with any one of the restaurant's famous sauces— Creole, barbecue, Caribbean lime–jalapeño, or several others. To start, try blackened sea scallops with a Louisiana rémoulade sauce or the crawfish bisque. Prices range from $23 to $29. It's BYOB. *Hours:* Mid-May to mid-October, daily 5 to 10pm.

Frescos, 412 Bank St. (☎ 609/884-0366), is all its name implies: lively, fun, and serving some up-to-the-minute Italian cuisine. Choose among half a dozen pastas—the richest is the shrimp and scallops in a champagne lobster cream sauce served over red and green pasta ribbons, while on the lighter side is the shrimp sautéed with feta, tomatoes, and fresh basil over fettuccine. There's always a risotto of the day. Heartier eaters will appreciate the well-prepared saltimbocca, the duck breast and fresh mission figs served with a port wine demi-glace, or the grilled fresh tuna with a smoked almond-basil pesto and sun-dried tomatoes. Prices range from $17 to $25. *Hours:* Mid-April to November, daily 5 to 10pm.

Peaches at Sunset, 1 Sunset Blvd. W. (☎ 609/898-0100), in a remodeled Victorian home, offers fine dining in a tropical ambience. The cuisine features fresh seasonal ingredients combined into richly flavored dishes that often contain Asian accents. For example, among the dozen entrees there might be pistachio-crusted salmon served with a beurre blanc flavored with Asian five-star spice and fresh lime juice, teriyaki pork chop served with crispy shallots, and breast of duck with a pear and coconut milk curry sauce flavored with fresh mint. Prices range from $18 to $26. The signature appetizer is the roasted garlic Gilroy, spread on sourdough bread along with mascarpone cheese; the clam chowder is a great favorite, too. *Hours:* May to mid-October, daily 4:30 to 9:15pm; mid-October to December and mid-February to April, Friday to Sunday only. Closed January to President's weekend.

Watson's Merion Inn, 106 Decatur St. (☎ 609/884-8363), is a Cape May tradition serving an updated American menu that features plenty of seafood—grilled swordfish with lime-cilantro butter served with mango salsa, grilled tuna with sesame-ginger glaze, and crab Imperial served in a giant scallop shell. Steak and additional chicken and veal dishes round out the menu. Prices range from $13 for penne with grilled vegetables and smoked mozzarella to $32 for surf and turf. The substantial atmosphere is created by the gilt portraits and pictures on the walls and the handsome sturdy cherry-and-oak bar. *Hours:* May to October, daily noon to 2:30pm and 5 to 10pm; April, Friday and Sunday noon to 2:30pm and 5 to 10pm.

My own choice for seafood would be **A & J Blue Claw,** Ocean Drive, south of the Wildwood Crest toll bridge (☎ 609/884-5878). The decor is plain and simple, but the fish is well cooked and this is one place where you can select your lobster from the tank. Specialties include lobster and crab cakes, plus such dishes as black sea bass cooked in parchment and served with a tomato fondue hollandaise. Steaks and pasta dishes round out the menu. Prices run $23 to $30. *Hours:* Summer, Sunday to Thursday 5 to 8:30pm, Friday and Saturday 5 to 10pm; rest of the year, Thursday to Sunday 5pm to closing.

For simple soups, salads, and a good filet mignon, steamed lobster, or poached salmon, try **Oyster Bay Steak and Seafood,** 615 Lafayette St. right across from the Acme supermarket (☎ 609/884-2111). Prices range from $14 to $22. Don't expect much decor, though. *Hours:* Open seasonally.

CAPE MAY AFTER DARK

During the summer, the **Mid-Atlantic Center for the Arts,** 1048 Washington St. (☎ 609/884-5404), offers musical and drama performances on their outdoor stage at the Physick Estate. Bring your own chair.

Relaxing **cocktail spots** include the schooner at the **Lobster House,** the **Washington Inn**'s porch and piano bar, the **Merion Inn**'s lounge bar, and the **King Edward Room** at the Chalfonte.

On the mall, locals often gather to gossip and catch some musical entertainment at the **Ugly Mug,** at 426 Washington Street Mall (☎ 609/884-3459), where the numerous mugs adorning the ceiling belong to Ugly Mug club members.

For loud raucous nightlife, you'll have to head for nearby **Wildwood.**

Cape May
Special & Recreational Activities

Beaches: The **town beaches** are pleasant and sandy, with a minimum of honky-tonk. Beach passes are required and readily available at the information center. More natural, secluded beaches, backed by high undulating dunes, are located at **Cape May Point;** take Cape Avenue off Sunset Boulevard. At **Sunset Beach,** not a particularly attractive sunning or swimming beach, you'll probably see a lot of people bent over double, scouring the sands for the famous and elusive Cape May diamonds. They're milky in color and, when polished, glitter like diamonds. Here you can also see the concrete bulkhead of the World War I SS *Atlantis* rising from the ocean. After several Atlantic crossings, this impractical vessel was sunk for use as a jetty.

Bicycling: At **Village Bike Rentals,** Elmira and Lafayette streets (☎ 609/884-8500), bikes rent for $4 per hour, $10 per day. There are also a couple of surreys for two or more that rent for $12 per hour. **Shields,** 11 Gurney St. (☎ 609/898-1818), rents bikes for $4 an hour and $9 a day.

Birding: Long before Cape May was famous as a resort, Audubon made it famous for its bird life. A million and half migrating shore birds pass through Cape May. Prime sights are the harlequin and eider ducks in winter, warblers in spring, herons and egrets in summer, and the largest raptor migration in the nation, which takes place in fall when as many as 88,000 hawks have been recorded massing.

In **Cape May State Park,** P.O. Box 107, Cape May Point, NJ 08212 (☎ 609/884-2159), blinds and platforms have been built for viewing the marsh and sea birds over the tall stately reeds. Turn left off Sunset Boulevard onto Lighthouse Avenue; the park is by the lighthouse.

At the **Cape May Bird Observatory and Sanctuary** overlooking Lily Lake, you'll find the offices of the Audubon Society (open daily 10am to 5pm). They sponsor weekend birding walks and other events. For their special weekends led by trained naturalists, contact the Cape May Bird Observatory, East Lake Drive (P.O. Box 3), Cape May Point, NJ 08212 (☎ 609/884-2736).

For special birding and other wildlife ventures, contact **Wildlife Unlimited,** P.O. Box 254, Cape May, NJ 08204 (☎ 609/884-3100). It operates early morning and sunset cruises through the wetlands to view the marine, plant, and bird life, plus an afternoon cruise to view osprey. The cruises are hosted by naturalists.

Camping: Cold Spring Campground, 541 New England Rd., Cape May, NJ 08204 (☎ 609/884-8717), has pleasant, secluded sites among sycamore, beech, and hickory. It's near Higbee Beach, where you can walk between 10-foot-high reeds to a small, albeit shingly, beach. Open May to Columbus Day, it charges $15 for two.

The closest wilderness camping can be found at **Belleplain Forest,** P.O. Box 450, Woodbine, NJ 08270 (☎ 609/861-2404), which has 169 sites and opportunities for bathing, boating (canoes/kayaks for $8 an hour), fishing (small stuff only), and hiking. Open all year.

Cruises: The 80-foot schooner **Yankee** (☎ 609/884-1919) gives 3-hour cruises leaving from the marina on Ocean Drive between Cape May and Wildwood. The ship usually leaves at 2 and 6pm, charging $28.50 per person.

The **Cape May–Lewes Ferry** that leaves from Lower Township, North Cape May on Lincoln Boulevard, is a fun, 70-minute trip to take from Cape May to Lewes in Delaware. It costs about $20 for a car and driver, $7 for bikes, $6.50 for passengers, $2 for children under age 5. For reservations call ☎ 800/643-3779; for information call ☎ 609/886-1725 or 302/426-1155.

Fishing: South Jersey Fishing Center (☎ 609/884-3800) is the dock to head for, with daily sailings from April to November for about $25 per person for 4 hours and $37 for 8 hours. Write P.O. Box 641, Cape May, NJ 08204.

Golf: Avalon Golf Club, 1510 Route 9 North (☎ 609/465-4389), is 18 holes, par 71. Semiprivate. Take Exit 13 off the Garden State Parkway.

Ice-skating: It's often fun when **Lily Lake** freezes.

Picnicking: Pick up staples in town at the supermarkets or main stores. There's a good fresh-produce stand just beyond Junction 607 on Sunset Boulevard en route to Cape May Point beaches, one of the prime picnic sites.

Kayaking: Aqua Trails (☎ 609/884-5600) offers several daily trips through bay and salt marsh. It costs $28 for a 1½-hour tour and $38 for 2½ hours.

Sailing: Cruise aboard **The Free Spirit,** a 27-foot yacht. The charge is $25 per person for a 2-hour cruise. Call ☎ 609/884-8347 between 8am and 1pm and 3 and 5pm. The captain takes a minimum of two and maximum of six people.

Tennis: The **William Moore Tennis Center,** on Washington Street just before the entrance to the Physick Estate (☎ 609/884-8986), has 4 all-weather and 12 clay courts. It charges $5 per person per hour.

Whale Watching: From April to December boats leave port in search of whales, dolphins, and sea birds. Contact either the **Cape May Whale Watch and Research Center,** 1286 Wilson Dr., Cape May NJ 08204 (☎ 609/898-0055), or **Cape May Whale Watcher,** Second Avenue and Wilson Drive, Cape May, NJ 08204 (☎ 609/884-5445). The latter operates three trips a day. The 1pm trip lasts 3 hours and goes out in search of whales and dolphins. It costs $26 adults, $12 children ages 7 to 12. A morning dolphin trip (2 hours) costs $17 adults and $8 children ages 7 to 12; the evening dolphin trip is $18 adults and $8 children and includes complimentary pizza and hot dogs.

PENNSYLVANIA
& DELAWARE

New Hope & Bucks County

New Hope ◆ *Lambertville, N.J.* ◆ *Phillips Mill* ◆ *Lumberville*
◆ *Point Pleasant* ◆ *Washington Crossing* ◆ *Fallsington* ◆
Stockton, N.J. ◆ *Milford* ◆ *Gardenville* ◆ *Holicong* ◆ *Buckingham* ◆
Doylestown ◆ *Frenchtown, N.J.* ◆ *Newtown* ◆ *Lake Nockamixon*

Distance in miles: Erwinna, 60; Upper Black Eddy, 65; New Hope, 78
Estimated driving time: 1½ hours

━◈━◈━◈━◈━◈━

Driving: For Upper Black Eddy, Erwinna, and Point Pleasant, take the
New Jersey Turnpike to Exit 10, Route 287 north to Exit 10, and then
Route 22 west to the Flemington-Princeton exit, onto Route 202 south. At the
Flemington circle, bear right onto Route 12 to Frenchtown and cross the river
to Route 32. For New Hope, continue down Route 202 south to Route 179,
which brings you to Lambertville and then across the river into New Hope.

Bus: Trans Bridge Lines (☎ 800/962-9135) goes to New Hope, Doylestown,
Buckingham, Lahaska, Lambertville, and Upper Black Eddy.

Further Information: Contact the **Bucks County Conference and Visitor's
Bureau**, 152 Swamp Rd., Doylestown, PA 18901 (☎ 215/345-4552), or the
New Hope Information Center, 1 West Mechanic St., New Hope, PA 18938
(☎ 215/862-5880).

━◈━◈━◈━◈━◈━

In the county of Buckinghamshire, England (known as beechy Bucks), is a
tiny village called Penn. From there, William Penn set out to settle in America.
He must have had his home county in mind when he named the valley
that borders the Delaware Bucks County. Like Bucks, England, it's a bucolic
landscape of woods and glades, gentle hills, and pleasant pastures.

In 1681 Penn granted the 1,000 acres that now constitute the borough of
New Hope to Thomas Woolrich, who never even saw the land because he
remained in England. Not until John Wells was licensed to operate a ferry in
1722 and to keep a tavern in 1727 did the town's life really begin. The tavern
was known as the Ferry Tavern, and if you visit the heart of the Logan Inn
you'll be standing in that early establishment. Whenever the ferry operator
changed, the name of the town changed. It was as Coryell's Ferry that the

New Hope & Bucks County

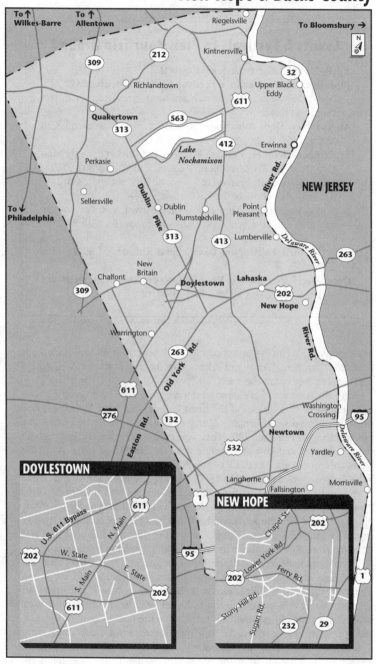

Events & Festivals to Plan Your Trip Around

April–May: Lambertville Shad Festival.

June: Bucks County Balloon Festival, Quakertown Airport (☎ 215/
538-3055)—hot-air-balloon race, aerobatics, airplane and helicopter
rides, and more.

August: New Hope Auto Show, New Hope. Second weekend. Call
☎ 215/862-5665.

September–October: Phillips Mill Art Exhibition runs through
October at the Phillips Mill Art Gallery. Call ☎ 215/862-0582.

October: State Craft Festival in Tyler State Park, Richboro (☎ 215/
579-5997), with more than 200 craftspeople.

   Bucks County Wine and Food Festival, a week of wines
and food from the area's restaurants and wineries. Call ☎ 215/
674-1047.

   Historic Fallsington Day (second Saturday). Call ☎ 215/
295-6567.

December: Reenactment of Washington's crossing of the Delaware
on Christmas Day. Call ☎ 215/493-4076.

community played an important part in the American Revolution, aiding the
retreating Continental Army and helping take them downriver to McConkey's
Ferry, where they began the march on Trenton.

After the American Revolution, the town prospered because of the river
and because of its location on the main Philadelphia–New York road. Real
prosperity arrived when Benjamin Parry established a flaxseed-oil mill and a
lumber factory here in the 1780s. They were destroyed by fire, and Parry rebuilt
only the lumber and gristmills, calling them the New Hope Mills. When the
Delaware Canal opened in 1832, it brought even greater prosperity. As many as
3,000 barges traveled the canal in 1860, carrying Bushmill's whisky and coal to
Bristol and returning to Easton with manufactured and imported goods.
Prosperity was brief, however, for in 1891 the railroad arrived on the other side
of the river, and New Hope slipped back into being a quiet backwater; but we
should be grateful for this, since it ensured the survival of the old inns and
buildings along Route 32 that make such delightful lodging places today.

At the turn of the century, the beauty of the area was discovered by a group
of landscape and impressionist artists. Edward Redfield, Daniel Garber, and
Charles Demuth made their homes in the area, turning New Hope into an art
colony of worldwide repute between 1905 and 1935. Their artistic ranks were
swelled when the old gristmill was turned into the Bucks County Playhouse
and opened in 1939, drawing the New York theater crowd. First came George
S. Kaufman, followed by his collaborator playwright, librettist, and director,
Moss Hart. His friends from the Algonquin Round Table, soon followed,
including Dorothy Parker and S. J. Perelman. In 1940 Oscar Hammerstein
settled down on a farm in Doylestown. In many ways the literati were the

vanguard of the tourists who flocked here later, turning New Hope into a very commercial, crowded weekend destination by the mid-1960s.

The town is still crowded on weekends and has succumbed to tourist honky-tonk, but New Hope is not the whole of Bucks County. Only a few miles outside of town you can experience the tranquillity of the banks along the Delaware River, the towpath along the canal, and the peace of the surrounding countryside. In nearby Doylestown you can ponder the eccentric brilliance of Henry Chapman Mercer, archaeologist, historian, anthropologist, and collector, and the legacy he left behind—a museum containing 40,000 preindustrial American tools, a tile-making factory, and a 39-room home, all built out of reinforced concrete. To the south lies Washington Crossing State Park, the site of Washington's dramatic crossing of the Delaware; Pennsbury, William Penn's 17th-century plantation; and, in contrast, Sesame Place, an ultra-20th-century playground for kids and parents alike.

Throughout the area are comfortable historic inns to stop at, antiques stores and art studios galore to browse through, haunted houses to visit, barge rides to enjoy, and all kinds of activities on the river and the canal. And wherever you look are trees and fields, the bucolic surroundings that first moved William Penn to remark on the valley's great beauty.

NEW HOPE ATTRACTIONS

Besides the pleasures afforded by the Delaware River and the grassy towpath of the historic Delaware Canal (great for hiking, picnicking, canoeing, and even cross-country skiing), New Hope has several attractions.

Start at the **New Hope Information Center,** at the corner of South Main and Mechanic streets (P.O. Box 141), New Hope, PA 18938 (☎ 215/862-5880), and obtain as much free information as possible. *Hours:* June to September, daily 10am to 6pm; October to May, Saturday and Sunday 10am to 6pm.

The best way to spend a lazy summer afternoon is gliding along the canal in a **mule-drawn barge** under leafy glades, past old inns and homes, an 11-mile journey from New Hope to Centre Bridge and back. For information, contact the **New Hope Canal Boat Company,** 149 S. Main St., New Hope, PA 18938 (☎ 215/862-0758). *Hours:* May to October, daily departures starting at noon. Call for full schedule. *Tickets:* $6.95 adults, $6.50 seniors and children under age 12.

You can then go from the canal age to the steam age by boarding the **New Hope & Ivyland Railroad** steam train, which leaves from New Hope's 1892 station, with its unusual witch's peak, for a 9-mile round-trip journey to Lahaska. For information, contact the New Hope & Ivyland Railroad, 32 W. Bridge St. (P.O. Box 634), New Hope PA 18938 (☎ 215/862-2332). *Hours:* Memorial Day to October and December 26 to January 1, daily 11am to 4pm; call for schedules at other times. *Tickets:* $8.95 adults, $7.95 seniors, $4.95 children ages 2 to 11, $1.50 children under age 2.

For a different kind of trip from June to November, you can sign up for a **Ghost Tour** of New Hope's many haunted sights. Contact **Ghost Tours,** P.O. Box 3354, Warminster, NY 18974 (☎ 215/957-9988). Tours are usually given on Saturday at 8pm and also on Friday in certain months. The charge is $8.

In town, between the historic Logan Inn and the Bucks County Playhouse stands the **Parry Mansion Museum** (☎ 215/862-5652), erected by mill owner Benjamin Parry in 1784. Each room is decorated to reflect the changes in interior design and lifestyle from colonial times to the early 1900s. *Hours:* May to December 10, Friday and Sunday 1 to 5pm. *Admission:* $4 adults, $3 seniors, $1 children under age 12.

Bucks County is also one of the few areas to have saved its **covered bridges**. There are 13 in the county, and the information center will gladly furnish you with a tour pamphlet.

Wine enthusiasts can visit the **Buckingham Valley Vineyard and Winery**, Route 413, Buckingham (☎ 215/794-7188), which offers a self-guided tour and tastings. *Hours:* Tuesday to Saturday 11am to 6pm, Sunday noon to 4pm.

And bear in mind that **Princeton** and **Trenton**, N.J., are only about 15 miles away—you can visit the tranquil groves of academia and the Princeton University Art Museum or the Capitol, planetarium, and art and natural history museum in Trenton.

Shopping

New Hope is full of gift, souvenir, and crafts shops. You may also want to take the shuttle bus (Saturday only) from New Hope that runs to the landscaped and heavily touristed **Peddler's Village** in Lahaska, which contains stores featuring everything from porcelain and crystal to crafts and apparel.

RIVER ROAD—ATTRACTIONS NORTH OF NEW HOPE

Whatever you do, don't miss driving Route 32, the undulating road that parallels the river and canal. Stop to browse in antiques stores or at farm stands, stay or dine in quaint country inns, or do whatever tickles your particular fancy. You'll pass through the tiny hamlet of **Phillips Mill**, where landscape painter William Lathrop made his home in 1900. In 1929 a group of area residents, many of them artists, formed an association and bought the mill to preserve it as a landmark and community center. Yearly art exhibitions, concerts, and theatrical productions were held, and Phillips Mill is still a cultural center.

Next door to the inn, **Bucks County Carriages**, West End Farm (☎ 215/862-3582), runs escorted trail and carriage rides on weekends. A 20-minute ride costs $12. Farther up the road is **Centre Bridge**, home of artist Edward W. Redfield at the turn of the century. At **Lumberville**, you'll want to stop at the old-fashioned country store that's been here since 1770 and walk across the footbridge over the river to **Bull's Island**, a New Jersey state park that's well known to birders for being the nesting ground of the cerulean and yellow-throated warbler. While you're here, stop in at the Black Bass.

The next community is **Point Pleasant**, the most popular base for canoeing the Delaware and the site of Ralph Stover State Park, great for swimming, fishing, camping, and hiking. A little farther north is **Erwinna**, where EverMay on the Delaware was a popular resort in the late 19th century, frequented by the Barrymore family. Pick up some Gentlemen Farmer jams at **River Road Farms** before heading for Upper Black Eddy, passing through **Uhlerstown**, where you'll find the only covered bridge over the canal at Lock 18. The final stop after Upper Black Eddy is **Riegelsville**, a small town with an inn, some antiques stores, and a few other shops nestled in beautiful countryside.

By the way, while traveling this route you may want to detour from Erwinna west to Perkasie to visit **Green Hills Farm**, on Dublin Road (☎ 215/249-0100), home of author Pearl S. Buck. Buck was the first American woman to win the Nobel Prize and the Pulitzer Prize for literature (for *The Good Earth*). She was born to missionary parents in China, but returned to the United States to live on this 60-acre farm, where she continued to write and raise her eight children. Today the Pearl S. Buck Foundation operates an adoption agency and assists displaced and Amerasian children. *Tours:* March to December, Tuesday to Saturday at 10:30am, 1:30pm, and 2:30pm, Sunday at 1:30 and 2:30pm. *Admission:* $5 adults, $4 seniors and children age 6 and up.

SOUTH (ROUTE 32) TO WASHINGTON CROSSING & PENNSBURY MANOR

Having suffered a string of defeats and retreated from the British across the Delaware safely to Pennsylvania, General George Washington reassembled his troops only a few miles south of New Hope. He desperately needed a victory to keep the American campaign alive. On Christmas Night he and 2,400 men made their famous Delaware crossing in a blinding snowstorm, negotiating their boats around ice floes, to his victory at Trenton on December 26, 1776.

The 500-acre area is now **Washington Crossing State Park**. The park is divided into two sections. The northern section, 2 miles south of New Hope, contains **Bowman's Tower**, a 110-foot observation tower marking the spot where the sentries watched the movements of the enemy. There's also a **wildflower preserve** (☎ 215/862-2924) here. On the east side of River Road, the **Thompson-Neeley House** was requisitioned during the campaign as a billet for officers. Among these was a young lieutenant, James Monroe, who was wounded at the Battle of Trenton, but survived to become the fifth president of the United States.

Farther south, near the point of embarkation, is the **Memorial Building**, which offers an old-fashioned recorded video and narration of the crossing; the **McConkey Ferry Inn**, where Washington supposedly ate his Christmas dinner before embarking; picnicking areas; and a bird sanctuary. For information, call ☎ 215/493-4076. *Hours:* Park, Tuesday to Saturday 9am to 5pm, Sunday noon to 5pm (to 4:30pm daily in winter).

In lower Bucks County, **Pennsbury Manor**, 400 Pennsbury Memorial Lane, Morrisville (☎ 215/946-0400), was the 17th-century residence/plantation of William Penn. He established this 8,400-acre estate in 1683, but did not live here very long—in fact, he visited Pennsylvania only twice during 1682–84 and in 1699–1701. Ill health and politics kept him in England. After his death the buildings decayed; by 1929 no trace of the originals survived. What you see today are reconstructions, built in the 1930s on this 43-acre site, in an effort to recapture the history and way of life of a typical 17th-century estate. Among the highlights are the reproduction of the barge that Penn used to reach Philadelphia from Pennsbury, a trip that took 5 hours; the manor house overlooking the Delaware; numerous outbuildings, including a bake-and-brew house, a smokehouse, and a joiner's shop; plus formal walled gardens, a kitchen garden, and orchards that also shelter a colony of honey bees in a keep. Special events and living history demonstrations are given. *Hours:* By tour only, Tuesday to Saturday 9am to 5pm, Sunday noon to 5pm. *Admission:* $5 adults, $4.50 seniors, $3 children ages 6 to 17.

Five miles northwest of Pennsbury Manor, **Historic Fallsington,** 4 Yardley Ave., Fallsington, PA 19054 (☎ 215/295-6567), represents historic preservation at its best. The village itself, an enduring Quaker community that has survived in the face of surrounding real estate development, consists of some 90 historic buildings dating from the 17th to the 19th century. Six of these buildings can be toured between May and October. They include a log cabin, a Federal residence, stagecoach tavern, schoolmaster's stone house, and a gambrel-roof meetinghouse. The best time to visit is the second Saturday in October, Historic Fallsington Day, when the village hosts an arts-and-crafts festival, a colonial dance and fashion show, plus Civil War reenactments and other entertainments. *Hours:* May to October, tours every hour on the hour Monday to Saturday 10am to 4pm, Sunday 1 to 4pm. *Admission:* $3.50 adults, $2.50 seniors, $1 children ages 6 to 17.

Sesame Place

Only a short distance west of Washington Crossing in Langhorne, **Sesame Place** (☎ 215/752-4900 or 215/752-7070) is a marvelous spot to spend the day with the whole family, exploring the 15 water adventures and the 50 stimulating play activities. Ride the Vapor Trail roller coaster or float down Big Bird's Rambling River. Romp down the Zoom Flume. Big Bird, Elmo, Cookie Monster, and other characters entertain in the Big Bird Theater, and other Muppet characters perform musical revues. Facilities include several cafes—you can eat your way through the Cookie Mountain and the Food Factory. *Hours:* June 18 to Labor Day, daily 10am to 8pm; Labor Day to early October, Saturday and Sunday 10am to 5pm. *Admission:* $27.95 adults (grandparents receive a 10% discount), $25.15 seniors, free for children age 2 and under. Parking is $5.

FROM NEW HOPE TO DOYLESTOWN & BEYOND

En route to Doylestown, you'll pass through the tiny village of **Holicong** and the town of **Buckingham,** where you might happen upon a farmer's market or flea market on a Saturday.

In **Doylestown** I suggest that you view the extraordinary landmarks created by archaeologist/anthropologist/dandy/bachelor Henry Chapman Mercer, who was considered something of an eccentric in his early years, but was awarded many academic honors in later life. Mercer was one of the first individuals to realize the unique properties of concrete—plasticity, fireproofness, and durability. All three of the structures you can visit are of poured, reinforced concrete built between 1908 and 1916, well before the medium became popular.

Fonthill, Mercer's 39-room home on East Court Street, was begun in 1908 when he was already 52 years old, and he designed it and supervised the construction. Today it illustrates his many accomplishments as an architect, an archaeologist, a tilemaker, a historian, and a creator of museums. The house is amazing in its conception: It contains 44 rooms, 18 fireplaces, 32 staircases, and 200 windows of different shapes and sizes. Even the bookcases, windows, steps, and pillars are constructed of concrete. Oddly enough, though, there's no formal dining room, for Mercer apparently preferred to dine wherever his whim decided at the moment.

The walls, columns, and vaulted ceilings in every room are covered with an incredible array of brilliantly colored tiles, collected from all over the world (Delft tiles, Chinese roof tiles, Persian tiles) or manufactured at his Moravian Pottery and Tile Works (see below). The rooms also contain treasures from Mercer's world travels and more than 900 prints.

Tours (mandatory; advance reservations necessary; call ☎ 215/348-9461): Monday to Saturday 10am to 5pm, Sunday noon to 5pm. *Admission:* $5 adults, $4.50 seniors, $1.50 children ages 6 to 17. Closed New Year's Day, Easter, July 4, Thanksgiving, and Christmas.

The **Moravian Pottery and Tile Works,** at Route 313 and East Court Street, is adjacent to Fonthill. Mercer had been moved to make tiles when he discovered that this old Pennsylvanian German art was dying. After several attempts, he succeeded in making a satisfactory tile, and by the turn of the century his tiles were in great demand. For example, they were installed in John D. Rockefeller's estate at Pocantico Hills, N.Y., in the Traymore Hotel in Atlantic City, and in the Isabella Stewart Gardner Museum in Boston. Most of the designs were adapted or copied from old German stove plates. Like Fonthill, this building is of concrete and looks like a Spanish mission. A short film precedes a self-guided tour on which you'll see the machinery, kilns, molds, tiles, and tools. The tiles are still manufactured according to Mercer's original formulas and methods, and you can purchase them in the store. For information, call ☎ 215/345-6722. *Hours:* Daily 10am to 4:45pm. Last tour at 4pm. *Admission:* $3 adults, $2.50 seniors, $1 children ages 6 to 17.

Mercer built the concrete **Mercer Museum** on Pine Street (☎ 215/345-0210) to house his collection of more than 50,000 preindustrial artifacts, tools, and folk art. He began to amass his collection when he realized that what most people considered junk was, in fact, the essence of history. These tools had cleared the forests of North America, opened a continent, and built a nation. In his museum he intended to illustrate America's history from a new point of view. Walk into the central court and you'll see a Conestoga wagon, an old stagecoach, whale boats, and antique fire engines suspended from the ceiling. There is a complete watch- and clockmaker's shop, a room filled with candy molds, another with redware pottery, and many more displaying the tools of over 60 early American crafts and trades. Among the folk art on display are cigar store figures, weather vanes, and decorated chests. *Hours:* Monday 10am to 5pm, Tuesday 10am to 9pm, Wednesday to Saturday 10am to 5pm, Sun noon to 5pm. *Admission:* $5 adults, $4.50 seniors, $1.50 children ages 6 to 17.

Another famous artist/author who was born in Doylestown is James Michener. The **James A. Michener Art Museum,** 138 S. Pine St. (☎ 215/340-9800), is located in the imposing old Bucks County prison and features 20th-century art and sculpture in changing exhibitions. Naturally, the collection includes a number of works by artists who made the area home: William Lathrop and Edward Redfield, who arrived in 1898, and the later New Hope group who lived at Cuttalossa in Lumberville around 1916—Daniel Garber, Charles Rosen, Robert Spencer, and Charles Sheeler among them. *Hours:* Tuesday to Friday 10am to 4:30pm, Saturday and Sunday 10am to 5pm. *Admission:* $5 adults, $4.50 seniors, $1.50 students, free for children ages 11 and under.

NEW HOPE & LAMBERTVILLE, N.J., LODGING & DINING

At the center of New Hope stands the impressive, 260-year-old **Logan Inn,** 10 W. Ferry St., New Hope, PA 18938 (☎ 215/862-2300), built by the first ferryman and originally known as the Ferry Inn. Friends of Moss Hart and members of the Algonquin Round Table—Dorothy Parker and George S. Kaufman, among others—and the theater crowd gathered here in the 1930s. The inn has hosted stars over the years, including Tallulah Bankhead and Robert Redford. It's still a favorite gathering place. The old tavern is a must. Or you can have a cocktail on the front terrace and dine either in the Greenhouse, brimming with plants, or in the more formal Colonial Room. The menu lists a variety of American/continental dishes—from filet mignon and chicken Valdostana (sautéed in vermouth and roasted garlic, topped with prosciutto and mozzarella cheese, and served with a tomato-cream sauce) to orange roughy broiled with lemon and olive oil.

The inn offers 16 air-conditioned guest rooms (all with baths, TVs, and phones) furnished in colonial style with four-poster canopied beds and other period pieces. Original art adorns the walls, and lace curtains and country flower baskets are set in the deep casement windows.

Rates: Weekends and in season, $105 to $160 double; weekdays off-season, $85 to $110 double. *Dining hours:* Daily 11am to 3:30pm, Sunday to Friday 4 to 9:30pm, Saturday 4 to 11pm.

The **Wedgwood Inn,** 111 W. Bridge St., New Hope, PA 18938 (☎ 215/862-2570; www.travelguides.com/bb/wedgwood), occupies three different homes encompassing 2 acres of landscaped grounds. The first is a gracious gabled 1870 Victorian with a large veranda decorated with scrolled-wood brackets and turned posts, the second a historic Classic Revival stone manor house (ca. 1833), and the third another Victorian. Pennsylvania Dutch–style surreys transport guests to and from New Hope. Carl Glassman and Nadine Silnutzer offer 18 rooms, all with baths, air-conditioning, and brass ceiling fans. One room has a spool bed with lilac lace ruffles, a treadle sewing machine, a towel rack, and an oak dresser; another well-lit room has a large bathroom and an iron bedstead with a candlewick spread; still another has a brass bed with a colorful quilt. On the ground floor, the grandest room boasts a four-poster with a lace canopy and more formal Federal-style highboy furnishings. There are also six suites, four with fireplaces—ask for rates. And in another Victorian, the Aaron Burr House just up the street, are another seven accommodations. At night you'll find your bed turned down and a complimentary carafe of amaretto awaiting you.

A breakfast of freshly squeezed juice, muffins, zucchini bread or croissants, and fruit salad is served out in the gazebo, on the back porch, or in your room. In summer, guests have swimming and tennis privileges at a nearby private club. In the evenings guests can settle into the Victorian chairs in front of the parlor fire and enjoy a quiet conversation. Carl and Nadine also operate an innkeeping school offering consultations, seminars, and even apprenticeship programs to anyone interested. And they're quick to offer information about Bucks County.

Rates (including breakfast): Weekends $115 to $215 double, weekdays $89 to $169 double.

Chimney Hill Farm, 207 Goat Hill Rd., Lambertville, NJ 08530 (☎ 609/397-1516), is a lovely 1820 stone-and-woodframe home atop a ridge with glorious views of the countryside. The 8 acres of grounds are well tended, and in summer the perennial gardens bloom in colorful abundance; there's even a boxwood maze. There are 12 guest rooms with baths; several have fireplaces. The Hunt Room contains an exotic canopied bed; the Terrace Room is decorated with lovely tapestry fabrics and offers a balcony. Four suites are located in the classic barn. The public rooms are extremely comfortable: The living room, for example, is furnished with Persian rugs and period reproductions, plus an antique baby grand piano. A full breakfast is served in the dining room—candlelit tables for two surround the fireplace and classical music plays in the background. In summer, breakfast can be enjoyed on the garden patio. Little extras that guests appreciate are the complimentary snacks and refreshments offered in the butler's pantry. The library and sunroom are other places to relax while looking out over the beautiful gardens. *Rates* (including breakfast): $105 to $225 double.

The **Inn at Lambertville Station**, 11 Bridge St., Lambertville, NJ 08530 (☎ 609/397-4400), is a brand-new accommodation right down by the Delaware River. The rooms (all with bath, phone, and color TV) are variously furnished to re-create the Victorian era and have been decorated to suggest particular places during that period—Hong Kong, New Orleans, Paris, and London. Some rooms have fireplaces; some have whirlpool tubs. *Rates* (including continental breakfast and complimentary newspaper): $95 to $145 double Sunday to Thursday, $145 to $195 double Friday, $165 to $240 double Saturday (discounted if you stay 2 nights).

LODGING & DINING ALONG THE RIVER ROAD (ROUTE 32)

The first accommodation you'll come to is the **Hotel du Village**, Phillips Mill Road and North River Road, New Hope, PA 18938 (☎ 215/862-9911). This estate, which most recently served as a girls' school, is quite lovely, set on spacious grounds studded with trees, shrubs, and flowers (some popped into tubs). The 19 air-conditioned guest rooms (all with bath) are in a large, rambling building. While they're not spectacular, they are good sized and fairly priced. Expect to find simplicity—like a king-size bed, a mahogany chest, an armchair, and a coat-and-hat stand. On the grounds there's a nicely landscaped secluded pool and two tennis courts. The dining room is extremely fetching and has a good reputation in the area. Oriental rugs cover the flagstone floors; rich chestnut paneling and fireplaces at each end of the room add warmth. There's also an outdoor flagstone dining area prettily arrayed with begonias and other plants and sheltered by a vine. It looks out onto a sylvan backdrop.

The menu might feature sole in curried butter, filet mignon with béarnaise sauce, duckling with cherry sauce, chicken with tarragon-cream sauce, and similar classic French dishes. To start, perhaps try escargots with garlic sauce, pâté maison, soup, or a salad. The desserts are always special, and so are the fresh vegetables and the bread that accompanies the meal. Prices range from $14 to $19. Breakfast brings coffee or tea, flaky croissants, and coffee cake or similar to your room. Dried-flower bouquets, hand-painted trays, and em-broidered clothes on the night tables are extra little touches.

Rates (including breakfast): $95 to $110 double. *Dining hours:* Wednesday to Thursday 5:30 to 9:30pm, Friday and Saturday 5:30 to 10:30pm, Sunday 3 to 9:30pm.

The **Inn at Phillips Mill,** 2590 N. River Rd., New Hope, PA 18938 (☎ 215/862-2984 for the inn, 215/862-9919 for the restaurant), is a small stone building (formerly a barn built around 1750) bedecked with ivy and other vines. The five charming guest rooms all have air-conditioning and are exquisitely furnished. One room, for example, has a four-poster, weathered barnboard paneling, a beamed ceiling, and colorful throw rugs on the plank floors; another has an unusual chest and a bath with a claw-foot tub (no shower). Godiva chocolates are placed in each room. Downstairs is a large parlor, with huge rough-hewn beams and a massive stone fireplace, where you can lounge on a leather couch. The original hand-cranked elevator is an affecting anachronism. The dining room has an excellent reputation for traditional French cuisine. The short menu features about six entrees ranging from duck with cranberry-orange sauce to brook trout with shiitake mushrooms and spinach. For vegetarians there's always a spring garden plate. Prices range from $14 to $21. In winter the fireplace makes the tiled dining room cozy, and in summer French doors open to an outdoor dining area. Bring your own wine. For a small additional charge you can secure a continental breakfast. *Rates:* $100 to $110. *Dining hours:* Sunday to Thursday 5:30 to 9:30pm, Friday and Saturday 5:30 to 10pm. Closed January and first week in February.

Although the whitewashed **Centre Bridge Inn,** 2998 N. River Rd., New Hope, PA 18938 (☎ 215/862-9139 or 215/862-2048), with maroon shutters and dormers, doesn't look particularly inviting (largely because it was built in the 1950s, after the 1706 structure had burned down), it's beautifully decorated inside with a mix of authentic antiques and reproductions; the rooms and terraces overlook the canal and the river. In summer, barges drift right by as you dine on the brick terrace graced with a fountain, hibiscus, and clematis. For guest use there's a parlor with a fieldstone fireplace, an oriental rug placed atop royal-blue carpeting, and Williamsburg blue-and-salmon sofas and wing chairs.

The grandest of the nine rooms is No. 9, on the ground floor, which has a large private terrace alongside the canal, a four-poster canopied bed with a colorful quilt, and a rocker. The spacious bath has double louvered closets and cedar (yes, cedar) paneling. This is also one of five rooms with a TV. While the other ground-floor room lacks the view, it has a separate sitting room, a fine marble Eastlake-style dresser, and a brass bed. In all rooms great attention is paid to quality products—the soap is Crabtree & Evelyn, the wallpapers from Schumacher. Upstairs, each of the more standard (but still large) rooms has sitting chairs, a chest, side tables, and a pretty decor.

The dining room is typically country, with a low, beamed ceiling and a fieldstone hearth; it serves well-prepared oven-roasted rack of lamb with horse-radish crust and mint sauce, pecan-crusted salmon with sorrel sauce, duck with pomegranate glaze and dried fruit couscous, and a daily fish and pasta special, among 10 or so items on the menu. The temptingly displayed desserts may include amaretto Bavarian cream pie, baked Alaska, and mocha-walnut pie. Prices for entrees run $19 to $27.

Rates: Weekends $110 to $160 double, weekdays $90 to $140 double. *Dining hours:* Monday to Thursday 5:30 to 9:30pm, Friday to Saturday 5:30 to 10pm, Sunday 11:30am to 2:30pm and 3:30 to 9pm.

STOCKTON, N.J., LODGING

On 10 acres surrounded by farmland, the **Woolverton Inn,** 6 Woolverton Rd. (R.D. Stockton), Stockton, NJ 08559 (☎ 609/397-0802), provides a pastoral retreat. It occupies a historic 1793 home built by industrialist John Prall as a wedding gift for his new bride, Amelia Coryell. The second owner, Maurice Woolverton, turned it into a Victorian by adding the mansard roofs and most of the architectural details—the elaborate scrollwork on the porch, the fanlight transom, and the wrought-iron cresting over the roof ridge. Whitney North Seymour, a leader of the American Bar Association for 50 years, added even more gingerbread and planted the formal gardens. St. John Terrell, who purchased it in 1957, hosted many of the celebrities who performed at his famous Lambertville "Music Circus" with lavish parties on the estate.

The house was converted into an inn in 1980, and innkeepers Elizabeth and Michael Palmer today continue the tradition of hospitality. From the sitting room—formally furnished with a grand piano, sofas, wing chairs, and French side chairs, all set around an Adam-style fireplace—you can step onto the porches and take in the view across the fields. A full breakfast is served either in the formal dining room or out on the flagstone patio. If you prefer, a continental breakfast can be served in your room. There are ten rooms (all with air-conditioning and private baths). Two have whirlpool tubs and three have fireplaces. Each is attractively furnished with a canopied bed, stenciled rockers, and stoneware lamps; a touch of whimsical charm is added to many rooms by the hand-painted decorations on the walls and ceilings. Note there are no TVs or phones. Croquet and horseshoes are available for guests. No children under age 14 and no pets are accepted.

Rates (including breakfast and afternoon tea): Weekends $115 to $210 double, weekdays $85 to $160 double.

Established in 1710, the **Stockton Inn,** 1 Main St. (Route 29, Box C), Stockton, NJ 08559 (☎ 609/397-1250), tucked away in the center of Stockton, inspired Richard Rodgers to write the song "There's a Small Hotel with a Wishing Well." The wishing well is still here, but the place has been completely renovated, while retaining an elegant old-world ambience. Two suites (each with a fireplace, a bath, a sitting room, a balcony, and a bedroom) and a cozy studio with a fireplace and bath are available in the inn. A suite and one large room with canopied beds and a shared veranda are in the carriage house. The Wagon House has two suites with canopied beds. An additional four rooms are across the street in the Federal House. Each room has a bath, and many have working fireplaces.

The restaurant, which serves contemporary American/continental cuisine, has two dining rooms. The original historic room has a formal ambience and some lovely murals depicting 18th-century life in Hunterdon County; the more modern Glass Room overlooks the garden. You can also dine in the garden itself, complete with a trout pond and waterfalls. Among the entrees might be horseradish-crusted grilled salmon with passion fruit vinaigrette, roast Long Island duckling with balsamic strawberry sauce, and Moroccan spiced rack of lamb with fresh mint chutney and cumin-scented lentils. Prices range from $17 to $27.

Rates (including continental breakfast): Weekends $115 to $180 double, weekdays $75 to $140 double. *Dining hours:* Monday to Saturday 11:30am to 2:30pm and 4:30 to 9:30pm, Sunday 11am to 2:30pm and 3 to 9:30pm.

LUMBERVILLE TO RIEGELSVILLE—LODGING & DINING

The **Black Bass Hotel**, 3774 River Rd. (Route 32), Lumberville, PA 18933 (☎ 215/297-5815; fax 215/297-0262; www.blackbasshotel.com), could be picked up and deposited in the English countryside and the locals would hardly notice. In this pre–American Revolution hostelry, the parlor fireplace is suitably blackened, Tudor-style settles keep the heat in, and portraits of Queen Victoria and Prince Charles stare down from the walls. Seven rooms have shared baths and the two suites private baths. All have air-conditioning. The room known as the Place Vendôme has a massive carved-oak Victorian bed, marble-top dressers, and side tables. The Grover Cleveland features a half-canopied bed, an Eastlake-style dresser, and a fireplace; a suite overlooking the river has a sleigh bed, a Victorian bed, and a separate sitting room. The tavern has a solid pewter bar rumored to be from Maxim's in Paris. In the dining room (☎ 215/297-5770) and also in the tavern, the owner displays his varied and large collection of Royal commemorative porcelain and china. The food is continental/American, offering everything from grilled lamb chops in a rosemary-jalapeño-mint sauce to seared Chilean sea bass in seafood gumbo sauce with fresh crawfish tails and jumbo lump crab. Prices run $20 to $27. The desserts are traditional—crème brûlée, strawberry shortcake, ice creams, sorbets, pies, and cheesecakes. *Rates* (including continental breakfast): Weekends $90 double, $160 to $185 suite; weekdays $75 double, $135 to $160 suite. *Dining hours:* Monday to Saturday 11:30am to 3pm and 5:30 to 10pm, Sunday 11am to 2:30pm and 4:30 to 8:30pm.

Tattersall, Cafferty Road (P.O. Box 569), Point Pleasant, PA 18950 (☎ 215/297-8233; fax 215/297-5093; www.bbhost.com/tattersallinn), is the name given to an early 1800s double-porched house standing among conifers and shade trees. Innkeepers Gerry and Herb Moss offer six air-conditioned rooms, each with a bath. The Highland Room (No. 1) has Black Watch plaid draperies and an Irish chain quilt on a mantle-style bed; Room 4 contrasts strongly—its walls are covered in lavender moiré silk, and a four-poster has a crocheted lace canopy. Many of the rooms have the original wainscoting, and two have gas fireplaces. Breakfast is served in the dining room, on the veranda, or in your room. Apple cider, coffee or tea, and cheeses are placed in front of the fireplace in the tavern in the midafternoon. Gerry's needlework and paintings can be seen throughout the house, and Herb enjoys demonstrating and talking about his old phonographs, which are displayed in the dining room. There's a small reading room and parlor with a beamed ceiling and a large fireplace. *Rates* (including breakfast): Weekends $95 to $140 double, weekdays $15 less.

For elegant romance, head for **EverMay on the Delaware,** River Road, Erwinna, PA 18920 (☎ 610/294-9100; fax 610/294-8249; www.evermay.com; e-mail: Moffly@evermay.com), an imposing Victorian mansion set well back from the road and approached via a semicircular drive. Built in the 1700s, it functioned as an elegant small hotel between the Civil War and the Great Depression, hosting vacationers like the Barrymores. It's now owned by Ronald Strouse and Frederick Cresson, who have restored it to its earlier glory. There are 16 rooms (all with baths, telephones, and air-conditioning), ranging from the large Colonel Erwin Room (with a towering Eastlake bed, needlepoint side chairs, Victorian velvet sofa, marble-top dresser, and fireplace) to the smallest room, the Edward Hicks (with a bed, a small chest, and a dresser). Fresh flowers, potpourri, and bowls of fruit and nougat are placed in each room, along with miniature bottles of liqueurs. Tea and sherry are served in the formal Victorian parlor with a grand piano, two fireplaces, and rare walnut paneling.

The dining room serves a $62 prix-fixe meal that begins with a champagne apéritif and hors d'oeuvres, followed by six courses. The menu changes daily, but the entrees might include poached salmon with citrus beurre blanc, grilled tuna with tomato-caper hollandaise, or roast loin of pork with Pommery mustard jus. These will be preceded by soups (shrimp bisque or roasted carrot and thyme, for example), Alsatian onion tart or wild mushroom and goat cheese strudel, and salads made with seasonal greens and other ingredients. Desserts are freshly made and might be double fudge torte or fresh fruit tart with a berry coulis.

Rates (including breakfast, tea, and sherry): $120 to $200 double, two-bedroom suite $300. *Dining hours:* Friday to Sunday and holidays at 7:30pm. Gentlemen are requested to wear jackets at dinner.

The **Golden Pheasant Inn,** River Road, Erwinna, PA 18920 (☎ 610/ 294-9595), is a lovely, historic inn nestled between the canal and the river (but lacking a view); it was built in 1857 to serve as an overnight stop for the bargemen traveling the canal. Now owned by Michel and Barbara Fauré, it offers fine hospitality in its 14 guest rooms and superb cuisine prepared by Michel, who trained at both La Tour d'Argent and Le Ritz in Paris and refined his expertise at Le Bec Fin and the Hotel duPont on this side of the Atlantic. All rooms are furnished with great flair. You might find a brass or cherry bed or a four-poster canopied bed, combined with appropriate antiques.

Each of the dining rooms is wonderfully atmospheric, too. The solarium, lit by candles only and with lights twinkling in the trees outside, is positively magical at night, while the French country dining room glows with copper pots, oriental rugs, and Barbara's Quimper collection. The cuisine is wonderful— roast duck with apricot-and-ginger sauce, roast pork loin with currant-and-cassis sauce, filet mignon with bordelaise sauce, and bay scallops with garlic, shallots, and tomatoes. Game is offered in season. Prices range from $17 to $23. Start with the pheasant pâté served with peach chutney or the richly flavored croustade of wild mushrooms with bordelaise sauce. For me, the only dessert is the Belgian white-chocolate mousse with raspberry coulis.

Rates (including continental breakfast): $120 to $155 double weekends, $105 to $135 double weekdays. *Dining hours:* Tuesday to Saturday 5:30 to 9pm, Sunday 11am to 3pm and 3 to 9pm.

Beatrice and Charles Briggs rescued the 1836 **Bridgeton House,** 1525 River Rd. (Route 32), Upper Black Eddy, PA 18972 (☎ 610/982-5856; www.bridgetonhouse.com), from decay and faithfully restored it, revealing the original fireplace and floorboards. They've furnished the living room with old pine chests and other Early Americana. At the back, French doors lead to a porch overlooking the river. The Briggs offer 11 rooms, many with screened-in porches and river views, all with baths and telephones. Throughout, Charles and Bea have decorated in their inimitable way, creating a variety of effects with murals and striking rich color palettes; the plank floors are covered with hooked rugs, rag rugs, or Chinese rugs. The furnishings are eclectically mixed, creating very warm, comfortable rooms.

Room 1 has a four-poster; Room 2 has an Eastlake look; Room 3 sports a four-poster with eyelet-lace pillows and sheets and a side table draped with a floor-length cloth. There are also several suites, the most spectacular being the third-floor penthouse, boasting a marble-and-mahogany bath with an oversize soaking tub, a fireplace, a TV, a separate dressing room, a bar, and a panoramic river view. Each room has fresh flowers, baskets of fruit, and chocolates, and there are British toiletries in the baths. A country breakfast of fresh fruit, omelets, waffles, and breads is served, and afternoon tea and cakes plus sherry are available in the sitting room. This is one of the few B&Bs right on the riverbank, where you can swim, fish, and even tube.

Rates (including breakfast, tea, and sherry): Weekends, $129 to $159 double, $209 to $299 suite or penthouse; weekdays, $109 to $209 double or suite.

MILFORD LODGING & DINING

Situated on the banks of the Delaware, **Chestnut Hill**, 63 Church St., Milford (☎ 908/995-9761), allows guests to relax and watch the river flow by. The inn occupies a handsome 1860 colonial Italianate house with gracious floor-to-ceiling windows on the first floor and a wraparound porch with handsome filigree work. There are seven guest rooms, all with private baths, telephones, and TVs. The Rose Garden Room is the largest. Each is decorated differently using country wallpapers and borders and such furnishings as Hitchcock rockers and other country pieces. You might find a maple four-poster covered with a pretty quilt combined with French-style armchairs and a German painted kas. The most private room is the Pineapple Room. There's also a cottage retreat with comfortable living room, bedroom, and full kitchen. In addition to the porch, which makes for a wonderful relaxing spot, there's a charming Victorian drawing room decked out with tufted Eastlake, elaborate patterning, jardinieres, lots of lace, and pictures hung from picture rails. A full breakfast is served in the formal dining room. Dishes range from delicious German apple pancakes and other sweet treats to traditional egg dishes. *Rates:* $100 to $150.

GARDENVILLE LODGING

Maplewood Farm, 5090 Durham Rd., Gardenville, PA 18926 (☎ 215/766-0477), is run by energetic and enthusiastic Cindy and Dennis Marquis. The stone farmhouse was built in 1792; the second story was added in 1826. Today it's surrounded by 5½ acres on which a flock of sheep graze and chickens roam—you can even pick your own eggs. Seven air-conditioned rooms (five with bath) are offered. The largest is the suite, featuring a sleeping loft (with a queen-size bed) that's reached by a fine tongue-and-groove oak staircase. Another room features an acorn four-poster combined with an oak dresser, a dry sink, a rocker, and a blanket chest to create a cozy, country ambience. Quilts and stenciled walls are found in all rooms. The full breakfast—of French toast, fluffy omelets, and similar fare—is served in the breakfast room, which is decorated with an inspiring "Tree of Life" mural painted by a local artist. Afternoon refreshments are also served, and guests may use a refrigerator that is stocked with beverages. The summer kitchen with its double walk-in fireplaces makes a great reading room, and the sun porch is an ideal spot for relaxing and chatting. Maplewood also has an outdoor pool. *Rates* (including breakfast): May to October, $120 to $165; November to April, $105 to $150.

FRENCHTOWN, N.J., LODGING & DINING

Across the river in Frenchtown, the **Frenchtown Inn,** 7 Bridge St. (☎ 908/996-3300), offers some of the finest cuisine in the area. The old, redbrick building contains a handsome bar on one side and an attractive dining room on the other. The high, beamed ceilings and natural elegance of the candlelit space enhance the dining experience. There's also an upstairs dining room with river views and a fireplace. The menu changes frequently, and the dishes will feature seasonal ingredients. You might start with chilled asparagus served with Coach Farm goat cheese, finished with a citrus vinaigrette, or sautéed jumbo shrimp in a brandied garlic butter with pink peppercorn sauce. The menu features about eight entrees, which often contain organic ingredients. Sample dishes might include a truly flavorsome roasted organic chicken breast wrapped in applewood-smoked bacon with natural jus, or roast herb-crusted rack of pork served with caramelized apples in Calvados and red wine jus, or a seafood bourride made with lobster, jumbo shrimp, and scallops served in a seafood anisette broth. Prices range from $20 to $28. Save some room for the signature dessert, the chocolate soufflé served with a raspberry chocolate truffle ice cream. *Hours:* Tuesday to Friday noon to 2pm and 6 to 9pm, Saturday noon to 2pm and 5:30 to 9:30pm, Sunday noon to 3pm and 5:30 to 8:30pm.

   Hunterdon House, 12 Bridge St., Frenchtown, NJ (☎ 908/996-3632), was built in 1865 by a local banker. The handsome Italianate house has seven guest rooms, all with baths (tub or shower). The most luxurious room is the Daisy Apgar Suite on the third floor, with an ornate cloverleaf window. The sitting area is furnished with wicker while the bedroom features an antique carved rosewood bed. In the Ruth Apgar Room you'll find an Eastlake dresser combined with a marble-top side table and a camelback sofa. The Lillian Apgar room features a carved canopied bed and has a decorative fireplace. A working fireplace is found in the William Apgar room, which is stylishly furnished with a high-back Eastlake bed. Guests can enjoy reading or watching TV in the parlor with its slate coal fireplace; there's also a shaded porch for relaxing and best of all, the belvedere for a quiet tête à tête. A full breakfast starting with fresh fruit and breads followed by a choice of three entrees (say, omelets or Belgian waffles) is served. Guest refrigerator and portable phones are welcome amenities. *Rates* (including breakfast): Weekends $120 to $175 double, weekdays $95 to $120 double.

NEWTOWN LODGING & DINING

Jean Pierre's, 101 S. State St. (☎ 215/968-6201), has a very French atmosphere and some fine French cuisine. Up front is a small bar and behind are two small dining rooms, including an upstairs room. The changing menu is supplemented by specials, which included fresh foie gras, quail Chinese style, and jumbo shrimp with balsamic vinegar when I visited. Among the 10 or so entrees might be a really fresh gingered fried red snapper in a miso broth flavored by lemongrass and shiitake mushrooms, fennel-crusted pork tenderloin with a Thai glaze served with golden apples and yellow turnips, or thyme-rubbed filet of beef with caramelized onion and elephant garlic in a red wine sauce. Prices range from $22 to $29. For an appetizer, try the quail salad with foie gras and truffle vinaigrette or the snails in garlic and parsley. On Sundays go for the $24 prix-fixe brunch, when you can select such dishes as an omelet made with lobster, tomato, red onion, and basil or Brioche French toast flavored with orange juice, Grand Marnier, and vanilla syrup. These dishes can be preceded by an assortment of smoked fish (trout, salmon, and whitefish) or caramelized grapefruit with brown sugar and sun-dried cranberries. *Hours:* Tuesday to Friday 11:30am to 2pm and 5:30 to 9pm, Saturday 5:30 to 9pm, Sunday 11:30am to 2pm and 4 to 8pm.

The **Temperance House,** 5–11 S. State St., Newtown, PA 18940 (☎ 215/860-0474), in the heart of town, combines a colonial stone building with two dormers and a Victorian. The 13 rooms have all the modern conveniences—baths, air-conditioning, TVs, and phones. They vary in color and decor. The Violetta is decorated in violet and contains white-painted furniture. The Benetz suite boasts a twig bed with a canopy, a Mission desk, an acorn chest, and even a comfortable chaise longue. The Granny McMinns features a Shaker four-poster with a crochet canopy. The Edward Hicks suite is more formal, with mahogany furnishings and walls hung with reproductions of the famous artist's work. A continental breakfast is served in the Checkers dining room.

There are three other dining rooms, plus the tavern, which offers a Dixieland brunch on Sunday afternoons. The Edward Hicks Dining Room has cherry tavern tables, two open hearths, and murals painted in Hicks's style. The menu is eclectic, featuring traditional and contemporary American fare, plus Italian dishes. You might find apple-smoked duckling served with a wild blackberry cognac sauce, horseradish- and Dijon-crusted salmon broiled with caramelized onion sour cream dill sauce, or pecan-encrusted venison with pineapple glaze. Four or so pasta dishes can be ordered as appetizers or main courses. Prices range from $13 to $33. In the fall and winter stop in for the lavish jazz buffet brunch.

Rates (including breakfast): $105 to $145 double. *Dining hours:* Monday to Friday 11:30am to 2pm and 4 to 10pm, Saturday 11:30am to 2pm and 6 to 10pm, Sunday 10am to 2pm and 4 to 9pm.

HOLICONG & BUCKINGHAM LODGING

A narrow, tree-lined lane, yellow with daffodils in spring, leads to **Barley Sheaf Farm,** Route 202 (P.O. Box 10), Holicong, PA 18928 (☎ 215/794-5104), one of my favorite lodgings anywhere. This 30-acre farm with sheep, chickens, and beehives was formerly playwright George S. Kaufman's residence. The barn, landscaped pool, pond, and majestic old trees round out the beautiful setting overlooking fields dappled with cattle and horses. The original part of the house dates from 1740, and the parlors and rooms contain comfortable antiques. There are five rooms and two suites in the main house, all with baths (including one Jacuzzi) and all furnished differently and attractively. Many have four-posters. The cottage, which used to be the ice house, contains three rooms with bath and a cozy living room with a fireplace and hooked rugs. One of the accommodations is known as the Strawberry Patch because of the wallpaper and comes with a handsome bed, plank floors covered with hooked rugs, a pie cupboard, and a Mexican-tiled bath. The bedroom has a French door, which opens onto a small flagstone terrace with a view over the pastures beyond. Two suites have been installed in the barn, all large enough to accommodate four. One has a wood-burning fireplace; the other has a fully equipped kitchen. Breakfasts are abundant—fresh juice, seasonal fruit, granola, followed by farm-fresh eggs scrambled with salmon or a frittata with sweet peppers and onions, plus a variety of baked Swiss breads, jams, and honey from the hives. Afternoon tea is also served, which might be scones and jam or cheese platters depending on the season.

Rates (including breakfast): Summer, weekends $150 to $225 double, midweek is $20 less; winter, weekends $120 to $205, midweek $20 less.

About 5 miles from New Hope, **Ash Mill Farm**, 5358 York Rd., P.O. Box 202, Holicong PA 18928 (☎ 215/794-5373; fax 215/794-9578), offers a tranquil retreat overlooking sheep-studded meadows. The circa 1790 plaster-over-stone house is set on 10 acres. There are three guest rooms and two suites, all comfortably furnished with a mixture of reproductions and family heirlooms. The largest and most private is the Ash Mill Suite on the third floor, which is furnished with a four-poster and has a comfortable sitting room, too. Other rooms might be furnished with Shaker reproductions or, say, a cherry pencil post. Guests gather around the Rumford fireplace in the living room, which seems particularly cozy in winter with its casement windows and plank flooring. Breakfast is served in front of the inglenook fireplace in the keeping room or on a patio overlooking the gardens. Rates: weekends $135 to $165, midweek $110 to $135.

Mike and Suella Wass run the **Whitehall Inn**, 1370 Pineville Rd. (R.D. 2), Buckingham, PA 18912 (☎ 215/598-7945), located 5 miles south of town. This 1794 home is set on 12 acres with an adjacent barn and stables. There are five air-conditioned guest rooms, all with private baths and four with fireplaces. All are attractively furnished. Extra touches include fine linens, Crabtree & Evelyn amenities, bathrobes, and chocolate truffles at turndown. The most sumptuous part of the experience is the four-course breakfast served by candlelight. Fresh fruit, freshly squeezed juice, and freshly made bread precede an entree like spinach-and-pine-nut tart or something similar. Afternoon tea is also served. The parlor provides a welcome retreat for guests who can relax in front of the fire and on the contemporary seating. There's a pool and horses for guests' pleasure. *Rates* (including breakfast and tea): $150 to $200 double.

Mill Creek Farm, P.O. Box 816, Buckingham, PA 18912 (☎ 215/794-0776), is a truly secluded retreat situated on 15 acres and surrounded by 100 more. Thoroughbred horses are raised on the property, giving it a real country feeling. Five well-appointed guest rooms, all with private baths and TVs, are offered in the 18th-century stone house. Each is decorated in a different color (peach, green, or pink) and furnished with antiques that might include cottage-style Victorian beds, marble-top dressers, wicker chairs, floor lamps, trunks, and similar pieces with character. A full breakfast is served in the sunroom overlooking the pond that's stocked with bass and serves as an ice-skating rink in winter. Facilities include an outdoor heated pool and tennis court. *Rates* (including breakfast): $155 double.

DOYLESTOWN AREA LODGING & DINING

The **Sign of the Sorrel Horse**, 4424 Old Easton Rd., Doylestown, PA 18901 (☎ 215/230-9999), dates to 1710 and was originally a gristmill. The dining room is rated highly for its cuisine, always artistically presented. Diners may choose from either the à la carte menu or from a seven-course tasting menu (costing $69.50). The first might offer a luscious boneless rack of lamb with cipollini onions and wild mushrooms; chicken stuffed with ricotta, roast peppers and prosciutto; nut-encrusted venison chops with a lingonberry and cassis sauce; or grilled tuna with tomato, pineapple salsa, cilantro, and tequila. The desserts are French classics. If you really want to spoil yourself, order the Deadly Sin—crème brûlée, chocolate-hazelnut terrine, and passion-fruit sorbet. Prices range from $15 to $26. A light menu is offered in the Waterwheel Lounge.

There are also five guest rooms available (three with bath). They're furnished with country pieces; a couple have canopied beds. The fireplace suite is a favorite; there's also a suite with a Jacuzzi.

Rates: $95 to $135 double, $160 to $185 suite. *Dining hours:* Wednesday to Saturday 5:30 to 9:30pm.

Highland Farms, 70 East Rd., Doylestown, PA 18901 (☎ 215/340-1354), was once the estate of lyricist Oscar Hammerstein. He was inspired to write some of his greatest hits here—*Oklahoma!, Carousel,* and *The King and I.* The stone house stands on 10 acres surrounded by sheep-filled meadows. Each of the rooms, decorated with great flair, is named after a musical. The *King and I* Room has bold floral wallpaper and an elaborate crown treatment over the bed. Among the furnishings is a love seat with a nearby floor lamp, making it an ideal reading place. The pink-and-sage *Carousel* Room has a carousel horse painted on the wall, the windows are draped with striking valances, and the bed is piled high with pillows. This room also features a fireplace and a comfortable love seat. Lovely bed treatments are found in the *Show Boat* Room, decorated with coral floral wallpaper. The *Oklahoma!* Room is a little more masculine, with a high-back oak bed, a wingback chair, and an acorn oak dresser.

The common rooms are welcoming, too. The original music room has been converted into the dining room, where a four-course breakfast of fruit, breads, cereal, and a hot entree like eggs Oscar is served. In summer, it's often served on the outdoor brick patio. The living room contains a grand piano, two comfortable sofas, and numerous books, plus a collection of great musical films. The sunroom, with flagstone floors and wicker furnishings, is a favorite spot for relaxing; so is the second-floor wraparound porch. Other facilities include a sylvan landscaped pool and a tennis court.

Rates (including breakfast): $145 to $205 double.

Past the gatehouse, a long driveway leads to the ivy-draped **Inn at Fordhook Farm,** 105 New Britain Rd., Doylestown, PA 18901 (☎ 215/345-1766), an entrancing building with diamond-paned leaded windows and several dormers along the roofline. It was built for W. Attlee Burpee of seed fame in 1880 and back then the estate was 100 acres; today it's only 60 acres. In the mid–19th century it served as a boys' school, but now it's a comfortable country inn where guests are welcomed by Carole Burpee. Some of the original Burpee furnishings—an Empire-style sofa, ormolu mirrors, a secretary, and ancestral Burpee portraits—adorn the large living room/parlor. Breakfast is served on Mrs. Burpee's china in front of the Mercer tile fireplace. It might start with poached pears and oatmeal or a similar cereal, baked items, fresh fruit, and French toast stuffed with cream cheese. Afternoon tea is served upon request in the living room or on the terrace shaded by 200-year-old linden trees. The study, added in 1903, is a wonderful place to withdraw and savor the surroundings—book-filled bookcases, leather chairs, a beamed ceiling, a large fireplace, and an immense world globe. Here W. Attlee Burpee wrote the first Burpee Seed catalogs.

There are five guest rooms and two rooms in the carriage house that share one bath. Each is well decorated with authentic antiques. The 18-by-22-foot Burpee Room contains a rice four-poster, a peer mirror, an Empire dresser, wing chairs, and fine paintings over the Mercer tile fireplace; it also has a private balcony. The Attlee Room boasts a brass bed, a working fireplace, and a private balcony. The third-floor Curtiss Room has sloping ceilings, a cannonball bed, a desk, a blanket chest, and stack bookcases, plus a tiny bath. The Carriage House is a large, self-contained suite with two bedrooms and the most striking room of all, the Great Room. This was Mr. Burpee's private library and is richly paneled in chestnut with chestnut beams, rafters, and bookcases and lit by Palladian windows.

Rates (including breakfast): Weekends $110 to $210 double, weekdays $110 to $185.

Pine Tree Farm, 2155 Lower State Rd., Doylestown, PA 18901 (☎ 215/348-0632), is set down an oak-shaded lane on 16 acres. The 1730 fieldstone farmhouse is a rambling place that has been added to over the years and is now operated as an inn by Ron and Joy Feigles. Joy was trained in hotel administration and always dreamed of opening an inn. She has filled the house with beautiful antique furnishings and her personal collections of redware and antique china. There are four guest rooms with bath, each furnished differently, but with an eye to guest comfort and convenience (a phone is available on request). For example, each has a writing desk and comfortable armchairs upholstered with fine fabrics. In one room you'll find a twig four-poster, in another a wrought-iron bed. Extra touches include nightly turndown and free morning paper with breakfast, which is served in the dining room or poolside. The breakfast may include such dishes as Grand Marnier French toast and omelets, plus fruit, muffins, and more. There are plenty of super-comfortable common rooms—from the keeping room with its blazing hearth to an upstairs sitting room, a library with a Mercer tile fireplace, and a bright solarium. In addition to the pool there's a tennis court.

Rates (including breakfast): $170 to $190 double.

State Street Cafe, 57 West State St., Doylestown (☎ 215/340-0373), is a casual and comfortable spot ideal for unwinding at the start of a weekend. What's great about it though, is the quality of the food. The menu offers a broad selection of about 10 dishes ranging from linguine with Italian sausage, kale, and roasted red peppers topped with smoked mozzarella to grilled chicken breast marinated in balsamic vinegar, honey mustard, and garlic served on a bed of brown-butter mashed potatoes. Prices range from $15 to $17. *Hours:* Tuesday to Saturday 11am to 3pm, Sunday 10am to 2pm; Tuesday to Saturday 5:30 to 10pm.

NEW HOPE AREA DINING

I've already discussed a couple of places that rank among the very best in the area, notably the **Inn at Phillips Mill** and the **Hotel du Village**. Other first-rate choices previously covered include the **Centre Bridge Inn**, the **Black Bass**, the **Golden Pheasant**, and the **Stockton Inn**.

Some of the best dining in the area lies across the river from New Hope in such New Jersey towns as Lambertville and Frenchtown.

Lambertville Dining

By the river, in a little cul-de-sac known as the Porkyard, **Hamilton's Grill Room**, 8 Coryell St. (☎ 609/397-4343), is a pretty local favorite. Up front is a raw bar and a fresh fish display in front of an open grill. The inner dining room is more formal, with a mirrored ceiling and trompe-l'oeil sky. The wood stove is garlanded with plants and flowers in summer. Among the eight or so entrees might be grilled striped bass with a delicious warm cilantro dressing, grilled rib-eye steak with green peppercorns and leeks, or pan-seared soft-shell crabs with roasted garlic and Dijon butter. Start with the grilled shrimp with anchovy butter or the wonderful salad of dandelion, breast of duck, aged chèvre, and pancetta dressing. Prices range from $18 to $30. *Hours:* Monday to Friday 6 to 10pm, Saturday 5 to 10pm, Sunday 5 to 9pm

Anton's at the Swan, 43 S. Main St. (☎ 609/397-1960), changes its menu monthly. The modern American cuisine uses the freshest local ingredients. The limited menu features only six or so entrees—seared skate with caramelized onions, grilled beef tenderloin on red beans and rice, or roast quail with an apple and cornbread stuffing. To start, you might find sautéed wild mushrooms in thyme crêpes or smoked duck with pears and baby greens. The ambience is warm, with wood paneling, brass sconces, and mirrors; a limited menu is served in the bar. *Hours:* Tuesday 6 to 9pm, Wednesday to Saturday 6 to 10pm, Sunday 4:30 to 8pm.

Manon, 19 N. Union St. (☎ 609/397-2596), is a small, pretty dining room decorated with old photographs and posters of Provence and fresh potted plants. The menu features hearty bistro and regional cuisine. The chicken breast is enhanced by a full-flavored roasted garlic cream sauce; a Roquefort sauce accompanies the filet of beef, while a thyme crust brings out the flavor of the rack of lamb. Seafood lovers will enjoy the bouillabaisse. The house pâté is a good start, or try the delicious salad of watercress and endive with walnuts, pear, and Roquefort. On Wednesday and Thursday a prix-fixe menu is usually offered for around $22; otherwise, prices range from $19 to $25. The desserts are classics—smooth, rich chocolate terrine with raspberry coulis or golden apple or pear tartin. BYOB. On Sunday an $18.50 prix-fixe brunch is served. You can start with soup or pâté or grilled shrimp with a red pepper coulis and follow with omelets, French toast, or a dish like grilled salmon with basil vinaigrette. *Hours:* Wednesday to Thursday 5:30 to 9:30pm, Friday and Saturday 5:30 to 10pm, Sunday 11:30am to 2:30pm and 5:30 to 9:30pm.

Back on Bridge Street at no. 23, **The Full Moon** (☎ 609/397-1096), is a casual spot with a light-oak and modern-graphics look. Here you can have a full breakfast (omelets, egg dishes) or savor a chocolate croissant or two. Salads, omelets, burgers, and sandwiches are the prime lunch items, and dinner features such dishes as walnut-breaded chicken with Dijon sauce, duck stuffed with apples and walnuts and served with either apple or cassis sauce, grilled salmon with mustard-dill sauce, and six or so pasta dishes. Prices run $14 to $17. BYOB. *Hours:* Monday and Wednesday to Thursday 8am to 3pm, Friday to Saturday 8am to 10pm, Sunday 9am to 3pm.

At the restored 1867 stone **Lambertville Station**, 11 Bridge St. (☎ 609/397-8300), there are a series of restaurants, a bar, and a lounge. Etched glass, oak, mirrors, period light fixtures, and Victorian furnishings create the atmosphere. About a dozen entrees are featured on the menu—grilled swordfish in a ginger-lime sauce, duckling with port wine and cranberry glaze, breast of chicken with sun-dried tomatoes and olive compote, and filet mignon with Merlot demi-glace. Prices range from $12 to $23. *Hours:* Monday to Thursday 11:30am to 3pm and 4 to 9pm, Friday and Saturday 11:30am to 3pm and 4 to 10pm, Sunday 10:30am to 3pm and 4 to 9pm.

New Hope Dining

Set in a condominium development known as Village 2, on a hill above New Hope, **La Bonne Auberge** (☎ 215/862-2462), a charming old stone inn, is a lovely surprise. The cuisine is prepared in a traditional French manner. Specialties include rack of lamb with Provençal herbs, veal with morels, and grilled salmon with lobster sauce. Prices range from $30 to $35. Among the luxurious appetizers are Beluga caviar and foie gras, along with simpler items like avocado vinaigrette. *Hours:* Wednesday to Saturday 6 to 10pm, Sunday 5:30 to 9pm.

Odette's, South River Road (☎ 215/862-3000), occupies a pretty stone house and offers several dining rooms overlooking the river. The atmosphere is warm and inviting, made even more so by the fireplace in the bar and the soft piano sounds (except Tuesday). In summer there's outdoor dining on the terrace, and on Friday, Saturday, and Sunday year-round there's cabaret and dancing in the Theater Room. The fare is contemporary American—roasted lamb chops with a rich tamarind sauce, pistachio-and-horseradish-encrusted chicken breast served with a roasted tomato and fresh basil coulis, filet mignon with three-peppercorn Madeira demi-glace, and Maryland crab cakes served with a red pepper rémoulade. Prices range from $15 to $25. *Hours:* Monday to Thursday 11:30am to 3pm and 5 to 10pm, Friday to Saturday 11:30am to 3pm and 5 to 11pm, Sunday 11:30am to 3pm and 4 to 9pm.

The Forager House, 1600 River Rd. (☎ 215/862-9477), is a refreshing change from many local dining rooms because the decor is sleek and modern. The cuisine offers a range of dishes from several ethnic traditions. For example, among the appetizers on the seasonal summer menu might be everything from crab spring roll with hoisin sauce to a roasted corn chowder, plus pan-seared mussels in garlic and herb butter. In addition to such main courses as wood-grilled salmon with roasted corn salsa and grilled beef tenderloin with red wine sauce, there are several pizzas and pasta dishes. Prices range from $8 to $23. *Hours:* Monday and Wednesday to Thursday 5:30 to 9pm, Friday 5:30 to 10pm, Saturday 1 to 10pm, Sunday 1 to 8:30pm.

The Landing, 22 N. Main St. (☎ 215/862-5711), offers, as its name implies, river-view dining in the dining room and on the patio in summer. The seasonal menu will likely offer a mixture of traditional continental dishes, plus some regional American and Asian-accented items. There could be pork tenderloin with gingered plum barbecue sauce, grilled salmon with a vodka-citrus-pineapple salsa with jalapeño and cilantro, or an 18-ounce porterhouse with caramelized mushrooms and onions stewed in Worcestershire, molasses, and fresh sage. Prices range from $19 to $27. To start there'll be a pâté and two soups of the day, plus several shellfish served on the half shell, as well as steamed mussels Portuguese-style in white wine, tomatoes, garlic, onion, and cilantro with Southwestern-spiced chicken sausage. Good lunch dishes include the mesquite grilled pork tenderloin sandwich topped with melted Gorgonzola; the traditional muffuletta filled with salami, ham, mortadella, provolone, and olive relish; and coconut shrimp served with coleslaw and corn on the cob. *Hours:* Sunday to Thursday 11am to 4pm and 5 to 10pm, Friday and to Saturday 11am to 4pm and 5 to 11pm.

For casual dining and great breakfasts and lunches in a warm rustic atmosphere, head for **Mother's**, 34 N. Main St. (☎ 215/862-9354). The breakfast choices, ranging from omelets to dishes like eggs Benedict, are perfect eye-openers. My favorite dish is the New Hope scramble made with sautéed mushrooms, asparagus tips, pimiento, prosciutto, cream cheese, and Parmesan and mozzarella cheeses. At lunch all kinds of sandwiches are available, from a crab melt to a filet mignon smothered with oyster and sherry sauce, plus such appetizers as spicy potstickers served with hoisin dipping sauce. Prices range from $6 to $12. Dinner brings more substantial dishes like champagne-glazed duck stuffed with orange mandarin rice, prime rib, steaks, and salmon marinated in and served with a lemon-soy vinaigrette—priced from $14 to $20. Desserts baked on the premises are also prime attractions. *Hours:* Monday to Thursday 9am to 9pm, Friday 9am to 10:30pm, Saturday 9am to 10:30pm, Sunday 9am to 9pm.

Lake Nockamixon Lodging & Dining

About 20 minutes north of New Hope between Erwinna and Ottsville, **Auldridge Mead**, 523 Geigel Hill Rd., Ottsville, PA 18942 (☎ 610/847-5842), is a unique bed-and-breakfast that offers tranquillity plus some other delights that reflect the enthusiasms of innkeeper Craig Mattoli. It stands on farmland that was purchased from William Penn in the late 18th century. Many of the buildings that comprise the inn date back to 1772. The heart of the inn is the stone farmhouse. Here, there are six guest rooms, two sharing a bath, two with private baths, and a three-room suite with a fireplace and private entrance. The rooms have been decorated in style, using a variety of painting techniques—sponging, marbleizing, crackling, and stenciling. Some of the rooms feature beds that have been hand-crafted by Craig in such fine woods as ebony, maple, and mahogany. These are made in the workshop in the granary building on the property. A rustic room on the third floor has a twig bed that was also created by Craig. The rooms are furnished with antiques. The three-room suite has a bedroom with fireplace, Jenny Lind bed, and plank floors, braided rugs, and a beamed ceiling that add to the ambience. Beams, pine floors, stone walls, and an inglenook fireplace set the tone of the living room/library, where guests gather to watch the large-screen TV/VCR. Extra luxuries include plush bathrobes and coffee and newspapers, placed outside your room in the morning. A full breakfast is served, and it includes freshly squeezed juices, sour cream pancakes, and applewood-smoked bacon minus nitrates, nitrites, or preservatives. Facilities include an attractive outdoor pool. In addition to the furniture workshop, there is a French Country Cooking School on the premises, and you can attend special cooking class weekends January through April. *Rates:* Weekend $125, midweek $110 for double with shared bath; weekend $165, midweek $125 to $145 for room with private bath; weekend $235, midweek $195 suite.

NEW HOPE AREA AFTER DARK

For theater entertainment, the **Bucks County Playhouse,** South Main Street (P.O. Box 313), New Hope (☎ 215/862-2041), stages musicals, including some Gilbert and Sullivan work, in a converted gristmill. The season runs Easter to mid-December. Over in Princeton, N.J., the **McCarter Theater,** 91 University Place (☎ 609/683-8000), presents a full season of professional drama, dance, music, and special events.

For jazz / blues lovers there's music Thursday to Sunday at the **Havana Bar and Restaurant,** 105 S. Main St., New Hope (☎ 215/862-9897).

In Lambertville, the **Swan Hotel,** 43 S. Main St. (☎ 609/397-3552), draws crowds regularly from as far away as Princeton to its typical English-style pub. It's open daily from 4pm to 2am. Other pleasant bars are found at the old inns stretching along Route 32 north, the **Golden Pheasant** and the **Black Bass.** Then, of course, there's the **Logan Inn** itself, whose tavern brings back so many memories from the 1930s. **Lambertville Station,** 11 Bridge St. (☎ 609/397-8300), has live jazz on Saturday and Sunday in the downstairs bar. There are other dancing spots around, some straight, some gay. Ask the locals for details.

New Hope Area
Special & Recreational Activities

Antiquing: The whole area is dotted with stores specializing in all sorts of items. Frenchtown has many good stores, and the road (Route 202) from New Hope to Lahaska is well stocked with stores.

Ballooning: Harrison Aire, Wertsville Road (P.O. Box 73), Hopewell, NJ 08551 (☎ 609/466-3389), offers daily balloon flights for $160 per person. They've been in business for more than 20 years. The whole experience lasts about 3 hours, though flight time is only 1 hour. After the flight champagne is served in the garden gazebo. Flights operate daily depending on the weather. On weekends you'll need to book 2 to 4 weeks in advance.

Canoeing & Rafting: Bucks County River Country, P.O. Box 6, Point Pleasant, PA 18950 (☎ 215/297-8823 or 215/297-5000), offers canoeing, kayaking, tubing, and rafting trips on the river. There are several options available—6-mile/2-hour and 13-mile/4-hour canoe trips costing $20 and $25 respectively, 6-mile/4-hour rafting trips at $15 per person, and tubing trips that are $15 for adults and children. On weekends, reservations are needed.

Golf: Five Ponds, 1225 W. Street Rd., Warminster (☎ 215/956-9727), is open to the public. Greens fees are $26 to $38 on weekends. You need to book a week in advance.

Hiking: There's a quiet, grassy towpath along the canal and some other trails in local state parks—for example, at Washington's Crossing, Bull's Run across the footbridge at Lumberville. See "State Parks," below.

Picnicking: Head for the **Bowman's Hill State Wildflower Preserve** or any state park, including the one along the towpath.

Shopping: Flemington, N.J., is famous for its outlets (☎ 908/806-8165)—close to 200 of them, ranging from Dansk and Reebok to Anne Klein, Calvin Klein, and Joan & David. For landscaped shopping, some people enjoy **Peddlers Village** (see above) at routes 202 and 263 in Lahaska (for confirmed tourists only).

State Parks: For state park information call ☎ 888/727-2757. **The Delaware Canal State Park,** R.R. 1, Box 615A, Upper Black Eddy, PA 18972 (☎ 215/982-5560), stretches along the canal that's the only intact remnant from the great canal-building era. It's ideal for biking, hiking, horseback riding, cross-country skiing, and picnicking. **Nockamixon State Park,** 1542 Mountain View Dr., Quakertown, PA 18951 (☎ 215/529-7300), offers picnicking, swimming, fishing, hiking, boat and bike rentals, sledding, iceboating, ice fishing, and skating in a 5,250-acre area. The 45-acre **Ralph Stover Park,** 6011 State Park Rd., Pipersville, PA 18947 (☎ 610/982-5560), has picnicking, fishing, hiking, sledding, and cross-country skiing. **Tyler State Park,** south of Washington Crossing at 101 Swamp Rd., Newtown, PA 18940 (☎ 215/968-2021), has close to 2,000 acres for picnicking, fishing, boating (canoe rentals available for $13 the first hour, $7 thereafter), hiking, bicycling, ice-skating and fishing, sledding, and cross-country skiing. **Bull's Island,** N.J., across the river at Lumberville, has camping, picnicking, and birding.

Swimming: See "State Parks," above, and the **Hotel du Village, Barley Sheaf,** and **Whitehall Farms.**

Tennis: The **Hotel du Village** and **Whitehall Farms** have courts. For other locations, call the chambers of commerce.

White-Water Rafting: See "Canoeing & Rafting," above. Call ☎ 215/297-8823 for information.

Greater Wilmington, the Brandywine Valley & Valley Forge

Downtown Wilmington ◆ *New Castle* ◆ *Brandywine River
Valley, including Winterthur, Longwood Gardens &
Chadds Ford* ◆ *Valley Forge* ◆ *Audubon*

Distance in miles: Valley Forge, 115; Wilmington, 121
Estimated driving time: 2½ hours

◄o►◄o►◄o►◄o►◄o►

Driving: For Wilmington, take the New Jersey Turnpike to I-95 to the Delaware Avenue exit (Exit 7). For Valley Forge, take the New Jersey Turnpike to the Pennsylvania Turnpike (I-76) to the Valley Forge exit.

Bus: Greyhound (☎ 800/231-2222) goes to Wilmington and King of Prussia.

Train: Amtrak (☎ 800/872-7245) runs to Wilmington. It also goes via Philadelphia to Harrisburg, stopping en route at the small town of Downingtown (southwest of Valley Forge).

Further Information: For more on the area, contact the following: the **Greater Wilmington Convention and Visitor's Bureau,** 100 W. 10th St., Suite 20, Wilmington, DE 19801-1661 (☎ 302/652-4088 or 800/422-1181 to request brochures); **Delaware Tourism,** 99 King's Hwy., Dover, DE 19901 (☎ 800/441-8846 or 302/739-4271); **Chester County Tourist Information,** 601 Westtown Rd., Suite 170, West Chester, PA 19382; or the **Valley Forge Country Convention and Visitors Bureau,** 600 W. Germantown Pike, Suite 130, Plymouth Meeting, PA 19462 (☎ 800/441-3549 or 610/834-1550).

◄o►◄o►◄o►◄o►◄o►

Most New Yorkers associate Brandywine with the battle of that name, but few have ever visited this lovely part of the country where the landscape is very much like the English countryside. The gently rounded hills, the old barns, the grazing horses, the roadside wildflowers, and the driftwood and willows along the Brandywine River's banks are all on a human scale. Besides the pleasant green landscape, the area is exceedingly rich in prime attractions—the finest

Events & Festivals to Plan Your Trip Around

February: Washington's Birthday Weekend reenactment of the winter of 1777–78 in Valley Forge Historic Park. Drilling, shooting, cooking demonstrations, and more (usually the third weekend).

April: Winterthur in the Spring, Winterthur Museum.

April to Mid-May: Blossom time in Valley Forge Park.

May: Winterthur Point-to-Point (first Sunday).

> **Devon Horse Show and Country Fair.** Contact Devon Horse Show and Country Fair, Route 30, Devon, PA 19333 (usually the last weekend). Call ☎ 610/964-0550

> **A day in Old New Castle,** 6 or so miles south of Wilmington (usually the third Saturday).

June: Festival of Fountains Longwood Gardens, which extends through the summer. Call ☎ 610/388-1000.

July: The Ice Cream Festival at Rockwood, Wilmington.

August: Goschenhoppen Folk Festival, authentic, noncommercial Pennsylvania Dutch Festival on Route 29, Green Lane (usually the second weekend).

September: Reenactment of the **Battle of the Brandywine.** Contact Brandywine Battlefield State Park, P.O. Box 202, Chadds Ford, PA 19317 (☎ 610/459-3342).

National Mushroom Festival in Kennett Square (usually the second weekend).

October: Chester County Day in West Chester—historic house tours, hunt, and hounds (first Saturday).

> **Laerenswert** ("worth doing"). Craftspeople demonstrate and invite audience participation at the Peter Wentz farmstead (usually the second Saturday).

November: Delaware Antiques Show at Winterthur.

December: Candlelight tours at Hagley, Winterthur, and Rockwood museums and of Historic Old New Castle.

collection of American furniture and decorative arts anywhere at Winterthur, an outstanding American garden at Longwood, a couple of truly fine art museums displaying the works of the school of painters inspired by the Brandywine River, a château to match any in France at Nemours, and a fascinating museum capturing part of America's early industrial history at Hagley. The Brandywine may be a narrow and short river, but it possesses a great and inspiring tradition.

There are a couple of ways to explore the area over a weekend. You can go to Wilmington and stay at the venerable Hotel duPont, which was ranked by the late Craig Claiborne in a class with London's Connaught and New York's Plaza, or you can anchor at Valley Forge, only about 45 minutes away from most of the attractions.

Wilmington & the Brandywine Valley

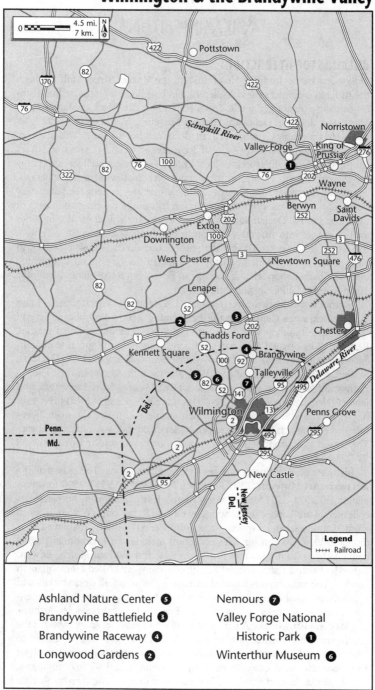

Legend
+++++ Railroad

Ashland Nature Center **5**

Brandywine Battlefield **3**

Brandywine Raceway **4**

Longwood Gardens **2**

Nemours **7**

Valley Forge National
Historic Park **1**

Winterthur Museum **6**

WILMINGTON

WILMINGTON ATTRACTIONS

Only a few blocks from the Hotel duPont, the **Market Street Mall** has been constructed around a series of splendid old buildings, including a fine 18th-century civic building, the **Old Town Hall,** in the 500 block of Market Street Mall. Next door the **Delaware History Museum,** 504 Market St. (☎ 302/655-7161), occupies a renovated art deco Woolworth store. The museum features changing exhibits of regional decorative arts, children's toys, and other subjects that highlight aspects of local history. On the second floor, kids enjoy the Discovery Center, which features hands-on activities like dress-up games, a market place, an old-time kitchen, and historic toys. Among the permanent treasures is one of the original chairs given by George Washington to each of the signers of the Declaration of Independence. The collection also includes an Early American primitive sculpture of Washington, carved to replace the one of King George III that the patriots tore down at Bowling Green in New York City, and which Senator T. Coleman du Pont found languishing outside a barber shop. *Hours:* Tuesday to Friday noon to 4pm and Saturday 10am to 4pm. Call for further information.

Farther down Market Street, at no. 818, stands the Grand Opera House (1871), Delaware's **Center for the Performing Arts,** a magnificent Second Empire–style building with a cast-iron facade resembling chiseled marble. Restored to its original Victorian splendor, it echoes to the applause of audiences enjoying a variety of programs—from Robin Williams and Marcel Marceau to the London Philharmonic and the Academy of St. Martin-in-the-Fields— as they did when such figures as actors Edwin Booth, Ethel Barrymore, and James O'Neill (father of Eugene O'Neill) performed here and Buffalo Bill brought his show. Tours of the building, which enable you to see the magnificent frescoed ceiling and lavish decor, can be arranged, but you must call ahead. The season runs from September to July. For tickets and information, call ☎ 302/658-7897.

Just outside Wilmington are several more attractions. The closest is the **Delaware Art Museum,** 2301 Kentmere Pkwy. (☎ 302/571-9590 for information, 302/571-9594 for tour reservations). It's internationally known for its collection of pre-Raphaelite paintings by Edward Burne Jones, William Holman Hunt, Dante Gabriel Rossetti, and John Everett Millais, displayed in a dramatic Victorian setting. The collection includes an exceptional pair of painted chairs from a suite of furniture created by William Morris, Edward Burne-Jones, and Dante Gabriel Rossetti for rooms at 17 Red Lion Square in London. The museum was founded on a core collection of 48 works by Howard Pyle, who established the Brandywine school of painting. It now has an extensive collection of works by N. C. Wyeth, Frank Schoonover, Stanley Arthurs, and Maxfield Parrish. The American art collection provides an overview of the development of American art from Winslow Homer and Thomas Eakins to John Sloan and Andrew Wyeth. Major works by contemporary international artists are also on display. To reach the museum, take I-95 to Wilmington Exit 7 (Route 52 north). *Hours:* Tuesday 9am to 4pm, Wednesday 9am to 9pm, Thursday to Saturday 9am to 4pm, Sunday 10am to 4pm. Closed

New Year's Day, Thanksgiving, and Christmas. *Admission:* $5 adults, $3 seniors, $2.50 students.

Rockwood, 610 Shipley Rd. (☎ 302/761-4340), is one of the few American examples of rural Gothic architecture and the Gardenesque school of landscape design. The house was built in 1851 by merchant banker Joseph Shipley, but it is the life of the Bringhurst family, who purchased it in 1892, that is portrayed at the house today. The interior is rich in decorative arts dating from the 17th to the mid–19th century. The house features a cast-iron and glass conservatory filled with plants that is one of the oldest still standing in the United States. The 6 acres of gardens make a wonderful setting for a series of events during the summer, including a concert series in June, an Irish Film Festival in March, an Ice Cream Festival in July, and many more. *Hours:* Guided tours of house, Tuesday to Saturday 11am to 4pm (the gardens can be toured during the same hours). *Admission:* $5 adults, $4 seniors, $2 children ages 5 to 16.

Named after the French ancestral home of the du Ponts, **Nemours** (☎ 302/651-6912) is an excellent example of a French château in this country. On this 300-acre country estate, Alfred I. du Pont had Carrère and Hastings of New York build a 102-room mansion, where he entertained lavishly. On arrival, you'll receive a glass of fresh juice, then you'll be ushered through the house to feast your eyes on the exquisite European art and furnishings. The ornate, wrought-iron gates were commissioned by Henry VIII; another set of gates came from Catherine the Great's palace in St. Petersburg; one of the many clocks was made for Marie Antoinette. There are tapestries, rugs, and paintings, some dating back to the 15th century. The rooms give a wonderful insight into the family's opulent lifestyle—vintage automobiles, a billiards room, a nine-pins alley, a bottling plant, and an ice plant. You'll notice personal items throughout and will learn about the character of the owner, who had the statuary washed every day and who personally inspected the boiler and heating system. The formal gardens are splendid, some of the finest examples of the French style to be found anywhere in America. The obligatory guided tours take about 2 hours. The mansion is on Rockland Road between routes 141 and 202, just north of Wilmington across the Brandywine River. *Tours:* May to November, Tuesday to Saturday at 9am, 11am, 1pm, and 3pm; Sunday 11am, 1pm, and 3pm. *Admission:* $10. Reservations are required and visitors must be age 16 or over. Contact the Nemours Mansion and Gardens, Reservations Office, P.O. Box 109, Wilmington, DE 19899 (☎ 302/651-6912).

WILMINGTON LODGING

The **Hotel duPont,** 11th and Market streets (P.O. Box 991, Rodney Square), Wilmington, DE 19899 (☎ 302/656-8121), is a venerable establishment where you immediately feel welcome. It's not in the least ostentatious—the luxury comes from service and attention to details: 24-hour room service; towels that are changed twice daily; a croissant, coffee, and a newspaper delivered to your room in the morning; turndown service; and a chocolate mint on your pillow and similar little touches. Each of the 206 large rooms features a service bar, a TV/VCR, a leather-inlaid desk, an in-room safe, and two phone lines with voice mail in three languages. Many famous personalities have bedded down here since it opened in 1913—Duke Ellington, Amelia Earhart, Eugene O'Neill, Tallulah Bankhead, Dorothy Gish, and even Ignacy Paderewski, who angered other guests by playing his piano well into the night.

Even if you don't stay here, you might think of attending the justly famous $29.50 brunch (reservations necessary), where you can treat yourself to a lavish spread of appetizers, then to a choice among several entrees, like a smoked salmon Florentine omelet, roasted tenderloin of beef with a Guinness beer sauce, and whole-wheat waffle with blueberry sauce. It's served in the formal Green Room, an imposing, oak-paneled space with majestic 18-foot Palladian windows draped and valanced in gold fabric, a coffered ceiling that's carved and gilded ornately, and gilt chandeliers and sconces; there's also a musician's loft. The tables are set with Rosenthal china.

At dinner the menu features such items as sesame-crusted tuna cooked and served in a lemongrass broth, grilled filet of beef in a delicious Merlot sauce, and a rack of lamb with dried cherry and green peppercorn sauce with rösti potatoes. Prices range from $24 to $29. My favorite desserts are the stuffed white-chocolate timbale with fresh fruit and orange sauce and the lemon crème brûlée with a cherry coulis. The Brandywine Room is richly paneled and enhanced with originals by Howard Pyle and three generations of Wyeths. It's noted for its fine cuisine, too—honey-roasted free-range chicken with thyme jus and roasted red pepper polenta, Chilean sea bass accented with dried tomato and olive tapenade, and grilled filet mignon topped with a mushroom ragoût and served on a rich Cabernet sauce. The lower-level grill serves cafeteria-style breakfast and lunch. Afternoon tea is also served. Facilities include fitness club and shopping arcade, but the most unusual facility is the plush Playhouse Theater.

Rates: Weekends $159 to $199 double, weekdays $239 to $309 double. Special weekend packages available.

Darley Manor Inn, 3701 Philadelphia Pike, Claymont, DE 19703 (☎ 302/792-2127), is a suburban B&B located in a rambling residence with a Dutch gable roof and a row of dormers. The main house, consisting of four rooms, was built in the 18th century and expanded substantially in the mid-19th century, when it was owned by illustrator Felix Darley. There are six rooms and a suite, all with private baths, cable TV/VCRs, and telephones. Furnishings will always include a comfortable recliner, desk, and good reading lights. The largest and most private is the Wren's Nest suite, which is decorated in classic colonial fashion, but my favorite is the North-South Writer's Suite tucked up on the third floor. It has a beamed, vaulted ceiling and such furnishings as a planter's desk along with decorative accents from the Civil War era—documents, art, and books. A couple of rooms have a fireplace. There are plenty of options for relaxing—on enclosed porch furnished with wicker and plants, in the back parlor (where you can entertain on the piano), and in the front parlor. Guests can also retreat to the garden gazebo or the benches and lawn swing. Breakfast is served in the formal dining room at a large dining table. Facilities include an exercise room containing a bike, treadmill, Nordic Trak, rower, and Universal equipment.
Rates: weekends $129 to $139, midweek $105 to $129.

The **Hilton**, I-95 and Naamans Road, Claymont, DE 19703 (☎ 302/792-2700), is on the outskirts of Wilmington (about 8 miles, or 10 minutes, from downtown) and offers modern rooms with full amenities. The Evergreens restaurant offers New American cuisine. There are 187 bed/sitting rooms and 7 suites. The seventh-floor executive rooms are spacious, with enough room for a desk, couch, and a coffee table. On the same floor is a convenient lounge area and plenty of business and other magazines to read. Whispers lounge is crowded, especially on weekends, when a DJ spins for dancing. The hotel has an outdoor, kidney-shaped pool.

Rates: From $166 double. Special weekend packages available.

The redbrick **Radisson Wilmington,** 4727 Concord Pike (Route 202), Wilmington, DE 19803 (☎ 800/325-3535 or 302/478-6000), offers 154 accommodations with modern furnishings. The hotel also has a restaurant, a lounge, an outdoor pool, and a fitness center. *Rates:* $159 double ($99 double on weekends).

WILMINGTON DINING

The brunch at the **Hotel duPont** (above) is the best known and an elegant treat.

The Silk Purse and the Sow's Ear, 1307 N. Scott St. (☎ 302/654-7666), is Wilmington's premier dining spot. In an obscure white-brick building, it provides an understated, elegant setting for fine cuisine. The menu changes daily, but offers a variety of dishes—pan-roasted Arctic char with ginger and lime broth, venison with soft mascarpone polenta and chili corn sauce, and grilled chicken breast with red-and-yellow tomato salsa. Prices range from $17 to $28. To start, select the shrimp and crab spring rolls with tamarind sauce or the grilled portobello mushrooms with smoked onion, arina cheese, and red pepper rouille. *Hours:* Tuesday to Saturday 5:30 to 9:30 or 10pm.

Sal's Place, 603 N. Lincoln St. (☎ 302/652-1200), in the heart of the city's Little Italy, is one of the top three restaurants. It looks like an Italian neighborhood place, and that's what a lot of people think it is when they stray in—until they see the prices and the fare on the menu. It's not exactly veal parmigiana territory. Instead, the menu features classics like steak au poivre flambée; duck with wild berry demi-glace and wild mushroom compote; rack of lamb roasted with rosemary, thyme, and port wine; and Dover sole meunière. Prices range from $19 to $28. To start, there's escargots bourguignonnes, pâté of venison and black truffles, and Gorgonzola-stuffed eggplant topped with tomato sauce. The decor is typical—plain red leatherette seating and undistinguished landscape paintings. *Hours:* Monday to Friday 11:30am to 2pm and 5 to 10pm, Saturday 5 to 10pm.

Carucci, 504 Greenhill Ave. (☎ 302/654-2333), in Wawaset Plaza, a small shopping center, is a sleek bistro. Black-and-white tile floors, black Breuer chairs, large bouquets, and modern lithographs set the scene for consistently good Italian cuisine, priced from $14 to $22. Dishes might include delicious roast rack of lamb with Barolo sauce; chicken Carucci, which is a breast of chicken pounded thin and layered with mozzarella, spinach, and prosciutto; a delicious zuppe di pesce; and a variety of pastas—like garlic and potato ravioli and penne with spicy tomato-basil sauce. *Hours:* Tuesday to Friday 11:30am to 2:30pm; Tuesday to Saturday 5:30 to midnight.

Dinardo's Seafood, Fourth and Lincoln streets (☎ 302/656-3685), is a traditional regional favorite for crabs, although, ironically, they actually come from Louisiana. Still, crabs here are steamed, sautéed, deviled, or Imperial.

Noncrab fanciers can sample clams and mussels as well as stuffed flounder and barbecued shrimp, from $12 to $20 (with king crab legs going for $34). The room is plain—wood tables and Hitchcock chairs—but it's a real Wilmington treat. *Hours:* Monday to Saturday 11am to 11pm, Sunday 3 to 10pm.

AN EXCURSION TO NEW CASTLE
New Castle Attractions

Only a 15-minute drive south of Wilmington lies historic New Castle, one of Delaware's oldest settlements and a lovely town to visit for a full day or just an afternoon. In 1631 the Dutch established the fishing settlement of Zwannendael (Valley of Swans) on the site of present-day Lewes. This settlement was destroyed by Native Americans, and so it was left to Sweden to establish the first settlement at the mouth of the Christina River in 1638. The Dutch took back the little colony in 1655 and renamed it New Amstel, a name the English changed to New Castle when they took over.

There's bound to be something happening on the **Green**—perhaps an arts or crafts show. Surrounding it, the beautiful historic buildings are all still used, and many are still fine residences. In May quite a few homes are open to the public (see the "Events & Festivals to Plan Your Trip Around" box at the beginning of this chapter). For details, call the **New Castle Historical Society** at ☎ 302/322-2794.

On the east side of the quadrangle is the **Academy** (1799). Adjacent to it, the oldest part of the handsome **Imanuel Episcopal Church** dates to 1703, although the congregation was established in 1689. Its graveyard contains many markers from the 1700s.

On the north side of the square are rows of old residences, including the **Old Dutch House** at 32 E. Third St. It was built around 1700 and is furnished with 17th- and 18th-century Dutch furniture including a kas, a courting bench, and a Dutch bible. *Hours:* March to December, Tuesday to Saturday 11am to 4pm, Sunday 1 to 4pm; January and February, Saturday 11am to 4pm, Sunday 1 to 4pm. *Admission:* $2 adult, $1 children.

Also on this side of the square is the **Old Library Town Museum,** 40 E. Third St., an interesting hexagonal structure designed by Frank Furness and built in 1892. The exhibits focus on Newcastle and Delaware history. *Hours:* Saturday 11am to 4pm, Sunday 1 to 4pm.

On the west side of the square stands the **Old Court House,** which was built in 1732. It also features exhibits on Delaware history. *Hours:* Tuesday to Saturday 10am to 3:30pm, Sunday 1:30 to 4:30pm.

The elegant **Amstel House** (1738) at the corner of 4th and Delaware was the home of Governor Van Dyke and is a splendid example of Georgian architecture. Here, George Washington attended the wedding of the Van Dykes' daughter to Chancellor Johns. It's furnished with period antiques. *Hours:* Tuesday to Saturday 11am to 4pm and Sunday 1 to 4pm. *Admission:* $2 adults, $1 children.

On the Strand, which was once the busy port of Newcastle, stand many fine historic homes including the **McWilliams House** (ca. 1720) and **George Read II's house,** at 42 (☎ 302/322-8411), a splendid 22-room, 14,000-square-foot mansion that was the largest house in Delaware when it was built in

1801. *Hours:* Tuesday to Saturday 10am to 4pm, Sunday noon to 4pm. Closed January and February except by appointment on weekdays. *Admission:* $4 adults, $3.50 seniors and students, $2 children ages 6 to 12.

There are many more historic buildings in Newcastle and the best way to enjoy them is to follow the **Newcastle Heritage Trail,** a map of which can be secured at the tourist information office. As you walk along the brick sidewalks, note the rise and fall of the pathway around the roots of the old trees that line the streets.

At a point not far from the Delaware River, a marker indicates the spot where William Penn landed on October 27, 1682. For additional information on New Castle, call ☎ 302/323-4453.

New Castle Lodging & Dining

The **David Finney Inn,** 216 Delaware St., New Castle, DE 19720 (☎ 302/322-6367), well known for its tavern/dining room and historic atmosphere, reopened in 1998 after it was severely damaged by fire a few years ago. The style and quality have been retained in the dining rooms and it's one of the best places to dine. The menu offers about 16 entrees that range from such traditional favorites as filet mignon with béarnaise sauce and Dover sole with a butter sauce noisette, to more contemporary fare like the shrimp marinated with garlic and toasted cumin and served with warm pineapple salsa, or the grilled pork tenderloin, which has been marinated with Dijon and sour mash bourbon. Prices range from $16 to $24. *Hours:* Sunday to Thursday 11am to 10pm, Friday to Saturday 11am to 11pm.

Serenely facing the tree-lined cobblestone street, with its back to the Green, is the **Arsenal on the Green,** 30 Market St. (☎ 302/328-1290). The two dining rooms. one decorated in cranberry, the other in Wedgwood blue, are lovely spots for sampling traditional American cuisine. The regional specialties are the Delaware crab cakes. There's also veal Arsenal with lemon sauce, pork medallions Creole with a Creole mustard sauce, and chicken Chesapeake—chicken breast topped with crab Imperial and hollandaise. Prices range from $14 to $30 (the higher price for surf and turf). For an appetizer, try the shrimp rémoulade or stuffed mushrooms. Some folks will want to try the traditional drinks like grog (rum, water, and sugar, served hot or cold) or the 18th-century favorite, Sangaree (Madeira with lemon and orange juices and a dash of soda). *Hours:* Monday to Saturday 11am to 2pm and 5 to 9pm, Sunday 11am to 2pm and 3 to 8pm.

THE BRANDYWINE RIVER VALLEY

AREA ATTRACTIONS

Three miles northwest of Wilmington, more of the du Pont legacy can be viewed at the 230-acre **Hagley Museum** (☎ 302/658-2400), bordering the Brandywine River. This is where Éleuthère Irénée du Pont established his first powder mills in 1802, according to family legend after hearing a retired artillery colonel complain about the inferiority of American gunpowder compared to European. These mills were simple stamping and rolling operations, where workers blended sulfur, saltpeter, and charcoal into black powder. Water was diverted from the river and channeled through a series of wooden waterwheels. Later, turbines provided power to turn the massive granite stones that ground the ingredients.

Today you can see this process as the powderman opens the millrace gates and lets the water do its work. In the 1850s steam engines were used, and the museum has one of these operating. In the main museum building, exhibits trace the change from water to giant steam-powered industries. At one time, 33 mills stretched along the river (part of 21 of them can now be seen). To minimize the devastation that an unexpected explosion could cause, the mills were designed with an opening over the river to direct a blast away from the du Pont home and the workers' cottages on the bluff above.

From the powder yards a bus takes you to **Eleutherian Mills,** a handsome Georgian residence built for E. I. du Pont in 1803; it has been furnished to reflect the changing tastes of the five generations of du Ponts who lived here until 1958. The modest office building can be seen, along with the workshop of Lammot du Pont, whose discovery of how to make explosives with Peruvian nitrate gave the Union forces superior firepower in the Civil War. On Blacksmith Hill, part of the workers' community has been restored. In the Gibbons House, you can see how a worker's family lived. The mills became obsolete after World War I and were closed in 1921. Allow 3 or 4 hours for a leisurely visit to explore the buildings, the gardens at the du Pont residence, and the grounds, which extend along the banks of the Brandywine River. *Hours:* Mid-March to December, daily 9:30am to 4:30pm; January to mid-March, Saturday to Sunday 9:30am to 4:30pm, one tour daily at 1:30pm on weekdays. Closed major winter holidays. *Admission:* $9.75 adults, $7.50 seniors and students, $3.50 children ages 6 to 14.

Kids always enjoy the **Delaware Museum of Natural History,** Route 52, Greenville (☎ 302/658-9111), which has, among other displays, a renowned shell collection of over a million items and possesses the egg of an elephant bird, which weighs 27 pounds! Exhibit highlights include a visit to an African water hole, a walk over the Great Barrier Reef, and an introduction to Delaware fauna. The dinosaurs are also a permanent exhibit, and there's a fun, interactive Discovery Room. *Hours:* Monday to Saturday 9:30am to 4:30pm, Sunday noon to 5pm. Closed New Year's Day, July 4, Thanksgiving, and Christmas. *Admission:* $5 adults, $4 seniors and children ages 3 to 17.

Winterthur

Antiques lovers, craftspeople, historians, and interior designers may want to spend a whole day at Winterthur (☎ 302/888-4600), 6 miles north of Wilmington, for this collection of furniture and decorative arts is extraordinary. It was amassed by Henry Francis du Pont, who began collecting in the 1920s and, before his death in 1969, had acquired a matchless collection of antiques made or used in America between 1640 and 1860. The collection includes furniture, textiles, paintings, prints, pewter, silver, ceramics, and glass. Highlights are a set of six silver tankards made by Paul Revere, John Trumbull's portrait of George Washington at Verplanck's Point, and Chinese export porcelain, including a 66-piece dinner set made for Washington. Du Pont also purchased interior architecture to use in several rooms, including the Port Royal Parlor from Frankford, Pennsylvania; a drawing room from Richmond County, Virginia; a commons room from a Delaware inn; the Montmorency staircase from a house in North Carolina; and a 17th-century room from Ipswich, Massachusetts.

The collection is displayed in two buildings, one containing 175 period rooms and another 3 exhibition galleries. The 175 period rooms are seen only on guided tours. As you go from room to room, you'll see beautifully crafted highboys and lowboys made by Townsend and Goddard, Shaker furniture, a stair hall filled with miniatures, exquisite pie-crust tables, lusterware, glass, and textiles. On a first visit you'll see only a fraction of the rooms.

The galleries offer a more traditional museum experience. On the first floor, "Perspectives on the Decorative Arts in Early America" in the Walter J. Laird Gallery introduces you to 200 years of American decorative arts. On the second floor, the Henry S. McNeil Gallery has three display areas focusing on furniture and traditions of craftsmanship. These galleries feature some inter-active exhibits.

The whole collection is at the home du Pont occupied until 1951. During his lifetime, Winterthur was a self-contained, nearly self-sustaining commu-nity with turkey and sheep farms, vegetable gardens, greenhouses, a golf course, a sawmill, a rail station, a post office, and a prize-winning herd of Holstein Friesian cattle. The estate covers nearly 1,000 acres today. Du Pont's first love was horticulture, and he designed the garden with an eye to color, shapes, and vista, planning it so that it would have color almost year-round. Spring presents the most glorious color show—lilacs, daffodils, azaleas, and dogwoods; summer is equally beautiful, while autumn offers the changing hues of the foliage.

There are two dining facilities. The Crossroads Cafe serves breakfast and lunch; the Garden Restaurant offers lunch, afternoon tea, and a Sunday brunch. You'll also want to stop at the museum stores in the Pavilion and on Clenny Run across from the museum for a selection of licensed reproductions, gifts, books, and plants. Special events include the Winterthur Point-to-Point races, the first Sunday in May, a large crafts festival on Labor Day weekend, and the Delaware Antiques Show, held in mid-November.

Hours: Monday to Saturday 9am to 5pm, Sunday noon to 5pm. Closed New Year's Day, Thanksgiving, Christmas. *Admission* (including a self-guided garden walk and the galleries): $8 adults, $6 seniors and students, $4 children ages 5 to 11. *Special Tours* (including general admission): Introductory tour of selected period rooms, $13 adults, $11 seniors and students, $9 children (reservations are recommended); 1-hour decorative arts tour, add $17 adults, $15 seniors and students (not available for children); 2-hour decorative arts tour, add $21 adults, $19 seniors and students (not available for children). Garden Walk is $13 adults, $11 seniors and students, and $9 children ages 5 to 11. Mid-November to January, holiday celebrations of the 18th and 19th centuries are highlighted on the annual Yuletide tour. Reservations required for the decorative arts tours.

Longwood Gardens & Environs

Longwood Gardens is on Route 1, over the state border in Kennett Square, PA (☎ 610/388-1000 for information, 610/388-6771 for the restaurant). I envy the curator of Longwood, for he can enjoy the beauty of the gardens in all seasons and weathers.

The conservatory is breathtaking year-round, but the outdoor gardens are in their prime during spring and summer, when they burst forth with magnolias, flowering crab apples, cherries, dogwoods, rhododendrons, wisteria, and thousands of annuals and perennials. The show continues through summer, when the formal Rose Garden blossoms and 5 acres of fountain gardens in front of the conservatory play, cooling the air with magnificent jets of water, and the other specialty gardens of topiary, vegetables, and wildflowers can be seen to full advantage.

The 4-acre **conservatory** is radiantly filled with the colors, scents, and textures of seasonal displays. Spring begins here in January, when cyclamen and narcissus bloom; followed by tulips, crab apples, and acacias in February; then magnolias, wisterias, azaleas, freesias, stocks, daffodils, hyacinths, primroses, Easter lilies, and velvet-sheen, and deep-red pocketbook flowers in March (a display that'll gladden any winter-wearied heart). November is the time for a fantastic display of 20,000 chrysanthemums; at Christmas the garden conifers sparkle with 400,000 lights and the conservatory is filled with red, pink, and white poinsettias and red-berried hollies.

Besides the special displays in the main conservatory, you can view orchids (6,000 plants are cultivated here, 1,200 or so hybrids or species, with only the best culled for display), centuries-old bonsai, all kinds of exotic tropical plants and cacti, and, at the center of it all, the **lily pond**—a true highlight—where lily pads as large as 7 feet in diameter float along with lilies that vary from tiny, perfect flowers to large orbs of deep purple, magenta, magnolia-pink, and yellow, many of which open even on the dullest of days. There's also a **children's garden** with a fun maze.

Longwood has other delights, like the 2,100-seat **theater**, inspired by the Villa Gori near Siena, Italy, and set amid a copse of trees. It hosts music, drama, and dance performances in summer. In place of the traditional curtain a brilliant screen is created by a row of illuminated fountains. After a performance, additional fountains in the stage floor rise as high as 50 feet into the trees. Tinted lights shine on the water to create a liquid kaleidoscope.

Another show is given in summer: For 3 nights a week the 5 acres of **fountains** in front of the conservatory are illuminated in all colors of the rainbow as they shoot 130 feet into the air, bringing to mind a marvelous, inverted Niagara Falls. After the show, visitors are free to wander through the conservatory and admire the exotic night-blooming water lilies, which are artfully lighted.

Finally, there's the old **Peirce-du Pont house,** open for self-guided tours. The Longwood property was granted to the Peirces by William Penn in 1700, and it was two Peirce brothers who laid out an arboretum of ornamental trees. The impending destruction of this arboretum prompted Pierre du Pont, great-grandson of founder Éleuthère, to purchase Peirce's Park (as it was called in 1906) and develop it into a horticultural showplace. The house is filled with photos and memorabilia tracing Longwood's history from 1700 to the present, with special emphasis on du Pont's accomplishments. Longwood is frequently open evenings for fountain shows; concerts that range from classical to jazz, folk, and pop; and holiday displays. There's also a mammoth pipe organ, played regularly October to April. For a current schedule of events, send a self-addressed stamped envelope to Schedule, Longwood Gardens, P.O. Box 501, Kennett Square, PA 19348. Longwood also has a very fine restaurant and self-service cafe.

Hours: April to October, conservatory, daily 10am to 6pm; outdoor gardens, daily 9am to 6pm. November to March, conservatory, daily 10am to 5pm; outdoor gardens, daily 9am to 5pm. The main fountain garden operates daily 9:30am to 5:45pm mid-April to mid-October with special 5-minute displays most days at noon, 2, and 4pm; 30-minute illuminated shows on Tuesday, Thursday, and Saturday evenings from Memorial Day to Labor Day. The Festival of Fountains runs from late May to Labor Day, and the Fireworks and Fountain spectacle on certain dates in July, August, and September (ticket reservations required, $18 for adults). *Admission:* $12 adults ($8 on Tuesday), $6 youths ages 16 to 20, $2 children ages 6 to 15.

The Mushroom Capital

While you're in the area you really should savor, or at least take home, some of the local delicacy—mushrooms. Kennett Square, known as the mushroom capital of the world, is only a half mile south on Route 1 from Longwood Gardens. Stop at **Phillips Mushroom Place**, 909 E. Baltimore Pike (☎ 610/388-6082), and pick up a basket (or baskets) of mushrooms—portobello, crimini, oyster, and shiitake. According to the wisdom of the place, you can partially cook and then freeze the mushrooms. (You may want to buy them *before* you go into the museum and discover the details of the growing process.) The store is also filled with all kinds of mushroomabilia. *Hours:* Daily 10am to 6pm.

CHADDS FORD

A few miles east along Route 1 you'll come to Chadds Ford, heart of the Brandywine Valley and home of the famous **Brandywine River Museum** (☎ 610/388-2700), an old gristmill that has been artfully converted to display American art, including the works of the region's most famous art family, the Wyeths. Around the mill the architect has wrapped several brick terraces and added dramatic towers of glass that give views over the creek and surrounding pastoral scenery. The plaster walls and hand-hewn beams of the galleries seem appropriate to the art, which is firmly rooted in a sense of place. On the second floor the works of several generations of Wyeths are displayed—those by N. C. (illustrator of *Kidnapped* and *Treasure Island*), his daughters Carolyn and Henriette, and his grandson James. On the first floor is a gallery devoted to the Brandywine River and its artists, including Howard Pyle, father of them all, Horace Pippin, W. T. Smedley, Frank Schoonover, and Maxfield Parrish. The third floor features a gallery devoted to works by the most famous of the Wyeths, Andrew, whose portraits of Christina generated much controversy. Another gallery is devoted to changing exhibitions. Special events are held throughout the year in the Belgian block to the paved courtyard.

Half a mile away from the museum, N. C. Wyeth's studio, built in 1911, has been restored as it was in 1945 when the artist died. Inside the space, lit by huge, north-facing windows, you can see easels, a paint smock, and a variety of costume props.

Hours: Museum, daily 9:30am to 4:30pm. Closed December 25. *Admission:* $5 adults, $2.50 seniors and children ages 6 and up. Studio, April through October, Wednesday to Sunday. *Admission:* $2.50; tickets must be purchased at the museum for specific tour times. The tour lasts about 40 minutes.

Just east of Chadds Ford is **Brandywine Battlefield Park,** Route 1 (☎ 610/459-3342). Great rounded hills with sturdy old trees overlook a brook that runs down toward a fieldstone Georgian-style church, whose weathered gravestones stand silently brooding. Although the Battle of Brandywine was fought around the church, it remained neutral, and no soldier from either side is buried here. Dioramas in the visitor center tell the story of the battle on September 11, 1777, while Washington's headquarters and the Marquis de Lafayette's quarters show life during the American Revolution. It makes a lovely setting for a picnic. *Hours:* Tuesday to Saturday 9am to 5pm, Sunday noon to 5pm. *Admission to the houses:* $3.50 adults, $1.50 children ages 6 to 12.

On Route 100 just north of Route 1, the **Christian Sanderson Museum** (☎ 610/388-6545) grants an intimate look at the history of a community. Chris Sanderson and his mother lived in the rear section of this house from 1937, and when the front section became available in 1959, friends and neighbors secured it for him and helped him set up a museum. Today all eight rooms in the house are used to display the eclectic collections that Chris and his mother amassed to preserve the artifacts of their day. A close friend of the Wyeth family, Chris kept everything that came into his hands—paintings, sketches, and personal memorabilia from every family member, including a very early Andrew Wyeth painting done for Chris's mother. Other collections include autographs, toys, dyed eggs, and personal, quirky oddments like melted ice from the South Pole, sand from the digging of the Panama Canal, and a piece from the bomber that crashed into the Empire State Building in World War II. It's a unique place, and many people leave commenting that they wish they had known him. *Hours:* Saturday to Sunday 1 to 4:30pm. *Admission:* By donation.

BRANDYWINE AREA LODGING & DINING

The **Fairville Inn,** Route 52 (Kennett Pike; P.O. Box 219), Mendenhall, PA 19357 (☎ 610/388-5900; fax 610/388-5902), has been completely restored by Ole Retlev, an experienced, Scandinavian-born Vermont innkeeper, and his wife, Patricia. They offer 13 rooms and 2 suites, pretty evenly distributed in three different buildings—Main House, Carriage House, and Spring House. Each room has air-conditioning, a private bath, hair dryer, TV, and phone; seven have fireplaces, and most have balconies. Though they are obviously new and are furnished with antique reproductions, the accommodations are attractive. All the cut-out lampshades were made by Patricia; the side tables are classic drop leaf. Some rooms have canopied beds; the wash basins are separate from the bath. Carriage House rooms are set well back from the road and have small decks overlooking a bucolic scene. A light continental breakfast is served in the main dining room between 7 and 10am or can be brought to your room. There's also the sitting room with a couple of sofas placed in front of a white-brick fireplace with a large copper coffee table in between. *Rates* (including breakfast and afternoon tea): $150 to $190 double.

Meadow Spring Farm, 201 E. Street Rd. (Route 926), Kennett Square, PA 19348 (☎ 610/444-3903), has been a family farm for over 50 years.

Anne Hicks and her daughter Debbie run the B&B, providing six accommodations. Each is nicely decorated and has a TV and air-conditioning. One room has a canopied bed; the quilt is stacked high with cushions, the plank floors are softened with rag rugs, and the furnishings include an Empire dresser and chest. The Fireplace Room boasts a fireplace, of course, and a high-back Victorian bed combined with a chaise longue. Character is bestowed throughout by the collections Anne displays, like her 100-plus dolls, some of which are over 75 years old. Orchids, too, can be found throughout the house. The kitchen is made cozy by beams hung with baskets and the cow figures that seem to be everywhere.

Breakfast is served in a fairly formal dining room with an Empire-style sideboard and Chippendale chairs set around an oval table. Anne's signature dish is a mushroom omelet, but you might also enjoy apple pancakes or French toast. In summer, breakfast is served on the porch. For relaxing, the sitting room with a fireplace is ideal, or even better are the pool in summer and the hot tub in winter. There's also a games room with a pool table and a Ping-Pong table, a pond for fishing, and plenty of fields for leisurely strolls. Kids love the cows, rooster, chickens, and rabbits. *Rates* (including full breakfast): $85 to $95 double.

Scarlett House, 503 W. State St., Kennett Square, PA 19348 (☎ 610/444-9592), occupies a solid, almost Richardsonesque stone house with a wraparound porch that was built in 1910 for State Senator Robert Scarlett. The interior features beautifully crafted chestnut elements—solid pocket doors in the parlor and a fireplace flanked by solid bookcases. There are four air-conditioned guest rooms, two with a bath. The Senator's Suite features an antique Jenny Lind walnut bed. The Victorian Rose Room, so named because of the rose-motif wallpaper, contains a high-back walnut Victorian bed. The Bayard Taylor Room has a mahogany canopied bed and Queen Anne–style furnishings. The Chanterell Room is ornamented with stenciling and offers a small sitting area. There are two Victorian parlors with fireplaces. One offers a cable TV. There's a small sitting area on the landing. The three-course breakfast is elegantly served and will probably include such delicious dishes as crabmeat omelet or baked French toast flavored with Grand Marnier and accompanied by seasonal fruit. *Rates* (including breakfast): $95 to $125 double, $145 suite.

Just down Route 52 not far from Winterthur, the **Mendenhall Hotel and Conference Center,** P.O. Box 208, Mendenhall, PA 19357 (☎ 610/388-1181), offers 70 hotel rooms furnished with North Carolina country pine furnishings. The front lobby is traditionally furnished with antique reproductions, and the place has a cozy ambience. The elegantly appointed dining room is candlelit at night. It serves classic country French and American cuisine—steaks and prime rib plus such dishes as chicken in a Dijon mustard, wild mushroom, and green peppercorn sauce; or duck glazed with Mandarin orange brandy sauce. Prices range from $16 to $30. Facilities include a fitness center. *Rates:* $125 double. Special packages available. *Dining hours:* Monday to Saturday 11:30am to 2pm and 5 to 9pm, Sunday 10am to 2pm and 4 to 7:30pm.

Sweetwater Farm, Sweetwater Road, Glen Mills, PA 19342 (☎ 610/459-4711), has to be one of the most idyllic inns I've ever visited. The large stone farmhouse on 50 acres was built in 1734 and expanded in 1815. Referred to as the Manor House, it contains six exquisite guest rooms, all with full bath or shower. The Lafayette Room, complete with a working fireplace, features a four-poster bed and a variety of antique furnishings—a comb-back Windsor chair, a cherry side table, and a blanket chest on which magazines are displayed. The Garden Room, my favorite, is in the oldest part of the house, where the ceilings are lower. It's furnished with a four-poster and colonial-style pieces. Additional accommodations are located in five attractive cottages (three with fireplace, and three with kitchen and washer and drier).

On the ground floor of the Manor House are two parlors, a library, and (best of all) an eat-in kitchen, all with fireplaces. An elegant country breakfast is served either in the formal, Queen Anne dining room or in the country kitchen at a harvest table. The beams are hung with baskets, and in winter a fire blazes in the brick hearth. From the back porch, furnished with wicker chairs, you can look out across the lawn to a well-landscaped pool and hay fields and meadows beyond. A truly special place.

Rates (including breakfast): $190 to $235 double, $300 for the two-bedroom cottage.

An elegant drive sweeps up to the forecourt of **Faunbrook,** 699 W. Rosedale Ave., West Chester, PA 19382 (☎ 610/436-5788). This marvelous, bracketed, Italianate Victorian features lovely wrought-iron work and carved woodwork. The seven rooms (one with bath) are nicely decorated with brass beds and other country pieces, plus a lot of paintings. One has a working fireplace. On cold days breakfast is served fireside in an inviting dining room. Guests have the run of the house, from the parlor (with a grand piano) to the library and the sunroom. Guests love to sit on the wraparound porches overlooking the beautifully landscaped grounds with their statuary. *Rates* (including breakfast): $92 to $130 double.

Pace One, Thornton Road (off Route 1), Thornton, PA 19373 (☎ 610/459-3702), is a cozy restaurant in a 250-year-old converted barn with hand-hewn beams, Shaker-style tin lanterns, and Brandywine scenes adorning the walls. Six guest rooms are offered, all with a bath, oak floors, rag rugs, chests, stoneware lamps, country wreaths, tattersall coverlets, and wrought-iron floor lamps. All have telephones.

A meal might begin with a selection from the chilled seafood bar or the smoked portobello mushroom that has been layered with roasted red peppers, mozzarella, and arugula and served on a red burgundy tomato sauce. Follow with a choice from such specialties as jerk-rubbed chargrilled mango-hazelnut chicken, veal tenderloin stuffed with crabmeat filling and served with hollandaise, and oatmeal-crusted salmon stuffed with apples and finished with a horseradish cream sauce. To finish there's chocolate fondue, kiwi crêpes with raspberry sauce, and a variety of pies and cakes (including a delicious bourbon pecan). Prices run $17 to $25. Brunch offers soup and dishes like broccoli, tomato, and ham rarebit; fresh fish marinated in soy, citrus, and parsley; broiled veal tenderloin stuffed with crabmeat; and egg dishes—for $7 to $15. Bring your own wine.

Rates: $85 to $105 double. *Dining hours:* Monday to Friday 11:30am to 2pm and 5:30 to 10pm, Saturday 5:30 to 10pm, Sunday 10:30am to 2:30pm and 5 to 9pm.

Hamanassett, Box 129, Lima, PA 19037 (☎ 610/459-3000), a wonderful old stone mansion capped with a Dutch gable roof, stands on top of a hill overlooking its 47-acre estate. It was built by Dr. Charles Meigs in the 18th century and remained in the Meigs family for many generations. Today it makes a handsome and tranquil retreat for visitors who want to enjoy country walks, pretty gardens, and some quiet time. The rooms are furnished with antiques, but also offer such modern amenities as private baths and TV/VCRs. You'll likely find a four-poster with a crochet canopy, oriental-style rugs on the floor, a couple of wing chairs, and such decorative accents as Federal mirrors and historic prints. On cold days guests gather around the Federal fireplace in the living-room library, with its well-stocked shelves. A full breakfast is served in a formal dining room or outside on the terrace overlooking the gardens, which are beautiful at any time of year. In winter the solarium is a welcome and often sunny retreat for guests. *Rates:* $100 to $135.

The **Inn at Montchanin Village,** Route 100 and Kirk Road, Montchanin, DE 19710 (☎ 302/888-2133), is a very special place, the result of a caring restoration project undertaken by Dan and Nancy G. Kitchell Lickle, a member of the du Pont family, to preserve a workers' village that was built between 1870 and 1910. Nine of the inn's buildings were once the homes of workers who labored at the du Pont powder mills. Clustered on a hillside, which has been attractively landscaped, they now contain 37 guest rooms featuring such luxuries as marble baths, two-line telephones, cable TVs, refrigerators, microwaves, coffeemakers, and wet bars. Some have sitting areas with gas fireplaces. They are furnished with a mixture of antiques and reproductions. Among the furnishings there might be wicker pieces along with funky painted chests and tables. Expect to find comfortable beds with the finest Frette linens and beautiful bedspreads as well. In the large bathrooms, most with separate tub and shower, you'll find such extras as towel warmers, lighted magnifying mirrors, and scales. A continental breakfast is included in the rates, or you can opt for such dishes as eggs Benedict, omelets, and bagels and smoked salmon for an additional charge.

The old village blacksmith's shop has been converted into Krazy Kat's, a fine dining room. It's a fun restaurant with its cat portraits in military garb on the walls and faux animal skin furnishings. The food is quite serious, though. At dinner you can select from about ten or so entrees. Each uses top-notch ingredients and aims to intensify their flavor. You might find a delicious Caribbean jerk-grilled pork tenderloin or pan-seared cod served with oven-roasted potatoes and braised leek beurre blanc. There will always be a vegetarian dish like the grilled vegetable lasagne, served with yellow pepper coulis. Prices range from $20 to $27. For dessert try the banana-and-white-chocolate bread pudding with a bourbon sauce and espresso chocolate chunk ice cream with chocolate sauce, or white-chocolate cheesecake with mango coulis. The inn is very conveniently located for Winterthur.

Rates: $160 to $180, suites from $190.

BRANDYWINE AREA DINING

The most comfortable place I know of in the area is the **Chadds Ford Inn,** at routes 1 and 100 (☎ 610/388-7361), where you may come across one of the members of the Wyeth family in the back tavern. You'll certainly encounter their work in each of the cozy low-ceilinged dining rooms, either placed between the deep-set windows or above the wainscoting of this 1703 building, which has served as a tavern since 1736. Butterfly Windsor chairs and pink-and-brown napery complete the comfortable ambience. The food is fine; there are usually several specials, plus a menu that offers a variety of small plates like shrimp and crab beignets or roasted-garlic hummus, and such entrees as duckling with a green apple glaze or grilled tuna with mango. Prices range from $11 to $26. A light tavern menu is offered from 2pm to closing, and brunch is served on Sunday. By the way, the colonial tavernkeeper here entertained the Americans before the Battle of Brandywine and was "plundered" when the British forces swarmed into the village. *Hours:* Monday to Thursday 11:30am to 2pm and 5:30 to 10pm, Friday to Saturday 11:30am to 2pm and 5 to 10pm, Sunday 11am to 2pm (brunch) and 4 to 9pm.

Buckley's Tavern, 5812 Kennett Pike (Route 52), Centreville (☎ 302/656-9776), is grander than it sounds. Oriental carpets cover the wide-plank floors, and molded panels and Queen Anne chairs give the dining room an elegant atmosphere. The cuisine is a mix of American traditional (Maryland crab cakes; a burger made with provolone, mushrooms, and bacon), and Italian continental dishes (penne with basil and feta in a garlic, tomato, and white wine sauce and grilled filet of beef with pancetta and balsamic demi-glace). Sandwiches and pizzas are also offered at dinner. Prices range from $6 to $20. Appetizers are equally eclectic—hummus, goat cheese bruschetta, and shrimp LeJon (a tangy dish of shrimp stuffed with horseradish, wrapped in bacon, and served with a mustard-horseradish sauce). Brunch offers a varied menu: eggs Benedict to cheeseburgers to seafood salad, priced from $7 to $12. *Hours:* Monday to Wednesday 11:30am to 2:30pm and 5:30 to 9pm, Thursday to Friday 11:30am to 2:30pm and 5:30 to 10pm, Saturday 11:30am to 3pm and 5 to 10pm, Sunday 11am to 9pm.

Appearances are deceptive at the **Lenape Inn,** routes 52 and 100, south of West Chester and convenient to Longwood Gardens (☎ 610/793-2005). Yes, the place is large. Yes, the people crowd in. Yes, you'd expect the food to be average—but it's not, because owner Michael Person keeps a close watch on the quality of the meats he serves, what the cattle are fed, and so on. The filet mignon my dinner partner sampled literally melted in the mouth. The rack of lamb was of equally high quality. On Sunday a raw bar displays oysters, clams, and shrimp. Among the other entrees you might find duckling with cherries, fillet of sole topped with lump crabmeat and served with a caper sauce, or veal medallions with prosciutto and shiitake mushrooms. Prices run $16 to $32 (the higher price for surf and turf). For dessert I highly recommend the linzertorte with Chambord sauce, served hot. There are plenty of other divine choices, too. The dining rooms have cathedral ceilings and overlook the grassy banks of the Brandywine. A resident gaggle of ducks parades by regularly, under what has to be one of the most perfectly shaped fir trees you could ever hope to see. *Hours:* Monday to Saturday 11:30am to 3pm and 4:30 to 11pm, Sunday 2 to 11pm.

For fancy dining there's the **Dilworthtown Inn,** Old Wilmington Pike, Dilworthtown (☎ 610/399-1390). You'll find it down a little country road off Route 202, near West Chester. The stone-and-brick inn, which functioned as a tavern in 1758, has been carefully restored to its original decor, even down to the wall stenciling. The rooms and the tavern with a large fireplace have been simply furnished with Early American art and furniture, appropriate for the traditional continental cuisine. Start with shrimp bisque flavored with

Armagnac, or the warm duck terrine with a cognac and green peppercorn sauce. Follow with such classics as pan-seared duck breast in a pear reduction, champagne mustard–encrusted rack of lamb flavored with rosemary and served in its natural juices, or salmon fillet napped with a lobster velouté. Traditional favorites like filet mignon béarnaise, Châteaubriand, and lobster tail are also available. Prices range from $18 to $29. *Hours:* Monday to Thursday 5:30 to 8:30pm, Friday 5:30 to 9:30pm, Saturday 5 to 9:30pm, Sunday 3 to 8:30pm.

The **Marshalton Inn**, 1300 W. Strasburg Rd. (Route 162), West Chester (☎ 610/692-4367), is an Early Federal landmark from 1793 and has been serving travelers since 1814, when it became a major overnight stop on the road from Philadelphia to Pittsburgh. Today it offers contemporary American cuisine, often with an Asian accent. Among the eight or so entrees you might find grilled brook trout with cider sauce, Thai crab cakes flavored with basil and ginger and served with green coconut curry sauce, filet mignon with a port wine caper sauce, and a lamb stew made with mushrooms, parsnips, shallots, and porter. Prices range from $15 to $19. Among the desserts may be chocolate-chip cheesecake, Black Forest cake, or raspberry torte, depending on the chef's whim and the season. *Hours:* Wednesday to Thursday and Sunday 5 to 10pm, Friday and Saturday 5 to 11pm

LODGING & DINING EN ROUTE TO VALLEY FORGE

The **Duling Kurtz House and Country Inn**, 146 S. Whitford Rd., Exton, PA 19341 (☎ 610/524-1830), is a romantic place to dine. The lodgings are lovely, but I'll begin with the restaurant and its seven dining rooms. Here's a rundown: an enclosed porch overlooking the formal gardens; a beamed tavern with a huge fireplace, rush-seated gatebacks, and wicker and rush objects hanging from the beams; fey Aunt Lena's Parlor, named after a legendary local woman with enough dramatic flair to play the musical saw in St. Peter's, and decorated with her hats and dashing dresses; the formal Chippendale-furnished Hunt Room; and several upstairs rooms, including a veranda that offers a beautiful view of sunsets over pastures. For $25 a night you can even rent the Duling Kurtz Room, affording you the privacy of a table with a closed curtain set in a bay window overlooking the gardens. The cuisine is classic French/continental. Among the dozen or so entrees you might find brook trout Sacramento sautéed with herbs and finished with tomatoes, avocadoes, and a sweet onion relish; hickory-smoked buffalo fillet with pearl onions and pine nuts; or veal chanterelles made with porcini and chanterelles and finished with cream. Prices range from $17 to $27.

Adjacent to the restaurant, the inn contains 15 rooms, all prettily turned out and furnished with antique reproductions. The Lincoln Suite, for example, has twin canopied beds with eyelet-lace linens, attractive fabric shutters, an oriental carpet, a small sitting room, and a courtyard for breakfast or cocktails. The Thomas Jefferson features a fireplace, while the George Washington suite has a four-poster and an old-fashioned claw-foot tub in the bathroom.

Rates (including continental breakfast): $75 to $130 double. *Dining hours:* Monday to Friday 11:30am to 2:30pm and 5 to 10pm, Saturday 5 to 11pm, Sunday 3 to 9pm.

Tucked away on Gordon Drive, just off Route 100 in Lionville, the **Vickers Tavern** (☎ 610/363-6336) offers fine food in five modestly sized dining rooms.

Each room is warmly country, lit by carriage lamps and Shaker-style tin chandeliers. In one, a high-beamed ceiling combined with brick and barn-board, comb-back Windsor chairs, a few landscapes, and farm implements evoke the atmosphere. Elsewhere, bold chintz and matching valances set the mood. Appetizers may include snails with a garlic and parsley emulsion or shrimp with wild mushrooms sautéed in garlic butter and white wine. The specialties are continental/American: beef Wellington, roast duck with fruit chutney, medallions of veal with morel-cream sauce, or Dover sole with lemon butter sauce. Finish with one of the fine flambéed desserts—crêpes Suzette, bananas Foster, or cherries jubilee. Entrees are $23 to $29. *Hours:* Monday to Friday 11:30am to 2:30pm and 5:30 to 10:30pm, Saturday 5:30 to 10:30pm.

Set on 4 acres, the **General Warren Inne,** Old Lancaster Highway, Malvern (☎ 610/296-3637; fax 610/296-8084; www.generalwarren.com), is an 18th-century inn offering accommodations plus dining in three candlelit, colonial-style dining rooms. The cuisine offered is classic continental: filet mignon with Roquefort butter, beef Wellington with mushroom duxelles and shallot demi-glace, and salmon fillet with a lemon beurre blanc, supplemented by more modern dishes like venison with caramelized onion and tomato with a veal glaze, and duck with mango pesto sauce. To start, try the shrimp dumplings with a caramelized ginger demi-glace or the Louisiana snapper soup served with sherry. Prices range from $20 to $28. There's a deck for summer dining and also a patio bar where you can enjoy cocktails and appetizers.

The inn has a rich history: It was built in 1745 and served as a major carriage stop. During the American Revolution it was owned by John Penn, loyalist and grandson of William Penn, and it was here that the Loyalists met and drew the maps that Howe and Cornwallis used to negotiate the valley and capture Philadelphia. The second and third floors feature eight two-room suites furnished with antique reproductions. Some have canopied or four-poster cherry beds; others feature cannonball beds. Two have fireplaces. The Franklin Suite contains two bathrooms, one with a whirlpool. All rooms have air-conditioning, cable TVs, phones, and hair dryers.

Rates (including continental breakfast): $110 to $160 double. *Dining hours:* Monday to Friday 11:30am to 2:30pm and 5 to 10pm, Saturday 5 to 10pm.

Wilmington & the Brandywine Valley
Special & Recreational Activities

Canoeing: Northbrook Canoe Company, 1810 Beagle Rd., West Chester (☎ 215/793-2279), offers 1-hour trips to full-day trips on the Brandywine River. Prices range from $24 to $55. They operate from late April to the end of October.

State Parks: The 271-acre **Bellevue State Park,** overlooking the Delaware River in North Wilmington, was last owned by William B. du Pont Jr. and his wife, Margaret Osborne. She was crazy about tennis (a former Wimbledon contender) and he was nuts about horses, and, as a consequence, the park is now blessed with eight outdoor clay courts and an equestrian center. Court time costs $12 an hour. Call the tennis center at ☎ 302/798-6686 for further details. At the equestrian center, unfortunately, your chances of landing a lesson on weekends are slim, and since most of the horses are privately owned and boarded here, no trail rides are given. A 1⅛-mile fitness track circles a fishing pond stocked with bass and catfish; there are also bike paths and hiking trails. This park is good for picnicking, too. Contact Bellevue State Park, 800 Carr Rd., Wilmington, DE 19809 (☎ 302/577-3390).

Brandywine Creek State Park offers 850 acres of rolling meadows and woodlands with Brandywine Creek flowing through the center. The Nature Center (☎ 302/655-5740) offers year-round interpretive programs and special events. You can also picnic and fish. Write to P.O. Box 3782, Greenville, DE 19807 (☎ 302/577-3534).

VALLEY FORGE

The historic park at Valley Forge is now surrounded by highways, shopping centers, and other suburban elements, a far cry from the time when you could look down across the hills and along the river to Philadelphia, as did the Continental troops while they waited through the winter of 1777–78. They were watching for the British, who were cavorting in Philadelphia, 18 miles downriver. Though the suburban development is dense, there are still some places to visit. But first, the park.

VALLEY FORGE HISTORIC PARK

"I lay there two nights and one day and had not a morsel of anything to eat all the time save half of a small pumpkin cooked by . . . making a fire on it." So wrote Private Joseph Martin in the winter of 1777. He was just one of the 11,000 soldiers who retreated here on December 19 after their defeat at Brandywine and a draw at Germantown—a raggle-taggle army General Anthony Wayne described as "sick and crawling with vermin" in March 1778. The winter was certainly cruel. Deep snow caused food shortages and starvation. Over 3,000 people died and, according to British reports, another 1,150 deserted. Hundreds of horses starved to death. Yet by June that same pathetic army was well drilled and ready to fight, and they marched out of Valley Forge on June 19, 1778, having won a victory of will and survival.

The visitor center of this 2,800-acre park houses various displays, including Washington's original battlefield tent. What you learn here will help you imagine the scene as you drive past the log cabin replicas, where 12 men were housed in 10-by-12-foot spaces during that long, frigid winter. From mid-April to October you can take a regular bus tour through the park or a self-guided tour past the monument to the soldiers who died in the American Revolution, down to the three-bedroom house that probably sheltered 25 to 30 people. One of these was Martha Washington, who provided food and shelter, aided by two or three servants. As you look at the rooms, imagine the inhabitants dining, playing cards, smoking, planning strategies, and whiling away the time before setting up their bunks in the rooms upstairs. Stop by the

Washington Memorial Chapel, in the parish of David and Julie Nixon Eisenhower, and hear the 58-bell carillon that rings regular recitals.

Besides the park's historic associations, it's a wonderful place to visit any time of year, but especially from late April to mid-May, when 50,000 dogwoods bloom. In summer it's filled with people picnicking, flying kites, biking, throwing Frisbees, and sunbathing on the rolling hills or down along the creek. Fall is magnificent, while winter can bring the most enthralling sight when snow carpets the ground and the ghosts of those soldiers tread softly, always looking downriver toward Philadelphia. The big event here is Washington's Birthday. The park is located at the junction of North Gulph Road and Route 23 (☎ 610/783-1000). Admission charged to enter Washington's headquarters is $2 for anyone over age 16. The park's hours are daily from 9am to 5pm.

NEARBY ATTRACTIONS

Closest to Valley Forge is **John James Audubon's Mill Grove**, Pawlings Road, in neighboring Audubon (☎ 610/666-5593). This was the first home Audubon occupied after he left France in 1803 at age 18. It may seem rather large and lavish for a boy, and, in fact, it belonged to his father; Audubon came to board with his father's tenants. In several rooms you can admire specimens of any number of shells, butterflies, and birds. There's a whole case of stuffed owls, all worthy characters, from the charming long-eared owl to the tiny saw whet and the awesome snowy owl. Besides the prints and watercolors from *The Birds of America,* examine the birds' nests and note the exquisite delicacy and dexterity that the swift exhibits in selecting, gathering, and gluing together with saliva the twigs for its nest. Early pictures and portraits of Audubon capture the young man who spent his days here happily "roaming the frontier seeking new birds and animals." Audubon hit upon a method of wiring animals or birds into lifelike positions and then painting them. You'll also discover (if you didn't already know) that Audubon had been born illegitimately in Haiti, but had been taken home to France and raised in the Loire Valley. From the house you can explore the nature trails on the 175 acres. It's especially beautiful at apple blossom time and at fall foliage time. *Hours:* Tuesday to Saturday 10am to 4pm, Sunday 1 to 4pm. Closed major holidays. *Admission:* By donation.

From the park, it's only a short ride up Route 363 to the **Peter Wentz Farmstead**, Worcester (☎ 610/584-5104), fascinating not only because Washington visited here before and after the Battle of Germantown but also for the ways restorers accomplished their detective work in uncovering the secrets of the house's construction and history. Built in 1758 in a Georgian style, the house has certain Germanic details—the blessing carved into the external wall in a German dialect, the beehive baking oven, and the dining room's fireplate stove. The house has been furnished with period pieces and restored to the way it looked in 1777. The staircase was reconstructed and the nails were placed in the same holes, which were still visible. The Washington Room, where the general planned the Battle of Germantown, still retains some of the original red milk paint, while in many places the original sponge painting can be seen. What will probably surprise visitors most are the vibrant colors—blue, yellow, and salmon—which appear as they would have in the 18th century. The summer kitchen is used for cooking demonstrations, and the surrounding gardens of seasonal herbs and vegetables, including flax, give some insight into the colonists' lives. Occasionally, on summer Saturday afternoons, the public is invited to participate in the craft program—weaving, wood carving, fireplace cooking, fraktur painting, and the like. Take Route 363 north to Route 73, the Skippack Pike, and turn right. *Hours:* Tuesday to Saturday 10am to 4pm, Sunday 1 to 4pm. *Admission:* By donation.

Shoppers and others fascinated by the advent of electronic retailing will want to take the studio tour at West Chester–based QVC. On the 1¼-hour tour visitors will see how products are sourced, tested, and then sold to millions of QVC customers. From the observation deck visitors can watch the shows being broadcast. Call ☎ 800/600-9900 for information.

VALLEY FORGE LODGING

The **Sheraton–Valley Forge,** North Gulph Road and First Avenue, King of Prussia, PA 19406 (☎ 800/325-3535 or 610/337-2000), is the area's most lively hostelry. Its Club 92.5 Country Music Saloon rocks from Tuesday to Saturday and on weekends is packed to its 750-person capacity. Lilly Langtry's (☎ 610/337-2000, ext. 601) features a Las Vegas–style revue with singing and dancing, and you can enjoy a meal before the show. The atmosphere is wonderfully gaudy—plenty of red velvet, brass, painted skylights, and waitresses scantily clad in black corsets and lace. The hotel's restaurants include Chumley's steak house, the Blue Grotto Italian bistro and bar, and the Sunflower coffee shop for casual dining. Sunday brunch in Lilly Langtry's (10am to 2pm) provides an all-you-can-eat buffet, loaded with everything from meatballs to omelets and other egg dishes, waffles, and pancakes.

The hotel offers 488 rooms and suites, including some exciting themed suites, just made for an exotic weekend experience. Each expresses a fantasy—Cleopatra's Tent, Love Parisian Style, Caesar's Palace, and the Titanic, which features portholes and cabin doors and is modeled after one of the staterooms as seen in the film. The Cave is a re-creation of a prehistoric cave complete with stalactites and cave art. Each suite has a loft with a small TV and phone, plus a downstairs area with a TV, a Murphy or hydraulic bed that descends from the ceiling, a stereo system, a wet bar, and an exotic hot tub or Jacuzzi in the bath. They're really fun, and you just might be lucky enough to obtain one on a weekend. Other hotel facilities include an outdoor pool, fitness center, and racquetball court.

Rates: $179 double; $260 suites on weekends, $195 midweek. Special packages available.

A quieter and stylish atmosphere can be found at the **Park Ridge at Valley Forge,** 480 N. Gulph Rd., King of Prussia, PA 19406 (☎ 800/337-1801 or 610/337-1800). The 265 large rooms are handsomely furnished, each with a balcony/patio overlooking the pool or the golf course. All rooms have unstocked refrigerators, desks with computer-compatible phones, cable TVs, full-length mirrors with high-intensity lights, and skirt hangers. The fourth-floor club level offers extra amenities and services—stocked minibars, bathrobes, a concierge, a private lounge, nightly turndown, and a continental breakfast. The Coppermill Harvest restaurant serves American cuisine. Mad Anthony's Tavern features light snacks and pool, darts, and alley bowling. Sports facilities include a landscaped outdoor pool, two tennis courts, and a fitness room. A public golf course is right across the street. *Rates:* Weekends $99 to $139 double, weekdays $189 double.

About 4 miles down Route 202 South, the **Valley Forge Marriott Suites,** 888 Chesterbrook Blvd., Wayne, PA 19087 (☎ 610/647-6700), is located in a redbrick building possessing a double atrium. All 230 accommodations are suites, set around one of the atriums. Each is equipped with air-conditioning, two TVs, three telephones, a stocked minibar, a coffeemaker, and a hair dryer. All have small sitting rooms. The bedroom is separated from the living room by the bathroom and a small open kitchen that has a refrigerator and sink. The faux-marble bath contains all the usual amenities.

Facilities include a restaurant offering steak and seafood. A couple of lobby lounges, an indoor pool with an outdoor terrace, and a fitness center with a rowing machine and Nautilus equipment plus jogging track complete the facilities. Services include room service, laundry/valet, and twice-daily maid service.

Rates (including full buffet breakfast and daily 5 to 7pm cocktail reception): $189 suite. Weekend packages available.

VALLEY FORGE AREA LODGING

About 30 minutes from Valley Forge and 20 minutes from New Hope, the **Joseph Ambler Inn,** 1005 Horsham Rd. (Route 463), Montgomeryville, North Wales, PA 19454 (☎ 215/362-7500), is a charming colonial inn set on 13 acres of lush woodland and pasture. It consists of four main buildings, the oldest being a 1734 stone farmhouse that was added to in 1820 and 1929. The small parlor to the left of the entrance is original, and here you'll find books and games, while the large sitting room to the right with the stone hearth is a reproduction built in 1929.

The inn offers 37 rooms including 5 suites. Each has a private bath, air-conditioning, TV, and telephone (with modem access) and is furnished attractively with antique reproductions. The suites also have fireplaces and whirlpools. Nine are in the farmhouse. The Ambler Room has an Empire-style mahogany bed with a Marseilles coverlet, a marble-top dresser, a gas fireplace, and random-width board floors covered with oriental area rugs. The Penn Suite, in the old part of the house, is two-level. The lower-level living room is furnished in Early American style and has a massive stone fireplace. Up the spiral staircase, the bedroom/bath has a sloping ceiling, a double-poster with a Marseilles coverlet, and a camelback sofa. The most luxurious is the Allman Room, which has a private entrance and French doors that open into a room with a Franklin stove and a rock-fall Jacuzzi. The four cranberry-colored cottage rooms in the Corybeck House (1929) are smaller, but decorated with four-posters with fishnet canopies, stenciled walls, wing chairs, and candle stands. The 13 rooms in the stone bank barn (1820) have a different feel, with their original exterior stone walls. They are furnished with wall-to-wall carpeting, decorative stenciling, and Williamsburg reproductions. The third-floor rooms have cathedral ceilings, and some have windows at elevated heights, like the particularly appealing Blue Bell Room. In the Thomas Wilson House (1850) innkeepers have retained the hardwood floors in the original part of the house, covering them with oriental area rugs. The addition to the house holds two suites, each with whirlpool tub and private patio, plus four rooms. All have wall-to-wall carpeting and are furnished in Victorian style.

A full breakfast, selected from a menu of eggs, omelets, French toast, and pancakes, along with fresh fruit, is served to overnight guests. In the restaurant, which is located in the barn, the house specialty is rack of lamb prepared in three ways. Other favorite dishes are the salmon en croûte set in a sherried lobster velvet sauce, tournedos of beef grilled with slivers of foie gras and mushroom ragoût, and filet mignon broiled in a Samuel Adams triple-bock beer sauce. Prices range from $19 to $26. The ambience is very country.

Rates (including breakfast): $110 to $185 double, $160 to $210 suites. *Dining hours:* Monday to Friday 6 to 10pm, Saturday 5 to 10pm, Sunday 5 to 9pm.

VALLEY FORGE AREA DINING

The **Baron's Inn,** 499 N. Gulph Rd., King of Prussia (☎ 610/265-2550), may not look like much from the outside, but the dining rooms have a plush European air and cuisine to match. The proprietor is an Austrian, and while some of the dishes, particularly the desserts, reflect that background, the food is new American. Featured specialties might include grilled filet mignon in Merlot wine sauce accompanied by a three-mushroom ragoût; sesame-crusted salmon fillet in a citrus-ginger-cilantro vinaigrette; or honey-roasted portobello Napoleon, a delicious combination of grilled vegetables, wilted spinach, and tomatoes served with roasted Vidalia onion confit and golden tomato vinaigrette. Prices run $16 to $26.

Start your meal with a delicious soup of tomatoes and roasted peppers, with shrimp and onions flambéed with vodka or gin and topped with crème fraîche and caviar or the smoked fish prepared in the seasonal style. Finish with a delicious Sacher torte, a poached pear, or chocolate decadence. All three dining rooms are atmospheric. The main Von Steuben Room has a warm atmosphere with its ruby-burgundy color scheme; the formal Washington Room has a crystal chandelier and burgundy velvet curtains; while the least formal is the den.

Hours: Monday to Friday 11am to 2:30pm and 5 to 10pm, Saturday 5 to 10pm.

Samuel's, in Spread Eagle Village, 503 W. Lancaster Ave., Wayne (☎ 610/687-2840), is one of the area's fine dining spots, popular with Main Liners. The restaurant offers a series of large dining rooms with well-spaced polished wood tables set with Villeroy & Boch. The waiters are aproned and the music is classical. The largest room has a stucco fireplace with a beam mantel and brick hearth. Narrow ceiling beams and valanced chintz curtains give a French provincial air to a smaller room. There's also an atrium dining room that sparkles with Mexican floor tiles. You can also eat in the large bar, where a less elaborate menu is served to the martini and cigar lovers who gather here.

The menu will likely include a dozen or so entrees, like sautéed striped bass with caramelized onion confit, aged balsamic vinegar, and vegetable risotto; grilled pork chops with a ginger soy hoisin glaze and grilled pineapple, or crispy roast duck with lingonberry sauce. Prices run $18 to $27. To start, try the tequila-cured salmon terrine. Desserts are made daily and worth sampling—orange crème caramel, peach tart, or chocolate-mousse cake could be on the tray. A simple grill menu is served in the bar from 6pm to closing. The wine list is extensive and there are several wines by the glass.

Hours: Daily 11:30am to 2:30pm, Sunday to Thursday 6 to 9pm, Friday to Saturday 6 to 10pm.

Villa Strafford, 115 Strafford Ave., Wayne (☎ 610/964-1116), is in a stone mansion with a classic portico supported by colonial revival pillars. The dining rooms are equally elegant. Forest-green velvet chairs are set at tables; burgundy drapes are cinched back gracefully. A bust of Schiller stands prominently on the mantel. A less formal room is in similar style. There's a comfortable bar for sipping drinks while waiting. The frequently changing menu features fresh, seasonal ingredients. The menu lists about 15 entrees ($19 to $30)—pork tenderloin with apples in a Calvados sauce; grilled salmon with a pesto tomato sauce; filet mignon with roasted shallots in a Barolo wine demi-glace; or delicious sautéed medallions of veal with wild mushroom, tomatoes, and Marsala wine. Several pasta dishes round out the menu. The appetizers consist mostly of shellfish dishes such as oysters with a vodka lime cocktail sauce or smoked salmon with horseradish cream sauce. *Hours:* Monday to Friday 11:30am to 2pm and 5:30 to 9:30pm, Saturday 6 to 10pm.

La Fourchette, 110 N. Wayne Ave., Wayne (☎ 610/687-8333), is the other contender for fine fare in this area. Lit by a row of tall, Palladian-style windows and graced by an elegant central balustered staircase, the room is distinctly decorated in French style. Dinner offers about eight entrees. There might be a rack of lamb finished with a green peppercorn beurre rouge, fillet of salmon with a citrus and port glaze, or roasted tenderloin of pork with apricot brandy reduction and golden raisins and currants. Prices range from $23 to $29. Choice appetizers are the fricassee of shrimp, scallops, and crab lightly sautéed with a thyme and white-wine cream sauce; or the trio of seasonal soups, which are presented in antique tea cups. The tempting desserts are made daily by the pastry chef—lemon tart, apple-hazelnut tart, or chocolate-praline torte, for example. *Hours:* Tuesday to Friday 11:30am to 2pm and 6 to 10pm, Saturday 5:30 to 10pm, Sunday 11:30am to 2pm and 5:30 to 9pm.

About 1700, William Penn and his daughter visited the Welsh Quakers at Gwynedd and stopped at the Thomas Evans home, which later became the **William Penn Inn,** Route 202 and Sumneytown Pike, Gwynedd (☎ 215/699-9272). Here you'll find two dining rooms: The Mayfair Room is lushly formal, with plush rose banquettes, brass sconces, a chandelier, forest-green napery, and large bouquets of fresh flowers; the typical colonial tavern contains booths and comb-back Windsor chairs. The Mayfair serves continentally inspired seafood, steaks, veal, and poultry—swordfish marinated in olive oil with red and green peppercorns and balsamic vinegar and served with a tomato, yellow pepper, and cilantro salsa; Dover sole sautéed in a lemon, caper, and butter sauce; Pommery-and-pine nut–encrusted rack of lamb served on a pool of balsamic vinegar demi-glace; or roasted duck glazed with orange juice, Grand Marnier, and champagne vinaigrette. Prices run $17 to $29. The tavern serves the same menu, except on Thursday night, when there's a special seafood buffet. *Hours:* Mayfair Room, Monday to Friday 11:30am to 2pm and 5 to 10pm, Saturday 11:30am to 2pm and 4:30 to 10pm, Sunday 2 to 8pm; tavern, Monday to Friday 11:30am to 1:45pm, Thursday 5:30 to 8:30pm, Friday 5:30 to 10pm, Saturday 5 to 10pm, Sunday 10:30am to 2pm.

In 1954 Edward Wallis Callahan turned his home into the **Coventry Forge Inn,** Route 23, Coventryville (☎ 610/469-6222)—it had been an inn earlier, from 1717 to 1818. This really is the most charming place to dine in the area—a series of low-ceilinged rooms, one with an original Franklin stove, that are lit by Shaker lanterns. The small tavern bar has wide-plank floors and a collection of fine flasks; it's particularly inviting in winter. The porch dining area is most pleasant in summer. The owners keep live trout and use local Muscovy duck for their special grilled breast of duck served with cherry–port wine sauce. Other menu items might include medallions of venison with a poivrade sauce, rack of lamb with port-rosemary sauce, and salmon steamed with fresh fennel. Prices range from $17 to $26. On Saturday a $38.50 four-course prix-fixe meal is served. These main dishes can be followed with classic desserts like a lemon sorbet, profiteroles, or white- and dark-chocolate mousse with raspberry coulis.

The accommodations in the adjacent guest house are spacious and attractive, with large baths. The windows look out onto a pastoral, wooded scene. Guests are requested to dine in the restaurant.

Rates (including continental breakfast): $75 to $85 a night, depending on room and day of the week. *Dining hours:* Tuesday to Friday 5:30 to 9pm, Saturday 5 to 10pm.

The **Roadhouse Grille,** Route 73, Skippack (☎ 610/584-4231), is a refreshing change from the many colonial decors that predominate in the area's restaurants. From the parking lot, a wooden footbridge and crazy paving path leads into the tavern room, which features an unusual tiled bar. A series of dining rooms, all small and intimate, are decorated with prints and copper lanterns and furnished with banquettes and cane Breuer chairs. The food is good and nicely presented; the menu is broad enough to satisfy many different tastes. Among the pasta dishes you might find both the traditional pad Thai or penne with smoked chicken, portobello mushroom, and asparagus in a tomato sauce. There are also seafood dishes like grilled striped bass with Tuscan style beans and herb-infused oil, plus such grilled meats as Asian barbecue–glazed pork tenderloin or meat loaf served with green peppercorn sauce. Prices range from $8 to $22. The desserts are traditional favorites like a hot-fudge sundae, chocolate mousse, and peach Melba. *Hours:* Monday to Thursday 11:30am to 2:30pm and 5 to 9pm, Friday and Saturday 11:30am to 2:30pm and 5 to 10pm, Sunday noon to 3pm and 4:30 to 8:30pm.

Back on the other side of Valley Forge is the **Jefferson House,** 2519 DeKalb Pike, Norristown (☎ 610/275-3407), a magnificent mansion (modeled after Jefferson's Monticello) overlooking a duck pond and gracious gardens. The cuisine is continental. Perhaps begin with the steamed mussels with white wine and capers or oysters on the half shell. Follow with any of the beef, poultry, veal, and many pasta dishes—salmon with horseradish crust with Cabernet Sauvignon–wine sauce; veal Oscar; or spaghetti albina made with shrimp, scallops, and crab in a white-wine sauce with clams. Prices range from $18 to $28. Take DeKalb Street (Route 202) north from Valley Forge. *Hours:* Monday to Friday 11:30am to 2:30pm and 4 to 10pm, Saturday 4 to 10pm, Sunday noon to 7:30pm.

Out east along Skippack Road (Route 73) you'll find the **Blue Bell Inn,** 601 Skippack Rd., Blue Bell (☎ 215/646-2010), a popular local favorite. The oldest part of the restaurant dates from 1743, but it has been extensively enlarged and now offers a series of large dining rooms. Here a traditional dinner menu is offered, featuring steaks and chops, plus such fish dishes as swordfish with black-bean mango salsa, sautéed scallops or crabmeat, plus other items like veal Marsala or calf's liver. Prices range from $16 to $29. There's also a pleasant piano bar containing a display of fine German steins. *Hours:* Tuesday to Saturday 11:30am to 2:30pm and 4:30 to 9:30pm.

Valley Forge
Special & Recreational Activities

Antiquing: Antiques stores are found in and around **Skippack Village** along Route 73.

Bicycling: Rentals are available in **Valley Forge Historical Park** from May to October.

Golf: General Washington Golf Club, 2750 Egypt Rd., Audubon (☎ 610/666-7602), charges $30 weekdays and $38 weekends; **Valley Forge Golf Club**, Route 363, King of Prussia (☎ 610/337-1776), charges $19 weekdays and $23 weekends to play the 18-hole par-71 course.

Horseback Riding: There's a 120-mile trail in **Valley Forge Historical Park**. Call the convention bureau at ☎ 610/834-1550 for nearby stables or call the park at ☎ 610/783-1077.

Picnicking: Valley Forge Historical Park makes a perfect spot.

Shopping: King of Prussia possesses one of the largest shopping centers in the country. Many foreigners fly here specifically to shop at Bloomingdale's, Saks, Lord & Taylor, Neiman Marcus, Nordstrom, and hundreds of other stores (365 in fact) in ease and comfort. The mall stays open until 9:30pm on Saturday. Dedicated shoppers will love it! It's at Exit 24 off the PA pike. For information call ☎ 610/265-5727 or 610/337-1210.

State Parks: Marsh Creek has 1,700 acres and offers picnicking, a pool, fishing, boat rentals, hiking, horseback trail riding, ice boating and fishing, skating, and sledding. Contact Marsh Creek, 675 Park Rd., Downingtown, PA 19335 (☎ 610/458-5119).

Tennis: Park Ridge has a couple of courts. At the **Gulph Mills Tennis Club**, 610 S. Henderson Rd., King of Prussia (☎ 610/265-3677), you can play for $30 to $40 per hour.

Lancaster & the Pennsylvania Dutch Country

Intercourse ◆ *Churchtown* ◆ *Gordonville* ◆ *Bird-in-Hand* ◆
Lancaster ◆ *Leola* ◆ *Strasburg* ◆ *Lititz* ◆ *Mount Joy* ◆
Manheim ◆ *East Petersburg* ◆ *Ephrata* ◆ *Adamstown*

Distance in miles: Lancaster, 153
Estimated driving time: 3 hours

◄O►◄O►◄O►◄O►◄O►

Driving: Take the New Jersey Turnpike to the Pennsylvania Turnpike west. Get off at Exit 22, where you can pick up Route 23 west. If you're in a hurry, take Exit 21 and Route 222 south.

Bus: Capitol Trailways (☎ 717/397-4861) travels to Lancaster daily from Philadelphia.

Train: Amtrak travels to Lancaster via Philadelphia. Call ☎ 800/872-7245 for information.

Further Information: For more about the state, contact the **Pennsylvania Center for Travel Tourism and Film**, Room 4, Forum Building, Harrisburg, PA 17120 (☎ 800/847-4872 or 717/787-5453). For specific information, contact the **Pennsylvania Dutch Convention and Visitors' Bureau**, 501 Greenfield Rd., Lancaster, PA 17601 (☎ 800/723-8824 or 717/299-8901).

◄O►◄O►◄O►◄O►◄O►

Although many visitors come to Lancaster County to see the rolling farmlands and to observe the lifestyles of the Amish and Old Order Mennonite communities, there are plenty of other fascinating things to do and see in this historic area that was settled by so many groups—Scottish Presbyterians, Quakers, French Huguenots, and many German sects, as well as Moravians, Roman Catholics, and German Jews. Their contributions to the arts and the agricultural and industrial development of the area can be viewed at many local historic and other museums—the National Clock and Watch Museum, the Landis Farm Museum, Robert Fulton's birthplace, Wright's Ferry Mansion, and many more.

    Lancaster itself is a lovely old historic town. Southeast of Lancaster, **Strasburg** offers a string of delights to railroad buffs—a trip aboard a real old iron horse, a collector's museum, a fine model-railroad museum, and even a

---

Events & Festivals to Plan Your Trip Around

May: Carriage and Sleigh Auction, Lebanon Fairgrounds (usually mid-May). Call ☎ 717/768-8108.

July: Kutztown Pennsylvania Dutch Festival—a 9-day celebration of the arts and crafts of the region (basketry, embroidery, woodworking, tinsmithing, decoy carving, wood whittling, toleware painting, sgraffito), along with food, music, and dancing (usually July 4th weekend). For information, contact the Kutztown Folk Festival, 461 Vine Lane, Kutztown, PA 19530 (☎ 800/447-9269 or 610/683-8707).

    Lititz—July 4th celebration, when thousands of candles are lit and reflect into the narrow waterways dotted with waterwheels in Lititz Springs Park. Contact the Lititz Borough Office, 7 S. Broad St., Lititz, PA 17543 (☎ 717/626-2044).

June–Labor Day: Crafts day and harvest days, Landis Valley Farm Museum. Call ☎ 717/569-0401.

December: Wheatland opens the dining room for punch and cookies in a **19th-century-style party.**

---

motel that's housed in 17 cabooses. On the northern side of Lancaster is the quiet, pretty Moravian town of **Lititz,** which possesses one of the most pleasant inns in the area, and **Ephrata,** site of a cloister and religious community—a historic example of the kind of groups and communities William Penn's tolerant state attracted and sheltered. For those who love to shop for antiques, the area has many stores and a fantastic collection of antiques emporiums and markets in nearby **Adamstown.** If discount shopping is on your mind, then the outlets at **Reading** (to which many New York–based corporations are taking their employees by the busload) are on the way to Lancaster. There are also the delights of Pennsylvania Dutch cooking and lively Pennsylvania Dutch markets and auctions, which are prime destinations on most visitors' agendas, along with those attractions that pretend to explain the local Mennonite and Amish communities.

The Pennsylvania Dutch The term *Pennsylvania Dutch* refers to the many groups who fled persecution in southern Germany and settled in Pennsylvania, in such places as Germantown, before fanning across the rest of the state to establish farms and communities. Their native language was German, or *Deutsch,* which probably became corrupted to *Dutch,* and their customs, traditions, and philosophies emphasized hard work and plain living. Among them are, of course, the Amish and the Mennonites, who are sort of cousins. Both groups, formed during the Reformation in Europe in the 1500s, were Anabaptists who sought a pure church, free from state control, open to adult believers from any religion. Because they preached the priesthood of all believers, there was no one leader among them, although Menno Simons, an ex-Catholic priest from Holland, became well known through his writings and gave his name to the

Lancaster & the Pennsylvania Dutch Country

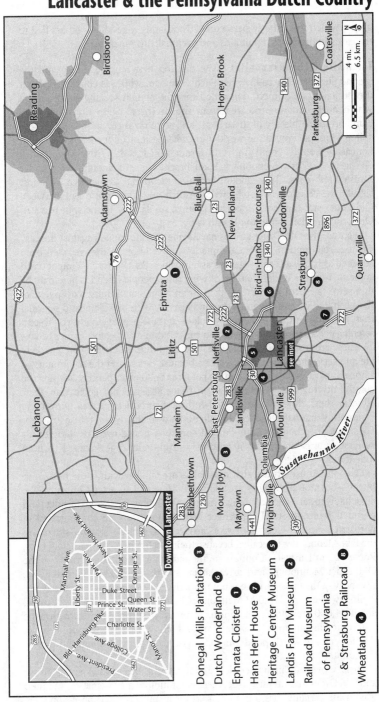

Donegal Mills Plantation ③
Dutch Wonderland ⑥
Ephrata Cloister ①
Hans Herr House ⑦
Heritage Center Museum ⑤
Landis Farm Museum ②
Railroad Museum
of Pennsylvania
& Strasburg Railroad ⑧
Wheatland ④

Downtown Lancaster

group, which was bitterly persecuted. Thousands were killed; others fled to the caves in the Swiss mountains and eventually to America.

The Amish & the Mennonites The division between the Amish and the Mennonites came in 1693, when Jacob Amman, who was concerned about the purity of the church, demanded that the church socially shun anyone who'd been excommunicated from the brethren. Such divisions were common in the history of these sects, and so today there are many different splinter groups around the world and in Lancaster County. For example, in Lancaster County you'll find Old Order Amish, Old Order Mennonites (Wenger), Old Order Mennonites (Pike), Beachy Order Mennonites, New Order Amish, Brethren in Christ, and the Lancaster Mennonite Conference. The most significant division is not between Amish and Mennonite but between Old Order and the more "modern" groups, similar, say, to the split between Orthodox and Reform in the Jewish faith.

Because the Old Order groups have made specific choices against the easy way of acculturation and the temptations of technology, they've often been attacked as backward and regarded as curiosities. As a visitor you might try to come to a deeper understanding of what these people intend. There may be things we can learn from them, like commitment, community, a deep love of the earth and its bounty, and living in harmony with life's daily and seasonal rhythms—in short, wholeness. If you look at these people closely, you'll see a serenity, peace, and contentment you can't find in many communities today.

These groups have chosen to live in communities where religion and daily life intersect. They have no use for cars because cars scatter the community—a horse can travel only about 8 miles per hour or 20 miles per day, keeping the community together. They believe in peace and will not go to war. They educate their children to live self-fulfilling, productive lives within the community, and believe in looking after their own elderly and refuse to accept Social Security benefits. Similarly, if someone is widowed or disabled or suffers some calamity, the neighbors and church come forward to help indefinitely.

The one Amish artifact that most of us are familiar with is the horse and buggy—but not all buggies are the same. Here in Lancaster County you're most likely to see Lancaster Amish carriages with gray tops, straight sides, and rounded roof corners. The Wenger Mennonites, who are concentrated in northern Lancaster County, drive a carriage with a black, straight-sided top; the Pike Mennonites (so-called because their meetinghouse is on the old pike, Route 322 in Lancaster County) are the oldest and most conservative of the Old Order Mennonites and drive carriages with no back or side windows. (By the way, the open carriage is not properly called a courting carriage at all.)

Today there are 313,000 Mennonites living in North America. Of these, about 34,000 are Old Order Amish. You may be surprised to learn that the fastest growing are the Old Order groups, both Amish and Mennonite, a fact that is certainly worth pondering on a visit to this lovely, bountiful part of the country.

Note: Obviously, many people are drawn to the area to gawk at the Amish and Old Order Mennonites. True, these communities are fascinating and their way of life certainly has lots to be said for it, but just imagine if you were suddenly to become the object of millions of staring people as you went about your daily business; and every activity from shopping and gardening to simply walking down the road was stared at, scrutinized, analyzed, and worse, photographed. The last is especially disturbing to the Old Order groups because their religious principles include the strict commandment that "thou shalt not make graven images." If you *must* take pictures, then please exercise some degree of sensitivity.

AMISH & PENNSYLVANIA DUTCH COUNTRY

AREA ATTRACTIONS

Driving along main roads like Route 30, you'll be assaulted by sign after sign screaming the word *authentic* and offering real buggy rides and so on. My advice is to try and sift the authentic from the chaff. One way to do this is to stay off Route 30 as much as possible. Instead, drive the routes that cut north-to-south like routes 772 and 860. Along these roads, go into the farms wherever you see a sign inviting you to buy eggs, quilts, vegetables, furniture, or whatever. I've tried to include only those places that will prove most rewarding. The best time to visit, for my money, is in the busy springtime of hoeing, plowing, and planting, when the farmers work night and day to beat the weather and get their crops in the ground. The other time to visit is in October, when the fall adds a colorful dimension to the whole rewarding scene of harvesting and thanksgiving. Summer is the most crowded. Plan to see all the Amish/Mennonite attractions on Saturday, for they're closed on Sunday. That applies to many Pennsylvania Dutch restaurants as well.

The best place to begin your visit is probably the **People's Place,** Intercourse (☎ 717/768-7171). See the 25-minute film *Who Are the Amish?* to get a very good and sympathetic idea of these people: their diversity, their practices, their traditions, and what has held them together through centuries. Afterward, walk upstairs, where there are a series of interactive exhibits that deal with the Amish and Mennonite way of life. These exhibits will tell you about the eight areas in which the Amish remain in tension with the rest of American society: (1) sense of time, (2) transportation, (3) dress, (4) education, (5) peace, (6) government aid, (7) energy, and (8) mutual aid.

Kids can enjoy the "Feeling Box"—dressing up, filling out an actual worksheet exercise in the one-room schoolhouse, and following Amos and Suzie through the 12 months of a typical Amish child's year. There are also several quizzes, which adults may find enlightening. The museum also features some wonderful, three-dimensional carved wooden paintings by Aaron Zook, each depicting a community scene—they're quite magnificent and deeply moving. You'll also find some watercolors and furniture designed by folk artist Henry Lapp, an Old Order Amish man. Downstairs you may want to browse in the bookstore and craft store.

Hours: Memorial Day to Labor Day, Monday to Saturday 9:30am to 8pm (with *Who Are the Amish?* showing continuously and an occasional Saturday 7pm showing of the film *Hazel's People,* with Geraldine Page); rest of the year, Monday to Saturday 9:30am to 5pm. Closed New Year's Day, Thanksgiving,

Christmas. *Admission:* For the film, $4 adults, $2 children; for the film and museum, $7 adults, $3.50 children.

While you're in Intercourse, you'll likely want to browse through the stores across the street from the People's Place and drop into Zimmerman's, which will likely have many buggies hitched out front.

For an overview of the history of the area and its settlers, you'd do well to visit the **Wax Museum,** Route 30, 4 miles east of Lancaster (☎ 717/ 393-3679). Although wax museums don't usually appeal to me, this one is artfully created and gives visitors an excellent grasp of the local history. Each diorama focuses on a particular period, event, or personality, from the arrival of the Mennonites and Amish through the Civil War. Some of the figures are made to speak, and some dramatic illusions are created—the whole tour capped by an impressive dramatization of a barn raising. It's fun and worth seeing. *Hours:* June to August, daily 9am to 8pm; March to May and September to October, daily 9am to 6pm; November to February, daily 9am to 5pm. *Admission:* $5.75 adults, $5.25 seniors, $3.25 children ages 5 to 11.

AN AMISH COUNTRY TOUR

For a quick trip through Amish country, take Route 772 out of Intercourse and turn left on Cat's Tail Road. All along here you can see the waterwheels and windmills that generate power for each farm. The road loops back to Route 340, which you can take west into Intercourse again. Then take Route 772 northwest for about a mile, turn right on Centerville Road and keep going until you come to the **Phillips Lancaster County Swiss Cheese** at no. 433 (☎ 717/354-4424). In this store you can see a video showing how the cheese is made and pick up some samples, of course. *Hours:* April to Christmas, Monday to Friday 8am to 5pm, Saturday 9am to 3pm.

While you're in the region you should also stop in at **Lapp's Ice Cream,** sold at a farm just off New Holland Road. It's also sold locally at such places as Kettle Village in Intercourse. Drive into the farmyard and purchase a really good creamy cone or sundae and enjoy it as the cows come and go, the turkey struts, and the dog barks wildly from the kennel.

Get back onto Route 340, heading for Intercourse. From Intercourse it's a short journey west on Route 340 to **Bird-in-Hand,** where there's a **farmer's market.** En route, if you want some handmade, hand-carved furniture, turn right on Weavertown Road and drive to the Red Barn and ask for **the furniture maker.** Bring your own design and he'll fashion whatever you want— even a whole dining table and chair set—for very reasonable prices. Continue west on Route 340 until you come to Witmer Road. Turn left and go down until you see a farm on the right with a QUILTS FOR SALE sign. Here you'll find some truly wonderful quilts and have the added enjoyment of seeing the farm and meeting Hannah Stoltzfoos, the mistress of the house. The quality of the work is superb, and the prices are fair. For me these are some of the highlights of the Amish country.

For informed tours along the back roads, head for the **Mennonite Information Center,** 2209 Millstream Rd., Lancaster (☎ 717/299-0954). For about $30 a Mennonite guide will accompany you in your car for 2 hours to explain the Pennsylvania Dutch ways. There's also a 20-minute film introducing the Amish and Mennonite communities. *Hours:* Monday to Saturday 8am to 5pm.

CHURCHTOWN, GORDONVILLE & BIRD-IN-HAND LODGING

The **Inn at Twin Linden**, 2092 Main St. (Route 23), Churchtown, PA 17555 (☎ 717/445-7619; fax 717/445-4656), occupies a 150-year-old frame house standing on 2 acres. Inside, guests discover a comfortable parlor with a blazing log fire in winter at one end of the room, and a TV area at the other, where you can also enjoy a brandy from the crystal decanter. There are seven rooms, all with baths. Each has been imaginatively decorated. The Polo Room has stencils of flying ducks on the walls, a Shaker four-poster with a canopy and Ralph Lauren quilt, and a sizable bath. The Linden Room has a canopied bed, a double whirlpool, and a gas fireplace. The most spectacular accommodation is the Palladian Suite, which has a private entrance, a fireplace/stove, a TV/VCR, a CD player, a double whirlpool, a wet bar with refrigerator, and a skylight. The Cottage Room has sloping ceilings and is decorated in a Laura Ashley style; the bath has a claw-foot tub and Mexican tile decor.

The inn is operated by Bob and Donna Leahy. Bob teaches at Temple University, while Donna is the chef, creating extra-special breakfasts and providing Saturday night dinners, served in the candlelit dining room or alfresco on the brick terrace. Breakfast brings such wonders as freshly baked croissants, cinnamon raisin buns, blueberry-peach cobbler, pesto eggs with leeks and asparagus, or walnut French toast with poached pears and Stilton cheese. On Saturday the four-course prix-fixe menu ($48) might offer the following menu: sweet corn, cheddar, and thyme soup; followed by fresh mozzarella and plum tomato with sweet basil; and a main dish like rack of lamb with caramelized onions, mustard, and rosemary pesto. The meal will conclude with a wonderfully fresh peach cobbler with homemade cinnamon gelato. It's BYOB. Guests enjoy wandering the gardens and relaxing on the rear porch, which looks across the gardens to farmland. The outdoor hot tub is fun, too.

Rates (including breakfast): $110 to $175 double, $220 suite.

The historic **Churchtown Inn**, 2100 Main St., Narvon, PA 17555 (☎ 717/445-7794; fax 717/445-0962), is a special place largely because the innkeepers extend a genuinely warm welcome to their guests. They have also taken the time to dream up some very engaging weekends, ranging from a "murder mystery weekend" to a full Victorian evening dress costume ball. There are even special fund-raising weekends for the Women's Shelter of Lancaster and other worthy causes. The inn is located in a delightful little town away from all the hubbub, yet in the center of the Amish country surrounded by rolling farmland. The 18th-century fieldstone mansion has an air of romance and is made even more so by the lush plantings, fountains, and swing seats at the back of the property. There are eight guest rooms (two sharing a bath), plus the large and exquisite Carriage House Suite. Both the James Griffin Room and the Carriage House Suite contain four-posters with crocheted canopies; the one in the Carriage House is dressed in a double-wedding-ring Amish quilt coordinated with swagged cherry drapes on the windows. The Edward Davis Room is decked out in purple and mauve, with a handsome crown-canopy fabric treatment draping the high-back bed.

In the double parlor furnished with Eastlake pieces guests can relax in front of the fire, play the grand piano, or, better yet, be entertained by inn-keeper Stuart Smith, who was the music director of a choir. You're in for a very moving experience when Stuart sits down at the piano and sings. Another parlor offers a cozy Victorian ambience with family portraits, china, and figurines on display, along with an old phonograph. Breakfast is a five-course feast of local fruit, oatmeal and cereal, homemade coffee cake, and such items as Grand Marnier French toast—all served on Royal Doulton china in a serene garden room that looks out across the lush gardens to a farm scene beyond. The innkeepers will also arrange for you to dine at an Amish/Mennonite home. A winning place indeed.

Rates (including breakfast): $75 to $115 double, $155 suite.

If you want to be in the heart of the Amish country and hear the gentle clop of horses' hooves as they go by, you can't beat the **Osceola Mill House,** 313 Osceola Mill Rd., Gordonville, PA 17529 (☎ 717/768-3758). It's a lovely 1766 stone house with maroon shutters set by a millstream and humpbacked bridge. A flower-lined brick path leads to the porch, and you may catch sight of one of the resident peacocks. You'll be welcomed into the parlor or into the beamed keeping room, furnished with Early American antiques.

Upstairs are three guest rooms, all with private baths, two with fireplaces. The Green Room offers an antique brass bed dressed in an Amish quilt and plank floors embellished with hooked rugs. The Blue room features a high canopied four-poster and a reproduction Queen Anne highboy. The Rose Room contains a hand-carved pine bed. The carriage house and keeping room, which rents as a separate unit, has a living room with a wood stove, kitchen, and private patio, with two bedrooms and a bath upstairs. It's equipped with TV/VCR and an unstocked refrigerator. It sleeps four people. A full breakfast is served in the dining room. It might bring eggs piccata or baked orange French toast served with fresh fruit and fresh breads and the local sausages—smoked, sage, or apple.

Rates (including breakfast): $95 to $145 double (higher price for fireplace rooms).

The **Village Inn of Bird-in-Hand,** 2695 Old Philadelphia Pike (P.O. Box 253), Bird-in-Hand, PA 17505 (☎ 717/293-8369), occupies an authentic 19th-century three-story building, with five bays fronted by a double porch with turned columns and fretwork railings. Guests stay in 11 comfortable rooms furnished with antique reproductions—Queen Anne chairs, Federal-style desks—combined with chintz wallpapers, lace curtains, and wall-to-wall carpeting. Four are suites, two have whirlpool baths, one has a wood-burning stove, and another has a fireplace. All have air-conditioning, TVs, and phones. Guests have free use of nearby indoor and outdoor pools and tennis courts. *Rates* (including continental breakfast): Late June to late October, $99 to $109 double, $129 to $149 suite; rest of the year, $79 to $89 double, $109 to $139 suite.

The **Bird-in-Hand Family Inn,** P.O. Box 402, Bird-in-Hand, PA 17505 (☎ 717/768-8271), is a well-kept and prettily landscaped motel accommodation. The rooms are attractive and modern. The restaurant is fine for breakfast or lunch, and you'll often find a number of locals, including Amish, sitting at the counter. A few hundred yards down the road you'll find the bakery, which I can heartily recommend for their buns, cookies, shoofly pies, and more. There's also tennis courts and an indoor pool. *Rates:* Summer, $90 to $96 double; winter, special lower rates apply.

PENNSYLVANIA DUTCH DINING

Groff's Farm Restaurant, Pinkerton Road, Mount Joy (☎ 717/653-2048), is a wonderful choice. The late James Beard and Craig Claiborne have both described Betty Groff's cooking as authentic Americana, and Betty certainly operates a restaurant where the ingredients are always fresh and the food is tasty and plentiful. Ideally, you'll arrive at the old stone farmhouse as the sun is sinking, and you can capture the silhouette of one of the swans gliding by on the farmyard pond against the pink-tinged sky of a Pennsylvania sunset. If you select the family-style menu, your meal will begin with a collection of relishes. Then comes your choice of soup or fruit salad, and the main course, served family style. You can choose any special combination of classic Pennsylvania Dutch fare—roast prime rib, hickory-smoked ham, a special seasonal seafood combination, or Betty's own famous chicken Stoltzfus, consisting of succulent chunks of chicken in cream sauce placed on a bed of light pastry. Whatever combination you choose, it'll be accompanied by several vegetables and a bowl of superb whipped potatoes. Want seconds? Just ask. If you have room for dessert, select from a variety of pies and ice creams included in the price of the meal. This family-style repast will cost $16 to $27, depending on your choices.

If Betty is there the night of your visit (she almost always is), she'll undoubtedly stop by and introduce herself, talking away in her effervescent manner, making sure everything is to your liking. At some point she may take out her trumpet to toast whoever happens to have a birthday or anniversary with a round or two of the "Anniversary Waltz" or "Happy Birthday."

Hours: Tuesday to Friday 11:30am to 1:30pm and 5 to 7:30pm, Saturday 11:30am to 1:30pm and dinner seatings at 5 and 8pm. Dinner is by reservation only.

One of the better and larger (capacity of 600) places to stop for Pennsylvania Dutch fare is the **Willow Valley Inn,** 2416 Willow Street Pike (☎ 717/464-2711), located south of Lancaster in a lovely setting overlooking a golf course. The breakfast buffet is vast. Spread before you are several tables, one piled with fruit salads and dried fruits, another with doughnuts and pastries, and still another with eggs, sausage, scrapple, waffles, home fries, and more. Help yourself, all for $7. Lunch and dinner offer equally large arrays of food, including the classic favorites associated with this part of the world: ham, beef, chow-chow, apple butter, shoofly pie. *Hours:* Monday to Saturday 6am to 8pm, Sunday 8am to 8pm. No liquor.

The **Stoltzfus Farms Restaurant,** on Route 772, just east of Intercourse (☎ 717/768-8156), is famous for its flavorsome sausages, which isn't surprising because the farming and butchering operation came first. The restaurant was an afterthought and a great one. Here you can enjoy family-style meals featuring sausage, ham loaf, roast chicken, chow-chow, apple butter, pepper cabbage, candied sweet potatoes, and all the other famous local treats for $12.95. No liquor. *Hours:* May to October, Monday to Saturday 11:30am to 8pm; April and November, Saturday to Sunday 11:30am to 8pm. Closed December to March.

The **Brownstown Restaurant,** 1 S. State St., Brownstown (☎ 717/656-0763), is another smaller (seating 200) dining room specializing in good, home cooking, served family-style (although it also offers a regular menu with dishes like veal cutlet, sandwiches, and haddock at very reasonable prices). The family-style platter includes roast beef, baked ham, chicken, or turkey, about four vegetables (corn, potatoes, and so on), dessert, beverage, and soup for only $9.95. Advance notice is required for the family-style meal. Good for breakfast. *Hours:* Monday to Saturday 6am to 8pm, Sunday 7am to 7pm.

Miller's Smorgasbord, 2811 Lincoln Hwy. E. (☎ 717/687-6621), is famous for its choice of 75 items at dinner. Here you can have the privacy of your own table. *Hours:* June to October, daily from 8am to 9pm; November to May, weekdays noon to 8pm, Saturday to Sunday from 8am.

Similar regional fare, family-style, can be found at the famous 600-seat **Good n' Plenty,** Route 896, Smoketown (☎ 717/394-7111). *Hours:* Monday to Saturday 11:30am to 8pm. Closed mid-December to first Friday in February.

SUNDAY DINING

In this area Sunday dining can be a problem. Here are a couple of establishments that are open on Sunday: the **Historic Strasburg Inn**, Route 896, Strasburg (☎ 717/687-7691), open from 7am to 9pm; and **Miller's Smorgasbord,** 2811 Lincoln Hwy. E. (☎ 717/687-6621), open from noon to 8pm.

LANCASTER

AREA ATTRACTIONS

Lancaster was the first inland settlement in Pennsylvania. During the American Revolution, it was capital for a day when the Continental Congress met here on September 27, 1777 while the British occupied Philadelphia. Lancaster is a lovely old town with streets lined with restored 18th- and 19th-century brick town houses. The old market downtown and the jail are impressive pieces of architecture.

For a full exploration of the city you can't beat the downtown **2-hour walking tours,** which are given from April to October, Tuesday, Friday, and Saturday at 10am, and daily at 1pm. Meet at 100 S. Queen St. (☎ 717/392-1776) for a short introductory film. The price is $5 for adults, $4 for seniors, and $2 for children ages 6 to 17. By the way, don't miss the ornate interior of the old Fulton Opera House.

The **Heritage Center Museum,** Penn Square at King and Queen streets (☎ 717/299-6440), displays objects relating to Lancaster's history—furniture, quilts, clocks, Pennsylvania rifles, and many kinds of folk art. *Hours:* May to December, Tuesday to Saturday 10am to 5pm. *Admission:* Free.

Just outside Lancaster stands **Wheatland,** 1120 Marietta Ave. (☎ 717/392-8721), the home of the only bachelor to gain possession of the White House—James Buchanan. He bought this house in 1848 for $6,750, primarily because it suited his aspirations, which were attained in 1857 when he entered the White House accompanied by his niece, Harriet Lee, who was then only 27 years old. Her portrait can be seen, along with other memorabilia, including a portrait of Buchanan's fiancée, Ann Coleman, who broke their engagement because he didn't pay enough attention to her. The 45-minute tour, given by costumed guides, provides insight into Buchanan's life and sensibility. *Hours:* April to mid-December, daily 10am to 4pm. *Admission:* $5.50 adults, $4.50 seniors, $3.50 students, $1.75 children ages 6 to 11.

Pennsylvania Dutch Markets

The market that has the reputation for being the most authentic is held in downtown Lancaster at **Center Square** (☎ 717/291-4723), on Tuesday and Friday from 6am to 4pm and Saturday from 6am to 2pm. It's the oldest market in the area, and from 1730 to 1889 it was held curbside, where farmers sold produce from their wagons. If you want to view the local farmers delivering their goods, you'll have to rise about 5am or earlier. Later in the day the market is bustling, and you'll see among the vendors Mennonite ladies selling their home-baked goods, fresh flowers, fancy-looking meats, and shoofly and whoopee pies.

If you have a lot of energy when you arrive on Friday night, you might plan to attend the **Green Dragon Market** in Ephrata, a huge affair. Dust whirls over the parking lot, which is filled with cars and a few buggies. Vendors of all sorts gather outside the main buildings selling clothes, flowers, cookies, fruits and vegetables, fast foods—all manner of items. In the main market building fresh meats, cheeses, homemade baked goods, books, and much more are sold. In the barn at around 6pm an auction of animals is held, and fat, frightened rabbits, chickens, goslings, hamsters, and all kinds of other small fry are held aloft as the auctioneer sing-songs his way to the final gavel and the animal is passed out over the heads of the crowd. Kids love the action and the whole rural ritual is fascinating to observe. Other auctions of the kind of merchandise you might expect to find at Odd Job Lot are held in other market buildings. Open Friday from 10am to 10pm.

Meadowbrook Market, on Route 23 just outside Leacock, is another good market to visit. The one in Bird-in-Hand is somewhat too modern and lacks any real character. On Tuesday from 2 to 9pm, **Roots Country Market and Auction,** between Manheim and East Petersburg off Route 72, is another fascinating market experience.

West of Lancaster in Columbia, on the east bank of the Susquehanna River, **Wright's Ferry Mansion,** at Second and Cherry streets (☎ 717/684-4325), is a stone house built in 1738 for the remarkable English Quaker Susanna Wright. The house, with its wonderful collection of early-18th-century furniture, glass, and ceramics, reflects the sophisticated tastes and interests of this woman, whose pursuits ranged from literature to raising silkworms. Well worth the visit. *Hours:* May to October, Tuesday to Wednesday and Friday to Saturday 10am to 3pm (last tour at 3pm). *Admission:* $5 adults, $2.50 children ages 6 to 18.

The **Watch and Clock Museum,** 514 Poplar St., just off Route 30 (☎ 717/684-8261), houses one of the nation's largest collections of precision watches, clocks, tools, and other related items. The museum is currently undergoing renovation and will reopen in fall 1999. *Hours:* May to September, Tuesday to Saturday 9am to 4pm, Sunday noon to 4pm; October to April, Tuesday to Saturday 9am to 4pm. Closed major holidays. *Admission:* $6 adults, $5 seniors, $4 children ages 6 to 12.

And farther south on Route 222 in Quarryville, New Yorkers may be surprised to discover **Robert Fulton's birthplace** (☎ 717/548-2679). The little stone house is a tribute to his diverse genius and inventive spirit; a room is devoted to exhibits showing some of Fulton's artistic and mechanical accomplishments. Among them are examples of Fulton's miniature portraits, some of the finest produced in this country. *Hours:* Memorial Day to Labor Day, Saturday 11am to 4pm, Sunday 1 to 5pm.

Fun for Kids

Kids probably won't let you escape without a visit to **Dutch Wonderland Family Amusement Park,** 2249 Lincoln Hwy. E., Lancaster (☎ 717/291-1888), where the monorail whisks them into a park with many rides—a stern-wheel riverboat, miniature auto rides, a wooden roller coaster, a merry-go-round, and a log flume. There are other entertainments, too, like the high diving show and more. *Hours:* Memorial Day to Labor Day, daily 10am to 8pm; Easter weekend to Memorial Day and Labor Day to Columbus Day, Saturday 10am to 6pm, Sunday 11am to 6pm. *Admission:* $19.95 adults (ages 6 and up), $14.95 seniors and children ages 3 to 5 (including unlimited rides).

Historic Rock Ford & Kauffman Museum

Just south of Lancaster, **Historic Rock Ford,** 881 Rockford Rd. (☎ 717/392-7223), is well worth visiting, and you may want to take along a picnic and enjoy it along the banks of the Conestoga River in Lancaster County Central Park.

This two-story brick mansion was the home of General Edward Hand and his family in the late 18th century and is one of the best-preserved late Georgian homes in North America. Begin your visit at the barn housing the Kauffman Collection, made up of more than 400 examples of fraktur, pewter, copper, tin, lehnware, shimmel figures, glassware, firearms, and furniture made by local artisans and craftsmen from 1750 to 1850. The collection includes some lovely bride's boxes and toleware. Then walk down to the house for a guided tour.

Edward Hand graduated from Trinity College, Dublin, in medicine and came to the American colonies in 1767 with an Irish regiment when he was 23 years old. He soon quit the British army, became a doctor in Lancaster County, and later joined the Continental Army, becoming George Washington's adjutant-general. The house was built in 1792, and you'll probably be shocked by the brilliance of the colors in these rooms. In fact, they're the blues and golds that would have been used at that time. On the tour you'll glean a lot of history about the house, the furnishings, and the personal quirks of Mr. Hand, who defied fashion by refusing to wear a wig (he considered such a practice "dirty"). Among the original pieces on display are the general's personal field desk with "secret" compartments and a special chair made to accommodate his 6-foot, 4-inch frame. Take Duke Street south and follow the signs. *Hours:* April to November, Tuesday to Friday 10am to 4pm, Sunday noon to 4pm (last tour at 3pm). Closed Thanksgiving. *Admission:* $4.50 adults, $3.50 seniors, $2.50 children ages 6 to 12.

The **Hans Herr House,** 1849 Hans Herr Dr., Willow Street (☎ 717/464-4438), is Lancaster County's oldest house, constructed in 1719. Those interested in the finer points of construction will find this an interesting place. There are few furnishings in the house—some of the more interesting are an ingenious ratchet lamp, a Swiss/German–style heating oven, and a kas (German-style wardrobe) that can be taken to pieces and doesn't contain a single nail. From Lancaster, take Route 222 south for 3 miles. Turn right onto Hans Herr Drive and the house is on the left. *Hours:* April to the first weekend in December, Monday to Saturday 9am to 4pm. Closed major holidays. *Admission:* $3.50 adults, $1 children ages 7 to 12.

From here, get back onto Route 222, taking it east to Lampeter and onto Route 741, which takes you all the way down to Strasburg, a railroad enthusiast's paradise in the heart of Amish country farmland.

LANCASTER LODGING

Gardens of Eden, 1894 Eden Rd., Lancaster, PA 17601 (☎ 717/393-5179; fax 717/393-7722), has an accurate name. In a beautiful, redbrick Victorian house built about 1867 by an ironmaster, it's set on 3½ acres overlooking the Conestoga with terraced grounds inhabited by scores of songbirds and carpeted with wildflowers (Dutchmen's breeches, coltsfoot, trout lilly), perennials, and woodsy trails. These gardens are the source of the many flowers and floral decorations that fill the house created by innkeeper Marilyn Ebel, who is a professional floral designer. There are four guest rooms with baths, all delightfully furnished. One has a sleigh bed and other Victorian pieces; another features a mahogany canopied bed. In each you'll find fetching floral wreaths and decorative framed needlework. In the Quilt Room a sampler quilt and several other quilts hang on the walls. The Beecher Cottage offers a bedroom upstairs and a living/dining area with a working fireplace and an efficiency kitchen downstairs. The sitting room in the main house is extraordinarily comfortable and cozy with its fireplace and plush seating, built-in bookcases, fine art on the walls, coffee table with small piles of magazines, and a grand piano displaying a collection of family portraits. Breakfast is taken on the porch or flagstone patio in summer to the sound of the nearby waterfall or in the country dining room at other times. Bill and Marilyn will also arrange a Saturday dinner at an Amish home and personal Dutch country tour. *Rates* (including breakfast): $105 to $120 double, $140 cottage.

A mile and half east, **Witmer's Tavern, Inn and Museum**, 2014 Old Philadelphia Pike, Lancaster, PA 17602 (☎ 717/299-5305), is the sole survivor of the 62 inns that once lined the old Philadelphia–Lancaster road, the route that led to the western frontier beyond the Susquehanna River. People stayed here while waiting for their Conestoga wagons and Pennsylvania rifles before heading out. The 1725 inn has been restored by Brant Hartung and offers seven rooms (two with bath, five with fireplace). First- and second-floor rooms share a bath; third-floor rooms have baths. The rooms are decorated in authentic colonial pumpkin and Wedgwood blue colors and are furnished with either high-back Victorian or brass beds, combined with painted cottage furniture, oak dressers, and similar pieces. Peg boards function as closets. In one room there's even an acorn pine rope bed and trundle covered with an antique quilt. Deep casement windows and shutters, wide-plank floors, and original hardware add historic character to each.

Downstairs, Brant's sister runs Pandora's Antiques, which occupies the earliest part of the house, and the two-room brick-floored tavern. The adjacent sitting room, which features a cast-iron stove and decorative corner cupboard, can be used by guests for reading or playing cards and other games.

Rates (including morning coffee, tea, and pastries): $70 to $100 double; add $20 for a room with a fireplace.

The **King's Cottage**, 1049 E. King St., Lancaster, PA 17602 (☎ 717/397-1017; fax 717/397-3447), is the name Karen and Jim Owens have given this marvelous Spanish Revival home that was built in 1913. Karen greets guests with genuine warmth. The interior has been beautifully decorated with antique reproductions and a fine eye for color and comfort. The floors are covered with oriental rugs, the windows given swag treatments, and sofas are set invitingly against the restful, sea-green walls of the parlors. The library has a TV. The Florida Room sports salmon-pink walls and upholstered wicker furnishings. Guests have access to a small kitchen. The inn offers nine very attractively decorated rooms. The King's Room in the front harbors a brass bed and a large walnut armoire, plus armchairs. Pink is the hue of the Queen's Room, which has an old-fashioned tub and a pedestal sink in the bathroom, plus some striking stained-glass windows. The peach-hued Duchess Room contains a hand-carved mahogany four-poster, a cherry secretary, and a swivel rocker. In the Carriage House is the most lavish of all the accommodations— a suite featuring a fireplace, a canopied king-size bed, a double Jacuzzi, refrigerator, microwave, and a handsome mahogany armoire inlaid with mother-of-pearl, and a walnut piecrust table. A full breakfast is served at a beautifully set table. *Rates* (including breakfast): $110 to $185.

The **Apple Bin Inn**, 2835 Willow Street Pike, Willow Street, PA 17584 (☎ 717/464-5881), is run by very warm and friendly Barry and Debbie Hershey, who offer four comfortably furnished guest rooms, all with private baths, cable TVs, and phones. One has a Shaker pencil four-poster covered in a down comforter and several ruffle-trimmed pillows, combined with an oak dresser, a wing chair, and a sofa. In summer a wonderful breakfast of German apple pancakes or French toast with pecan sauce is served on the patio or on pine tables in the dining room. Guests have use of a sitting room with an upright piano for anyone inspired to play; it also features several apple checkerboards made by Barry. There's also a suite in the carriage house—the living room has a gas fireplace, wing chairs, and a love seat, and the bedroom is furnished with an acorn poster bed and other country pieces. There are TVs in both rooms. *Rates* (including breakfast): $105 double, $145 carriage house.

In downtown Lancaster, the **Hotel Brunswick**, at Chestnut and Queen streets (P.O. Box 749), Lancaster, PA 17604 (☎ 717/397-4801), looks like a rather unattractive slab of concrete, but it offers a good location if you're looking for easy access to fine dining, cocktail spots, and some evening entertainment. The rooms are typically modern, and facilities include a restaurant/lounge, an indoor pool, free parking, and an adjacent movie theater. *Rates:* $89 to $125 double.

On the outskirts, the **Best Western**, 222 Eden Rd. (Route 30 and the Oregon Pike), Lancaster, PA 17601 (☎ 717/569-6444), has 230 rooms set around a courtyard or the pool; they're furnished in typical modern style. Other facilities include an outdoor pool, a health club, and a games room. *Rates:* In season, $149 double; off-season, $129 double.

Lancaster Resorts

Out on Route 222 south, the **Willow Valley Inn**, 2416 Willow Street Pike, Lancaster, PA 17602 (☎ 800/444-1714 or 717/464-2711), is a well-landscaped family resort run by the Thomas family, who "believe deeply in the Anabaptist way of life." There's a nine-hole golf course, outdoor lighted tennis courts, a special children's playground, rental bicycles, and one outdoor and two indoor pools. The 170 rooms are very pleasantly appointed. Facilities include two restaurants. *Rates:* Mid-June to Labor Day, $119 to $159 double; rest of the year, $89 to $149 double. MAP rates and packages available.

Lancaster Host Resort, 2300 Lincoln Hwy. E., Lancaster, PA 17602 (☎ 800/233-0121 or 717/299-5500), is a full-facility resort with 18-hole golf course, eight indoor tennis courts, four lighted outdoor courts, jogging trails, an exercise-fitness center, a games room, four pools, and kids programs, too. The 330 rooms are modern, and each is fully equipped with a refrigerator, a wet bar, a coffeemaker or tea maker, and a TV. Facilities include two restaurants, a bar, and a nightclub. *Rates:* July to Labor Day, $149 to $179 double; Labor Day to November and April 2 to June, $109 to $149 double; December to April 1, $99 to $139 double. Special packages available.

LANCASTER DINING

At **Jethro's,** 659 First St., at Ruby Street (☎ 717/299-1700), three-piece-suited characters rub elbows with students in jeans and rumpled professors from nearby Franklin and Marshall College in a comfortable relaxed atmosphere. At the front is a long, narrow bar with a couple of gray-upholstered booths for dining; the room in the back, seating only about 30 people, is simple, but takes on a special air of elegance and even romance at night.

The food is excellent. Any one of the eight entrees will feature prime ingredients and be packed full of flavor, whether it's the breast of duck with plum sauce; the shrimp Provençal with tomato, olives, and capers; or the filet mignon with port and rosemary sauce. Prices range from $14 to $22. The menu also offers some light dishes, including a burger served with port wine–rosemary or béarnaise sauce and a Cajun shepherd's pie, which is served with Creole sauce. These are priced from $7 to $11. All the desserts are homemade, and the real specialty of the house is the alluring death by chocolate—a dark-chocolate Grand Marnier terrine served with orange crème anglaise. To find Jethro's, take Orange Street West (it's one-way) to Ruby Street and turn left. Go down 1 block to First Street; the restaurant's on the corner. *Hours:* Monday to Thursday 5 to 10pm, Friday to Saturday 5 to 10:30pm.

Portofino, 254 E. Frederick St. (☎ 717/394-1635), has a sleek look and serves some very fine cuisine indeed. Beyond the bar lit by lights with pink-fringed shades you'll find a dining room filled with black tables set with pink and gray, and black moderne chairs. The menu offers a broad selection. Among the main courses try the chicken sautéed with pine nuts, sun-dried tomatoes, black olives, garlic, and parsley. Veal Christine is a house specialty, made with veal and jumbo shrimp sautéed with shallots, basil, sun-dried tomatoes, and shiitake mushrooms in a vermouth cream sauce. Chicken piccata and veal parmigiana are among the more traditional favorites. Prices range from $11 to $29. *Hours:* Sunday to Thursday 11am to 4pm and 5 to 10pm, Friday to Saturday 11am to 4pm and 5 to 10:30pm.

Located upstairs, **The Loft,** at the corner of North Water and West Orange streets (☎ 717/299-0661), affects a country atmosphere, with an occasional farm implement or piece of wicker hanging around or above the cozy booths. The management is gracious and considerate of its customers to the extent that it has installed a special mechanical chairlift for those unable to climb the stairs. At lunch expect a wide choice: salads, hamburgers, London broil with mushroom sauce, stuffed shrimp, and delicious crab sandwiches, all under $10. At dinner, candlelight provides the setting for steaks, including a filet mignon stuffed with crabmeat, plus veal with brandied morels and cream sauce, venison with juniper cream sauce, roast duck with raspberry-tamarind glaze, and poached salmon with hollandaise. Prices range from $13 to $24 rising to $32 for the broiled seafood combination with filet mignon. *Hours:* Monday to Friday 11:30am to 2pm and 5:30 to 9pm, Saturday 5:30 to 9pm.

In downtown Lancaster, overlooking the splashing fountains, trees, and brick courtyard of Steinman Park, is **The Press Room**, 26–28 W. King St. (☎ 717/399-5400). The cuisine touches base with most American favorites taken from a variety of cuisines—tuna with citrus butter, blackened catfish, filet mignon with parsley garlic butter, and chicken sautéed with wild mushrooms and honey-smoked bacon with a veal demi-glace. Prices at dinner range from $14 to $22. Pizza and pasta dishes priced from $8 to $10 are also available. *Hours:* Monday to Saturday 11:30am to 3:30pm, Tuesday to Thursday 5 to 9:30pm, Friday to Saturday 5 to 10:30pm.

Market Fare, in the Hager Arcade, 25 W. King St. (☎ 717/299-7090), directly across from the Market Building, is a fine lunch, brunch, or dinner spot. Upstairs, the atmosphere is cafelike, and the menu is light—salads, sandwiches, soups—while downstairs is more formal (cushioned armchairs and 19th-century paintings). Downstairs, a full menu of seven pasta dishes and about a dozen entrees is available. Among the favorites are steak-and-seafood combinations and veal topped with asparagus and crab imperial and baked. Prices range from $14 to $23. Start with a sampler of tapas (Cajun shrimp, cheese puffs on tomato coulis, and mushrooms stuffed with crabmeat). The brunch menu lists such items as mushroom-crab omelet, French toast with apple-almond topping, and eggs Oscar, priced from $10 to $13. *Hours:* Monday 11am to 2:30pm and 5 to 9pm, Tuesday to Saturday 11am to 2:30pm and 5 to 10pm, Sunday 11am to 2pm and 5 to 9pm.

Although it's large and lacks any real atmosphere or decor, locals still swear by the **Stockyard Inn**, 1147 Lititz Ave., on routes 501 and 222 (☎ 717/394-7975), for prime rib, steaks, and seafood at moderate prices—$14 to $25. *Hours:* Tuesday to Friday noon to 9pm, Monday and Saturday 4 to 9:30pm.

If you enjoy diners, try **Zinn's Diner**, on Route 272 in Denver, 5 miles north of Ephrata (☎ 717/336-2210), famous for the statue of an Amish man standing upright with a pitchfork in hand. It's a popular place for Pennsylvania Dutch meals, with daily specials like pork mit kraut and Wienerschnitzel, priced from $6 to $13. *Hours:* Daily 6am to 11pm.

LEOLA DINING

A really wonderful find for the area, if somewhat difficult to locate, is **The Log Cabin**, off Route 272 at 11 Lehoy Forest Dr., in Leola (☎ 717/626-1181). Tucked away in the woods and reached by the Rose Hill covered bridge spanning Cocalico Creek (as befits a spot built during Prohibition), the Log Cabin offers good food—primarily steaks—in a series of comfortable, convivial rooms. The original log-cabin room now has brass chandeliers and plenty of mirrors. Cozy booths provide the seating in another room, while Windsor chairs and a selection of portraits accent another; then there's a room with barn siding, beams, and plush armchairs. A meal begins with a hot loaf of bread and a plate of crackers and cheese. The food is straightforward: steaks, double-cut lamb chops, roast duck, lobster, and stuffed flounder with crabmeat. Entrees run $19 to $30, topping out at $38 for surf and turf. The selection of appetizers includes smoked brook trout with strawberry-horseradish sauce, clams Provençal, and fried calamari. For dessert, try a standard like chocolate mousse, cheesecake, or carrot cake. Upstairs is a lounge area with a pianist/singer entertaining. *Hours:* Monday to Saturday 5 to 10pm, Sunday 4 to 9pm.

LODGING & DINING ACROSS THE SUSQUEHANNA

The **Accomac Inn**, Wrightsville (☎ 717/252-1521), is located in a 200-year-old stone building down by the Susquehanna River, a peaceful spot with a screened-in porch where tables are covered with blue gingham. The dining rooms are formal: Tables set with white cloths, pewter candlesticks and plates, fresh flowers in pewter mugs; Queen Anne–style chairs; gilt-framed landscapes and portraits; and a white fieldstone hearth create the ambience. The bar is equally formal, in Chippendale style. The menu offers classic French/American cuisine—pan-fried brook trout in a bacon tomato beurre blanc, pecan-crusted breast of chicken with a thyme-flavored jus, and crêpes filled with fresh seasonal ingredients. Prices range from $20 to $29. The luscious desserts might include key lime tart, and chocolate mousse fantasy, which is a rich chocolate terrine served on a Godiva white-chocolate sauce. The $22.95 champagne brunch is spectacular. You'll begin with assorted breads and either soup du jour or fresh seasonal fruit salad. A selection from about a dozen entrees will follow. There might be French toast and maple sausage with warm bananas in a Jamaican rum brown sugar syrup, eggs Benedict, and a petite fillet in a rich Madeira sauce with shallots and mushrooms served with rösti potatoes. The meal will conclude with a choice of dessert from such wonderful items as chocolate peanut butter cup to something called a gold brick, which is vanilla ice cream covered with chocolate pecan butter sauce. *Hours:* Monday to Saturday 5:30 to 9:30pm, Sunday 11am to 2:30pm (brunch) and 4 to 8:30pm.

STRASBURG

STRASBURG ATTRACTIONS

Summer is the time to ride the **Strasburg Railroad**, Route 741, east of Strasburg (☎ 717/687-7522), and recapture the days when the great iron horses, their bells and whistles sounding, traveled round the mountain in a billowing cloud of coal-fired smoke. On the way you can stop off, enjoy a picnic, and hop the train back. The trip is 9 miles round-trip (45 minutes) from Strasburg to Paradise. Every car in the train has a history, but one is especially appealing—an open coach featured in the Barbra Streisand film *Hello, Dolly!* At the Railroad Museum next door you can see a large collection of the old iron characters. *Hours:* April to October, train operates daily; the rest of the year, weekends only. Closed first 3 weeks in January. *Admission:* $8 adults, $4 children ages 3 to 11.

At the **Railroad Museum,** Strasburg (☎ 717/687-8628), the history and technology of the railroad industry from the earliest steam locomotives to 20th-century innovations are preserved and interpreted through exhibits and daily programs. The collection possesses 80 railroad engines and cars. Visitors may enter the cab of a steam locomotive, view the stateroom of a private car, see the interior of a Pullman sleeper, and walk under No. 1187—the 62-ton class of locomotive swept downstream for nearly a mile during the 1889 Johnstown flood. *Hours:* July and August, Monday to Thursday 9am to 5pm, Friday and Saturday 9am to 7pm, Sunday 11am to 5pm. May to June and September to October, Monday to Saturday 9am to 5pm and Sunday 11am to 5pm. Closed Monday November to April and certain holidays. *Admission:* $6 adults, $5 seniors, $4 children ages 6 to 12.

At the **National Toy Train Museum,** Paradise Lane, Strasburg (☎ 717/687-8976), headquarters for the Train Collectors Association, you'll find the nation's largest nonprivate collection of toy and model trains. In the historical hall are exhibits of toy trains from the last half of the 19th century to the present. Toy train buffs will especially appreciate the classic 1928 Blue Comet set, while the average viewer will definitely note the pink girl's train pulling pink, turquoise, and lavender freight cars, which Lionel produced in the late 1950s (and which totally bombed in the marketplace). Kids and dads will love the operating layouts, reminiscent of department-store displays from the first half of this century, while wives and others can commiserate with the poor female featured in the nostalgic movie that's shown every 30 minutes or so. *Hours:* May to October, daily 10am to 5pm; April, November and December, Saturday to Sunday 10am to 5pm. *Admission:* $3 adults, $1.50 children ages 5 to 12.

Kids will also love the model railroad drama at the **Choo-Choo Barn,** Route 741, Strasburg (☎ 717/687-7911), complete to the finer details of motor cars running on the roads, animated figures at work, and even a "fire" in a home attended to by the fire department. *Hours:* June to August, daily 10am to 6pm; April to June and September to December, daily 10am to 4:30pm. Closed January to March. *Admission:* $4 adults, $2 children ages 5 to 12.

STRASBURG AREA LODGING
Staying on a Farm
Since 1968 Ellen Neff has been welcoming visitors to **Neffdale Farm,** 604 Strasburg Rd. (on Route 741, east of Strasburg), Paradise, PA 17562 (☎ 717/687-7837), a 160-acre dairy farm that also keeps sheep. Her six guest rooms (three with bath and three with unstocked refrigerator) are spick-and-span and comfortable; some have TVs. You're welcome to help milk the cows at 5:30am or 5pm. No breakfast is served. *Rates:* $38 to $50 double.

Rayba Acres Farm, Black Horse Road (R.D. 1), Paradise, PA 17562 (☎ 717/687-6729; fax 717/687-8386; www.800padutch.com/rayba.html), is off Route 741 east of Strasburg. Since 1971 Reba Ranck has been illustrating a "different way of life" to urban visitors on her farm. She maintains four rooms in the main redbrick farmhouse (all with double beds and shared bath), accommodations over the garage (which include a double with a bath and TV and a large family room with two double beds and a couch, which can sleep up to eight), and four additional rooms with bath. Morning coffee is available free—just help yourself. The 100-acre farm is a dairy and chicken operation, with a few sheep "for atmosphere." From the windows you'll look out across the flat landscape. You can set up picnics in the backyard with views over the fields. There's a swing for the kids. No breakfast is served. *Rates:* $36 to $60 double.

Other Strasburg Area Lodging & Dining

The **Timberline Lodges,** 44 Summit Hill Dr., Strasburg, PA 17579 (☎ 717/ 687-7472), are set on a wooded hillside outside Strasburg and provide seclusion on 15 acres. The cabins are all different. Yours might contain two double beds and a pine chest in the bedroom; a fully equipped kitchen; a sitting room furnished with a couch, two armchairs, a TV, and a fieldstone fireplace; a full bath; and sliding glass doors that open onto a wooden deck. There are also some new deluxe rooms (with small decks, TVs, and tasteful furnishings) and some motel-style units available. Facilities include a fine country restaurant decorated in earth tones that glow in winter. The limited prix-fixe menu changes every 3 weeks. It offers a choice of three items like crab cakes served with a champagne vanilla sauce, marinated grilled flank steak served with mushrooms, and pork tenderloin with hunter's-style sauce made with peppers, onions, and tomatoes. The adjacent bar/lounge is one of the few convivial watering holes in the woods—a rare find around here. Facilities include a pool and games room. Take Route 896 south, off Route 30, to Strasburg. Then continue into Strasburg, picking up Route 896 going east and following the signs. *Rates:* $110 to $170 cabin for two (depending on number of bedrooms); summer, $70 double; off-season, $60 double.

A fine time was had by the original owner, Donald Denlinger, when he was trying to get 19 25-ton hulks of rolling stock he'd purchased on a lark from Gordonville, Pennsylvania, to their current resting place. Down in Strasburg, they now form the **Red Caboose Motel,** P.O. Box 102, Strasburg, PA 17579 (☎ 717/687-6646).

Yes, you'll be sleeping in one of these red cabooses, built in the early 1900s. Inside each you'll find a double bed covered in velveteen with an engineer's lantern swinging over it, a TV atop a potbellied stove, and a bath with sink and stall shower. The larger cabooses have bunk beds as well. The rooms are small and cozy, as you'd expect—hope for a warm, still night or you'll be gently rocked by the wind. At the motel you'll also find a dining car (complete with brass Pullman lanterns and gold-tasselled red velvet curtains; open March to November) and a gift shop filled with all kinds of railroad memorabilia and trains, priced from a few hundred dollars to $39,000 for a large, custom-built outdoor model locomotive. *Rates:* Summer, $75 to $85 small caboose for two, $95 to $100 double unit with four bunks; rest of the year, $55 to $65 small caboose for two, $65 to $85 double unit with four bunks.

The **Historic Strasburg Inn,** Route 896, Strasburg, PA 17579 (☎ 717/ 687-7691), is a replica of the Strasburg Washington House that served travelers from 1793 to 1921. Although it exudes all the imitation "charm" that such reconstructions inevitably seem to possess, the rooms are tasteful and comfortable, with chintz wallpaper, chair rails, Lapp furniture, and Hitchcock rockers. The large dining room serves breakfast, lunch, and dinner daily, plus a Sunday brunch buffet. Dinner items like braised veal loin with wild mushrooms, pearl onions, and caramelized garlic in a Madeira sauce; duck with apricot brandy served on top of oranges and apricots; and crab cakes served over a Dijon cream sauce range from $20 to $30. There's an outdoor pool, and bicycles are available free of charge. *Rates:* Mid-June to October, $139 to $149 double; April to mid-June and November to March, $119 to $129 double; many weekend packages are offered. *Dining hours:* Monday to Thursday 7 to 10am, 11:30am to 2pm, and 5 to 9pm; Friday to Saturday 7 to 10am, 11:30am to 2pm, and 4:30 to 9:30pm; Sunday 7 to 10am, 11am to 2pm, and 4 to 9pm.

LITITZ, MOUNT JOY & ENVIRONS

AREA ATTRACTIONS

Only 8 miles north of Lancaster is the village of Lititz, a charming, undisturbed town that was a Moravian community until 1855.

Stop at the **Sturgis Pretzel House**, 219 E. Main St. (☎ 717/626-4354), and try to twist your own pretzel. Find out where and how the first pretzel was made, watch what it symbolizes, and see them being baked at the first pretzel bakery in the United States. *Hours:* Monday to Saturday 9am to 5pm. *Admission:* $2.

Walk through the village and browse in the antiques stores and around Moravian Square, which was the town's hub in the 1700s. Here you'll find the **Brethren's House,** built in 1759, which was used as a hospital during the American Revolution; the **Sisters' House,** built in 1758 and now part of **Linden Hall,** the oldest girls' residence school in the country. Here also stands the **Moravian Church**, built in 1787 but rebuilt several times. The July 4th weekend is special here: a pageant of the Queen of Candles is held as more than 5,000 candles burn in Lititz Springs Park. The main street is also lined with crafts and antiques stores worth browsing.

From Lititz it's only a short drive over to Mount Joy and East Petersburg, where there are several fine accommodation and dining establishments, including Groff's farm, where you ought to plan for an evening meal (see "Pennsylvania Dutch Dining," above).

Tours and wine tastings are offered at the **Nissley Winery** in Bainbridge, off Route 441, via Wickersham Road (☎ 717/426-3514), along with a variety of special events. The place is appealing—an 18th-century-style stone building and plenty of acreage for a quiet picnic lunch (washed down by a bottle of wine, of course). *Hours:* Self-guided tours and tastings, Monday to Saturday 10am to 5pm, Sunday 1 to 4pm. Closed major winter holidays and Easter.

LITITZ LODGING

The **General Sutter Inn,** 14 E. Main St., Lititz, PA 17543 (☎ 717/626-2115), a handsome three-story brick edifice overlooking the town square, has been famous for its unique feather beds, good food, and prohibition of dancing, cursing, gossip, and bawdy songs since it was founded in 1764 by the Moravian Church as the *Zum Anker* ("The Sign of the Anchor"). It's named after John Augustus Sutter, who discovered gold in California. The forty-niners trampled his livestock and crops, bringing him close to ruin, and he retreated to Lititz, hoping to find peace and a cure for arthritis in the town's famed mineral springs. He died in 1880 and is buried in the Moravian Cemetery. Today the inn is known for being one of the area's quieter retreats. Enter into the downstairs parlor with a Louis XIV medallion-backed sofa, a carved marble-top coffee table, and a parlor organ, which are just part of the ultra-Victorian atmosphere.

The upstairs corridors, with oriental throw rugs, lead to 14 individually decorated rooms, all with baths, air-conditioning, phones, and TVs. Ornate Victorian beds with inlaid work, shaving stands, and other eclectic pieces of Victorian, country-style furniture add dash to the rooms. The 1764 dining room is as richly decorated in deep cranberry, accented with old-fashioned gas lights and antique accessories. It serves typical American/continental fare— crab cakes with lemon caper rémoulade; roast duck with saffron, honey, pear, and sun-dried cherry sauce; and lamb chops marinated in basil, Worcestershire sauce, and herbs, priced from $16 to $25. There's a pleasant cocktail lounge, too. On the Broad Street side guests can enjoy sitting on the brick patio by the fountain.

Rates: $85 to $115 double, suites $115 to $150. *Dining hours:* Daily 7am to 3pm, Monday to Thursday 5 to 9pm, Friday to Saturday 5 to 9:30pm, Sunday noon to 8pm.

The **Alden House**, 62 E. Main St., Lititz, PA 17543 (☎ 800/584-0753 or 717/627-3363; www.aldenhouse.com), is an 1850 brick Victorian with olive-green shutters and a gambrel portico. It has three rooms and three two-room suites, all with a bath and cable TV. The Lilac and Lace Suite contains a four-poster with a lace canopy, window seats under the bay window, and a sitting area. A full breakfast is served in the dining room or on one of the porches. *Rates* (including breakfast): $95 to $130 double.

Swiss Woods, 500 Blantz Rd., Lititz, PA 17543 (☎ 717/627-3358), is indeed in the woods, overlooking Speedwell Forge Lake, and is styled like a Swiss chalet. This appealing place offers seven modern rooms with private entrances. The rooms are furnished with country pine four-posters and armoires, armchairs, and such country accents as twig wreaths and lamps bearing stenciled shades. The most luxurious room is the Lake of Geneva, named because it has a view of the lake; it also offers a Jacuzzi in the bath. The focal point of the common room is the sandstone fireplace. Open beams, natural woodwork, hand-crafted furniture, and cowbells give it a distinctly Swiss air. In the mornings proprietor Debrah Mosimann prepares specialties like cinnamon-raisin French toast stuffed with strawberry cream cheese and eggs Florentine along with birchermuesli, a Swiss fruit-and-yogurt dish. Werner tends the gardens that overflow with annuals and perennials and flowers that attract hummingbirds and butterflies. *Rates* (including breakfast): $107 to $157 double.

MOUNT JOY & MANHEIM LODGING

The **Olde Square Inn**, 127 E. Main St., Mount Joy, PA 17552 (☎ 717/653-4525; fax 717/653-0976), is on the town's square in a handsome 1917 two-story home with dormer windows and an elegant side porch. There are four rooms with baths, each decorated in a different color scheme—the Charleston Room in dark-blue wallpaper with sprays of pink and white flowers and a bathroom with a double shower, the Garden Room in soft green and furnished with an iron canopy bed and featuring a whirlpool tub in the bathroom. The Ivy Room contains furniture painted by a local artist. The Royal Room is splendidly decorated in red-and-blue wallpaper. All rooms have TV/VCRs, phones, and air-conditioning. The most lavish accommodation is in the Carriage House. Here you'll find a suite featuring a double whirlpool tub with a fireplace beside it and such additional amenities as a stereo system, wet bar, refrigerator, and microwave, plus a private patio. The bedroom features an iron bed made up lavishly with comforter. Guests use the living room with fireplace and the porch, a favorite spot for breakfast in summer. *Rates* (including breakfast): $95 to $105 double, $155 to $185 suite.

At **Rocky Acres Farm**, Pinkerton Road (R.D. 3), Mount Joy, PA 17552 (☎ 717/653-4449), Mrs. Eileen Benner will give you a really warm welcome and provide a room and breakfast. Over a humpback bridge, along a twisting road beside a brook you'll suddenly come upon the farm around a corner. There are five rooms with baths in this 200-year-old farmhouse. If you're lucky, you'll be given the large front room with a fireplace; it's furnished with a colossal carved and painted Victorian bed. Other rooms are pleasantly and modestly furnished with cannonball beds and perhaps a marble-top chest, pegboards serve as closets, and the bathroom is shared. There's also an efficiency on the third floor and a private apartment that sleeps seven people, with two upstairs bedrooms, a bath, a living room, and a fully equipped kitchen. Kids'll love helping milk or feed the cows or watch the calves being born; there's also a Victorian dollhouse for them to play with and a small horse for them to ride.

You'll be treated to a superb country breakfast. Although the fare may vary, there'll always be heaps of it. Plates are piled high with scrambled eggs, ham, pancakes, and the best home fries anywhere, all accompanied by applesauce, sugar cake, home-baked bread or muffins, jams, fresh milk, and coffee. There's plenty of surrounding groves and fields for walking and a creek to tube down if you wish. Eileen will steer you to all the authentic attractions in the region and can even arrange for you to have dinner in a real Amish home.

To get there, take Route 30 west, to Route 283 west, to Route 230 west, which will bring you into Mount Joy. In Mount Joy, take Route 772 west a short distance only, to Pinkerton Road. Turn left and follow the road about 3 miles over the stone arch bridge. *Rates* (including breakfast Monday to Saturday): $85 double. Extra adult $10; extra child $5.

When you stay at Country Comforts of **Ionde Lane Farm**, 1103 Auction Rd., Manheim, PA 17545 (☎ 717/665-4231), you really are part of the Nissley family—John, Elaine, and their four children who run this farm. At breakfast as many as 18 to 20 people will probably sit down at the table in the kitchen to a farm breakfast of orange juice, eggs, bacon, toast, homemade bread or doughnuts, and coffee or tea. There are six rooms available, three with private baths. All rooms are well suited to families: One has a double bed with twin bunks; the others have doubles or two singles and a crib. The quilts were all made by Elaine. Calves, chickens, pigs, goats, sheep, and ponies are added attractions. A full breakfast is served Monday to Saturday, and a continental version on Sunday. *Rates* (including breakfast Monday to Saturday): $55 to $75 double, children $7.50 in parents' room.

MOUNT JOY LODGING & DINING

The **Cameron Estate Inn**, Donegal Springs Road (R.D. 1, Box 305), Mount Joy, PA 17552 (☎ 717/653-1773), is an inviting redbrick Victorian mansion set on 15 acres; it once belonged to Simon Cameron, secretary of war to President Abraham Lincoln. It has been carefully restored and lavishly furnished with antique reproductions. The 17 rooms (7 with fireplaces) are large and spread over three floors. In each you'll most likely find a canopied four-poster or brass bed, porcelain lamps, two wing chairs, a writing desk, and oriental rugs. All have telephones with data ports.

Downstairs, the lounge has been made luxuriously comfortable with a brocade-covered couch, Martha Washington chairs, assorted books, and a TV. Breakfast is served on an enclosed porch overlooking the lovely gardens, which include a formal rose and herb garden. It will consist of fresh fruit, cereals, and baked items plus such hot dishes as Belgian waffles, brunch casseroles, and French toast. An afternoon tea is also served. Children under age 14 are discouraged. *Rates* (including breakfast): $140 to $200.

Bube's Brewery, 102 N. Market St. (☎ 717/653-2160), is as much fun as it sounds, located in an old brewery. There are three distinct areas: Stone walls and rafters and thousands upon thousands of empty bottles characterize the Bottling Works (☎ 717/653-2160). Downstairs, the Catacombs (☎ 717/653-2056) is precisely that—the old cellar area—now a romantic candlelit dining room, and Alois's (☎ 717/653-2057), a plush Victorian dining room with lots of stained glass, overstuffed chairs and sofas, and oak chairs.

Steaks, light dinners, sandwiches, and subs are served in the Bottling Works. Dinner prices are $4 to $17. The Catacombs, where you'll be greeted by a serf in a medieval costume, offers traditional steak and seafood dishes like coquilles Catacombs (bay scallops, onions, tomatoes, garlic, and white-wine sauce), filet mignon with herb butter, and stuffed chicken breast, priced from $16 to $22. Medieval feasts are held twice a month. At Alois's prices range from $20 to $27. Cocktails and appetizers are served in the parlor before diners move into one of the dining rooms. A sample menu offers veal Dijon, roast duck with orange-marmalade glaze, steak Diane, and spiced scallops and cashews in tomato sauce. These will be preceded by an appetizer, a soup, a salad, and a sorbet, then followed by a dessert like crème Kahlúa or chocolate-chip/banana cake.

Hours: Bottling Works, Monday to Thursday 11am to 2pm and 5:30 to 10pm, Friday 11am to 2pm and 5pm to midnight, Saturday 5pm to midnight, Sunday 5 to 10pm. Catacombs, Sunday to Thursday 5:30 to 9pm, Friday 5 to 9:45pm, Saturday 4:45 to 9:45pm. Alois's, Thursday to Sunday 5:30 to 9pm.

A Special Dining Place in East Petersburg

Haydn Zugs, Center Square, 1987 State St., East Petersburg (☎ 717/569-5746), offers traditional dining. Both dining rooms are elegant, with Queen Anne–style chairs, pewter settings, pink napkins, and a Williamsburg-blue background. The menu emphasizes steaks and meats, including Lancaster County smoked pork chops with fresh horseradish and blackened breast of duckling with a Grand Marnier sauce. Fish offerings might include grilled salmon with maître d' butter or grilled shrimp with lobster sauce. Among the more unique dishes is Norwegian chicken—sautéed breasts of chicken with smoked salmon, capers, onions, tomatoes, and white wine. Prices range from $16 to $23. To start, you'll find such tasty morsels as grilled portobello mushrooms with a Parmesan crust, and bacon-wrapped scallops. Finish with the bananas Foster or one of the other tempting sundaes. *Hours:* Tuesday to Friday 11:30am to 2pm, Tuesday to Saturday 5 to 9pm. Closed 1 week around July 4.

FROM LANCASTER TO EPHRATA & ADAMSTOWN

AREA ATTRACTIONS

From Lancaster, take Route 501 to Route 272/222, which will lead you all the way past the Landis Farm Museum to Ephrata, site of a fascinating religious community, and then to Adamstown, a well-known center for antiques— a journey of 19 miles, which makes a perfect Sunday.

Henry and George Landis were avid collectors of farm and related machinery and gadgetry, and they used their collection to found the **Landis Valley Museum**, 2451 Kissel Hill Rd. (☎ 717/569-0401), in 1924. The collections are housed in 22 buildings, some original and some newly constructed, which have been laid out as a village. During summer, such crafts as tinsmithing, flax and wool spinning, and weaving are demonstrated; but whatever time you visit the museum will provide insight into rural and 19th-century American life, offering much to marvel at from our 20th-century viewpoint. For example, did you know that 1 acre of land is required to keep one sheep, that one sheep is required for one person's clothing, that between 1750 and 1850 it took roughly 25 days to go 320 miles (or from Philadelphia to Pittsburgh)? Did you know that a sickler could cut only three-quarters of an acre a day, compared to the grain cradle introduced in the 1780s, which could cut 2 to 2½ acres per day, or the reaper of the mid-1800s, which could cut 10 to 12 acres a day?

To get here, take the Oregon Pike (Route 272 north) exits off either Route 22, 230-30 (the Bypass), or 72. Entrance to the parking area is off Landis Valley Road opposite the Landis Valley Resort Inn. *Hours:* Monday to Saturday 9am to 5pm, Sunday noon to 5pm. Closed November to early April. *Admission:* $7 adults, $6.50 seniors, $5 children ages 6 to 12.

German Pietist Conrad Beissel founded the **Ephrata Cloister**, 632 Main St., Ephrata (☎ 717/733-6600), a religious communal society consisting of three orders—two celibate and a married order of householders—in 1732. From 1735 to 1750 about 300 souls lived on 250 acres as a fully self-supporting community, complete with mills, craft shops, and so on. The celibates lived in the 10 restored medieval-style buildings you can see today. The doorways, which are extremely low, were meant to ensure a bowed head, an expression of a proper sense of humility. The spartan monastic cells, where the celibates slept on wooden benches with wooden blocks as pillows, and the nearly masochistic strictures of the community testify to the cultlike dedication that these followers felt for their leader, Conrad Beissel.

Beissel combined ideas from pietist, Kelpian, Jewish, Roman Catholic, Anabaptist, mystic, inspirationist, and Rosicrucian faiths. His followers rose at 5am for private devotions, and they passed the day alternating study periods with work periods of basket making, printing, bookmaking, carpentry, and paper making until their 6pm vegetarian meal. This was followed by singing and music school, and retirement to bed at 9pm. At midnight the bell was sounded for 2 hours of worship followed by additional sleep from 2 to 5am.

After Beissel died in 1768, the practices became less austere and the community declined; when the last celibate member died in 1814, the married congregation formed the German Seventh Day Baptist Church. Members continued to live and worship at the cloister until 1934. The order was famous for the original music and hymns Beissel composed, the singing and music schools, the art of fraktur, and the many important books that were printed here. Tours are given of the sisters' house and the meetinghouse, and then you're free to explore the other buildings and the graveyards. A small museum shows archaeological fragments that were recovered when the buildings were restored, along with fraktur and documents.

Take Route 272 north to Ephrata, then turn right onto Route 322. *Hours:* Tours hourly, Monday to Saturday 9am to 5pm, Sunday noon to 5pm. *Admission:* $5 adults, $4.50 seniors, $3 children ages 6 to 12.

If you enjoy shopping for handmade craft items, including jewelry and quilts, go to the **Artworks at Doneckers,** 100 N. State St., Ephrata (☎ 717/738-9503), a restored shoe factory building that now contains 30-plus studios, galleries, and specialty shops. Closed Wednesday.

If you have time, stay over until Monday and head out to New Holland for the regular weekly **horse auction** at New Holland Sales Stables, Fulton Street (☎ 717/354-4341)—an exciting event for any visitor from 10am to 1pm. Here, the local farmers and Amish and Mennonites bid for work horses and other animals. Later in the week the auctions are for pigs, sheep, and other livestock.

EPHRATA LODGING

The **Inns at Doneckers,** 318–324 N. State St., 301 W. Main St., 251 N. State St., and 287 Duke St., Ephrata, PA 17522 (☎ 717/738-9502), offer some of the area's most comfortable and best-decorated rooms. The accommodations are in four buildings: The largest (with 20 rooms) is the Guesthouse; the second largest is the 1777 House (with 12 rooms), which once belonged to famous clock maker and member of Ephrata, Jacob Gorgas; the Gerhart (5 rooms) and the Homestead (4 rooms) are the smallest.

Each room is different. In the Guesthouse, the Wheatland Suite features stained glass in the bay window, inlaid wood floors, and a Jacuzzi in the bathroom; it has a private entrance. In the Rock Ford Suite are lovely individualized stenciling, a fireplace, a comfy sitting area, and a Jacuzzi. The Traveler's Berth is small, but still appealing, with exposed brick walls, a blanket chest, and a wing chair among the furnishings. In the 1777 House, the Jacob Gorgas Suite contains a love seat in front of the original green marble fireplace; the Peter Miller Suite is heavily stenciled and has a handsome kas among the furnishings (its bath features the original stone masonry and a Jacuzzi); the Blacksmith's Loft bursts with color—blue-green, mustard, and spicy red—and features a loft sitting room, a fireplace, and a Jacuzzi. Rooms in the Gerhart House tend to have either iron, canopied, or cannonball beds; in the Homestead, Melba's Suite contains a unique four-poster iron bed, the original limestone fireplace, and a sitting area in the bay window.

Guests are served a buffet breakfast at long harvest tables—baked apples, croissants, cheese, fruit, and cereal. The inn also has a fine restaurant (☎ 717/738-9501), where the cuisine applies French traditions to fresh local ingredients. Additional amenities include the store, which has great home furnishings and men's and women's fashions, plus the Artworks, an old warehouse that's been converted into artists' studios and galleries selling a variety of fine art, quilts, jewelry, and designer crafts—some of the best the region has to offer.

Rates (including breakfast): Weekends $95 to $220, midweek $79 to $205; higher prices for suites. *Dining hours:* Monday to Tuesday and Thursday to Saturday 11am to 10pm.

Smithton, 900 W. Main St., Ephrata, PA 17522 (☎ 717/733-6094), is a B&B offering charming rooms with bath and fireplace. What can be finer for romance than a candlelit room with the strains of chamber music playing in the background and a fire in the hearth? That's what you'll find here, plus some good books and a refrigerator to store the champagne. In addition, each room has a sitting area, comfortable leather chairs, reading lamps, and a writing desk. The beds are covered with bright Pennsylvania Dutch quilts. The Red Room contains a four-poster that's covered with a magnificent handmade quilt. Ball-fringe curtains, rag rugs, fresh flowers, and stenciling accent the country look. Among the Blue Room's furnishings, the rope four-poster with a velvet canopy stands out. On the third floor is a small suite— four skylights, beams, a Franklin stove, and a Red Star quilt give it wonderful character. This is one of the quietest rooms, along with the Red Room.

Guests are welcome to use the attractive living room with its stucco-brick fireplace, comfy armchairs, valanced curtains, and country knickknacks in the windows, or to relax and read in the study filled with books. Breakfast (homemade waffles, fruits, coffee, and tea) is served at a harvest table in a room that has a number of quilts, stuffed animals, and folk art for sale. There's also a brick fireplace here. In summer the back brick patio is a favorite haven.

Rates (including breakfast): $85 to $165 double, $155 to $185 suite.

Glenn and Mildred Wissler operate **Clearview Farm**, 355 Clearview Rd., Ephrata, PA 17522 (☎ 717/733-6333), an 1814 limestone house with Turkey red shutters. It's a fully working farm of 200 acres planted with crops. There are five rooms (all with private baths): The Garden Room is a floral celebration with black-and-rose curtains; its furnishings include an iron-and-brass bed with a crown canopy, wicker rockers, a marble dresser, and a trunk filled with quilts. The Princess Room is very Victorian, with a hooped four-poster canopied bed, a cottage-style marble-top dresser, and upholstered Victorian side chairs. The Royal Room is appropriately decorated in red and gilt, with a carved walnut Victorian bed. My favorite is the Washington Room, which is tucked up in the attic: It contains a Shaker four-poster with a ball-fringe canopy and a pretty dahlia quilt; the walls are of stone and the ceilings display the original pegged rafters, and additional comforts include wing chairs and a table with a lamp for reading.

The comfortable sitting room overlooks the pond and fields, and an appealing stone patio is adjacent to the well-manicured lawns and flower beds. A full breakfast is served on fine china. Glen likes to collect chocolate pots, and these are on display in the cabinet he converted from an armoire. *Rates* (including breakfast): $145 double weekends, $105 double weekdays.

LANCASTER COUNTY AFTER DARK

Lancaster County is hardly nightlife country. Farm folk rise early, work hard, eat well, and retire early to rest for an early start to the next day. The rhythm is completely different from the urban pace New Yorkers are used to. However, Lancaster has several bars, a prime historic theater, cinemas, and good restaurants.

America's oldest continuously operating theater is the **Fulton Opera House,** 12 N. Prince St., Lancaster (☎ 717/397-7425), a National Historic Landmark that was restored to its Victorian splendor in 1995. It hosts a season of theater and musicals from September to June. Tours of the marvelous gilt-and-red interior are available.

At the **Mount Gretna Playhouse,** Pennsylvania Avenue, Chautauqua side (P.O. Box 578), Mount Gretna, PA 17064 (☎ 717/964-3627), the Gretna Theatre produces plays and musicals. **Music at Gretna** presents chamber music and jazz concerts in the summer.

Franklin and Marshall College's **Green Room Theater** on College Avenue (P.O. Box 3003), Lancaster, PA 17604, also puts on good theater and dance productions. Famous alumni include Roy Scheider. Call ☎ 717/291-4015 for information.

Drinking spots include the **Lancaster Dispensing Company,** 33–35 N. Market St. (☎ 717/299-4602), which features bands Friday and Saturday along with a large selection of beers served in a decor of stained and etched glass, a 1960s marble bar, bentwood cane chairs, and lots of greenery. **Jethro's** (see "Lancaster Dining," above) is another good spot.

Lancaster County
Special & Recreational Activities

Antiquing: Adamstown is a great center, boasting 1,500 dealers every Sunday of the year at several large markets. The most famous is probably **Ed Stoudt's Black Angus** (☎ 717/484-4385), with over 200 dealers and a convenient steak house. **Lititz** and vicinity is another, much smaller hunting ground—there are several stores downtown. **New Holland** has four or five stores.

Bicycling: Rental or free bicycles are available at certain accommodations— the **Strasburg Inn** and **Host Farm,** for example.

Golf: Hawk Valley Golf, R.D. 1, Denver (☎ 717/445-5445), charges $40 to play the course; **Overlook Golf Course,** 2040 Lititz Pike, Lancaster (☎ 717/569-9551), charges $31.

Picnicking: You can picnic on the **Strasburg Railroad trip** or in **Lancaster County Central Park, Lititz Springs Park,** or **Burchmiller State Park** on Route 222 south. See also "State Parks," below.

Shopping the Reading Outlets: En route to or from the Dutch country, you can stop (or spend a whole day) at the shopping outlets at Reading for shoes, sportswear, linens, tools, jewelry—you name it, it's here being sold at a discount. For more information, call ☎ 610/376-0206.

Shopping for Quilts & Crafts: Quilts have a history and symbolism and offer the quilters an opportunity to express their creative side and love of color. Many of the patterns are derived from the natural patterns of the fields, the interplay of sunshine and shadow, the bounty of the earth, and the celestial bodies.

Among the better commercial places to shop for local crafts, including quilts, is the **Studio at Donecker's** in Ephrata and also the **Old Country Store** across from People's Place in Intercourse. According to the locals, the latter accepts work only from the very best, rejecting as much as 40%. Best of all, though, is to shop at the farms wherever you see a QUILTS FOR SALE sign. One of my favorites is **Hannah Stoltzfoos's farm** at 216 Witmer Rd., which is off Route 340 just west of Smoketown. Hannah stocks many fine, quality quilts. **Dotty Lewis** is known for her talent in traditional weaving; find her by calling ☎ 717/872-2756.

State Parks: Susquehannock, % Gifford Pinchot State Park, 2200 Rosstown Rd., Lewisberry, PA 17339 (☎ 717/432-5011), has picnicking and hiking areas. **Samuel S. Lewis State Park,** % Gifford Pinchot State Park, 2200 Rosstown Rd., Lewisberry, PA 17339 (☎ 717/432-5011), has picnicking and hiking. **French Creek State Park,** 843 Park Rd., Elverson, PA 19520 (☎ 610/582-9680), has over 7,000 acres for picnicking, an Olympic-size swimming pool, fishing, boating (rentals in summer), hiking (32 miles of trails), ice fishing and skating, sledding, and nongroomed cross-country skiing. There are also 318 camping sites. **Gifford Pinchot State Park** (☎717/432-5011), which is located between York and Harrisburg, has 340 camping sites

Swimming: There's a pool in **Lancaster County Park** on Broad Street (☎ 717/392-4621 or 717/299-8215). See also "State Parks," above.

Tennis: Six tennis courts are available in **Burchmiller Park** on Route 222, south of Lancaster. Four are available in **Lancaster County Park** (☎ 717/299-8215).

INDEX

Page numbers in italics refer to maps.

LODGING

FROMMER'S® COMPLETE TRAVEL GUIDES

FROMMER'S® DOLLAR-A-DAY GUIDES

FROMMER'S® PORTABLE GUIDES

FROMMER'S® NATIONAL PARK GUIDES

Family Vacations in the National Parks	National Parks of the American West	Yosemite & Sequoia/ Kings Canyon
Grand Canyon	Yellowstone & Grand Teton	Zion & Bryce Canyon

FROMMER'S® GREAT OUTDOOR GUIDES

New England	Southern California & Baja
Northern California	Pacific Northwest

FROMMER'S® MEMORABLE WALKS

Chicago	New York	San Francisco
London	Paris	Washington D.C.

FROMMER'S® IRREVERENT GUIDES

Amsterdam	London	New Orleans	San Francisco
Boston	Manhattan	Paris	Walt Disney World
Chicago			Washington, D.C.

FROMMER'S® BEST-LOVED DRIVING TOURS

America	Florida	Ireland	Scotland
Britain	France	Italy	Spain
California	Germany	New England	Western Europe

THE COMPLETE IDIOT'S TRAVEL GUIDES

Boston	Las Vegas	New York City
Cruise Vacations	London	San Francisco
Planning Your Trip to Europe	Mexico's Beach Resorts	Walt Disney World
Hawaii	New Orleans	Washington D.C.

THE UNOFFICIAL GUIDES®

Branson, Missouri	Florida with Kids	Las Vegas	New York City
California with Kids	The Great Smoky &	Miami & the Keys	San Francisco
Chicago	Blue Ridge	Mini-Mickey	Skiing in the West
Cruises	Mountains	New Orleans	Walt Disney World
Disney Companion			Washington, D.C.

SPECIAL-INTEREST TITLES

Born to Shop: Caribbean Ports of Call	Israel Past & Present
Born to Shop: France	Monks' Guide to California
Born to Shop: Hong Kong	Monks' Guide to New York City
Born to Shop: Italy	New York City with Kids
Born to Shop: New York	New York Times Weekends
Born to Shop: Paris	Outside Magazine's Guide
Frommer's Britain's Best Bike Rides	to Family Vacations
The Civil War Trust's Official Guide	Places Rated Almanac
to the Civil War Discovery Trail	Retirement Places Rated
Frommer's Caribbean Hideaways	Washington, D.C., with Kids
Frommer's Europe's Greatest Driving Tours	Wonderful Weekends from Boston
Frommer's Food Lover's Companion to France	Wonderful Weekends from New York City
Frommer's Food Lover's Companion to Italy	Wonderful Weekends from San Francisco
Frommer's Gay & Lesbian Europe	Wonderful Weekends from Los Angeles